THE PROBLEMS OF

MW01074493

Genocide is not only a problem of mass death but also of how, as a relatively new idea and law, it organizes and distorts thinking about civilian destruction. Taking the normative perspective of civilian immunity from military attack, A. Dirk Moses argues that the implicit hierarchy of international criminal law, atop which sits genocide as the "crime of crimes," blinds us to other types of humanly caused civilian death, like bombing cities, and the "collateral damage" of missile and drone strikes. Talk of genocide, then, can function ideologically to detract from systematic violence against civilians perpetrated by governments of all types. *The Problems of Genocide* contends that this violence is the consequence of "permanent security" imperatives: the striving of states, and armed groups seeking to found states, to make themselves invulnerable to threats.

A. DIRK MOSES is the Frank Porter Graham Distinguished Professor of Global Human Rights History at the University of North Carolina, Chapel Hill. He is the coeditor of *Decolonization, Self-Determination, and the Rise of Global Human Rights Politics* (2020) and *The Holocaust in Greece* (2018).

Edited by

Stefan-Ludwig Hoffmann, University of California, Berkeley
Samuel Moyn, Yale University, Connecticut

This series showcases new scholarship exploring the backgrounds of human rights today. With an open-ended chronology and international perspective, the series seeks works attentive to the surprises and contingencies in the historical origins and legacies of human rights ideals and interventions. Books in the series will focus not only on the intellectual antecedents and foundations of human rights, but also on the incorporation of the concept by movements, nation-states, international governance, and transnational law.

A full list of titles in the series can be found at:
www.cambridge.org/human-rights-history

THE PROBLEMS OF GENOCIDE

Permanent Security and the Language of Transgression

A. DIRK MOSES

University of North Carolina, Chapel Hill

CAMBRIDGE
UNIVERSITY PRESS

CAMBRIDGE
UNIVERSITY PRESS

University Printing House, Cambridge CB2 8BS, United Kingdom

One Liberty Plaza, 20th Floor, New York, NY 10006, USA

477 Williamstown Road, Port Melbourne, VIC 3207, Australia

314–321, 3rd Floor, Plot 3, Splendor Forum, Jasola District Centre, New Delhi – 110025, India

79 Anson Road, #06–04/06, Singapore 079906

Cambridge University Press is part of the University of Cambridge.

It furthers the University's mission by disseminating knowledge in the pursuit of education, learning, and research at the highest international levels of excellence.

www.cambridge.org
Information on this title: www.cambridge.org/9781107103580
DOI: 10.1017/9781316217306

First published 2021

A catalogue record for this publication is available from the British Library.

Library of Congress Cataloging-in-Publication Data
Names: Moses, A. Dirk., author.
Title: The problems of genocide : permanent security and the language of transgression / A. Dirk Moses, University of North Carolina, Chapel Hill.
Description: New York, NY : Cambridge University Press, 2021. | Series: Human rights in history | Includes bibliographical references and index.
Identifiers: LCCN 2020023793 (print) | LCCN 2020023794 (ebook) | ISBN 9781107103580 (hardback) | ISBN 9781107503120 (paperback) | ISBN 9781316217306 (epub)
Subjects: LCSH: Genocide–Prevention. | Atrocities–Prevention. | Genocide intervention. | Genocide—Law and legislation. | Human rights.
Classification: LCC HV6322.7 .M68 2021 (print) | LCC HV6322.7 (ebook) | DDC 364.15/1–dc23
LC record available at https://lccn.loc.gov/2020023793
LC ebook record available at https://lccn.loc.gov/2020023794

ISBN 978-1-107-10358-0 Hardback
ISBN 978-1-107-50312-0 Paperback

CONTENTS

PREFACE

The Problems of Genocide has been a bit too long in the making. Editing anthologies and the *Journal of Genocide Research* over the years took me off the career-conscious path of rapid book completion, often against the advice of friends and colleagues who warned against distracting collaborative projects. In the end, I feel it was time well spent. The side-tracks led to new scholarly landscapes and expanded my horizons, while the extra time allowed the argument to crystallize. Grant applications require that the "research plan" is stipulated in linear terms and that "outputs" are clearly enumerated. But most academics know that the high road of intellectual creativity and productivity is marked less by prescribed milestones than surprising twists and unexpected turns.

I understand that this "output" will not be to everyone's liking. The dissonance is intended. The book casts doubt on the belief that adjustments to the international system can solve the problem of genocide. Given the common comparison between the campaigns to abolish slavery in the nineteenth century and to banish the "scourge of genocide" today, I address those who believe in the right of (usually Western) intervention to effect the latter: in other words, many liberal and conservative political scientists, legal scholars, politicians, and activists. To them I say: if we want to promote the norm of "never again" – namely, stopping the killing of lots of people – then we need to think about the problem of genocide beyond prevention activism. My hope is that, upon reaching its end, readers of this book might be open to the proposition that the concept of genocide is part of the problem of civilian destruction rather than its solution.

I have accumulated many debts in this journey. Donald Bloxham suggested I combine my interests in colonial genocide, intellectual history, and international law as we strolled through New York's Washington Square in early 2005. I appreciated the encouragement and eventually followed the advice. At length, I decided to articulate my misgivings about "genocide" as an idea, a law, and a claim-making praxis via a historical account of its "origins." Such an account, I determined, could not be another exercise in biographical reconstruction that dominated the field and to which I, alas, had also fallen prey. A non-teleological intellectual history was required that exposed genocide's problematic function in obscuring the logic of "permanent security" in what I call the "language of transgression." Doing so meant reconstructing (a) diachronically: the historically rooted discursive conditions of genocide's thinkability and (b) synchronically: the political conditions of its break-through since the 1940s, when it was invented. I suggested such a critical theory of genocide already in 2008 in an essay in the *Online Encylopaedia of Mass Violence*, then edited by Jacques Sémelin (www.sciencespo.fr/mass-vio-lence-war-massacre-resistance/en/document/toward-theory-critical-genocide-studies.html). The permanent security argument was first expressed in a keynote address for the International Network of Genocide Scholars confer-ence at the University of Sussex in 2010, and appeared in part in an article on "Revisiting a Foundation Assumption of Genocide Studies" in 2011.

I am happy to record my thanks to the many friends and colleagues who shared insights, gave feedback, and/or afforded hospitality in the course of my research: Laura Downs, Regina Grafe, Pieter Judson, Lucy Riall, Federico Romero, Corinna Unger, and Jennifer Welsh at the European University Institute (EUI) in Florence, where I worked from January 2011 to December 2015; Alon Confino at the University of Tel Aviv in 2007 and the University of Virginia in 2010; Paul Betts, Gerhard Wolf, and Gideon Reuveni at the University of Sussex in 2008 and 2013; Martin and Anabel Shaw in Brighton, Vieussan and IBEI in Barcelona, where I trialled an early version of Chapter 8 in 2012; Pavel Kolář at the EUI and University of Konstanz, Germany, with Kornelia Kończal and little Klara in 2020; Martin van Gelderen and Antoinette Saxer at the EUI, San Bavello, and finally at the Lichtenberg-Kolleg in Göttingen that Martin directs and where I completed the manuscript in the European winter of 2019–2020; Nehal Bhuta and Nida Alahmad at the EUI and at Edinburgh University, where Nida organized two events on draft chapters in 2020; Michael Geyer and Tara Zahra at the Forced Migration and Humanitarianism in Global History conference at the University of Chicago in 2013; Bernard Struck at St Andrews in 2013 when Chapter 8 was also presented; Geoff Eley, Gina Morantz-Sanchez, Ron Suny, Fatma Müge Gögçek, Julia Hell, George Steinmetz, and Melanie Tanielian in Ann Arbor, where Chapters 1, 8, and part of Chapter 10 was given a going over in 2012 and 2015; Nadera Shalhoub-Kekorkian, Bashir Bashir, Amos Goldberg, and Raef Zreik in Jerusalem, Tel Aviv, Haifa, and Nazareth in 2013; Alison Bashford and Shruti Kapila at the Cambridge Global Intellectual History Seminar in 2015, Lyndsey Stonebridge and Cathie Carmichael (also a long-time editorial chum at the *Journal of Genocide Research*) in Norwich in 2015; Alex Hinton and Nela Navarro at Rutgers-Newark; Levent Yilmaz, Ayhan Aktar, Heghnar Watenpaugh, and Hülya Adak at The Armenian Genocide Concepts and Comparative Perspectives conference in Istanbul in 2015; Andrew Woolford, Adam Muller, and Umut Özsu in Winnipeg in 2016; Azar Dakwar and Maria Mälksoo in the Interrogating our Multiple Crises lecture series at the Brussels School of International Studies in 2017; Penny Green and Wayne Morrison at Queen Mary, London, in 2017; Eric Weitz, Rajan Menon, and Bruce Cronin at the Human Rights Seminar at City College, New York, which subjected the Introduction to exacting discussion in late 2017; John Torpey at the Ralph Bunche Institute for International Studies, CUNY Graduate Center in 2017; Philippa Hetherington, Alex Drace Francis, and Dejan Djokic, who had me in their Rethinking Modern Europe seminar at the Institute of Historical Research in London in 2017; Vimalin Rujivacharakul, Eve Buckley, and James M. Brophy for the David Warnock invited lecture at the University of Delaware in 2018; Uğur Ümit Üngör at the Genocide after 1948: 70 Years of Genocide Convention conference in Amsterdam in 2018; Susanne Hilman and Lisa Lampert in the Holocaust Living History program at UC San Diego in 2019; Raz Segal at Stockton in 2019; Dieter Gosewinkel and Matthias Kumm at the Wissenschaftszentrum Berlin für Sozialforschung where I was a visiting fellow in late 2019; Robert Gerwarth, William Mulligan, and Mark Jones in Dublin in 2020; Alanna O'Malley in Leiden where Eelco van der Maat gave an expert commentary on the Introduction in 2020; Alex Hinton and Nela Navarro at Rutgers-Newark whose Center for the Study of Genocide and Human Rights hosted me on various occasions; Volker Berghahn and Marion Berghahn, Mark Mazower, and Matthew Connelly who hosted talks over the years at Columbia; Taner Akçam, Thomas Kühne, and Debórah Dwork at the Strassler Center, Clark University, who gave me a forum several times; Stefan-Ludwig Hoffmann, Norma von Ragenfeld-Feldman, Martin Jay, John Connelly, Cathy Gallagher, Carla Hesse, and Tom Laqueur in Berkeley, where I aired early iterations of the argument more than once since graduating from there in 2000.

I am also grateful to friends and colleagues who made invaluable suggestions on draft chapters or oral presentations: Maartje Abbenhuis, Mohammed Abed, Yutaka Arai, Avril Alba, Francesca Antonini, Steven E. Aschheim, David Brophy, Marco Duranti, Carole Fink, Andrew Fitzmaurice, Sheila Fitzpatrick, Max Friedman (who gave repeated and extremely helpful feedback on the Introduction and Chapter 10), Chris Hilliard, Yotam Hotam, Douglas Irvin-Erickson, Claudia Kraft, Gili Kugler, Eric Kurlander, Nathan Kurz, Konrad Kwiet, William Levine, Mark Lewis, Shiru Lim, Kerstin von Lingen, James Loeffler, Stefan Malinowski, Eyal Mayroz, Maria Mälksoo, Elliot Neaman, Sophie Rigney, Weronika Romantik, Andrew Sartori, Ann-Sophie Schoepfel, Daniel Marc Segesser, Alexa Stiller, Damien Short, Glenda Sluga, Adam Storry, Lorenzo Veracini, Florian Wagner, Stephen Wertheim, Natasha Wheatley, Martin Woessner, Gerhard Wolf, the greatly missed Patrick Wolfe, and Greg Zuschlag. Needless to say, there is no suggestion that they agree with my arguments or bear responsibility for any remaining errors. Apologies to anyone I have inadvertently overlooked.

Others accompanied me on the journey and helped in ways they may not realize: Tony Barta in Melbourne; Warren Breckman and Cordula Grewe in Philadelphia and at Penn; Antonio Feros, Ben Nathans, Sophie Rosenfeld, and Beth Wenger also at Penn; Neil Levi and Beth Drenning in Jersey City; Seth Anziska, Jane Burbank, and Fred Cooper in New York; Dirk Rupnow, Greta Anderl, Éva Kovács, Béla Rásky, Dean Vuletic, Berthold Molden, Anais Angelo, and Jakob Lehne in Vienna; Mark Roseman in Bloomington; Geoff Levey, Jisuk Han, Oliver Frankel, Nick and Helen Doumanis, Rawan Arraf and Alaa Arraf in Sydney; Michael Laffan, Vanita Neelakanta, and Shel Garon in New Jersey; Jie-Hyun Lim in Seoul; Azar Dakwar and Mayse Khoury in Leuven; Dan Stone (likewise at the *Journal of Genocide Research*), Damien Short, Christina von Hodenberg and Dan Wilson, Jens Meierhenrich and Shan Lam, Dan Lee and Liz Marcus in London; Saadi Nikro, Yassin El-Haj Saleh, Linh Nguyen Vu, Robin Celikates, and Ayla in Berlin; Omer Bartov, Anne Berg, Vivian Berghahn, Diana Dumitru, Federico Finchelstein, Peter Holquist, Karl Jacoby, Mark Levene, Barbara Keys, Rob Manne, Małgorzata Mazurek, Sam Moyn, Saadi Nikro, Devin Pendas, Nadia Oweidat, Rebecca Sheehan, Richard Steigmann-Gall, Jess Whyte, Ihab Shalbak, Brad Simpson, Keith Watenpaugh, and Jürgen Zimmerer; Glenda Pryor, Rob Wheatley, Warren Percy, Jarrod Wheatley, and Luisa Krein in Wentworth Falls; Rolf Moses and Maryla Rutyna in Brisbane and Miami Beach on the Gold Coast; and of course my parents John and Ingrid in Canberra.

Several cafes provided de facto office space for sustained reading and writing. I can't list them all, but Black Market Roasters in Enmore, Sydney; Rojos Roastery in Palmer Square, New Jersey; Ultimo Coffee in Center City, Philadelphia; and the Kaffeehus in Göttingen warrant mention for their cheerful toleration during the final push. Likewise essential then were Frances Tanzer's Unsent Postcards. Finally, thanks go to the editors at Cambridge University Press, Michael Watson and Emily Sharp, who waited patiently for me to deliver the manuscript and indulged me over its unexpected length.

Between 2009 and 2010, this project was supported by the Australian Research Council (ARC) Discovery Project: DP098759 "Genocide: Critical History of an Idea" when I was working at the University of Sydney. Given the subsequent scandalous political inference in the ARC's decision-making processes by conservative federal ministers of education, it is uncertain whether it would be awarded today. The ARC is effectively the only game in town for Australian social scientists and humanities scholars, so its integrity must be guaranteed.

Parts of Chapter 5 appear in *Genocide: Key Themes*, ed. Donald Bloxham and A. Dirk Moses (Oxford: Oxford University Press, 2021). A version of Chapter 8 is published in *Decolonization, Self-Determination, and the Rise of Global Human Rights Politics*, ed. A. Dirk Moses, Marco Duranti, and Roland

Burke (Cambridge: Cambridge University Press, 2020). Chapter 9 draws on "Partitions, Hostages, Transfer: Retributive Violence and National Security," in *Partitions: A Transnational History of Twentieth-Century Territorial Separatism*, ed. Arie Dubnov and Laura Robson (Stanford: Stanford University Press, 2019).

~

Introduction

The Problems of Genocide

Genocide is a problem in two ways: not only the terrible fact of mass death, but also how the relatively new idea and law of genocide organizes and distorts our thinking about civilian (that is, noncombatant) destruction. Taking the normative perspective of civilian immunity from military attack that international law and norms ostensibly prioritize, this book argues that their implicit hierarchy, atop which sits genocide as the "crime of crimes," blinds us to other types of humanly caused civilian death, like bombing cities and the "collateral damage" of missile and drone strikes, blockades, and sanctions.[1] In other words, talk of genocide functions ideologically to detract attention from systematic violence against civilians perpetrated by governments, including Western ones. *The Problems of Genocide* also contends that this violence is the consequence of "permanent security" imperatives: the striving of states, and armed groups seeking to found states, to make themselves invulnerable to threats. Permanent security is the unobtainable goal of absolute safety that necessarily results in civilian casualties by its paranoid tendency to indiscriminate violence. To solve the problem of genocide concealing permanent security, this book proposes replacing the former with the latter: permanent security should be illegal.

Indiscriminate is aerial bombing, which is no trivial matter if protecting noncombatants is a "civilized" norm, as long claimed by Western states. The United States (US) dropped eight times more bomb tonnage in Indochina – over two million tons on Laos alone – in the Vietnam War than during World

---

[1] In her important genealogical analysis of the category of "civilian," Helen Kinsella shows that the distinction between combatant and noncombatant is neither natural nor stable, but its endurance as a normative category enables assessment of any state or para-state's actions. Helen M. Kinsella, *The Image before the Weapon: A Critical History of the Distinction between Combatant and Civilian* (Ithaca, NY: Cornell University Press, 2011). See also: Sahr Conway-Lanz, *Collateral Damage: Americans, Noncombatant Immunity, and Atrocity after World War II* (London and New York: Routledge, 2006); Nicola Foote and Nadya Williams, eds., *Civilians and Warfare in World History* (London and New York: Routledge, 2017).

War II, killing two to three million people, mainly civilians.[2] When Western publics recoiled in horror from the often-televised destructive scenes of this war, air forces moved to more accurate technologies, namely guided missiles. Even then, military strategists and lawyers acknowledge that the "collateral damage" of "surgical strikes" – which drone operators cynically call "bugs-plat" – is unavoidable, if regrettable.[3] It is no surprise, then, that US forces were responsible for almost half the civilian casualties in Afghanistan in 2019, dropping more ordnance on the country that year than in all previous ones, hoping to bomb the enemy to the negotiation table as they did in Vietnam in the early 1970s.[4] The weapons may have differed, but the tactics, strategy, and civilian destruction continues as before.

In the spirit of making careful distinctions, commentators insist that such civilian destruction cannot be compared to genocide because the purpose of the latter is to destroy peoples, whereas military action aims only to defeat enemies, even if killing some civilians in the process is inevitable.[5] To this objection, I respond thus: why privilege the intention of states and their armed forces? I dispute the "doctrine of double effect" that permits the killing of innocents as a side-effect of a moral end, like self defense.[6] What does it matter to civilians if they are killed by violence inflicted with genocidal or military intent? And what if global policing is intrinsic to national security policy, thereby entailing constant military action – the "infinity," "forever," "endless," or "permanent" wars in which some states are engaged?[7] Such wars are

---

[2] Marilyn B. Young, "Bombing Civilians: From the Twentieth- to the Twenty-First Centuries," in *Bombing Civilians A Twentieth-Century History*, ed. Yuki Tanaka and Marilyn B. Young (New York: Free Press, 2010), 157; John Tirman, *The Deaths of Others: The Fate of Civilians in America's Wars* (Oxford: Oxford University Press, 2011).

[3] Brian D. Laslie, *The Airforce Way of War: US Tactics and Training after Vietnam* (Lexington: University of Kentucky Press, 2016); Bruce Cronin, *Bugsplat: The Politics of Collateral Damage in Western Armed Conflict* (Oxford: Oxford University Press, 2018), and the forum on this book in the *Journal of Genocide Research* 21, no. 2 (2019): 263–98; Mark Grimsley and Clifford J. Rogers, eds., *Civilians in the Path of War* (Lincoln: University of Nebraska Press, 2002).

[4] Julian Borger, "US Dropped Record Number of Bombs on Afghanistan Last Year," *The Guardian*, January 28, 2020. Kaamil Ahmed, "'Zero Accountability': US Accused of Failure to Report Civilian Deaths in Africa," *The Guardian*, April 2, 2020.

[5] Symptomatic are Israel Charny, "Foreword," to Eric Markusen and David Kopf, *The Holocaust and Strategic Bombing: Genocide and Total War in the Twentieth Century* (Boulder, CO: Westview Press, 1995), and the reviews of this book by Malham M. Wakin in *Armed Forces and Society* 23, no. 2 (1996): 299–301, Joe Ross in *Air Power History* 43, no. 4 (1996): 60, and David Cesarani in *Studies in Contemporary Jewry* 14 (1998): 271–3.

[6] Alison McIntyre, "Doing Away with Double Effect," *Ethics* 111, no. 2 (2001): 219–55. Thanks to Knox Peden for discussion on this point.

[7] Sam Moyn and Stephen Wertheim, "The Infinity War," *Washington Post*, December 13, 2019; Danny Sjursen, "America's First 'Endless War' Was Fought in the Philippines," *The*

enabled by the use of drones and missiles, which shifts risk from armed personnel to enemy noncombatants, resulting in "repeated 'small massacres' of civilians."[8]

Drone and missile use have increased since late 2001 with the US's "Global War of Terror" in the Middle East and Asia, in which 801,000 people have died, of whom some 335,000 were civilians.[9] In its interventions there, the US also applies collateral damage considerations to nonarmed (nonwar) contexts, like Pakistan and Sudan, where the ban on extrajudicial killing should apply. Then, in cases of doubt, the US military presumes people are combatants rather than noncombatants, making them drone-strike targets.[10] In these circumstances, *the continuous killing of civilians becomes the norm rather than confined to occasional wars*: they are casualties of "mowing the grass," as Israeli security analysts call the "long-term strategy of attrition designed primarily to debilitate the enemy capabilities" in their "protracted intractable conflict" with Hamas. In practice, civilian casualties are routinely and cumulatively caused by this strategy. Some scholars say that "mowing the grass" has effectively become not only the "new Western way of war," but of modern warfare itself, as the Russian and Syrian bombing of targets in Syria also indicates.[11] This book argues that such practices are not so new: they are intrinsic to the global

Nation, December 18, 2019; Mark Danner, *Spiral: Trapped in the Forever War* (New York: Simon and Schuster, 2016); Mary L. Dudziak, *War Time: An Idea, Its History, Its Consequences* (Oxford: Oxford University Press, 2012); and Marilyn B. Young, "Permanent War Positions," *East Asia Cultures Critique* 13, no. 1 (2005): 177–94.

8 Martin Shaw, *War and Genocide* (Cambridge: Polity, 2003), 239.

9 Neta C. Crawford and Catherine Lutz, "Human Cost of Post-9/11 Wars," Costs of War project, Watson Institute of International and Public Affairs, Brown University, November 13, 2019, https://watson.brown.edu/costsofwar/files/cow/imce/papers/2019/Direct%20War%20Deaths%20COW%20Estimate%20November%2013%202019%20FINAL.pdf. 21 million Afghans, Iraqis, Pakistanis, and Syrians have been made refugees by the violence, https://watson.brown.edu/costsofwar/papers/summary.

10 Gabor Rona, "Much More Iceberg Below the Surface on Civilian Casualties," *Just Security*, May 15, 2018, www.justsecurity.org/56133/letter-editor-iceberg-surface-civilian-casualties/; Ryan Goodman, "Does the US 'Deliberately Misinterpret' the Laws of War? A Response to Gabor Rona," *Just Security*, May 15, 2018, www.justsecurity.org/56217/united-states-deliberately-misinterpret-laws-war-a-response-gabor-rona/; Mary L. Dudziak, "Death and the War Power," *Yale Journal of Law and the Humanities* 30, no. 1 (2018): 25–61; Rosa Brooks, *How Everything Became War and the Military Became Everything: Tales from the Pentagon* (New York: Simon and Schuster, 2019).

11 Efraim Inbar and Eitan Shamir, "Mowing the Grass in Gaza," *Jerusalem Post*, July 22, 2014; Daniel Byman, "Mowing the Grass and Taking Out the Trash," *Foreign Policy*, August 25, 2014; Michael Shkolnik, "'Mowing the Grass' and Operation Protective Edge: Israel's Strategy for Protracted Asymmetric Conflict with Hamas," *Canadian Foreign Policy Journal* 23, no. 2 (2017): 185–9; Shaw, *War and Genocide*.

settler colonial expansion of Europe and its state model since the late-fifteenth century.[12]

The principle of civilian immunity is the presumption of civilian innocence. Military thinkers and international lawyers have wrestled with the conundrum of observing that twentieth-century warfare was total, whether in enlisting entire populations in the two world wars or internal armed conflict like civil wars. Total warfare, they suggest, means that, say, factory workers and their families contribute to the war effort as much as soldiers on the front: they are not so innocent, and thus legitimate targets. To insist on the tidy distinction between combatants and civilians is outmoded, they conclude.[13] But, if civilians are not immune, they are presumed guilty by association with enemy combatants – including neutral humanitarian personnel providing medical assistance to designated terrorists, not to mention so-called human shields.[14] Then we verge on the mental world of genocide: entire peoples as enemies whose members are collectively guilty, or at least expendable.[15] Is it to conceal this murderous assumption in military strategy and international law that civilian destruction needs to be genocidal to "shock the conscience of mankind," to invoke the antiquated language of humanitarian declarations? And, furthermore, is that why such mass violence needs to resemble the Holocaust to be recognizable as genocide?

[12] Markus Gunneflo, *Targeted Killing: A Legal and Political History* (New York: Cambridge University Press, 2016) argues that Israeli targeted killing practices can be traced to Zionist paramilitary operations in the Mandate period and is paradigmatic of current US practices, but as Chapter 6 of this book elaborates such constitutive violence is intrinsic to settler colonialism and the permanent necessity of crushing resistance to the extractive logic of originary (primitive) accumulation in general. State protection cannot be counterposed to settler colonialism as Gunneflo argues (34).

[13] Alex J. Bellamy, *Massacres and Morality: Mass Atrocities in an Age of Civilian Immunity* (Oxford: Oxford University Press, 2012); Thomas Hippler, *Bombing the People: Giulio Douhet and the Foundations of Air-Power Strategy, 1884–1939* (Cambridge: Cambridge University Press, 2013); Julius Stone review of *International Law, A Treatise*, 2 Vols. *Disputes, War and Neutrality*, by Lassa Oppenheim, 7th ed. by Hersh Lauterpacht (London: Longmans, Green and Co., 1952), in the *Sydney Law Review* 17 (1954): 270–5.

[14] Dustin A. Lewis, Naz K. Modirzadeh, and Gabriella Blum, *Medical Care in Armed Conflict: International Humanitarian Law and State Responses to Terrorism*, Harvard Law School Program on International Law and Armed Conflict, Legal Briefing and Compendium, September 2015, https://pilac.law.harvard.edu/mcac-report//4-impartial-wartime-medical-care-concerning-terrorists-under-ihl-two-sets-of-key-protections.
Thanks to Boyd van Dijk for sharing this source. On human shields, see Neve Gordon and Nicola Perugini, *Human Shields: A History of People in the Line of Fire* (Berkeley: University of California Press, 2020).

[15] See the nuanced discussion in Charles S. Maier, "Targeting the City: Debates and Silences About the Aerial Bombing of World War II," *International Review of the Red Cross* 87, no. 859 (2005): 429–44.

These are some of the problems of genocide. But there are others. United Nations (UN)-related investigations adhere so strictly to international law's narrow definition of genocide that cases like Darfur in Sudan, which closely resemble the Armenian Genocide of 1915, are effectively downgraded to the less grave legal category of "crimes against humanity."[16] More recently, in June 2016, the Independent International Commission of Inquiry on Syria issued a report accusing *Daesh* ("Islamic State") of genocide against the Yazidi minority in Iraq and Syria.[17] Pursuant to a UN Human Rights Council mandate to investigate violations of international human rights law in Syria, the Commission had issued other reports critical of all civil war players, but only this one made headlines.[18] The genocide determination captured attention more because of its special status and rarity than to *Daesh*'s spectacular atrocities or lawyer Amal Clooney's offer to represent Yazidi survivors.[19]

As is so common in international relations, accusing geopolitical rivals of genocide is politically expedient.[20] Only when it appeared that the Assad regime might win the civil war with its Russia-supported siege of Aleppo in the second half of 2016 did Western liberal internationalists invoke

---

[16] "Sudan's Darfur Crimes Not Genocide, Says UN report," *The Guardian*, February 1, 2005. Report of the International Commission of Inquiry on Darfur to the United Nations Secretary-General, Pursuant to Security Council Resolution 1564 of September 18, 2004 (Geneva, January 25, 2005), 2; Kerstin von Lingen, *"Crimes against Humanity": Zur Ideengeschichte der Zivilisierung von Kriegsgewalt, 1864–1945* (Paderborn: Schoeningh, 2018).

[17] "They Came to Destroy": ISIS Crimes against the Yazidis," www.ohchr.org/Documents/ HRBodies/HRCouncil/CoISyria/A_HRC_32_CRP.2_en.pdf; "UN Commission of Inquiry on Syria: ISIS Is Committing Genocide against the Yazidis," June 16, 2016, www.ohchr.org/EN/NewsEvnts/Pages/DisplayNews.aspx?NewsID=20113&LangID=E.

[18] Independent International Commission of Inquiry on the Syrian Arab Republic, "About the Commission of Inquiry," www.ohchr.org/EN/HRBodies/HRC/IICISyria/Pages/ AboutCoI.aspx; Matt Brown, "Islamic State Militants Committing Genocide Against Yazidis in Syria, Iraq: UN Investigation," *ABC News*, June 17, 2016, www.abc.net.au/ news/2016-06-17/islamic-state-committing-genocide-against-yazidis-un/7518978; Fazil Moradi and Kjell Anderson, "The Islamic State's Êzîdî Genocide in Iraq: The Sinjâr Operations," *Genocide Studies and Prevention* 10, no. 2 (2017), https://doi.org/10.3138/ gsi.10.2.02; Adam Chandler, "How Meaningful Is the ISIS 'Genocide' Designation?" *The Atlantic*, March 19, 2016.

[19] "Amal Clooney 'Will Represent Yazidi Survivor and Isil Genocide Victims,'" *The Telegraph*, June 9, 2016. Updated information is provided by Vaeria Cetorelli et al, "Mortality and Kidnapping Estimates for the Yazidi Population in the Area of Mount Sinjar, Iraq, in August 2014: A Retrospective Household Survey," *PLOS Medicine*, May 9, 2017, http://journals.plos.org/plosmedicine/article?id=10.1371/journal.pmed.1002297.

[20] Another current example is Turkey's highlighting of the genocide of Herero and Nama people by Imperial German forces in 1904–1905 in retaliation for the German Parliament's recognition of the Armenian Genocide in 2016. See the comments from historian Jürgen Zimmerer, in "Historiker wirft Bundestag Doppelmoral vor," *Der Spiegel*, June 3, 2016.

"extermination" and the history of modern genocide. "Aleppo will join the ranks of those events in world history that define modern evil, that stain our conscience decades later," declared Samantha Power, the US ambassador to the UN, listing the sites synonymous with genocide: "Halabja, Rwanda, Srebrenica, and, now, Aleppo."[21] Until then, Western diplomats limited themselves to accusing the Syrian state of the still-less-sensationalist category of "war crimes" although it killed far more civilians than *Daesh*.[22]

Excusing allies is equally expedient. There was no rhetorical invocation of genocide, or even of international crimes, by Samantha Power and British diplomats when various agencies reported that the West's lucrative arms customer, Saudi Arabia, was killing thousands of civilians in its relentless bombing of Yemen, or that its blockade of the country's main port town condemned 85,000 children to death by starvation.[23] Nor did the Western

---

[21] Samantha Power, "Remarks at a UN Security Council Emergency Briefing on Syria," New York City, December 13, 2016, https://usun.state.gov/remarks/7607; Leon Wieseltier, "Aleppo's Fall is Obama's Failure," *Washington Post*, December 15, 2016; Martin Schram, "Genocide in Aleppo a Failure of Obama's Foreign Policy," *Australian Financial Review*, December 15, 2016. The journalist Patrick Cockburn called the comparison of Aleppo with Rwanda and Srebrenica a "gross exaggeration": Cockburn, "Who Supplies the News?" *London Review of Books*, February 2, 2017. Needless to say, the thousands of Syrian and Iraqi civilians killed by United States-led coalition airstrikes against *Daesh* positions and shelling of Mosul are not central parts of the international legal conversation about criminal transgressions despite the efforts of Amnesty International. Jared Maslin, "Civilian Casualties From American Airstrikes in the War Against ISIS Are at an All-Time High," *Time Magazine*, March 27, 2017, http://time.com/4713476/isis-syria-iraq-casualties-us-airstikes; Amnesty International, *At Any Cost: The Civilian Catastrophe in West* Mosul, Iraq, July 11, 2017, www.amnesty.org/en/latest/campaigns/2017/07/at-any-cost-civilian-catastrophe-in-west-mosul-iraq.

[22] David Blair, "Syria War Crimes Investigators Amass Strongest Evidence 'Since Nuremberg' Against Bashar al-Assad," *The Telegraph*, April 12, 2016. On civil society action to prosecute the Syrian state, see Melinda Rankin, "The Future of International Criminal Evidence in New Wars? The Evolution of the Commission for International Justice and Accountability (CIJA)," *Journal of Genocide Research* 20, no. 3 (2018): 392–411.

[23] Harriet Agerholm, "Boris Johnson says 'we do not think the threshold has been crossed' by Saudi Arabia's bombing of Yemen," *The Independent*, December 4, 2016; Bethan McKernan, "Yemen: Up to 85,000 Young Children Dead From Starvation," *The Guardian*, November 21, 2018. The British government resisted UN moves to investigate the Saudi bombing: Jeff Farrell, "UK Refuses to Back UN Inquiry into Saudi 'War Crimes' Amid Fears it Will Damage Trade," *The Independent*, September 28, 2017. A UN report issued in August 2018 criticizing all parties to the Yemen civil war, but especially Saudi bombing, did lead to a Pentagon warning that it might reduce aid should the Saudis not limit civilian casualties. See Barbara Star, "US warns Saudi Arabia it may withdraw support over civilian casualties in Yemen," *CNN*, August 27, 2018, https://edition.cnn.com/2018/08/27/politics/us-saudi-arabia-warning-yemen/index.html; and Report of the United Nations High Commissioner for Human Rights containing the findings of the Group of Independent Eminent International and Regional Experts and a summary of

envoys highlight the possibility that Syrian Shia civilians might be victims of *Daesh* genocide, an accusation that might benefit Syria and Iran.[24] Such is the genocide concept's stigmatic aura that states are reluctant to name conflicts as genocide if they are disinclined to intervene, if their clients are the perpetrators, if their enemies' clients are the victims, or if it is otherwise diplomatically inconvenient.[25]

This political problem is founded on a conceptual one: distinguishing genocide from noninternational armed conflict (civil war: rebellion, insurgency, and belligerency) and international armed conflict (interstate war).[26] Since its appearance in international law in the late 1940s, genocide has been conceived as a crime committed by one state or para-state's forces against another's civilians or against a hapless ethnic minority within its own borders. According to the UN Convention on the Punishment and Prevention of Genocide (1948), it is the "intent to destroy in whole or in part a national, ethnical, racial, or religious group as such."[27] That means political enemies like, say, communists, are not covered by the Convention, leading scholars to engage in contentious conceptual innovation to subsume political violence in the genocide category.[28]

technical assistance provided by the Office of the High Commissioner to the National Commission of Inquiry. A/HRC/39/43 (August 17, 2018), www.ohchr.org/EN/HRBodies/HRC/Pages/NewsDetail.aspx?NewsID=23479&LangID=E.

24 Walaa Chanine, "It's Time to Acknowledge Shi'ite Genocide," *Huffington Post*, April 18, 2017, www.huffingtonpost.com/entry/its-time-to-acknowledge-shiite-genocide_us_58f3deb6e4b0156697225082; Ranji Alaaldin, "The Isis Campaign against Iraq's Shia Muslims is not Politics: It's Genocide," *The Guardian*, January 6, 2017.

25 Gareth Evans, "Crimes against Humanity: Overcoming Indifference," *Journal of Genocide Research* 8, no. 3 (2006): 325–39; David Scheffer, "Defuse the Lexicon of Slaughter," *New York Times*, February 23, 2012; Robert Fisk, "It Was Bizarre to Watch Samantha Power at the UN Conveniently Forget to Mention all the Massacres Done in America's Name," *The Independent*, December 15, 2015. Advancing a case for genocide in Yemen is Jeffrey S. Bachman, "A 'Synchronised Attack' on Life: The Saudi-Led Coalition's 'Hidden and Holistic' Genocide in Yemen and the Shared Responsibility of the US and UK," *Third World Quarterly* 40 (2019): 1–19.

26 Robert McLaughlin, *Recognition of Belligerency and the Law of Armed Conflict* (Oxford: Oxford University Press, 2020).

27 Convention on the Punishment and Prevention of Genocide, Adopted by Resolution 260 (III) A of the United Nations General Assembly on December 9, 1948, www.hrweb.org/legal/genocide.html.

28 In Argentina, for example, the stretching of the genocide concept has gone so far as to include the leftist victims of the authoritarian military regime between 1974 and 1983. Based on the work of Argentine sociologist Daniel Feierstein, this approach is really analyzing the modalities of permanent security (discussed below). Instead of understanding the Holocaust in terms of security, as I do in this book, it assimilates the Argentine case to the Holocaust to lend it gravitas. See Daniel Feierstein, "Political Violence in Argentina and Its Genocidal Characteristics," *Journal of Genocide Research* 8, no. 2 (2006): 149–68. For analysis of this interpretation in Latin American schoolbooks, see

Although there are no legal barriers to identifying genocide within civil wars – in fact, genocidal violence is most likely during and immediately after civil wars[29] – political discourse commonly distinguishes between them because armed conflict suggests belligerent symmetry whereas genocide is imagined as asymmetrical violence against the civilian members of ethnic groups. Thus, the governments of Nigeria and Pakistan rejected the genocide claim leveled by Biafran and East Pakistan (Bangladesh) secessionist movements in the late 1960s and 1971 respectively, insisting that they were confronting internal rebellions that were no business of the international community. Most members of the UN agreed, despite widespread public support for the independence cause and acceptance that genocidal violence was taking place.[30]

Ulrike Capdepón, "La representación del Holocaustoen libros escolares de historia chilenos,españoles y argentinos:¿haciala inscripción de los Derechos Humanosen un marco universal?," in *La enseñanza del Holocausto en América Latin: Los desafíos para los educadores y leg isladores* (Paris: UNESCO, 2017), 174–83. On genocide of political groups, see Beth Van Schaak, "The Crime of Political Genocide: Repairing the Genocide Convention's Blind Spot," *Yale Law Journal* 106, no. 7 (1996): 2259–91; Andrei Gomez-Suarez, "Perpetrator Blocs, Genocidal Mentalities and Geographies: The Destruction of the Union Patriotica in Colombia and Its Lessons for Genocide Studies," *Journal of Genocide Research* 9, no. 4 (2007): 637–60; Robert Cribb, "Genocide in Indonesia, 1965–1966," *Journal of Genocide Research* 3, no. 2 (2001): 219–39; Robert Cribb, "Political Genocides in Postcolonial Asia," in *The Oxford Handbook of Genocide Studies*, ed. Donald Bloxham and A. Dirk Moses (Oxford: Oxford University Press, 2010), 445–66; David L. Nersessian, *Genocide and Political Groups* (Oxford: Oxford University Press, 2010); Annie Pohlman, "Incitement to Genocide against a Political Group: The Anti-Communist Killings in Indonesia," *Journal of Multidisciplinary International Studies* 11, no. 1 (2014): 1–22; Jess Melvin, *The Army and the Indonesian Genocide: Mechanics of Mass Murder* (London and New York: Routledge, 2018).

[29] Matthew Krain, "State-Sponsored Mass Murder: The Onset and Severity of Genocides and Politicides," *Journal of Conflict Resolution* 41, no. 3 (1997): 331–60; Holly Nyseth Brehm, "Re-Examining Risk Factors of Genocide," *Journal of Genocide Research* 19, no. 1 (2017): 61–87; Angela D. Nichols, "The Origins of Genocide in Civil War," *Trames* 22, no. 1 (2018): 89–101; Daniel Krcmaric, "Varieties of Civil War and Mass Killing: Reassessing the Relationship between Guerrilla Warfare and Civilian Victimization," *Journal of Peace Research* 55, no. 1 (2018): 18–31.

[30] A. Dirk Moses and Lasse Heerten, eds., *Postcolonial Conflict and the Question of Genocide: The Nigeria-Biafra War, 1967–1970* (Abingdon: Routledge, 2018); A Dirk Moses, "Civil War or Genocide? Britain and the Secession of East Pakistan in 1971," in *Civil Wars in South Asia: State, Sovereignty, Development*, ed. Aparna Sundar and Nandini Sundar (New Delhi: Sage India, 2014), 142–64. Political scientists who persist in distinguishing the logics of political and genocidal violence are Gary Uzonyi, "Civil War Victory and the Onset of Genocide and Politicide," *International Interactions* 41, no. 2 (2015): 365–91, and Gary Uzonyi and Victor Asai, "Discrimination, Genocide, and Politicide," *Political Research Quarterly* 73, no. 2 (2020): 352–65.

The distinction between genocide and political violence blinds us to civilian destruction in general and the circumstances that produce it.[31] To ensure that the Hutu killed by Hutu extremists are downgraded in status, the Rwandan government pushed through a UN resolution in 2018 that changed the title of the UN commemoration day from "International Day of Reflection on the 1994 Genocide in Rwanda" to "International Day of Reflection on the 1994 Genocide against the Tutsi in Rwanda." In doing so, the Rwandan government claims it is combatting negationist and revisionist arguments that suggest a symmetry of civil war violence (a "double genocide"). However understandable this motivation, noteworthy is how this presentation of the conflict tries to copy the common understanding of the Holocaust as a nonpolitical crime driven only by race hatred: Tutsis murdered solely for being Tutsis. By fixating on the genocidal features of the conflict in Rwanda and surrounding countries in 1994, the approach occludes the mass violence against Hutu civilians along with the broader civil war context in which all civilian destruction took place.[32]

Alternatively, state violence can be excused as legitimately political – that is, motivated by security concerns – rather than illegitimately ethnic in motivation. That is, by defining genocide in such narrow terms, governments can undertake drastic measures against population groups in the name of security, self-preservation, "military necessity," and opposing "terrorists." The Assad regime in Syria has been doing so for years, just as the Sudanese government attacked a section of its population in the Darfur region in 2005.[33]

---

[31] Sigall Horovitz, "Rwanda's Kabgayi Trial between International Justice and National Reconciliation," in *International Practices of Criminal Justice: Social and Legal Perspectives*, ed. Mikkel Jarle Christensen and Ron Levi (Abingdon and New York: Routledge, 2017), 228–50. Carrie Booth Walling's analysis of UN Security Council (UNSC) humanitarian debates underscores this point. The UNSC was inclined to vote for intervention when conflicts could be depicted as "intentional," meaning clear victims and perpetrators are identifiable. It was less likely to support intervention when conflicts were "inadvertent" and "complex," that is, they were "multifaceted, complicated, and tragic situations in which multiple and often fragmenting groups are responsible," in which case intervention was unlikely to be seen as efficacious. Carrie Booth Walling, *All Necessary Measures: The United Nations and Humanitarian Intervention* (Philadelphia: University of Pennsylvania Press, 2013), 23–6.

[32] Scott Straus, "The Limits of a Genocide Lens: Violence against Rwandans in the 1990s," *Journal of Genocide Research* 21, no. 4 (2019): 504–24; "General Assembly Designates 7 April International Day of Reflection on 1994 Genocide against Tutsi in Rwanda, Amending Title of Annual Observance," United Nations Meeting Coverage and Press Releases, January 28, 2018, www.un.org/press/en/2018/ga12000.doc.htm. The distorting attempt of victim groups leaders and intellectuals to cast their experiences in Holocaust-like terms is examined in Chapters 11 and 12.

[33] Yassin El-Haj Saleh, "State Extermination, Not a Dictatorial Regime," *Aljumhuriya*, June 18, 2018, www.aljumhuriya.net/en/content/state-extermination-not-%E2%80%9Cdictatorial-regime%E2%80%9D.

The prosecutor of the International Criminal Court (ICC) who issued an indictment against the Sudanese head of state, Omar al-Bashir, for genocide in 2008 denounced his counterinsurgency justification as an "alibi," effectively buying into the genocide-civil war distinction. On this ubiquitous logic, the government's policies could not be both genocidal and a counterinsurgency.[34] Consequently, in response to the accusation that the Myanmar is committing genocide by driving some 730,000 Rohingya into Bangladesh with wanton violence, its leaders denounce them as "Bengali terrorists" because of the Arakan Rohingya Salvation Army's attacks on 30 police stations. Based on a government-commissioned report into the violence, issued in January 2020, the state concluded no genocidal intent could be discerned: "The ICOE has not found any evidence suggesting that these killings or acts of displacement were committed pursuant to an intent or plan to destroy the Muslim or any other community in northern Rakhine State." On the contrary, the Rohingya had provoked the state into an "internal armed conflict."[35] Some Western commentators effectively agreed with the Myanmar state by insisting on the purity of the genocide concept – meaning its approximation to the Holocaust. It was wrong to pin the genocide label on the campaign against the Rohingya, declared the former *New York Times* journalist and foreign policy pundit, Stephen Kinzer: "Not all atrocities are genocide."[36] This was a civil war-like rather than genocidal conjuncture, these commentators imply.

The vexed relationship between the categories of genocide and civil war (or "non-international armed conflict," as Common Article 3 of the four Geneva Conventions refers to the latter) is an urgent problem given that the majority of post–World War II conflicts have been internal to states, and that civilians are now the majority of victims of armed conflict.[37] This conceptual problem

---

[34] International Criminal Court, "ICC Prosecutor Presents Case against Sudanese President, Hassan Ahmad AL BASHIR, for Genocide, Crimes against Humanity and War Crimes in Darfur," Press Release, July 14, 2008, www.icc-cpi.int/Pages/item.aspx?name=a.

[35] "Bangladesh FM: Violence against Rohingya 'Is Genocide,'" Al Jazeera, September 11, 2017, www.aljazeera.com/news/2017/09/bangladesh-fm-violence-rohingya-genocide-170911023429604.html. Michael Safi, "Myanmar Treatment of Rohingya Looks Like 'Textbook Ethnic Cleansing', says UN," *The Guardian*, September 12, 2017; Thu Thu Aung and Poppy McPherson, "Myanmar Government-Appointed Panel Finds 'War Crimes' but No 'Genocide' against Rohingya," *UK Reuters*, January 20, 2020, https://uk .reuters.com/article/uk-myanmar-rohingya-idUKKBN1ZJ105.

[36] Stephen Kinzer, "Not All Atrocities Are Genocide," *Boston Globe*, January 19, 2017. A balanced assessment of the situation is Ken Maclean, "The Rohingya Crisis and the Practices of Erasure," *Journal of Genocide Research* 21, no. 1 (2019): 83–95.

[37] International Committee of the Red Cross, "Non-International Armed Conflict," https:// casebook.icrc.org/glossary/non-international-armed-conflict; Scott Gates et al., "Trends in Armed Conflict, 1946–2014," *Conflict Trends* 1 (2016): www.prio.org/utility/ DownloadFile.ashx?id=15&type=publicationfile.

is particularly intractable in the "new wars" that emerged after the collapse of the Soviet Union. With their multiple, internal and external state and private actors, driven by predatory political economies of semiorganized criminality, these wars do not map onto the melodramatic binary of victims ("goodies") and perpetrators ("baddies") required by the genocide optic.[38] For this reason as well, the multidirectional violence in Congo that has resulted in over three million deaths and four and half million refugees is all but ignored by scholars of genocide.[39] Overall, patterns of civilian destruction since World War II resemble more the violence of imperial expansion and consolidation that has marked human relations for millennia.

Yet, international law since World War II takes genocide as the threshold of mass violence to be proscribed and prosecuted.[40] As a consequence, journalists feel compelled to make genocidal allusions to gain humanitarian attention for suffering of civilians in the bombings of besieged cities in the Middle East.[41] They do so because a narrow definition of genocide downgrades, if not screens out, more common and equally destructive human losses. Indeed, as I argue in these pages, the fetish of genocide as the "crime of crimes" effectively licences

Anthony Cullen, *The Concept of Non-International Armed Conflict in International Humanitarian Law* (Cambridge: Cambridge University Press, 2010); Max Roser, "War and Peace," *Our World in Data*, 2018, I.5 War and Peace after 1945, https://ourworldindata.org/war-and-peace#war-and-peace-after-1945; Human Security Report Project, *Human Security Report 2013* (Vancouver: Human Security Press, 2014); Andrew Barros and Martin Thomas, eds., *The Civilianization of War: The Changing Civil-Military Divide, 1914–2014* (Cambridge: Cambridge University Press, 2018); Christi Siver, *Military Interventions, War Crimes, and Protecting Civilians* (Basingstoke: Palgrave Macmillan, 2018).

[38] Mary Kaldor, *New and Old Wars: Organized Violence in a Global Era*, 3rd ed. (Cambridge: Polity, 2013); Christine Chinkin and Mary Kaldor, *International Law and New Wars* (Cambridge: Cambridge University Press, 2017); Michael Mann, "Have Wars and Violence Declined?" *Theory and Society* 47, no. 1 (2018): 37–60. That is why political scientists use the category of "mass violence": Joan Esteban, Massimo Morelli, and Dominic Rohner, "Strategic Mass Killings," *Journal of Political Economy* 123, no. 5 (2015): 1087–132.

[39] Council on Foreign Relations, "Violence in the Democratic Republic of Congo," Global Conflict Tracker, February 10, 2020, www.cfr.org/interactive/global-conflict-tracker/conflict/violence-democratic-republic-congo Jason Stearns, *Dancing in the Glory of Monsters: The Collapse of the Congo and the Great War of Africa* (New York: Public Affairs, 2011); Michela Wrong, *In the Footsteps of Mr. Kurtz: Living on the Brink of Disaster in Mobutu's Congo* (New York: Harper Collins, 2000).

[40] Michael Bazyler, *Holocaust, Genocide, and the Law: A Quest for Justice in a Post-Holocaust World* (Oxford: Oxford University Press, 2016).

[41] Simon Tisdall, "Eastern Ghouta Is Another Srebrenica, We Are Looking Away Again," *The Guardian*, February 20, 2018.

rather than proscribes many forms of mass violence against civilians.[42] Rare is the case of Myanmar in which the UN-sponsored International Fact Finding Mission could infer the necessary intent to destroy from the military chain of command; with its easily identifiable Rohingya victims, this case was legible as genocide or at least as ethnic cleansing despite government denials.[43]

Finally, the concept of genocide presumes the existence of identity-based groups as the building blocks of humanity that are targeted on the basis of this identity: by racial, ethnic, or religious hatred. In this categorization, populations comprise ethnic majorities and minorities as political facts. They are understood as political agents with ontological status rather than as the outcomes of complex processes of racialization. This presupposition of fixed identities flies in the face of the fact that people have multiple, layered identities. It also ignores the dynamic that, say, religious difference, only becomes a public, political identity in particular circumstances. When politics is imagined in sectarian terms, as ethnic struggle, we are inhabiting the mental world of genocide rather than thinking beyond it. Another problem of genocide, then, is its participation in the discursive construction of identity-based violence against civilians.[44]

Given these problems, I suggest in this book that the genocide concept should be replaced with the more general crime of "permanent security." To that end, we need to understand how our categories and imagination of mass criminality produced this moral hierarchy, the lamentable hair-splitting in discussions about civilian destruction, and the occlusion of permanent security: these problems of genocide.

---

[42] Rebecca Jinks, *Representing Genocide: The Holocaust as Paradigm?* (New York: Bloomsbury, 2016); David MacDonald, *Identity Politics in the Age of Genocide: The Holocaust and Historical Representation* (New York: Routledge, 2008), 4.

[43] International Fact-Finding Mission on Myanmar (August 27, 2018), A/HRC/39/CRP.2, www.ohchr.org/EN/HRBodies/HRC/MyanmarFFM/Pages/ReportoftheMyanmarFFM .aspx. See Chris Sidoti, "Personal Reflections on the Law of Genocide," *Journal of Genocide Research* 21, no. 2 (2019): 227–37. On January 23, 2020, in a suit filed by The Gambia, the International Court of Justice determined that it could take "provisional measures" before a determination of whether genocide had taken place. It required Myanmar to abide by the UN Genocide Convention by taking "all measures within its power to prevent the commission of all acts within the scope of Article II of the Convention": Application of the Convention on the Punishment and Prevention of the Crime of Genocide (The Gambia v Myanmar), www.icj-cij.org/files/case-related/178/178-20200123-ORD-01-00-EN.pdf.

[44] For a version of this argument in relation to Syria, see Yassin El-Haj Saleh, "The Dark Path of Minority Politics," The New Century Foundation, April 18, 2019, https://tcf.org/ content/report/dark-path-minority-politics. On racialization, see Michael Omi and Howard Winant, *Racial Formation in the United States: From the 1960s to the 1990s* (New York: Routledge, 1986); Robert Miles and Malcolm Brown, *Racism* (London: Routledge, 2003).

The Flawed Solution of Genocide

When, how, and why did these problems arise? In 1943, in the depths of World War II, the Polish-Jewish lawyer, Raphael Lemkin (1900–1959), invented a new concept for the destruction of human groups: genocide, a combination of *genos*, from the Greek word for race or tribe, with *cide*, the Latin for killing. This alien-sounding term hardly captured the imagination when it debuted a year later in his book, *Axis Rule in Occupied Europe*, a dense legal commentary on Nazi conquest.[45] Although working for the US government at the time, Lemkin was unable to convince the American delegation to the International Military Tribunal (IMT) in Nuremberg to take his neologism seriously. In prosecuting leading Nazis, the natural caution of lawyers predisposed them to prefer "war crimes," based on the Hague Conventions of 1899 and 1907. And, instead of using "genocide" to cover various crimes against civilians, they preferred "crimes against humanity," a notion that the Entente powers (Great Britain, France, and Russia) had leveled against the Ottoman Empire for its massacre of Armenians during World War I.[46]

The General Assembly of the UN, which first met in early 1946, was more amenable to Lemkin's energetic lobbying.[47] By then, awareness of Nazi criminality had been horrifically visualized in images of the liberated concentration camps.[48] At the end of the year, the Assembly passed a resolution calling for a new international law to outlaw genocide, declaring that "denial of the right of existence of entire human groups... shocks the conscience of mankind" and is condemned by the "civilized world." After UN committees thrashed out a

---

[45] Lemkin completed the book in late 1943 but it appeared a year later. Raphael Lemkin, *Axis Rule in Occupied Europe: Laws of Occupation – Analysis of Government – Proposals for Redress* (Washington, DC: Carnegie Endowment for International Peace, 1944). A new edition with an introduction by Samantha Power was published by the Law Book Company in 2008.

[46] See Chapter 5, and Alexa Stiller, "The Mass Murder of the European Jews and the Concept of 'Genocide' in the Nuremberg Trials: Reassessing Raphael Lemkin's Impact," *Genocide Studies and Prevention* 12, no. 1 (2019): 144–72.

[47] The most comprehensive and analytical treatment is Douglas Irvin-Erickson, *Raphaël Lemkin and the Concept of Genocide* (Philadelphia: University of Pennsylvania Press, 2016).

[48] Raymond Daniell, "War-Crimes Court Sees Horror Films," *New York Times*, November 30, 1945; Dan Stone, *The Liberation of the Camps: The End of the Holocaust and Its Aftermath* (New Haven: Yale University Press, 2015); Sharon Sliwinski, *Human Rights in Camera* (Chicago: University of Chicago Press, 2011), ch. 4; Toby Haggith, "The Filming of the Liberation of Bergen-Belsen and Its Impact on the Understanding of the Holocaust," *Holocaust Studies* 12, nos. 1–2 (2006): 89–122; Jeremy Hicks, *First Films of the Holocaust: Soviet Cinema and the Genocide of the Jews, 1938–1946* (Pittsburgh, PA: University of Pittsburgh Press, 2012).

formal definition, the same body approved the *Convention on the Prevention and Punishment of Genocide* on November 9, 1948.[49]

The publicity of the UN's deliberations and its blessing of the hybrid term immediately launched genocide as an ideological weapon to level accusations in the age of decolonization. All sides alleged genocide during the partition of India in 1947, and it featured four years later in the African-American Civil Rights Congress petition to the UN, "We Charge Genocide: The Crime of Government Against the Negro People."[50] Algerians held France guilty of genocide for its brutal repression of the national liberation struggle between 1954 and 1962, indeed for its massacre in Sétif in 1945.[51] Having gained sovereignty, some new African and Asian countries were wracked by secessionist conflicts in which the genocide accusation also featured, as noted above, in the Nigeria-Biafra war between 1967 and 1970, and in the conflict in East Pakistan in 1971.[52]

The Cold War also afforded opportunities for mutual accusation. American Jewish organizations alleged a Soviet "spiritual genocide" of Jews for its persecution and assimilation policies during the 1970s. Leaders of Baltic and Slavic peoples living in the West likewise accused the Soviet Union of genocide for suppressing their national culture and deporting or murdering their political and religious elites. In response, when the US raised the question of discrimination against Soviet Jews in the UN Human Rights Commission, the Soviet representative denounced its Cold War rival as a "racist Babylon" for

---

[49] General Assembly Resolution 91(1), "The Crime of Genocide," December 1, 1946, https:// documents-dds-ny.un.org/doc/RESOLUTION/GEN/NR0/033/47/IMG/NR003347.pdf? OpenElement; Matthew Lippman, "The Drafting and Development of the 1948 Convention on Genocide and the Politics of International Law," in *The Genocide Convention: The Legacy of 60 Years*, ed. Harmen van de Wilt et al. (Leiden: Brill, 2012), 15–25.

[50] On "We Charge Genocide," see Carol Anderson, *Eyes of the Prize: The United Nations and the African American Struggle for Human Rights, 1944–1955* (Cambridge: Cambridge University Press, 2003); Stephen Leonard Jacobs, "'We Charge Genocide': A Historical Petition All but Forgotten and Unknown," in *Understanding Atrocities: Remembering, Representing and Teaching Genocide*, ed. Scott W. Murray (Calgary: University of Calgary Press, 2017), 125–43.

[51] The accusation has not been dropped: "Algerian Minister: France Will Admit to Its Crimes in Algeria Sooner or Later," *Middle East Monitor*, April 24, 2014, www .middleeastmonitor.com/20150424-algerian-minister-france-will-admit-to-its-crimes-in-algeria-sooner-or-later. Turkey supports Algeria in this matter: "Turkey Accuses France of Genocide in Colonial Algeria," *BBC News*, November 23, 2011, www.bbc.co.uk/news/ world-europe-16314373.

[52] On East Pakistan, see the special issue of the *Journal of Genocide Research* 13, no. 4 (2012).

genocide against Native Americans, African Americans, and the Vietnamese.[53] The Soviet representative was likely referring to complaints by African American leaders that neglect of inner-city neighborhoods and attempts to stem supposedly high African American birth rates were tantamount to genocide.[54] Within decades, genocide had become a global keyword despite the UN's reluctance to use the term.[55]

After the Cold War, when Security Council consensus on genocide was less impossible to reach, the UN definition of genocide was adopted by the ad hoc international criminal tribunals for Rwanda in 1993 and the former Yugoslavia in 1994, founded to prosecute those suspected of committing mass crimes in those territories. The new International Criminal Court likewise incorporated the same formulation in its founding statute in 1998, half a century after the UN General Assembly passed the Genocide Convention.[56] The court crowns the international legal order's capacity to punish genocidal perpetrators, and is offered by many as the solution to what the Convention's preamble calls the "odious scourge" of genocide.[57]

Buttressing these legal developments and ubiquitous genocide rhetoric was the emergence of Holocaust memory after the Eichmann Trial in 1961, constituted by the widespread civilizational shock about Nazi crimes in general and its genocidal polices toward Jews in particular. This shock gave rise to a politics of recognition and entitlement indexed to group trauma, in which the Holocaust represents the maximal mass crime.[58] Although particularly prevalent in Western countries, this memory regime became a global

---

[53] The advertisement by Doubleday publishers for two books on antisemitism in the Soviet Union was headlined with "Spiritual Genocide – Soviet Outrage," *New York Times*, February 18, 1971, 26; Thomas J. Hamilton, "U.S., at U.N. Parley, Attacks Soviet Policy on Jews," *New York Times*, February 27, 1971, 3.

[54] Harry Schwartz, "The Fear That Birth Control May Mean 'Genocide,'" *New York Times*, May 2, 1971, E7; "Group Was Set Up to Protest Cuts: 'Black Coalition' Appeals to U.N. on Genocide," *New York Times*, May 6, 1971, 28; Robert D. McFadden, "State Leaders Invited to see 'Genocide' in Brownsville Area," *New York Times*, May 8, 1971, 59.

[55] Anton Weiss-Wendt, *A Rhetorical Crime: Genocide in the Geopolitical Discourse of the Cold War* (New Brunswick, NJ: Rutgers University Press, 2018).

[56] Rome Statute of the International Criminal Court, http://legal.un.org/icc/statute/99_corr/ preamble.htm.

[57] "BEING CONVINCED that, in order to liberate mankind from such an odious scourge, international co-operation is required," Convention for the Prevention and Punishment of the Crime of Genocide, December 9, 1948, third preambular paragraph, https://treaties .un.org/doc/publication/unts/volume%2078/volume-78-i-1021-english.pdf. William A. Schabas, "The 'Odious Scourge': Evolving Interpretations of the Crime of Genocide," *Genocide Studies and Prevention* 1, no. 2 (2006): 93–106; Adam Jones, ed., *The Scourge of Genocide: Essays and Reflections* (Abingdon: Routledge, 2013).

[58] Jeffrey C. Alexander, "On the Social Construction of Moral Universals: The 'Holocaust' From War Crime to Trauma Drama," *European Journal of Social Theory* 5, no. 1 (2002): 5–85; Jeffrey C. Alexander, *Remembering the Holocaust: A Debate* (Oxford: Oxford

phenomenon, indicated by the many references to the Holocaust in colonial and postcolonial conflicts since the 1950s.[59] The UN underlined this universality when, in 2005, it instituted an "International Day of Commemoration in Memory of the Victims of the Holocaust."[60] Not for nothing do scholars now talk about the "globalization" of Holocaust memory, even of "global Holocaust culture."[61] Together, these interlocked legal and memory regimes present widely believed "lessons of history": genocide, conceived as a race-hate crime distinct from civil war, must be prevented ("never again") by promoting ethnic and religious toleration and intervening in intolerant non-Western countries.[62]

Ethnicizing and Depoliticizing Genocide

This book disputes such supposed solutions and lessons. It questions the comforting story of moral and legal progress sketched out above that dominates academic and public understandings of mass criminality and international order. Neither does it subscribe to the heroic narrative of Lemkin's "struggle for the Genocide Convention."[63] Unlike these accounts of the genocide concept and associated jurisprudence, which suppose they are gradually taming Leviathan, I argue that the Genocide Convention at once preserved "military

---

University Press, 2009); Martin Shaw, *What Is Genocide?* (Cambridge: Polity Press, 2007), 44–45.

[59] Michael Rothberg, *Multidirectional Memory: Remembering the Holocaust in the Age of Decolonization* (Stanford: Stanford University Press, 2009); Berthold Molden, "Vietnam, the New Left and the Holocaust: How the Cold War Changed Discourse on Genocide," in *Memory in a Global Age: Discourses, Practices, and Trajectories*, ed. Aleida Assmann and Sebastian Conrad (Basingstoke and New York: Palgrave Macmillan, 2010), 79–96; Emma Kuby, *Political Survivors: The Resistance, the Cold War, and the Fight against Concentration Camps after 1945* (Ithaca, NY: Cornell University Press, 2019).

[60] The Holocaust and the United Nations Outreach Programme, www.un.org/en/holocaustremembrance.

[61] Daniel Levy and Natan Sznaider, *The Holocaust and Memory in the Global Age* (Philadelphia: Temple University Press, 2005); Claudio Fogu, Wulf Kansteiner, and Todd Presner, eds., *Probing the Ethics of Holocaust Culture* (Cambridge, MA: Harvard University Press, 2016). Critical of the Levy-Sznaider argument are contributors to Amos Goldberg and Haim Hazan, eds., *Marking Evil: Holocaust Memory in the Global Age* (New York and Oxford: Berghahn Books, 2015).

[62] Symptomatic: Irwin Cotler, "The Lessons of Nuremberg: Stand up to Hate, and Remember Hate's Victims," *Edmonton Jewish News*, September 25, 2015.

[63] Samantha Power, *"A Problem from Hell": America and the Age of Genocide* (New York: Basic Books, 2002); William Korey, *An Epitaph for Raphael Lemkin* (New York: Blaustein Institute for the Advancement of Human Rights, 2002); John Cooper, *Raphael Lemkin and the Struggle for the Genocide Convention* (Basingstoke: Palgrave Macmillan, 2008); Philippe Sands, *East West Street: On the Origins of "Genocide" and "Crimes against Humanity"* (London: Weidenfeld & Nicolson, 2016).

necessity" in the conduct of warfare and the ability of states to suppress domestic opposition. Contrary to the proclaimed historical lessons about ubiquitous, deadly identity-based violence, a broader view of civilian destruction indicates that declarations of national emergencies and proclamations of security threats are its driver. Yet, politically motivated violence does not "shock the conscience of mankind."

This outcome was not implicit in Lemkin's claim that civilian immunity was his basic premise. He began his justification of the genocide concept in promising terms when he declared that the distinction between civilians and combatants was elemental to the crime. Genocide was:

> the antithesis of the Rousseau-Portalis Doctrine, which may be regarded as implicit in the Hague Regulations. This doctrine holds that war is directed against sovereigns and armies, not against subjects and civilians. In its modern application in civilized society, the doctrine means that war is conducted against states and armed forces and not against populations.[64]

Here Lemkin declared that criminality was defined as warfare waged against populations rather than armies: today, customary international humanitarian law refers to the "principle of distinction" (or discrimination). Indeed, Westerners have long declared that their mode of warfare was "civilized" and "humanitarian" because of this distinction.[65] But then he, and the UN, specified genocide as a *national, ethnic, racial, and religious* crime, excluding other categories of civilians. The Convention thus defines genocide as the "intent to destroy, in whole or in part, a national, ethnical, racial or religious group" by a variety of means affecting their physical-biological existence.

Although UN delegates did not use the term "Holocaust," they were acutely conscious of the Nazis' extermination policies against Jews, and defined genocide to capture their extremity and, above all, racial focus and ideological motivation. Leaders of "smaller" European nations subject to Nazi occupation also regarded German policies as an attack on their nationality. Using this imagery of ultimate criminality, genocide was depoliticized by being defined as murderous attacks on people solely on the basis of their hated group membership: merely for who they are. This definition ensured that a state could avoid committing genocide by claiming to act for political-strategic purposes. As a consequence, we think more about the victims of genocide during World War II

---

[64] Lemkin, *Axis Rule in Occupied Europe*, 80. On civilian immunity, see Igor Primoratz, ed., *Civilian Immunity in War* (Oxford: Oxford University Press, 2010).

[65] International Committee of the Red Cross, "Rule 1. The parties to the conflict must at all times distinguish between civilians and combatants. Attacks may only be directed against combatants. Attacks must not be directed against civilians." Customary IHL, "Rule 1. The Principle of Distinction between Civilians and Combatants," https://ihl-databases.icrc.org/customary-ihl/eng/docs/v1_cha_chapter1_rule1.

than the overall civilian casualties – a staggering 30 million. While the targeting of nationalities "as such" accounts for much of this number, they were as much victims of all powers' "strategies of annihilation," namely of permanent security, a point I elaborate below.[66]

What is more, Lemkin and his supporters ignored the international debate since the 1920s about the efficacy of a new technology with terrifying potential: aerial warfare. The strategic bombing of civilian populations was intended to destroy enemy industrial capacity and morale, meaning that the enemy was conceptualized as a national whole, thereby eliding the distinction between civilians and combatants. He likewise passed over the similarly intensive and significant debate in the League of Nations about wartime blockades of countries that led to mass starvation, as in Germany and Lebanon during World War I.[67] Instead of following his premise about the Rousseau-Portalis Doctrine (civilian immunity) in the face of epochal changes in the relationship between warfare and civilians, Lemkin fixated on ethnic or national groups as victims of massive hate crimes. Consequently, he did not develop a framework that also included the targeting of entire peoples as military objectives in armed conflict. As we see in Chapter 3, his imaginary of humanity as an ensemble of peoples with unique national "spirits" was a product of his Zionism, itself a version of "small nations" consciousness and its intense attachment to vulnerable cultural identity. We have adopted this ethnic-national human ontology and made it the barely acknowledged basis of the hierarchy of criminality. This adoption is one of the problems of genocide.

Genocide as a Hate Crime

The ethnic definition of genocide is compounded by its conceptualization as an irrational hate crime: innocent, blameless victims are attacked for racial rather than for political reasons – for who they are, not for what they (or members of the group) have done. Primordial antipathy or ideologically driven racism, instead of rational political considerations, are supposed to motivate the perpetrator. In law and popular culture, genocide is a crime against identity. This understanding of genocide is indexed to its archetype, the Holocaust. If the Holocaust is unique, as often asserted, it is because

---

[66] Thomas Zeiler, *Annihilation: A Global History* (Oxford: Oxford University Press, 2014); Norman Davies, *Europe: A History* (New York: Oxford University Press, 1996). For a study about the politics of victimhood in modern warfare, see Svenja Goltermann, *Die Wahrnehmung von Krieg und Gewalt in der Moderne* (Frankfurt am Main: S. Fischer, 2017).

[67] Nicholas Mulder and Boyd van Dijk, "Why Did Starvation Not Become the Paradigmatic War Crime in International Law?" in *Contingency and the Course of International Law*, ed. Kevin Jon Heller and Ingo Venzke (Oxford: Oxford University Press, 2021).

European Jews were not engaged in an uprising against Nazi rule; their agency consisted variously in escaping, resisting, surviving, and retaining dignity in the attempt to exterminate them. They were politically innocent, heightening the evil of their persecution: they did not provoke it. They were murdered out of pure hate.

No state or para-state admits a hateful motivation, of course. Instead, they claim that they kill and deport opponents who are threatening and dangerous – for defensive, political reasons. Even the Nazis did so. Security and racial animus intersect, as I demonstrate in this book. This misleading binary thus distinguishes between genocide and armed conflict in the following way: whereas genocide is understood as asymmetrical warfare against a passive ethnic group or people who are thus deemed to be innocent, civil war and insurgency are armed conflicts in which all parties possess agency and are thus not entirely blameless for violence that befalls them. In doing so, this distinction effectively criminalizes entire groups, although the vast majority of its members will be noncombatants. What is more, in reality, as I elaborate below, security and hatred accompany one another. Unfortunately, this specious distinction causes scholars and activists to pose misleading questions: are deportations and killings acts of "military necessity," or is state security merely an "excuse for genocide"?[68] Instead, one might ask whether military necessity and state security imperatives lie at the heart of state transgressions.

The "Crime of Crimes"

Politically rather than racially defined victims are effectively assigned a lower status in the hierarchy of criminality. International law and popular culture regard genocide – and its archetype, the Holocaust – as the ultimate violation. The result is not only to trivialize war crimes and crimes against humanity, but also to exclude the aerial bombing of civilians, which likewise violates the principle of distinction, and is often deadlier. Few recall that the US relentlessly bombed North Korean cities and transport infrastructure during the war on the Korean peninsula between 1950 and 1953, killing over 20 percent of the population, leading one authority to characterize the campaign as genocidal.[69]

---

[68] Edward J. Erickson, "The Armenian Relocations and Ottoman National Security: Military Necessity or Excuse for Genocide?" *Middle East Critique* 20, no. 3 (2011): 291–8. An analysis that questions this distinction is Douglas Irvin-Erickson, "Genocide Discourses: American and Russian Strategic Narratives of Conflict in Iraq and Ukraine," *Politics and Governance* 5, no. 3 (2017): 130–45.

[69] Bruce Cumings, *The Korean War: A History* (New York: Random Hose, 2010), 161, 172; Alexander Downes, "Creating a *Cordon Sanitaire*: US Strategic Bombing and Civilians in Korea," in *The Civilization of War and the Unpredictable Civil-Military Divide, 1914–2014*, ed. Andrew Barros and Martin Thomas (Cambridge: Cambridge University Press, 2018), 196–220; Sahr Conway-Linz, "Bombing Civilians after World War II: The

The Holocaust exercised a profound effect in establishing this hierarchy, superseding another diplomatic vocabulary. Two days after the UN General Assembly voted for the famous genocide resolution in December 1946, it passed another affirming the principles of the IMT in Nuremberg, thereby approving its core indictment, crimes against peace.[70] Also called the crime of aggression, it was the superordinate violation of international law beneath which lay war crimes and crimes against humanity. Justice Robert Jackson declared it the core of the case, the "crime which comprehends all lesser crimes," indeed "the supreme international crime differing only from other war crimes in that it contains within itself the accumulated evil of the whole."[71] If there was a crime of crimes in the mid-1940s, it was the crime of aggression.[72]

But not for long. The Cold War and unwillingness of states to relinquish the right of anticipatory self-defense hamstrung international agreement about a definition of aggression until 2010.[73] What is more, the discovery of incriminating Nazi documentation led to 12 successor trials of Nazi *Einsatzgruppen* officers, military planners, and doctors (among others) conducted by the US military (the Nuremberg Military Tribunal) between 1946 and 1949, at which crimes against humanity were less dependent on the nexus with aggressive warfare than at the IMT. Consequently, the prosecutors focused more on various mass crimes against civilians – extermination, genocide, and other crimes against humanity, inaugurating what Lawrence Douglas calls the "atrocity paradigm" in international criminal law. Henceforth, civilian destruction due to Nazi-like racial hatred rather than interstate aggression

---

Persistence of Norms against Targeting Civilians in the Korean War," in *The American Way of Bombing: Changing Ethical and Legal Norms, from Flying Fortresses to Drones*, ed. Matthew Evangelista and Henry Shue (Ithaca, NY: Cornell University Press, 2014), 47–63.

[70] Antonio Cassese, "On Some Problematical Aspects of the Crime of Aggression," *Leiden Journal of International Law* 20 (2007): 842.

[71] Kirsten Sellars, *"Crimes against Peace" and International Law* (Cambridge: Cambridge University Press, 2013), 114–5; Franz B. Schick, "Crimes against Peace," *Journal of Criminal Law and Criminology* 38, no. 5 (1948): 447.

[72] R. W. Cooper, *The Nuremberg Trial* (Harmondsworth and New York: Penguin, 1947), 293–300; Jonathan A. Bush, "'The Supreme... Crime' and Its Origins: The Lost Legislative *History* of the *Crime* of Aggressive War," *Columbia Law Review* 102, no. 8 (2002): 2324–424.

[73] Mauro Politi, "The ICC and the Crime of Aggression: A Dream that Came through and the Reality Ahead," *Journal of International Criminal Justice* 10, no. 1 (2012): 267–88; Carrie McDougall, *The Crime of Aggression under the Rome Statute of the International Criminal Court* (Cambridge: Cambridge University Press, 2013); Noah Weisbrod, *The Crime of Aggression: The Quest for Justice in an Age of Drones, Cyberattacks, Insurgents, and Autocrats* (Princeton: Princeton University Press, 2019).

captured the judicial and popular imaginations.[74] Such is the Holocaust's hold on our imagination that the ICC prosecutor of Sudanese leader al-Bashir felt compelled to invoke Holocaust analogies in making the case for genocide. "These 2.5 million people are in camps. They [Sudanese authorities] don't need gas chambers because the desert will kill them." In the camps, internal refugees live "under genocide conditions, like a gigantic Auschwitz."[75]

As I show in the first two chapters, public concern about atrocities was in fact well developed before World War II. Scandals about oppression and exploitation in European conquest and colonial rule punctuated metropolitan life. However, unlike the post-Holocaust era to which Douglas refers, contemporaries recognized that civilian destruction occurred for practical-political reasons of suppressing anticolonial rebellions or in vicious systems of labor extraction rather than for nonpolitical reasons of racial or religious hatred. The postwar depoliticization of atrocity occurred with the breakthrough of genocide in this paradigm. It can be traced to the opening address of the *Einsatzgruppen* trial by the young prosecutor, Benjamin Ferencz (b. 1920). He had read the damning cables of *Einsatzgruppen* officers detailing their body counts, and then convinced senior US officials to prosecute them. He also studied Raphael Lemkin's book, *Axis Rule*, after the latter thrust it in his hand while stalking the halls to importune anyone who might utilize his neologism.[76] Ferencz told the court that "the killing of defenseless civilians during a war may be a war crime, but the same killings are part of another crime. A graver one, if you will – genocide, or a crime against humanity."[77] Although he named genocide as a species of crime against humanity, his hierarchy was clear: genocide was the worst crime. The Nuremberg judges ultimately imprisoned Nazis convicted of crimes against peace, whereas those guilty of crimes against humanity were executed; at this moment, genocide was not one

---

[74] Lawrence Douglas, "Crime of Atrocity, the Problem of Punishment and the *Situ* of Law," in *Propaganda, War Crimes Trials and International Law: From Speakers' Corner to War Crimes*, ed. Predrag Dojcinovic (Abingdon and New York: Routledge, 2012), 272. This term also features in the work of the philosopher Claudia Card, *The Atrocity Paradigm: A Theory of Evil* (Oxford: Oxford University Press, 2002), which defines atrocity more broadly.

[75] Peter Walker and James Sturcke, "Darfur Genocide Charges for Sudanese President Omar al-Bashir," *The Guardian*, July 14, 2008; "Omar al-Bashir Charged with Darfur Genocide," *The Guardian*, July 13, 2010.

[76] Benjamin B. Ferencz, "Origins of the Genocide Convention," *Case Western Reserve Journal of International Law* 40, nos. 1–2 (2008): 27; Hilary Earl, *The Nuremberg SS-Einsatzgruppen Trial, 1945–1958: Atrocity, Law and History* (Cambridge: Cambridge University Press, 2009); Michael J. Bazyler and Frank M. Tuerkheimer, *Forgotten Trials of the Holocaust* (New York and London: New York University Press, 2014), ch. 6.

[77] Douglas, "Crime of Atrocity," 273; Roger S. Clark, "Nuremberg and the Crime against Peace," *Washington University Global Studies Law Review* 6 (2007): 527–50.

of the indictments and was mentioned as the most extreme crime against humanity.[78]

Ever since, genocide has come to enjoy the status as the "crime of crimes" in the developing atrocity paradigm.[79] The District Court of Jerusalem hearing the trial of Adolf Eichmann in 1961 followed Ferencz's reasoning. "It is hardly necessary to add that the 'crime against the Jewish people,' which constitutes the crime of 'genocide,'" it declared, "is nothing but the gravest type of 'crime against humanity.'"[80] *The Economist* magazine called genocide the "ultimate crime," echoing a UN report from 1985 that pronounced it "the gravest violation of human rights it is possible to commit."[81] This conventional wisdom is repeated by lawyers, diplomats, and politicians: "Genocide is a crime on a different scale to all other crimes against humanity and implies an intention to completely exterminate the chosen group," averred the Belgian former secretary general of *Médecins Sans Frontières*, Alain Destexhe, in the wake of the Rwandan genocide.[82] Before him, in 1994, the Rwandan representative to the UN Security Council referred to genocide as the "crime of crimes," as did trial chambers of the International Criminal Tribunals for the former Yugoslavia and Rwanda. "The crime of genocide is unique," said the judges in Arusha, Tanzania, where the latter tribunal deliberated, "because of its element of *dolus specialis* (special intent) which requires that the crime be committed with the intent 'to destroy in whole or in part, a national, ethnic, racial or religious group as such.'" Consequently, they continued, "genocide constitutes the crime of crimes, which must be taken into account when deciding the sentence."[83] While the Appeals Chamber rejected such a

---

[78] William A. Schabas, *War Crimes and Human Rights: Essays on the Death Penalty, Justice and Accountability* (London: Cameron May, 2008), 864.

[79] William A. Schabas, *Genocide in International Law: The Crime of Crimes*, 2nd ed. (Cambridge: Cambridge University Press, 2009); Janine Natalya Clark, "The 'Crime of Crimes': Genocide, Criminal trials and Reconciliation," *Journal of Genocide Research* 14, no. 1 (2012): 55–77; Bazyler, *Holocaust, Genocide, and the Law*; Nicole Rafter, *The Crime of All Crimes: Towards a Criminology of Genocide* (New York and London: New York University Press, 2016).

[80] The Attorney-General of the Government of Israel v. Eichmann, *American Journal of International Law* 56, no. 3 (1962): 821.

[81] "The Uses and Abuses of the G-word: Genocide Is the Ultimate Crime," *The Economist*, June 2, 2011; Benjamin Whitaker, Revised and Updated Report on the Question of the Prevention and Punishment of the Crime of Genocide, Sub-Commission on Prevention of Discrimination and Protection of Minorities, UN Doc. E/CN.4/Sub.2/1985/6, para. 14.

[82] Alain Destexhe, *Rwanda and Genocide in the Twentieth Century* (London: Pluto Press, 1995), 4.

[83] Manzi Bakuramutsa, UN Doc. S/PV.3453 (November 8, 1994), 15; Prosecutor v. Kambanda, Case No. ICTR-97-23-A, 1998, para. 16; Claus Kreß, "The International Court of Justice and the Elements of the Crime of Genocide," *European Journal of International Law* 18 no. 4 (2007): 621.

hierarchy, it agreed that "genocide in itself is a crime that is extremely grave."[84] The Rome Statute of the International Criminal Court, for its part, does not stipulate the sentencing provisions but disqualified the defense of superior orders available for those accused of genocide and crimes against humanity, though not war crimes.[85]

The strictly legal consensus, then, tends to place genocide and crimes against humanity on the same plane. Even so, UN officials still suggest that racial-civilian destruction is worse than political-civilian destruction. Of *Daesh*'s actions, the UN Secretary-General's Representative for Iraq told the Security Council in May 2016 that they may "constitute crimes against humanity, war crimes and *even* genocide."[86] Speaking of the campaign against Rohingya in Myanmar, the UN special advisor for the prevention of genocide, Adama Dieng, likewise reiterated the consensus that murder and forcible transferal of people "in a widespread or systematic manner" could constitute ethnic cleansing and crimes against humanity, which "can be the precursor to all the egregious crimes – and I mean genocide."[87] Crimes motivated by ethnic or racial rather than political consideration were the most serious, he was saying, although why identity-based civilian destruction is worse than others is never explained. The media reporting of Bosnian Serb leader Radovan Karadžić's prosecution in The Hague fixated on the genocide verdict, although he was found guilty on more counts of war crimes and crimes against humanity.[88]

This status is buttressed by other legal traditions. The venerable phrase of the UN Genocide Convention, "shocking the conscience of mankind," has long been a synonym for moral turpitude in Anglo-Saxon jurisprudence,

---

[84] International Criminal Tribunal for Rwanda, Appeal Chamber. The Prosecutor vs. Clément Kayishema and Obed Ruzindana, Case No. Case No. ICTR-95-1 (June 1, 2001), http://unictr.unmict.org/sites/unictr.org/files/case-documents/ictr-95-1/appeals-chamber-judgements/en/010601.pdf.

[85] Article 33 of the Statute of the International Criminal Court. For discussion on this point, see Paola Gaeta, "The Defence of Superior Orders: The Statute of the International Criminal Court versus Customary International Law," *European Journal of International Law* 10 (1999): 172–91, and William A. Schabas, "Penalties," in *The Rome Statute of the International Criminal Court*, Vol. 2, *International Criminal Proceedings*, ed. Antonio Cassese, Paola Gaeta, and John R.W.D. Jones (Oxford: Oxford University Press, 2002), 1497–534.

[86] "Political Impasse Adds 'New Layer of Complications' to Iraq's Complex Challenges – UN Envoy," UN News Center, May 6, 2016, www.un.org/apps/news/printnews.asp?nid=53874. Emphasis added.

[87] Liam Cochraine, "Myanmar Could Be on the Brink of Genocide, UN Expert Says," *ABC News*, September 6, 2017, www.abc.net.au/news/2017-09-06/myanmar-on-brink-of-genocide-un-expert-say/8879858.

[88] Julian Borger and Owen Bowcott, "Radovan Karadžić Sentenced to 40 years for Srebrenica Genocide," *The Guardian*, March 25, 2016.

denoting acts that are "inherently base, vile, or depraved, and contrary to the accepted rules of morality and the duties owed between persons or to society in general." Samantha Power made use of it in the UN Security Council in identifying violations that "stain our conscience decades later." International law refers to such norms as "peremptory," meaning crimes universally condemned that are thus binding and nonderogatable (*jus cogens*: "binding law"), namely genocide, aggression, slavery, piracy, and torture.[89]

Genocide stands at the top of this list by virtue of its "special intent" (*dolus specialis*) requirement that effectively incorporates the antique notion of "malice aforethought." This is the specific intention (*mens rea*) of premeditation required in some common law jurisdictions for aggravated forms of murder ("in the first degree"). Aggravated offences are more serious than basic versions of a crime by distinguishing features like the attributes of the perpetrator (when in a position of trust), the victim (when particularly vulnerable), the mode of perpetration (use of weapons and infliction of injury), and motivation (to benefit a criminal enterprise). This special intent is also analogous to the "grave" or "serious" breaches provisions of the Geneva Conventions and their Additional Protocols, which proscribe specified acts that are committed "wilfully" and "wantonly."[90]

Many scholars echo these views. According to a prominent legal academic, genocide is "the worst crime of all, and the crime whose very name was coined to describe the systematic murder of 6 million Jews," while a political scientist declared that "No crime matches genocide in the moral opprobrium that it generates."[91] Challenging this status, international lawyer Payam Akhavan doubts that transgressions with apparently ineffable, even mysterious, qualities

---

[89] The Vienna Convention on the Law of Treaties (1969), Article 53. Miles Jackson, *Complicity in International Law* (Oxford: Oxford University Press, 2015), 173. As we see in Chapter 3, Lemkin referred to this normative standard in proposing "barbarism" and "vandalism" as international crimes.

[90] Nate Carter, "*Shocking the Conscience* of Mankind: Using International Law to Define 'Crimes Involving Moral Turpitude' in Immigration Law," *Lewis and Clark Law Review* 10, no. 4 (2006): 959; International Committee of the Red Cross, "How 'Grave Breaches' are Defined in the Geneva Conventions and Additional Protocols," June 4, 2004, www.icrc.org/eng/resources/documents/faq/5zmgf9.htm; Marko Divac Öberg, "The Absorption of Grave Breaches into War Crimes Law," *International Review of the Red Cross* 91 (March 2009): 163–83; Louis Blom-Cooper and Terence Morris, *With Malice Aforethought: A Study of the Crime and Punishment for Homicide* (Oxford and Portland: Hart Publishing, 2004).

[91] Alan Dershowitz, "Black Lives Matter Must Rescind Anti-Israel Declaration," *Boston Globe*, August 12, 2016; George J. Andreopoulos, "The Calculus of Genocide," in *Genocide: Conceptual and Historical Dimensions*, ed. George J. Andreopoulos (Philadelphia: University of Pennsylvania Press, 1997), 1.

can be captured by a rational and rigid legal definition with slogan-like appeal.[92] But, even on this reading, genocide possesses special status as a negative sublime. This outcome would have pleased Lemkin who, in his tussle with the rival notions of human rights and crimes against humanity in the late 1940s, insisted that genocide is the "most heinous of all crimes. It is the crime of crimes."[93] Now, 70 years later, this notion is the conventional wisdom and the central pillar of contemporary politics. Almost without fail, those claiming to speak for an ethnic or national group invoke genocide to draw attention to apparent persecution, expulsion, and destruction.[94] Genocide captures public attention in a way that war crimes or crimes against humanity do not. Clearly, the deliberate destruction of a people is a terrible crime; but why is it worse than the foreseeable destruction of many people?

As a consequence of genocide's depoliticization by ethnicization and hier-archization, it is convenient for actors to demarcate genocide from civil war and insurgency, as well as from warfare proper.[95] However problematic the distinction between ethnic and political violence, Article 2 of the UN Charter forbids intervention in noninternational armed conflicts unless they threaten peace (Chapter VII of the UN Charter), meaning that international interdic-tion of the mass killing of foreign civilians is illegal in most circumstances. As before the so-called human rights revolution in the late 1940s, states can violently repress their own civilians during proclaimed national emergencies.[96] They can also legally kill the civilians of other states using the cover of military necessity, proportionality, and collateral damage. According to the Yemen Data Project, 48 percent of recorded airstrikes in Yemen hit nonmilitary targets, Saudi missiles have killed more than 9,000 there in just two years, more than 5,000 Iraqi civilians have died in Russian and Coalition air strikes, over 2,000 Gazan civilians perished from Israeli ordnance in three operations since 2008, while the number of civilians killed by indiscriminate government

---

[92] Payam Akhaven, *Reducing Genocide to Law: Definition, Meaning, and the Ultimate Crime* (Cambridge: Cambridge University Press, 2012).

[93] Raphael Lemkin, "Genocide as Crime Under International Law," *United Nations Bulletin*, no. 4 (January 15, 1948): 70.

[94] Oliver Walton, "Framing Disputes and Organizational Legitimation: UK-Based Sri Lankan Tamil Diaspora Groups' Use of the 'Genocide' Frame since 2009," *Ethnic and Racial Studies* 38, no. 6 (2014): 959–75; Christian Axboe Nielsen, "Surmounting the Myopic Focus on Genocide: The Case of the War in Bosnia and Herzegovina," *Journal of Genocide Research* 15, no. 1 (2015): 21–39. The temptation affects human rights workers as well, as Alex De Waal lays out superbly in "Writing Human Rights and Getting it Wrong," *Boston Review*, June 6, 2016, http://bostonreview.net/world/alex-de-waal-writing-human-rights.

[95] On the history of the concept of civil war, see David Armitage, *Civil Wars: History in Ideas* (Cambridge, MA: Harvard University Press, 2017).

[96] Sandesh Sivakumaran, *The Law of Non-International Armed Conflict* (Oxford: Oxford University Press, 2012).

shelling (not to mention the crimes committed by the separatist Liberation Tigers of Tamil Eelam) in the final phase of the Sri Lankan civil war in 2009 remains disputed.[97] To ensure their technological advantage in the early years of the Cold War, the American and British governments conspired to exclude nuclear weapons from regulation by the Fourth Geneva Convention of 1949.[98]

Fatally, then, Lemkin and the UN monumentalized only depoliticized racial destruction, thereby attenuating the principle of distinction that he himself invoked when defining a "crime of crimes." The UN Genocide Convention then entrenched the virtually untrammelled sovereignty of states in their internal affairs and a relatively free hand in waging aerial warfare abroad. It was inconceivable for the "community of nations" to protect civilians in general when they met to effect the human rights revolution in the second half of the 1940s, because that would entail both proscribing their own conduct during World War II and tying their hands in defending their empires and/or waging the predicted war with ideological opponents.

I have become increasingly troubled not only by how the depoliticizing effect of the genocide concept enables states to legally kill civilians in the name of *raison d'etat*, but also how the institutionalization of genocide-prevention policies and toleration pedagogy implies that Non-Governmental

---

[97] Yemen Data Project, http://yemendataproject.org; Bel Trew, "'Irresponsible and Incoherent': British-Backed Bombing Raids Destroy UK Aid in Yemen," *The Independent*, November 2, 2018; Airwars, "Civilian and 'Friendly Fire' Casualties"; https://airwars.org/civilian-casualty-claims/; B'Tselem, "Operation Cast Lead, 27 Dec. '08 to 18 Jan. '09," June 1, 2011, www.btselem.org/gaza_strip/castlead_operation; "B'Tselem's Findings: Harm to Civilians Significantly Higher in Second Half of Operation Pillar of Defense," May 8, 2013, www.btselem.org/press_releases/20130509_pillar_of_defense_report. Russian forces in Syria will claim their presence as invited, not as an invitation. "50 Days: More than 500 Children: Facts and Figures on Fatalities in Gaza, Summer 2014," July 20, 2016, www.btselem.org/press_releases/20160720_fatalities_in_gaza_conflict_2014. Bruce Cronin, "Reckless Endangerment Warfare: Civilian Casualties and the Collateral Damage Exemption in International Humanitarian Law," *Journal of Peace Research* 50, no. 2 (2013): 175–87: Taylor B. Seybolt, Jay D. Aronson, and Baruch Fischhoff, *Counting Civilian Casualties: An Introduction to Recording and Estimating Nonmilitary Deaths in Conflict* (Oxford: Oxford University Press, 2013); Michael N. Schmitt, "The Principle of Discrimination in 21st Century Warfare," *Yale Human Rights and Development Law Journal* 2 (1999): 143–82; Michael Lippman, "Aerial Attacks on Civilians and the Humanitarian Law of War: Technology and Terror from World War I to Afghanistan," *California Western International Law Journal* 33, no. 1 (2002): 1–68; Eric Schmitt, "Saudi Arabia Tries to Ease Concerns Over Civilian Deaths in Yemen," *New York Times*, June 14, 2017; Charles Haviland, "Sri Lanka Government Publishes War Death Toll Statistics," *BBC News*, February 24, 2012, www.bbc.com/news/world-asia-17156686.

[98] Boyd van Dijk, *Preparing for War: The Making of the Geneva Conventions* (Oxford: Oxford University Press, forthcoming).

Organizations (NGOs), states, and the UN have correctly identified the illness and devised a remedy. In view of the egregious violence in which millions of civilians have died since 1948, there are good reasons to ask whether the house of international criminal law was built on shaky conceptual foundations. Concepts like genocide, crimes against humanity, and war crimes do not possess ontological status, no matter what black-letter lawyers may think. They are neither naturally given, nor do they enjoy timeless validity. They are products of history: of particular conjunctures of ideas and interests.[99]

Although Lemkin himself understood the genocide concept as a constructed artifice – a composite violation that bundled existing crimes on the basis of their underlying intention – he thought that it reflected a recurring reality: the destruction of ethno-cultural groups as a historical reality. In doing so, he did not understand that genocide is in fact a generative notion. Through the "magic of concepts," scholars *create* their object of inquiry by retrospectively imposing Lemkin's (or the UN's) ideal-typical definition on the past, thereby "discovering" cases. In this way, supposed instances of a stable phenomenon can be traced throughout history, "from Sparta to Darfur," giving the illusion of continuity and objectivity to arbitrary choices made in the present.[100] For example, why are the cases of Biafra and East Pakistan routinely excluded from genocide studies but Cambodia included, let alone the almost unimaginable mortality of the Chinese Great Leap Forward? Most civilian destruction in the second half of the twentieth century is excluded by fixating on genocide as a nonpolitical crime of racial hatred.[101]

Lemkin did not foresee that his creation would distort our criminal vocabulary with its paralyzingly monumental status as the "crime of crimes" that screens out other violations of the principle of civilian distinction. We ask, then: why have we inherited genocide, crimes against humanity, war crimes, and crimes against peace as the vocabulary of criminal transgression?

---

[99] Historians have long operated on these assumptions, which constructivist international relations scholars also share. Cf. Charlotte Epstein, *The Power of Words in International Relations: Birth of an Anti-Whaling Discourse* (Cambridge, MA: MIT Press, 2008), ch. 1.

[100] On the distortion caused by hypostasized concepts, whether of "the economy" or "Third World women," see Rebecca E. Karl, *The Magic of Concepts: History and the Economic in Twentieth-Century China* (Durham, NC: Duke University Press, 2017) and Chandra Talpade Mohanty, "Under Western Eyes: Feminist Scholarship and Colonial Discourses," *Boundary 2* 12, no. 3 (1984): 333–58. The key text that exposes this operation of concepts is of course Theodor W. Adorno, *Negative Dialectics*, trans. E. B. Ashton (New York and London: Continuum, 1973). Symptomatic is Ben Kiernan, *Blood and Soil: A World History of Genocide and Extermination from Sparta to Darfur* (New Haven: Yale University Press, 2007).

[101] Mark Mazower, "Violence and the State in the Twentieth Century," *American Historical Review* 107, no. 4 (2002): 1158–78; Vinay Lal, "The Concentration Camp and Development: The Pasts and Future of Genocide," *Patterns of Prejudice* 39, no. 2 (2005): 220–43.

How was this vocabulary constructed and what are its consequences? In answering these questions, we will see that the Western tradition of categorizing mass atrocities against civilians since the sixteenth century became formulated in legal propositions immediately after World War II. This legalization dramatically *narrowed* the inherited imagination of transgression, creating a memory regime at the center of which stands the Holocaust. In other words, our current imagination is *impoverished* compared to its nineteenth-century and interwar predecessors. Whereas the gravest acts of violence were once understood as political as well as ethnic, now we fixate on the latter. What is more, the fixation on ethnic/racial difference preserves this limited imagination of criminality, inadvertently heightening the potency of race in the public sphere – even as those who do so argue that "race" is biologically meaningless.

The Language of Transgression

In tracing this development, I focus on what I call the *language of transgression* from which Lemkin confected his new word. The language of transgression determines the upper threshold of mass criminality. It is the matrix of words and concepts used to define and police that threshold. Actions that transgress this threshold "shock the conscience of mankind," to use the common phrase. As *The Problem of Genocide* makes clear in Chapters 1 and 2, "shocking," "conscience," "mankind" (or "humanity"), "civilization," and "barbarism" are the keywords in the language of transgression that index the particular moral imaginary in which the crime of genocide makes sense.

In returning to the period before World War II, we can peel back the scaffolding of this moral and linguistic architecture to a point before it crystallized into its present form, before a "crime of crimes." This conceptual excavation reveals that international observers used the vocabulary of transgression to refer to political sources of mass violence, located in slavery and in civil-war-like conflict, generally in imperial contexts. The connection between state oppression and national liberation struggles seemed self-evident before 1945, and it was reflected in the vocabulary of transgression: enslaving people and destroying "native peoples" and "small nations" was shocking. Labor exploitation was regarded as the outcome of economic greed, and intergroup violence was a manifestation of political conflict, like conquest and resistance, rather than solely as expressions of bigotry. Until the UN Genocide Convention in 1948, the language of transgression did not place various crimes – slavery, expulsion, assimilation, mass murder – in a hierarchy. Each shocked "civilized conscience" in its own way. And to repeat: their political and economic contexts were also readily apparent – they occurred in liberation struggles, and liberation struggles occurred because of oppressive occupations that frustrated national ambitions or attempted to obliterate national characteristics of peoples that Europeans regarded as worthy of autonomy or self-government. Racial hatred was incidental to, and not the driver of, civilian destruction.

In 1946, the UN General Assembly referred to shocking "the conscience of mankind" for what one could call the "transgression effect": the impact of norm violation so egregious that public opinion insists they be stopped and/or transgressors punished. That effect had belonged to the Armenian genocide until the 1940s; thereafter, it has become the Holocaust. The difference is that Armenians were ascribed political agency in advancing a national project whereas Jews were understood as agentless, targeted solely on racial grounds. So, while Jews referred to the Armenian genocide to understand their experiences until the early 1940s, now advocates for recognition of the Armenian genocide portray Armenian victims like Jewish victims of the Holocaust. As a consequence, as I show in Chapter 11, Armenians are stripped of agency and our understanding of those historical events is depoliticized.

This memory regime undergirds the conventional, uplifting story of international criminal law's steady, if halting, march toward perfecting the language of transgression. After the Hague Conventions in 1899 and 1907, this story narrates the failed trials of the Young Turk leaders and German officers in 1918 and 1919 for crimes committed during the war as a way station to the full realization of liberal internationalism in the human rights revolution after 1945: the Nuremberg Trials, the Genocide Convention, and the Universal Declaration on Human Rights. Only with these instruments, so the teleological argument goes, was the vocabulary of transgression conceptually clarified to form the basis of the "new justice."[102] In fact, international society after World War I was conceptually equipped to prosecute the Ottoman leaders using the

---

[102] Vahakn N. Dadrian, "The Historical and Legal Interconnections between the Armenian Genocide and the Jewish Holocaust," *Yale Journal of International Law* 23, no. 2 (1998): 504, 553; Yves Beigbeder, *Judging War Criminals: The Politics of International Justice* (Basingstoke: Palgrave, 1999), 28; M. Cherif Bassiouni, *Crimes against Humanity in International Criminal Law*, 2nd rev. ed. (The Hague: Kluwer Law International, 1999), 73–4; James F. Willis, *Prologue to Nuremberg: The Politics and Diplomacy of Punishing War Criminals of the First World War* (Westport, CT: Greenwood, 1982); Laurence Douglas, *The Memory of Judgement: Making Law and History in the Trials of the Holocaust* (New Haven: Yale University Press, 2001); Vahakn N. Dadrian and Taner Akçam, *Judgement at Istanbul: The Armenian Genocide Trials* (Oxford and New York: Berghahn Books, 2011); Kevin Jon Heller and Gerry Simpson, eds., *The Hidden Histories of War Crimes Trials* (Oxford: Oxford University Press, 2013). Challenging this teleology is Samuel Moyn, *The Last Utopia: Human Rights in History* (Cambridge, MA: Belnap Press of Harvard University Press, 2010) and Stefan-Ludwig Hoffmann, ed., *Human Rights in the Twentieth Century* (New York: Cambridge University Press, 2011). Mark Lewis coins the notion of "new justice," in his brilliant, nonteleological book: Mark A. Lewis, *The Birth of the New Justice: The Internationalization of Crime and Punishment, 1919–1950* (Oxford: Oxford University Press, 2014).

relatively new concept of crimes against humanity.[103] Only the American and
Japanese objection to the term – because there was "no fixed and universal
standard of humanity" embedded in a treaty – excluded crimes against
humanity from postwar trial indictments.[104] Even so, a new justice could have
broken through after 1919 rather than after 1945.

To be sure, such a breakthrough would have been highly ambivalent.
Although the language of transgression recognized the political dimensions
of ethnic and national conflict, its Eurocentric rhetoric about civilization and
barbarism was indexed to a global order of empires that divided the world
into racial hierarchies.[105] The language of "shocking" civilized "conscience"
was ubiquitous in the Western press in relation to Ottoman and Russian
empires in the nineteenth century, to slavery and the excesses of their own
or others' empires – like Belgian King Leopold II's Congo – when Europeans
exploited and murdered non-Europeans, thereby violating Western civilizational norms. It was, and remains, an Orientalist idiom of humanitarian
empire, a colonialism shorn of scandalous excesses, but colonialism all the
same. This discourse was largely deaf to the millions of Muslim refugees
caused by the Russian conquest of the Caucasus, the successive national
liberations of the Christian Balkan states in the nineteenth century, and during
and after the Balkans Wars of 1912–1913.[106] Without this language, the
contemptuous disregard of indigenous people's aspirations is impossible to
imagine: in, say, the British proposition to partition Palestine in 1937, which is
analyzed in Chapters 8 and 9.

This is the language of transgression out of which the genocide concept
evolved. Because of its Orientalist baggage, this language – whether before or

---

[103] Michelle Tusan, "'Crimes against Humanity': Human Rights, the British Empire, and the
Origins of the Response to the Armenian Genocide," *American Historical Review* 119,
no. 1 (2014): 47–77; Peter Holquist, "By Right of War: Imperial Russia and the
Development of the Law of War," paper presented to the History of the Laws of War
workshop, European University Institute, January 23, 2015.

[104] *Violation of the Laws and Customs of War: Reports of Majority and Dissenting Reports
of American and Japanese Members of the Commission of Responsibilities, Conference of
Paris 1919* (Oxford: Clarendon Press, 1919), 73; Gary J. Bass, *Stay the Hand of
Vengeance: The Politics of War Crimes Tribunals* (Princeton: Princeton University
Press, 2000).

[105] Susan Pedersen, "Back to the League of Nations," *American Historical Review* 112, no. 4
(2007): 1091–117; Tusan, "'Crimes against Humanity'."

[106] Umut Özsu, *Formalizing Displacement: International Law and Population Transfers*
(Oxford: Oxford University Press, 2015); Keith David Watenpaugh, *Bread from
Stones: The Middle East and the Making of Modern Humanitarianism* (Berkeley:
University of California Press, 2015), 12; Isa Blumi, *Ottoman Refugees, 1878–1939*
(London: Bloomsbury, 2013).

after the Holocaust – is inadequate to the task of analysing the causes of mass violence against civilians. Lemkin's conceptual evolution exemplifies the problem. In 1933, he suggested "barbarism" and "vandalism" as new international crimes. Then, a decade later, in *Axis Rule*, he claimed to combine them to form his neologism, genocide. His new term was intended to further the process of "civilization" by proscribing wars against populations that, he thought, returned the world to the barbarous conflicts of Antiquity and the Middle Ages.[107] The loaded language of barbarism and civilization is embedded in the concept of genocide with problematic consequences.

Writing the History of a Concept

Despite genocide's prominence in the language of transgression, it has not been studied as a concept or keyword. The famous multivolume German "history of concepts" (*Begriffsgeschichte*) project omits both genocide and human rights.[108] So does the pioneering book, *Keywords*, by Welsh scholar Raymond Williams, even though genocide was well established by the 1970s when its first edition was published. Keywords are the building blocks of political discourse, constituting "general vocabulary ranging from strong, difficult and persuasive words in everyday usage to words which, beginning in particular specialized contexts, have become quite common in descriptions of wider areas of thought and experience." They are "significant, binding words in certain activities and their interpretations" and "indicative... in certain forms of thought."[109] Williams' subtitle indicates the reasons for the omission of genocide: *A Vocabulary of Culture and Society*. As a Marxist, he sought to catalogue the historical semantics of words like class, art, industry, and democracy that registered capitalism's dramatic transformations of Western societies. The fact that Williams, a veteran of World War II, excluded those terms that have become central for articulating contemporary experience – genocide as well as Holocaust and human rights – points to a Western Eurocentrism concerned more with the legacy of capitalism than the piles of corpses produced by the war and subsequent decolonization struggles.

---

[107] Lemkin, *Axis Rule in Occupied Europe*; Irvin-Erickson, *Raphaël Lemkin and the Concept of Genocide.*

[108] Otto Brunner Werner Conze, and Reinhart Koselleck, ed., *Geschichtliche Grundbegriffe: Historisches Lexikon zur politisch-sozialen Sprache in Deutschland*, 8 Vols. (Stuttgart: Klett-Cotta Verlag, 1972–1997).

[109] Raymond Williams, *Keywords: A Vocabulary of Culture and Society* (London: Collins, 1976, 1983), 14–5. Holocaust and human rights but not genocide are included in Tony Bennett, Lawrence Grossberg, and Meaghan Morris, eds., *New Keywords: A Revised Vocabulary of Culture and Society* (Malden, MA, and Oxford: Wiley-Blackwell, 2005); Kelly Fritsch, Clare O'Connor, and AK Thompson, eds., *Keywords for Radicals: The Contested Vocabulary of Late-Capitalist Struggle* (Chico, CA: AK Press, 2016).

The same could be said of the *Begriffsgeschichte* volume editors who loyally served the Nazi regime as academics or soldiers.[110]

For all that, Williams's approach left open the possibility for genocide's inclusion in the pantheon of contemporary keywords. He was well aware that the meaning of words varies over time and between classes of people, and he would have surely welcomed keywords that reflected non-European structures of experience.[111] Although, as a term of such recent provenance, genocide cannot be equated with the ancient elements of Western thought like, say, reason and its siblings, reasonableness and rationality, the apparently inevitable development of its immutable meaning can be questioned. Rather than tracing how origin strands crystallized into a seemingly ideal-type definition, we need to reconstruct the varying intersections of human experience, power, and language at distinct moments.[112] That is the task of Chapters 3, 4, and 5 in particular. My questions, then, are not when genocide was authentically defined or whether events qualify as genocide, but how its criteria were determined and whose interests they served. How and why was the "truth" – rather than the violent reality – of genocide constructed?[113]

Williams also highlighted the importance of understanding keywords in clusters: as related to and overlapping with other terms that gesture to, inform, and articulate particular structures of feeling. They cannot be understood in isolation; their meanings are mutually constituted in complex interaction. To understand the genocide keyword, then, we need to insert it into the semantic field from which it emerged and in the memory regime to which it contributes.[114] As we will see in Chapters 1 and 2, the most relevant semantic field is that concerning Western imperialism and state-building, with its familiar trinity of savagery, barbarism, and civilization. While Lemkin regarded himself as speaking for history's victims and thus defined genocide broadly, he necessarily drew on the available language of transgression when he began writing about group destruction between the world wars. Consequently, a term intended to articulate victims' experience emerged within a semantic field occupied by history's victors, the "civilized" colonial powers. The victims' challenge is to inflect available rhetorical tools with critical meaning.[115]

Lemkin's contemporaries spoke this language when they denounced Nazism as a reversion to barbarism, whether as a throwback to pre-Christian Europe, to

---

[110] Thomas Etzemüller, *Werner Conze und die Neuorientierung der westdeutschen Geschichtswissenschaft nach 1945* (Munich: De Gruyter Oldenbourg, 2001).

[111] Williams, *Keywords*, 24.

[112] Michel Foucault, "Nietzsche, Genealogy, History," in *Foucault*, Aesthetics, Method, and Epistemology, ed. James D. Faubion (New York: New Press, 1998), 371.

[113] Srdjan Vucetic, "Genealogy as a Research Tool in International Relations," *Review of International Studies* 37, no. 3 (2011): 1295–312.

[114] Williams, *Keywords*, 23.   [115] Thanks to Umut Özsu for discussions on this point.

the wars of religion or, for British Prime Minister Winston Churchill, to "the Mongol invasions of the thirteenth century."[116] British Foreign Secretary Anthony Eden, speaking for the UN (as the Allied powers called themselves), told the House of Commons in 1942 that he had read reports "regarding the barbarous and inhuman treatment to which Jews are being subjected in German-occupied Poland."[117] In the same year, the prominent North American legal scholar, Ellery Stowell, invoked the history of international law to condemn the Nazis' abuse of military norms. He quoted with approval US Civil War officer, Henry Halleck (1815–1872), who averred that "inconsiderate retaliation removes belligerents farther and farther from the mitigating rules of regular ways, and by rapid steps leads them nearer to the internecine war of savages." Regular warfare, Halleck explained, was fought by "civilised governments and among all Christian people." Stowell agreed, suggesting that Nazi warfare was savage.[118]

Following this wartime rhetoric, the prosecutors at the Nuremberg Trials also spoke of Nazi crimes in terms of civilization and barbarism, as did UN delegates. When members of the UN signed up to the new genocide prevention regime in the same year, they did so in the firm conviction that their states did not commit genocide, and never had: that was a crime committed by the Nazis, standing in a posited barbarous lineage featuring Genghis Khan. Genocide is what *they* did. In this dominant mode, they tied genocide to the language of power by enabling victorious states to stigmatize the vanquished.[119] Lemkin concurred. As we know, the preamble to the UN Universal Declaration on Human Rights of 1948 echoed the 1899 Hague Convention in referring to "barbarous acts which have outraged the

---

[116] Winston Churchill, *Into Battle: Speeches by the Right Hon Winston S Churchill* (London: Cassell, 1941) 87; George Steiner, *Language and Silence* (New York: Athenaeum, 1977), viii; Philip Smith, "Barbarism and Civility in the Discourses of Fascism, Communism, and Democracy: Variations on a Set of Themes," in *Real Civil Societies: Dilemmas of Institutionalization*, ed. Jeffrey C. Alexander (London: Sage, 1998), 115–37.

[117] United Nations Declaration, House of Commons Debates, December 17, 1942, Vol. 385, cc2082, http://hansard.millbanksystems.com/commons/1942/dec/17/united-nations-declaration.

[118] Ellery C. Stowell, "Military Reprisals and the Sanctions of the Laws of War," *American Journal of International Law* 36, no. 4 (1942): 649–50.

[119] Ayşe Zarakol, "What Made the Modern World Hang Together: Socialisation or Stigmatisation?" *International Theory* 6, no. 2 (2014): 311–32; Mark B. Salter, *Barbarians and Civilization in International Relations* (Chicago: University of Chicago Press, 2002) thinks that the civilization-barbarism binary unraveled during the two world wars because of intra-European violence and Nazi crimes, but the evidence suggest that it was reinforced by understandable Allied stigmatization of the Nazis.

conscience of mankind."[120] We are still speaking this language, but not only does it conceal as much as it reveals, it enables widespread violence against civilians.

Permanent Security and Civilian Destruction

Some scholars have attempted to redefine genocide to include civilian destruction in general – in particular nuclear warfare – but this conceptual stretch inevitably runs into the problem of genocide's archetype, the Holocaust, with its emphases on strict intentionality and ethnic identity.[121] Instead, I argue, we should develop an alternative category to name and explain the criminality that the genocide concept only partially captures. Genocide, like war crimes and crimes against humanity, obscures a deeper source of transgression better covered by the notion of *permanent security*. Despite its possibly anodyne connotations, permanent security is a deeply utopian and sinister imperative that has not been satisfactorily examined by the extensive security studies literature.[122] The term is not my invention. The Nazi commander of *Einsatzgruppe D, SS-Führer* Otto Ohlendorf (1907–1951), coined it for the rationale of his troops' mass murder of Jews in southern Ukraine, Moldova, and the Caucasus. Security thinking saturated his political imagination. He joined the Nazi Party in 1925, and after studying economics took a job in the Security Service of the SS in 1936, assuming leadership of its domestic section (*Sicherheitsdienst-Inland*) in 1939. The *Einsatzgruppen* embodied security imperatives in the field. They were four special action units, totaling some 3,000 men, established by the Security Service and Security Police of the Imperial Security Main Office (*Reichssicherheitshauptamt*), for the invasion of the Soviet Union in 1941. Their orders were to ensure the security of

---

[120] General Assembly resolution 260 A (III) of December 9, 1948, www.ohchr.org/EN/ ProfessionalInterest/Pages/CrimeOfGenocide.aspx; Universal Declaration of Human Rights, www.un.org/en/documents/udhr/. Cf. Mark Mazower, "The End of Civilization and the Rise of Human Rights: The Mid-Twentieth-Century Disjuncture," in Hoffmann *Human Rights in the Twentieth Century*, 29–44.

[121] Robert Jay Lifton and Eric Markusen, *The Genocidal Mentality: The Nuclear Holocaust and Nuclear Threat* (New York: Basic Books, 1990); Eric Markusen and David Kopf, *The Holocaust and Strategic Bombing: Genocide and Total War in the Twentieth Century* (Boulder, CO: Westview Press, 1995). I analyze the debate on this question in Chapters 10 and 11. On conceptual stretching, see Giovanni Sartori, "Concept Misformation in Comparative Politics," *American Political Science Review* 64, no. 4 (1970): 1033–53; David Collier and James E. Mahon, Jr., "Conceptual 'Stretching' Revisited: Adapting Categories in Comparative Analysis," *American Political Science Review* 87, no. 4 (1993): 845–55.

[122] Barry Buzan and Lene Hansen, *The Evolution of International Security Studies* (Cambridge: Cambridge University Press, 2009).

territory conquered by the German Army by exterminating political enemies. These were not clearly itemized at the outset but came to denote Bolshevik functionaries and perceived threats, including Jews and "Gypsies."[123]

Believing himself innocent of criminal intentions at his trial in 1947, Ohlendorf did not cite superior orders to escape the hangman's noose: he justified them in the name of "necessity." When asked about murdering Jewish children, he maintained that they would grow up to resist the occupation when they understood that Germans had murdered their parents. Realizing that he was advancing an unconventional argument, Ohlendorf explained that the Germans sought more than military security: their aim was what he called "permanent security." In this regard, Hitler set the tone in a speech after the conquest of Poland in October 1939. He declared that German policy should include, among other measures, "The pacification (*Befriedung*) of the entire area in the sense of producing tenable peace and order," and "the absolute guarantee of security not only of imperial territory but of the entire sphere of interest." In the rest of the speech, he spoke at length about the "feeling of security" (*Gefühl der Sicherheit*) that would attend the ethnic reordering of the continent when minorities were eliminated by population transfer, including "the attempt to order and regulate the Jewish problem."[124]

This security imagination – permanent security – entailed a radically new temporal structure. It was concerned not only with eliminating immediate threats but also with future threats. Governed by a logic of prevention (future threats) as well as preemption (imminent threats), it strove to close the gap between perceived insecurity and permanent security. The latter thereby entails a fatally restless and dynamic process indentured to a paranoid subject who not only perceives grave threats but manufactures circumstances in which they become self-fulfilling prophecies; for example, attacking others who are thereby driven into a hostile (defensive) posture. Herewith, Ohlendorf expressed a truth about state and para-state thinking and behavior that rarely speaks its name. At times, articulate mass murderers can give devastatingly clear accounts of their motivations that we ignore because of their provenance.[125]

---

[123] Helmut Krausnick, *Hitlers Einsatzgruppen: Die Truppe des Weltanschauungskrieges 1938–1942* (Frankfurt am Main: Fischer, 1998), 135.

[124] Adolf Hitler, "Entgegennahme einer Erklärung der Reichsregierung," Verhandlungen des Deutschen Reichstags (October 6, 1939), 56, 61, www.reichstagsprotokolle.de/Blatt2_n4_bsb00000613_00052.html.

[125] Not for nothing does one scholar observe that such practices possess a "strategic logic" that can culminate in "final solutions": Benjamin A. Valentino, *Final Solutions: Mass Killing and Genocide in the Twentieth Century* (Ithaca, NY: Cornell University Press, 2004); Wolfgang Sofsky, *The Order of Terror: The Concentration Camp*, trans. William Templer (Princeton, NJ: Princeton University Press, 1996), 21, warns against taking *ex post facto* statements in legal proceedings as authentic expressions of what perpetrators

The analytical point is not to adopt Ohlendorf's perspective but to turn the concept back onto him and his ilk: to expose the terrible implications of what he was saying about the Nazi project as a whole, not just on the Eastern Front. As Israeli historian Saul Friedländer pointed out, the Nazis regarded Jews "as an *active threat*, for all of Aryan humanity in the long run, and in the immediate future for a Reich embroiled in a world war," meaning that "the Jews had to be exterminated before they could harm 'Fortress Europe' from within or join forces with the enemy coalition they had themselves set against the Reich."[126] If the regime was deeply irrational when viewed from the outside, its extermination policies made perfect sense to its followers as applications of permanent security.[127] Ohlendorf's defense counsel called his actions "putative self-defense" (or "putative necessity"). His US prosecutors, which starred Benjamin Ferencz, wrestled with the disjunction between subjective and objective perspectives and, understandably, discounted the former as untenable. To accept it would be to allow abrogation of the laws of war because of outlandish threat perceptions, they said.[128] But, in doing so, they set a trap for future American strategic planners whose forces killed millions of civilians with bombs in combatting communism in Korea and Indochina, far from US shores.

My point, then, is also to expose the deadly reasoning of Ohlendorf's Nuremberg prosecutors, who had no answer to his provocation that Allied bombing knowingly killed German children, as we see in Chapter 5.[129] If our premise is to distinguish noncombatants from military targets, then their intended or indiscriminate largescale destruction as a matter of policy is highly problematic, because it continues until victory. And if war becomes permanent, then so does civilian destruction. Usually associated with fascist regimes, especially Nazi warfare and strategic ambitions, we see below that

---

thought they were doing when they committed their crimes, but Ohlendorf was not avoiding responsibility for his actions; he was explaining why they were rational and legitimate in his eyes.

[126] Saul Friedländer, *The Years of Extermination: Nazi Germany and the Jews, 1939–1945* (New York: HarperCollins, 2007), 557. Emphasis in original.

[127] On the thesis of Nazi irrationality, see Dan Diner, *Beyond the Conceivable: Studies on Germany, Nazism, and the Holocaust* (Berkeley: University of California, 2000). I discuss the paranoia entailed in this belief system in Chapter 7.

[128] Trials of the War Criminals before the Nuremberg Military Tribunals, Vol. 4, The "Einsatzgruppen Case." October 1946–April 1949 (Washington DC: US Government Printing Office, 1949). United States of America vs. Otto Ohlendorf, et al. (Case No. 9), 346–55, 463–6.

[129] Because I am adapting rather than adopting the term, I do not place quotation marks around it in this book.

permanent warfare is shared by all forms of permanent security.[130] From the perspective of non-Europeans conquered, colonized, and exploited by Europeans since the sixteenth century, permanent warfare seems an apt description of what they have endured, as we see in Chapters 1, 2, and 6. We also need to consider noninternational armed conflicts, whether civil wars, internal repressions, or internal upheavals associated with forced development like the Chinese Great Leap Forward that cost the lives of 20–30 million people.[131] All told, they have accounted for far more civilian deaths than the narrowly defined cases of genocide. Whether committed by militaries or paramilitaries, there are two, related modalities of permanent security: illiberal and liberal.

Illiberal Permanent Security

This modality entails preventative killing of presumed future threats to a particular ethnos, nation, or religion, in a bounded "territoriality."[132] To invoke the term of the Syrian dissident intellectual, Yassin El-Haj Saleh, such regimes are "genocratic," because they represent the rule of a "genos" rather than the "demos," and wield state terror to entrench their power.[133] Scholars have long identified such practices in the targeting of political and ethnic groups, like communists in Latin America and Indonesia, or national minorities in countless cases. The Nazi genocide of Jews – the Holocaust – is the most notorious case of illiberal permanent security. Illiberal permanent security disregards international law and claims of universal morality and thus does not distinguish between civilians and combatants: peoples as a whole are enemies.[134]

Killing children as future threats is a sure sign of illiberal permanent security aspirations. The Biblical book of Exodus recounts how the Egyptian pharaoh ordered midwives to drown Hebrew baby boys to weaken the captive Jewish people. Surviving this murderous security policy, this author's

---

[130] Miguel Alonso, Alan Kramer, and Javier Rodrigo, "Introduction," in *Fascist Warfare, 1922–1945*, ed. Miguel Alonso, Alan Kramer, and Javier Rodrigo (Basingstoke: Palgrave Macmillan, 2019), 14.

[131] Lal, "The Concentration Camp and Development"; Jean-Louis Margolin, "Mao's China: The Worst Non-Genocidal Regime?" in *The Historiography of Genocide*, ed. Dan Stone (Basingstoke: Palgrave Macmillan, 2008), 438–67.

[132] Charles S. Maier, *Once Within Borders: Territories of Power, Wealth, and Belonging since 1500* (Cambridge: MA: Harvard University Press, 2016).

[133] Yassin al-Haj Saleh, "Terror, Genocide, and the 'Genocratic' Turn," *Aljumhuriya*, September 19, 2019, www.aljumhuriya.net/en/content/terror-genocide-and-%E2%80%9Cgenocratic%E2%80%9D-turn.

[134] Alan Kramer, *Dynamics of Destruction: Culture and Mass Milling in the First World War* (Oxford: Oxford University Press, 2007), 329–30.

namesake (but not relative), Moses, went on to lead the Jews out of slavery and exile to the "promised land."[135] Centuries later, as if acting on precedent, King Herod, the Roman-appointed ruler of Judea, is said to have felt so threatened by the infant Jesus as the prophesied "king of the Jews" that he had baby boys in Bethlehem murdered in the infamous "massacre of the innocents," inaugurating an enduring subject in the Jewish and Christian artistic imaginations.[136] To likewise eliminate potential rivals, the eldest son of a deceased sultan in the early Ottoman court would imprison and ultimately execute his brothers, even if they were infants.[137]

The practice of killing perceived future threats is all-too modern as well. Young Turk leader Talaat Pasha explained the deportations of Armenians in these terms in an interview with a German newspaper in 1916: "We have been reproached for making no distinction between the innocent Armenians and the guilty: but that was utterly impossible in view of the fact that those who are innocent today might be guilty tomorrow."[138] North American settlers justified murdering Indian children with the argument that "nits make lice."[139] More recently, the former director of Guatemala's Peace Archives told the national court prosecuting military leaders for various crimes against indigenous people in the 1990s that "The army's objective with the children was to eliminate the seed for future guerrillas."[140]

After killing 160 children on a military base in Peshawar, Pakistan, in 2014, a Taliban spokesman said that they "killed children in [the] army school because they would join [the] army in the future." Likewise, a landlord militia leader in India admitted that "We kill children because they will grow up to become Naxalites [Maoist insurgents] and we kill women because they will

[135] Exodus 1: 22: "Every Hebrew boy that is born you must throw into the Nile, but let every girl live." New International Version. Baby girls were held to be unthreatening because they could be married off and assimilated, an example of the patriarchal assumption about gender and nationhood so common in the pattern of genocidal attacks over the centuries.

[136] Matthew 2:16–18; Laura Jacobus, "Motherhood and Massacre: The Massacre of the Innocents in Late-Medieval Art and Drama," in *The Massacre in History*, ed. Mark Levene and Penny Roberts (Oxford: Berghahn Books, 1999), 39–54.

[137] Günhan Börekçi, "Mustafa I," in *Encyclopedia of the Ottoman Empire*, ed. Gábor Ágoston and Bruce Alan Masters (New York: Facts on File, 2009), 409. Thanks to Umut Özsu for this point.

[138] Quoted in Vigen Guroian, "Collective Responsibility and Official Excuse Making: The Case of Turkish Genocide of the Armenians," in *The Armenian Genocide in Perspective*, ed. Richard G. Hovannisian (New Brunswick, NJ: Transaction Publishers, 1986), 143.

[139] Katie Kane, "Nits Make Lice: Drogheda, Sand Creek, and the Poetics of Colonial Extermination," *Cultural Critique*, no. 42 (1999): 81–103.

[140] Jo-Marie Burt, "From Heaven to Hell in Ten Days: The Genocide Trial in Guatemala," *Journal of Genocide Research* 18, nos. 2–3 (2016): 149–50.

give birth to Naxalites."[141] When the children of an Islamic home school group in upstate New York asked why a man, Robert Doggart, arrested for plotting to attack their mosque wanted to kill them, they did not understand his paranoid logic: he saw the children as future Islamic terrorists in the US, so he sought to eliminate them in an act of anticipatory self-defense.[142]

That was also the logic of two rabbis in a West Bank settlement when they wrote *The King's Torah*, in which they stated that Jewish law licensed killing Palestinian babies and children because "it is clear that they will grow to harm us."[143] The Australian terrorist who murdered 51 praying Muslims in Christchurch, New Zealand, in March 2019, shared this logic. Children "will one day become teens, then adults, voting against the wishes of our people, practicing the cultural and religious practices of the invaders, taking other people's lands, work, houses and even attacking and killing our children," he declared. The necessary action is inescapable: "You burn the nest and kill the vipers, no matter their age."[144]

Liberal Permanent Security

Ironically, and fatally, condemning illiberal permanent security with the language of transgression often initiates a dialectic that leads to *liberal permanent security*. For the righteous speakers of this language can all too easily place the objects of condemnation beyond the realm of humanity, as

---

[141] Pawel Iskra Parashar, Facebook post, December 17, 2014, www.facebook.com/pawel .parashar/posts/1021391037878340. See also "Day after massacre, Taliban says kids killed because they were future soldiers," *Southeast Asia Post*, December 18, 2014, www.southeastasiapost.com/index.php/sid/228653759, and "Sunday Anchor: Army of Assassins," *The Hindu*, August 23, 2015, www.thehindu.com/sunday-anchor/sunday-anchor-army-of-assassins/article7569720.ece.

On the landlord militias, see Gaurva Bhatnagar, "Confessions from Bihar's Killing Fields Set to Singe BJP, and Nitish Too," *The Wire*, August 17, 2015, http://thewire.in/ 2015/08/17/confessions-from-bihars-killing-fields-set-to-singe-bjp-and-nitish-too-8661.

[142] Remarkably, US law does not categorize Doggart's intent as terroristic, because terrorism is drastically limited in definition in domestic circumstances. Chris Sommerfeldt, "Tenn. Man Who Plotted NY Mosque Attack Won't Face Terror Charges," *New York Daily News*, February 14, 2017.

[143] Dan Estrin, "The King's Torah: A Rabbinic Text or a Call to Terror?" *Ha'aretz*, January 22, 2010. Their book was endorsed by a senior national-religious rabbi, Dov Lior, who became involved in teaching police recruits in the "Believers in the Police" program. On how stoking fears plays into the development of a "security theology," see Nadera Shalhoub-Kevorkian, *Security Theology, Surveillance and the Politics of Fear Security Theology, Surveillance and the Politics of Fear* (Cambridge: Cambridge University Press, 2015).

[144] Brenton Tarrant, *The Great Replacement: Towards a New Society, We March Ever Forwards* (2019), 52. See A. Dirk Moses, "'White Genocide' and the Ethics of Public Analysis," *Journal of Genocide Research* 21, no. 2 (2019): 201–13.

"barbarians," "savages," and "enemies of humanity," to justify the permanent extension of their own power to oppose and even eliminate them. In this way, genocidal perpetrators become *hostes humanis generis* – enemies of all human-ity, the ultimate evil – which is of course the same category used by genocidal perpetrators.[145] Whereas illiberal permanent security aspires to a bounded territoriality, the liberal version envisions the world as the territory to be secured in the name of "humanity."[146] A fitting example is nineteenth-century British politician W. E. Gladstone, who in his famous pamphlet, *The Bulgarian Horrors* (1876), attacking the Ottoman repression of a Bulgarian uprising, demonized the Turks as a particularly dangerous "racial" type of Muslim and "the one great anti-human specimen of humanity." They had earned his invective for many atrocities and destroying civilization; they were an "advancing curse that menaced the whole of Europe."[147] He was drawing on venerable arguments about pirates as outlaws and "enemies of humanity."

Having profited from the slave trade for centuries, Britain opposed it in the nineteenth century when humanitarians, and eventually the state, regarded slave-traders and pirates in these terms, and believed that extending British imperial rule or writ was coterminous with abolishing slavery and piracy.[148] By the end of the century, this fusion of humanitarianism and empire became a European liberal project: the "Scramble for Africa" was justified by ending slavery there and introducing the emoluments of civilization, commerce, and Christianity.[149] These are instances of liberal permanent security because of the pretence to universal values and commitment to a metanarrative of human progress based on freedom and material improvement, all of which are predicated on the colonial civilizing missions of European and North American powers.[150]

The intrinsic relationship between settler colonialism and liberal permanent security was neatly expressed in 1938 by US President Franklin D. Roosevelt in

---

[145] Alette Smeulers, "Punishing the Enemies of All Mankind," *Leiden Journal of International Law* 21 (2008): 974.

[146] Maier, *Once Within Borders*.

[147] W. E. Gladstone, *Bulgarian Horrors and the Question of the East* (New York and Montreal: Lovell, Adam, Wesson and Co., 1876), 10.

[148] This proposition is elaborated in Chapter 1.

[149] Amalia Ribi Forclas, *Humanitarian Imperialism: The Politics of Anti-Slavery Activism, 1880–1940* (Oxford: Oxford University Press, Oxford 2015); Daniel Laqua, "The Tensions of Internationalism: Transnational Anti-Slavery in the 1880s and 1890s," *International History Review* 33, no. 4 (2011): 705–26.

[150] Matthew Dillon and Julian Read, *Liberal Way of War: Killing to Make Life Live* (London: Routledge, 2009); Duncan Bell, *Reordering the World: Essays on Liberalism and Empire* (Princeton: Princeton University Press, 2016); Jennifer Pitts: *Boundaries of the International: Law and Empire* (Cambridge, MA: Harvard University Press, 2018).

praising the white settler pioneers of the Ohio Company: they were "seeking *permanent security* for men and women and children and homes." He hinted at the violence that enabled this colonization by mentioning "the scouts and the skirmishers of the great American migration" who did not recoil at the sight of "Indians and redcoats [British soldiers]," because they "had held their beloved wilderness for themselves – and for us – with their own bare hands and their own long rifles." Then followed the settler families, "the first battalions of that organized army of occupation which transplanted... whole little civilizations that took root and grew." Although he appropriately invoked a military metaphor to express the notion that civilization proceeded by conquest and occupation, Roosevelt also stressed the role of the state in the settlers' "genius for organized colonization, carefully planned and ordered under law."[151] As significant as the reference to (always defensively understood) violence was the unstated assumption of the Europeans' right to displace and replace the inferior noncivilization of the indigenous people.[152]

Military campaigns in which civilian casualties are intended or accepted as incidental to the military objective in the context of permanent states of emergency are also signs of liberal permanent security: in aerial bombings, starvation blockades, and population expulsions. A political scientist calls the outcome of such campaigns "civilian victimization," defining the concept thus: "Civilian victimization is a military strategy chosen by political or military elites that targets and kills noncombatants intentionally or which fails to discriminate between combatants and noncombatants and thus kills large numbers of the latter."[153] A more apt term to capture this strategic logic is "civilian destruction," for even if the total destruction of an enemy's civilians is not the aim, the entire population is targeted as killable. The issue of so-called collateral damage that international law permits is central to this modality of permanent security. It is the incidental but entirely foreseeable deaths of civilians in the vicinity of military targets, the scale of which is limited only by proportionality principles: the greater the significance of the military target, the more extensive the legally permissible civilian deaths. When this

---

[151] Franklin D. Roosevelt, Address at Marietta, Ohio, July 8, 1938, The American Presidency Project, www.presidency.ucsb.edu/documents/address-marietta-ohio. Emphasis added.

[152] This assumption continues in paeans to settlers today. See David McCullough, *The Pioneers: The Heroic Story of the Settlers Who Brought the American Ideal West* (New York: Simon and Schuster, 2019).

[153] Alexander B. Downes, *Targeting Civilians in War* (New York: Cornell University Press, 2008), 13. This definition resembles R. J. Rummel's notion of "democide," but Rummel was uninterested in fatalities caused by democracies: R. J. Rummel, *Death by Government* (New Brunswick, NJ: Transaction Publications, 1994); Rummel, *Power Kills: Democracy as a Method of Nonviolence* (New Brunswick, NJ: Transaction Publishers, 1997). Also see Hugo Slim, *Killing Civilians: Method, Madness and Morality in War* (London: Hurst, 2007).

calculation becomes integrated into permanent warfare, the continuous, serial killing of civilians becomes the rule, not the exception.[154]

The Criminality of Permanent Security

As I elaborate in Part II of this book, permanent security is a praxis in which human groups – civilians – are targeted collectively and preventatively as security threats. When a "national, ethnical, racial or religious group," to use the UN Genocide Convention list, is targeted, its members are *racialized* by those who ascribe racial meaning to social, political, and cultural processes and events. Members of groups can also self-racialize. Permanent security implicates racialization when it is combined with *securitization*: identifying a group as threatening. Persecution does not occur without securitization even if victims experience their persecution as the outcome of hatred, because that is the emotion they discern in the perpetrators. The social fact of racial or religious difference or even prejudice does not cause genocidal violence, however. The securitization of groups, whether racialized or otherwise defined, is the driver of excessive violence.[155]

Permanent security is the underlying criminality that unites the triumvirate of genocide, crimes against humanity, and war crimes as well as collateral damage. These security imperatives inhere in the absolute claims of any state, para-state, or international grouping to assert the interests of either a particular ethnos (illiberal permanent security) or "civilized humanity" (liberal permanent security). Whether liberal or illiberal, permanent security is an impossible and immoral aspiration that drives states and para-states to kill innocent people in the name of ending vulnerability by imposing their regime – forever. The paranoid and hubristic quest for permanent security escalates routine state and (para)military security practices to sanction violating the principle of distinction in massive and/or cumulatively persistent

---

[154] Theodor Meron, "The Humanization of Humanitarian Law," *American Journal of International Law* 94, no. 2 (2000): 239–78; David Kennedy, *Of Law and War* (Princeton: Princeton University Press, 2006); Valerie Epps, "Civilian Casualties in Modern Warfare: The Death of the Collateral Damage Rule," *Georgia Journal of International and Comparative Law* 41, no. 2. (2013): 307–55. Historical background: Grimsley and Rogers, *Civilians in the Path of War*. On the contemporary scene, Jason Ralph, *America's War on Terror: The State of the 9/11 Exception from Bush to Obama* (Oxford: Oxford University Press, 2013).

[155] Aliya Saperstein, Andrew M. Penner, and Ryan Light, "Racial Formation in Perspective: Connecting Individual, Institutions, and Power Relations," *Annual Review of Sociology* 39 (2013): 359–78. Among the many publications on securitization, see David Mofette and Shaira Vadasaria, "Uninhibited Violence: Race and the Securitization of Immigration," *Critical Studies on Security* 4, no. 3 (2016): 291–305.

attacks: killing, incarcerating, or deporting civilians, including collaterally, with the aim of ending resistance to their rule, and thus politics; indeed of stopping time itself. In the case of liberal permanent security, one famous scholar spoke of the "end of history" after the fall of communism and seeming victory of the capitalist West.[156] Yassin El-Haj Saleh's observation about the Assad regime can be universalized: they seek to "make 'eternity' – and the endless war against the future that it requires – a principal objective of their rule."[157] When a regime crushes alternative visions of human collective existence – other political options – human history is imperilled.

What is more, the effort to impose permanent security, whether liberal or illiberal, provokes the very resistance that it seeks to exterminate, leading to never-ending wars against "terror" in the name of peace as well as to the civilian casualties it claims to seek to prevent. These operations are not only dispersed in international law's various criminal categories, but are also obscured by its prosecution of individuals rather than the concrete abstractions – states – in whose name masses of people are killed.[158]

This book is a plea against the civilian destruction caused by the aspiration for permanent security: the illegitimacy of killing civilians for the sake of a state, whether in the name of an ethnos or humanity (or both) that it claims to defend.[159] What is the experiential difference between a victim of genocide and a victim of collateral damage? Both are innocent. That they can be regarded as legitimately killed by one interpretation or another in the name of safety *ad finitum* indicates the presence of permanent security.

This Book

There are two bundles of problems regarding the concept of genocide, then, the first relating to diagnosis, the second to remedy. First: by constructing a hierarchy of mass crimes with genocide at its apex, the hegemonic legal and memory regimes make subgenocidal violence less grave and the protection and commemoration of its victims less urgent. Similarly, by depoliticizing genocide as a monumental hate crime, most mass violence against civilians is not considered as gravely criminal. Civilians become collateral victims of civil war – whether of the Assad government's bombing of "rebel" areas, opposition

---

[156] Francis Fukuyama, *The End of History and the Last Man* (New York: Free Press, 1992).

[157] Yassin El-Haj Saleh, "Assad's 'Eternal Rule': The Long Prelude to Genocide," October 7, 2019, www.yassinhs.com/2019/10/07/assads-eternal-rule-the-long-prelude-to-genocide.

[158] Mark Drumbl, *Atrocity, Punishment, and International Law* (New York: Cambridge University Press, 2007); Martti Koskenniemi, "Between Impunity and Show Trials," *Max Planck Year Book of United Nations Law* 6 (2002): 1–35.

[159] Jonathan Glover, *Humanity: A Moral History* (New Haven: Yale University Press, 2001).

attacks on government-controlled areas, or the coalition's bombing of *Daesh* areas. As the chapters in this book show, genocide and civil war became conceptually sundered. Because of these distinctions, and because Holocaust victims are cast as the universal or archetypal victim, other victims feel compelled to cast the violence they endure as Holocaust-like in nature, thereby framing – or "redacting" – the facts and usually failing in the attempt, thereby reaffirming their invisibility.[160]

Second: banal "lessons of history" reinscribe the old imperial hierarchy by presenting genocidal violence as the product of "barbaric" race or ethnic hatred, simultaneously marking out "civilization" by its attributes of tolerance and diversity. An ostensibly depoliticized preoccupation with atrocity prevention thereby licences foreign interventions, even wars of aggression in the name of humanitarianism and human rights; in Libya in 2011 for example.[161] These "lessons" also reinforce dangerous assumptions about the supposedly natural home of a people within "its" state, and thus the relationship between majorities and minorities, on which security imperatives feed, ironically sustaining a racist imaginary while officially outlawing racism. Furthermore, they monopolize the hermeneutic potential of reflection on genocide by concealing the actual criminal nature of much state – and often aspirational para-state military – behavior, namely their drive for permanent security, including by states that pride themselves on implementing history's apparent lessons.

The Problems of Genocide does not pretend to be a comprehensive history of the genocide keyword and permanent security. Part reconstruction, part critique of our inherited vocabulary, it presents episodes in concept formation by laying bare the deep intellectual and political structures that enabled the formulation of this new keyword and that determine its conventional meaning. The second aim of this book is to show that the criminality underlying our vocabulary of transgression – genocide, crimes against humanity, war crime, and collateral, each with their distinct jurisprudential traditions – is the drive

---

[160] On how redaction is intrinsic to the constitutions of victims and perpetrators, see Alexander Laban Hinton, *Man or Monster? The Trial of Khmer Rouge Torturer* (Durham and London: Duke University Press, 2016). An example: Paul B. Miller, "Just Like the Jews: Contending Victimization in the Former Yugoslavia," in *Lessons & Legacies IX. Memory, History, Responsibility: Reassessments of the Holocaust, Implications for the Future*, ed. John K. Roth, Jonathan Petropoulos, and Lynn Rapaport (Evanston, IL: Northwestern University Press, 2010), 251–68.

[161] Symptomatic: Lawrence Douglas, "From IMT to NMT: The Emergence of the Jurisprudence of Atrocity," in *Reassessing the Nuremberg Military Tribunals: Transitional Justice, Trial Narratives, and Historiography*, ed. Kim C. Priemel and Alexa Stiller (New York and Oxford: Berghahn Books, 2012), 286; Analysis: Rajan Menon, *The Conceit of Humanitarian Intervention* (Oxford: Oxford University Press, 2016); Steven Hopgood, *Endtimes for Human Rights* (Ithaca: Cornell University Press, 2013); Mark Swatek-Evenstein, *A History of Humanitarian Intervention* (Cambridge: Cambridge University Press, 2020).

for permanent security. The three aims are related: the genocide keyword evolved from the early-modern period to (mis)name the phenomenon of permanent security that underlay the imperial violence intrinsic to the growth of the European state.

Part I contains five chapters on the language of transgression. Chapter 1 begins with its crystallization in the heated sixteenth-century debate about Spanish imperialism in the Americas, and delineates its keywords of "shock," "conscience," and "humanity" until the 1890s. The next chapter demonstrates the remarkable stability of this language into the interwar years. It also highlights central tropes of unprecedented violence and scandal ("the worst in history") that featured in colonial scandals. While these chapters show how the invocation of "humanity" to ameliorate abuses licensed and sanitized imperial rule, they also reveal that the language of transgression recognized the economic context of labor exploitation in slavery, and the political nature of violence against civilians, namely in national liberation struggles and civil wars.

The next chapters on the semantic competition to name mass criminality examines how Raphael Lemkin and his contemporaries, especially leaders of Central European "small nations," grappled with the question of state violence. Was it driven by political factors such as imperial expansion, or nonpolitical motivations like hate? Their answers to this question during the World War II varied depending on circumstances, but the inclination of Lemkin and the World Jewish Congress, which was advocating for special Jewish representation at the Nuremberg Trials, was to argue that racial hatred alone – antisemitism – accounted for what later became known as the Holocaust. This interpretation was then enshrined in the 1948 Genocide Convention because it suited the interests of states: most old and new states in the UN depoliticized the concept so it could not be used to challenge their sovereignty and colonial empires, especially at the onset of the Cold War and decolonization.

Part II concerns permanent security until the immediate postwar years. Chapter 6 presents an account of the praxis of permanent security in world history. It focuses largely on imperial and settler-colonial violence necessary to impose Western empires since the fifteenth century, the former embodying illiberal permanent security, and the latter the liberal permanent security of the settler colonial formations that drove globalizing capitalism and that are synonymous with "liberal internationalism." In Chapter 7, I present the apogee of illiberal permanent security, the Nazi regime, to show how Hitler drew on the history of permanent security practices carried out by previous empires to make Germans great and safe again. Chapters 8 and 9 argue that an alternative order of liberal permanent security based on human rights and atrocity prevention was imagined by Germany's opponents. They planned partitions and "population exchanges" of land and populations in Palestine, India, and Germany to found stable and peaceful nation-states after the war, but countenanced considerable violence to this end. For many statesmen and commentators, human rights and ethnic cleansing were not only compatible, but necessary, to produce and secure ethnically homogeneous nation-states that so many equated with progress and modernity.[162] This style of thinking was prevalent among South Asian and Zionist elites in imagining the security of their imagined nations.

Part III takes the analysis from the late 1940s until the present day. Since the postwar order is based on the permanent security afforded by massive population expulsions, the human rights revolution, including the law of genocide, needed to exclude its workings. In Chapter 10, I show how Lemkin and Hannah Arendt did the bidding of their adopted home, the US, by defining genocide in terms of the Holocaust and by distinguishing the Holocaust from other forms of mass violence by its nonpolitical motivation of irrational race hatred. Both figures furnished the arguments that justified liberal permanent security – that is, the West's settler colonial and imperial conquest of the world – by distinguishing the Holocaust from its imperial context. As they were writing, however, other intellectuals were contesting their Cold War centralization of the Holocaust by identifying the arms race and possibility of nuclear extinction as the major issue in the international system. In doing so, they proposed an exacting critique of permanent security by exposing the workings of the US "national security state," its "permanent war machine," and serial interventions in other countries that anticipates similar arguments today. As Chapter 11 details, these critiques became sidelined in the 1990s when the West won the Cold War and the new field of Genocide Studies (initially Comparative Genocide Studies) moved the agenda to genocide prevention, particularly in light of its failure in Rwanda and Bosnia. The new field adapted Lemkin and Arendt's argument to justify a new interventionism, thereby becoming a handmaiden of liberal permanent security. The chapter revisits the complex causes and baleful consequences of this depoliticization in misleading "lessons of history" and the distinction between genocide and civil war. The concluding chapter highlights the problems of genocide today by examining the distorting effect of a particular mode of victim-identification and Holocaust memory in particular. *The Problems of Genocide* asks its readers to look beyond the confines of our inherited legal and moral categories to recognize the persistence of liberal and illiberal permanent security practices that confront us today.

---

[162] Mark Mazower, *Dark Continent: Europe's Twentieth Century* (London: Penguin, 1998).

PART I

The Language of Transgression

1

The Language of Transgression, 1500s to 1890s

Introduction

A striking consistency of terms and phrases characterizes discussions of mass criminality. Genocide "shocks the conscience of mankind" and is condemned by the "civilized world," declared the UN General Assembly in 1946. Versions of this statement peppered the subsequent two years of debate about the Genocide Convention in UN committees, in which delegates spoke about civilization, mankind and "his" shocked public conscience, universal conscience, and world conscience. Meanwhile, at the Nuremberg Trials, the chief US prosecutor said of the defendants' crimes that they "are things which have turned the stomach of the world and set every civilized hand against Nazi Germany." Then, in 1948, the UN General Assembly approved the Universal Declaration on Human Rights, whose preamble refers to "barbarous acts which have outraged the conscience of mankind." Three years later, the International Court of Justice used the same rhetoric in its judgment on reservations to the Genocide Convention. Fresh in memory, Nazi crimes in particular had shocked, outraged, and turned the stomachs of those engaged in UN and international legal deliberations.[1]

Lest this language be regarded as a relic of the immediate postwar years, consider the preamble to the Rome Statute that established the International Criminal Court in 1998. It states: "Mindful that during this century millions of children, women and men have been victims of unimaginable atrocities that deeply shock the conscience of humanity." At the same time, the ad hoc criminal tribunals for the former Yugoslavia and Rwanda likewise had

---

[1] General Assembly Resolution 91(1), "The Crime of Genocide," December 1, 1946, https://documents-dds-y.un.org/doc/RESOLUTION/GEN/NR0/033/47/IMG/NR003347.pdf? OpenElement; Hirad Abtahi and Philippa Webb, eds., *The Genocide Convention: The Travaux Preparatoires*, 2 vols. (Leiden: Martinus Nijhoff, 2008), *passim*; Universal Declaration of Human Rights, December 10, 1948, www.un.org/en/universal-declaration-human-rights; Lawrence Douglas, *The Memory of Judgment: Making Law and History in the Trials of the Holocaust* (New Haven: Yale University Press, 2001), 83l. Reservation to the Convention on the Prevention and Punishment of the Crime of Genocide, Advisory Opinion, May 28, 1951, *ICJ Reports* (1951): 15.

recourse to these terms, declaring how crimes against humanity and genocide "shock the collective conscience."[2] The welcome replacement of "mankind" with the gender-neutral "humanity" has not entirely supplanted the old terminology, however. In 2013, the Estonian ambassador to the UN implored "all actors to renew their commitment to the cause of eradicating from our shared earth the scourge of the most serious crimes that shock the conscience of mankind."[3] One eulogy for Kofi Annan by an erstwhile colleague referred to him as "a custodian world conscience" despite his "conscience-shocking" failures as a UN official during the Rwandan Genocide in 1994 and genocide of Bosnians in Srebrenica in 1995.[4] These formulaic and hackneyed phrases pass the lips of diplomats and officials of international organizations as easily today as they did seventy years ago.

The vocabulary of civilization and barbarism likewise retains its utility for the transgression effect. While Western ally Saudi Arabia visited destruction upon the civilians of Yemen in September 2016, the British, French, and US representatives to the UN Security Council condemned Russia and the Assad government in familiar terms for bombing Aleppo. "Aleppo is to Syria what Sarajevo was to Bosnia, or what Guernica was to the Spanish war," declared the French diplomat, invoking iconic atrocities: "this week will go down in history as the one in which diplomacy failed and barbarism triumphed." His US counterpart, Samantha Power, concurred: "what Russia is sponsoring and doing is not counterterrorism. It is barbarism."[5] The British envoy sang from the same song sheet when he told the Security Council that "you might think that the [Assad] regime has had its fill of barbarity – that its sick bloodlust against its own people has finally run its course."[6] Adding a memorable phrase to the language of transgression, Power announced that Russian action "creeps you out a little bit."[7]

Conscience, shock, humanity, barbarism, civilization: the fact that diplomats resort to this vocabulary so readily today means they are still speaking

---

[2] Prosecutor v. Kambanda, Case No. ICTR 97-23-S, Judgment and Sentence (September 4, 1998), 14, http://hrlibrary.umn.edu/instree/ICTR/KAMBANDA_ICTR-97-23/KAMBANDA_ ICTR-97-23-S.html.

[3] International Criminal Court, "'Victims Now Have a Voice': UN High Commissioner for Human Rights Navi Pillay commemorates International Criminal Justice Day," Press Release, July 8, 2013, www.icc-cpi.int/legalAidConsultations?name=pr928.

[4] Ramesh Thakur, "Kofi Annan's Achievement," *Project Syndicate*, August 20, 2018, www .project-syndicate.org/commentary/kofi-annan-remembered-by-ramesh-thakur-2018-08. Annan was the former UN secretary-general who died in 2018.

[5] Julian Borger and Kareem Shaheen, "Russia Accused of War Crimes in Syria at UN Security Council Session," *The Guardian*, September 26, 2016.

[6] Caroline Mortimer, "Western Powers Accuse Russia of Barbaric War Crimes Before Shock UN Walkout," *The Independent*, September 26, 2016.

[7] Samantha Power, "Remarks at a UN Security Council Emergency Briefing on Syria," December 13, 2016, https://2009-2017-usun.state.gov/remarks/7607.

about political evil with the venerable language of transgression. Many international lawyers, political scientists, and ethicists also routinely invoke these keywords as natural categories. If they have histories, they are constituents of an imagined civilizing process that culminates in the contemporary legal regime regulating armed conflict.[8] They ask: what shocks our civilized consciences today? Instead, we ask: who defines these categories? From which vista does "humanity" look out across the global landscape of transgression? According to what hierarchy of values and assumptions does it orient its conscience, and according to what constellation in the history of emotions does it feel this shock? What are the cultural and geopolitical processes that constitute their contested meanings? Who has the ability to arrogate to themselves the right to incarnate and define humanity and civilized conscience? Which actions and processes are screened out by setting an upper level of transgression that "shocks the conscience"? In sum: how is the greatest political evil named and defined?

This chapter and the next one answer these questions by historicizing the intersecting keywords of the language of transgression since the early-modern period when, I argue, we can locate its operation for the first time. The analysis focuses on Western empires. Certainly, drawing distinctions between the civilized and the savage was not limited to Europeans. The Ottoman Empire (c. 1299–1922) and Chinese Qing Dynasty (1644–1912) also expanded their holdings based on a hierarchy between their civilized core and uncivilized peripheral peoples. They too possessed "civilizing missions." Of the later Japanese empire, one scholar has suggested its internalization of Western civilizational discourse represented a form of "mimetic imperialism."[9]

---

[8] Payam Akhaven, *Reducing Genocide to Law: Definition, Meaning, and the Ultimate Crime* (Cambridge: Cambridge University Press, 2012); Peter Sutch, "Evil in Contemporary International Political Theory: Acts That Shock the Conscience of Mankind," in *Evil in Contemporary Political Theory*, ed. Bruce Haddock, Peri Roberts, and Peter Sutch (Edinburgh: Edinburgh University Press, 2011), 101–23; Michel Veuthey, "Public Conscience in International Humanitarian Law Today," in *Crisis Management and Humanitarian Protection: In Honour of Dieter Fleck*, ed. Horst Fischer et al. (Berlin: Berliner Wissenschafts-Verlag, 2004), 611–42; Michal Walzer, "The Argument about Humanitarian Intervention," *Dissent* (Winter 2002), www.dissentmagazine.org/article/the-argument-about-humanitarian-intervention; W. R. Smyser, *The Humanitarian Conscience: Caring for Others in the Age of Terror* (New York and Basingstoke: Palgrave Macmillan, 2003).

[9] Robert Eskildsen, "Of Civilization and Savages: The Mimetic Imperialism of Japan's 1874 Expedition to Taiwan," *American Historical Review* 107, no. 2 (2002): 388–418; Shogo Suzuki, *Civilization and Empire: China and Japan's Encounter with European International Society* (Abingdon: Routledge, 2009); Sebastian Conrad, "Die Zivilisierung des 'Selbst': Japans koloniale Moderne," in *Zivilisierungsmissionen: Imperiale Weltverbesserung seit dem 18. Jahrhundert*, ed. Boris Barth and Jürgen Osterhammel (Constance: UVK Verlagsgesellschaft, 2005), 245–68; Ussama Makdisi, "Ottoman Orientalism," *American*

Even so, the Western maritime empires that colonized the Americas, Oceania, and later Africa made the most extensive contact with indigenous peoples, and were the drivers of economic globalization based on the trans-Atlantic slave trade.

We will see that this language could be spoken by different people in different ways to different ends. Because we are interested in laying out the linguistic context from which Lemkin invented "genocide," as well as the vested interests that went into its restricted legal meaning, this chapter highlights its operation and development as an instrument of power. The focus is on European and white North American actors. It would take another book to reconstruct in detail the subaltern idioms of resistance that inverted and challenged its dominant registers, although anticolonial critique is noted here. Moreover, the chapter emphasizes linguistic continuity over contextual distinctions. It goes without saying that the notion of "humanity" varied between Greeks, Romans, Christians, early-modern international jurists, and nineteenth-century humanitarians. They excluded "barbarians" from "humanity" in different ways. "Slaves" were excluded in Antiquity while explicitly included in the late imperial and humanitarian discourse. Those who allegedly refused to work and declined participation in capitalism were placed outside early international law and high imperialism, if not by humanitarians. Civilization was restricted to economic development for some, and was extended to education and "uplift" for others. What is more, these keywords in the language of transgression were naturally open to interpretation. And yet, a common feature in all their uses was the framing of exploitative and violent excesses – atrocities – as "barbaric." Significantly, atrocities were understood not only as punctual events but as the outcomes of corrupt political and economic processes. If the non-European perpetrator was the cruel despot, the European one was the imperial tyrant who enslaved non-Europeans, provoked or put down their rebellions, and otherwise abused power.

Although critical when applied against imperial excess, this language rarely questioned European rule and capitalism as such. Westerners attacked savage capitalism and mismanaged colonial (often private) enterprises that undermined the ability of the system to reproduce and ethically justify itself. As a sustainable alternative, internal or external critics of an empire's atrocities usually entreated "gentle" versions of imperial expansion and colonial rule.

Historical Review 107, no. 3 (2002): 768–96; Mostafa Minawi, *The Ottoman Scramble for Africa* (Stanford: Stanford University Press, 2016); Kenneth Pomeranz, "Empire and 'Civilizing' Missions, Past and Present," *Daedalus* 134, no. 2 (2005): 34–45; Laura Hostetler, *Qing Colonial Enterprise: Ethnography and Cartography in Early Modern China* (Chicago: University of Chicago Press, 2001).

With few exceptions, non-Europeans, like Haitian liberation leader Toussaint Louverture (1743–1803) and Trinidadian historian and writer, C. L. R. James (1901–1989), rejected Western colonial rule altogether.[10] Both types of critics had to contend with imperial apologists who accused indigenous people of atrocities against one another and Europeans to justify colonial rule.

If the continuing circulation of terms like shock, conscience, and mankind – including the recurring trope of the "worst crime in history" – suggests the language of transgression's relative semantic stability over almost 500 years, we will see in Chapters 5, 10, and 11 that the Holocaust led to its depoliticization.[11] After 1945, the greatest evil was driven by racial hatred alone, an identity crime devoid of political logics. Slave-like exploitation fell from view. What is more, whereas the label "unprecedented crime" was regularly attached to the latest outrage of the day before the World War II, thereafter it became firmly affixed to the Holocaust, freezing the fluidity of meaning into a rigid hierarchy of criminality. Any atrocity now must analogize with the Holocaust to be registered as shocking, thereby limiting the capacity of trauma to be legible as supreme emergencies.

Raphael Lemkin spoke this language and was instrumental in mediating, if not completing, the transition of its meaning. Reconstructing these developments can unfreeze the language of transgression so it becomes truly global and polyvalent, a source of insight rather than blindness. As noted above, because I am exploring the complicity of humanitarian political rhetoric with empire, my focus is the European and North American speakers of this language, although we also hear from the non-Europeans who spoke back. Remarkable is the shared vocabulary among all parties to imperial encounters, whether in expanding the notion of civilization to include non-Europeans or in branding Westerners as the barbarians.

Empire and Critique

The formative moment for the language of transgression is the confrontation in 1550 and 1551 between two Spanish Roman Catholic priests about their country's conquest of the Aztec and Inca empires of Mexico and Peru, which had been underway for several decades. Their debate turned on just-war theory in relation to non-Europeans: when can war justifiably be waged on barbarians and their lands conquered? Bartolomé de las Casas (1484–1566)

---

[10] Benedikt Stuchtey, *Die europäische Expansion und ihre Feinde: Kolonialismuskritik vom 18. bis in das 20. Jahrhundert* (Munich: Oldenbourg Verlag, 2010).

[11] On semantic stability, see Reinhart Koselleck, "Linguistic Change and the History of Events," *Journal of Modern History* 61, no. 4 (1989): 649–66, and idem, "Introduction and Prefaces to the Geschichtliche Grundbegriffe," *Contributions to the History of Concepts* 6, no. 1 (2011): 1–37.

indicted Spanish rule in his *A Short Account of the Destruction of the Indies*, written in 1542.[12] His opponent was Juan Ginés de Sepúlveda (1494–1573), who defended Spanish conquest and rule. This celebrated encounter is unnecessary to recount in detail; pertinent for the language of transgression is their invocation of excessive violence – atrocity. The legitimacy of Spanish arms, argued Sepúlveda, lay in its purpose as a humanitarian intervention, to use today's term: to prevent the Amerindians' scandalous violations of natural law: idolatry, sodomy, human sacrifice, cannibalism, and internecine warfare. These were "considered by the philosophers to be the most ferocious and abominable perversities." The Amerindians were not guided by reason, he declared, but by passion, rendering them children and natural slaves. The Spanish, for their part, embodied civilized morality – he spoke about the "gentleness and humanity of our people" – and the right to effectively police the world to stamp out injuries to humanity by "savage and cruel races." Consequently, Amerindian resistance to the Spanish Christianizing entreaties was illegitimate.[13]

By contrast, Las Casas was shocked by the Spanish massacres and exploitation of Indians, and he reported that listeners were similarly "deeply shocked" by what he had witnessed and learned.[14] He thus inverted the image of civilized Europeans who followed the laws of nature and barbarians who violated them by trying to shock the Spanish ruling class to reform its new American holdings. Even if his reform campaign did little to ameliorate conditions on the ground, Las Casas's polemics against the Spanish enslavement and massacres of Amerindians, and those like Sepúlveda who excused or trivialized them, instigated a sustained scandal. His book was quickly translated into many European languages, in part because it provided a rich source for Protestant empires to criticize their rival, inaugurating a centuries-long

---

[12] Bartolomé de Las Casas, *A Short Account of the Destruction of the Indies*, ed. and trans. Nigel Griffin, intro. Anthony Pagden (New York: Penguin, 1992), 3; Peter Stamatov, *The Origins of Global Humanitarianism: Religion, Empires, and Advocacy* (New York: Cambridge University Press, 2013); Thomas Weller, "Humanitarianism Before Humanitarianism? Spanish Discourses on Slavery from the Sixteenth Century to the Nineteenth Century," in *Humanity: A History of European Concepts in Practice from the Sixteenth Century to the Present*, ed. Fabian Klose and Mirjam Thulin (Göttingen: Vandenhoeck and Ruprecht, 2016), 151–68; Tzvetan Todorov, *The Conquest of America: The Question of the Other* (New York: Harper and Row, 1984).

[13] Daniel R. Brunstetter and Dana Zartner, "Just War against Barbarians: Revisiting the Valladolid Debates between Sepúlveda and Las Casas," *Political Studies* 59, no. 3 (2011): 737; Ellen Meiksins Wood, *Liberty and Property: A Social History of Western Political Thought from the Renaissance to the Enlightenment* (London: Verso, 2012), 102; Lewis Hanke, *All Mankind Is One: A Study of the Disputation between Bartolomé de Las Casas and Juan Ginés de Sepúlveda in 1550 on the Intellectual and Religious Capacity of the American Indians* (DeKalb: Northern Illinois University Press, 1974).

[14] Las Casas, *A Short Account of the Destruction of the Indies*, 3.

debate about the "black legend" of Spanish conquest. Las Casas has been cited by liberals and humanitarians ever since as representing Christian-European conscience.[15]

By virtue of this reception, Las Casas inaugurated a new version of the language of transgression: to criticize rather than to justify empire, although this did not mean opposing European rule over others. What is more, this language lent itself to attacking other empires in order to exculpate one's own. Centuries later, in 1835, French writer Alexis De Tocqueville echoed Las Casas in condemning the Spanish for committing "unparalleled atrocities which bring an indelible shame upon themselves" while he justified the French conquest of Algeria.[16] Intrinsic to this debate was mutual observation and criticism of empires, which led to a consistent pattern of interpreting atrocities: rival empires provoked uprisings by their despotism and misrule, while the unpolitical criminal motives of bandits and fanatics drove rebellion in one's own realm.

We can identify six elements that recur in the Las Casasian language of transgression.

First, although his book relied on Christian and classical motifs, it marked a departure by basing its truth claims on direct or proximate reportage of the described events.[17] The witness-writer who related graphically-told atrocity stories lent the text authenticity. Not only was the detail difficult to dispute, it made a vicarious witness of the reader. The effect was heightened by the use of images, even in Las Casas's day. Translations of his book contained graphic illustrations of atrocities sketched by the Flemish engraver, Theodore de Bry.[18]

Second: Las Casas described the emotional response to atrocity in now familiar terms: "if one were to set out in detail all the atrocities he committed," he wrote of one conquistador, "they would make a very weighty tome indeed,

---

[15] Benjamin Keen, "The Black Legend Revisited: Assumptions and Realities," *Hispanic American Historical Review* 49, no. 4 (1969): 703–19. As we see in Chapter 3, Lemkin relied heavily on Las Casas for his views of what he called the "Spanish American Genocide." See also Christopher Schmidt-Nowara and John M. Nieto-Phillips, eds., *Interpreting Spanish Colonialism: Empires, Nations, and Legends* (Albuquerque: University of New Mexico Press, 2005).

[16] Alexis De Tocqueville, *Democracy in America*, trans. Gerald Bevan (London: Penguin, 2003), 397; idem, *Writings on Empire and Slavery*, ed. Jennifer Pitts (Baltimore, MD, and London: Johns Hopkins University Press, 2001).

[17] Anthony Pagden, "Introduction," in Las Casas, *A Short Account of the Destruction of the Indies*, xiii–xIi; Daniel Castro, *Another Face of Empire: Bartolomé de Las Casas, Indigenous Rights, and the Ecclesiastical Imperialism* (Durham: Duke University Press, 2007), xxxii–xxxiii.

[18] Patricia Gravatt, "Rereading Theodore de Bry's Black Legend," in *Rereading the Black Legend: The Discourses of Racial and Religious Difference in the Renaissance Empire*, ed. Margaret R. Greer, Walter D. Mignolo, and Maureen Quilligan (Chicago: University of Chicago Press, 2007), 225–43.

and one which would truly shock the world." Another incident, he repeated, "proved sufficiently grave to shock the whole world." Alternatively: "the atrocities, barbarities, murders, clearances, ravages and other foul injustices" committed by the Spanish "would stagger not only contemporaries but future generations."[19] Thanks to Las Casas's writings, Europeans would use words like shock and stagger to describe their own outraged affects in relation to criminality they witnessed or perceived.

Roland Barthes's theory of what he calls "shock photos" illuminates the affirmative cultural work of this emotional reaction. He distinguishes between images that can be registered by the viewer's interpretative capacity, and those that exceed and punctuate them.[20] The latter were not "shock photos," however. The effect of shock is not to exceed or punctuate, but to reveal an unconscious connection: they "shout" but do not wound. In other words, the "scandal of horror," as he described the effect of "shock photos," was not the traumatic irruption of novelty but the reiteration of established, if half-forgotten, culturally predetermined emotional repertoires.[21]

Third: to signal these crimes' excessive character, Las Casas depicted them as virtually sublime forms of violence beyond human comprehension. They were "too many and too dreadful to recount," indeed they "beggared" description, anticipating the Rome Statute's reference to "unimaginable crimes" half a millennium later.[22] Similarly, to emphasize the totality of destruction, he referred to the "desert" that Spaniards had made of Indian lands, evoking Tacitus's ironic description of *Pax Romana* as a polity based on the destruction of conquered people.[23] The device of "unprecedented" criminality served the same purpose. The Spanish "outrages," wrote Las Casas, "[were] of a truly fiendish nature and on a quite unprecedented scale." Their crimes went "far beyond" others in the New World and elsewhere.[24] "Peru," he declared, "daily witnesses acts of a spine-chilling barbarity unequalled by anything seen before, either in the New World or anywhere else on earth, the upshot being that not only have entire indigenous populations been wiped out and their kingdoms

---

[19] Las Casas, *A Short Account of the Destruction of the Indies*, 63, 90, 100, 54. Emphasis added.

[20] He describes it as an image that "rises from the scene, shoots out of it like an arrow, and pierces me": Roland Barthes, *Camera Lucida: Reflections on Photography*, trans. Richard Howard (New York: Hill and Wang, 1982), 26.

[21] Ibid., 32, 41; Roland Barthes, "Shock-Photos," in *The Eiffel Tower and Other Mythologies* (Berkeley: University of California Press, 1997), 73; Michael Fried, "Barthes's Punctum," *Critical Inquiry* 31, no. 3 (2005): 539–74; Dan Stone, "The Sonderkommando Photographs," *Jewish Social Studies* 7, no. 3 (2001): 132–48; Nicolas Chare and Dominic Williams, *The Auschwitz Sonderkommando: Testimonies, Histories, Representations* (Basingstoke: Palgrave Macmillan, 2016), ch. 3.

[22] Las Casas, *A Short Account of the Destruction of the Indies*, 42, 65, 68, 104.

[23] Ibid., 55, 123.   [24] Ibid., 51, 69, 116, 55.

abandoned."[25] It is easy to see why Lemkin thought Las Casas was describing a genocide.[26]

Fourth: still another trope to communicate excess was the inversion of civilizational hierarchies. Not the Indians but the Spaniards were "barbarians": they committed the "outrages," "enormities," "abominations," "carnage," and "butchery." He referred to the Moors who had dominated Spain to specify barbarity. Now the Spanish were behaving like the hated Muslim occupier, "more inhumane and more vicious than savage tigers, more ferocious than lions or than ravening wolves."[27] Las Casas went so far as to denounce the Spanish as "enemies of humanity," the legal categorization of pirates and tyrants, deemed to be waging private warfare against humankind in general, who could therefore be killed by anyone.[28] In doing so, he anticipated later European views of Ottoman Muslims, and provided the script for nineteenth-century humanitarians and the Western representatives on the UN Security Council condemning Russia and Syria in 2016.[29] As we will see, this script has been put to different uses over the centuries, but as remarkable as the twists and turns in its restaging and reinterpretation is the fact of its continuity.

Fifth: of equal significance was Las Casas's identification of economic and political motives and dynamics in the Spaniards' conquest. Their crimes were de facto slavery and massacre, the two issues that have exercised humanitarians since the late eighteenth century. Economic exploitation – greed – not racial or religious contempt motivated the Spanish, who made impossible demands of Indians. If the latter did not immediately obey orders, "they were dubbed outlaws and held to be in rebellion against His Majesty," thereby licensing exterminatory violence against them.[30] This point was also taken

---

[25] Ibid., 129. Emphasis added.

[26] This tradition of proclaiming atrocities as unprecedented continued, for example, in Nathan Hanover's eyewitness account of Cossack massacres of Jews in Eastern Europe in the middle of the seventeenth century. "Some ten thousand souls perished by the most terrible deaths the world has ever witnessed," he wrote. Nathan Nata Hanover, *Abyss of Despair: The Famous 17th Century Chronicle Depicting Jewish Life in Russia and Poland during the Chmielnicki Massacres of 1648–49*, trans. Abraham J. Mesch, foreword William B. Helmreich (New Brunswick, NJ: Transaction Publishers, 1983), 63. Thanks to Omer Bartov for discussion on this point.

[27] Las Casas, *A Short Account of the Destruction of the Indies*, 96. I take this point from Pagden, "Introduction," xxxviii.

[28] Las Casas, *A Short Account of the Destruction of the Indies*, 17.

[29] This continuity is doubted by some scholars, but I argue below that Stoic themes of shared reason as the basis of a common humanity unite classical, Christian, later humanitarian traditions. Skeptical is Konstantinos Delikostantis, *Der moderne Humanitarismus: Zur Bestimmung und Kritik einer zeitgenössischen Auslegung der Humanitätsidee* (Mainz: Matthias-Grünewald-Verlag, 1982). Thanks to Umut Özsu for drawing my attention to this book.

[30] Las Casas, *A Short Account of the Destruction of the Indies*, 13, 53, 113.

up by Lemkin, who also saw through the cynical and self-serving Spanish assumption of the right to trade with the Indians as a pretext to wage war on them. In this regard, Las Casas differed from his fellow Spanish priest, Francisco de Vitoria, who likewise criticized Spanish rule and invested Indians with natural rights, but argued that the Indians were in rebellion when they resisted the Spanish right of natural partnership and communication (*naturalis societatis et communicationis*) – in effect, trade and missionary work – thereby justifying violent practices of permanent security as self-defense, indeed as just war.[31]

Sixth: like later humanitarians, Las Casas was moved by conscience to act: "it would constitute criminal neglect of my duty to remain silent about the enormous loss of life."[32] Here he invoked his individual Christian conscience, also refusing absolution to conquistadors unless they were penitent and made restitution for their crimes.[33] It was unnecessary for Las Casas to invoke the "conscience of mankind" that UN conventions and declarations used 400 years later, because he could draw on established concepts from classical thought. By "shocking the whole world," he did not limit his appeal to Christendom but recalled the cosmopolitan solidarity of all people. Socrates had declared himself a "citizen of the world" – of the cosmos – not just of Athens and Greece. Later, the Stoic philosophers, who were influential in Greece and Rome, also rejected the distinction between Greek and barbarian by enjoining people to act as if they were members of a common human family by virtue of their shared capacity to reason.[34] Roman writers like Cicero quoted Socrates's famous self-identification, extending it to the "citizen of the *whole* world" (*civis totius mundi*), to underline its universality, a status available to the philosopher who recognized the "nature of all things."[35] Cicero translated this

---

[31] See Andrew Fitzmaurice, "The Problem of Eurocentrism in the Thought of Francisco de Vitoria," in *At the Origins of Modernity: Francisco de Vitoria and the Discovery of International Law*, ed. José María Beneyto and Justo Corti Varela (Basel: Springer, 2017), 77–93.

[32] Las Casas, *A Short Account of the Destruction of the Indies*, 5, 3; Castro, *Another Face of Empire*, 108–9.

[33] Brian P. Owensby, "The Theater of Conscience in the 'Living Law' of the Indies," in *New Horizons in Spanish Colonial Law: Contributions to Transnational Early Modern Legal History*, ed. Thomas Duve and Heikki Pihlajamäki, Vol. 3 (Frankfurt am Main: Max Planck Institute for European Legal History, 2015), 125–49.

[34] Melissa Lane, *Greek and Roman Political Ideas* (London: Penguin, 2014), 315. I am grateful to Andrew Fitzmaurice for discussions on this subject.

[35] Tamara T. Chin, "What Is Imperial Cosmopolitanism? Revisiting *Kosmopolitēs* and *Mundanus*," in *Cosmopolitanism and Empire: Universal Rulers, Local Elites, and Cultural Integration in the Ancient Near East and Mediterranean*, ed. Myles Lavan, Richard E. Payne, and John Weisweiler (Oxford: Oxford University Press, 2016), 138. Emphasis added.

notion into *jus gentium*, the law of nations that regulated interaction with non-Romans.[36]

The priests Las Casas and Vitoria also included Stoic themes in their thinking. Las Casas invoked Cicero in pronouncing that Amerindians were "men like us," indeed that "there is only one definition of each and every man, and that is that he is rational ... and thus all the races of human kind are one."[37] Vitoria imported the notion into the *jus gentium* by declaring that "The whole world, which is in a sense a commonwealth, has the power to enact laws which are just and convenient to all men; and these make up the law of nations."[38] The notion of a common humanity was of course intrinsic to the Christian cosmology as well.[39] To shock the world, then, was to suggest that the delicate tissue of human solidarity – in this case, the God-given, universal natural rights of Amerindians – had been violated to an extent that human community itself was imperilled. To injure part of humanity was to injure the rest, a theme that Lemkin took up. This was the transgression effect.

For all that, Cicero did not regard himself as a citizen of no place; he was emphatically Roman. Indeed, for him the whole world, *orbis terrarum*, entailed the expansion of Roman rule to others: the extension of its law spread civilization.[40] Las Casas followed in this tradition. He did not oppose Spanish rule as such, still less the spread of Christianity. His *Short Account* was addressed to the king to prompt him to assert imperial authority over the colonial elites exploiting the Indians. Las Casas himself held the title of the first "Protector of the Indians" and even recommended the introduction of slaves from Africa to ameliorate Amerindian labor conditions.[41] Much like liberal nineteenth-century imperialists, he thought Indians would be better off in a regulated empire as free vassals of the king rather than as virtual slaves of Spanish entrepreneurs. Such an empire would incorporate the Americas into the incipiently globalizing economy by its simultaneous respect of Amerindian

---

[36] Gordon E. Sherman, "Jus Gentium and International Law," *American Journal of International Law* 12, no. 1 (1918): 56–63. Stephen C. Neff, "International Law and the Critique of Cosmopolitan Citizenship," in *Cosmopolitan Citizenship*, ed. Roland Dannreuther and Kimberly Hutchings (Basingstoke: Palgrave, 1999), 106.

[37] Garrett Wallace Brown and David Held, "Editors' Introduction," in *Cosmopolitanism Reader*, ed. Garrett Wallace Brown and David Held (Cambridge: Polity Press, 2010), 6.

[38] Georg Cavallar, *The Rights of Strangers: Theories of International Hospitality, the Global Community and Political Justice Since Vitoria* (Abingdon: Routledge, 2016), 91–2.

[39] Katell Berthelot and Matthias Morgenstern, eds., *The Quest for a Common Humanity: Human Dignity and Otherness in the Religious Traditions of the Mediterranean* (Leiden: Brill, 2011).

[40] Anthony Pagden, "Stoicism, Cosmopolitanism, and the Legacy of European Imperialism," *Constellations* 7, no. 1 (2000): 3–22.

[41] Castro, *Another Face of Empire*, 153; Ian Haywood, *Bloody Romanticism: Spectacular Violence and the Politics of Representation, 1776–1832* (Basingstoke: Palgrave Macmillan, 2006), 146.

property rights, and the right of the Spanish to trade with them, as Vitoria insisted.[42] He objected to savage colonialism, not to private property, its universalization, and sovereignty backed by a theory of just war. A well-ordered empire would also be a more efficient converter of souls to Christianity.

The language of transgression was rarely put to anti-imperial uses, then: it justified humanitarian empire. The language of transgression thus highlighted some systems of exploitation while condoning actions and processes that fell below Las Casas's threshold of shocking: they were acceptable forms of exploitation. The issue, then, is not "humanitarianism or imperialism?" as one scholar posed the dichotomy, but the marriage of imperialism and humanitarianism.[43]

Empire, Commerce, Corruption

Spain's Protestant rivals, the English and Dutch, took up Las Casas's and Vitoria's themes in their imperial ideologies, which they developed in negation to Spanish conquest and its rapacious reputation. Notions of commerce and land cultivation – as opposed to Iberian plunder and exploitation – as the drivers of civilization, and humanity and public conscience as a normative horizon, were central to these justifications of empire. Together, they became the keywords of humanitarian colonial projects and the language of transgression. The latter justified the former as the answer to Spanish-like excesses.

Tudor and early Stuart English expansion was to be benign, "humility" and "self-restraint" in encounters with indigenous people vouchsafing its legitimacy. Commerce and/or settlement rather than domination and exploitation were the ideals.[44] As a peaceful praxis of human interaction, commerce between nations instantiated a civilizing process by dissolving parochial prejudices and binding humans in a cosmopolitan order. Commerce – which entailed private property and colonial settlement – thereby realized the Stoic ideal of human communication and sociability on which neo-Thomists like Vitoria set so much store and that Samuel Pufendorf (1632–1692), John Locke (1632–1704), and Adam Smith (1732–1790) later made the centrepieces of

---

[42] Martti Koskenniemi, "Empire and International Law: The Real Spanish Contribution," *University of Toronto Law Journal* 61, no. 1 (2011): 28; Stuchtey, *Die europäische Expansion und ihre Feinde*, 119.

[43] Gary J. Bass, *Freedom's Battle: The Origins of Humanitarian Intervention* (New York: Knopf, 2008), ch. 1, "Humanitarianism or Imperialism?"

[44] Christopher Hodgkins, *Reforming Empire: Protestant Colonialism and Conscience in British Literature* (Columbia, MI: University of Missouri Press, 2002), 78; David Armitage, *The Ideological Origins of the British Empire* (Cambridge: Cambridge University Press, 2000), 61–99; Andrew Fitzmaurice, *Humanism and Empire: An Intellectual History of English Colonisation, 1500–1625* (Cambridge: Cambridge University Press, 2003).

their visions.[45] Free trade in particular led to world peace because a global market promised expansion rather than the zero-sum calculation of mercantilism. In 1848, when free market principles were changing English laws and institutions, John Stuart Mill (1806–1873) extolled the virtues of Smith's political economy in terms of permanent security:

> It is commerce which is rapidly rendering war obsolete, by strengthening and multiplying the personal interests which are in natural opposition to it. And it may be said without exaggeration that the great extent and rapid increase of international trade, in being the principal guarantee of the peace of the world, is the great permanent security for the uninterrupted progress of the ideas, institutions, and the character of the human race.[46]

Mill was also repeating the views of Dutch jurist Hugo Grotius (1583–1645) who elaborated the relationship between commerce and sociability in a hugely influential memorandum for the Dutch East India Company that disputed the Spanish and Portuguese claim to exclusive rights in Asia in the name of free trade on the oceans. By restricting access to competitors, the Iberians were rupturing the "bond of human fellowship," because God "wished human friendship to be engendered by mutual needs and resources" that commerce embodied.[47] These were arguments about natural sociability and communication that Vitoria had made in the service of Spanish access to trade in the Americas and, implicitly, the globe. In reasoning later enforced by British and US naval power, Grotius claimed that the oceans belonged to no-one or, rather, were public commons, so the Dutch military enforcement of free trade served a universal interest: "the cause of the Dutch is the more reasonable, because their advantage in this matter is bound up with the advantage of the whole human race," wrote Grotius, "an advantage that the Portuguese are trying to destroy."[48] An informal empire of commerce carried on by private corporations like the Dutch East India Company benefited all peoples.

---

[45] Pagden, "Stoicism, Cosmopolitanism, and the Legacy of European Imperialism"; Richard Tuck, *The Rights of War and Peace: Political Thought and the International Order from Grotius to Kant* (Oxford: Oxford University Press, 1999), 167–72; Istvan Hont, *Jealousy of Trade: International Competition and the Nation-State in Historical Perspective* (Cambridge, MA: Belnap Press of Harvard University Press, 2005); Jennifer Pitts, *A Turn to Empire: The Rise of Liberalism in Britain and France* (Princeton: Princeton University Press, 2005), ch. 2.

[46] John Stuart Mill, *Principles of Political Economy* (New York: Longmans, Green, 1909), 582.

[47] Hugo Grotius, *The Freedom of the Seas, or the Right Which Belongs to the Dutch to Take Part in the East Indian Trade*, ed. James Brown Scott, trans. Ralph Van Deman Magoffin (New York: Oxford University Press, 2016), 7–8.

[48] Grotius, *The Freedom of the Seas*, 70; Eric Wilson, *Savage Republic: De Indis of Hugo Grotius, Republicanism and Dutch Hegemony within the Early Modern World-System (c. 1600–1619)* (Leiden: Brill, 2008), 251.

The notion of the "whole human race" led to the abstraction of "humanity."[49] In another famous treatise, *The Laws of War and Peace*, Grotius referred to "humanity" as the norm that moderated warfare, likely drawing on his slightly older contemporary, the Protestant Italian professor of law at Oxford, Alberico Gentili (1552–1608). Gentili liberally invoked the "right of humanity," the "common sentiments of humanity," and "common law of humanity" as the values underlying the law of nations, thereby repeating the Stoic conviction that their violation injured all mankind.[50] Like Las Casas before him, he mentioned piracy as a prime example of such a violation. Because pirates thereby became enemies of mankind, just war could be made against them by anyone.[51] Those who campaigned against piracy also served a universal purpose, argued French political leaders and thinkers justifying the occupation of Algeria in 1830, just as US leaders declare a "global war on terrorism" in the name of "civilization."[52]

By the eighteenth century, jurists like the Swiss Emerich de Vattel (1714–1767) used this terminology to condemn slavery as a "disgrace to humanity." The French thinker Baron de Montesquieu (1689–1755) thought likewise in his famous *Spirit of the Laws* (1748). But they were relatively isolated voices at the time; slavery was not illegal in the law of nations, and even Vattel did not criminalize the enslavement of prisoners. There was no antislavery movement when they were writing although by then about five million Africans had been forcibly taken to British, French, Dutch, Spanish, and Portuguese plantations in the Americas and Cape Colony of southern Africa.[53] Trade in African slave labor was not so shocking to most Europeans

---

[49] Generally, see Klose and Thulin, *Humanity*.

[50] Theodore Meron, "Common Rights of Mankind in Gentili, Grotius and Suarez," *American Journal of International Law* 85, no. 1 (1991): 110–6.

[51] See the discussion in Alexis Heraclides and Ada Dialla, *Humanitarian Intervention in the Long Nineteenth Century* (Manchester: Manchester University Press, 2015); Claire Vergerio, "Alberico Gentili's *De iure belli*: An Absolutist's Attempt to Reconcile the *jus gentium* and the Reason of State Tradition," *Journal of the History of International Law* 19, no. 4 (2017): 429–66.

[52] Paul A. Silverstein, *The New Barbarians: Piracy and Terrorism on the North African Frontier* (Ithaca: Cornell University Press, 2005); Michael Kempe, "'Even in the remotest corners of the world': Globalized Piracy and International Law, 1500–1900," *Journal of Global History* 5, no. 3 (2010): 353–72.

[53] Emerich de Vattel, *The Law of Nations: Or, Principles of the Law of Nature, Applied to the Conduct of Nations and Sovereigns*, ed. and intro. Bela Kapossy and Richard Whatmore (Indianapolis: Liberty Fund, 2008), 556; Diana J. Schaub, "Montesquieu on Slavery," *Perspectives on Politics* 34, no. 2 (2010): 70–8; Mark W. Janis, *America and the Law of Nations 1776–1939* (Oxford: Oxford University Press, 2010), 93; Jean Allain, "The Nineteenth Century Law of the Sea and the British Abolition of the Slave Trade," *British Yearbook of International Law* 78, no. 1 (2007): 346; David Eltis and Stanley L. Engerman, eds., *The Cambridge World History of Slavery*, Volume 3, AD 1420–AD 1804 (Cambridge: Cambridge University Press, 2011).

until the second half of the eighteenth century, when the nonconformist Protestant and Enlightenment emphasis on free, private conscience could be joined with the developing notion of public opinion to challenge established religion and absolutism. Until then, "public conscience" had expressed statist priorities, echoing Thomas Hobbes's (1588–1679) coining of the term "public conscience" to uphold the authority of law over the potential anarchy of private judgment: "the law is the publique Conscience, by which he hath already undertaken to be guided."[54]

Such restrictions were intolerable for an incipient middle class that sought a share in government and claimed public conscience as a combination of reason and morality informed by public debate. Because law was motivated by justice, it was an expression of the public good, of binding norms like the *jus gentium*, the law of nations. To invoke public conscience came to refer to other universal abstractions like humanity and civilization in the law's protection of the individual freedom and the common good.[55]

These ideals did not necessarily entail a critical posture to empire. Condemning atrocities could justify conquest in the first place as Sepúlveda's example indicates. Pointing to indigenous crimes covered up the violence of conquest. A classic case is the lurid depiction of the "Black Hole of Calcutta," when a victorious Indian leader incarcerated British subjects in a prison where many perished in 1756, a year before the Battle of Plassey in which the East India Company consolidated its grip of the South Asian continent. "The annals of the world cannot produce an incident like it in any degree or proportion to all the dismal circumstances attending it," declaimed one survivor in the familiar terms of the language of transgression.[56] Indian barbarism rather than the British East India Company's incremental conquest and exploitation of the subcontinent was the scandal. Two decades later, American colonists would mythologize massacres of settlers by "savage Indians" to legitimate their anti-British and murderous anti-indigenous campaigns. Their Declaration of Independence in 1776 condemned King George III for exciting "insurrections" by "the merciless Indian savages, whose known rule of warfare is an undistinguished destruction of all ages, sexes, and conditions."[57] The shared fear of Indians by European settlers,

---

[54] Thomas Hobbes, *Leviathan*, ed. Richard Tuck (Cambridge: Cambridge University Press, 1997), 223.

[55] David Dyzenhaus, "The Public Conscience of the Law," *Netherlands Journal of Legal Philosophy* 43, no. 2 (2014): 115–25; Larry May, "Hobbes, Law, and Public Conscience," *Critical Review of International Social and Political Philosophy* 19, no. 1 (2016): 12–28.

[56] Nicholas B. Dirks, *Scandal of Empire: India and the Creation of Modern Britain* (Cambridge, MA: The Belknap Press of Harvard University Press, 2006), 1.

[57] John R. Wunder, 'Merciless Indian Savages' and the Declaration of Independence: Native Americans Translate the Ecunnaunuxulgee Document," *American Indian Law Review* 25, no. 1 (2000/2001): 65–6; Haywood, *Bloody Romanticism*, ch. 4.

otherwise divided along religious and national lines, in fact united them into a settler community that came to prize its tolerance of ethnic difference.[58]

These possibilities in the language of transgression were publicly staged with an intensity not witnessed since Las Casas in the celebrated and controversial impeachment trial of the East India Company director, Warren Hastings (1732–1818), between 1788 and 1795. The prosecution case was led by Whig politician and writer Edmund Burke (1730–1797), who played the role of Las Casas, a figure he would have known from his cowritten history of Christopher Columbus.[59] Like his Spanish predecessor, Burke was no enemy of empire, but the East India Company's oppression and exploitation of Indians scandalized him just as its infiltration of the British political system by rampant bribery sounded the tocsin about domestic corruption. His main charge was that the East India Company was behaving like a rogue state, waging war on Indians and plundering their resources. His recounting of atrocities, like public flogging inflicted in extorting money from Indians, also resembled Las Casas's graphic style. Indian rebellion was thus understandable, legitimate, and legal, in his eyes, thereby following Vattel's view that even heathens enjoyed the right of resistance against tyranny. Hastings responded by arguing the right to put down illegitimate insurgencies, because he had inherited the sovereign rights of Indian rulers who he had either defeated or with whom he had signed treaties, and was thus responsible for security.[60]

In the event, the House of Lords acquitted Hastings, although the sustained scandal led to greater Parliamentary oversight of the East India Company's activities. Empire's legitimacy had been questioned but came to be reconfigured as part of a morally governed empire. In effect, the stench of illegitimacy entrenched government regulation, binding India closer to Britain and thereby consolidating imperial rule, a process that culminated in 1857 after the Indian uprising prompted Parliament to end company rule. The new terms of legitimacy were no longer conquest but civilizational hierarchy: Britain ruled by right of its higher standing. Scandalous now were barbarous Indian cultural practices rather than British economic exactions, serving as objects of reform for humanitarians, missionaries and administrators.[61]

---

[58] Peter Silver, *Our Savage Neighbours: How Indian War Transformed Early America* (New York: W. W. Norton, 2008).

[59] Sora Sato, *Edmund Burke as Historian: War, Order and Civilisation* (Basingstoke: Palgrave Macmillan, 2018), ch. 4.

[60] Dirks, *Scandal of Empire*, 111; Mithi Mukherjee, "Justice, War, and the Imperium: India and Britain in Edmund Burke's Prosecutorial Speeches in the Impeachment Trial of Warren Hastings," *Law and History Review* 23, no. 3 (2005): 589–630.

[61] Dirks, *Scandal of Empire*, 21–23, 34; Mukherjee, "Justice, War, and the Imperium"; Camilla Boisen, "The Changing Moral Justification of Empire: From the Right to Colonise to the Obligation to Civilise," *History of European Ideas* 39, no. 3 (2013): 335–53; Boisen,

The keywords of the Enlightenment – humanity and civilization – pointed in two directions. On the one hand, some Enlightenment figures like Denis Diderot (1713–1784), Immanuel Kant (1724–1804), and Johan Gottfried Herder (1733–1803) advocated the values of cultural diversity and human equality to attack empire as systems of domination and exploitation. Theirs was an "enlightenment anti-imperialism," in the words of one scholar, the first sustained intellectual opposition to imperialism. On the other hand, this language signalled human hierarchy, both within European countries and in relation to their colonial possessions and geopolitical rivals. It expressed a deep-seated commitment to highly Eurocentric, and in many cases essentially racist, conceptions of state formation and international order.[62] By the middle of the eighteenth century, Westerners understood the unfolding of history as the development of civilization from the barbarous past, and they employed the triad of the civilized, the barbarous, and the savage to structure relations between whites and nonwhites, and between elites and nonelites within white society. Indigenous ("native") people were seen as savages who committed savage acts – atrocities – while Asians, who stood slightly higher on the civilizational ladder, were barbaric, though savagery and barbarism were used interchangeably.[63]

Even liberals like John Stuart Mill, who worked for the East India Company for decades, justified British rule in India in these terms, defended British despotism in India because of its civilizing motives and effects: "Despotism is a legitimate mode of government in dealing with barbarians, provided the end be their improvement." For that reason, he approved of the French intervention in Algeria; far from violating Algerian self-determination, it brought good government to people oppressed by local despots.[64]

"Triumphing Over Evil: Edmund Burke and the Idea of Humanitarian Intervention," *Journal of International Political Theory* 12, no. 3 (2016): 276–98.

[62] Jakob Lehne, "The Glittery Fog of Civilization: Great Britain, Germany, and International Politics, 1854–1902" (PhD diss., European University Institute, 2015); Jacinta O'Hagan, "The Role of Civilization in the Globalization of International Society," in *The Globalization of International Society*, ed. Tim Dunne and Christian Reus-Smit (Oxford: Oxford University Press, 2017), 185–203; Brett Bowden, *The Empire of Civilization: The Evolution of an Imperial Idea* (Chicago: University of Chicago Press, 2009).

[63] Ann Thomson, *Barbary and Enlightenment: European Attitudes towards the Maghreb in the 18th Century* (Leiden: Brill, 1987); Gerry Simpson, *Great Powers and Outlaw States: Unequal Sovereigns in the International Legal Order* (Cambridge: Cambridge University Press, 2004).

[64] Mark Tunick, "Tolerant Imperialism: John Stuart Mill's Defense of British Rule in India," *Review of Politics* 68, no. 4 (2006): 586–611; Georgios Varouxakis, "Empire, Race, Euro-Centrism: John Stuart Mill and his Critics," in *Utilitarianism and Empire*, ed. Bart Schultz and Georgios Varouxakis (Lanham, MD: Lexington Books, 2005), 137–54; Uday Singh Mehta, *Liberalism and Empire: A Study in British Liberal Thought* (Chicago: University of Chicago Press, 1999); Bhikhu Parekh, "Liberalism and Colonialism: A Critique of Locke

The hierarchical view prevailed over that of idealistic philosophers, whose condemnations of slavery failed to make an impact in the eighteenth century, the highpoint of transatlantic slavery. Few were the critics like Kant who ironically invoked civilization to suggest that it made Europeans the more efficient barbarians. He shared the cultural relativism of the French essayist, Michel de Montaigne (1533–1591), who long before had mocked the proposition that the cannibalism of Brazilian Indians was any more barbaric than some European practices, like torture. At least the consumed enemies were dead.[65] Equally few were listening when the African slaves who had expelled the French from Haiti in 1804 denounced their former masters as "barbarians who have bloodied our land for two centuries" while styling themselves as "a people, free, civilized and independent."[66] These minority views would be echoed by subaltern voices and radical British critics of empire in the second half of the nineteenth century.

By the late-eighteenth century, the slave trade had provoked concerted opposition in the name of European ideals of humanity and conscience, civilization and barbarism, which imperilled European hegemony, just as Spanish excesses in the Americas had imperilled its claims there in the sixteenth century.[67] As before, the answer to such practices was not to end

and Mill," in *The Decolonization of Imagination: Culture, Knowledge and Power*, ed. Jan Nederveen Pieterse and Bhikhu Parekh (London: Zed Books, 1995), 81–98; Lynn Zastoupil, *John Stuart Mill and India* (Stanford: Stanford University Press, 1994); Abram L. Harris, "John Stuart Mill: Servant of the East India Company," *Canadian Journal of Economics and Political Science* 30, no. 2 (1964): 185–202; On the Indian Uprising, see Kim Wagner, *The Great Fear of 1857: Rumours, Conspiracies and the Making of the Indian Uprising* (Bern: Peter Lang, 2010). This did not mean that he condoned arbitrary violence. He opposed colonial repressions during theIndian uprising in 1857 and Governor Eyre's widespread use of flogging and hangings to put down a rebellion in Jamaica eight years later.

[65] Immanuel Kant, *Toward Perpetual Peace and Other Writings on Politics, Peace, and History*, ed. Pauline Kleingeld, trans. David L. Colclasure (New Haven: Yale University Press, 2006), 79; Michel de Montaigne, "On Cannibals," in *Michel de Montaigne: The Complete Essays*, ed. trans., and intro., M. A. Screech (New York: Penguin, 1993), 228–41. For "Enlightenment anti-imperialism, see Sankar Muthu, *Enlightenment against Empire* (Princeton: Princeton University Press, 2003); Pauline Kleingeld, *Kant and Cosmopolitanism: The Philosophical Ideal of World Citizenship* (Cambridge: Cambridge University Press, 2011); Derek Heater, *World Citizenship and Government: Cosmopolitan Ideas in the History of Western Political Thought* (Basingstoke: Macmillan, 1996); Jacqueline Taylor, "Hume on the Importance of Humanity," *Revue Internationale de Philosophie* 263, no. 1 (2013): 81–98; Claus Offe, "Modernity and Barbarism," *Constellations* 2, no. 3 (1996): 354–77.

[66] Liliana Obregón, "The Civilized and the Uncivilized," in *The Oxford Handbook of the History of International Law*, ed. Bardo Fassbender and Anne Peters (Oxford: Oxford University Press, 2012), 923.

[67] On the settlement dimension, see James Belich, *Replenishing the Earth: The Settler Revolution and the Rise of the Anglo-World, 1783–1939* (Oxford: Oxford University Press, 2009).

European empire and reverse the European penetration of the globe; it was, rather, to end slavery and regulate the lawless colonialism of private corporations like the East India Company, to reform empire in light of those ideals of humanity, conscience, and civilization, and to promote its chief vehicles, commerce and Christianity.[68] The British Empire's attempt to temper the arbitrariness of local governors and settlers via investigative commission and the imposition of imperial legal authority in the nineteenth century represented nothing less than a "rage for order."[69] Britain annexed Fiji in 1874 to protect the locals from British settlers who were trafficking them as forced labor in Fiji, Queensland, and Peru. "The settlers had so disrupted the Fijian polity," noted one historian, "that their security and the peace of the islands depended on the presence of the Royal Navy."[70] Implementing reform by imposing order drove imperial consolidation and expansion in the nineteenth century.

Humanitarianism and Slavery

The emergence of a humanitarian movement in England in the late eighteenth century was predicated on monumental transformations: the industrial revolution and the growth of a politically assertive middle class that placed a premium on public debate and public opinion in its struggle with the gentry; a culture of reading sentimental texts that elicited empathy with the pain of others; an evangelical Christian revival preoccupied with civic conscience that understood cruelty as barbaric and that felt obligated to the needy; the changes in perception wrought by the globalizing market that enabled the identification of causal connections and tracing of moral responsibility; the founding of the second British empire, which offered proselytization possibilities; and the scandal of the British East India Company's misrule in India that promoted the ideal of empire as trusteeship.[71]

---

[68] See generally Andrew Sartori, "The British Empire and Its Liberal Mission," *Journal of Modern History* 78, no. 3 (2006): 623–42.

[69] Lauren Benton and Lisa Ford, *Rage for Order: The British Empire and the Origins of International Law, 1800–1850* (Cambridge, MA: Harvard University Press, 2016), 1, 11.

[70] W. D. McIntyre, "Anglo-American Rivalry in the Pacific: The British Annexation of the Fiji Islands in 1874," *Pacific Historical Review* 29, no. 4 (1960): 371; Tracy Banivanua-Mar, *Violence and Colonial Dialogue: The Australian-Pacific Indentured Labor Trade* (Honolulu: University of Hawaii Press, 2007); Lorenzo Veracini, "'Emphatically not a white man's colony': Settler Colonialism and the Construction of Colonial Fiji," *Journal of Pacific History* 43, no. 2 (2008): 189–205.

[71] Peter Marsh, "Conscience and the Conduct of Government in Nineteenth-Century Britain," in *The Conscience of the Victorian State*, ed. Peter Marsh (Syracuse, NY: Syracuse University Press, 1979), 10–3; Lynne Hunt, *Inventing Human Rights: A History* (New York: Penguin, 2007); Thomas Haskell, "Capitalism and the Origins of Humanitarian Sensibility," *American Historical Review* 90 (1985), pt. 1, 339–61, and pt. 2, 547–66;

Nothing galvanized the humanitarian movement more than ending the slave trade; indeed, humanitarianism and abolitionism were effectively coterminous. Elements of Las Casas's language of transgression now crystallized into a rhetorically powerful movement that succeeded in convincing the British state to end its slave trade by 1807. The trade was, as Prime Minister Grenville announced, "contrary to the principles of justice, humanity, and sound policy."[72] The invocation of "humanity" was not new; British Protestants had invoked it in the early eighteenth century to advocate for coreligionists persecuted in European Roman Catholic countries.[73] By the end of the century, British abolitionists were shocked by stories of African slaves' suffering, as they were in the US, where whites could more easily witness their mistreatment. They were moved to action as much by outrage as adherence to abstract principles.[74] Pamphlet literature emphasized gratuitous cruelty like the dismemberment of African families. Distressing images made for vicarious witnessing, especially as the "humanity" of Africans was vouchsafed by former slaves like Ignatius Sancho (1729–1780), who became a celebrated man of letters in England.[75] Theologically objectionable was African slaves' lack of liberty, which prevented their ability to make moral choices and lead an authentically Christian life. All imperial subjects, declared abolitionists, had the right to be "free born." In short, slavery was a "national crime."[76]

Sounding like Las Casas in his vivid depictions of slavery's effects on Africans, the American statesman, James Madison (1751–1836), reprised the Enlightenment argument against slavery in claiming that it violated the "laws of humanity."[77]

Thomas Lacquer, "Bodies, Details and the Humanitarian Narrative," in *The New Cultural History*, ed. Lynn Hunt (Berkeley: University of California Press, 1989), 176–204; Michael Barnett, *Empire of Humanity: A History of Humanitarianism* (Ithaca, NY: Cornell University Press, 2009); Lynn Fester, "Humanity without Feathers," *Humanity* 1, no. 1 (2010): 3–27.

[72] David Brion Davis, *Inhuman Bondage: The Rise and Fall of Slavery in the World* (New York, Oxford University Press, 2006); Seymour Drescher, *Econocide: British Slavery in the Era of Abolition* (Chapel Hill: University of North Carolina Press, 2010); Ian Clark, *International Legitimacy and World Society* (Oxford: Oxford University Press, 2007), 40.

[73] Catherine S. Arnold, "Affairs of Humanity: Arguments for Humanitarian Intervention in England and Europe, 1698–1715," *English Historical Review* 133, no. 533 (2018): 835–65.

[74] James L. Huston, "The Experiential Basis of the Northern Antislavery Impulse," *Journal of Southern History* 56, no. 4 (1990): 609–40.

[75] Margaret Abruzzo, *Polemical Pain: Slavery, Cruelty, and the Rise of Humanitarianism* (Baltimore: The Johns Hopkins University Press, 2011); Brycchan Carey, "'The Extraordinary Negro': Ignatius Sancho, Joseph Jekyll, and the Problem of Biography," *Journal for Eighteenth-Century Studies* 26, no. 1 (2003): 1–13.

[76] Catherine Hall, *Civilising Subjects: Metropole and Colony in the English Imagination, 1830–1867* (Oxford: Oxford University Press, 2002), 310–11.

[77] James Madison, "Second Annual Message, December 5, 1810," in *The Writings of James Madison*, ed. Gaillard Hunt, 9 Vols. (New York and London: G. P. Putnam's Sons, 1908), 8: 127.

These ideals could of course be mobilized by their objects of European condescension. The African slave leader of the celebrated rebellion against French rule in Saint Domingue (now Haiti) in 1791, Toussaint Louverture, drew on Enlightenment thought and the French Revolutionary ideals to point out French hypocrisy in running slave plantations. Three year later, the French National Convention abolished slavery, but the truly universal application of its ideals was instantiated in the constitution that Louverture drew up in 1801.[78] "In this territory slaves cannot exist; servitude is permanently abolished. All men within it are born, live, and die free and French," proclaimed one article, while another declared that only "virtues and talents" distinguished residents, not color.[79] Louverture's successor, Jean-Jacques Dessalines (1758–1806), went much further, instigating a massacre of up to 5,000 white residents in 1804 and proclaiming a constitution a year later that, among other measures, categorized as "black" the children of white women and black men: such women who married black men would be spared.[80]

British antislavery advocates were unwilling to go that far. The rights of slaves were not a given, but granted by Europeans, and entreaties against their cruel treatment did not necessarily entail equality. Although an early supporter of abolition, Edmund Burke declared that "the cause of humanity would be far more benefited by the continuance of the trade and servitude, regulated and reformed than by the total destruction of both or either."[81] The humanity at issue was not necessarily that of slaves, whose wretched suffering depicted in abolitionist literature bordered on their animalization: they were human foremost in their experience of pain. It was above all the Europeans' humanity that was vouchsafed by his or her sympathy and abolitionist activism. As an 1818 musical called *The Slave* put it, "Humanity is Britain's

---

[78] Malick W. Ghachem, *The Old Regime and the Haitian Revolution* (Cambridge: Cambridge University Press, 2012).

[79] Robin Blackburn, "Haiti, Slavery, and the Age of the Democratic Revolution," *William and Mary Quarterly* 63, no. 4 (2006): 647; C. L. R. James, *The Black Jacobins: Toussaint L'Ouverture and the San Domingo Revolution*, 2nd rev. ed. (New York: Vintage Books, 1963); Laurent Dubois, *Avengers of the New World: The Story of the Haitian Revolution* (Cambridge, MA: Harvard University Press, 2004); "The Haitian Declaration of Independence," in David Armitage, *The Declaration of Independence: A Global History* (Cambridge, MA: Harvard University Press, 2009), 193–8; David Geggus, "The Haitian Revolution in Atlantic Perspective," in *The Oxford Handbook of the Atlantic World, c.1450–1850*, ed. Nicholas Canny and Philip Morgan (Oxford: Oxford University Press, 2011), 533–49.

[80] Philippe R. Girard, *The Slaves Who Defeated Napoleon: Toussaint Louverture and the Haitian War of Independence 1801–1804* (Tuscaloosa: University of Alabama Press, 2011); 1805 Constitution of Haiti: http://faculty.webster.edu/corbetre/haiti/history/early haiti/1805-const.htm.

[81] Dirks, *The Scandal of Empire*, 33.

glory – Pity, and protect the slave!"[82] After the loss of the American colonies in 1783, the abolitionist cause represented an issue with which the British could burnish their credentials as sentinels of liberty and gain a moral advantage over the slave-owning rebels.[83]

Neither did abolitionists think ending slavery entailed Europeans withdrawing from the parts of the globe they had penetrated. On the contrary, the solution was a well-governed empire of commerce operating as a trust for non-Europeans. For non-Europeans were heathens in thrall to superstitions and barbarous customs who would benefit from reform and uplift. Christianity in particular could contribute to this civilizing process.[84] Evangelicals analogized between free trade and freedom to spread the word, for where commerce could spread, so could missionaries. What is more, commerce imparted Christian virtues of private property and the dignity of work. Early and mid-Victorian Christians, like the missionary, antislavery campaigner, and explorer of Africa, David Livingstone (1813–1873), in his famous Cambridge lectures in 1857 promoting commerce, civilization, and Christianity, saw both as elements of the British Empire's civilizational mission.[85]

Noteworthy is the abolitionists' understanding of the atrocity of slavery: it was a trade – a system of exploitation motivated by profit – that needed to be outlawed in the first instance, because states could more easily interdict human trafficking than interfere in slave owners' private property rights. By the early nineteenth century, the humanitarian lobby convinced the British state to make global abolition official policy. In the Final Act of the Congress of Vienna in 1815, which concluded the Napoleonic wars, signatories committed themselves to end the slave trade with the language of transgression,

---

[82] Fester, "Humanity without Feathers," 7, 12, 15; Karen Halttunen, "Humanitarianism and the Pornography of Pain in Anglo-American Culture," *American Historical Review* 100, no. 2 (1995): 303–34; Joyce E. Chaplin, "Slavery and the Principle of Humanity: A Modern Idea in the Early Lower South," *Journal of Social History* 24, no. 2 (1990): 299–315.

[83] Christopher L. Brown, *Moral Capital: Foundations of British Abolitionism* (Chapel Hill: University of North Carolina Press, 2006).

[84] Hall, *Civilising Subjects*, 297, 301–2.

[85] William Monk, ed., *Dr. Livingstone's Cambridge Lectures*, pref. Allan Sedgwick (Cambridge: Deighteon, Bell, and Co., 1858); Brian Stanley, "'Commerce and Christianity': Providence Theory, the Missionary Movement, and the Imperialism of Free Trade, 1842–1860," *Historical Journal* 26, no. 1 (1983): 71–94; Andrew Porter, "'Commerce and Christianity': The Rise and Fall of a Nineteenth-Century Missionary Slogan," *The Historical Journal* 28, no. 3 (1985): 597–621; Andrew Porter, *Religion versus Empire? British Protestant Missionaries and Overseas Expansion, 1700–1914* (Manchester: Manchester University Press, 2004).

condemning it "as repugnant to the principle of humanity and universal morality," and as a "scourge which has so long desolated Africa, degraded Europe, and afflicted humanity."[86] Having abjured slavery, it was in Britain's economic interests that other states do so as well. Joining Britain's geopolitical interest with humanity's advantage was not an innovation. During the Napoleonic wars, abolitionists had advanced their case in terms of national security, arguing that banning the trade would weaken British enemies. With the Vienna Treaty setting the norm, Britain concluded bilateral treaties about visitation (inspection) rights with Latin American states that were not geographically limited, leading one historian of international law to observe that they marked "an initial step towards an international police authority of the British fleet upon all of the world's oceans."[87] For the British Navy began patrolling African and Brazilian coasts for slave ships and prosecuting their captains – except French and Americans ones, and Spanish ships south of the equator – in mixed commissions, that is, international courts, in Sierra Leone, Cuba, Brazil, and Suriname, established by the bilateral treaties.[88]

As might be expected, the French, sensing British self-interest, rejected its arrogation of humanity and civilization as the driving force of the antislave-trade campaign.[89] Equally predictably, the British disavowed cynicism, portraying their empire as a force for universal good: they made immoral nations take the high road of abolition. Humanity was Britain's main consideration, declared Foreign Secretary Lord Palmerston (1784–1865): ending slavery was a "moral duty" for Britain, which stood "at the head of moral, social, and political civilisation" by embodying liberty – the rule of law, property rights, and Parliament's guarantee of subjects' freedom, unlike those of other states.[90] Palmerston drove the pursuit of Portuguese ships and destruction of slave infrastructure in Brazil in the 1830s. Legally dubious, there was nothing the weaker Portugal could do, and the great powers acquiesced because of the new

[86] Clark, *International Legitimacy and World Society*, 55; Edith F. Hurwitz, *Politics and the Public Conscience: Slave Emancipation and the Abolitionist Movement in Britain* (London: George Allen & Unwin, 1973).

[87] Wilhelm Grewe, *The Epochs of International Law*, trans Michael Byers (New York: Walter de Gruyter, 2000), 561.

[88] Clark, *International Legitimacy and World Society*, 49; William Mulligan and Maurice Bric, *A Global History of Anti-Slavery Politics in the Nineteenth Century* (Basingstoke: Palgrave Macmillan, 2013).

[89] Paul Michael Kielstra, *The Politics of Slave Trade Suppression in Britain and France, 1814–1848: Diplomacy, Morality and Economics* (Basingstoke: Palgrave Macmillan, 2008), 1, 20, 24, 256.

[90] Jenny S. Martinez, *The Slave Trade and the Origins of International Human Rights Law* (Oxford: Oxford University Press, 2012), 139; R. J. Vincent, *Nonintervention and International Order* (Princeton: Princeton University Press, 1974), 92; Armitage, *The Ideological Origins of the British Empire*, 8.

antislavery consensus.[91] The crusading rhetoric was intended for public consumption, as much domestic as international, thereby placating the humanitarian lobby. Apart from a small number of crusading officials, the British state apparatus would only enforce antislavery policy when it aligned with strategic and financial interests. However, antislavery had become so intrinsic to British self-understanding, and thus its justification of the imperial mission, that ideals and interests were difficult to prise apart entirely in public debate.[92]

Some scholars today regard this global campaign as the birth of international human rights justice, because the slave traders were depicted as pirates subject to universal jurisdiction, and because American legal scholar Henry Wheaton (1785–1848) called slavery a "crime against humanity" in 1842.[93] In fact, slaves' rights were not at issue; they were regarded by all as "prize" – as cargo. Nor were slave-ship captains prosecuted as pirates under universal jurisdiction, which the great powers rejected as an intolerable British infringement on their sovereignty. Wheaton disavowed a British right to stop and search US ships. That is why the British Navy operated under the auspices of bilateral treaties struck with compliant powers on varying terms. If anything, the ensuing "mixed commission" courts functioned as an extension of the British state, asserting imperial authority over slave traders and colonial governments that indulged them, much as Las Casas urged the Spanish king to correct abuses in the Americas. Over time, the British allowed these commissions to run down, replacing them with their own admiralty courts.[94]

Moreover, it was not as if emancipated slaves suddenly enjoyed unadulterated freedom. Attentive to West Indian plantation owners' economic

---

[91] Maeve Ryan, "The Abolition of the West African Slave Trade," in *Humanitarian Intervention: A History*, ed. Brendan Simms and D. J. B. Trim (Cambridge: Cambridge University Press, 2011), 244–46.

[92] William Mulligan, "British Anti-Slave Trade and Anti-Slavery Policy in East Africa, Arabia, and Turkey in the Nineteenth Century," in Simms and Trim, *Humanitarian Intervention*, 257–280; Kielstra, *The Politics of Slave Trade Suppression in Britain and France, 1814–1848*, 6, 217, 263, 266; Chaim D. Kaufmann and Robert A. Pape, "Explaining Costly International Moral Action: Britain's Sixty-year Campaign Against the Atlantic Slave Trade," *International Organization* 53, no. 4 (1990): 631–68. Taking the self-interest angle is Joel Quirk, *The Anti-Slavery Project: From Slave Trade to Human Trafficking* (Philadelphia: University of Pennsylvania Press, 2011).

[93] Martinez, *The Slave Trade and the Origins of International Human Rights Law*.

[94] Lauren Benton, "Abolition and Imperial Law, 1790–1820," *Journal of Imperial and Commonwealth History* 39, no. 3 (2011): 355–74; Fabian Klose, "Enforcing Abolition: The Entanglement of Civil Society Action, Humanitarian Norm-Setting, and Military Intervention," in *The Emergence of Humanitarian Intervention: Ideas and Practice from the Nineteenth Century to the Present*, ed. Fabian Klose (Cambridge: Cambridge University Press, 2016), 97; Leslie Bethell, "The Mixed Commissions for the Suppression of the Transatlantic Slave Trade in the Nineteenth Century," *Journal of African History* 7, no. 1 (1966): 79–93.

demands, British authorities sweetened the bitter pill of abolition within the empire in 1833 with financial compensation, importing indentured laborers from India, and establishing an "apprenticeship" regime that tied younger workers to employers until 1838.[95] To be sure, humanitarian reformers condemned this private recruitment as a "coolie slave trade," arguing that only genuinely free labor was consistent with a market economy. The manifest abuses of the system led to its abolition in 1839, but it was reintroduced with government regulation after drastic declines in sugar production, justified by humanitarian arguments that indentured laborers were really free and served the cause of emancipation by improving both the workers and the country in which they worked: indentured labor could be viewed as training workers for freedom. Henceforth, it was normalized and opposed only when abuses came to light, as they had in other parts of the empire, like southern Africa.[96]

Most humanitarians thus drew an artificial distinction between free and unfree labor, when in fact a continuum of semi-free practices continued in the colonies, some preceding and coexisting with chattel slavery – whether bonded labor, convicts, military conscripts, and settlers – others developing in its wake. For example, Chinese coolies worked side by side with African slaves in Cuba in the 1870s, and were treated in the same way irrespective of their differing legal status.[97] As we will see in the next chapter, the requirement that "free" laborers work on public infrastructure and in military service continued beyond the World War I on the insistence of Western colonial powers, blessed by the League of Nations.[98] In sum: the language of transgression bought into

---

[95] Thomas C. Holt, *The Problem of Freedom: Race, Labor, and Politics in Jamaica and Britain, 1832–1938* (Baltimore, MD: Johns Hopkins University Press, 1992); K. Marshall Woodville "The Termination of the Apprenticeship in Barbados and the Windward Islands: An Essay in Colonial Administration and Politics," *Journal of Caribbean History* 2, no. 1 (1971): 1–45; O. Nigel Bolland, "Systems of Domination after Slavery: The Control of Land and Labor in the British West Indies after 1838," *Comparative Studies in Society and History* 23, no. 4 (1981): 591–619; Alex Tyrrell, "The 'Moral Radical Party' and the Anglo-Jamaican Campaign for the Abolition of the Negro Apprenticeship System," *English Historical Review* 99, no. 392 (1984): 481–502.

[96] Jonathan Connolly, "Indentured Labour Migration and the Meaning of Emancipation: Free Trade, Race, and Labour in British Public Debate, 1838–1860," *Past & Present* 238, no. 1 (2018): 85–119.

[97] Lisa Yun, *The Coolie Speaks: Chinese Indentured Laborers and African Slaves in Cuba* (Philadelphia: Temple University Press, 2008).

[98] Zoë Laidlaw, "Investigating Empire: Humanitarians, Reform and the Commission of Eastern Inquiry," *Journal of Imperial and Commonwealth History* 40, no. 5 (2012): 749–68; Clare Anderson, "After Emancipation: Empires and Imperial Formations," in *Emancipation and the Remaking of the British Imperial World*, ed. Catherine Hall, Nicolas Draper, and Keith McClelland (Manchester: Manchester University Press, 2014), 113–27; Clare Anderson, "Transnational Histories of Penal Transportation: Punishment, Labour and Governance in the British Imperial World, 1788–1939," *Australian Historical Societies* 47, no. 3 (2016): 381–97; Andrea Major, "The Slavery of

the strict binary between free and unfree labor that occluded the continuum of coercive labor practices on which colonial and imperial economies relied. The language was thus deaf to practices that fell below its threshold, thereby bolstering empire's ethical self-image.

The extension of imperial writ was also justified by the universal benefit of commerce and free trade. The abolition of slavery in the 1830s, however fitful in practice, coincided with the breakthrough of free trade in Britain, signalled by the scrapping of the Corn Laws in 1846. Championed by Richard Cobden (1804–1865), who also opposed slavery, the free trade cause also entailed the abolition of British bases abroad, because the theory abjured force and presumed peaceful commerce between states. But, for statesmen like Palmerston, freedom of the seas required the British Navy, meaning that the universal human interest was advanced by the British one.[99] From the 1820s to the 1840s, the British Navy asserted itself in stamping out the so-called white slave trade in European prisoners conducted by the Barbary pirate states in North Africa, while also destroying pirate bases in Crete, Borneo, and Oman. The US Navy was doing the same in the West Indies to also make the seas safe for trade.[100] Gradually, Britain sought to end privateering, as the practice threatened its merchant fleet and continental powers could increasingly circumvent blockades.[101] Protecting British commerce rather than free trade as such was the imperative. Either way, the language of transgression was a vehicle for humanitarian empire justified by the abolition of slavery and extension of commerce that supposedly enriched all.

The Protection of Small Nations and "Native" Peoples

As the abolition campaigns peaked in the 1830s, two other questions preoccupied the liberal press, humanitarians, and statesmen that bore on the language

'East and West': Abolitionists and 'Unfree' Labour in India, *1820–1833*," *Slavery and Abolition* 31, no. 4 (2010*)*: 501–25; Tom Brass and Marcel van der Linden, eds., *Free and Unfree Labour: The Debate Continues* (Bern: Peter Lang, 1997).

[99] Anthony Howe, "Free Trade and Global Order: The Rise and Fall of a Victorian Vision," in *Victorian Visions of Global Order*, ed. Duncan Bell (Cambridge: Cambridge University Press, 2007), 26–46; Simon Morgan, "The Anti-Corn Law League and British Anti-Slavery in Transatlantic Perspective, 1838–1846," *Historical Journal* 52, no. 1 (2009): 87–107; Bernard Semmel, *The Rise of Free Trade Imperialism: Classical Political Economy the Empire of Free Trade and Imperialism 1750–1850* (New York: Cambridge University Press, 1970); John Gallagher and Ronald Robinson, "The Imperialism of Free Trade," *Economic History Review* 6, no. 1 (1953): 1–15.

[100] Ethan Nadelmann, "Global Prohibition Regimes: The Evolution of Norms in International Society," *International Organization* 44, no. 4 (1990): 479–526; Klose, "Enforcing Abolition."

[101] Jan Martin Lemnitzer, *Power, Law and the End of Privateering* (Basingstoke: Palgrave Macmillan, 2014).

of transgression: European peoples subject to continental empires and "native" peoples within the British Empire. Palmerston's contention that Britain was to be "the champion of justice and right" extended to the protection of vulnerable European nationalities, a principle also enshrined in the Treaty of Vienna in 1815.[102] This principle derived from a British self-understanding as a unity of small, free countries that shared more attributes with minor European republics than with large, absolutist empires. Britain sought to maintain the survival of Europe's small states to enhance its reputation as the guarantor of liberty and to preserve the continental balance of power against the overweening ambitions of powerful states.[103] Accordingly, the British, with French help, insisted that the powers that had partitioned Poland in the late-eighteenth century – Russia, Prussia, and Austria – agree to recognize Polish national rights, the first time such rights, as opposed to religious ones, were accorded this status. Besides guaranteeing free trade and communication within 1772 prepartition frontiers, the treaty also stipulated institutions of Polish national representations. Because there were no enforcement mechanisms, the partitioning powers grudgingly agreed.[104]

The British Parliamentary debate in 1833 about the Russian repression of the Polish uprising in 1830 indicated that members of Parliament understood the political context in which nationality was imperiled: in despotic continental empires. Their indignant declamations of Russian behavior exhibited the language of transgression in all its dimensions: "humanity commanded that the blood should cease to flow," declared one member. Instead of showing clemency to the Poles, the Czar had determined on "their extirpation as a people." The Russians were engaging in a "war of extermination – nothing could end it, but the intervention of the other powers of Europe."[105] Recognizing the political logics of repression, a member said that Russia was "not at liberty to destroy the nationality of a whole people for the offences of a few."[106] Palmerston referred to this international agreement in his identification of Russia's crimes:

> The Treaties of 1815 ... clearly stipulate that the nationality of the Poles shall be preserved. But statements have reached His Majesty's Government which, if true, tend to show a deliberate intention on the

[102] Vincent, *Nonintervention and International Order*, 93; Carol Fink, *Defending the Rights of Others: The Great Powers, the Jews, and International Minority Protection, 1878–1938* (Cambridge: Cambridge University Press, 2004), 7.

[103] Richard Whatmore, "'Neither Masters nor Slaves': Small States and Empire in the Long Eighteenth Century," in *Lineages of Empire: The Historical Roots of British Imperial Thought*, ed. Duncan Kelly (Oxford: Oxford University Press, 2009), 54–81.

[104] Andre Liebich, "Minority as Inferiority: Minority Rights in Historical Perspective," *Review of International Studies* 34, no. 3 (2008): 243–63; Piotr S. Wandycz, *The Lands of Partitioned Poland, 1795–1918* (Seattle: University of Washington Press, 1975), 65.

[105] Parliamentary Debates (Hansard), Official report, Vol. 19, July 9, 1833, 413–4.

[106] Ibid., 429.

part of the Russian Government to break down the nationality of Poland, and to deprive it of everything which, either in outward form or in real substance, gives to its people the character of a separate nation.[107]

His listing of the Russian acts anticipated those of the Allied indictment of the Central Powers in the World War I, and then of Lemkin's genocide concept.

> Abolition of the Polish colors; the introduction of the Russian language into public acts; the removal to Russia of the national library; the suppression of schools and other establishments for public instructions; the removal of a great number of children to Russia on the pretense of educating them at the public expense; the transportation of whole families to the interior of Russia; the extent and severity of the military conscriptions; the large introduction of Russians into the public employments in Poland; the interference with the National Church; all these appear to be symptoms of a deliberate intention to obliterate the political nationality of Poland and gradually to convert it into a Russian province.[108]

The oppression was compounded by the fact that the Poles were civilized; indeed, according to *The Times* writing about a later uprising, they were "vanguards of progress" in a backward region who could push the West's "loftier civilization eastwards" if the Russians only got out of the way.[109]

Not so the lowly "native" peoples within Britain's empire. But they too required protection, in this case against British settlers' loftier civilization, as Charles Darwin (1809–1882) observed: "When civilized nations come into contact with barbarians, the struggle is short, except where a deadly climate gives aid to a native race."[110] Humanitarian sympathy followed accordingly from the 1820s as stories of Maori and Aboriginal suffering in New Zealand and New South Wales led to a Parliamentary select committee investigation and report on British settlement in 1837 and the formation of the Aborigines Protection Society, whose membership comprised middle-class professionals and businessmen committed to free trade. Again, the political context was apparent: settler colonialism pushed indigenous peoples off their land and led to myriad problems. Because it was impossible to abolish settlement in the same way as slavery without contradicting the commitment to the humanitarian civilizing mission, most humanitarians agreed on an anodyne "protection" policy: the radical recommendation of the report to oppose the colonization of

---

[107] Ellery C. Stowell, *Intervention in International Law* (Washington, DC: John Byrne and Co., 1921), 116–7.

[108] Ibid., 117–8.

[109] K. S. Pasieka, "The British Press and the Polish Insurrection of 1863," *Slavonic and East European Review* 42, no. 98 (1963): 22.

[110] Charles Darwin, *The Descent of Man* (London: John Murray, 1871), 190.

New Zealand was rejected.[111] The "moral imperialism" of humanitarians was predicated on extending protection and expecting loyalty in return, with the implication of violent reprisal in the case of resistance.[112] As with Las Casas, the humanitarian agenda was formal colonization: it regularized relations between the races to ensure "native" welfare, based on the assumption of their supposed inability to govern themselves on the one hand, and Europeans' productive use of the land according to commercial precepts on the other.[113] The conclusion that aberrant settlers rather than empire itself was to blame for indigenous suffering was shared by Lemkin when he wrote his accounts of colonial Tasmania, based in part on the 1837 parliamentary report.[114]

The blindness of the humanitarian agenda led to more trenchant and sustained criticisms of the British Empire when it appeared as unjust and wrong as any of the continental empires: after the Second Opium War between 1856 and 1860, for example. Although the pretext for the British declaration of war on China was impounding illicitly imported opium and insulting British honor, it is clear that free trade meant less open competition for all than the enforcement of open markets for British opium producers in India, especially with China from which it imported far more (silk, tea, ceramics) than it exported. Opium exports were vital for the British economy, and militarily ensuring their legality could be justified by appeal to free trade principles.[115] The war demonstrated the customary confluence of violent commercial self-assertion with the rhetoric of law and justice that Palmerston embodied.[116]

[111] Charles Swaisland, "The Aborigines Protection Society, 1837–1909," *Slavery and Abolition* 21, no. 2 (2000): 265–80; Zoë Laidlaw, "Imperial Complicity: Indigenous Dispossession in British History and History Writing," in Hall, Draper, and McClelland, *Emancipation and the Remaking of the British Imperial World*, 131–48.

[112] Elizabeth Elbourne, "Violence, Moral Imperialism and Colonial Borderlands, 1770s–1820s: Some Contradictions of Humanitarianism," *Journal of Colonialism and Colonial History* 17, no. 1 (2016).

[113] Tony Ballantyne, "Humanitarian Narratives: Knowledge and the Politics of Mission and Empire," *Social Sciences and Missions* 24, nos. 2–3 (2011): 233–64; Alan Lester and Fae Dussart, *Colonization and the Origins of Humanitarian Governance: Protecting Aborigines Across the Nineteenth-Century British Empire* (Cambridge University Press, Cambridge, 2014).

[114] Raphael Lemkin, "Tasmania," in *Genocide and Colonialism*, ed. A. Dirk Moses and Dan Stone (Abingdon and New York: Routledge, 2007), 74–100.

[115] Julia Lovell, *The Opium War: Drugs, Dreams, and the Making of Modern China* (Cambridge, MA: Harvard University Press, 2011); Robert Bickers, *The Scramble for China: Foreign Devils in the Qing Empire 1832–1914* (London: Allen Lane, 2011); Glenn Melancon, *Britain's China Policy and the Opium Crisis: Balancing Drugs, Violence and National Honour, 1833–1840* (Aldershot: Ashgate, 2003); John Y. Wong, *Deadly Dreams: Opium, Imperialism, and the Arrow War (1856-1860) in China* (Cambridge: Cambridge University Press, 1998).

[116] E. D. Steele, *Palmerston and Liberalism, 1855–1865* (Cambridge: Cambridge University Press, 1991), 361.

The brutal suppression of the Indian uprising in 1857 and the bloody denouement of the Morant Bay uprising in Jamaica in 1865 were harder to justify in those terms. Even members of the judiciary like the Lord Chief Justice invoked the "sentiments of humanity" in his misgivings about the excessive executions in Jamaica.[117] By identifying with the colonized peoples as equals rather than as wards, radical journalists, writers, and politicians decried British misrule as despotism – whether of the East India Company in India or British landlords in Ireland – that inevitably provoked uprisings. On the continent, they supported the struggle of the Polish and Italians for independence from Russia and Austria respectively, and the rights of Christian minorities in the Ottoman Empire. Domestically, they sought democratic reform as the antidote to imperialism, which radicals denounced as the elite's plunder of local and foreign resources supported by a manipulated mob.[118] Tory Prime Minister Disraeli's (1804–1881) vision of imperial expansion and grandeur based on realpolitik rather than principle in the second half of the 1870s scandalized them. In the Victorian debate about the rights of small and large nations, radicals sided with the former, while Tories argued that the latter were more legitimate by virtue of their "greatness."[119] On these bases, radical lawyer and historian Frederic Harrison (1831–1923) denounced the empire as "this huge crime against humanity."[120]

---

[117] Richard Huzzey, "Minding Civilisation and Humanity in 1867: A Case Study in British Imperial Culture and Victorian Anti-Slavery," *Journal of Imperial and Commonwealth History* 40, no. 5 (2012): 807–25; Bernard Semmel, *Jamaican Blood and Victorian Conscience: The Governor Eyre Controversy* (Westport, CT: Greenwood Press, 1962). On the unease caused by brutal British reprisals, see Christopher Herbert, *War of No Pity: The Indian Mutiny and Victorian Trauma* (Princeton: Princeton University Press, 2007). The contemporary debate about its legality is analyzed in Rande Kostal, *A Jurisprudence of Power: Victorian Empire and the Rule of Law* (Oxford University Press, 2005).

[118] Peter Cain, "Radicals, Gladstone, and the Liberal Critique of Disraelian 'Imperialism,'" in Bell, *Victorian Visions of Global Order*, 215–38; George Claeys, "The 'Left' and the Critique of Empire c 1865–1900: Three Roots of Humanitarian Foreign Policy," in Bell, *Victorian Visions of Global Order*, 239–66; Eugenio F. Biagini, "The Politics of Italianism: *Reynold's Newspaper*, the Indian Mutiny, and the Radical Critique of Liberal Imperialism in Mid-Victorian Britain," in *Evil, Barbarism and Empire: Britain and Abroad, c.1830–2000*, ed. Tom Crook, Rebecca Gill, and Bertrand Taithe (Basingstoke: Palgrave Macmillan, 2011), 99–125.

[119] Georgios Varouxakis, "'Great' versus 'Small' Nations: Size and National Greatness in Victorian Political Thought," in Bell, *Victorian Visions of Global Order*, 136–58.

[120] H. S. Jones, "The Victorian Lexicon of Evil: Frederic Harrison, the Positivists and the Language of International Politics," in Crook, Gill, and Taithe, *Evil, Barbarism and Empire*, 129. See also Gregory Claeys, *Imperial Sceptics: British Critics of Empire, 1850–1920* (New York: Cambridge University Press, 2010); Antoinette Burton, *The Trouble with Empire: Challenges to Modern British Imperialism* (Oxford: Oxford

Liberal politicians mobilized elements of this radical critique against the Tory vision of empire. Opposition leader William Gladstone's (1809–1898) famous pamphlet, *Bulgarian Horrors and the Question of the East* (1876), contested the British government's pro-Turkish position in the conflict between Russia and the Ottoman Empire. There was a Bulgarian insurgency, he conceded, but no civil war-like circumstances of symmetrical violence. The Turks' repression was grossly disproportionate and they had provoked the Bulgarian nationalist movement with their "terrible misgovernment" and "anarchical misrule."[121] To further disqualify the Turkish and British position, he expressed "astonishment and horror" at Ottoman crimes, which were the "basest and blackest outrages upon record within the present century, if not within the memory of man," repeating classical Las Casasian rhetoric.[122]

Deeply Christian, Gladstone proclaimed an empire of principle that ruled for the benefit of its subjects. Like Palmerston, this conviction manifested itself in a self-confident civilizing mission that equated British and universal interests: "We have a true superiority, as to moral questions, in European affairs, over the other great Powers in this part of the globe."[123] Gladstone thereby advocated the protection of such minorities, subject European nations, and the colonial subjects that humanitarians had advocated since the 1830s. This protective ambition extended to Jews in Eastern Europe and the Middle East as a vulnerable people without a protective state of their own. In the words of the *Manchester Daily Examiner* in 1867, there are "cases in which it becomes the duty of all who have a share in guiding or expressing public opinion to raise their voice against the perpetration of wrong which are an outrage upon humanity and a disgrace to the civilisation of the age."[124] The newspaper was referring to atrocities against Jews in Romania, thereby echoing the standard terms used to refer to persecuted Jews in the infamous Damascus Affair of 1840, when British Jewish leader Moses Montefiore (1784–1885) invoked them to draw the Empire's attention to a ritual murder allegation and riot against Damascene Jews.[125]

University Press, 2015); Priyamvada Gopal, *Insurgent Empire: Anticolonialism and the Making of British Dissent* (London: Verso, 2019).

[121] W. E. Gladstone, *Bulgarian Horrors and the Question of the East* (New York and Montreal: Lovell, Adam, Wesson and Co., 1876), 13, 20, 31. Generally: Donald Bloxham, *Genocide, the World Wars and the Unweaving of Europe* (London: Vallentine Mitchell, 2008), ch. 7. R. T. Shannon, *Gladstone and the Bulgarian Agitation 1876* (London: Nelson, 1964).

[122] Gladstone, *Bulgarian Horrors and the Question of the East*, 8.

[123] Cain, "Radicals, Gladstone, and the Liberal Critique of Disraelian 'Imperialism,'" 227.

[124] Abigail Green, "Intervening in the Jewish Question, 1840–78," in Simms and Trim, *Humanitarian Intervention*, 156.

[125] Ibid.

Since Britain represented the interests of humanity and civilization, it fell to the *Pax Britannica* to expand informal empire and commerce for the common good. The liberal press supported Gladstone's combination of moral indignation and civilizing mission. For example, *The Times* condemned the Russian suppression of the Polish rebellion in 1863 as "eastern barbarism" and the behavior of its troops as akin to "the hordes of Tamerlane and Genghis Khan." The government, it continued, had "a right and a duty to remonstrate against acts of barbarism and cruelty which are a dishonour to a civilized Government, and which disgrace the age in which they are committed."[126] Even Disraeli, prime minister during the Russo-Turkish war, agreed that Britain should become Armenians' official protector with the 1878 Treaty of Berlin, which settled the Russian-Ottoman conflict.[127]

For all that, he was not entreating national liberation from empire. Disraeli's advocacy of British rule in Egypt was based on the proposition that the locals could not manage a modern state and economy.[128] While Gladstone abhorred Ottoman, Austrian, and Russian misrule over what he regarded as culturally superior nations, he did not believe in their national independence as a right: he was no supporter of Mazzini or Garibaldi. Differing from radicals on this question, he believed that subject peoples needed to demonstrate the capacity for self-government. Regional stability was paramount: there was no reason to break up a well-governed empire.[129]

Subject peoples like Ottoman Armenians were at once objects of fascination and condescension for Gladstone's contemporaries, sympathetic as ancient Christians but requiring civilizational uplift after enduring aeons under the dead hand of Ottomanism.[130] Both the British and Russians took a special interest in their welfare. Contemporaries identified several violations against them in the absence of the genocide concept. One was the exploitation of and discrimination against Armenians, especially tribal Kurdish depredations in

[126] Pasieka, "The British Press and the Polish Insurrection of 1863," 23.
[127] Donald Bloxham, *The Great Game of Genocide: Imperialism, Nationalism, and the Destruction of the Ottoman Armenians* (Oxford: Oxford University Press, 2005) ch. 1; Arman Dzhonovich Kirakossian, *British Diplomacy and the Armenian Question: From the 1830s to 1914* (Princeton and London: Gomidas Institute Books, 2003), ch. 3.
[128] Cain, "Radicals, Gladstone, and the Liberal Critique of Disraelian 'Imperialism,'" 232.
[129] Deryck M. Schreuder, *Gladstone and Kruger: Liberal Government and Colonial Home Rule, 1880–1885* (London: Routledge, 1969); Keith A. P. Sandiford, "W. E. Gladstone and Liberal-Nationalist Movements," *Albion* 13, no. 1 (1981): 27–42.
[130] Jo Laycock, *Imagining Armenia: Orientalism, Ambiguity and Intervention* (Manchester, Manchester University Press, 2009); Mark Toufayan, "Empathy, Humanity, and the 'Armenian Question' in the Internationalist Legal Imagination," *Revue québécoise de droit international* 24, no. 1 (2011): 171–91.

Anatolia, where they competed for land.[131] The destruction of group culture was an associated transgression as well: Armenians and other Christian peoples were unable to flourish was the view despite evidence to the contrary. Another transgression was massacre, especially since the mid-1890s with the terrible "Hamidian" pogroms – named after Sultan Abdülhamid II – when 80,000 to 200,000 Armenians and other Christians were murdered. The 1895 massacre of Armenians in Trabzon "shocked the whole civilized world," said the British consul; they were "the hugest and foulest crimes that have ever stained the pages of human history," declared an Armenian advocate in England.[132] The prominent radical English journalist and newspaper man, William Stead (1849–1912), typified the energetic English lobby of the Anglo-Armenian Society and Friends of Armenia in his booklet *The Haunting Horrors in Armenia* (1896). Roused by Gladstone's *The Bulgarian Horrors*, he advocated for the small Christian nations of the Ottoman Empire and, as we see in the next chapter, transferred this identification to the Boers of southern Africa when conflict broke out with Britain a few years later.[133]

This was the immediate context of the debate about "humanitarian intervention," a term coined in 1880 by the English lawyer, William Edward Hall (1835–1894): "intervention for the purpose of checking gross tyranny or of helping the efforts of a people to free itself."[134] Interventions against tyranny had been discussed in Europe at least since the early-modern period, and oppressing a nationality – that characteristically nineteenth-century notion – was evidence of tyranny.[135] The right to intervene was invoked by any power that claimed to represent civilization. Fyodor Martens (1845–1909), the

---

[131] Michael A. Reynolds, *Shattering Empires: The Clash and Collapse of the Ottoman and Russian Empires, 1908–1918* (Cambridge: Cambridge University Press, 2011).

[132] Davide Rodogno, *Against Massacre: Humanitarian Interventions in the Ottoman Empire, 1815–1914* (Princeton: Princeton University Press, 2012), 197; E. J. Dillon, "Armenia: An Appeal," *Contemporary Review*, January 19, 1896, quoted in Michelle Tusan, "'Crimes against Humanity': Human Rights, the British Empire, and the Origins of the Response to the Armenian Genocide," *American Historical Review* 119, no. 1 (2014): 56.

[133] William T. Stead, *The Haunting Horrors in Armenia* (London, 1896). The Christian missionary perspective is expressed by Edwin Munsell Bliss, *Turkey and the Armenian Atrocities: A Reign of Terror* (Philadelphia: Hubbard 1896); Michelle Tusan, *The British Empire and the Armenian Genocide: Humanitarianism and the Politics of Empire from Gladstone to Churchill* (London: I.B. Tauris, 2017).

[134] William Edward Hall, *A Treatise on International Law* (Oxford: Clarendon, 1880), 303.

[135] On the nationality principle: Pasquale Fiore, *International Law Codified and Its Legal Sanction*, trans. Edwin Borchard (New York: Baker, Voorhis, and Co., 1918), 41. On intervention: Simon Chesterman, *Just War or Just Peace? Humanitarian Intervention and International Law* (Oxford: Oxford University Press, 2001), ch. 1; David Trim, "Intervention in European History, c1520–1850," in *Just and Unjust Military Intervention: European Thinkers from Vitoria to Mill*, ed. Stefano Recchia and Jennifer Welsh (Cambridge: Cambridge University Press, 2013), 21–47; Mark Swatek-Evenstein,

Russian diplomat and professor at the University of St Petersburg, referred to the Russian intervention in Bulgaria as undertaken in "the interests of humanity": "to safeguard the interests recognized as worthy of sympathy by all the civilized nations," meaning the "life and honour of Christians." The principles of intervention, he added, were "not applicable to relations between civilized powers."[136] The common threshold was expressed by French scholar Antoine Rougier (1877–1927) in 1910 when he wrote that "a collective intervention can take place only in exceptionally grave cases, as when the life of an entire population is menaced, or when the barbaric acts are often repeated, or when the particularly horrible character violently shocks the universal conscience."[137] Lemkin followed this line of thinking, writing in 1945 that humanitarian "interventions are based essentially on considerations of international morality" that genocide codified in law.[138]

Of the great powers concerned with their rights of intervention in the Ottoman Empire, none was more assertive than Russia. Late-nineteenth-century reform plans culminated in 1913 with a Russian plan of minority protection. Its author, André Mandelstam (1869–1949), a Russian diplomat, indeed the Dragoman in the Russian embassy in Constantinople, and Martens's personal secretary at the 1907 Hague Convention, foresaw the creation of a new and large consolidated province for Armenians in Asia Minor that would be largely self-governing and under European supervision. Needless to say, it was contested by the Ottoman state and its diplomatic supporter, Imperial Germany, as a new violation of its sovereignty and a suspected prelude to partition. The outbreak of the war vitiated its implementation.[139]

A History of Humanitarian Intervention (Cambridge: Cambridge University Press, 2020).

[136] Alexis Heraclides, "Humanitarian Intervention in International Law 1830–1939: The Debate," *Journal of the History of International Law* 16, no. 1 (2014): 42–3.

[137] Ibid., 52; Antoine Rougier, "Théorie de l'intervention d'humanité," *Revue générale de droit international public* 17 (1910): 468–526.

[138] Raphael Lemkin, "Genocide as a Crime in International Law," *American Journal of International Law* 41, no. 1 (1945): 146

[139] The ultimate agreement, signed in February 1914, was a much watered-down version. Hans-Lukas Kieser, Mehmet Polatel, and Thomas Schmutz, "Reform or Cataclysm? The Agreement of 8 February 1914 Regarding the Ottoman Eastern Provinces," *Journal of Genocide Research* 17, no. 3 (2015): 285–384; Reynolds, *Shattering Empires*, 16–17; and Umut Özsu, *Formalizing Displacement: International Law and Population Transfers* (Oxford: Oxford University Press, 2015), ch. 1. On Mandelstam, see Helmut Philipp Aust, "From Diplomat to Academic Activist: André Mandelstam and the History of Human Rights," *European Journal of International Law* 25 no. 4 (2015): 1105–21. On Turkish opposition to his plans, Hülya Adak, "The Legacy of André Nikolaievitch Mandelstam (1869–1949) and the Early History of Human Rights," *Zeitschrift für Religion- und Geisteswissenchaft* 70, no. 2 (2018): 117–30.

The Belgian international lawyer and cofounder of the *Institut de Droit International*, Gustave Rolin-Jaequemyns (1835–1902), likewise took a keen interest in Armenians as objects of protection by Christian powers.[140] The *Institut* was an international network of lawyers established in Brussels in 1873 that purported to embody "the legal conscience of the civilized world": the rule of international law would regulate – and thus humanize – relations between states and between states and nonstate peoples based on the presumption of Western superiority. Its manifesto was explicitly reformist, born at the humanitarian moment when the Red Cross was founded with the Geneva Convention on treating wounded and captured soldiers in 1864. Its program was that of nineteenth-century liberalism: the abolition of slavery and servitude of all types, freedom of association, and so forth. In effect, its ambition was to legally codify the language of transgression.[141]

Shocking Europe's moral sense inhered in coercive assimilation policies and preventing legitimate self-determination as well as massacre. For sober lawyers, the political context was always apparent. A. G. Stapleton, author of the 1866 book on interventions, referred to a "war of extermination" to describe the Ottoman response to the Greek war of liberation in the 1820s in terms that anticipate the genocide of Armenians almost 90 years later: "wherever there was the slightest resistance," he wrote, the Pacha "massacred all the males, and sent the women and children into slavery in Egypt. He was labouring to blot out of existence a whole Christian people."[142] "War of extermination" and "civil war of extermination" – these predecessors to genocide – occurred in repressing rebellions: they were politically motivated, even if excessive acts of state.[143]

To be sure, nonpolitical interpretations of such violence were also discernible by the 1890s. Advocates for Armenians portrayed them as a "victim nation" suffering a "passive victimhood," foregrounding the suffering of women in particular (unpolitical) to contest the Ottoman focus on insurgent men (political).[144] By contrast, British diplomats relied on local reports to paint a more complex picture that revealed the political dynamics of the

---

[140] M. G. Rolin-Jaequemyns, *Armenia, the Armenians and the Treaties* (London: John Heywood, 1891).

[141] Martti Koskenniemi, *The Gentle Civilizer of Nations: The Rise and Fall of International Law 1870–1960* (Cambridge: Cambridge University Press, 2001).

[142] Augustus Granville Stapleton, *Intervention and Non-Intervention or, the Foreign Policy of Great Britain, 1790–1865* (London: Murray, 1866), 32.

[143] Heraclides, "Humanitarian Intervention in International Law 1830–1939," 46; Rodogno, *Against Massacre*, 206; Bass, *Freedom's Battle*.

[144] Laycock, *Imaging Armenia*, 119, 125–32; Irvin Cemil Schick, "Christian Maidens, Turkish Ravishers: The Sexualization of National Conflict in the Late Ottoman Period," in *Women in the Ottoman Balkans: Gender, Culture and History*, ed. Irvin Cemil Schick and Amila Buturovic (London: I.B. Tauris, 2007), 273–306.

conflict while not excusing Ottoman excesses. A Foreign Office analysis from 1895 is worth quoting at length:

> The view held at numerous meetings in England on behalf of the Armenians that they were suffering solely on account of their religion was not correct, at all events in the first instance. The action of the Turkish Government was undoubtedly directed against a political movement which was promoted by certain agitators and a secret propaganda, though the nature and importance of the movement may have been greatly exaggerated. The measures taken by the local authorities and the attitude of the Mussulman population were in no doubt too frequently dictated by religious antipathy, which intensified though it had not originated the evil.[145]

The sultan thought there was "widespread sedition among his Armenian subjects" based on misleading reports of Armenian rebellion, and "in a moment of panic or irritation, gave orders to stamp out the movement and destroy the villages." In fact, the memorandum continued, there was no insurrection, and Armenian villages had to defend themselves against a Kurdish "campaign of extermination." The diplomats could see how violence that seemed framed in religious-sectarian terms originated in political logics of local anarchy, self-defense, and repression.[146]

As always, imperial officials found it difficult to fathom the reason for challenges to their rule. It was inconceivable to the British, for example, that their well-governed empire could provoke legitimate resistance, unless they could ascribe responsibility to a rogue actor, like the British East India Company in its later years. Sounding much like their Ottoman counterparts, officials in India denounced Indian killings of British as "murderous outrages," ascribing them to the apolitical categories of "fanaticism" and banditry.[147] Understandably, the Turkish sultan said he had as much the right to repress rebellion as the British did in India and Egypt.[148] In keeping with this self-serving interpretation of locals' violence, British security officials in the 1920s were convinced that Bolshevik opposition to imperial rule in India was

---

[145] The National Archives, UK, FO 881/6645, "Summary of Correspondence Relating to the Armenian Question," August 3, 1895.

[146] Ibid., 25–6.

[147] Mark Condos, *The Insecurity State: Punjab and the Making of Colonial Power in British India* (Cambridge: Cambridge University Press, 2017), 174; Condos, "Licence to Kill: The Murderous Outrages Act and the Rule of Law in Colonial India, 1867–1925," *Modern Asian Studies* 50, no. 2 (2016): 479–517; Condos, "Fanaticism" and the Politics of Resistance along the North West Frontier of British India," *Comparative Studies in Society and History* 58, no. 3 (2016): 717–45.

[148] Rodogno, *Against Massacre*, 193.

based on the unpolitical atavism of "racial hatred" of the British that threatened their rule.[149]

King Leopold II's Congo

Ideals of protection and good governance combined in striking harmony at the Berlin Conference of late 1884 and early 1885 when the great powers reconciled their growing trade rivalries in Africa by effectively chartering Belgian King Leopold II's own company to administer the Congo as a free trade and navigation protectorate based on precedents of smaller exploitative and privatized European business-polities in Africa.[150] Like the Dutch, Belgium styled itself as a "small" nation in Europe – particularly with its neutrality – while seeking to be a "giant" abroad.[151] Although money-making was the priority, the Italians and British, prompted by their domestic antislavery lobbies, sought the moral high ground by seeking to criminalize slavery by Africans, that is, by "Arab" or "Muslim" traders, as they were called.[152] The other powers demurred because of the impracticality of ending a trade that extended deep into the African interior, so ultimately a nonbinding article to end its maritime aspect was written into the General Act of the Berlin Conference. It was thus all the more important that the act's rhetorical justification was humanitarian.

[149] David Petrie, *Communism in India, 1924–27* (Calcutta: Editions India, 1972), 291–92; Richard J. Popplewell, *Intelligence and Imperial Defence: British Intelligence and the Defence of the Indian Empire, 1904–1924* (London: Frank Cass, 1995), 79, 91, 303; Durba Ghosh, *Gentlemanly Terrorists: Political Violence and the Colonial State in India, 1919–1947* (Cambridge: Cambridge University Press, 2017).

[150] Steven Press, *Rogue Empires: Contracts and Conmen in Europe's Scramble for Africa* (Cambridge, MA: Harvard University Press, 2017); Andrew Fitzmaurice, "The Justification of King Leopold II's Congo Enterprise by Sir Travers Twiss," in *Law and Politics in British Colonial Thought*, ed. Shaunnagh Dorsett and Ian Hunter (Basingstoke: Palgrave Macmillan, 2010), 109–26.

[151] H. L. Wesseling, "The Giant That Was a Dwarf or the Strange Case of Dutch Imperialism," in H. L. Wesseling, *Imperialism and Colonialism: Essays on the History of European Expansion* (Westport, CT.: Greenwood Press, 1997). The relevant Belgian theorist was Émile Banning (1836–1898), who provided Leopold with the humanitarian and free-trade arguments for his scheme, and who represented Belgium at the Berlin conference: Émile Banning, *Africa and the Brussels Geographical Conference*, trans. Henry Richard Major (London: S. Low. Marston, Searle & Rivington, 1877). Thanks to Florian Wagner for this reference.

[152] Stig Förster, Wolfgang J. Mommsen, and Ronald Robinson, eds., *Bismarck, Europe, and Africa: the Berlin Africa Conference, 1884–1885 and the Onset of Partition* (Oxford: Oxford University Press, 1988); Olivier Pétré-Grenouilleau, ed., *From Slave Trade to Empire: European Colonisation of Black Africa 1780s–1880s* (London and New York: Routeldge, 2004); H. L. Wesseling, *Divide and Rule: The Partition of Africa, 1880–1914* (Westport, CT: Greenwood, 1996).

Article 6 crystallized the civilizing mission commenced in the Treaty of Vienna's antislavery rhetoric in 1815:

> All the Powers exercising sovereign rights or influence in the aforesaid territories bind themselves to watch over the preservation of the native tribes, and to care for the improvement of the conditions of their moral and material well-being, and to help in suppressing slavery, and especially the slave trade. They shall, without distinction of creed or nation, protect and favour all religious, scientific or charitable institutions and undertakings created and organized for the above ends, or which aim at instructing the natives and bringing home to them the blessings of civilization.[153]

Judging by Lemkin's writings on genocide in Africa, he would have subscribed to this statement.[154] Leopold's lawyers supported his self-presentation as a philanthropist against ensuing British criticisms of his administration of the Congo, indeed that the colonization of Africa was "decreed by the double law of conservation and progress that is the proper law of humanity."[155] Although Gustave Rolin-Jaequemyns preferred state rather than private-concession control of the enterprise, he praised the king's aspirations and the Berlin Act's free trade and navigations provisions, lending the good name of his international law institute to the enterprise.[156]

These were not isolated sentiments. The campaign to abolish the slave trade in Africa was driven by Christian activism across Europe, this time with slavery conveniently localized as an Arab-Muslim sin in Africa after the abolition of the trans-Atlantic trade in the 1860s.[157] Whereas the African had been the enslaved victim, now he was the enslaving tyrant who inhibited commerce in the "dark continent." The "mission to civilize" to promote good governance was also based on the proposition that Africans – and Asians – not only mistreated one another but also massacred and committed atrocities against Europeans when possible, as in the Indian uprising in 1857: anticolonial resistance was "terrorism."[158] The General Act of Brussels of 1890,

---

[153] "General Act of the Conference of Berlin concerning the Congo," *American Journal of International Law* 3, no. 1, Supplement: Official Documents (1909): 12.

[154] Dominik J. Schaller, "Raphael Lemkin's View of European Rule in Africa: Between Condemnation and Admiration," in *The Origins of Genocide: Raphael Lemkin as a Historian of Mass Violence*, ed. Dominik J. Schaller and Jürgen Zimmerer (Abingdon: Routledge, 2009), 87–94.

[155] Koskenniemi, *The Gentle Civilizer of Nations*, 162.   [156] Ibid., 156–7.

[157] Frederick Cooper, "Conditions Analogous to Slavery: Imperialism and Free Labor Ideology in Africa," in *Beyond Slavery: Explorations of Race, Labor, and Citizenship in Postemancipation Societies*, ed. Frederick Cooper, Thomas C. Hold, and Rebecca J. Scott (Chapel Hill and London: University of North Carolina Press, 2000), 115.

[158] Andreas Eckert, "Abolitionist Rhetorics, Colonial Conquest, and the Slow Death of Slavery in Germany's African Empire," in *Humanitarian Intervention and Changing Labor Relations*, ed. Marcel van Linden (Leiden: Brill, 2010), 351–68; Frederick Cooper

which expanded the Berlin Act's provisions, encapsulated the self-serving Western self-perception for imperial expansion: the negation of predatory rule of both African chiefs and Spanish-style rule excoriated by Las Casas, namely "putting an end to the crimes and devastations engendered by the traffic in African slaves, of efficiently protecting the aboriginal population of Africa, and of securing for that vast continent the benefits of peace and civilization."[159]

Fittingly, in 1894, a new international association was founded, again in Brussels, by members of colonial associations in European countries: the *Institut Colonial International* (ICI). It determined to place colonialism on a scientific footing by exchanging and publishing expert opinion on the standard issues of humanitarian colonial reform: economic development, labor supply, the alcohol and opium trade, and sanitation. By seeking to transcend imperial rivalry, the ICI made reformed colonialism an explicitly European project. The Aborigines Protection Society supported the British presence in Egypt to protect the peasantry from exploitative landlords and authorities.[160] On the pretext of stamping out slavery, the French established a protectorate in Tunisia in 1881 and the British set up the British Central Africa Protectorate in 1889, having already expanded into Egypt, Sudan, and East Africa – Lagos was annexed already in 1861 – on humanitarian pretexts. European powers carved up Africa in the name of ending slavery and promoting "ordered liberty."[161]

"Africa in a Capitalist World," in *Crossing Boundaries: Comparative History of Black People in Diaspora*, ed. Darlene Clark Hine and Jacqueline McLeod (Bloomington: Indiana University Press, 1999), 399–418; H. Hazel Hahn, "Heroism, Exoticism, and Violence: Representing the Self, 'the Other,' and Rival Empires in the English and French Illustrated Press, 1880–1905," *Historical Reflections* 38, no. 3 (2012): 62–83; Isaac Land, ed., *Enemies of Humanity: The Nineteenth-Century War on Terrorism* (New York and Basingstoke: Palgrave Macmillan, 2008); Alice Conklin, *A Mission to Civilize: The Republican Idea of Empire in France and West Africa, 1890–1930* (Stanford: Stanford University Press, 1997).

[159] *Convention Relative to the Slave Trade and Importation into Africa of Firearms, Ammunition, and Spiritous Liquors* (General Act of Brussels), July 2, 1890, *Preamble*, 135, www.loc.gov/law/help/us-treaties/bevans/m-ust000001-0134.pdf.

[160] The only book-length study is Florian Wagner, *Colonial Internationalism: How Cooperation Among Experts Reshaped Colonialism (1880s–1950s)* (Cambridge: Cambridge University Press, forthcoming); Samera Esmeir, *Juridical Humanity: A Colonial History* (Stanford: Stanford University Press, 2012), 156.

[161] Amalia Ribi Forclaz, *Humanitarian Imperialism: The Politics of Anti-Slavery Activism, 1880–1940* (Oxford: Oxford University Press, 2015); Daniel Laqua, "The Tensions of Internationalism: Transnational Anti-Slavery in the 1880s and 1890s," *International History Review* 33, no. 4 (2011): 705–26; Bertrand Taithe "Evil, Liberalism and the Imperial Designs of the Catholic Church, 1867–1905," in Crook, Gill, and Taithe, *Evil, Barbarism and Empire*, 147–71; Suzanne Miers, "Slavery and the Slave Trade as International Issues, 1890–1939," in *Slavery and Colonial Rule in Africa*, ed. Suzanne Miers and Morton A. Klein (London: Frank Cass, 1999), 16–37; Huzzey, "Minding

These traditional justifications of empire were soon destabilized when the missionaries in Congo, their European counterparts, and the Aborigines Protection Society signalled disquiet with the conditions under Leopold's rule after 1890. Far from allowing free trade, the country's rubber industry was controlled by concessions that exacted forced labor from Africans with the local gendarmes, the notoriously brutal *Force Publique*. Violating the Berlin Act in every respect, Leopold's Congo led to the deaths of millions of Congolese.[162] In fact, Leopold had studied and applied Spanish and Dutch models of forced plantation labor in their colonies, although he realized the need to present his scheme in philanthropic terms to gain international approval.[163] The international protest movement that developed in the first decade of the twentieth century crystallized a century of abolitionism in technologically more advanced conditions. Activists like English radical E. D. Morel (1873–1924), a founder of the Congo Reform Movement in 1904, utilized wrenching photographs of floggings and mutilations in his books on the subject, while large evangelical audiences in Great Britain beheld such images in lantern slide shows. Eyewitnesses to these atrocities were quoted in the voluminous pamphlet literature, including in a major report by British-Irish consul Roger Casement (1864–1916). Together, they built up such pressure that the king was forced to hand over the Congo's administration to the Belgian state in 1908.[164] Casement's work in the Putumayo region of the Amazon in 1910, about which he reported in what one historian

Civilisation and Humanity in 1867"; Mulligan, "British Anti-Slave Trade and Anti-Slavery Policy in East Africa, Arabia, and Turkey in the Nineteenth Century," 271; Peter J. Cain, "Character, 'Ordered Liberty,' and the Mission to Civilise: British Moral Justification of Empire, 1870–1914," *Journal of Imperial and Commonwealth History* 40, no. 4 (2012): 557–78; Kirsten Manne, *Slavery and the Birth of an African City Lagos, 1760–1900* (Bloomington: Indiana University Press, 2007), ch. 3.

[162] Martin Ewans, *European Atrocity, African Catastrophe: Leopold II, the Congo Free State and its Aftermath* (London: Curzon, 2002); Dean Clay, "Transatlantic Dimensions of the Congo Reform Movement, 1904–1908," *English Studies in Africa* 59, no. 1 (2016): 18–28; Adam Hochschild, *King Leopold's Ghost: A Story of Greed, Terror and Heroism in Colonial Africa* (New York: Mariner, 1998); David van Reybrouck, *Congo Epic: History of a People* (New York: HarperCollins, 2014). On the paradoxical function of the Berlin Act in enabling system of exploitation inimical to free trade in the rhetorical effort to promote the latter, see Matthew Craven, "Between Law and History: the Berlin Conference of 1884–85 and the Logic of Free Trade," *London Review of International Law* 3, no. 1 (2015): 31–59.

[163] Florian Wager, "Private Colonialism and International Co-operation in Europe, 1870–1911," in *Imperial Co-operation and Transfer, 1870–1930*, ed. Volker Barth and Roland Cvetkovski (London: Bloomsbury, 2015), 85–6.

[164] Dean Pavlakis, *British Humanitarianism and the Congo Reform Movement, 1896–1913* (Farnham: Ashgate, 2015); John Peffer, "Snap of the Whip/Crossroads of Shame: Flogging, Photography, and the Representation of Atrocity in the Congo Reform Campaign," *Visual Anthropology Review* 24 (2008): 55–77; Andrew Porter, "Sir Roger

calls a "measured observational style," detailed the virtual enslavement of Indians by the British-financed Peruvian Amazon Company, again in rubber harvesting. Casement's revelations also caused public scandal and a Parliamentary ("rubber atrocities") inquiry.[165]

This literature exemplified the language of transgression by highlighting the systematic nature of the criminality, which entailed both slavery and extermination. The root cause of the Congo atrocities, charged Morel, was that the terms of the Berlin Act had been violated: free trade was thwarted by monopolies supported by the military terrorism of the gendarmes. Arguing like reformers before him, he observed that Africans' land rights had been taken away, and thus their capacity for economic agency. Here was a system of exploitation that was inimical to commerce, "the greatest civilizing agent."[166] As an officer of the Congo Reform Association put it, "The essential issue had ceased to be one of 'atrocities' and had become one of the fundamentals of the Congo administration."[167] Demonstrating the alliance between commerce and reform, radical politician Charles Dilke (1843–1911) declared that "The Aborigines Protection Society and the merchants of Liverpool and Manchester are now able to join together in a final condemnation of the Congolese authorities."[168]

The highly charged rhetoric of condemnation reprised Las Casasian themes. In his exposé of the Congo system, *Red Rubber* (1906), Morel frequently mentioned the "extermination" of Africans, adding for emphasis that "Crime so awful, scandal of such magnitude, tragedy so immeasurable – the world surely has never seen this like in combination." Reviewers concurred. Dilke wrote that "It can safely be asserted that never in history has there been a more fiendish cruelty," while one newspaper called the Congo a "stupendous crime

Casement and the International Humanitarian Movement," *Journal of Imperial and Commonwealth History* 29 (2010): 59–74; Dean Clay, "Transatlantic Dimensions of the Congo Reform Movement, 1904–1908," *English Studies in Africa* 59, no. 1 (2016): 18–28; Kevin Grant, *A Civilised Savagery: Britain and the New Slaveries in Africa, 1884–1826* (London: Routledge, 2005); Andrew Porter, "Sir Roger Casement and the International Humanitarian Movement," *Journal of Imperial and Commonwealth History* 29 (2010): 59–74; W. Roger Louis, "Roger Casement and the Congo," *Journal of African History* 5, no. 1 (1964): 99–120.

[165] Robert M. Burroughs, *Travel Writing and Atrocities: Eyewitness Accounts of Colonialism in the Congo, Angola, and the Putumayo* (New York and Abingdon: Routledge, 2011), 56; Suzanne Miers, *Slavery in the Twentieth Century: The Evolution of a Global Problem* (Walnut Creek, CA: Altamira Press, 2003), 54–5. The inquiry recommended consular reform to improve oversight rather than prosecutions.

[166] Bernard Porter, *Critics of Empire: British Radicals and the Imperial Challenge* (London: Macmillan, 1968), 258.

[167] John Daniels, "The Congo Question and the 'Belgian Solution,'" *North American Review* 188 (December 1908): 892.

[168] Henry Richard Fox Bourne, *Civilisation in Congoland: A Story of International Wrong-Doing* (London: P. S. King & Son, 1903), xv.

against humanity."[169] Arthur Conan Doyle (1859–1930), author of the Sherlock Holmes novels, lent his pen to the campaign in *Crime of the Congo* (1909), which likewise condemned "the sack of a country, the spoliation of a nation, the greatest crime in all history."[170] By adding that the crime was "the greater for having been carried out under an odious pretense of philanthropy," Doyle was candid about the multidimensional Belgian criminality. Leopold's Congo was an outlaw state for these critics.

As might be expected, Belgian lawyers rushed to defend their king's enterprise in the face of what Ernest Nys (1851–1920), a longtime member of the Institut de Droit International, called "exaggerations and generalisations skilfully arranged."[171] While not denying that abuses had occurred, he insisted they were exceptional and that the Congo state had "spared no sacrifice to realise the humanitarian wishes of the Berlin Conference of 1884–1885, and of that of Brussels of 1889–90." Indeed, to question its civilizing achievements was "to cast doubt on the progress of the world" itself, by which he meant ending slavery, spreading European civilization ("the noblest civilisation that has ever prevailed on this planet"), promoting work, and the arbitration of disputes. The latter was dear to his heart as a member of the Permanent Court of Arbitration established by the Hague Convention in 1899.[172]

In the event, both critique and defense of King Leopold II's Congo shared a commitment to empire. The problem with the shock literature and these images was not, as supposed by some, that they confined engagement with atrocity to depoliticized outrage rather than to complex analysis, or that they deadened sensibilities with repetition; in fact, Congo critics contextualized the violence in systems of exploitation, their indignation did not diminish, nor did that of their audiences.[173] The issue was that spectatorship of distant suffering created an illusion of a community of solidarity that enabled continuing faith in humanitarian empire.[174] King Leopold II's crime was that he sullied the

---

[169] E. D. Morel, *Red Rubber: The Story of the Rubber Slave Trade Which Flourished on the Congo for Twenty Years, 1890–1910*, new rev. ed. (London: The National Labour Press, 1919), 35, 136, 137, 194, xv, xvi.

[170] Arthur Conan Doyle, *The Crime of the Congo* (New York: Doubleday, Page, and Co, 1909), 126. On Nys, see Koskenniemi, *The Gentle Civilizer of Nations*, 160–2.

[171] Ernest Nys, *The Independent State of the Congo and International Law* (Brussels: J. Lebègue & Co. 1903), 61.

[172] Ibid., 59, 62.

[173] Barthes, "Shock-Photos"; Susan Sontag, *On Photography* (New York: Farrar, Straus & Giroux, 1973), 14–5.

[174] Symptomatic: Sharon Sliwinski, *Human Rights in Camera* (Chicago: Chicago University Press, 2011). Perceptive: Wendy S. Hesford, *Spectacular Rhetorics: Human Rights Visions, Recognitions, Feminisms* (Durham, NC: Duke University Press, 2011).

"conscience of Europe." Doyle concluded by calling for punishment for those "who by their injustice and violence have dragged Christianity and civilization in the dirt."[175] The Belgians had betrayed the European civilizing mission. "Under enlightened and enlightening leadership, firm but generous," wrote the secretary of Aborigines Protection Society, Henry Richard Fox Bourne (1837–1909), in his ironically titled *Civilisation in Congoland* (1903), Africans "might have been made prompt disciples and capable partners with as much benefit to themselves as to the newcomers."[176] The notion of the "preservation of the native tribes" in the Berlin Act was consistent with humanitarian protests about "coolie" labor in Africa because of the supposedly pernicious effects of introducing aliens, like Chinese and Indians.[177] Self-determination for Africans was not envisaged.

The conceit of these ideals was the enduring rescue mission: "saving the races of Central Africa from the grip of the modern slavers," as Morel put it in reminding his readers ("the British conscience") that "the great Congo tragedy synchronises with the Centenary of the most noble act which our historical annals record," namely the abolition of the slave trade in 1807.[178] The condescension about Africans was also evident in the depiction of the *Force Publique*, which epitomized African savagery.[179] Basing his account of the Congo on the humanitarian literature, Lemkin shared this view, writing that guards "were chosen for their savage character, and killed and tortured the natives according to the barbaric customs prevalent among primitive peoples."[180] Casement's account of the Putumayo people as childlike and innocent also partook of enduring colonial stereotypes. He too proposed that Christian missionaries take up work among them as a remedy against their exploitation.[181] The language of transgression was based on a subjectivity that experienced shock, thereby vouchsafing its humanity and ability to assess the level of civilization of others. It was, and remains, the subject that intervenes for humanity.

[175] Doyle, *The Crime of the Congo*, 126.   [176] Bourne, *Civilisation in Congoland*, 298–9.
[177] Swaisland, "The Aborigines Protection Society, 1837–1909"; Laidlaw, "Imperial Complicity."
[178] Morel, *Red Rubber*, 183.
[179] Robert M Burroughs, "'Savage Times Come Again': Morel, Wells, and the African Soldier, c.1885–1920," *English Studies in Africa* 59, no. 1 (2016): 40–51.
[180] Raphael Lemkin, "Congo," Raphael Lemkin Papers, New York Public Library, Reel 3, Box 2, Folder 7, 89.
[181] Lesley Wylie, "Rare Models: Roger Casement, the Amazon, and the Ethnographic Picturesque," *Irish Studies Review* 18, no. 3 (2010): 315–30.

Conclusion

As so often, critique of imperial practices did not imply rejection of empire. Writing in 1833, Alex de Tocqueville was perturbed by France's ruthless warfare on Algeria. "For my part," he concluded, "I returned from Africa with the distressing notion that we are now fighting far more barbarously than the Arabs themselves. For the present, it is on their side that one meets with civilization."[182] Nonetheless, he had no doubts about the necessity and justice of the French project there. In a half-conscious way, Rudyard Kipling's paean to the Western civilizing mission in his iconic poem, "The White Man's Burden" (1899), also registered this ambivalence when he coined the memorable phrase, "savage wars of peace."[183] But neither did Kipling think that imperial excesses invalidated the colonial enterprise. He was at once one of his empire's greatest proponents and icons. The ends ultimately justified the means, even if the means led to occasional uneasiness.

Their application of the language of transgression was not uncontested. African-American intellectual W. E. B. Du Bois (1868–1963) concluded the first Pan African Convention, held in London in 1900, in a speech addressed "To the Nations of the World." He pleaded that they recognize Africans as members of "the great brotherhood of mankind," invoking the Stoic ideal of a shared humanity. Mentioning the keywords of civilization, conscience, progress, and abolition, he concluded by flattering Westerners' self-perception to elicit the desired effect: "with boldness and confidence [I appeal] to the Great Powers of the civilized world, trusting in the wide spirit of humanity, and the deep sense of justice and of our age, for a generous recognition of the righteousness of our cause."[184] His was an adroit mediation between condemning the terms by which civilization was spread – namely by "War, murder, slavery, extermination, and debauchery" – and the universal possibilities that inhered in the development of human capacities.[185]

---

[182] Alexis de Tocqueville, *Writings on Empire and Slavery*, ed. Jennifer Pitts (Baltimore, MD and London: Johns Hopkins University Press, 2001), 70.

[183] Rudyard Kipling, "The White Man's Burden: The United States and the Philippine Islands," in *The Norton Anthology of English Literature*, ed. Stephen Greenblatt, Carol T. Christ, and Deidre Shauna Lynch, 2 Vols. 8th ed. (New York: W. W. Norton and Co., 2006), 2: 1821–1822. The term has inspired apologists for empire ever since. Max Boot, *The Savage Wars of Peace: Small Wars and the Rise of American Power* (New York: Basic Books, 2002).

[184] W. E. B Du Bois, "To the Nations of the World," in *W.E.B. Du Bois Speaks: Speeches and Addresses 1920-1963*, ed. Philip S. Foner (New York: Pathfinder, 1970), 124-7.

[185] W. E. B Du Bois, *Souls of Black Folk*, ed. and intro Brent Hayes Edwards (Oxford: Oxford University Press, 2007), 111.

DuBois's was a minority voice at the time, as were those of lawyers who criticized the legal basis of King Leopold's claim to the Congo.[186] The voices of empire, whether triumphant or agonized, predominated abroad as they did at home. French elites, for instance, regarded the Parisian communards of 1871 and other revolutionary actors as political savages, metropolitan corollaries of the New Caledonian "Kanaks."[187] "Unruly women" in particular offended their sensibilities. "In the midst of the atrocious scenes that shock Paris," reported the *Paris-Journal*, "the women are particularly distinguished by their cruelty and rage."[188] The discursive connection between the empire and metropole was realized during the dramatic events in Paris when the ruler of the Kabyle region of Medjana in Algeria began an insurgency, and Algerian nationalists joined the commune in solidarity. For the ultimately victorious French republican forces, crushing the commune and the Algerian uprising were one and the same endeavor: ensuring that civilization prevails over savagery and barbarism.[189]

The language of transgression, with its insights and blindnesses, reached its apogee in the final year of the nineteenth century and the beginning of the next with the consequences of the "new imperialism": US intervention in Cuba, the Boer War, German colonial crimes in Africa and, of course, the World War I and its atrocities. The ideals of humanity, commerce, conscience, colonial rule, the protection of small nations and vulnerable peoples continued the Las Casasian themes as the legitimating ideals of a Western-dominated commercial civilization even as it was globalized in the League of Nations in the interwar years. As historian Frederick Cooper rightly observes, "The reformist critique of imperialism gone wrong emphasized the morality and normalcy of colonial rule."[190]

---

[186] Andrew Fitzmaurice, *Sovereignty, Property and Empire, 1500–2000* (Cambridge: Cambridge University Press, 2014), 290–301.

[187] Alice Bullard, *Exile to Paradise: Savagery and Civilization in Paris and the South Pacific, 1790–1900* (Stanford: Stanford University Press, 2001).

[188] Gay L. Gullickson, *Unruly Women of Paris: Images of the Commune* (Ithaca and London: Cornell University Press, 1996), 174.

[189] Abdelmajid Hannoun, *Violent Modernity; France in Algeria* (Cambridge, MA: Harvard University Press, 2010), 94–136. Thanks to Lorenzo Veracini for pointing out this connection.

[190] Frederick Cooper, *Decolonization and African Society: The Labor Question in French and British Africa* (Cambridge: Cambridge University Press, 1996), 27.

2

The Language of Transgression, 1890s to 1930s

The language of transgression has been multidirectional from its beginnings. Just as European elites denounced the Spanish in the sixteenth century, so they attacked one another as barbaric in the nineteenth and early twentieth centuries. Germans were wont to condemn Anglophone settlers for their treatment of Native Americans, often identifying with the latter as fellow victims of the British, and regarding themselves as the better colonizers. When it came to German rule in Africa and Samoa later in the nineteenth century, British administrators and missionaries denounced its harshness in similar terms. French textbooks similarly referred to Prussians as barbarians after defeat at their hands in 1871. In turn, Imperial Germany complained bitterly about the French use of African troops during World War I, which it said violated the code of civilized warfare. Soon after, the Allies adjudged that Germans' abuse, indeed "extermination," of Africans before the war disqualified them as a civilizing–colonial power, meaning that the colonies should pass into the victors' hands.[1]

The Allies (or Entente) could strip Germany of its colonies because Germany lost the war. Applying normative pressure with the language of transgression was the tactic until then, as in the campaign to stop the system of labor exploitation in the Congo in the name of humanity and civilization. Violating the sovereignty of another European power's colonial possessions was another. Yet so pervasive was the language of transgression that it could justify such a drastic intervention. The state that purported to represent

---

[1] H. Glenn Penny, *Kindred by Choice: Germans and American Indians since 1800* (Chapel Hill: University of North Carolina Press, 2013); Jörg Lehmann, "Civilization versus Barbarism: The Franco-Prussian War in French History Textbooks, 1875–1895," *Journal of Educational Media, Memory, and Society* 7, no. 1 (2015): 51–65; Kenneth Mackenzie, "Some British Reactions to German Colonial Methods, 1885–1907," *Historical Journal* 17, no. 1 (1974): 165–75; John N. Horne and Alan Kramer, *German Atrocities, 1914: A History of Denial* (New Haven: Yale University Press, 2001); Jeremy Silvester and Jan-Bart Gewald, eds., *Words Cannot Be Found: German Colonial Rule in Namibia: An Annotated Reprint of the 1918 Blue Book* (Leiden: Brill, 2003); Rotem Giladi, "The Phoenix of Colonial War: Race, the Laws of War, and the 'Horror on the Rhine,'" *Leiden Journal of International Law* 30, no. 4 (2017): 847–75.

human freedom in general could align universal ideals with its interests. In this respect, Britain's rival was less Germany than the US, whose developing naval power and trading capacity combined with its anticolonial self-understanding and republican civilizing mission to produce world-ordering aspirations.[2] These would be realized in the League of Nations when "international conscience" and the "public mind" were joined in the reformist imperial project of tutelage over "primitive peoples" in its mandates system.

Warfare and Civilization

US President William McKinley's (1843–1901) justification for invading Cuba in 1898 encapsulates the alignment of ideals and interests in unexpected ways. Reports of Spanish atrocities against Cubans fighting for independence incensed US public opinion, which identified with the rebels. Despite business leaders who urged caution lest their investments be threatened, McKinley felt compelled to follow the general sense of indignation, condemning the Spanish in the venerable terms of the black legend: "the chronic condition of disturbance there [in Cuba], which so deeply injures the interests and menaces the tranquillity of the American nation by the character and consequences of the struggle thus kept at our doors, besides shocking its sentiments of humanity." Again, American humanity was at stake: "all through the war we have mingled with our heroism our splendid and glorious humanity." Congress concurred: the Spanish repression "shocked the moral sense of the people of the United States, have been a disgrace to Christian civilization."[3] While the invasion was justified in anti-imperial terms, Cuba effectively became part the US empire, which repeatedly intervened in its domestic affairs after independence in 1902.[4]

The war with Spain extended to the Philippines, which the Americans annexed on a humanitarian pretext, as an "obligation" and owing to the "dictates of humanity." It provoked a colonial campaign against the Filipino independence forces that was as brutal as the war the Americans had accused the Spanish of waging against Cubans.[5] Restraint need not be exercised against uncivilized rebels who were criminalized as irregulars to be summarily

[2] Greg Grandin, "The Liberal Traditions in the Americas: Rights, Sovereignty, and the Origins of Liberal Multilateralism," *American Historical Review* 117, no. 1 (2012): 68–91.

[3] William McKinley, *Speeches and Addresses of William McKinley, from March 1, 1897 to May 30, 1900* (New York: Doubleday and McClure, 1900), 79–80, 108.

[4] Frank Schumacher, "Embedded Empire: The United States and Colonialism," *Journal of Modern European History* 14, no. 2 (2016): 202–4.

[5] Mike Sewell, "Humanitarian Intervention, Democracy, and Imperialism: The American War with Spain, 1898, and After," in *Humanitarian Intervention: A History*, ed. Brendan Simms and D. J. B. Trim (Cambridge: Cambridge University Press, 2011), 305–9.

executed in counterinsurgency operations. In a telling linkage, President Roosevelt denounced these Filipinos as treacherous like "our Arizona Apache."[6]

Hobbes's state-centric public conscience became penetrated by the notion of public opinion during the nineteenth century: its meaning was now determined in the force-field between the state and the people, a proposition exemplified by jurist Albert Venn Dicey's (1835–1922) *Lectures on the Relation between Law and Public Opinion in England during the Nineteenth Century* in 1905. Far from fickle *mass* opinion, *public* opinion was the outcome of extensive debate in the press, resulting in a "national common sense." Dicey was clear that this common sense was now intensely imperial. Analogously, international law was thought to manifest *international* public opinion, although the international public was limited to "civilized" states, reflecting the geopolitical asymmetries of the time.[7]

Government delegations at The First Hague Conference in 1899 to regulate warfare were acutely conscious of their national public opinion's expectations of peaceful arbitration to prevent international conflict.[8] The conference focused particularly on occupation regimes. It codified the language of transgression at the high point of imperial rule, setting the norms of civilized warfare. However, smaller European states, led by Belgium, could not agree with the larger imperial powers about the rights of occupying powers and of occupied European peoples. As might be expected, the continental powers with large land armies, Germany and Russia, demanded the right to change local laws, import their own public servants, and levy taxes while disputing the occupied population's right of resistance that smaller nations naturally defended. As a compromise, the signatories agreed to the Russian diplomat Fyodor Martens's suggestion to insert a new paragraph in the preamble that set a general standard of conduct until positive agreement could be reached. It was sufficiently vague to satisfy Germany and Russia, while smaller nations

---

[6] Paul A. Kramer, *The Blood of Government: Race, Empire, and the United States and the Philippines* (Chapel Hill: University of North Carolina Press, 2006), 90, 101, 136–7; Stuart Creighton Miller, *Benevolent Assimilation: The American Conquest of the Philippines* (New Haven, CT: Yale University Press, 1984), 88; Christopher J. Einolf, *America in the Philippines, 1899–1902: The First Torture Scandal* (Basingstoke: Palgrave Macmillan, 2014).

[7] A. V. Dicey, *Lectures on the Relation between Law and Public Opinion in England during the Nineteenth Century* (London: Macmillan and Co., 1905). Dicey's imperial commitments are elaborated in Dylan Lino, "Albert Venn Dicey and the Constitutional Theory of Empire," *Oxford Journal of Legal Studies* 36, no. 4 (2016): 751–80; James Thompson, *British Political Culture and the Idea of "Public Opinion," 1867–1914* (Cambridge: Cambridge University Press, 2013).

[8] Maartje Abbenhuis, *The Hague Conference and International Politics, 1898–1915* (Cambridge: Cambridge University Press, 2018).

were reassured by its invocation of standards that supplemented the specific articles of the convention:

> Until a more complete code of the laws of war is issued, the High Contracting Parties think it right to declare that in cases not included in the Regulations adopted by them, populations and belligerents remain under the protection and empire of the principles of international law, as they result from the usages established between civilized nations, from the laws of humanity and the requirements of the public conscience.[9]

The language of transgression was thus split between the Convention's specific prohibitions and the imprecise requirements of the preamble. As we will see in Chapter 5, the former – "laws and customs of war" – enjoyed the status of settled law and would be called "war crimes" (the Convention used that term only once) while the latter became named as crimes against humanity and genocide during World War II. Lemkin and his continental contemporaries in particular referred to both dimensions of the convention while wrestling with Germans' mass crimes in their occupied homelands.

The question of public opinion and peace was thrust onto the agenda immediately after the Hague meeting with Britain's conduct in the Second Boer War (1899–1902). There was no avoiding the stark asymmetry of the world's mightiest empire ranged against Afrikaner settlers in Transvaal and Orange Free State. Confronting the Boers' guerrilla tactics entailed the drastic countermeasures used by the Spanish in Cuba and Americans in the Philippines in their colonial warfare: destroying villages and interning the civilian population to isolate the insurgents. International and domestic commentators invoked the Hague regulations to condemn the British warfare as uncivilized while the British state insisted it was law-abiding.[10] Liberal and radical critics in Britain spoke the language of transgression against the New Imperialism of the Tory government, in particular idealizing small nations. Pro-Boer critics adopted the mantle of Gladstonian liberalism against the Tory government, even mentioning "extermination," as Congo critics like Morel would soon thereafter. Liberal politician Henry Campbell-Bannerman (1836–1908) instructed Conservatives in Parliament with a classic defense of national culture that evoked Palmerston's denunciation of the Russian treatment of Poles in the 1830s and that by decades anticipates Lemkin's notion of cultural genocide:

---

[9] Theodor Meron, "The Martens Clause, Principles of Humanity, and Dictates of Public Conscience," *American Journal of International Law* 94, no. 1 (2000): 78–89; Kerstin von Lingen, "Fulfilling the Martens Clause: Debating 'Crimes against Humanity,' 1899–1945," in *Humanity: A History of European Concepts in Practice from the Sixteenth Century to the Present*, ed. Fabian Klose and Mirjam Thulin (Göttingen: Vandenhoeck and Ruprecht, 2016), 187–208.

[10] Abbenhuis, *The Hague Conference and International Politics, 1898–1915*, ch. 5.

The object of the Government is not, he says, to exterminate the Boers in the sense of destroying men, women and children among them. No one means that. But there is something short of that which will still come under the general name of extermination – not the removal of them from the face of the earth, but to obliterate them and reduce them and deprive them of their national identity. This is the old spirit of racial ascendancy, the old spirit which, wherever it has been applied in the experience of the world, has brought serious and deadly evils with it. This is what the world at large discerns in the recent policy, which was the policy of His Majesty's Government from the first, and I fear in the face of the facts it will not be easy to disown.[11]

Critics underlined this point. The British were guilty of a "crime against nationality" with its "policy of exterminating the Boer States," which was hypocritical given Britain's earlier support for Polish uprisings against Russia. Welsh and Scottish opponents of the war saw in the Boers an analogy with their relationship to English hegemony, which violated what one of them called "the doctrine of nationality" that they traced to Gladstone. Irish voices went further still, declaring Britain a "Great Pirate" for attempting to destroy the Boers as it had the Irish Celts.[12] As always, piracy marked ultimate criminality in the language of transgression.

Such oppression, particularly of women and children in small nations, was tantamount to barbarism. William Stead, the journalist who had helped popularize the news of massacres of Armenians in 1896, titled his popular pamphlet about British conduct in the Boer War *Methods of Barbarism* to underline the point. It concentrated a sustained debate about the morality and legality of Britain's counterinsurgency tactics, which other publicists, notably Arthur Conan Doyle, defended as consistent with Hague regulations, indeed as a war "waged with humanity."[13] International opinion – both diplomatic and public – sided with Stead despite government efforts, which included reprinting 300,000 copies of Doyle's booklet, *The War in South Africa: Its Cause and Conduct*, in seven

---

[11] John S. Ellis, "'The Methods of Barbarism' and the 'Rights of Small Nations': War Propaganda and British Pluralism," *Albion* 30, no. 1 (1998): 58.

[12] Ellis, "'The Methods of Barbarism' and the 'Rights of Small Nations,'" 58–61.

[13] William T. Stead, *Methods of Barbarism: The Case for Intervention* (London: Review of Reviews, 1901); Abbenhuis, *The Hague Conference and International Politics, 1898–1915*, 104–5; Ingrid Hanson, "'God'll Send the Bill to You": The Costs of War and the God Who Counts in W. T. Stead's Pro-Boer Peace Campaign," *Journal of Victorian Culture* 20, no. 2 (2015): 168–85; Stephanus B. Spies, *Methods of Barbarism? Roberts, Kitchener and Civilians in the Boer Republics: January 1900–May 1902* (Johannesburg: Jonathan Ball, 2001); Arthur Conan Doyle, *The War in South Africa: Its Cause and Conduct* (New York: McClure, Phillips & Co., 1902), preface.

languages. The Hague regulation's normative statements codified the language of transgression in law and lent it harder edges.[14]

The same alignment of international opinion and domestic criticism existed regarding Imperial Germany's African colonies after 1884 via concessions in what is now Namibia (German Southwest Africa) and Tanzania (German West Africa). British observers noted sarcastically that the German mode of spreading civilization entailed savage violence, which provoked rebellions by its disregard for local custom and exploitation.[15] German leftists and humanitarians assailed the explorer, Carl Peters (1856–1918), leader of the German East Africa Company, whose outrages against Africans in the 1890s suggested to them, and to colonial officials and the media, that he had become a savage as well.[16] Of the genocidal campaign against the Herero and Nama in German Southwest Africa between 1904 and 1907, socialist politician August Bebel advanced the same arguments as English radicals: the African rebels were not criminal bandits, but patriots trying to liberate their country. Not that he opposed colonialism as such, only its excesses. Other Social Democrats used the classical inversion tactic inaugurated by Las Casas: the German Army had sunk "down to the moral level of the Hottentots."[17] Lemkin shared these views, basing his two chapters on German colonial rule in Africa largely on British anti-German atrocity literature published during and after World War I. Indeed, he explicitly endorsed the British views and leftist criticisms expressed in the Reichstag.[18]

---

[14] Abbenhuis, *The Hague Conference and International Politics, 1898–1915*.

[15] Kenneth Mackenzie, "Some British Reactions to German Colonial Methods, 1885–1907," *Historical Journal* 17, no. 1 (1974): 165–75.

[16] Arne Perras, *Carl Peters and German Imperialism 1856–1918: A Political Biography* (Oxford: Clarendon, 2004), 216; Frank Bösch, *Öffentliche Geheimnisse: Skandale, Politik und Medien in Deutschland und Großbritannien 1880–1914* (Munich: Oldenbourg Verlag, 2009), 142.

[17] Helmut Walser Smith, "Talk of Genocide, the Rhetoric of Miscegenation: Notes on Debates in the German Reichstag concerning Southwest Africa, 1904–14," in *German Colonialism and its Legacy*, ed. Sara Friedrichsmeyer, Sara Lennox, and Susanne Zantorp (Ann Arbor: University of Michigan Press, 1998), 107–23. Generally see Jürgen Zimmerer and Joachim Zeller, eds., *Genocide in German South-West Africa: The Colonial War of 1904–1908 and Its Aftermath* (Monmouth: Merlin Press, 2008); Dominik Schaller, "From Conquest to Genocide: Colonial Rule in German Southwest Africa and German East Africa," in *Empire, Colony, Genocide: Conquest, Occupation, and Subaltern Resistance in World History*, ed. A. Dirk Moses (New York and Oxford: Berghahn Books, 2008), 296–324.

[18] Raphael Lemkin, "The Germans in Africa," in *Lemkin on Genocide*, ed. Stephen L. Jacobs (Lanham, MD: Lexington Books, 2012), 189–222; Lemkin, "Herero," American Jewish Archives, Collection 60, Box 6, 20–1. The last two pages of "The Germans in Africa" were lifted almost verbatim from Africanus, *The Prussian Lash in Africa: The Story of German Rule in Africa* (London: Hodder and Stoughton, 1918), 18–9.

World War I and the Language of Transgression

With Liberals in government when Britain went to war with Germany in 1914, the language of transgression could again be spoken on behalf of *Pax Britannica*. Germany's violation of Belgian neutrality, which triggered a British treaty obligation, combined with stories of German atrocities to galvanize the moral case for war. Britain was fighting to defend "Little Belgium" and the rights of small nations from the barbaric steamroller of Prussian militarism. Pro-Boer arguments against British imperialism were now applied to Germany. Liberal leader David Lloyd George (1863–1945), who was prime minister between 1916 and 1922, summarized the case: "Many of us have opposed war before on the ground of the extinction of small nationalities. But everyone who believes in the preservation of the smaller nationalities and their freedom must endeavour to prevent Germany from trampling on them."[19] In his pamphlet, *The Value of Small States*, Liberal politician and historian Herbert Fisher (1865–1940) expressed this viewpoint in terms that Lemkin would repeat:

> Almost everything which is most precious in our civilization has come from small states, the Old Testament, the Homeric poems, the Attic and Elizabethan drama, the art of the Italian Renaissance, the common law of England. Nobody needs to be told what humanity owes to Athens, Florence, Geneva, or Weimar. The world's debt to any one of these small states far exceeds all that has issued from the militant monarchies of Louis XIV, of Napoleon, of the present Emperor of Germany.[20]

He excluded Britain from the list of militant monarchies and conveniently omitted the Boer War. By virtue of "its capacity to preserve the small state in the great union," Britain was a force for good, its imperial success lying in "the wise and easy tolerance" of cultural difference after earlier mistakes in Ireland.[21] Invoking the Hague Conventions, the British defended their war aims in internationalist and humanitarian terms: to honor the Treaty of London (1839) that guaranteed Belgian neutrality and that Germany dismissed as a "scrap of paper," and to protect civilians from German barbarism.[22]

---

[19] Ellis, "'The Methods of Barbarism' and the 'Rights of Small Nations,'" 67.
[20] H. A. L. Fisher, *The Value of Small States* (Oxford: Oxford University Press, 1914), 9.
[21] Ibid., 22–3.
[22] Nicoletta F. Gullace, "Sexual Violence and Family Honor: British Propaganda and International Law during the First World War," *American Historical Review* 102, no. 3 (1997): 714–47; Isabel V. Hull, *A Scrap of Paper: Breaking and Making International Law during the Great War* (Ithaca, NY: Cornell University Press, 2014).

This conception of the war was shared by the Russian diplomat and legal scholar, André Mandelstam, who became an important proponent of minority and human rights during the interwar years. A protégé of Martens, he was posted in Istanbul until the war's outbreak, and continued to concern himself closely with Armenian and Ottoman questions, which he regarded as a particular Russian imperative. Although he supported US President Wilson's self-determination rhetoric, he did not think it should apply to the Baltic states and Ukraine, which were "Russia's vital interest."[23] Like his British and French counterparts, Mandelstam's notion of international society during the war was firmly imperial: civilized powers had the right to intervene in uncivilized entities that committed massacres and other atrocities. He would agree with them to dismember the Ottoman Empire because its elites had disqualified themselves from ruling over minority nations. Needless to say, he was attacked by Turkish writers for double standards; valuing Christian lives over Muslim ones.[24]

Mandelstam's example demonstrated that squaring the lofty rhetoric about small nations with Russia's multinational empire was a propaganda challenge. As an intrinsic member of the Entente, Russia's record was vulnerable to exploitation. The German Foreign Office thus sponsored the third conference of the Union of Nationalities (*L'Union des Nationalités*), founded by a Lithuanian nationalist in 1912, and the newly formed League of Nation-Russian Peoples, to highlight despotic Russian rule and Germany's intention to grant these small nations independence after its victory. Although representatives of other nationalities participated, those from the Russian Empire dominated the meeting in Lausanne, in neutral Switzerland, in June 1916. Availing itself of the dominant idiom, the League appealed "to the whole civilized world" for assistance against Russian oppression, and hailed Germany as "protector of the rights of the oppressed."[25] Germany would

[23] Mandelstam quoted in Dzovinar Kevonian, "André Mandelstam and the Internationalization of Human Rights (1869–1949)," in *Revisiting the Origins of Human Rights*, ed. Pamela Slotte and Miia Halme-Tuomisaari (Cambridge: Cambridge University Press, 2015), 249.

[24] André Mandelstam, *Le sort de l'Empire ottoman* (Lausanne and Paris, Librairie Payot, 1917); Hülya Adak, "The Legacy of André Nikolaievitch Mandelstam (1869–1949) and the Early History of Human Rights," *Zeitschrift für Religion- und Geisteswissenchaft* 70, no. 2 (2018): 117–30.

[25] Carole Fink, *Defending the Rights of Others: The Great Powers, the Jews, and International Minority Protection, 1878–1938* (Cambridge: Cambridge University Press, 2004), 79; Seppo Zetterberg, *Die Liga der Fremdvölker Russlands 1916–1918: Ein Beitrag zu Deutschlands antirussischem Propagandakrieg unter der Fremdvölkern Russlands im Ersten Weltkriegs* (Helsinki: Suomen Historiallinen Seura, 1978); Alfred Erich Senn, "Garlawa: A Study in Émigré Intrigue, 1915–1917," *Slavonic and East European Review* 45, no. 105 (1967): 411–24; Senn, *The Russian Revolution in Switzerland, 1914–1917* (Madison: University of Wisconsin Press, 1972): 185–8.

continue this posture in the interwar period, when it championed minority protection treaties in the new states with German minorities.

Both Entente and Central powers predictably instrumentalized atrocity propaganda and colonial excesses. The German "rape of Belgium," with the sacking of Leuven in August 1914, was the first salvo in an effective campaign that intensified the outrage by utilizing gendered imagery of violated women.[26] By December, liberal Viscount James Bryce (1838–1922), who had opposed the Boer War, was appointed to chair an investigative committee that issued its "Report of the Committee on Alleged German Outrages" in May 1915. It followed in the Las Casasian tradition of quoting witnesses, invoking the standard of civilization, mentioning "shocking" crimes, and their lack of precedent.

> In the present war ... and this is the gravest charge against the German army – the evidence shows that the killing of non-combatants was carried out to an extent for which no previous war between nations claiming to be civilised (for such cases as the atrocities perpetrated by the Turks on the Bulgarian Christians in 1876, and on the Armenian Christians in 1895 and 1896, do not belong to that category) furnishes any precedent.[27]

The class of murder that was "altogether unprecedented" was the killing of civilian inhabitants of villages from which shots had been fired on German troops: Germany was outraging fellow Europeans rather than Africans or other non-Europeans.[28] The Imperial German Army had been particularly sensitive to partisan warfare – hostilities conducted by irregulars, or *Franc-tireurs* (free shooters) – from the Franco-Prussian War of 1870–1871, when it also executed many civilians.[29] Partisans were not protected by the Hague Conventions of 1899 and 1907, but shooting civilians without judicial proceedings violated their stipulations. The report added that "this killing was

---

[26] Nicoletta F. Gullace, *The Blood of Our Sons: Men, Women, and the Renegotiation of British Citizenship during the Great War* (Basingstoke: Palgrave Macmillan, 2002); Horne and Kramer, German Atrocities, 1914; John Horne, "Atrocities and War Crimes," in *Cambridge History of the First World War*, Vol. 1, *Global War*, ed. Jay Winter (Cambridge, Cambridge University Press, 2014), 561–83.

[27] *Report of the Committee on Alleged German Outrages appointed by His Britannic Majesty's government and presided over by the Right Hon. Viscount Bryce* (London: HMSO, 1915), 40; Trevor Wilson, "Lord Bryce's Investigation into Alleged German Atrocities in Belgium, 1914–1915," *Journal of Contemporary History* 14, no. 3 (1979): 369–83.

[28] *Report of the Committee on Alleged German Outrages*, 43. See also *Germany's Violations of the Laws of War, 1914–1915*, trans. and intro. J. O. P. Bland (London: William Heinemann, 1915), where The Hague conventions feature as the normative and legal yardstick by which to assess German actions.

[29] Isabel V. Hull, *Absolute Destruction: Military Culture and the Practice of War in Imperial Germany* (Ithaca, NY: Cornell University Press, 2005).

done as part of a deliberate plan," a phrase that we will see recur in Lemkin's condemnation of German rule nearly 30 years later.[30]

The report did not mention the fact that such collective punishment, in fact annihilation, was routine in colonial warfare, and occasionally in intra-European warfare, indeed that the British bombed Afghan civilians during World War I: the outrage it was stoking was based on the violation of treating Europeans like non-Europeans.[31] The report also coincided with the British policy of stifling imports of goods and foodstuffs to Germany by blockading neutral ports. This policy led indirectly to the deaths of between 300,000 and 424,000 civilians due to malnutrition, which constituted 10 times the casualties caused by well-publicized German atrocities against civilians and infractions of international law.[32] The Allied blockade of Ottoman Eastern Mediterranean contributed to the deaths of up to 300,000 in Mount Lebanon and half the population of Beirut.[33] The British were far more scrupulous in debating the legalities of its economic warfare than the Germans but, like their enemy, were prepared to ignore or bend international maritime law, which was vague and contested, to suit their war aims when they felt national survival was at stake.[34]

David Lloyd George was acutely conscious that "transport on sea and land" would be "vital" for the supply of munitions and food. Food shortages on the continent threatened his ally, Russia, as much as Austria-Hungary and Germany. After the decisive battles of 1916, he noted in his memoir, "the belligerents were confronted with a war of starvation." The policy conclusions were manifest: "If we maintained control of the seas without actually breaking on shore, the Central Powers could in the end be starved into surrender." It goes without saying that he did not admit to seeking to cause civilian deaths, because, he reasoned, "no people will die of hunger rather than relinquish conquests of foreign territory." But civilians did starve, and he admitted the

---

[30] *Report of the Committee on Alleged German Outrages*, 40.

[31] A. E. Borton, "The Use of Aircraft in Small Wars," *Journal of the Royal United Service Institute* 65 (May 1920): 310–319; J. B. Glubb, "Air and Ground Forces in Punitive Expeditions," *Royal United Service Institution Journal* 71 (August 1926): 777–84; Michael Paris, "Air Power in Imperial Defence, 1880–1918," *Journal of Contemporary History* 24, no. 2 (1989): 209–25.

[32] Hull, *A Scrap of Paper*, 169; Benjamin Ziemann, review of Hull, *A Scrap of Paper*, in H-Soz-u-Kult (May 2015), www.h-net.org/reviews/showrev.php?id=44367. On German atrocities, see Horne and Kramer, German Atrocities, 1914.

[33] Melanie S. Tanielian, *The Charity of War: Famine, Humanitarian Aid, and World War I in the Middle East* (Stanford: Stanford University Press, 2017).

[34] Hull, *A Scrap of Paper*, and Alan Kramer, "Blockade and Economic Warfare," in *The Cambridge History of the First World War*, Vol. II, *The State*, ed. Jay Winter (Cambridge: Cambridge University Press, 2014), 460–89, give the British the benefit of any doubt. For background on international law, see Scott Andrew Keefer, *The Law of Nations and Britain's Quest for Naval Security: International Law and Arms Control, 1898–1914* (Basingstoke: Palgrave Macmillan, 2016).

policy "was a ruthless calculation, but war is organized cruelty." In the end, he reasoned with surprising candor, much like the Germans in their curt dismissal of the international laws of war: "Those who think they can restrict its barbarities will find in the end that savagery is of its essence and that civilised warfare only means that men have changed the instruments and methods of torture."[35]

No sooner had Bryce's report appeared than the escalating Ottoman attack on its Armenian subjects in late April 1915, commencing what is now known as the Armenian genocide, triggered another episode of atrocity reporting. Within a month, the Allies issued a joint declaration accusing Turkey of "new crimes ... against humanity and civilization," the first time this term had appeared in official diplomatic communication.[36] Bryce was thereupon commissioned to conduct another Parliamentary inquiry. Much of the work was carried out by the young historian, Arnold Toynbee (1889–1975), from political intelligence in the Foreign Office. He wove together many eyewitness accounts and analysis in *The Treatment of Armenians in the Ottoman Empire: 1915–16*, the 733-page report published the next year.[37]

Toynbee added three booklets of his own: *Armenian Atrocities: The Murder of a Nation* (1915), *The Destruction of Poland: A Study in German Efficiency* (1916), and *The Murderous Tyranny of the Turks* (1917). In his preface to *Armenian Atrocities*, Bryce observed that the rounding up and sifting of the Armenian population was "exceedingly systematic," the men separated off at various points for murder, while the women and children were marched into the desert where they were to expire. Toynbee reminded readers that the Armenians had suffered before: "the unprecedented Armenian massacres under official direction, that horrified the civilized world in 1895 and 1896, and evoked from Gladstone the last public speech of his old age." The wartime campaign of massacre and deportation represented a radicalization: "the intermittent sufferings of the Armenian race have culminated in an organised,

[35] David Lloyd George, *War Memoirs of David Lloyd George, 1916–1917* (Boston: Little, Brown, and Co., 1934), 43–6.

[36] Sévane Garibian, "From the 1915 Allied Joint Declaration to the 1920 Treaty of Sèvres," *Armenian Review* 52, nos. 1–2 (2010): 87–102. On the genocide, see Taner Akçam, *The Young Turks' Crime against Humanity: The Armenian Genocide and Ethnic Cleansing in the Ottoman Empire* (Princeton: Princeton University Press, 2012); Ronald Grigor Suny, *"They Can Live in the Desert but Nowhere Else": A History of the Armenian Genocide* (Princeton, NJ: Princeton University Press, 2015).

[37] Viscount Bryce, *The Treatment of Armenians in the Ottoman Empire: 1915–16* (London: G. P. Putnams's Sons, 2016); Michelle Tusan, "James Bryce's Blue Book as Evidence," *Journal of Leventine Studies* 5, no. 2 (2015): 35–50; Tusan, *The British Empire and the Armenian Genocide: Humanitarianism and Imperial Politics from Gladstone to Churchill* (London: I. B. Tauris, 2017); David Monger, "Networking against Genocide during the First World War: The International Network Behind the British Parliamentary Report on the Armenian Genocide," *Journal of Transatlantic Studies* 16, no. 3 (2018): 295–316.

cold-blooded attempt on the part of its Turkish rulers to exterminate it once and for all by methods of inconceivable barbarity and wickedness." Toynbee concluded by quoting the *New York Tribune*, which attacked Germany for enabling this destruction, thereby bringing "us all back in the Twentieth Century to the condition of the dark ages."[38] Based on the Blue Book, the Archbishop of Canterbury told the House of Lords that these attacks on Armenians were "unspeakable outrages" and "an outrage on civilization without historical parallel in the world."[39]

These were classic instantiations of the language of transgression, sharing with Bryce's report on German atrocities the emphasis on systematic planning and execution that befitted the capacities of the modern state. Underplayed in analyses of this atrocity literature is Bryce's emphasis on the Turks' political rather than racial or religious motivations, mirroring British diplomats' analysis from the 1890s.

> There was no Moslem passion against the Armenian Christians. All was done by the will of the Government, and done not from any religious fanaticism, but simply because they wished, for reasons purely political, to get rid of a non-Moslem element which impaired the homogeneity of the Empire, and constituted an element that might not always submit to oppression.[40]

Further detracting from the focus on interreligious strife was Britain's ascription of blame for the anti-Armenian atrocities on Imperial German support for the Ottomans.[41] Even if Bryce's intention was not to inflame Muslim subjects in India and other parts of the empire, as German propaganda was encouraging them to rise up against Allied imperial rule, the refusal to depoliticize violence as racial–religious conflict is striking.

British colonial officials also desired a political analysis of German rule in Africa to discredit it as a civilized colonial power. An excessive emphasis on atrocities, of which there were many, could be more easily dismissed as sensationalism, like its report from 1916, *German Atrocities, and Breaches of*

---

[38] Viscount Bryce, "The Armenian Massacres," in Arnold Toynbee, *Armenian Atrocities: The Murder of a Nation* (London: Hodder and Stoughton, 1915), 8–9; Toynbee, *Armenian Atrocities*, 21, 17, 117; Toynbee, *The Murderous Tyranny of the Turks* (New York: Doran, 1917).

[39] Michelle Tusan, "'Crimes Against Humanity': Human Rights, the British Empire, and the Origins of the Response to the Armenian Genocide," *American Historical Review* 119, no. 1 (2014): 62.

[40] Bryce, "The Armenian Massacres," in Toynbee, *Armenian Atrocities*, 7. Michelle Tusan, whose invaluable work drew my attention to this passage, is the exception: Tusan, *The British Empire and the Armenian Genocide*.

[41] Donald Bloxham, *The Great Game of Genocide: Imperialism, Nationalism, and the Destruction of the Ottoman Armenians* (Oxford: Oxford University Press, 2005).

the Rules of War in Africa, which dined out on tales of savagery and brutality. So, officials welcomed the *Report on the Natives of South-West Africa and Their Treatment by Germany* by the Union of South Africa after its invasion of the German colony in 1915.[42] It was reprinted as a Blue Book in 1918 amid the British determination to retain the German territories one way or another. In addition to photographs of executions and Africans in cruel leg-irons, including many mentions of "extermination" regarding the crushing of the Herero uprising between 1904 and 1907, the report purported to demonstrate that Germany was violating Article 6 of the Berlin Act of 1885 and the Brussels Conference on Slavery in 1890.[43]

In this way, it closely resembled the reports about Congo abuses underway at the same time. Indeed, one senior British politician noted the resemblance, but powerful Germany was not the comparatively weaker Belgium. Great Britain and Germany were uneasy colonial partners in ruling southern Africans before World War I, the former aiding the latter in hunting down Herero insurgents while ensuring stability in the border region.[44] The British were well aware of the exterminatory counterinsurgency against the Herero and then Nama, but were more concerned with potential effects on Boers who were recruited by the Germans.[45] And there were uncomfortable connections. The German use of camps to incarcerate Herero, with deadly effects, was inspired by the British camps used for Boer civilians only a few years before; the Germans believed they were the more civilized because they interned Africans rather than Europeans.[46]

The calculus changed dramatically during the war when highlighting German colonial cruelty and misrule became the diplomatic priority. The British Colonial Secretary reminded his listeners about the moral case for the war in December 1918 to justify keeping German colonies: "We said we have fought the war for the liberty of small nations," so he questioned whether

---

[42] *German Atrocities, and Breaches of the Rules of War in Africa* (London: Stationery Office, Darling and Son, 1916); *Words Cannot Be Found: German Colonial Rule in Namibia: An Annotated Reprint of the 1918 Blue Book*, ed. Jeremy Silvester and Jan-Bart Gewald (Leiden and Boston: Brill, 2003). See the analysis in Christina Twomey, "Atrocity Narratives and Inter-Imperial Rivalry: Britain, Germany and the Treatment of 'Native Races,' 1904–1939," in *Evil, Barbarism and Empire: Britain and Abroad, c.1830–2000*, ed. Tom Crook, Rebecca Gill, and Bertrand Taithe (Abingdon: Routledge, 2011), 201–25.

[43] *Words Cannot Be Found*, 9, 33.

[44] David Bargueño, "Humanitarianism in the Age of Empire Deutsch-Südwestafrika & L'Ètat Indépendant du Congo," *Journal of Namibian Studies* 9 (2011): 17–60.

[45] Mads Bomholt Nielsen, "Selective Memory: British Perceptions of the Herero–Nama Genocide, 1904–1908 and 1918," *Journal of Southern African Studies* 43, no. 2 (2017): 315–30.

[46] Jonas Kreienbaum, "Deadly Learning: Concentration Camps in Colonial Wars Around 1900," in *Imperial Co-operation and Transfer, 1870–1930: Empires and Encounters*, ed. Volker Barth and Roland Cvetkovski (London: Bloomsbury, 2015), 226–9.

it was plausible or tenable "if we thrust back the natives tribes of Africa against their will to the tyranny of the German power?"[47] Arthur Balfour (1848–1930), who as foreign secretary had written to British Zionists in 1917 promising Palestine to the Zionist movement, was a year later telling Parliament that Germany had forfeited its right to colonies because it threatened commerce.

> What I object to is giving back to Germany at the end of the War an instrument so powerful for universal evil as a great colonial empire would, Germany being as she is at present, undoubtedly put into her hands. No greater instrument for disturbing the peace of the world or increasing the miseries of humanity could be conceived, in my opinion, than giving Germany a great Central African dominion, to be used as Germany would know how to use it – for offence within the continent of Africa and, offence, perhaps even more perilous, to all the great arteries of trade that join civilised nations together.[48]

He, too, mentioned the ideology of small nations, human communication, and advance of civilization.[49]

Depictions of the Ottoman Empire tended in the same direction in justifying the war as a moral crusade. At the Paris Peace Conference in 1919, the French President, Raymond Poincaré, hailed the surviving "captive nationalities" and "oppressed people" who sided with the Entente. They – "Yugo-Slavs the Armenians, the Syrians and Lebanese, the Arabs" – had suffered "outraged consciences":

> Thus, the war gradually attained the fulness of its first significance, and became, in the truest sense of the term, a crusade of humanity for Right; and, if anything can console us, in part at least, for the losses we have suffered, it is assuredly the thought that our victory is also the victory of Right.[50]

In direct response to the British campaign to keep the German colonies, Germany produced its own report on British misrule in 1918, *The Treatment of Native and Other Populations in the Colonial Possessions of Germany and*

---

[47] Twomey, "Atrocity Narratives and Inter-Imperial Rivalry," 214; Nielsen, "Selective Memory."

[48] Arthur Balfour, *House of Commons Debates on War Aims, 8 August 1918, Vol. 109, cc1633–1634*, http://hansard.millbanksystems.com/commons/1918/aug/08/war-aims#S5CV0109P0_19180808_HOC_397.

[49] Ibid. Generally, see Jason Tomes, *Balfour and Foreign Policy: The International Thought of a Conservative Statesmen* (Cambridge: Cambridge University Press, 1997).

[50] Preliminary Peace Conference, Protocol No. 1, Session of January 18, 1919. *Papers Relating to the Foreign Relations of the United States, The Paris Peace Conference, 1919*, Volume III, *Paris Peace Conf.* Department of State, https://history.state.gov/historicaldocuments/frus1919Parisv03/d3.

England. It mocked the British Blue Book as a "pathetic and melodramatic chamber of horrors" with which the British "strove to shock the whole world" about German colonialism. Humanitarian reports and the British and American press were quoted at length throughout, just as the British cited German humanitarians, politicians, and the press on German excesses before the war. Its basic point was encapsulated in a late chapter entitled "The 'Pax Britannica' a Mere Fiction." Another chapter covered Australia, exposing "The Extermination and Enslavement of Natives in Queensland" and "The Extermination of the Tasmanians, 1823 to 1876." In addition to elaborations of British misrule of India, the book contained damning information about the British suppression of the African revolts and of course the incarceration of Boer civilians in camps. The conclusion laid out the symmetrical logic of atrocity, although suggesting that British capitalism and hypocrisy were the worse:

> The Putumayo atrocities, one of the most terrible instances of the capital-istic extermination of a poor, defenceless people, which has ever blackened civilization, would more than outweigh whatever excesses may have been committed in the German protectorates. The mere fact that after the frightful disclosures which resulted from investigations made by Sir Roger Casement, the British Government undertook no steps whatever to prevent these indescribable tortures of human beings being perpetrated in the interests of British finance, might furnish occasion for luminous comment upon the quality of British justice.[51]

As always with imperial accusations, it was expedient to argue that the rival's misrule had provoked the uprising while unrest in one's own colonies was caused by fanaticism and criminality or perhaps the forces of nature. Thus, the British were shocked by the Shona-Ndebele revolts of 1896–97, unable to see that rule by the British South Africa Company and settlers had led to excessive taxation, sequestration of cattle, and forced labor services that heightened millenarian appeal in circumstances of environmental stress.[52] Such blindness enabled postwar deliberations about war crimes.

---

[51] German Colonial Office, *The Treatment of Native and Other Populations in the Colonial Possessions of Germany and England* (Berlin: Hans Roberts Engelmann, 1919), 19, 77–8, 83, 237–42, 286–90, 308–9; Susanne Kuss, *German Colonial Wars and the Context of Military Violence*, trans. Andrew Smith (Cambridge, MA: Harvard University Press, 2017), 228; Nielsen, "Selective Memory," 323.

[52] Suzanne Dawson, "The First Chimurenga: 1896–1897 Uprising in Matabeleland and Mashonaland and Continued Conflicts in Academia," *Constellations* 2, no. 2 (2011): 144–53; Terence Ranger, *Revolt in Southern Rhodesia 1896–97: A Study in African Resistance* (Evanston: Northwestern University Press, 1967); Richard Price, *Making Empire. Colonial Encounters and the Creation of Imperial Rule in Nineteenth-Century Africa* (Cambridge: Cambridge University Press, 2008).

War Crimes

The crusade of humanity for justice continued after the war in the attempt to prosecute international crimes committed by Central Powers. To that end, the Entente established a *Commission on the Responsibility of the Authors of the War and Enforcement of Penalties*, whose members included, among others, the leading personalities of interwar international law, some representing "small nations" ravaged by Germany and Turkey during the war: American international lawyer James Brown Scott (1866–1943), Greek foreign minister Nicolas Politis (1872–1942), and Belgian Edouard Rolin-Jaequemyns (1863–1936), who followed in his father's footsteps at the *Institut de Droit International.* US Secretary of State Robert Lansing (1864–1928) chaired proceedings, with French international lawyer Albert de Lapradelle (1871–1955) acting as secretary.[53] It is noteworthy that Brown Scott, with Ernest Nys, led the campaign to institute Vitoria and the Salamanca School of theologians and jurists noted in the previous chapter, as the founders of international law, rather than Grotius. In this way, they could emphasize international law's humanitarian dimension, perfectly compatible with empire. Pacifying the world for commerce also led them to involvement in the Permanent Court of Arbitration established at The Hague in 1899.[54]

The Commission's deliberations and final report featured the keywords of the language of transgression. The French representative and future prime minister, André Tardieu (1876–1945), commenced proceedings by asking rhetorically whether, "before the tribunal of the universal conscience," they could fail to prosecute "the authors of the attack to which the whole world has been a victim?"[55] The final report copiously referenced Hague law, especially the famous Martens Clause in the preamble of the 1899 Convention that invoked the "dictates of humanity." The Axis Powers, the report stated, had violated "international morality" and "piled outrage upon outrage":

---

[53] The unpublished deliberations of the commission can be found at the British National Archives, FO 608/245 and FO 608/246.

[54] James Brown Scott, *The Spanish Origin of International Law: Francisco De Vitoria and His Law of Nations* (Oxford: Clarendon Press, 1934); Peter Fitzpatrick, "Latin Roots: Imperialism and the Making of Modern Law," in Fitzpatrick, *Law as Resistance: Modernism, Imperialism, Legalism* (Aldershot: Ashgate, 2008), 275–92; Martti Koskenniemi, "Colonization of the 'Indies': The Origin of International Law?" in *La idea de América en el Pensamiento Ius Internacionalista del Siglo XXI*, ed. Yolanda Gamarra (Zaragoza: Institución Fernando el Católico, 2010), 44; Benjamin Allen Coates, *Legalist Empire: International Law and American Foreign Relations in the Early Twentieth Century* (Oxford: Oxford University Press, 2016).

[55] Minute of the First Meeting held February 3, 1919, British National Archives, FO 608/245, *Peace Conference (British Delegation) 1919*, 144.

> Violations of the rights of combatants, of the rights of civilians, and of the rights of both, are multiplied in this list of the most cruel practices which primitive barbarism, aided by all the resources of modern science, could devise for the execution of a system of terrorism carefully planned and carried out to the end. Not even prisoners, or wounded, or women or children have been respected by belligerents who deliberately sought to strike terror into every heart for the purpose of repressing all resistance.[56]

This list to which the Commission referred was compiled from memoranda submitted by the Belgian and Greek delegations, the latter also including one on behalf of the stateless Armenians. The resemblance to Lord Palmerston's list from 1834, quoted in Chapter 1, is readily apparent.

(1) Murders and massacres; systematic terrorism.
(2) Putting hostages to death.
(3) Torture of civilians.
(4) Deliberate starvation of civilians.
(5) Rape.
(6) Abduction of girls and women for the purpose of enforced prostitution.
(7) Deportation of civilians.
(8) Internment of civilians under inhuman conditions.
(9) Forced labor of civilians in connection with the military operations of the enemy.
(10) Usurpation of sovereignty during military occupation.
(11) Compulsory enlistment of soldiers among the inhabitants of occupied territory.
(12) Attempts to denationalize the inhabitants of occupied territory.
(13) Pillage.
(14) Confiscation of property.
(15) Exaction of illegitimate or of exorbitant contributions and requisitions.
(16) Debasement of the currency, and issue of spurious currency.
(17) Imposition of collective penalties.
(18) Wanton devastation and destruction of property.
(19) Deliberate bombardment of undefended places.
(20) Wanton destruction of religious, charitable, educational, and historic buildings and monuments.
(21) Destruction of merchant ships and passenger vessels without warning and without provision for the safety of passengers or crew.
(22) Destruction of fishing boats and of relief ships.

---

[56] "Report of the Commission on Responsibility of the Authors of the War and Enforcement of Penalties," in *Violation of the Laws and Customs of War, Reports of Majority and Dissenting Reports of American and Japanese Members of the Commission of Responsibilities*, Conference of Paris, 1919 (Oxford: Clarendon, 1919), 1, 17.

(23) Deliberate bombardment of hospitals.

(24) Attack on and destruction of hospital ships.

(25) Breach of other rules relating to the Red Cross.

(26) Use of deleterious and asphyxiating gases.

(27) Use of explosive or expanding bullets, and other inhuman appliances.

(28) Directions to give no quarter.

(29) Ill-treatment of wounded and prisoners of war.

(30) Employment of prisoners of war on unauthorized works.

(31) Misuse of flags of truce.

(32) Poisoning of wells.[57]

As the first annex to the report made clear, this list included atrocities against the Central Powers' own citizens, for example massacres of Ottoman Armenians, meaning they were not strictly speaking war crimes according to the Hague Conventions. This expansive approach was advocated by Politis during the commission deliberations; he argued that "criminal acts ... should not be considered from the technical point of view, that is to say as limited to acts characterized as crimes or punished as such by penal law." It was important to include "the massacres organised by Turkish authorities," namely "prosecutions of an international character in respect of acts which violated what might be called the law of humanity or the general moral law."[58] This was, of course, the crime that the Entente Powers denounced as "crimes against humanity and civilization" in 1915. As we will see in Chapter 4, the report's introduction of "terror" and "terrorism" as synonyms for atrocities would be used to describe the Nazis a generation later. Key elements of the list also made their way into the charter of the Nuremberg Trial in 1945 where "crimes against humanity" were defined as "murder, extermination, enslavement, deportation, and other inhumane acts committed against any civilian population, before or during the war, or persecutions on political, racial or religious grounds."[59]

The Commission concluded that the Central Powers waged war "by barbarous or illegitimate methods in violation of the established laws and customs of war and the elementary laws of humanity."[60] Following its wartime propaganda about the rights of small nations, the British then pushed for an international tribunal to place the German Kaiser on trial. One of its

---

[57] Ibid., 17–18.

[58] Minute of the Second Meeting held on February 7, 1919, British National Archives, FO 608/245, Peace Conference (British Delegation) 1919, 152.

[59] *Agreement for the Prosecution and Punishment of the Major War Criminals of the European Axis, and Charter of the International Military Tribunal.* London, August 8, 1945. Charter – II: Jurisdiction and general principles – Article 6(c), https://ihl-databases .icrc.org/ihl/WebART/350-530014?OpenDocument.

[60] "Commission on the Responsibility," 64.

representatives on the Commission, British Solicitor General Sir Ernest Pollock (1861–1936), endorsed "Politis' remarkable speech" and declared that the peace conference represented "the whole of civilisation" and had "the necessary authority and weight to bring up to date the idea of right from the international point of view," meaning prosecuting those "responsible for gross violations of the principle of humanity."[61] Despite American and Japanese objections, the Commission also recommended that a "High Tribunal" prosecute those "guilty of offences against the laws and customs of war and the laws of humanity," which would include Armenians who, as Ottoman citizens, were not covered by the Hague regime.[62]

Ottoman attempts to reenter the society of civilized states by pointing to their own trials of war criminals were summarily rebuffed. The Turkish conduct of war, the Entente put it in 1919, was "accompanied by massacres whose calculated atrocity equals or exceeds anything in recorded history," echoing familiar statements heard during the previous century.[63] The Treaty of Sèvres of 1920, signed by the defeated Ottoman Empire with the three (France, Great Britain, Italy) Entente Powers, referred to the wartime government as a "terrorist regime," and to its massacres and deportations (Articles 142, 144, and 230). Dissatisfied with the Turks' prosecution of wartime perpetrators, the treaty stipulated that Turkey should hand them over for trial in keeping with the Entente's 1915 note (Part VII).

While the Commission's conception of transgression was broad and sensitive to the political nature of Turkish crimes – note the reference to repressing resistance – only violations "of the laws and customs of war" was included in the Treaty of Sèvres (Article 226). The Americans objected that to invoke the "laws and principles of humanity" entered uncharted territory and reeked of retrospective justice: the phrase "crimes against the laws of humanity" thus did not make its way into either the Sèvres or Versailles treaties.[64] In other words, the Americans restricted war crimes to those stipulated in the Hague Conventions and omitted the supplementary potential contained in the Martens Clause, with its vague but promising reference to "the usages established between civilized nations, from the laws of humanity and the requirements of the public conscience." In the end, too, the effort to establish an

---

[61] Commission on the Responsibility for the War, Minute No. 7. Meeting held at the Ministry of the Interior, March 17, 1919, British National Archives, FO 608/245, Peace Conference (British Delegation) 1919, 219.

[62] "Commission on the Responsibility," 25.

[63] British Foreign Office, *Documents on British Foreign Policy, 1919–1939*, 1st series, vol. 4, ed. W. L. Woodward and Rohan Butler (London: HMSO, 1952), 645.

[64] "Commission on the Responsibility," 64; *Treaty of Peace with Turkey*, Signed at Sèvres, August 20, 1920 (London: HMSO, 1920), http://treaties.fco.gov.uk/docs/pdf/1920/ts0011 .pdf; Garibian, "From the 1915 Allied Joint Declaration to the 1920 Treaty of Sèvres," 87–102.

independent tribunal to prosecute German war criminals was abandoned after the Netherlands refused to allow the extradition of the Kaiser, who had fled there after the war. The trials of middle- and lower-ranked personnel were left to the Germans, with predictable results.[65] The American and British foreign policy establishments continued this legal separation of the language of transgression in the early 1940s when they resisted attempts by small nations and the World Jewish Congress to prosecute Nazi practices before World War II.

Regarding the Turks' claim that they had ruled harmoniously over a heterogeneous polity until the state had been captured by a ruthless clique – that is, the Committee of Union and Progress – the Entente disputed their "capacity to rule over alien races." Its note stated: "The experiment has been tried too long and too often for there to be the least doubt as to its result."[66] Turkish elites had failed to meet the standard of civilization. Accordingly, their defeat meant that the Entente Powers had the "heavy duty of determining the destiny of the various populations in her heterogeneous Empire."[67] The note concluded with the calculated insult that "To thinking Moslems throughout the world, the modern history of the Government enthroned at Constantinople can be no source of pleasure or pride."[68] Accordingly, Part III of the treaty stipulated the partitioning of the empire with Arab provinces as League of Nations mandates, the Armenian provinces becoming "a free and independent State," and Kurds receiving "local autonomy."[69] Writing at the time, André Mandelstam also disqualified Turkey from ruling over other nations: the empire should be dismantled for the sake of stability and good governance. "Turkey having violated the Rights of Man and of the Nation regarding the non-Turkish peoples under its domination, the international community has to declare that it has no right anymore to the tutelage over these people."[70]

If the language of transgression could be used to disqualify Turkey from running an empire, those claiming to be victims could try to found one at Turkey's expense. Greek Prime Minister Eleftherios Venizelos (1864–1936) made a claim for Greek expansion into western Turkey (Asia Minor), where "Hellenism" could be found, on the basis of wartime civilian suffering. In a

---

[65] William A. Schabas, *The Trial of the Kaiser* (Oxford: Oxford University Press, 2018); Gary J. Bass, *Stay the Hand of Vengeance: The Politics of War Crimes Tribunals* (Princeton: Princeton University Press, 2000); James F. Willis, *Prologue to Nuremberg: The Politics and Diplomacy of Punishing War Criminals of the First World War* (Westport, CT: Greenwood, 1982).

[66] *Documents on British Foreign Policy, 1919–1939*, 646.   [67] Ibid.   [68] Ibid., 647.

[69] *Treaty of Peace with Turkey*, Articles 88 and 62.

[70] Daniel Marc Segesser, "Dissolve or Punish? The International Debate amongst Jurists and Publicists on the Consequences of the Armenian Genocide for the Ottoman Empire, 1915–23," *Journal of Genocide Research* 10, no. 1 (2008): 107.

letter to his British counterpart, Lloyd George, in November 1918, he made the link between military service and national losses as the currency of sympathy and recompense.

> It would be neither just nor politic that the Powers should concern themselves with the Arabs, the Syrians and the Armenians, and neglect the future of the Greeks in the Ottoman Empire.
>
> The Armenians deserve the sympathy of the whole civilized world, and we could not contemplate any settlement of the Eastern Question which does not ensure their future. But the Greeks are also worthy of the same sympathy.
>
> They are as numerous as the Armenians, and have been the victims of the same kind of maltreatment, while an enormous number of them have been exterminated. Further, tens of thousands of Greek volunteers took part in the war in Macedonia, and formed a very important part of the Army of National Defence which I organised as head of the Salonica Government.
>
> The settlement of the future of the Greek portion of the Western part of Asia Minor by its annexation to Greece is the sole method by which Greece would be able appreciably to extend her territories, at this moment when Serbia and Roumania are respectively completing their national unity.[71]

Lloyd George was sympathetic to Venizelos's case for Greater Greece (the *Megali* [great] idea) and gave the green light for the Greek occupation of Smyrna in May 1919. Not anticipated was the violent behavior of Greek forces, which produced a flood of complaints and pressure for yet another inter-allied commission of inquiry. This one, which met between August and October, painted such a damning picture of the Greek excesses that Lloyd George had to bury it.[72] Needless to say, the issue was hardly buried for Turkish nationalists, for whom Greek expansionism and atrocities were of a piece with the Entente partition plans to establish independent Armenian and Kurdish entitites in the core Turkish province of Anatolia. These plans were a rallying cry for nationalist resistance against both the Entente Powers and the Ottoman government that signed the Treaty of Sèvres.[73]

---

[71] Venizelos Memorandum, November 2, 1918, David Lloyd George Papers, F/147/8/11, UK Parliamentary Archives.

[72] Peter M. Buzanski, "Interallied Investigation of the Greek Invasion of Smyrna, 1919," *Historian*, 25, no. 3 (1963): 325–43; Erik Goldstein, "Great Britain and Greater Greece," *Historical Journal* 32, no. 2 (1989): 339–56.

[73] Willis, *Prologue to Nuremberg*, 155; Taner Akçam, "Another History on Sèvres and Lausanne," in *Der Völkermord an den Armeniern und die Shoah/The Armenian Genocide and the Shoah*, ed. Hans-Lukas Kieser and Dominik J. Schaller (Zurich: Chronos, 2002), 281–99.

Turkish opposition to Sèvres was hardly surprising for other reasons. Its Article 261 stipulated the reintroduction of the capitulatory regime that impinged on Turkish sovereignty, while Part IV was devoted to "The Protection of Minorities," taking up where the great powers had left off in 1913.[74] The impression of inimical civilizational hierarchies was difficult for Turks to swallow, especially the atrocity rhetoric in view of ruthless European expansion into Muslim territories during the nineteenth century, whether in the French conquest of Algeria in 1830, the Russian penetration of the Caucasus with the consequent refugee flows into the Ottoman Empire, and the genocidal Dutch conquest of Aceh in the 1870s, which led the Achenese to request humanitarian intervention by the Ottomans.[75] For decades, the sultan had responded to European protests about the treatment of Ottoman Christians by pointing out that they had a right to suppress rebellions like the British did in its territories, say in India in 1857.[76] Muslim intellectuals could note that Christian subjects in the Ottoman Empire enjoyed more rights than the Muslim subjects in British India. The fact that the Ottoman Empire had lasted for centuries and hosted the caliphate made it a source of prestige rather than shame for the newly imagined Muslim world.[77] Indeed, Muslims like the Indian anti-imperial activist, Shaikh Mushir Hosain Kidwai (1878–1937), insisted that "the record of the Turks is clean from the stain of such butcheries as have been committed in the Congo, or in British Colonies over indentured labourers, or in German Africa to enrich the European capitalists and profiteers."[78] The partition of the Ottoman Empire, he insisted, was hypocritical in view of Britain's refusal to grant independence to Muslims

---

[74] Cf. Philip Marshall Brown, "From Sèvres to Lausanne," *American Journal of International Law* 18, no. 1 (1924): 113–16; Brown, "Elements of a Just and Durable Peace," *Annals of the American Academy of Political and Social Science* 17 (1917): 76–83.

[75] William Gallois, *A History of Violence in the Early Algerian Colony* (Basingstoke: Palgrave Macmillan, 2013); Robert Geraci, "Inner Colonialism and the Question of Genocide in Imperial Russia and the Soviet Union," in Moses, *Empire, Colony, Genocide*, 343–71; Emmanuel Kreike, "Genocide in the Kampongs? Dutch Nineteenth Century Colonial Warfare in Aceh, Sumatra," in *Colonial Counterinsurgency and Mass Violence: The Dutch Empire in Indonesia*, ed. Bart Luttikhuis and A. Dirk Moses (Abingdon: Routledge, 2014), 45–63.

[76] Davide Rodogno, *Against Massacre: Humanitarian Interventions in the Ottoman Empire, 1815–1914* (Princeton: Princeton University Press, 2011), 193; Cemil Aydin, "Globalizing the Intellectual History of the Idea of the 'Muslim World,'" in *Global Intellectual History*, ed. Samuel Moyn and Andrew Sartori (New York: Columbia University Press, 2013), 166, 175.

[77] Aydin, "Globalizing the Intellectual History of the Idea of the 'Muslim World,'" 173.

[78] Lerna Ekmekcioglu, "Republic of Paradox: The League of Nations Minority Regime and the New Turkey's Step-Citizens," *International Journal Middle East Studies* 46 (2014): 668. On the financial support that Indian Muslims lent the Kemalists, see Azmi Özcan, *Pan-Islamism: Indian Muslims, the Ottomans and Britain, 1877–1924* (Leiden: Brill, 1997).

in India, and its denial of Indian self-government while the Ottoman Empire included all subject peoples in its governance structures.[79] As usual, such arguments were not heard in the halls of the Versailles palace.

The League of Nations and the Language of Transgression

We know that Western advocacy for Ottoman Christians was tinged with Orientalist paternalism. This posture continued in the Entente's desire to have the US govern Armenia as a League of Nations mandate.[80] The 12th US President, Woodrow Wilson's Fourteen Points – his statement of principles for the postwar peace – stated, *inter alia*, that while "The Turkish portion of the present Ottoman Empire should be assured a secure sovereignty ... other nationalities which are now under Turkish rule should be assured an undoubted security of life and an absolutely unmolested opportunity of autonomous development."[81] The Armenian cause was an element of Wilson's wartime vision expressed in his ideal of self-determination and famous speech, "Making the World Safe for Democracy," that explained the American decision to join the Allies in 1917. He reiterated the language of transgression's entailment to free trade and its negation, piracy, by declaring Germany's "submarine warfare against commerce is a warfare against mankind. It is a war against all nations." He continued that the German violation of international law, especially "upon the seas ... the free highways of the world," paraphrasing Grotius's attacks on the Portuguese arrogation to restrict free trade, is "a challenge to all mankind." The decision for war, concluded Wilson, "was accomplished ... with a clear view ... of what the heart and

---

[79] Ekmekcioglu, "Republic of Paradox"; Cemil Aydin, *The Politics of Anti-Westernism in Asia: Visions of World Order in Pan-Islamic and Pan-Asian Thought* (New York: Columbia University Press, 2007), 133–4.

[80] Jay Winter, ed., *America and the Armenian Genocide of 1915* (New York and Cambridge: Cambridge University Press, 2003).

[81] President Woodrow Wilson's Fourteen Points, January 8, 1918, http://avalon.law.yale .edu/20th_century/wilson14.asp. Despite Wilson's campaign for the mandate, the US Senate rejected it, and Turkish forces prevailed on the ground, vitiating Sèvres' recognition of an Armenian state in eastern Turkey. By contrast, the King-Crane Commission supported a US mandate over Armenia while questioning a British one over Palestine. "Report of the American Section of the International Commission on Mandates in Turkey," in *Papers Relating to the Foreign Relations of the United States: The Paris Peace Conference 1919*, vol. 12 (Washington: United States Government Printing Office, 1947), 751; Harry N. Howard, *The King-Crane Commission: An American Inquiry in the Middle East* (Beirut: Khayats, 1963); and Leonard V. Smith, "Wilsonian Sovereignty in the Middle East: The King-Crane Commission Report of 1919," in *The State of Sovereignty: Territories, Laws, Populations*, ed. Douglas Howland and Luise White (Bloomington: Indiana University Press, 2009), 56. Thanks to Umut Üszu for references and communications regarding the commission.

conscience of mankind demanded." He, too, now joined the Entente rhetoric about "the rights and liberties of small nations" and proclaimed a "universal dominion of right by such a concert of free peoples as shall bring peace and safety to all nations and make the world itself at last free."[82] This was a departure from the US aversion to involvement in European affairs. Until then, he had said that joining the war would be a "crime against civilization" and that it was the American flag, not a European one, which flew for "humanity."[83]

International Conscience and the Public Mind

Here was the moment when the US began to replace the British as humanity's avatar, its public conscience. "America has a cause which is not confined to the American continent. It is the cause of humanity itself," declared Wilson in defending the US annexations of Hawaii, Puerto Rico, and the Philippines. They were "part of the domain of public conscience and of serviceable and enlightened statesmanship."[84] Through a process of syllogistic reasoning, Wilson regarded himself as speaking for the US and thereby for humanity and international conscience. Confiding to his diary in 1889, he wrote "Why may not the present age write, through me, its political autobiography?"[85] Leaders should shape public opinion to accord with international conscience that only they really divined, he thought.[86]

Wilson's liberal internationalism was a continuation of the US Open Door trade policy that insisted on open markets abroad, its version of the

---

[82] Woodrow Wilson, "Making the World Safe for Democracy: 'Address of the President of the United States Delivered at a Joint Session of the Two Houses of Congress, April 2, 1917,'" *American Journal of International Law Supplement: Official Documents* 11 (1917): 143–51; Lloyd E. Ambrosius, *Woodrow Wilson and American Internationalism* (New York: Cambridge University Press, 2017); Thomas Knock, *To End All Wars: Woodrow Wilson and the Quest for a New World Order* (Princeton: Princeton University Press, 2019).

[83] Adam Tooze, *The Deluge: The Great War, America and the Remaking of the Global Order, 1916–1931* (New York: Penguin, 2015); Ambrosius, *Woodrow Wilson and American Internationalism*, 245.

[84] Mary E. Stuckey, "'The Domain of Public Conscience': Woodrow Wilson and the Establishment of a Transcendent Political Order," *Rhetoric and Public Affairs* 6, no. 1 (2003): 15–16.

[85] Stephen Wertheim, "Reading the International Mind: International Public Opinion in Early Twentieth Century Anglo-American Thought," in *The Decisionist Imagination: Sovereignty, Social Science, and Democracy in the Twentieth Century*, ed. Nicholas Guilhot and Daniel Bessner (New York: Berghahn Books, 2018), 44.

[86] Stephen Wertheim "The Wilsonian Chimera: Why Debating Wilson's Vision Hasn't Saved American Foreign Relations," *White House Studies* 10, no. 4 (2011): 343–59.

imperialism of free trade.[87] The American so-called isolationism during the interwar years, when it turned away from the League of Nations he championed, did not mean forsaking global investment and trade; on the contrary, American business invested far and wide, in oil in Mesopotamia to Latin America and Europe. The turn to formal empire in 1898 was an aberration based on the Republican Party's commitment to protectionism in the late-nineteenth century.[88] Whether formal empire or the informal empire of economic domination, however, US elites were beginning to think in global terms. It was the imperial president, Theodore Roosevelt (1858–1919), who had declared in his State of the Union Address in 1904 that the US could exercise "international police power" to maintain order, at least in the Americas, in keeping with the Monroe Doctrine.[89]

No expression of American global leadership – or the craving for it – was more ardently stated than in American philosophy professor John M. Mecklin's article on "international conscience," published in 1919. It articulated the tethering of the language of transgression to power as a world-historical mission in all its partiality. By international conscience, he meant "simply a body of sentiments and ideas shared by all peoples that will assure a peaceful solution of international differences," embodied particularly in law. Wilson was his hero, whom he quoted liberally on public opinion and the rule of law, "which draws its sanctions from an enlightened conscience"; these Mecklin contrasted with the arbitrary "power of armaments" incarnated by Prussia and the German will to power.[90] The former was the legacy of Rome, the *Pax Romana*, which, echoing Cicero, preceded "*jus gentium*, or the idea of a law of the nations, binding upon all alike because it reflected the organised opinion of mankind, the tested political experience of the *orbis terrarium*."[91] Only nations "sympathetic towards the international attitude," like Great Britain and the US, which "have found scope for expansion and free untrammelled self-expression," by which he implied maritime empires without the need for a large standing army – he omitted to mention the large

---

[87] William Appleman Williams, *The Tragedy of American Diplomacy* (Cleveland: World Publishing, 1959).

[88] Marc-William Palen, *The "Conspiracy" of Free Trade: The Anglo-American Struggle over Empire and Economic Globalisation, 1846–1896* (Cambridge: Cambridge University Press, 2016); Stephen Wertheim, "Reluctant Liberator: Theodore Roosevelt's Philosophy of Self-Determination and Preparation for Philippine Independence," *Presidential Studies Quarterly* 39, no. 3 (2009): 494–518.

[89] Frank Ninkovich, "Theodore Roosevelt: Civilization as Ideology," *Diplomatic History* 10, no. 3 (1986): 221–45.

[90] John M. Mecklin, "International Conscience," *International Journal of Ethics* 29, no. 3 (1919): 284–93.

[91] Ibid., 286.

British Army stationed in India – are properly responsive to "the demands of international conscience."[92]

Repeating H. A. L. Fisher's arguments about "England's championship of the balance of power, the rights of the smaller nations, the freedom of the seas, and democracy," Mecklin urged Americans to follow its example of global empire, which he figured as "the solution of the problem of international peace." Unlike "the German gospel of force," the *Pax Britannica* exhibited an exemplary "moral and spiritual solidarity," and its "economy ... points the way to a possible *pax orbis terrarum.*"[93] Given the manifest racial inequalities of the empire, he was likely referring to the white settler colonies as connected communities of moral and spiritual solidarity, while gesturing to non-Europeans whom Britons governed in Africa and Asia in terms of the generous British recognition of difference: "of incorporating alien races, without trying to disintegrate them, or to rob them of their individuality."[94] He acknowledged the empire's dark sides – the Opium and Boer wars – but identified with their domestic critics who exemplified England's idealism that the Germans lacked: "the conscience of the English people has been made sensitive to the rights of weaker nations, though even here idealism and realism are mingled."[95] Like many before him, Mecklin posited human ethical development and free trade guaranteed by a global hegemon: "England won for herself moral emancipation by policing the world and protecting our [US] trade." He concluded by calling on the US to take up the British burden to shoulder the world's problems:

> America, the young Hercules among the nations, stands at the parting of the ways. Has she the moral courage to work out her national salvation through the stern discipline of the great international role opened up to her by this war? Or will she return to the isolation and the selfish economic nationalism of other days where the sheer glut of her own prosperity will in time inevitably undermine her character?[96]

That is precisely what Wilson wanted via a new international organization, the League of Nations, to supersede the old empires and great power diplomacy as

---

[92] Ibid., 287.   [93] Ibid., 289.

[94] Ibid., 291. Duncan Bell, *Reordering the World: Essays on Liberalism and Empire* (Princeton: Princeton University Press, 2016); Bell, *The Idea of Greater Britain: Empire and the Future of World Order, 1860–1900* (Princeton: Princeton University Press, 2007); Jeanne Morefield, "'An Education to Greece': The Round Table, Imperial Theory and the Uses of History," *History of Political Thought* 28, no. 2 (2007): 328–61; Marilyn Lake and Henry Reynolds, *Drawing the Global Colour Line: White Men's Countries and the International Challenge of Racial Equality* (New York: Cambridge University Press, 2008).

[95] Mecklin, "International Conscience," 290–1.   [96] Ibid., 293.

"the moral force of the public opinion of the world."[97] Among its duties was the administration of mandates over former Ottoman and German colonies, which he insisted could not be annexed by the war's victors. The humanitarian ideal of trusteeship was his loadstar. "We must administer them for the people who live in them and with the same sense of responsibility to them as toward our own people in our domestic affairs," he declared. It would be a "conscience for the world."[98]

To a striking extent, this language won through in international law despite the premature ending of Wilson's presidency due to a stroke and the US disengagement with the League of Nations. The Statute of the Permanent Court of International Justice, established in 1920, listed "general principles of law recognized by civilized nations" as one of its four sources of law.[99] The preamble to the 1925 Geneva Protocol on chemical and biological weapons, organized by the League, states that they have "been justly condemned by the general opinion of the civilized world" and that their prohibition in international law is "binding alike the conscience and the practice of nations."[100] By then, the British understood that their imperial influence could be better maintained by working with rising American power through an international organization rather than by fighting a rear-guard action in favor of annexations like the French; the League's notion of trusteeship was compatible with, indeed a vehicle for, liberal empire, even if its institutional apparatus eventually took on an unexpectedly intrusive life of its own for Mandatory powers.[101] Accordingly, Article 22 of the League's covenant reiterated the language of humanitarian empire for a supposedly decolonizing world, replete with references to tutelage and civilization like the Berlin Act of 1885, but this time as a colonial reform project to create sovereign entities out of backward peoples.[102]

> To those colonies and territories ... inhabited by peoples not yet able to stand by themselves under the strenuous conditions of the modern world, there should be applied the principle that the well-being and development of such peoples form a sacred trust of civilization ...

---

[97] Wertheim, "Reading the International Mind," 37.

[98] Stuckey, "The Domain of Public Conscience," 15–16; Ambrosius, *Woodrow Wilson and American Internationalism*, 202.

[99] Statute of the Permanent Court of International Justice, December 16, 1920, Article 38 (c), www.refworld.org/docid/40421d5e4.html.

[100] 1925 Geneva Protocol for the Prohibition of the Use in War of Asphyxiating, Poisonous or Other Gases, and of Bacteriological Methods of Warfare, www.un.org/disarmament/wmd/bio/1925-geneva-protocol/; Michael Veuthey, "Public Conscience in International Humanitarian Action," *Refugee Survey Quarterly* 22, no 4 (2003): 197–224.

[101] Susan Pedersen, *The Guardians: The League of Nation and the Crisis of Empire* (Oxford: Oxford University Press, 2015).

[102] Antony Anghie, *Imperialism, Sovereignty and the Making of International Law* (Cambridge: Cambridge University Press, 2005), ch. 3.

> The best method of giving practical effect to this principle is that the tutelage of such peoples should be entrusted to advanced nations who by reason of their resources, their experience or their geographical position can best undertake this responsibility, and who are willing to accept it, and that this tutelage should be exercised by them as Mandatories on behalf of the League.

The familiar language of antislavery and commerce was repeated for those regarded as particularly backward, like the inhabitants of the C-Class mandates in Central Africa: the "Mandatory must be responsible for the administration of the territory under conditions which will guarantee ... the prohibition of abuses such as the slave trade, the arms traffic and the liquor traffic ... and will also secure equal opportunities for the trade and commerce of other Members of the League.[103] It was no accident that many members of the Permanent Mandates Commission (PMC) established to oversee the system were former colonial officials and members of the International Colonial Institute who spoke openly about "inferior races" and "degenerate Europeans" who might threaten "the best results of western civilization." The British one, Sir Frederick Lugard (1858–1945), traced the mandates system to the Berlin Conference of 1884–1885 international agreements on slavery and trade.[104]

His much-cited book, *The Dual Mandate in British Tropical Africa*, published in 1922, became the commission's "bible."[105] It justified mandates as a mutually beneficial arrangement of development and governance via indigenous authorities, which he famously called "indirect rule." Humanitarian empire was still empire, though, and Lugard's purpose was to defend it in the face of British Labour Party criticisms of European imperialism as avarice driven by financial capitalism. He had to admit that philanthropy alone did not suffice to bring Europeans to Africa. Empire afforded opportunities of "independent initiative" for "every class of the youth of England," it provided the raw materials for improved British living standards, and it secured access to these materials through political control of territory. Lugard thereby implicitly argued for the continuation of wartime protectionist measures that ensured African products were headed to Britain rather than sold on the open

---

[103] The Covenant of the League of Nations, 1920, Yale Law School, Avalon Project: Documents in Law, History and Diplomacy, http://avalon.law.yale.edu/20th_century/leagcov.asp.

[104] Pedersen, *The Guardians*, 107–108. On France: Ben T. White, "Rhetorical Hierarchies in France and Syria during the Mandate," *Chronos: Revue d'Histoire de l'Université de Balamand* (2008): 105–23.

[105] Pedersen, *The Guardians*, 110; Frederick D. Lugard, *The Dual Mandate in British Tropical Africa* (Edinburgh and London: William Blackwood and Sons, 1922).

market, to the detriment of African producers.[106] These entirely legitimate undertakings, averred Lugard, could be not stigmatized as "common greed," as the Labour Party alleged: these were not base motives but the material necessities of a democratic people.[107]

Labour's criticisms, continued Lugard, also ignored the fact that Britain was in Africa in part to stamp out slavery and enable missionary work – hardly exploitative motivations. The enduring protective and uplift rhetoric also justified empire's civilizing mission.

> In all these cases a higher civilisation was brought into contact with barbarism, with the inevitable result, as history teaches, that boundaries were enlarged in the effort to protect the weak from the tyranny of the strong, to extend the rule of justice and liberty, to protect traders, settlers, and missions, and to check anarchy and bloodshed on our frontiers, even though territorial expansion was not desired. Nor must we ignore the very real desire of the people of this country to assist in the suppression of slavery and barbarous practices.[108]

What is more, Lugard continued in a Lockean vein, Europeans had a right to African resources not only because they needed them more but because they could develop them better: "These [natural] products lay wasted and ungarnered in Africa because the natives did not know their use and value ... Who can deny the right of the hungry people of Europe to utilise the wasted bounties of nature, or that the task of developing these resources was, as Mr Chamberlain expressed it, a 'trust for civilisation' and for the benefit of mankind?" This mutually advantageous arrangement was the dual mandate: "Europe benefited by the wonderful increase in the amenities of life for the mass of her people which followed the opening up of Africa at the end of the nineteenth century. Africa benefited by the influx of manufactured goods, a rudimentary welfare state, and the substitution of law and order for the methods of barbarism."[109] In fulfilling this mandate, the colonial administrator was following in Roman footsteps, civilizing Africa as Rome civilized Britain, "endeavouring to teach the native races to conduct their own affairs with justice and humanity, and to educate them alike in letters and in industry."[110] This renovation of the traditional civilizing mission for a democratic

---

[106] David Killingray, "The Empire Resources Development Committee and West Africa 1916–20," *Journal of Imperial and Commonwealth History* 10, no. 2 (1982): 194–210.

[107] Lugard, *The Dual Mandate in British Tropical Africa*, 613.   [108] Ibid., 612–13.

[109] Ibid., 615.

[110] Ibid., 616–17. More generally on this sort of thinking at the time, see Jeanne Morefield, *Covenants without Swords: Idealist Liberalism and the Spirit of Empire* (Princeton: Princeton University Press, 2004), Mark Mazower, *No Enchanted Palace: The End of Empire and the Ideological Origins of the League of Nations* (Princeton: Princeton

age was hard to distinguish from French and Italian imperial rhetoric from before World War I.[111] Much the same language pervaded the renewed Belgian justification of enlightened colonial rule after King Leopold handed over his Congo to the state in 1908.[112] As before, humanitarian rhetoric justified imperial rule.

The Congo campaigner, E. D. Morel, had grown skeptical about this rhetoric after studying the results in Africa.[113] He was so dismayed by the great powers' cynical disregard of the Berlin Treaty as a meaningless "scrap of paper" that he thought the German dismissal of the Entente treaty guarantee of Belgian neutrality as refreshingly, if brutally, honest. To be sure, he was no friend of Germany, whose "diplomacy has been as immoral, as short-sighted, as treacherous as any other," but they were not the only culprit. Thus inured to the jingoism of World War I, he declared it "a catastrophe which has over-whelmed civilisation," as peace activists had long argued.[114] Unlike Roger Casement, he limited himself to writing rather than to participation in an anti-British insurrection, and thus survived the war to continue his advocacy. In 1920, he published *The Black Man's Burden*, a trenchant settling of accounts with what he called the "capitalistic exploitation" of Africans by European chartered corporations and by states' military conscription. He doubted that the League's mandates system could guarantee the "equitable treatment" of Africans as an "international concern," because they were tantamount to annexations. What is more, *pace* Lugard, Europeans were driven primarily by economic motives, favoring the interests of the "alien capitalist," which resulted in "the exploitation and impoverishment of the

University Press, 2009), and Karuna Mantena, *Alibis of Empire Henry Maine and the Ends of Liberal Imperialism* (Princeton: Princeton University Press, 2010).

[111] Alice L. Conklin, "Colonialism and Human Rights, A Contradiction in Terms? The Case of French West Africa, 1895–1914," *American Historical Review* 103, no 2 (1998): 419–42; Vanda Wilcox, "The Italian Soldiers' Experience in Libya, 1911– 1912," in *The Wars before the Great War: Conflict and International Politics before the Outbreak of the First World War*, ed. Dominik Geppert, William Mulligan, and Andreas Rose (New York: Cambridge University Press, 2015), 41–57.

[112] Matthew G. Stanard, *Selling the Congo: A History of European Pro-Empire Propaganda and the Making of Belgian Imperialism* (Lincoln: University of Nebraska Press, 2012).

[113] On this rhetoric, see David Spurr, *The Rhetoric of Empire: Colonial Discourse in Journalism, Travel Writing, and Imperial Administration* (Durham, NC: Duke University Press, 1993).

[114] E. D. Morel, *Truth and the War* (London: National Labour Club Press, 1916), xvi, xiii; William Mulligan, *The Great War for Peace* (New Haven, CT: Yale University Press, 2014).

native population."[115] Apart from making Africa a neutral continent so European conflicts could not be played out there, he suggested a charter of rights for tropical Africa. The balance between European and African needs could be struck "provided that native rights in land are preserved, and provided the natives are given the requisite facilities for cultivating and exploiting the raw material which it is Europe's economic purpose to secure." This was the proposition about which Morel hoped "to convince the public mind."[116]

Although he imagined empire as the cause of harm rather than its remediation, Morel continued to promote abolitionism's protective and free labor ideology. Nor was this commitment inconsistent with racism. In the same year, 1920, he wrote a bitter condemnation of the French policy of using African troops to occupy the Rhineland when Germany failed to meet its reparations obligations. Relying on information from German women's organizations, his *The Horror on the Rhine* and newspaper articles reproduced German racist propaganda by highlighting alleged rapes of local women by sexually uncontrollable occupation soldiers.[117] Africans should stay in Africa to produce for a world market, if on their own terms, in true "open door" conditions, as the third of Wilson's Fourteen Points had stipulated. To guarantee this outcome, the League should establish a permanent African Commission to oversee the mandates "and to create an international conscience with regard to tropical Africa which does not now exist."[118] International oversight would realign racial economic relations, converting exploitation to active, if not equal, participation. "For the first time in the history of contact between the white races and the black," Morel concluded his book hopefully, "the black man's burden would be lifted from the shoulders which for five hundred years have bent beneath its weight."[119] Like Las Casas 500 years before him, a legitimate order was a global economy with the protection of native rights. If the empires could not guarantee those rights, international conscience, the public mind, and an international organization

---

[115] E. D. Morel, *The Black Man's Burden* (Manchester: National Labour Press, 1920), 216, 228, 234.

[116] Ibid., 232.

[117] E. D. Morel, "Black Scourge in Europe, Sexual Horror Let Loose by France on Rhine, Disappearance of Young German Girls," *Daily Herald*, April 9, 1920; Morel, *The Horror on the Rhine* (London: Union of Democratic Control, 1920); Robert C. Reinders, "Racialism on the Left: E. D. Morel and the 'Black Horror on the Rhine,'" *International Review of Social History* 13, no. 1 (1968): 1–28; Peter Campbell, "'Black Horror on the Rhine': Idealism, Pacifism, and Racism in Feminism and the Left in the Aftermath of the First World War," *Histoire sociale / Social History* 47 (June 2014): 471–93.

[118] Ibid., 239–40.   [119] Ibid., 240.

would do so. But could they regulate one of the most pressing issues in the mandates: the question of forced labor?

Free and Unfree Labor

The language of transgression targeted slavery as much as massacre. Already during World War I, Britain, France, and Belgium wanted the Berlin and Brussels Acts to better regulate their African colonies. A new agreement in 1919 abolished slavery in "all its forms," though without defining it, also doing away with the Acts' supervisory empowerment. Into this breach stepped the new International Labor Organization (ILO), founded in 1919 under the League's auspices, and the Treaty of Versailles, which obliged signatories to apply ratified labor conventions to their dependent territories.[120] Consensus on slavery was easy to achieve in the 1926 Slavery Convention, which continued the nineteenth-century abolitionist spirit. But what of grey-zones of slave-like conditions on which most empires depended economically? The legendary consul-general of Egypt, Evelyn Baring (Lord Cromer, 1841–1917), had defended compulsory labor as a regrettable necessity in circumstances when the community would otherwise suffer without it. Indeed, although the late-nineteenth century conquests of Africa were justified by ending slavery, Europeans soon discovered they had to indulge their local allies' economic investment in slavery to ensure victory and then stability. If they eventually did away with large-scale slave-raiding and trade, they turned a blind eye to slave labor.[121] Ever since emancipation, European businesses had sought cheap labor legally distinguishable from slavery that could function as its disciplined equivalent. In plantation and mining enterprises, in particular, sourcing and affixing labor was a major challenge.[122]

After the war, British authorities now found it increasingly difficult to defend forced labor in view of the scandals, like in Putomayo, that exercised the antislavery lobby. Taking the lead against the practice was also a means of

---

[120] Suzanne Miers, *Slavery in the Twentieth Century: The Evolution of a Global Problem* (Walnut Creek, CA: Altamira Press, 2003), 61–62; Michael Callahan, *Mandates and Empire: The League of Nations and Africa, 1914–1931* (Brighton: Sussex Academic Press, 1999); Sandrine Kott and Joëlle Droux, eds., *Globalizing Social Rights: The International Labour Organization and Beyond* (Basingstoke: Palgrave Macmillan, 2013).

[121] Andreas Eckert, "Abolitionist Rhetorics, Colonial Conquest, and the Slow Death of Slavery in Germany's African Empire," in *Humanitarian Intervention and Changing Labor Relations*, ed. Marcel van Linden (Leiden: Brill, 2010), 351–68.

[122] Esmeir, *Juridical Humanity*, 94; Florian Wagner, *Colonial Internationalism: Expert Cooperation and the Reshaping of Colonialism* (Cambridge: Cambridge University Press, forthcoming); Richard A. Goodridge, "The Issue of Slavery in the Establishment of British Rule in Northern Cameroon to 1927," *African Economic History*, no. 22 (1994): 19–36.

squeezing Portuguese, Belgian, and French plantation economies in Africa, much as British abolitionism in the nineteenth century had been utilized to squeeze these same rivals. An ILO Committee of Experts formulated a Forced Labour Convention in 1930. Like humanitarians, missionaries, and scholars, these experts engaged in a political analysis: forced labor immiserated Africans and caused violence.[123] Predictably, France, Belgium, and Portugal abstained; even the convention's exceptions for public necessity and military service were too narrow for them. France did not ratify the convention until 1937, and forced labor lived on in its empire for another nine years. In practice, most colonies persisted with it because they reasoned that economic development and famine relief could not occur without compulsion. They even used "indirect rule" (or "association" as the French called the governing modality) to argue that forced labor recruitment was an indigenous practice that required protection under mandate norms. In Ghana's Northern Territories, for instance, the convention's loopholes regarding forced labor in the "direct interest of the community" for "minor communal services" became a normalized state of affairs. As Morel had feared, the League, in the form of the PMC, let the mandatories get away with such ruses.[124] The military services exception also enabled Britain to make extensive use of African labor and armed service during World War II, while the *deuxième portion*, introduced in 1926, meant the French could exploit African conscripts deemed unfit for the army for labor both in peace- and wartime.[125]

[123] J. P. Daughton, "Behind the Imperial Curtain: International Humanitarian Efforts and the Critique of French Colonialism in the Interwar Years," *French Historical Studies* 34, no. 3 (2011): 503–28; Luis Rodríguez-Piñero, *Indigenous Peoples, Postcolonialism, and International Law: The ILO Regime (1919–1989)* (Oxford: Oxford University Press, 2006), ch. 1; S. James Anaya, *Indigenous Peoples in International Law*, 2nd ed. (Oxford: Oxford University Press, 2004).

[124] Frederick Cooper, *Decolonization and African Society: The Labor Question in French and British Africa* (Cambridge: Cambridge University Press, 1996), 27–29; Pedersen, *The Guardians*, 257; Alice Wiemers,"'It Is All He Can Do to Cope with the Roads in His Own District: Labor, Community, and Development in Northern Ghana, 1919–1936," *International and Working Class History* 92 (2017): 89–113; Dennis D. Cordell and Joel W. Gregor, "Labour Reservoirs and Population: French Colonial Strategies in Koudougou, Upper Volta, 1914 to 1939," *Journal of African History* 23, no. 2 (1982), 205–24; Kwabena Opare Akurang-Parry, "Colonial Forced Labor Policies for Road-Building in Southern Ghana and International Anti-Forced Labor Pressures, 1900–1940," *African Economic History*, no. 28 (2000): 1–25.

[125] Kenneth P. Vickery, "The Second World War Revival of Forced Labor in the Rhodesias," *International Journal of African Historical Studies* 22, no. 3 (1989): 423–37; David Johnson, "Settler Farmers and Coerced African Labour in Southern Rhodesia, 1936–46," *Journal of African History* 33, no. 1 (1992): 111–28; Hamilton Sipho Simelane, "Labor Mobilization for the War Effort in Swaziland, 1940–1942," *International Journal of African Historical Studies* 26, no. 3 (1993): 541–74; Hals Brands, "Wartime Recruiting Practices, Martial Identity and Post–World War II

The antislavery lobbies were unhappy about such fudging, but their free market and free labor ideals did not necessarily entail worker freedom either. When feudal domains were privatized under British rule in Egypt, workers were no longer subject to state regulation, and their conditions deteriorated accordingly in conditions of hyper-exploitation.[126] While the ILO defended indigenous workers' rights, it continued to believe in colonial rule and, as we know, forced labor in some circumstances was condoned.[127] Similarly, Western scholars and travelers to the colonies who were troubled by local suffering – whether caused by the spread of disease due to new commerce, introduced Western vices like alcohol, the loss of land to white settlers and their enterprises, labor exploitation, or the suppression of uprisings – continued the Las Casasian approach of urging empire's reform rather than its abolition.[128] They never really questioned whether the extractive industries on which Europeans relied were ultimately compatible with Africans' welfare; the question was how to align them. "Basically the problem of the Europeans in Africa is to secure the economic development of the natural resources and trade possibilities without exploiting, exterminating, and degrading the natives," wrote a University of Chicago historian in 1929. Theoretically, both imperatives should be possible, he continued in a Lugardian manner, but practically "translating this policy into specific terms" was the difficulty.[129] Indeed, Europeans, whether a humanitarian or colonial official, could never decide "between *helping* the African become a more productive peasant and *forcing* him to be a worker."[130]

Depoliticizing the Language of Transgression: The Question of Violence and Refugees

Deferring such tension was also intrinsic to European rule before the war when colonial sex scandals rather than the violence of conquest excited metropolitan attention.[131] Famine in India and the system of camps the

---

Demobilization in Colonial Kenya," *Journal of African History* 46, no. 1 (2005): 103–25; Cooper: *Decolonization and African Society*, 38.

[126] Esmeir, *Juridical Humanity*, 221–3; Roger Owen, *Cotton and the Egyptian Economy, 1820–1914: A Study in Trade and Development* (Oxford: Clarendon Press, 1969).

[127] Daughton, "Behind the Imperial Curtain," 518.

[128] Raymond Leslie Buell, *The Native Problem in Africa*, 2 Vols. (New York: Macmillan, 1928); Nicola Cooper, "Colonial Humanism in the 1930s: The Case of Andrée Viollis," *French Cultural Studies* 17, no. 2 (2006): 189–205.

[129] Arthur P. Scott, Review of Raymond Leslie Buell, *The Native Problem in Africa*, 2 Vols. (New York: Macmillan, 1928), in *American Journal of Sociology* 35, no. 1 (1929): 128.

[130] Cooper, *Decolonization and African Society*, 34. Emphasis in the original.

[131] Frank Bösch, "Are We a Cruel Nation? Colonial Practices, Perceptions and Scandal," in *Wilhemine Germany and Edwardian Britain: Essays on Cultural Affinity*, ed. Dominik

British instituted across the empire in the name of hygiene and security did not merit much attention either.[132] Colonial violence was less difficult to ignore after 1918, however. The war stimulated independence aspirations among colonial subjects, hundreds of thousands of whom had served their imperial masters during the global conflict, and who understood Wilson's Fourteen Points as a call for universal self-determination when, in fact, he stood in the Gladstonian tradition of entreating self-government for qualified peoples.[133] Wilson and the mainly Western delegates at the Paris Peace Conference had no intention of dissolving their empires. On the contrary, most wanted to annex or control former German and Ottoman territories; mandates were the compromise. Frustration with enduring European rule led to almost a decade of unrest from North Africa to the Middle East, including the Egyptian Revolution and Amritsar Massacre in India in 1919, the Iraqi revolt against British occupation in 1920, the Rif War with Spain in Morocco between 1920 and 1927, and the Syrian revolt against French rule in 1925.[134]

What states did in their own empires was their business under international law. Adverse press coverage was an irritant but not a threat. Matters were different in their mandates because of PMC oversight and the expectation of mandates' eventual independence. Even so, the language of transgression's stability is the striking feature of the period. When, in September 1922, South African forces preemptively suppressed a feared Bondelswart/Nama uprising in their German Southwest African mandate with aerial bombing, which killed women and children, the League's "sacred trust" was tarnished and required polishing. In response to the international outcry and pressure from the antislavery lobby, the customary hierarchical protection measures were instituted: native practices would be preserved against the white settler's

---

Geppert and Robert Gerwarth (Oxford: Oxford University Press, 2008), 115–42; Rebekka Habermas, *Skandal in Togo: Ein Kapitel deutscher Kolonialherrschaft* (Frankfurt am Main: S. Fischer Verlag, 2016).

[132] Mike Davis, *Late Victorian Holocausts: El Niño Famines and the Making of the Third World* (London: Verso, 2000); Aidan Forth, *Barbed-Wire Imperialism: Britain's Empire of Camps, 1876–1903* (Berkeley: University of California Press, 2017).

[133] Erez Manela, *The Wilsonian Moment: Self-Determination and the International Origins of Anticolonial Nationalism* (Oxford: Oxford University Press, 2007); Trygve Throntveit, "The Fable of the Fourteen Points: Woodrow Wilson and National Self-Determination," *Diplomatic History* 35 (2011): 445–81.

[134] Giorgio Potì, "Imperial Violence, Anti-Colonial Nationalism and International Society: The Politics of Revolt Across Mediterranean Empires, 1919–1927" (PhD diss., European University Institute, 2016); Robert Gerwarth and Erez Manela, eds., *Empires at War, 1911–1923* (Oxford: Oxford University Press, 2014); Martin C. Thomas, Bob Moore, and L. J. Butler, eds., *Crises of Empire: Decolonization and Europe's Imperial States, 1918–1975* (London: Hodder Education, 2008); Nick Lloyd, "The Amritsar Massacre and the Minimum Force Debate," *Small Wars and Insurgencies* 21, no. 2 (2010): 382–403.

ultraexploitation that had provoked the Bondelswart unrest, and "racial" contact and "hybridization" would be limited to prevent detribalization and concomitant destabilization.[135]

Unlike the African mandates, Syria-Lebanon was an A-Class mandate assigned to France in the Treaty of Sèvres in 1920 and violently imposed on the Syrian population that year. Conflict broke out again five years later, during which the French engaged local minorities against the insurgents and ended up shelling central Damascus. While they predictably criminalized their opponents as bandits, European observers saw a war of national liberation by a civilized people.[136] French counterinsurgency was excessive. "European pres-tige among the more civilized races of the Near East cannot possibly be enhanced by such an imitation of the grotesque barbarity of primitive peoples," pronounced the London *Times* in a classic instance of Las Casas's inversion of values.[137] Besides rhetorical chastisement, the French suffered no consequences for their misrule. The PMC was not in the business of divesting powerful empires of their possessions, even ones overseen by an international organization.

Few were the voices that questioned the terms of the *Times*'s analysis. One of them was Arnold Toynbee, now radicalized by the Greek invasion of Turkey in 1919. Shocked by Greek reprisals, he compared them to Turkish treatment of Armenians four years earlier: this was a "war of extermination against unarmed civilians – like the C.U.P's extermination of the Armenians."[138] The venerable assumption of Western moral superiority was overturned. Ever the scholar, Toynbee ascribed violence in the Ottoman Empire in part to the "revolutionary process of Westernisation," that is, the destabilization of their "indigenous civilizations" due to "intrusive influences of the West" rather than "endemic" problems with Islam or Turks. Atrocities – which he usefully defined as attacks on civilians unconnected to military objectives – could occur in Europe as elsewhere.[139] He was presenting an analysis of political violence with universal application.

Where the political origins of violence were unmistakable in the postwar wave of colonial unrest and repression, the humanitarian reaction to the refugee crises caused by the war led ultimately to its depoliticization. Already during the war, humanitarian organizations from the neutral US (till 1917), above all the American Red Cross (ARC), mobilized to deliver food and

---

[135] Pedersen, *The Guardians*, 113–40.   [136] Ibid., 157.

[137] "The Damascus Troubles," *The Times*, October 27, 1927.

[138] Rebecca Gill, "'Now I Have Seen Evil, and I Cannot Be Silent About It': Arnold J. Toynbee and His Encounters with Atrocity, 1915–1923," in Cook, Gill, and Taithe, *Evil, Barbarism, and Empire*, 180.

[139] Arnold Toynbee, *The Western Question in Greece and Turkey: A Study in the Contact of Civilisations* (Boston: Houghton Mifflin, 1922), 260–7.

aid to German-occupied Belgium, one of those small nations that Wilson eventually swore to protect. American organizations dominated postwar relief as well due to their vastly superior resources and organizational acumen. In the main, they portrayed military conflicts as natural disasters, depoliticizing humanitarian aid in two ways: the political causes of war were ignored, thereby obviating the difficult question of responsibility on the one hand, while civilians were accordingly framed as innocent victims who incarnated the apolitical ideal of humanity on the other. In this way, they hoped their interventions in postwar societies were above politics, although in practice host states often regarded them suspiciously as threats to their sovereignty. Not for nothing did Wilson view the ARC as an extension of the American mission to redeem the world.[140]

The Armenian refugee crisis drove the depoliticization of the language of transgression after the failure of a political solution. The victorious powers initially treated Armenians not only as victims of war but as survivors of a concerted attempt to exterminate and denationalize them. Their rights were imagined collectively and articulated in political – that is, communal national – terms. The Paris Peace Conference and League of Nations – in the form of the Treaty of Sèvres – thus envisaged the return of refugees to Turkey, now safeguarded by minority rights, and an American mandate for a new Armenian state. But when the Turkish nationalist forces pushed out invading Greeks and overran Armenian territory by 1922, the League was forced to depoliticize Armenian (as well as other) refugees by treating them as stateless, and granting them League travel documents – the famous "Nansen passport," invented for (White) Russian refugees from the Russian Civil War – that enabled only legal residence in their country of refuge. The Armenian problem was supposed to be solved by assimilation into new societies, like Syria and Lebanon.[141]

All the while, those charities concerned with Armenians – Near East Relief, Save the Children, the Quakers – had been underlining this depoliticization process in part by design, in part due to outside pressure. Their turn to film to reach larger audiences to dramatize Armenians' plight for fundraising purposes was an adroit publicity tactic but exposed them to the censor.

---

[140] Julia F. Irwin, "The Disaster of War: American Understandings of Catastrophe, Conflict and Relief," *First World War Studies* 5, no. 1 (2014): 15–28; Davide Rodogno, "The American Red Cross and the International Committee of the Red Cross' Humanitarian Politics and Policies in Asia Minor and Greece (1922–1923)," in ibid., 82–99.

[141] Keith Watenpaugh, *Bread from Stones: The Middle East and the Making of Modern Humanitarianism* (Berkeley: University of California Press, 2015); Ben T. White, "Refugees and the Definition of Syria, 1920–1939," *Past and Present*, no. 235 (2017): 131–78.

A revolutionary film, *Auction of Souls* (or *Ravished Armenia*), made in 1919, depicted graphic imagery of violated Armenian women, dead and mutilated bodies. In the familiar trope, the film presented a "vivid picture of almost unbelievable barbarism, persecution and inhumanity such as the world has never known." Troubling for British authorities was the film's depiction of Turks that could offend Muslim feeling just as the empire was dealing with security emergencies. Scenes thought "obscene" and politically sensitive were cut, further depoliticizing the film's message by focusing solely on the victims without any sense of why they were persecuted. Film makers got the message and focused similarly on hungry victims, especially children, to reach audiences.[142] In general, the League's humanitarian campaigns tended to a very general definition of victims, ranging from civilian refugees to maimed war veterans, driven by an ethic of care without distinction.[143]

The Language of Transgression

Whether in appeals to conscience and shocked sensibilities, or invocations of unprecedented criminality, the endurance and stability of the language of transgression is the remarkable feature of the Western and, by the interwar period, international normative vocabulary. This linguistic stability entailed the continuity of the terms civilization, barbarism, and savagery to denote gradations of humanity, usually to favor Westerners but also with the potential for reversed signs. In a liberal reading, the American internationalist, Raymond B. Fosdick (1883–1972), who Wilson appointed the first Under-Secretary of the League of Nations, echoed Kant in his 1928 book, *The Old Savage in the New Civilization*, which decried the development of modern destructive capacities without humanity's commensurate development beyond its savage instincts. He was no outsider, of course, promoting US engagement with the League as president of the Rockefeller Foundation from 1936 to 1948.[144] Outsiders wanting to become insiders were Egyptian, Indian, and Korean national liberation leaders who petitioned Wilson and the great

---

[142] Michelle Tusan, "Genocide, Famine and Refugees on Film: Humanitarianism and the First World War," *Past and Present*, no. 237 (2017): 197–235. On the British landscape, Tehila Sasson, "From Empire to Humanity: The Russian Famine and the Imperial Origins of International Humanitarianism," *Journal of British History* 55, no. 3 (2016): 519–37; Emily Baughan, "The Imperial War Relief Fund and the All British Appeal: Commonwealth, Conflict and Conservatism within the British Humanitarian Movement, 1920–25," *Journal of Imperial and Commonwealth History* 40, no. 5 (2012): 845–61.

[143] Bruno Cabanes, *The Great War and the Origins of Humanitarianism, 1918–1924* (Cambridge: Cambridge University Press, 2014).

[144] Raymond B. Fosdick, *The Old Savage in the New Civilization* (New York: Doubleday Doran, 1928); Theodore M. Brown and Elizabeth Fee, "Raymond B. Fosdick

powers at the Paris Peace Conference in 1919 to grant them independence by virtue of their ancient civilizations and their contemporary level of development. For its part, Japan insisted on racial parity with the Europeans and Americans. Far from challenging the international order, they hoped to join it and contribute to the international civilizing mission.[145]

Outsiders or new insiders thus invoked the language of transgression in their bids for or defenses of statehood. In his appeal to the League of Nations in response to the Italian invasion of Ethiopia in 1936, its president, Haile Selassie (1892–1975), challenged Mussolini's claims that Italy was ending the "cruel reign of the arbitrary" and "millennial slavery" in Ethiopia, thereby bringing civilization.[146] Invoking Las Casasian themes, he accused Italy of unprecedented violence and attempted "extermination": "there has never before been an example of any Government proceeding to the systematic extermination of a nation by barbarous means, in violation of the most solemn promises made by the nations of the earth that there should not be used against innocent human beings the terrible poison of harmful gases." The Italians' was the most refined "barbarism," namely "carrying ravage and terror" by aerial bombing to urban areas far from the front. The outrage was all the greater, he continued, because the League was working with Ethiopia "to help her to reach a higher level of civilization." As a consequence, "the country is more united and the central power is better obeyed."[147]

Colonial nationalists likewise spoke this language in criticizing Western imperial indulgence of the Italian conquest of Ethiopia. So dismayed was the West African Civil Liberties and National Defence League by Britain's "condonation [sic.] of the barbarous aggression of Italy against Abyssinia" in violation of "all international laws of war and adverse to all human conceptions, morality and justice" that it passed a resolution withdrawing cooperation in the planned commemoration of the World War I armistice, an embarrassing situation for the British authorities *in situ*.[148] Similarly, the legendary leader of the Rif war against Spanish-French forces in Morocco between 1921 and 1926, Abd al-Karim (1882–1963), who united different tribes in the anticolonial struggle, thought that allowing local autonomy

---

(1883–1972): Ardent Advocate of Internationalism," *American Journal of Public Health* 102, no. 7 (2012): 1285.

[145] Manela, *The Wilsonian Moment*.

[146] Marie-Anne Matard-Bonucci, "Italian Fascism's Ethiopian Conquest and the Dream of a Prescribed Sexuality," in *Brutality and Desire: War and Sexuality in Europe's Twentieth Century*, ed. Dagmar Herzog (Basingstoke: Palgrave Macmillan, 2009), 91–108.

[147] Haile Selassie, "Appeal to League of Nations," June 1936, www.mtholyoke.edu/acad/intrel/selassie.htm.

[148] S. K. B. Asante, "The Italo-Ethiopian Conflict: A Case Study in British West African Response to Crisis Diplomacy in the 1930s," *Journal of African History* 15, no. 2 (1974): 297.

"would return the country to the worst conditions of anarchy and barbarism."[149] Not that he shared the Spanish and French denunciations of the Tarifit people in northern Morocco as barbarians, which was an easy word play on their Berber identity: Berber deriving from the Greek *bárbaros*, while *barabira* meant the same in Arabic.[150] Those seeking statehood spoke the language of transgression, addressing a Western-dominated international sphere, as Algerian nationalists managed so successfully in the 1950s.[151] Mobilizing domestic struggle against imperial domination, especially rural rather than urban populations more attuned to religious idioms, by contrast, required speaking indigenous languages of resistance, like jihahdists in Muslim lands.[152]

The outsiders who, like nineteenth-century radicals, inverted the hierarchies of the language of transgression were European and non-European opponents of Western imperialism. Rosa Luxemburg (1871–1919) famously posed the choice between socialism and barbarism in an antiwar pamphlet published in 1916. Quoting Friedrich Engels, she wrote that "Capitalist society faces a dilemma, either an advance to Socialism or a reversion to Barbarism": bourgeois society was equated with imperialism, militarism, and world war that she predicted would lead, ultimately, to "the destruction of all culture, and, as in ancient Rome, depopulation, desolation, degeneration, a vast cemetery."[153] Luxemburg was all too prescient, although she could not have imagined the scale of Europe's devastation.

With varying degrees of distance from the Soviet experiment – whose excesses the Western press decried in usual manner – these writers shared

[149] C. R. Pennell, "Women and Resistance to Colonialism in Morocco: The Rif 1916–1926," *Journal of African History* 28, no. 1 (1987): 117. On the Rif War, see C. R. Pennell, *A Country with a Government and a Flag: The Rif War in Morocco, 1921–1926* (Wisbech: Middle East and North African Studies Press, 1986).

[150] Bruce Maddy-Weitzman, "Berbers and the Nation-State in North Africa," in *Oxford Research Encyclopedia of African History*, ed. Thomas Spear (New York: Oxford University Press, 2017).

[151] Matthew Connelly, *A Diplomatic Revolution: Algeria's Fight for Independence and the Origins of the Post-Cold War Era* (Oxford: Oxford University Press, 2003); Jeffrey James Byrne, *Mecca of Revolution: Algeria, Decolonization, and the Third World Order* (Oxford: Oxford University Press, 2016).

[152] George Joffé, "Nationalism and the Bled: the Jbala from the Rif War to the Istiqlal," *Journal of North African Studies* 19, no. 4 (2014): 475–89; C. R. Pennell, "Ideology and Practical Politics: A Case Study of the Rif War in Morocco, 1921–1926," *International Journal of Middle East Studies* 14 (1982): 19–33.

[153] Rosa Luxemburg, *The Crisis in the German Social-Democracy (the "Junius" pamphlet)* (New York: Socialist Publication Society, 1919), 18. See J. P. Nettl, *Rosa Luxemburg: The Biography* (London and New York: Verso, 2019), 630–2; Rosemary H. T. O'Kane, *Rosa Luxemburg in Action: For Revolution and Democracy* (London and New York: Routledge, 2015), 87–9; Norman Geras, *The Legacy of Rosa Luxemburg* (London: Verso, 1983), ch. 1.

the Marxist understanding of fascism as a radicalized form of capitalist rule, although they differed on the identity of the revolutionary subject. Non-European Marxists like the Trinidadian historian and writer, C. L. R. James (1901–1989), ascribed far greater agency to Africans and African-Americans in challenging capitalism than European Marxists.[154] In either case, though, the language of transgression could speak back to power. In his famous history of the Haitian revolution, *The Black Jacobins*, written in 1938, James cast the French as the *génocidaires* who determined to "exterminate mulattoes and confiscate their property." While he acknowledged the reciprocal violence of the revolutionary slaves and Mulattoes, he insisted that "the white planters began it" and, in familiar turn of phrase, claimed that they "exceeded all rivals in barbarism, being trained in violence and cruelty by their treatment of the slaves." What is more, the French planters "passed a series of laws which for maniacal savagery are unique in the modern world, and (we would have said up to 1933) not likely to be paralleled again in history."[155] James used the language of Las Casas not to plea for a reformed empire but to announce its bankruptcy and to celebrate the self-emancipation and sovereignty of enslaved Africans. This rejection of the Western civilizing mission was shared by African-Caribbean intellectuals who joined the Black radicals and the communist movement in the US: Pan-Africanists like George Padmore (1903–1959) in London, and African and Asian intellectuals who congregated in Paris in the interwar period.[156]

German-Jewish Marxists came to similar, if Eurocentric, conclusions, by experiencing the violence of Western civilization in the form of German fascism in the 1930s. German-Jewish literary critic Walter Benjamin (1892–1940) famously declared in 1940 that "there is no document of culture

---

[154] Andrew Smith, *C.L.R. James and the Study of Culture* (Basingstoke: Palgrave Macmillan, 2010).

[155] C. L. R James, *The Black Jacobins: Toussaint L'Ouverture and the San Domingo Revolution*, 2nd rev. ed. (New York: Vintage Books, 1963), 20, 40, 64, 358–9, 370, 375.

[156] Cedric J. Robinson, *Black Marxism: The Making of the Black Radical Tradition* (London: Zed Press, 1983); Minkah Makalani, *In the Cause of Freedom: Radical Black Internationalism from Harlem to London, 1917–1939* (Durham, NC: North Carolina University Press, 2014); Penny von Eschen, *Race against Empire: Black Americans and Anticolonialism, 1937–1957* (Ithaca, NY: Cornell University Press, 1997); Leslie James, *George Padmore and Decolonization from Below: Pan-Africanism, the Cold War, and the End of Empire* (Basingstoke: Palgrave Macmillan, 2014); Hakim Adi, *Pan-Africanism and Communism: The Communist International, Africa and the Diaspora, 1919–1939* (Trenton, NJ: Africa World Press, 2013); Susan Pennybacker, *From Scottsboro to Munich: Race and Political Culture in 1930s Britain* (Princeton: Princeton University Press, 2009); Marc Matera, *Black London The Imperial Metropolis and Decolonization in the Twentieth Century* (Berkeley: University of California Press, 2015); Michael Goebel, *Anti-Imperial Metropolis: Interwar Paris and the Seeds of Third World Nationalism* (Cambridge: Cambridge University Press, 2015).

that is not also a document of barbarism."[157] For leftists like Benjamin, the violent dialectic of civilization could be transcended only by socialism; otherwise civilization would cannibalize itself as it did during World War I. Drawing on Luxemburg and Benjamin during the next war, Max Horkheimer (1895–1973) and Theodor W. Adorno (1903–1969) from the Frankfurt School of critical theory thus set out to undertake "nothing less than the discovery of why mankind, instead of entering into a truly human condition, is sinking into a new barbarism."[158]

Leftists were not alone in denouncing fascist imperialism in these terms. Liberal commentators, including Raphael Lemkin, also figured Nazism as a form of savagery and barbarism. For him, the notion of genocide encapsulated 500 years of Western thinking about atrocity: the language of transgression concentrated into a single word. How and why he engaged in this creative linguistic operation is the subject of the next chapter.

[157] Walter Benjamin, "Theses on the Philosophy of History," in Walter Benjamin, *Illuminations*, ed. Hannah Arendt, trans. Harry Zohn (New York: Schocken, 1968), 256.
[158] Max Horkheimer and Theodor W. Adorno, *Dialectic of Enlightenment*, trans. John Cumming (New York: Continuum, 1976), xi.

3

Raphael Lemkin and the Protection
of Small Nations

Raphael Lemkin beguiles humanitarian scholars and activists – unsurprisingly. His life story and creative response to the mass atrocities committed by the Nazi regime and its allies offer rich material for identification and empathy. Born to a rural Jewish family in the Russian Empire in 1900, he studied at the Polish University of Lwów (now Lviv in Ukraine) and pursued a law career in Warsaw in the 1930s, mixing in international legal circles. It was cut short by the German invasion of Poland in 1939, when Lemkin fled to Sweden and eventually to the US, where he worked intermittently for the government and various law schools. Having collected occupation decrees and regulations by Germany and its allies, he analyzed them and coined the word "genocide" in his book *Axis Rule in Occupied Europe*, finished in 1943 but published in late 1944. He then lobbied tirelessly for the inclusion of his neologism in the Nuremberg Trials indictments and for its codification in international law. After a fleeting moment of fame in the second half of the 1940s, when the United Nations (UN) debated and passed an international convention against genocide, he disappeared from view and died penniless in New York in 1959, his law a virtual dead letter when the US declined to ratify it. And yet, so the story goes, he left an enduring legacy of world-historical significance: a law against destruction of peoples that realizes for everyone the maxim of "never again."[1]

The academic "Pioneers of Genocide Studies," who rediscovered Lemkin in founding a new academic field in the 1980s, saw themselves as his epigones. Seeking to redeem his memory, honor his achievement, and hallow his name, they anointed him a humanitarian icon and prophet of genocide prevention.[2] With increasing posthumous fame, Lemkin soon became the subject of plays and documentaries, while biographers equated his journey with concept

---

[1] Stanley A. Goldman, "The Man Who Made Genocide a Crime: The Legacy of Raphael Lemkin," *Loyola Los Angeles International and Comparative Law Review* 34 (2011–2012): 295–300; Annette Becker, *Messagers du désastre: Raphaël Lemkin et Jan Karsk* (Paris: Fayard, 2018).

[2] Steven Leonard Jacobs and Samuel Totten, eds., *Pioneers of Genocide Studies* (New Brunswick, NJ: Transaction Publishers, 2002).

formation. As a "hero of humankind" and "unsung hero of modern humanitarianism," Lemkin's person was held to be coeval with the "origins of genocide" and the "struggle for the Genocide Convention." Written as an epic battle against cynical *realpolitik* and jealous rivals, these hagiographies celebrate Lemkin's triumph in the UN Genocide Convention in 1948 as his new concept vanquished the contenders of war crimes, crimes against humanity, and crimes against peace – when genocide became the "crime of crimes." This consummation was rendered all the more poignant – even sacrificial – by his exilic life, lonely death, and subsequent obscurity, an exhausted martyr of international justice.[3]

This common approach confuses biography with historical explanation. An actual intellectual history of genocide might attend more to Lemkin's context and contemporaries, discerning in his creation greater derivation than originality, and contingency than inevitability. As we will see, his conception of humanity as comprising distinct nationalities did not originate in the liberal cosmopolitanism he postulated upon arriving in the US, but in a lifelong Zionist commitment to Jewish statehood in Palestine. This trajectory is not apparent in his highly stylized autobiography, *Totally Unofficial*, which casts his life as an apolitical quest to criminalize genocide in international law.[4] A draft chapter of his autobiography was entitled "A Pole Discovers America," perhaps an unsurprising choice given the Christian context of his first port of call in the US: North Carolina and Duke University, originally Trinity College, with its cross emblem and motto of *Eruditio et Religio* ("Knowledge and Religion").[5] Nor does the autobiography tell readers that he wrote mainly on

[3] The plays are Catherine Filloux, *Lemkin's House* (New York: Playscripts, 2005), and Robert Skloot, *If the Whole Body Dies: Raphael Lemkin and the Treaty against Genocide* (Madison: Parallel Press, 2006). The documentary is *Watchers of the Sky* (2014): http://watchersofthesky.com/. The literary and musical event is *East West Street: A Song of Good and Evil* by Philippe Sands, based on his book, *East-West Street: On the Origins of "Genocide" and "Crimes against Humanity"* (London: Weidenfeld and Nicolson, 2016). Other symptomatic biographical treatments are Samantha Power, *"A Problem from Hell": America and the Age of Genocide* (New York: Basic Books, 2002); William Korey, *An Epitaph for Raphael Lemkin* (New York: Blaustein Institute for the Advancement of Human Rights, 2002); Agnieszka Bieńczyk-Missala and Sławomir Dębski, eds., *Rafał Lemkin: A Hero of Humankind* (Warsaw: Polish Institute of International Affairs, 2010); Michael Ignatieff, "The Hunger Artist: The Unsung Hero of Modern Humanitarianism," *New Republic*, September 16, 2018, 46–51; and John Cooper, *Raphael Lemkin and the Struggle for the Genocide Convention* (Basingstoke: Palgrave Macmillan, 2008). Lemkin's rival, Hersch Lauterpacht, is the hero for others: Philippe Sands "My Legal Hero: Hersch Lauterpacht," *The Guardian*, November 10, 2010.

[4] Raphael Lemkin, *Totally Unofficial: The Autobiography of Raphael Lemkin*, ed. Donna-Lea Frieze (New Haven: Yale University Press, 2013).

[5] Ibid., 228. Thanks to Ernest Zitser for conversations on this topic. See his "A White Crow: Raphael Lemkin's Intellectual Interlude at Duke University, 1941–1942," *North Carolina Historical Review* 96, no. 1 (2019): 34–66. Historian James Loeffler has discovered a

economic and business jurisprudence in the 1930s, and that until the 1950s he ignored the Soviet repression of Ukrainians and other mass crimes unfolding just across Poland's border.[6]

There was nothing inevitable or natural about Lemkin's coining of the genocide concept. But for the Nazi occupation of Europe, he would have had no reason to do so. Likewise, as Chapter 5 details, had the Nuremberg Trials prosecuted prewar crimes against humanity instead of insisting on a nexus with waging an illegal war, it is hard to imagine a consensus forming to fill a nonexistent gap in international law.[7] On the few occasions that he addressed large-scale criminality during the 1930s – in international legal debates about terrorism – he contributed to depoliticizing the language of transgression and obscuring permanent security. Famously, he proposed "barbarism" and "vandalism" in 1933 as new crimes in response to fascism, only to be ignored. He combined them a decade later in his neologism "genocide," he claimed, to underline the continuity of his trajectory. In fact, as we will see in the next two chapters, the military context of the early 1940s demanded reference to an entirely different body of law, namely that of military occupation in the Hague Conventions of 1907. Barbarism and vandalism had only vague rhetorical connections to his invention of genocide, and were in any event common terms at the time.

The immediate circumstances of the early 1940s determined Lemkin's conceptualization of genocide rather than those of the early 1930s. He was shocked by Western public apathy about the Nazis' murderous persecution of Jews in Poland. If Allied leaders were not blind to the specific Nazi targeting of Jews despite the representations of Jewish organizations and the trickle of

---

Hebrew-language essay that Lemkin published in *Ha-boker*, the newspaper of the Revisionist Zionists, in Israel in 1952. Personal communication, June 26, 2018.

[6] Raphael Lemkin, *La réglémentation des paieanents internationaux* (Paris: A. Pedone, 1939); Lemkin, *Valutareglering och clearing* (Stockholm: P. A. Norstedt and Söner, 1941). Lemkin's ignoring of the Soviet case is all the more remarkable in view of the fact that he studied the Soviet penal code in various publications. His essay on the Ukrainian genocide was commissioned by a US-Ukrainian organization in the early 1950s while he was campaigning for the Genocide Convention's ratification, and does not necessarily reflect his thinking 20 years before. See Anton Weiss-Wendt, "Hostage of Politics: Raphael Lemkin on 'Soviet Genocide,'" *Journal of Genocide Research* 7, no. 4 (2005): 551–9; Douglas Irvin-Erickson, *Raphaël Lemkin and the Concept of Genocide* (Philadelphia: University of Pennsylvania Press, 2017), 38–9, and Marek Kornat, "Polish Interpretations of Bolshevism and Totalitarian Systems (1918–1939)," in *Totalitarian and Authoritarian Regimes in Europe: Legacies and Lessons from the Twentieth Century*, ed. Jerzy Wojciech Borejsza and Klaus Ziemer (New York and Oxford: Berghahn Books, 2006), 98.

[7] William A. Schabas, "Core Crimes of International Criminal Law: Evolving Conceptions from the Time of Vespasian V. Pella," *Romanian Journal of International Law* 6 (2008): 224–44.

news from Europe, they did little beyond issue declarations. Until late 1944, Western publics understood Nazi criminality as visited upon all the occupied nations of Europe where Christians were the principal victims.[8] To mobilize action about Jews, as we see in Chapters 4 and 5, it made strategic sense to link the fate of Jewish and non-Jewish victims of Nazis under a single conceptual umbrella. This is the task that Lemkin's genocide concept was designed to perform. Far from unthinkingly eliding the differences between Jewish and non-Jewish victims as supposed by Lemkin's critics decades later, uniting them was the point of the concept. To retain the necessary distinctions, however, he distinguished between the logics of destruction of Jews and non-Jews *within* his genocide concept: Jews (and Roma) were attacked on racial grounds alone, that is, for nonpolitical reasons of identity. By contrast, the genocide of the other "small nations" of Christian Poles, Serbs, and so forth was driven by Nazi security imperatives, namely for political reasons.[9]

This nuance in his thinking has been unrecognized to date, leading to considerable misunderstanding about the concept. As its early reception demonstrates, Lemkin's contemporaries were also confused by his opportunistic mediation between the generic (genocide) and the specific (Jews and Roma targeting). After the war, conceptual ambiguity was partially removed by associating genocide solely with the Holocaust, namely as a nonpolitical crime of racial hatred. Again arguing opportunistically, Lemkin participated in this conceptual narrowing by playing down his concern with cultural genocide and by dismissing the claims of some African-American advocates, who in 1951 claimed that Blacks were victims of genocide in the US. Genocide in these reduced terms – the "crime of crimes" as he boasted – then became that which "shocks the conscience of mankind." Slavery and its legacies disappeared from the language of transgression. Whereas Jews had to resemble Christians to gain attention via genocide claims until the 1940s, now the reverse obtains: non-Jews need to resemble Jews because of the force of the Holocaust archetype. As this and the next chapter relate, if anyone is to blame for the problems of genocide, it is Lemkin.

---

[8] Typical is René Kraus, *Europe in Revolt* (London: Jarrolds, 1942).

[9] For these misplaced criticisms, see Uriel Tal, "On the Study of the Holocaust and Genocide," *Yad Vashem Studies* 13 (1979): 24–46; Yehuda Bauer, "The Place of the Holocaust in History," *Holocaust and Genocide Studies* 2, no. 2 (1987): 209–20; Steven T. Katz, *The Holocaust in Historical Context*, Vol. 1 (Oxford: Oxford University Press, 1994), 129–30; Dan Michman, "The Jewish Dimension of the Holocaust in Dire Straits? Current Challenges of Interpretation and Scope," in *Jewish Histories of the Holocaust: New Transnational Approaches*, ed. Norman J. W. Goda (New York and Oxford: Berghahn Books, 2014), 17–38; and Cooper, *Raphael Lemkin and the Struggle for the Genocide Convention*. Unlike Lemkin, Jacob Robinson opposed the coupling of Roma and Jews; this point is discussed in Chapter 4.

From Zionism to the Protection of "Small Nations"

Lemkin was raised in an Ashkenazi Jewish religious and cultural environment imbued with a deep ritualized memory culture of collective persecution and physical destruction as a routine and ongoing threat to Jewish survival. These included Passover and Purim, but also the First Crusade and the 1648–1649 Chmielnicki massacres. Jews were still fasting twice a week and, on specific days, several times a year to commemorate these attacks of centuries past – along with the older layers of memory about violence and victimhood and the vicissitudes of history.[10] The survival of Jews over the millennia, the mainten-ance of their traditions, their cultural flourishing in the lands of the former Polish-Lithuanian Commonwealth and Russian Empire, where the vast major-ity of world Jewry lived and, equally, the intense consciousness that peoples and their memories could be entirely erased – this was the cultural milieu and drama in which Lemkin was steeped. This consciousness was likely impressed on the young Lemkin who – he recounts in his autobiography – heard about pogroms, like that in Białystok, 50 miles away, in 1906, when he was six years old.[11]

Lemkin's commitment to Zionism as a young man in the 1920s thus should come as no surprise. James Loeffler's important research demonstrates his avid support for a Jewish state in Palestine, sometimes expressed with robust organic-blood metaphors, along with impassioned pleas for Zionist political unity. "A state consists of three factors," Lemkin wrote in 1927: "Land, people, and political sovereignty," entailing "colonization work" in Palestine.[12] He also published his translation from Hebrew into Polish of a short romantic story by Zionist writer Chaim Bialik (1873–1934), who was famous for reviving Hebrew and who had migrated to Palestine in 1924. Like his mentor, the preeminent thinker of cultural Zionism, Ahad Ha'am (1856–1927), Bialik sought to fashion a national identity for dispersed Jews by immersion in the Bible, rabbinic texts, and medieval Hebrew poetry: these were sources of the "soul of the nation." Such contact with Jewish literary and religious traditions would also guard against assimilation into surrounding Christian culture.[13]

[10] See Stephen Leonard Jacobs, "The Jewishness of Raphael Lemkin," in *The Highest Form of Wisdom: A Memorial Book in Honor of Professor Saul Friedman (1937-2013)*, ed. Jonathan C. Friedman and Robert D. Miller II (Hoboken and Jerusalem: Ktav Publishing House, 2016), 93–109.

[11] Lemkin, *Totally Unofficial*, 17.

[12] James Loeffler, "Becoming Cleopatra: The Forgotten Jewish Politics of Raphael Lemkin," *Journal of Genocide Research* 19, no. 3 (2017): 340–60.

[13] *Bialik Hayyim Nahman, Noach i Marynka*, przetłumaczył i wstępem zaopatrzył Rafał Lemkin (Lwów: Snunit, 1926), cited in Adam Redzik, *Rafał Lemkin (1900-1959): Co-Creator of International Criminal Law*, trans. Julian J. Bakowski (Warsaw: Oficyna Allerhanda, 2017), 15. Eliezer Schweid, "The Rejection of the Diaspora in Zionist

Lemkin's thinking at the time closely resembled that of the slightly older Lithuanian Zionist and lawyer, Jacob Robinson (1889–1977), who was likewise influenced by Bialik and made a case for Jewish national – and not just religious – identity in terms of language and culture.[14] Robinson thought it necessary for Jews to de-assimilate by relinquishing the "disease of multilingualism" and reviving the Hebrew language for national renewal. Far from advocating tribal particularism, though, he was echoing the Herderian view that nations were the vehicle of what he called "universal human values."[15] After their nationalization, Jews would contribute to the universal human values of world civilization, which he conceived as a concatenation of national cultures: "The Jewish Torah, Indian Buddhism, Greek philosophy and art, Roman law, Arabic Islam, Roman Catholic theocracy, Italian humanism, German Reformation, the French Revolution – all of these created universal human values from within particular boundaries through the power of nationhood."[16] For Zionists like Robinson and Lemkin's slightly older contemporary at the Jan Kazimierz University in Lwów (and later an illustrious professor of international law at Cambridge University), Hersh Lauterpacht (1897–1960), Zionism was simultaneously a form of nationalism and internationalism because it posited Jews as a globally dispersed nation with international quasi-legal personality.[17] They were not alone in this style of thinking. Making culture, nations, and religions rather than states the protagonists of history was common among leaders of stateless, subaltern, and colonized people at the time. African-American intellectual W. E. B. Du Bois advanced

Thought: Two Approaches," *Studies in Zionism* 5, no. 1 (1984): 43–70; Adam Rubin, "'Like A Necklace of Black Pearls Whose String Has Snapped': Bialik's 'Aron ha-sefarim' and the Sacralization of Zionism," *Prooftexts* 28, no. 2 (2008):157–96. He is regarded as Israel's "national poet."

[14] Omry Kaplan-Feuereisen and Richard Mann, "At the Service of the Jewish Nation: Jacob Robinson and International Law," *Osteuropa* 58, nos. 8–10 (2008): 157–70.

[15] Yaakov Robinzon, *Yediat amenu: Demografyah ve-natsiologyah* (Berlin, 1923), 133, quoted in James Loeffler, "'The Famous Trinity of 1917': Zionist Internationalism in Historical Perspective," *Simon Dubnow Yearbook* 15 (2016): 11. Liora R. Halperin, *Babel in Zion: Jews, Nationalism, and Language Diversity in Palestine, 1920–1948* (New Haven: Yale University Press, 2015). On the significance of J. H. Herder for Eastern European thinking about culture and culture, see John Connelly, *From Peoples into Nations: A History of Eastern Europe* (Princeton, NJ: Princeton University Press, 2020). On the harmony between nationalism and internationalism, see Glenda Sluga, *Internationalism in the Age of Nationalism* (Philadelphia: University of Pennsylvania Press, 2015).

[16] Loeffler, "The Famous Trinity of 1917," 10–11.

[17] James Loeffler, "The 'Natural Right of the Jewish People': Zionism International Law and the Paradox of Hersch Zvi Lauterpacht," in *The Law of Strangers Jewish Lawyers and International Law in the Twentieth Century*, ed. James Loeffler and Moria Paz (Cambridge: Cambridge University Press, 2019), 23–42.

similar arguments about each people's unique cultural contributions to world civilization in a famous essay from 1897, "The Conservation of Races."[18]

We do not know if Lemkin read Robinson's manifesto in the 1920s, but he clearly imbibed the same Bialikian message about nations constituting the building blocks of humanity, as well as Robinson's hostility to multinational subjectivities. It is also likely that he mixed in the same Zionist student circles as Lauterpacht. It was a "bitter thought," declared Lemkin in 1925, that Jews were indifferent to their national language, Hebrew.

> In the universities of Europe and beyond, we have learned all the languages of the world, ancient and modern. We have absorbed many cultures. We have drunk of the beauties of Japheth in large gulps, while our own people's language, our great and beautiful culture, we have forsaken and abandoned.[19]

Like other Zionists at the time, Lemkin seems to have regarded the Zionist project in Palestine as a national redemption that would allow Jews to reenter the history of nations, and that would also offer a safe haven for Jews in an increasingly dangerous Europe. It made perfect sense to be working with the British Empire, that upholder of international law, to this end. It is unclear how he imagined that the small Jewish minority in Palestine (about 10 percent of the population at the end of World War I) would become the deciding majority, but he does not seem to have considered the tension between opposing ethno-nationalism in Europe and supporting it in Palestine. Nor do we yet know what he thought of Palestinian nationalism. He may have shared the view of other Zionists that it was another manifestation of the antisemitism they encountered in Europe.[20]

What is more, as Loeffler also shows, Lemkin's original concern with group survival was likely not the boyhood reading about the persecution of Christians, as he later claimed, but experiencing the Christian persecution of Jews in interwar Poland. The primal motive to outlaw the destruction of human groups came not from abstract universalism but from his interpretation of Sholem Shvartsbard's murder of a Ukrainian nationalist in Paris in 1927 for pogroms in which Shvartsbard's family members had perished. Commentating on Shvartsbard's trial at the time, Lemkin called the murder

---

[18] W. E. B. Du Bois, "The Conservation of Races (1897)," in *The Problem of the Color Line at the Turn of the Twentieth Century: The Essential Early Essays*, ed. Nahum Dimitri Chandler (New York: Fordham University Press, 2007), 51–65.

[19] Loeffler, "Becoming Cleopatra," 343.

[20] Thanks to James Loeffler for discussions on this point. See his *Rooted Cosmopolitans: Jews and Human Rights in the Twentieth Century* (New Haven: Yale University Press, 2018).

a "beautiful crime" that "avenged the blood of his people."[21] For Lemkin, justice inhered in Shvartsbard's "pure" motive, his act committed on behalf of a people, indeed for humanity:

> Such a crime can only be executed by people with sublime feelings, pure souls and huge hearts, who take upon themselves the pain of their brothers, often of all of humanity, even of entire generations. And the legal conscience of the nations, which expresses itself together with their culture and is not too tightly locked into the strict confines of a law code, has declared of these people: One cannot judge them solely on the basis of rigid formulas and outdated theses; one must make law out of the living, pulsating national conscience, that which is truly alive to every pain and injury; that which is simply spontaneous in its feelings and judgements.[22]

The young lawyer, Lemkin was invoking the language of transgression for Zionism. Lemkin's later recounting narrated the article into his crusade to criminalize genocide from an early age. He did not complain about the lack of such a law at the time, however. Instead, he asserted the right of Shvartsbard's vigilante justice on the basis of higher law.[23] This notion could be advanced in terms of distinctions made in international legal thinking at the time. Lemkin is likely to have read Lassa Oppenheim's (1858–1919) canonical book, *International Law: A Treatise*, in which the author distinguished between international law and international conscience: on the one hand, the "Law of Nations" characterized by the enforceable "body of rules of international conduct" consented to by "civilized States ... and public opinion of the whole of civilized humanity" and, on the other hand, the "rules of international morality and courtesy which are left to the consideration of the conscience of nations."[24] Here Lemkin was drawing on the famous Martens clause to the 1899 Hague Conventions discussed in the previous chapter. He pleaded for the "conscience of the nations" to reflect "the living, pulsating national conscience," namely that of the Jewish nation. As we will see below, this is what he eventually codified as genocide.

In the retrospective constructions of his autobiography, Lemkin claimed that this moment was preceded by debate with his university professors about the trial of the Armenian, Soghomon Tehlirian (1896–1960), for murdering

---

[21] Ibid., 348. Cf. Lemkin, *Totally Unofficial*, 21; Katrin Steffen, *Jüdische Polonität: Ethnizität und Nation im Spiegel der polnischsprachigen jüdischen Presse 1918–1939* (Göttingen: Vandenhoeck und Ruprecht, 2004).

[22] Loeffler, "Becoming Cleopatra," 348.   [23] Ibid.

[24] Lassa Oppenheim, *International Law: A Treatise*, 2 vols. (London: Longman Green, 1905), 1: 12–13. Lemkin cites the 1935 edition in Raphael Lemkin, *Axis Rule in Occupied Europe: Laws of Occupation, Analysis of Government, Proposals for Redress* (Washington, DC: Carnegie Endowment for International Peace, 1944), 24.

Talaat Pasha (1874–1921), the Turkish architect of the Armenian genocide.[25] A Berlin court acquitted Tehlirian on the grounds of insanity, but Lemkin took him as acting "as the self-appointed legal office for the conscience of mankind."[26] While we can find him mentioning the Armenian genocide from the 1940s when he was invoking the distant and recent past to popularize his new legal concept, historians have not yet found mention of the case in his writings in the 1920s and 1930s. Given the unreliability of his memoir, we cannot yet determine whether the wartime Ottoman mass murder and deportation of Armenians motivated him to launch a crusade to criminalize genocide, nor verify whether the massacre of Assyrians by the new Iraqi state in 1933 inspired him to criminalize "barbarism" and "vandalism," as he claimed in postwar interviews. However, it is not unlikely given the widespread discussion of the Armenian plight – which persisted as a refugee crisis – in the 1920s.[27]

We do not yet know about Lemkin's Zionist activities in the 1930s, but he maintained close associations with Jewish organizations, teaching at a rabbinical seminary in Warsaw while practicing as a private lawyer. In his postwar campaign to popularize his genocide concept, however, he downplayed its Jewish origins by hitching his cart to the ideal of "small (Christian) nations." This ideal was consistent with his Zionism that, we recall from Robinson, imagined humanity as a tapestry of nations, preferably each with their own state. Lemkin claimed he met the Czechoslovak foreign minister, Jan Masaryk (1886–1948), at the UN in 1946 and expressed admiration of his father, Tomáš G. Masaryk (1850–1937), Czechoslovakia's first president. "Your Excellency, I have studied the writings of your father . . . who devoted his life to explaining the cultural personality of nations," gushed Lemkin, hoping to win Masaryk Jr's backing of the Genocide Convention.[28] Even if the story is apocryphal, Lemkin's invocation of Masaryk's ideas indicates his chosen intellectual heritage. For Masaryk's writings articulated the perspective of Central European

---

[25] Hans-Lukas Kieser, *Talaat Pasha: Father of Modern Turkey, Architect of Genocide* (Princeton: Princeton University Press, 2018).

[26] Lemkin, *Totally Unofficial*, 19–22; Sands, *East-West Street*, 149–52; Patrizia Resta, "The Revenge of Soghomon Tehlirian," *Journal on European History of Law* 7 (2016): 45–53.

[27] Peter Balakian, "Raphael Lemkin, Cultural Destruction, and the Armenian Genocide," *Holocaust and Genocide Studies* 27, no. 1 (2013): 57–89; Stephen L. Jacobs, "Raphael Lemkin and the Armenian Genocide," in *Looking Backward, Looking Forward: Confronting the Armenian Genocide*, ed. Richard G. Hovannisian (New Brunswick, NJ: Transaction Publishers, 2003), 125–36; Keith Watenpaugh, *Bread from Stones: The Middle East and the Making of Modern Humanitarianism* (Berkeley: University of California Press, 2015); Michelle Tusan, "Genocide, Famine and Refugees on Film: Humanitarianism and the First World War," *Past and Present* 237 (2017): 197–235.

[28] Lemkin, *Totally Unofficial*, 127; Irvin-Erickson, *Raphaël Lemkin and the Concept of Genocide*, 67, 155.

"small nations," a term he took from British wartime rhetoric; he invoked the liberals H. H. Asquith (1852–1928) and H. A. L. Fisher discussed in the previous chapter. Lemkin shared the British aversion to Pan-Germanism's enduring imperative to dominate the land between Germany and Russia, which he traced to medieval German colonization in the region.

The adoption of the "small nations" discourse made sense to Eastern Europeans imbued with the Herderian spirit of cultural nationality. Pervasive in the early decades of the twentieth century, it cast smaller European nations subject to foreign-imperial rule as bearers of cultural virtues produced despite powerlessness. Their independence was claimed to guarantee European civilization.[29] National culture was also prioritized because of long-denied statehood. For Central Europeans, resisting German colonization – whether by German settlers or by German culture – was a central trope. The Czechoslovak foreign minister-in-exile, Jan Masaryk, told a London Jewish audience in 1943 that culture was elemental to nationality, indeed a vehicle to "humanity." In explaining that the destruction of his state enabled a "concentrated attack on the Czech language and culture," he referred not only to the obvious situation of the Nazi regime but also to the "Germanising influence of the Hapsburg Empire," suggesting a centuries-long Teutonic assault on Slavic culture.[30]

Central Europe was the region that English historian Lewis Namier in 1915 called "The European 'Middle East,' the district of small nationalities and scattered German settlements."[31] A year later, in his famous lecture on "The Problem of Small Nations in the European Crisis" at the University of London, Masaryk averred the value of nationality – what Lemkin called "cultural personality of nations" – of small peoples against states and empires. A plea to Britain's planners to grant Czechoslovak independence after the war, the lecture identified a swathe of small nations in what he identified as Europe's "central zone" – the Austria-Hungarian Empire, the northern and western parts of the Russian Empire, and the Balkans – that deserved statehood. Such a reorganization would stabilize this part of Europe, he argued,

---

[29] Siniša Malešević, *Grounded Nationalisms: A Sociological Analysis* (Cambridge: Cambridge University Press, 2019), ch. 10. Malešević argues the "small nations" discourse was a "strategic narrative" to challenge imperial rule – like the Irish claim against the British – rather than reflecting geopolitical reality; Balkan states, for instance, which were smaller than Ireland, were expansionist and portrayed themselves as great nations. Malešević is criticizing Miroslav Hroch, *Social Preconditions of National Revival in Europe: A Comparative Analysis of the Social Composition of Patriotic Groups among the Smaller European Nations* (New York: Columbia University Press, 1985).

[30] Jan Masaryk, *Minorities and the Democratic State*, Lucien Wolf Memorial Lecture (London: Jewish Historical Society of England, 1943), 8; Yohanan Cohen, *Small Nations in Times of Crisis and Confrontation*, trans. Naftali Greenwood (Albany: State University of New York, 1989).

[31] Lewis B. Namier, *Germany and Eastern Europe* (London: Duckworth, 1915), xiii.

which was a "danger-zone" because of unresolved nationality questions and "a very great variety of national and racial fragments."[32] The Allies, he suggested, could realize the aspirations of small nations while advancing their own interests by resolving these nationality questions in the form of new states.

Ten years later, the Czechoslovak Foreign Minister, Edvard Beneš (1884–1948), addressed the "The Problem of the Small Nations after the World War," likewise identifying the cause of small nations with Britain, the US ("where the policy of democracy is carried out in the name of the ideals of humanity"), Italy, and France, against autocratic continental empires. Now the Allies' "humanitarian and democratic ideals" were continued by the League of Nations, whose covenant, he continued breathlessly, "is, and will always remain, one of the most celebrated memorials of political wisdom and the finest expression of the philosophy of humanitarianism and of the ideas of modern democracy in the sphere of international politics."[33] The new interwar order drew on the same vocabulary as the language of transgression, both avowing liberal internationalism with its rhetoric of social progress and minority protection. As we will see in Chapter 9, this language applied to population "transfers" that were supported by figures like Beneš, who invoked a new term in the language of transgression: human rights.

As a Pole, Lemkin could sympathize with the Czechoslovak aversion to German Central European aspirations. He noted in *Axis Rule* that the Germans and their allies banned and burned the writings of Masaryrk and Beneš because they represented the Czechoslovak "national spirit" and "emphasized national elements."[34] Lemkin's unpublished world history of genocide written after World War II adopted this perspective by including chapters on the genocidal effects of German settlement in Eastern Europe since the Middle Ages. Indeed, Germany was the "classical country of genocide practices," he wrote in 1947.[35] Lemkin also shared Masaryrk and Beneš's avocation of the symbiosis between Western powers and the small nations of Central Europe with their commitment to internationalism and humanitarian ideals.

To appeal to Christian ears, Lemkin opportunistically invoked alternative forms of Jewish politics, namely the nonnationalist Jewish autonomy movement popular in Poland and Lithuania, and the idiom of criminal and

---

[32] Thomas G. Masaryk, *The Problem of Small Nations in the European Crisis* (London: King's College, Council for the Study of International Relations, 1916); Masaryk "Pangermanism and the Zone of Small Nations," *New Europe* 1, no. 9 (December 14, 1916): 271–7; Masaryk, "The Slavs after the War," *Slavonic Review* 1, no. 1 (1922): 2–23.

[33] Edward Beneš, "The Problem of the Small Nations after the World War," *Slavonic Review* 4, no. 11 (1925): 257–77.

[34] Lemkin, *Axis Rule in Occupied Europe*, 138.

[35] Raphael Lemkin, "Genocide as a Crime under International Law," *American Journal of International Law* 41, no. 1 (1947): 151.

international law, which exemplified a common concern for small nations. It is associated with the Russian-Jewish historian, Simon Dubnow (1860–1941), who summarized the project thus: as "a spiritual or historical-cultural nation, deprived of any possibility of aspiring to political triumph, of seizing territory by force or of subjecting other nations to cultural domination, it [the Jewish nation] is concerned only with one thing: protecting its national individuality and safeguarding its autonomous development in all states everywhere in the Diaspora."[36] Lemkin claims he paid homage to Dubnow on his flight from Poland, although the meeting cannot be verified because the Nazis murdered Dubnow. Whether true or not, Lemkin mentioned the story to fashion a non-Zionist lineage for his ethno-national imaginary.

This non-Zionist movement retained Lemkin's youthful national aversion to assimilation and preference for Hebrew over Yiddish, but strove neither to colonize lands nor to found an ethno-state. Indeed, its focus was surviving the colonization of other nations. That is why, in *Axis Rule*, he told readers not to confuse nationalism (bad) with "the idea of the nation" (good), and later approvingly cited the Italian national liberation leader, Giuseppe Mazzini (1805–1872), and John Stuart Mill's (1806–1873) criticism of German nationalism as chauvinism.[37] The imperative for local autonomy and self-rule coincided with Austro-Marxist thinking about reconciling contending nationalities in single-state structure, although its main proponent, Otto Bauer (1881–1938), regarded "national spiritualism" as bourgeois sentimentalism, indeed a "romantic ghost" that ignored the material conditions of nationality.[38] In 1950, Lemkin alleged an affinity with Austro-Marxism's nationality ideas in a typically obsequious letter to one of its major figures, Karl Renner (1870–1950), the first president of postwar Austria, in seeking his support for the Genocide Convention.[39]

Lemkin's casting of his mission as a cosmopolitan ideal led him to invoke particular Biblical sources, especially for non-Jewish audiences. Thus, in his autobiography, he refers to the ancient Hebrew prophetic tradition to which he says his teacher introduced him as a boy. He felt drawn to the prophets' example and message of solidarity with the poor and downtrodden: suffering

---

[36] Simon Dubnow, *Nationalism and History: Essays on Old and New Judaism*, ed. and intro Koppel S. Pinson (Philadelphia: Jewish Publication Society of America, 1958), 97; Simon Rabinovitch, "The Dawn of a New Diaspora: Simon Dubnow's Autonomism, from St. Petersburg to Berlin," *Leo Baeck Institute Yearbook* 50 (2005): 267–88.

[37] Lemkin, *Axis Rule in Occupied Europe*, 91n51; Lemkin, "Introduction to Part I: The New Word and the New Idea," n.d., Reel 3, Box 2, Folder 2, 8, Raphael Lemkin Papers, MssCol 1730, New York Public Library, New York.

[38] Otto Bauer, *The Question of Nationalities and Social Democracy*, trans. Joseph O'Connell, intro. Ephraim Nimni (Minneapolis: University of Minnesota Press, 2000 [1907]), 24.

[39] Raphael Lemkin to Karl Renner, March 29, 1950, American Jewish Archives, Lemkin Papers, Box 1, Folder 15.

for their struggle.[40] From Isaiah's call to "Cease to do evil; learn to do well; relieve the oppressed; judge the fatherless; plead for the widow" (Isaiah 1:17), he drew a redemptive conclusion that appealed to humanitarian consciousness: it "sounded to me so urgent, as if the oppressed stood now outside our door. The appeals for peace by converting swords into ploughshares seemed to recreate his presence."[41] In this self-fashioning, his advocacy for the genocide concept linked it to the Jewish tradition of *Tikkun Olam* – healing the world and caring for all the oppressed – rather than to what he feared others might regard as a tribal imaginary.[42]

To underline his postwar self-presentation, Lemkin wrote in his autobiography that, as a schoolboy, he read widely about the persecution of human cultural groups since antiquity, beginning with Roman Emperor Nero's attempted extermination of Christians. By learning about the travails of many ethnic groups over the centuries – the Huguenots of France, Catholics in Japan, Muslims in Spain – he concluded that ethnic destruction was a general and enduring problem, linking Jewish and non-Jewish experiences. While the persecution of Jews was part of this sorry tale – indeed, he later called them "that classical victim of genocide"[43] – he indicated that his sympathies were for people everywhere; their suffering was part of the same human story: "A line, red from blood, led from the Roman arena through the gallows of France to the pogrom of Białystok."[44]

Lemkin thus couched his appeal to end genocide in relation to the small nations ideal of world civilization blended with stoic notions of universal human solidarity. This ideal allowed him to appeal to non-Jews while remaining faithful to his Zionist ontology of humanity.

> I identified myself more and more with the sufferings of the victims, whose numbers grew, and I continued my study of history. I understood that the function of memory is not only to register past events, but to stimulate human conscience. Soon contemporary examples of genocide followed, such as the slaughter of the Armenians. It became clear to me that the diversity of nations, religious groups and races is essential to civilization because every one of these groups has a mission to fulfill and a contribution to make in terms of culture. To destroy these groups is opposed to the will of the Creator and to disturb the spiritual harmony

---

[40] Lemkin, *Totally Unofficial*, 16–17.   [41] Ibid., 16.

[42] The full phrase is *Tikkun olam b'malchut Shaddai*: repairing a [broken] world beneath God's sovereignty. Gilbert S. Rosenthal, "Tikkun ha-Olam: The Metamorphosis of a Concept," *Journal of Religion* 85, no. 2 (2005): 214–40.

[43] Raphael Lemkin, "Genocide in Economics," New York Public Library, Raphael Lemkin Collection, N.D.

[44] Lemkin, *Totally Unofficial*, 17.

of mankind. I have decided to become a lawyer and work for the outlawing of Genocide and for its prevention through the cooperation of nations. These nations must be made to understand that an attack on one of them is an attack on them all.[45]

As we see in the next two chapters, mobilizing support for his new concept required enlisting the representatives of small nations whose leaders understood themselves as cultural nations seeking to found or consolidate a new state.[46] If genocide was the destruction of nations, and nations were cultural entities, then attacking bearers of culture and its symbols was genocide. That is why the cultural dimension of genocide included the intention to "cripple" as well as to "destroy" a people, Lemkin wrote in 1947 when the inclusion of "cultural genocide" was being debated in UN committees.[47]

At the same time, the biological assumptions in Lemkin's thinking also flowed into his conception of nationhood. In 1934, he wrote about the biological propensity of criminals and the virtues of "criminal biology" in relation to the 1932 Polish Penal Code, which concerned him as a public prosecutor. To be sure, as a liberal, he also stressed social factors causing criminality, and advocated that law seek the resocialization of offenders; on that basis, he criticized the Nazi criminal law reform for its deterrent rather than rehabilitative intent.[48] And yet, the shared belief in the biological-hereditary basis of antisocial conditions like "work shyness" is impossible to overlook. Ten years later, he continued to write about "biological forces" and the "biological structure" of nations as analytical categories while complaining that the Nazis conceived of nations solely in biological terms.[49] Lemkin contributed to the problems of genocide by combining biological and cultural dimensions of nationhood in a single concept.

---

[45] Raphael Lemkin, "Autobiography," New York Public Library, Raphael Lemkin Collection, Box 1, Reel 2, Folder 36, 2. This quotation was excluded from Lemkin, *Totally Unofficial*.

[46] On the distinction between cultural and political nations, common at the time, see Friedrich Meinecke, *Cosmopolitanism and the National State*, trans. Robert B. Kimber (Princeton: Princeton University Press, [1908] 1970).

[47] Lemkin, "Genocide as a Crime Under International Law," 147.

[48] Rafał Lemkin, "O wprowadzenie ekspertyzy kriminalo-biologicznej do procesu karnego" [On the Introduction of Criminal-Biological Expertise in the Criminal Trial], *Głos Prawa Lwów* 11, no. 3 (1934): 137–44; Lemkin, "Reforma prawa karnego w Niemczech," *Wiadmości Literackie* 30 (1934): 7. Thanks to James Loeffler and Claudia Kraft for sharing these articles and their thoughts about them. For a contemporary analysis of Nazi law reform, see Karl Loewenstein, "Law in the Third Reich," *Yale Law Journal* 5, no. 2 (1936): 779–815.

[49] Lemkin, *Axis Rule in Occupied Europe*, xi, 80–1.

Barbarism, Vandalism, and the Political

Soon after penning his plea for Shvartsbard, Lemkin became involved in international legal penal reform as the prodigy of the Polish vice president of the International Association of Penal Law, Professor Emil Stanisław Rappaport (1877–1965), his former mentor at the Jan Kazimierz University in Lwów. By coincidence, the association met in Warsaw in 1927. A number of issues concerned the League of Nations and leading international lawyers like Rappaport, Romanian Vespasien V. Pella (1897–1952) and Frenchman Henri Donnedieu de Vabres (1880–1952): establishing an international criminal court and universal jurisdiction, outlawing interstate aggression and incitement to war, defining and criminalizing terrorism and instituting the category of "international crimes." Pella and de Vabres were giants in the field, drafting the first version of the UN Genocide Convention with Lemkin in 1947, while de Vabres served as a Nuremberg judge. Both influenced Lemkin. Neither are mentioned in his autobiography. In the main, historians have been seduced by Lemkin's melodramatic narrative by casting him as the intrepid discoverer of genocide in the face of these largely forgotten rivals. In fact, he was less the isolated creative genius than a minor participant in a general effort to forge a "new justice" after World War I. His status at the time has been exaggerated in biographical treatments of his role in international legal forums.[50]

In his autobiography, Lemkin claims that he prefigured the genocide concept with the introduction of "barbarism" (massacres) and "vandalism" (destruction of cultural property) at an international law conference on terrorism in 1933. Scholars, including the present writer, have taken Lemkin at his word, following him in lamenting that the failure of the conference to take up his suggestion left European nations and minorities legally vulnerable to Nazi mass crimes a few years later. In this telling, the 1933 conference in Madrid is at once a conceptual waystation to the full realization of Lemkin's thinking in *Axis Rule*, and a fatal missed opportunity to outlaw the destruction of groups and their culture before World War II. While he did suggest these crimes, however, they were less original than he boasted.

---

[50] This observation does not apply to Mark Mazower's brief portrait in *No Enchanted Palace: The End of Empire and the Ideological Origins of the United Nations* (Princeton: Princeton University Press, 2009), 124–33, nor to Mark A. Lewis, *The Birth of the New Justice: The Internationalization of Crime and Punishment, 1919–1950* (Oxford: Oxford University Press, 2014), which surveys the activities of international lawyers in the interwar and immediate postwar period, during which Lemkin was a minor player until the later 1940s. Also see Nathaniel Berman, *Passion and Ambivalence: Colonialism, Nationalism, and International Law* (Leiden: Brill 2011); Umut Öszu, *Formalizing Displacement: International Law and Population Transfers* (Oxford: Oxford University Press, 2015).

Lemkin's predecessors and mentors were thinking about pressing international legal issues, namely prosecuting war criminals and defending minorities, while he was still a student. The denouement of World War I set the interwar international legal agenda. The Commission on Responsibility report of 1919 identified two major transgressions: provoking the world war and violating "the laws and customs of war and the laws of humanity."[51] Outlawing aggressive warfare and what was called "racial persecution" became priorities. A draft reply by the Council of Four (Britain, France, the US, and Italy) to German objections to punitive measures in the Treaty of Versailles stated baldly that the war "was the greatest crime against humanity and the freedom of peoples that any nation, calling itself civilised, has even consciously committed."[52] The various crimes that German forces committed were folded into the general category of the war to dominate the small nations of Europe. Article 227 of the Treaty of Versailles declared that the Allies "publicly arraign" the former German emperor, William II, for "a supreme offence against international morality and the sanctity of treaties," meaning the outbreak of the war.[53] The League of Nations preamble also reflected the emphasis on interstate relations in making its aim the promotion of "international co-operation and to achieve international peace and security."[54]

The Commission on Responsibility report also condemned German "systematic terrorism" against civilians and of course the Turkish massacres of Armenians. The concern for civilians continued in international conversations about the novel technology of the imprecise bombing from aircraft in the Hague Draft Rules on Air Warfare of 1923. Article 22 prohibited "Aerial bombardment for the purpose of terrorizing the civilian population, of destroying or damaging private property not of military character, or of injuring non-combatants."[55] The ad hoc international Commission of Jurists that drew

---

[51] "Report of the Commission on Responsibility of the Authors of the War and Enforcement of Penalties," in *Violation of the Laws and Customs of War, Reports of Majority and Dissenting Reports of American and Japanese Members of the Commission of Responsibilities*, Conference of Paris, 1919 (Oxford: Clarendon, 1919).

[52] Paul Mantoux, ed., *The Deliberations of the Council of Four (March 24–June 28, 1919): From the Delivery of Peace Terms to the German Delegation to the Signing of the Treaty of Versailles*, trans. Arthur S. Link, 2 Vols. (Princeton: Princeton University Press, 2000), 2: 406.

[53] Treaty of Versailles, June 28, 1919, Yale Law School, Avalon Project," Documents in Law, History, and Diplomacy, http://avalon.law.yale.edu/imt/partvii.asp.

[54] Preamble to the Covenant of the League of Nations found before Article 1 of the Treaty of Versailles, June 28, 1919, ibid.

[55] Heinz Markus Hanke, "The 1923 Hague Rules of Air Warfare: A Contribution to the Development of International Law Protecting Civilians from Air Attack," *International Review of the Red Cross* 33 no. 292 (1993): 17; "Hague Rules of Air Warfare," *American Journal of International Law* 17, supplement (1923).

up the rules explicitly recalled World War I's effects on civilians in terms of the language of transgression.

> The experiences of the recent war have left in the mind of the world at large a lively horror of the havoc which can be wrought by the indiscriminate launching of bombs and projectiles on the non-combatant populations of towns and cities. The conscience of mankind revolts against this form of making war in places outside the actual theatre of military operations, and the feeling is universal that limitations must be imposed.[56]

In reality, whatever the commission said about the conscience of mankind, the revulsion was not universal among state elites, especially powerful imperial ones, like the humanitarian British and French, who wanted to reserve the right to bomb in the name of the reprisal doctrine. They did not adopt these Hague Rules, which remained a dead letter. Even so, they could not admit the right to terrorize civilians as a matter of policy despite their practice of doing so in colonial warfare. The principles of humanity in the Martens Clause remained a powerful rhetorical standard in the language of transgression.[57] The fate of the Draft Hague Rules demonstrated that reconciling this norm with state sovereignty usually entailed asserting that states represented humanity.

This was the context in which Nicolas Politis, Pella, and de Vabres proposed laws to criminalize aggression and to establish an international tribunal to prosecute those who broke them. Disappointed by the outcome of the trials of war criminals by the Germans in Leipzig and Ottomans in Istanbul, they sought to implement the agenda of placing German and Ottoman leaders on trial after the war, as Sir Ernest Pollock had urged.[58] The Geneva Protocol of 1924 for the Pacific Settlement of International Disputes, drafted by Politis and Edvard Beneš, and signed by 47 League members, devised a mechanism to

---

[56] Commission of Jurists to Consider and Report upon the Revision of the Rules of Warfare, *American Journal of International Law* 32, Supplement (1938): 2. The commission also explicitly invoked the Martens Clause at 53. The commission comprised delegations from Italy, France, Great Britain, the Netherlands, the US, and Japan. Amanda Alexander "The Genesis of the Civilian," *Leiden Journal of International Law* 20 no. 2 (2007): 359–76 argues that the commission effectively invented the category of "civilian," femininizing it as vulnerable and lacking agency.

[57] Ben Saul, *Terrorism in International Humanitarian Law* (Oxford: Oxford University Press, 2008), 272–3.

[58] Vespasian V. Pella, *La Coopération des États Dans la Lutte Contre le Faux Monnayage: Rapport et Projet de Convention Présenté à la Société des Nations* (Paris: A. Pedone, 1928); Lewis, *The Birth of the New Justice*, 46.

define aggressive warfare by binding them to a system of arbitration.[59] In *La Criminalité Collective des États et le Droit Pénal de l'Avenir* (The Collective Liability of Sates and the Criminal Law of the Future, 1925), Pella advocated the criminal responsibility not only of individuals but of states for wars of aggression. Confident in the justice of the postwar order, he and his colleagues proposed to make states – that is, potentially revisionist states – liable for prosecution.[60] Three years later, Politis gave a series of lectures at Columbia University in which he decried aggression as the "greatest spectacle of immorality offered by the international community."[61] In the same year, 1928, the French convinced the Americans and 61 other nations to sign the General Treaty for Renunciation of War as an Instrument of National Policy (Kellog-Briand Pact).[62] Whether this treaty made waging an aggressive war an international crime was debated in the early 1940s, as we see in Chapter 5, but there was no doubt that the winners at Versailles were developing a norm against revisionist warfare.

Proponents of humanitarian intervention, these jurists also invoked what they called "racial massacres" in general and "the Armenian massacres" in particular as crimes so grave as to justify violating the principle of state sovereignty in the interests of "restoring the moral order which must reign in the whole of humanity."[63] Henri Donnedieu de Vabres wrote about "attacks on humanity that might be perpetrated in a country under the influence of race hatred" in the mid-1920s, while his Spanish colleague, Quintiliano Saldaña (1878–1938), who Pella often cited, wrote of "acts of savagery, such as major political or racial massacres" in reference to "the massacres of

---

[59] Nicholas Tsagourias, "Nicolas Politis' Initiatives to Outlaw War and Define Aggression, and the Narrative of Progress in International Law," *European Journal of International Law* 23 no. 1 (2012): 255–66.

[60] Vespasien V. Pella, *La Criminalité Collective des États et le Droit Pénal de l'Avenir* (Bucarest: Imprimerie de l'État, 1925); Mark A. Lewis, "The History of the International Association of Penal Law, 1924–1950: Liberal, Conservative, or Neither?" in *Historical Origins of International Criminal Law*, Vol. 4, ed. Morten Bergsmo et al. (Brussels: Torkel Opsahl Academic EPublisher, 2015), 615.

[61] Nicolas Politis, *The New Aspects of International Law* (Washington, DC: Carnegie Endowment for International Peace, 1928), 32–48.

[62] Oona Hathaway and Scott Shapiro, *The Internationalists: And Their Plan to Outlaw War* (New York: Allen Lane, 2017).

[63] Pella, *La Criminalité Collective des États et le Droit Pénal de l'Avenir*, 145–6. On the question of repressing "race massacres," he cited the Spanish jurist, Quintiliano Saldaña, *La Défense Sociale Universelle* (Coueslant: Cahors, 1924), 25. Florian Jeßberger, "The Modern Doctrinal Debate on the Crime of Aggression," in *The Crime of Aggression: A Commentary*, ed. Claus Kreß and Stefan Barriga (Cambridge: Cambridge University Press, 2017), 291–2; Schabas, "Core Crimes of International Criminal Law," 226.

Christian-Armenians and Russian Jews."[64] These common nineteenth-century and early-twentieth-century phrasings about religiously or racially motivated mass atrocities increased in circulation due to the experiences of Armenians during the war, and Jews in Russia and Poland after they were subject to widespread pogroms.[65] Lemkin would naturally have been aware of anti-Jewish violence at the time, and he later wrote about it in his unpublished history of genocide.[66]

The Armenian case was well known in Francophone circles thanks in part to the steady stream of publications by Russian émigré diplomat and jurist André Mandelstam (1869–1949), who joined the *Institute de droit international* after fleeing the Russian Revolution. His intellectual development in the interwar years demonstrates how the nexus of empire and humanitarian concern transitioned into the idiom of universal human rights. As a Russian diplomat, he represented that empire as a civilized power that arrogated to itself the right to supervise how Armenians were treated in the Ottoman Empire.[67] Toward the end of World War I, in 1917, he published *Le Sort de l'Empire Ottoman* (The Fate of the Ottoman Empire), in which he joined Entente voices in calling for the breakup of the Ottoman Empire – depriving Turkey "of its guardianship over non-Turkish peoples" – in the name of human rights and punishment of wartime leaders for the crimes against Armenians.[68] His rhetoric encapsulated the language of transgression at its

[64] Cited in John Quigley, *The Genocide Convention: An International Law Analysis* (Aldershot: Ashgate: 2006), 3. Donnedieu de Vabres, "La Cour Permanente de Justice Internationale et sa Vocation en matière criminelle," *Revue internationale de droit penal* 1, no. 19 (1924–1925): 186; Quintiliano Saldaña, "La Justice pénale internationale," *Recueil des cours* 10 (1925): 369; Saldaña, "La Défense Sociale Universelle," *Revue Internationale de Sociologie* (March–April 1925): 145–74.

[65] William W. Hagen, *Anti-Jewish Violence in Poland, 1914–1920* (Cambridge: Cambridge University Press, 2018).

[66] Raphael Lemkin, "The Jews in Poland," New York Public Library, Raphael Lemkin Collection, Box 2, Folder 8.

[67] On Imperial Russia's civilized self-understanding, see Peter Holquist, "The Russian Empire as a 'Civilized State': International Law as Principle and Practice in Imperial Russia, 1874–1878," Unpublished paper, The National Council for Eurasian and East European Research, July 2014, www.ucis.pitt.edu/nceeer/2004_818-06g_Holquist.pdf.

[68] André Mandelstam, *Le Sort de l'Empire Ottoman* (Lausanne and Paris: Librarie Payot et Cie, 1917), ix–xi; Mandelstam, *La Société des Nations et les Puissances devant le Problème Arménien* (Paris: A. Pedone, 1926); Mandelstam, *Das Armenische Problem im Lichte des Völker-und Menchenrechts* (Berlin: Stilke, 1931); Mandelstam, "Der internationale Schutz der Menschenrechte und die New-Yorker Erklärung des Instituts für Völkerrecht," *Zeitschrift für ausländisches öffentliches Recht und Völkerrecht* 2 (1931): 335–77. Dzovinar Kévonian, "André Mandelstam and the Internationalization of Human Rights (1869–1949)," in *Revisiting the Origins of Human Rights*, ed. Pamela Slotte and Miia Halme-Tuomisaari (Cambridge: Cambridge University Press, 2015), 239–66.

most strident. Indeed, he claimed to speak for civilization itself to appear before "the court of history," namely as a "tribunal of civilization against the Ottoman Empire." Rejecting the German theory that rights inhered in the state, he proclaimed the sovereignty of law above the state. In the name of "human rights," then, civilized powers had the right of "humanitarian intervention."[69] In "the legal consciousness of peoples of the Entente" was an "intuitive right" to "fulfill a duty, to contribute in the measure of our forces to the establishment of the truth" and the "law of peace." An imperial servant, Mandelstam spoke on behalf of small nations. "Greater than the hatred for the vampire that is the Ottoman Empire, is our love for the races it oppresses. It is the love for the weak, eternal, boundless love that has guided our pen." Because the Entente represented universal values, he implied fancifully, his was not "a political book."[70]

In view of these commitments and his prewar advocacy of Armenian autonomy in the Ottoman Empire, Mandelstam was an understandable proponent of the League of Nations minority protection regime. This regime comprised treaties between the victorious Allies and 14 states either established after the war or ones that were rewarded with new territory, thereby acquiring large minority populations, like Greece. Provisions to protect the rights of minorities – such as school instruction and legal proceedings in their language, proportional rights of public expenditure, and so forth – were built into the general peace treaties as well as those recognizing independence and new borders. Although the treaties empowered the League of Nations to supervise the provisions, little was done for minorities, which could send petitions to the League but not place their complaints on the official agenda. Nonetheless, their existence rankled the affected states, which blamed their minorities for conspiring with international enemies to compromise their hard-won sovereignty and territorial integrity. Poland eventually renounced its treaty in 1934.[71]

During the 1920s, Mandelstam saw the logic of the objection by small nations that the treaties were selectively applied. The great powers, including defeated Germany, were not subject to such treaties. The French, for instance, said they had no minorities to protect, and no state liked the notion of special rights for any section of its citizenry. What is more, he was already suspicious of states as such. Mandelstam concluded that the rights of individuals might coax more states to sign onto an international regime of protection; rather than some states' sovereignty being porous, every state's should be, even if a

---

[69] Among other jurists, he relied on Rougier mentioned in Chapter One. Mandelstam, *Le Sort de l'Empire Ottoman*, 451–66.

[70] Ibid., x–xi.

[71] Carole Fink, *Defending the Rights of Others: The Great Powers, the Jews, and International Minority Protection, 1878–1938* (Cambridge: Cambridge University Press, 2004).

little. In view of Imperial Russia's demise and his experience as an exiled member of a class criminalized by the Bolsheviks, he transposed the universal values of civilization onto the League of Nations as the guarantor of human rights.[72]

Mandelstam was not the only international lawyer trying to influence the League of Nations. With Greek scholar Antoine Frangulis (1888–1975) – also a refugee from dictatorship – he established an International Diplomatic Academy (*Academie Diplomatique Internationale*) in 1926. Together with another member, Edvard Beneš, they set out to investigate human rights protection, arguing in a 1928 academy report that the minorities treaties amounted to "the international protection of the Rights of Man." A year later, Mandelstam drafted a "declaration on the international rights of man" that was adapted by the *Institute de droit international.* Invoking the "juridical conscience of the civilized word," its six articles ascribed to states the duty to protect various individual rights, including those mentioned in the minorities treaties, like the freedom of religion and to use one's language in public instruction. These lawyers were replacing the language of group minority protection with that of protecting individual rights to achieve the same outcome; and they could apply to victims of the Greek and Soviet dictatorships, unlike Lemkin's narrow ethnic formulation. The "ethical minimum," as Mandelstam put it, of the minorities treaties was generalizable to all states, thereby overcoming the objection that it was an imperial imposition, as it once was. Besides, he wrote in 1931, the example of the Soviet Republics showed that minorities could oppress majorities.[73] In 1933 and 1934, Frangulis, as Haiti's representative at the League, tabled a resolution for the adoption of the Institute's declaration as the basis of a convention to protect human rights, but decided against putting it to a vote when he discerned little support in the League's Assembly. Whether this was a turning point in the manner of Lemkin's claim about the failure to adopt his proposed crimes of "barbarism" and "vandalism" at the same time is difficult to say, because international conventions were hardly likely to deter totalitarian regimes. We do know that Mandelstam remains virtually unknown despite proposing human rights

---

[72] Andre Mandelstam, "La protection des minorites," *Recueil des Cours de Academie de droit international* 1 (1923): 368–519; Mandelstam, *Le Sort de l'Empire Ottoman*, 444.

[73] Mandelstam, "Das Problem der Menschen- und Bürgerrechte im *Institut de Droit International*," *Die Friedens-Warte* 28 (1928): 350–4. Paul Gorden Lauren, *The Evolution of International Human Rights Visions Seen*, 2nd ed. (Philadelphia: University of Pennsylvania Press, 2003), 130–1; Jan-Herman Burgers, "The Road to San Francisco: The Revival of the Human Rights Idea in the Twentieth Century," *Human Rights Quarterly* 14, no. 4 (1992): 450–9; Helmut Philipp Aust, "From Diplomat to Academic Activist: André Mandelstam and the History of Human Rights," *European Journal of International Law* 25 no. 4 (2015): 1105–21.

protections well before Lemkin proposed such measures.[74] As we will see in the next chapters, the separate debate about Nazi war crimes propelled the genocide concept into prominence.

Also before Lemkin, Rappaport, at the International Association of Penal Law conference in 1927, suggested that propaganda inciting warfare be categorized as "a new international crime," not only to defend state security, but also for the protection "of a *new international good – of the safety of culture and the world civilization.*" Invoking the familiar vocabulary of the language of transgression, he declared that such a law "imposes itself on the public conscience."[75] Again, it was the (revisionist) state that, at least regarding warfare, was imperiling culture and world civilization. He deemed culture and world civilization "a new international good," gesturing to the relationship between the two that we saw in Victorian liberals and Robinson from whom Lemkin drew this ideal. Rappaport and his colleagues in the Association were implicitly importing from the domain of the laws of war the Hague Convention's and Commission on Responsibility's invocation of "the laws of humanity" and concern for civilians into international criminal law. A balanced, non-Lemkin-centric reading of the origins of genocide could draw a line from their conceptualization about state criminality against races, culture, and civilization in the 1920s to Pella's and de Vabres's involvement in the UN formulation of the Genocide Convention 20 years later. Such a reading is all too rare.[76]

Terrorism and Political Crimes

For these lawyers, the postwar order was threatened not only by renewed warfare waged by revisionist states unhappy with the Treaty of Versailles's new borders, but also by terrorism: attacks on states by communists and anarchists inspired by the Bolshevik victory in Russia. The problem was compounded by the fact that revisionist states sponsored or at least tolerated terrorist groups that carried out acts abroad. Most Ustaša Croatian fascists, for instance, lived abroad, mainly in Italy, Hungary, and Germany. With a Macedonian terrorist group that also wanted to secede from Yugoslavia, they participated in the assassination of its Serb King in Marseilles, France, in 1934.[77] Assassinations

---

[74] Herman Burgers, "André Mandelstam, Forgotten Pioneer of International Human Rights," in *Rendering Justice to the Vulnerable*, ed. Fons Coomans et al. (The Hague: Kluwer, 2000), 69–82.

[75] E. S. Rappaport, "Presente au sujet de le propaganda de la guerre d'agression," in *Conférence internationale d'unification du droit pénal (Varsovie, 1er-5 novembre 1927)* (Paris: Recueil Sirey 1929), 40. Emphasis in original.

[76] Lewis, *The Birth of the New Justice.*

[77] R. W. Seton-Watson, "King Alexander's Assassination: Its Background and Effects," *International Affairs* 14, no. 1 (1935): 20–47; Max Bergholz, *Violence as a Generative*

of officials and sabotage of infrastructure was thus international lawyers' main concern. Accordingly, legal reforms that underwrote state security rather than the civil and political rights of citizens was their predominant concern.[78] At its 1927 meeting, the International Association of Penal Law resolved to contrive the category of "international crimes (*delictum juris gentium*)" that presented a "common danger" to all states, like piracy, slavery, pornography, the drugs trade, counterfeiting money, disrupting international communication, and spreading diseases. As we know, some of these had been long the subject of international agreements, and constituted *jus cogens*, or peremptory, norms of general international law from which it is impossible to derogate.[79]

Central to the question of terrorism was the law and practice of extradition. Already in 1926, Pella broached the problem of terrorists fleeing to another state that would not extradite them. Buried in the question of extradition was the thorny question of political crimes for, since the French Revolution, European states generally would not extradite individuals accused of criminal acts with political motivations. In this way, political crimes were removed from the category of common criminality, with the exception of assassins (successful or not): the criminal and the political were distinct categories. The language of transgression both enabled and limited this construction. Thus the 1927 French extradition law adopted the 1892 resolutions of the Institute of International Law in blocking the extradition of parties to insurrection or civil war unless their "acts constitute acts of odious barbarity and of vandalism forbidden by the laws of war." The law thereby introduced the standards of international armed conflict into domestic ones as Rappaport did the same year with his declaration of a new international good.[80]

The category of the political became progressively restricted after the world war, especially in relation to anarchist crimes, effectively criminalizing revolutionary activity. The general view was that acts cannot be political if accompanied by atrocities, signaled by the mention of barbarism and

---

Force: Identity, Nationalism, and Memory in a Balkan Community (Ithaca, NY: Cornell University Press, 2016), 61–2.

[78] Lewis, *The Birth of the New Justice*, 123–4; Claudia Kraft, *Europa im Blick der polnischen Juristen: Rechtsordnung und juristische Profession im Spannungsfeld zwischen Nation und Europa 1918–1939* (Frankfurt: Klostermann, 2002), 304.

[79] For the construction of these as "international crimes," see Paul Knepper, *The Invention of International Crime: A Global Issue in the Making, 1881–1914* (Basingstoke: Palgrave Macmillan, 2010); Umut Özsu, "An Anti-Imperialist Universalism? *Jus Cogens* and the Politics of International Law," in *International Law and Empire: Historical Explorations*, ed. Martti Koskenniemi, Walter Rech, and Manuel Jiménez Fonseca (Oxford: Oxford University Press, 2016), 295–314.

[80] Lora L. Deere, "Political Offenses in the Law and Practice of Extradition," *American Journal of International Law* 27 (1933): 247–8, 262–3; Hersch Lauterpacht, "Revolutionary Activities by Private Persons against Foreign States," *American Journal of International Law* 22, no. 1 (1928): 105–30.

vandalism: they were terroristic. These terms reflected the Eurocentrism of the language of transgression: barbarism onomatopoeically reproduced the primitive language of non-Greeks ("bar-bar"), while vandalism referred to the Eastern Germanic peoples (the Vandals) who conquered Rome – civilization itself – in the fifth century, BC.[81] Pella mentioned the categories of savagery and vandalism during the League of Nations deliberations about an anticounterfeiting convention in 1929, distinguishing them from the nonviolent but equally terroristic effect of forging currency. He insisted that counterfeiting could not be considered a political offence because it was not "directed exclusively against the political and social organisation of a particular State."[82] The policy intentions of this demarcation were sound, he thought, namely to render illegitimate the conduct of politics by excessive violence or attacks on the common good, like undermining a currency, which Pella said "affected the interest which every country had in ensuring the security of international circulation."[83] The significant conceptual operation was that actions deemed terroristic – whether authored by state or nonstate actors – were not categorized as political but as criminal, instead of both.

Some tried to limit criminality to nonstate actors. Quintiliano Saldaña distinguished political crimes from terrorism by ascribing the former to citizens and the latter to aliens: "the political criminal will necessarily be a subject of the State, a national, while the terrorist is often a foreigner, sometimes a stateless person, anarchist, or nomad, shirker, expelled by all parties as undesirable, a mercenary."[84] This strict demarcation made sense for states that engaged in liberal permanent security: the violent potential of their self-preservation could be hidden from view by criminalizing terrorist actors and regimes but reserving the right to extralegal action in exceptional circumstances in the name of humanity and civilization.

Having placed international crimes on the agenda in 1927, the International Association for Penal Law spent subsequent years deliberating about their

---

[81] David Kazanjian, "Re-flexion: Genocide in Ruins," *Discourse* 33, no. 3 (2011): 367–70. The author excoriates Lemkin for excluding European colonial violence from his notion of civilization, but in fact Lemkin wrote extensively on the subject. See Dominik J. Schaller and Jürgen Zimmerer, eds., *The Origins of Genocide: Raphael Lemkin as a Historian of Mass Violence* (Abingdon and New York: Routledge, 2009).

[82] League of Nations, Proceedings of the International Conference for the Adoption of a Convention for the Suppression of Counterfeiting Currency, Geneva, 9th April to 20th April 1929 (Series of League of Nations Publications, II: Economic and Financial, 1929), 53; Lewis, *The Birth of the New Justice*, 188.

[83] Proceedings of the International Conference for the Adoption of a Convention for the Suppression of Counterfeiting Currency, 53.

[84] Chris Millington, "Immigrants and Undesirables: 'Terrorism' and the 'Terrorist' in 1930s France," *Critical Studies on Terrorism* 12, no. 1 (2019): 40–59.; Quintiliano Saldaña, "Le terrorisme," *Revue international de droit pénal* 13 (1936): 26–38.

definition and codification. The Belgian delegate introduced the notion of "terrorism" for such general dangers at the Brussels conference in 1930, linking the creation of common danger with "manifesting or achieving political or social ideals." Lemkin, who was no opponent of assassinations carried out in the right spirit, argued at the 1931 meeting in Paris that the question of the terrorist's intention should be disregarded; it was the creation of a "common danger" to human communications (postal, telegraphic, transport, etc.) that mattered. He followed Pella and others in maintaining that "political and social terrorism" could not protect a perpetrator from extradition, indeed, the common criminal and political fanatic were as dangerous when committing the same violations of international security.[85] Terrorism was effectively not a political crime, irrespective of the motivations.

Lemkin continued this line of argument two years later in his well-known submission to the association's Madrid conference. (In fact, his supplementary report, discussed below, is the more quoted text because it elaborates his insertion of barbarism and vandalism into the list of international crimes.[86]). In keeping with the imperative of international solidity, he also published articles on Nazi law that criticized its claims that law expressed the *völkisch* particularities of a people, an argument that had echoes among nationalist Poles who emphasized their national legal traditions.[87] A member of the Jewish minority, he was compelled to advocate for international and universal legal norms despite his own Zionist commitment to Jewish cultural particularity. And given rising antisemitism in Europe, including Poland, it is no surprise that Lemkin combined the common vocabulary of barbarism and

---

[85] "Rapport de M. Lemkin," in *Actes de la IV Conférence pour l'Unification du Droit Penal* (Paris: A. Pedone, 1933), 65; Claudia Kraft, "Völkermord als *delictum iuris gentium*: Raphael Lemkins Vorarbeiten für eine Genozidkonvention in der Zwischenkriegszeit," *Simon Dubnow Institute Yearbook* 4 (2005): 79–98; Daniel Marc Segesser and Miriam Gessler, "Raphael Lemkin and the International Debate on the Punishment of War Crimes (1919–1948)," *Journal of Genocide Research* 7, no. 4 (2005): 453–68; Lewis, *The Birth of the New Justice*, 123.

[86] The original is Raphael Lemkin, "Rapport et projet de textes" (sometimes titled "Terrorisme" or "Le terorisme") in *Acte de la V-me Conférence pour l'Unification du Droit Penal (Madrid, 19–20 October 1933)*, ed. Luis Jimenez de Asua, Vespasien Pella, and Manuel Lopez-Rey Arroyo (Paris: A. Pedone, 1935), 48–56. The supplement is called "Les actes constituant un danger general (interétatique) consideres comme delites des droit des gens": Explications additionelles au Rapport spécial présentè à la V-me Conférence pour l'Unification du Droit Penal à Madrid (14-20.X.1933) (Paris: A. Pedone, 1935). The English translation by James T. Fussell, "Acts Constituting a General (Transnational) Danger considered as Crimes under International Law," appears at www.preventgenocide .org/lemkin/madrid1933-english.htm. There is also an abridged German translation of the supplement published as "Akte der Barbarei und des Vandalismus als *delicta juris gentium*," *Internationales Anwaltsblatt* 6 (1933): 117–19.

[87] Kraft, *Europa im Blick der polnischen Juristen*, 315; Kraft, "Völkermord als *delictum iuris gentium*," 17.

vandalism used by Pella with Rappaport's new "international good" to protect minorities threatened by fascist regimes – even by the Polish one that renounced its minority treaty in 1934.

Vandalism and Barbarism

In his 1933 formulation, Lemkin defined vandalism as "the evil destruction of works of art and culture," that is, "great" art of international significance. Such violations, he concluded in familiar language, "demonstrated not only a highly anti-social behavior but also a specific savagery that places its author outside the entire civilized world."[88] He then moved on to "acts of barbarism," in which he invoked a recent paper by Pella that effectively reprised the 1919 Commission on Responsibility: "massacres, pogroms, collective cruelties against women and children, treatment of people that violates their dignity and humiliates them." The violence must be systematic, be directed against at a specific collective that is helpless and defenseless, and it must be intended to intimidate the population. Particularly savage attacks "evoke therefore a vivid reaction in the conscience of the entire civilized world," he continued in the customary idiom of international lawyers. "The opinion of the entire world despises it and worries about the future of world culture." Such indignation crossed borders: "Humanitarianism, like ferocity, has its spatial expansion."[89]

For all the high-octane rhetoric, it is striking how Lemkin's earlier objections to the political definition of terrorism dominate his exposition. He doubted whether criminalizing terrorism made sense because it was a political rather than legal concept that would sow discord among states that inevitably differed in their assessment of terrorist motivations. It was better, he thought, to enumerate particular crimes or the criterion of representing a general danger to the international community. Their universal repression would ensure that "international solidarity" and "civilized humanity" were not disrupted.[90] This was an argument Lemkin overturned 10 years later when he proposed genocide as a generic, legal concept.

The discussion of his innovation amounts to one-and-a-half pages of his nine-page text, and the two new articles were added after two familiar ones about international communication: they were not the focus of his initial submission. It is for this reason perhaps that the supplementary essay elaborated and prioritized his innovation. In it, Lemkin again underlined the importance of highlighting crimes that presented a transnational danger to several states and their populations: "international crimes" and not just a "public danger" as suggested at the 1927 Warsaw conference. To offend the

---

[88] Lemkin, "Rapport et projet de textes," 54.   [89] Ibid., 55.
[90] Ibid., 52. Kraft, *Europa im Blick der polnischen Juristen*, 312–14.

law of nations, the international community itself needed to be imperiled, he argued, invoking Stoic themes. In the place of terrorism, he now proposed a more dramatic amendment to those crimes listed in Warsaw, beginning with his innovations[91]:

a) acts of barbarity
b) acts of vandalism
c) provocation of catastrophes in international communications
d) intentional interruption of international communications
e) propagation of human, animal or vegetable contagions.

Attacks on individuals' human rights did not qualify as barbarity unless they also pertained to their relationship to collectivities; that is, barbarity entails attacking individuals because of their group membership. "Offenses of this type bring harm not only to human rights," he explained, "but also and most especially they undermine the fundamental basis of the social order."[92] They present a transnational danger because, like a "social psychosis" and "epidemics, they can pass from one country to another," triggering the need for "consecutive responses." The invocation of refugee flows and consequent economic disruption was a concrete threat to the international order. To the "acts of extermination" that he listed in his previous report, he added "actions undertaken to ruin the economic existence of the members of a collectivity, etc.," and specified the target: "ethnic, religious or social collectivities whatever the motive (political, religious, etc.)."[93] He likewise added further detail to his notion of vandalism. It meant "systematic and organized destruction of the art and cultural heritage in which the unique genius and achievement of a collectivity are revealed in fields of science, arts and literature." Vandalism counted as an international crime because it violated "world culture as a whole." As with barbarism, the stoic notion of an international community was as much the victim as an individual person or culture.[94]

Although Lemkin mentioned political motives, the thrust of the argument was to depoliticize the crimes by using the loaded notion of "hatred" in the formal definition of barbarism and vandalism: "Whoever, out of hatred towards a racial, religious or social collectivity or with the goal of its extermination ..." The criminal, as opposed to political motivations, were likewise underlined in his summary of the new crimes in the classical terms of the language of transgression:

> In the acts of barbarity, as well as in those of vandalism, the asocial and destructive spirit of the author is made evident. This spirit, by definition,

---

[91] Lemkin, "Acts Constituting a General (Transnational) Danger considered as Crimes under International Law."
[92] Ibid.   [93] Ibid.   [94] Ibid.

is the opposite of the culture and progress of humanity. It throws the evolution of ideas back to the bleak period of the Middle Ages. Such acts shock the conscience of all humanity, while generating extreme anxiety about the future. For all these reasons, acts of vandalism and barbarity must be regarded as offenses against the law of nations.[95]

Confusingly, he listed these crimes, in which the perpetrator would be states, with others about disrupting communications and transport in which perpetrators would be terrorists attacking states. Lemkin's importation of rhetoric from the laws of armed conflict into this domain of international law did not resonate with his colleagues, and his proposal was omitted from the commission's agenda.[96] Even so, Lemkin was attacked by both nationalists in Poland and the Soviets, who felt they were the objects of his innovation; he was forbidden from attending the Madrid meeting, and lost his position at the Warsaw prosecutors office at a time when the Polish state was pushing Jews out of state employment.[97]

Lemkin did take up these themes in *Axis Rule* 11 years later, but there was no straight line despite his claims to the contrary. In view of the Madrid rebuke and the initiative of the League of Nations to formulate a convention on terrorism after dramatic assassinations of state leaders in 1934, Lemkin dropped the stipulations of barbarism and vandalism in his conference presentation in 1935. He was now concerned above all to distinguish between domestic and international terrorism, both of which were directed against the state and populations: "Terrorism in the broadest sense of this term is to intimidate people with acts of violence," he wrote.[98] He followed Pella in supporting efforts to promote peace and criminalize warfare. In many ways, he followed his senior peers.[99]

---

[95] Ibid.

[96] Segesser and Gessler, "Raphael Lemkin and the International Debate on the Punishment of War Crimes (1919–1948)," 458.

[97] Kraft, "Völkermord als *delictum iuris gentium*," 18; Irvin-Erickson, *Raphaël Lemkin and the Concept of Genocide*, 48; Anton Weiss-Wendt, *The Soviet Union and the Gutting of the Genocide Convention* (Madison and London: University of Wisconsin Press, 2017), 12.

[98] Raphael Lemkin, "Terrorisme," in *VI Conférence internationale pour l'unification du droit pénal (Copenhagen 31 August–2 September 1935)* (Paris: A. Pedone, 1938), 189. See also Bartolomé Clavero, *Genocide or Ethnocide, 1933–2007: How to Make, Unmake, and Remake Law with Words* (Milan: Giuffrè Editore, 2008), 25.

[99] Raphael Lemkin, *Terrorisme: Extrait des actes de la VIIème Conférence Internationale pour l'Unification du Droit Pénal, Copenhague, août-septembre, 1935* (Paris: A. Pedone, 1938); Lemkin, *La protection de la paix par le droit pénal, Rapport présenté au IVe Congrès International de Droit Pénal (Paris, 26–31 Juillet, 1937)* (Paris: Librairie Marchal et Billard, 1938); Ryszard Szawlowski, "Raphael Lemkin (1900–1959): The Polish Lawyer Who Created the Concept of 'Genocide,'" *Polish Quarterly of International Affairs*, no. 2 (2005): 115–17; Marek Kornat, "Rafał Lemkin's Formative Years and the Beginning of

Conclusion: Blindspots

Lemkin depoliticized the language of transgression by promoting the notion of hatred and racial categories, while evacuating terrorism of political content. It is no surprise that a biological assumption in Lemkin's thinking was there from the outset and flowed into his conception of nationhood. In 1934, he wrote about the biological propensity of criminals and the virtues of "criminal biology."[100] That is why he did not think assimilation was tantamount to genocide, arguing in *Axis Rule* that it treats "mainly the cultural, economic, and social aspects of genocide, leaving out the biological aspect, such as causing the physical decline and even destruction of the population involved." Nations, he continued, had a "biological essence."[101]

His legal proposals also offered no political explanation for state excesses other than "hatred," a force he presumably identified with the antisemitism and Pan-Germanism that he opposed. Nor were they as original as commonly supposed. From his contemporaries, Lemkin took the notions of barbarism, vandalism, the protection of culture, and international crimes. Before them, the Commission on Responsibility report, like the Hague Draft Rules on Air Warfare, also referred to terrorizing civilians. If anything, Lemkin was adapting – and simplifying and racializing – familiar themes in the language of transgression.

What is more, Lemkin's ethnic-tribal ontology of the human and related preoccupation with racial hatred led him to ignore other sinister developments that threatened to terrorize civilians. By the mid-1930s, fears of rivals' capacity to deliver a "knock-out blow" in preemptive bomber strikes on cities haunted military and civilian authorities.[102] Like Lemkin, American jurist John Bassett Moore (1860–1947), who chaired the Hague Commission in December 1922 considering international legal regulation of radio and aircraft, affirmed that, since the Middle Ages, civilization rested in part on distinguishing between combatants and civilians in warfare. Unlike Lemkin, he lamented

---

International Career in Inter-War Poland (1918–1939)," in Bieńczyk-Missala and Dębski, *Rafał Lemkin*, 59–73; Lewis, *The Birth of the New Justice*, 130, 190; Ben Saul, "The Legal Response of the League of Nations to Terrorism," *Journal of International Criminal Justice* 4 (2006): 78–102.

[100] Lemkin, 'O wprowadzenie ekspertyzy kriminalo-biologicznej do procesu karnego,' 137–44.

[101] Lemkin, *Axis Rule in Occupied Europe*, 80–1.

[102] Brett Holman, *The Next War in the Air: Britain's Fear of the Bomber, 1908–1941* (Farnham: Ashgate, 2014); Paul K. Saint-Amour, "Air War Prophecy and Interwar Modernism," *Comparative Literature Studies* 42, no. 2 (2005): 130–61; James S. Corum, "Airpower Thought in Continental Europe between the Wars," in *The Paths of Heaven: The Evolution of Airpower Theory*, ed. Phillip S. Meilinger (Maxwell Air Force Base: Air University Press, 1997), 151–81.

that World War I and the advent of modern weapons had eroded this basic principle.[103] The reasons for this erosion were explicate and supported by the American lawyer and air force pilot, Frank Quindry, in 1931:

> Considering the economic structure of a nation during a modern war and the conscriptive systems which will probably be employed by all nations, it is difficult to determine whether the civilian who helps supply the fighting forces is any less dangerous to the success of the opposing army than the soldier who operates the mechanical instruments of destruction.[104]

In fact, Quindry had no doubt about the matter, continuing that "history discredit[s] the idea of a distinction between combatants and non-combatants . . .. Logically, there is no reason to regard him as less an offender than the soldier, or sailor or airmen who wields the weapons of destruction."[105] For many military thinkers, civilians were dangerous "offenders" and thus military objectives. However squeamish some leaders were about strategic bombing of cities, and thus civilians, because the civilized norm prohibited "terrorizing the civilian population" as a policy objective, the collective guilt argument would be too tempting to resist in the next world war.[106]

International lawyers resisted this reasoning. Representative was James W. Garner (1871–1938), a prodigious commentator on legal issues pertaining international armed conflict who taught at the University of Illinois. Reflecting on the Hague Draft Rules on Air Warfare in 1924, he observed that the bombing of civilians, civilian infrastructure, private property, and historical monuments during World War I "aroused a feeling of horror against which the conscience of mankind everywhere revolted."[107] Already then, he had discerned that "terrorization of the civilian inhabitant" was strategic bombing's aim, and that, far from demoralizing the enemy, by "their very barbarity is rather more likely to intensify the hatred of the people against whom they are directed." Thus, while he recognized that workers in arms manufacture

---

[103] John Bassett Moore, *International Law and Some Current Illusions and Other Essays* (New York; Macmillan, 1924), viii–ix, 3–6, 200–1.

[104] Frank E. Quindry, "Aerial Bombardment of Civilian and Military Objectives," *Journal of Air Law and Commerce* 2, no. 4 (1931): 494–5.

[105] Ibid., 495. A study of the US air force's view of bombing as progressive and humane, see Mark Clodfelter, *Beneficial Bombing: The Progressive Foundations of American Air Power, 1917–1945* (Lincoln: University of Nebraska Press, 2010).

[106] Article 22, The Hague Rules of Air Warfare, 1923: https://wwi.lib.byu.edu/index.php/The_Hague_Rules_of_Air_Warfare.

[107] James W. Garner, "Proposed Rules for the Regulation of Aerial Warfare," *American Journal of International Law* 18, no. 1 (1924): 64.

could be a legitimately targeted, he feared the logic of escalating reprisal would "cause war to degenerate into a struggle of reciprocal barbarism."[108]

This important debate about civilian immunity, so portentous for the next world war and the nuclear age, bypassed Lemkin completely. He did not respond to the obvious implications of the practices of "total war" during World War I – the bombing of cities and blockades that led to the starvation of hundreds of thousands – that a military thinker like German general Erich Ludendorff (1865–1937) systematized in his *Der totale Krieg* (*Total War*) in 1935.[109] During the next world war, 600,000 civilians would die from aerial bombing, and another million would be maimed, while European cities lay in ruins. Some 400,000 Japanese perished from US bombing.[110] Death by starvation due to sieges, like the German siege of Leningrad (September 1941 to January 1942), also resulted in hundreds of thousands more civilian deaths, and were not regarded as war crimes by the American judges after the war because they did not violate the Hague Convention of 1907.[111]

Lemkin's ignoring of these developments is not surprising given that the British and French had vehemently resisted the efforts of neutral countries and the Red Cross in 1921 to limit the right of blockade that the British had used to great effect against Germany during World War I. Like the air-war theorists, defenders of blockades argued that civilian starvation was more humane than trench warfare; if it led to an earlier cessation of hostilities, the price was worthwhile. They also argued that blockade was a legitimate sanction for the League of Nations to apply to recalcitrant states. It was thus an instrument of enforcing international law and agreements rather than representing a

---

[108] Ibid., 65. See generally Thomas Hippler, *Bombing the People: Giulio Douhet and the Foundations of Air-Power Strategy, 1884–1939* (Cambridge: Cambridge University Press, 2013).

[109] Erich Ludendorff, *Der totale Krieg* (Munich: Ludendorrfs Verlag, 1935); Richard Overy, *The Bombing War: Europe, 1939–1945* (London: Penguin, 2013), i.

[110] Ian Patterson, *Guernica and Total War* (Cambridge, MA: Harvard University Press, 2007); Yuki Tanaka and Marilyn Young, eds., *Bombing Civilians: A Twentieth-Century History* (New York: New Press, 2009); Andrew Barros, "The Problems of Opening Pandora's Box: Strategic Bombing and the Civil–Military Divide, 1916–1939," in *The Civilization of War: The Changing Civil–Military Divide, 1914–2014*, ed. Andrew Barros and Martin Thomas (Cambridge: Cambridge University Press, 2018), 165–80; John W. Dower, *War without Mercy: Race and Power in the Pacific War* (New York: W. W. Norton, 1986), 41. Thanks to Sheldon M. Garon for clarification on these statistics. See his "On the Transnational Destruction of Cities: What Japan and the United States Learned from the Bombing of Britain and Germany in the Second World War," *Past and Present* (February 19, 2020): 1–38, https://doi.org/10.1093/pastj/gtz054.

[111] United Nations War Crimes Commission, *Law Reports of the Trials of War Criminals*, Vol. XII, *The German High Command Trials* (London: HMSO, 1949), 84, 563; David Marcus, "Famine Crimes in International Law," *American Journal of International Law* 97, no. 2 (2003): 245–81.

perfidious means of civilian destruction that should be criminalized.[112] The Western powers were thus happy to elide the distinction between combatants and civilians in enforcing international rules that suited them. On the eve of World War II, the future architect of the British welfare state, William Beveridge (1879–1963), pressed home this point in arguing that "totalitarian warfare" implicated the entire population, which was thus targetable. Besides, he continued, any blame for starvation was attributable to how the blockaded state distributed food rather than to the blockading state.[113]

Likewise, that the Hague Rules on air war that Moore's commission proposed in 1923 were not ratified by states, especially Britain and the US, is a turning point in international law not mentioned in the same breath as the failure of League of Nation organizations to criminalize the destruction of their minorities: certainly not by Lemkin.[114] He regarded these powers as progressive forces in history, and was thus blinded to their liberal permanent security measures in which they enjoyed a comparative advantage: aerial warfare and naval blockades that were driven by the same logic of military necessity – killing enemy civilians until the enemy state surrendered. As we will see in Chapters 5, 10, and 11, defenders of this logic distinguished it from genocide by referring to the greater good of "civilization" (or antitotalitarianism).

Lemkin also missed another development in illiberal permanent security: the fascist mode of conducting war in the 1930s: the Japanese invasion of China, the Italian invasion of Abyssinia in 1935, and the Spanish Civil War. These were effectively wars of extermination that targeted the enemy population as a whole with aerial bombing, murderous mistreatment of prisoners, and, in the Japanese and Italian cases, extensive settlement projects that aimed to replace the local populations by deportation and starvation measures. The Japanese forced resettlements in northern China cost the lives of 2.3 million locals, while up to 10 million Asian civilians died at the hands of Japanese imperial ambitions. The Italians built concentration camps, bombed villages, and used poison gas against civilians, killing or causing the death by starvation of over 10 percent of the population of 800,000. German military elites carefully observed these campaigns in developing their own radical conception of annihilatory warfare that disregarded both international treaties and the

---

[112] Nicholas Mulder and Boyd van Dijk, "Why Did Starvation Not Become the Paradigmatic War Crime in International Law?" in *Contingency and the Course of International Law*, ed. Kevin Jon Heller and Ingo Venzke (Oxford: Oxford University Press, 2021).

[113] William Beveridge, *Blockade and the Civilian Population* (Oxford: Clarendon Press, 1939), 26–7, 31. Thanks to Boyd van Dijk for drawing my attention to this book.

[114] Hanke, "The 1923 Hague Rules of Air Warfare." Some states initially adhered to the Rules voluntarily, but this restraint soon disappeared as World War II dragged on.

Geneva and Hague Conventions. They were particularly interested in Italian fascist settlement projects in North Africa.[115] Lemkin had nothing to say about these dramatic projects that were so devastating to civilians, but it was not as if others ignored them. When Germany invaded Poland in 1939, the US president, Franklin Delano Roosevelt (1882–1945) warned belligerents not to bombard "civilian populations or . . . unfortified cities," because such "ruthless bombing" in the recent past was a "form of barbarism" and had "profoundly shocked the conscience of humanity."[116]

By contrast, Lemkin was more interested in intrastate violence against minorities, like Jews, and state terrorism. He wanted to make these international crimes, rather than the laws of war that were the basis for the prosecution of Nazis. His own later writing in *Axis Rule*, with its conception of genocide, ended up having to draw on these laws, and had little legally to do with his 1933 formulation.

---

[115] Sven Reichardt, "National Socialist Assessments of Global Fascist Warfare (1935–1938)," and Amedeo Osti Guerrazzi, "Cultures of Total Annihilation? The German, Italian, and Japanese Armies During the Second World War," in *Fascist Warfare, 1922–1945*, ed. Miguel Alonso, Alan Kramer, and Javier Rodrigo (Basingstoke: Palgrave Macmillan, 2019), 51–72, 119–42.

[116] Quoted in Sahr Conway-Lanz, "The Ethics of Bombing Civilians After World War II: The Persistence of Norms Against Targeting Civilians in the Korean War," *Asia-Pacific Journal* 12, no. 1 (2014): 2.

4

The Many Types of Destruction

British codebreakers intercepted German cables detailing mass executions of civilians, especially of Jews, soon after the German invasion of the Soviet Union in June 1941. Two months later, British Prime Minister Winston Churchill made a BBC broadcast to condemn them: "Since the Mongol invasions of Europe, there has never been methodical, merciless butchery on such a scale or approaching such a scale," he declared. "We are in the presence of *a crime without a name*." This famous rhetorical flourish has often been taken to refer to the Holocaust, with Lemkin naming that crime as "genocide." But Churchill mentioned "Soviet patriots," meaning the civilian population in general rather than Jews in particular.[1]

These crimes actually did have a name, even names. Terrorism was the common term in the language of transgression to refer to excesses against civilians. It had featured in the Commission on Responsibility report as the first listed crime: "Murders and massacres; systematic terrorism."[2] Not for nothing did contemporaries calls Nazis "terrorists" who committed atrocities

---

[1] Michael Smith, "Bletchley Park and the Holocaust," in *Understanding Intelligence in the Twenty-First Century: Journeys in Shadows*, ed. Peter Jackson and L. V. Scott (London: Routledge, 2004), 113. Emphasis added. Prominent examples of this view are Samantha Power, *"A Problem from Hell": America in the Age of Genocide* (New York: Basic Books, 2002), ch. 2, and William A. Schabas, *Genocide in International Law*, 1st ed. (Cambridge: Cambridge University Press, 2000), 14. Churchill's decision not to mention Jews, although he even circled the word "Jews" in the reports, is the subject of historiographical debate. The salient factors include the limitation of information to police reports, which did not necessarily reveal a broader exterminatory plan, and the desire not to let the Germans know that their code had been broken. Impatient with such rationalizations is Richard Breitman, *Official Secrets: What the Nazis Planned, What the British and Americans Knew* (New York: Hill and Wang, 1999), 92–6. See also Stephen Budiansky, *Battle of Wits: The Complete Story of Codebreaking in World War II* (New York: Simon and Schuster, 2002), 199–201, and Michael Fleming, *Auschwitz, the Allies and Censorship of the Holocaust* (Cambridge: Cambridge University Press, 2014), ch. 5.

[2] "Report of the Commission on Responsibility of the Authors of the War and Enforcement of Penalties," in *Violation of the Laws and Customs of War, Reports of Majority and Dissenting Reports of American and Japanese Members of the Commission of Responsibilities*, Conference of Paris, 1919 (Oxford: Clarendon, 1919), 17.

and war crimes. Soviet Foreign Minister Molotov's diplomatic note to the Allies in January 1942 referred to the German Army's "bloody terrorism" in repeating, almost verbatim, Las Casian phrases about tortured Soviet prisoners.[3] A few months before, in October 1941, the US president Roosevelt condemned German reprisal killings of hostages as "terrorism," likewise denouncing the "frightfulness" of their quest for "*lebensraum* and *new order*."[4] The common assumption was that such atrocities occurred when terrorists took over states and made them instruments of their will. The Nazis provided plenty of evidence for this interpretation, whether by terrorizing designated regime opponents after 1933 or in the brutal invasion of Poland in 1939.[5] Other states soon came under the Nazi heel. The entirety of Czechoslovakia was occupied that year after the annexation of the Sudetenland region in 1938, and France was defeated in 1940. In November that year, the Polish government and Provisional Czechoslovak government issued a declaration about the "destruction of our two ancient nations" that listed many crimes and ended with the familiar hyperbole from the language of transgression:

> the expulsions of the native population from large areas of its secular homelands, the banishing of hundreds of thousands of men and women to the interior of Germany as forced labour, mass executions and deportations to the concentration camps, the plundering of public and private properties, the extermination of the intellectual class and of all manifestation of the culture life, the spoliation of the treasure of science and art and the persecution of all religious beliefs – are unparalleled in all human history.[6]

The governments were echoing the spirit of Churchill, who a few days before condemned German atrocities in occupied Europe, "and above all

---

[3] V. M. Molotov, *Notes and Statement by the Soviet Government on the German Atrocities* (Moscow: Foreign Languages Publishing House, 1943), 3–8.

[4] Franklin D. Roosevelt, *The Public Papers and Addresses of Franklin D. Roosevelt, Vol. 11, Humanity on the Defensive, 1942, Foreword and Compiled by Samuel I. Rosenman* (New York: Random House, 1950), 331. Emphasis in the original. The US ambassador in London likewise wrote of "German terrorism." The Ambassador in the United Kingdom (Winant) to the Secretary of State, December 7, 1942, in Foreign Relations of the United States, 1942, Vol. I, General, The British Commonwealth, The Far East (Washington, DC: Government Printing Office, 1980), 66. He referred to the newspaper article, "Terror Against Jews: European Pogrom," *The Times*, December 7, 1942, 3.

[5] Alexander B. Rossino, *Hitler Strikes Poland: Blitzkrieg, Ideology, and Atrocity* (Lawrence: University of Kansas Press, 2002).

[6] "Declaration issued by the Polish Government and the Provisional Czechoslovak Government, November 1940," Robert H. Jackson Papers, Library of Congress, Nuremberg War Crimes Trial, Pre-Trial Material, Declarations of Intent to Punish War Criminals.

behind the German front in Russia," as surpassing "anything that has been known since the darkest and most bestial ages of mankind."[7]

The representatives of these and other occupied or invaded states who convened at the Inter-Allied Conference in St James Palace in London on January 13, 1942 also resorted to this vocabulary.[8] Their St James Declaration leant on the 1919 Commission on Responsibility report and the Molotov Note in decrying the German "policy of aggression" and "regime of terror." Consisting of "imprisonments, mass expulsions, execution of hostages and massacres," the German actions violated "the convention signed at The Hague in 1907 regarding laws and customs of land warfare."[9] Hague law, that is war crimes, was the legal category to understand and prosecute Nazi criminality in other countries. These leaders often complained that the failure to convict German war criminals after World War I emboldened their powerful neighbor to launch the current war. They would not permit a repetition of this failure, and for this reason they called their declaration "Punishment for War Crimes."[10]

The state leaders also signalled an expansive agenda at St James Palace: reforming international law by broadening the definition of war crimes. In denouncing the German aggression, they sought to criminalize the Nazi invasion as such: not just the mode of warfare (*jus in bello*), but its declaration (*jus ad bellum*), which had been the right of states for centuries.[11] What is more, conventional notions of war crimes did not fully cover Germany's permanent security policies: the German mode of occupation was bent on destroying their nations. The Czechs insisted that this process began with the

---

[7] Winston Churchill, "The Slaughter of Hostages," in *The Unrelenting Struggle: War Speeches by the Right Hon. Winston S. Churchill* (Boston: Little Brown and Co., 1942), 296.

[8] They were Belgium, the Free French National Committee, Greece, Luxemburg, Poland, Norway, the Netherlands, Czechoslovakia, and Yugoslavia. See "The Inter-Allied Conference, January 13, 1942," *Bulletin of International News* 19, no. 2 (1942): 50–3. Great Britain and its Dominions, the US, Soviet Union, China, and India were observers. On the governments in exile, see Daniel Bell and Leon Dennen, "The System of Governments in Exile," *Annals of the American Academy of Political and Social Science*, no. 232 (1944): 134–47, and Pavol Jakubec, "Together and Alone in Allied London: Czechoslovak, Norwegian and Polish Governments-in-Exile, 1940–1945," *International History Review* 42, no. 3 (2020): 465–84.

[9] "The Inter-Allied Conference, January 13, 1942," 50–1.

[10] *Punishment for War Crimes: The Inter-Allied Declaration Signed at St. James Palace, London, on* 13th *January, 1942 and Relative Documents* (London: HMSO, 1942).

[11] Signatories of the Kellog-Briand Pact (General Treaty for Renunciation of War) of 1928 renounced aggressive warfare, but many international lawyers disputed whether it constituted an international crime. See Oona Hathaway and Scott Shapiro, *The Internationalists: How a Radical Plan to Outlaw War Remade the World* (New York: Simon and Schuster, 2017). The January 1942 declaration echoed the Inter-Allied St James Agreement of June 1941 that referred to the "menace of aggression." See St James Agreement, June 12, 1941, http://avalon.law.yale.edu/imt/imtjames.asp.

German annexation of the Sudetenland territory of their country in 1938. Already in 1941, its government-in-exile had published an account of the German occupation that detailed "Germanisation," the persecution of the Christian Churches and Jews, "economic enslavement and robbery," and the "destruction of Czech schools and persecution of Czechoslovak cultural life."[12] In a phrase that would appear in Lemkin's writings, the St James Declaration's introduction noted that Nazi "crimes intended to cripple the vital forces of the nations they have temporarily subjugated."[13] The Greek prime minister's speech described "the methods of extermination practised in cold blood … with the object of bringing about, with famine as their grim ally, the destruction of the Greek population in order that Italians and Bulgars may establish themselves permanently."[14] These state leaders were convinced that their small nations were being destroyed.

A few months later, foreign ministers of these states wrote in similar terms to the US secretary of state: "the barbaric and unrelenting character of the occupational regime will become more marked, and may even lead to the extermination of certain populations."[15] These crimes, the Czech prime minister had said at the St James Conference, "cannot be classified either as acts of war or political crimes": indeed, this conviction was contained in the Declaration itself: "that acts of violence thus perpetrated against civilian populations are at variance with accepted ideas concerning acts of war and political offenses as these are understood by civilized nations." They were so extreme, concluded the Greek prime minister, that the excuse of obeying orders could be no defense: henceforth "A new principle of International Penal Law has come into being." For these reasons, stated his Polish counterpart, "the Declaration resolutely turns International Law in a new direction," even if "establishing all the details" would occur later.[16] Those details would bedevil inter-allied relations for the next three years, as did confusion about whether Nazi permanent security policies were political or nonpolitical. Aggression, crippling, enslavement, destruction, and extermination thus accompanied terrorism and war crimes as the terms for a prospective expansion of international law to cover the actions of Germany and its allies. There was little hope for "terrorism" to become the vehicle of this ambition, however, when the 1937 League of Nations Convention for the Prevention and

---

[12] Czechoslovak Ministry of Foreign Affairs, Department of Information, *Two Years of German Oppression in Czechoslovakia*, pref. Edvard Beneš (London: Unwin, 1941).
[13] *Punishment for War Crimes*, 3.   [14] Ibid., 10.
[15] The Netherlands Ambassador (London), the Luxembourg Minister (Le Callais), and the Yugoslav Minister (Fotitch) on behalf of the inter-allied governments to the US secretary of state, Washington, July 30, 1942, in Foreign Relations of the United States, 1942, Vol. I, *General, The British Commonwealth, The Far East* (Washington, DC: Government Printing Office, 1980), 46–7.
[16] *Punishment for War Crimes*, 9, 10, 5.

Punishment of Terrorism pertained to antistate terrorism and was not ratified.[17]

Raphael Lemkin screened out this discursive context to his invention of genocide so he could propose it as a miraculous creation, entirely of his imagination. He began the mythmaking about the origins of the genocide concept in May 1941 when he told a North Carolina Bar Association meeting of his dramatic appearance at the 1933 Madrid conference that rejected his barbarism and vandalism proposal. In fact, he had not been present. And while he spoke to the assembled North Carolina lawyers about the German occupation of Europe, he mentioned its mass transfer of property and other illegalities rather than mass violence.[18] The mythmaking continued two years later in *Axis Rule in Occupied Europe*, in which he referred to his 1933 formulation as tantamount "to the actual conception of genocide."[19] In establishing this lineage, Lemkin not only conveniently omitted his intellectual debts to Rappaport and Pella, but also disguised the fact that his new term derived from a different legal context. Whereas the terrorism debates of the League pertained to actions committed by states against their citizens and residents, Nazi crimes in neighboring countries related to the law of international armed conflict that were governed by the Hague and Geneva Conventions. That is why he chose the title *Axis Rule* for the book in which he introduced the genocide concept.[20] Its title and method reflected commonplace themes at the time.

Extending the Limits of International Law

The postwar coalition of inter-allied small nations and Jewish groups was neither inevitable nor natural given that the minority protection treaties were opposed by the former and supported by the latter.[21] The tension continued during the war when these states declined Jewish requests to contribute to

[17] On the convention, see Ben Saul, "The Legal Response of the League of Nations to Terrorism," *Journal of International Criminal Justice* 4 (2006): 78–102.

[18] Raphael Lemkin, "Law and Lawyers in the European Subjugated Countries," *Proceedings of the Forty-Fourth Annual Session of the North Carolina Bar Association*, ed. Allston Stubbs (Durham: Christian Printing Company, 1942), 112. He implies his presence at the Madrid meeting in his curriculum vitae at the time: "Raphael Lemkin, JD, Curriculum Vitae," no date, Duke University Archives, Box 9, School of Law Records, Dean Horack Correspondence, 1934–1947.

[19] Raphael Lemkin, *Axis Rule in Occupied Europe: Laws of Occupation, Analysis of Government, Proposals for Redress* (Washington, DC: Carnegie Endowment for International Peace, 1944), xiii, 91–2.

[20] See generally Anson Rabinbach, "The Challenge of the Unprecedented: Raphael Lemkin and the Concept of Genocide," *Jahrbuch des Simon-Dubnow-Instituts* 4 (2005): 397–420.

[21] Carole Fink, *Defending the Rights of Others: The Great Powers, the Jews, and International Minority Protection, 1878–1938* (Cambridge: Cambridge University Press, 2004).

deliberations at St James Palace, still less to recognize that "Jews [were] special victims of [the] inhuman and criminal policy of oppression of [the] civilian population," as the World Jewish Congress (WJC) put it.[22] To distinguish Jewish citizens in this way would be to play into the Nazi division of their population, reasoned state leaders. A publication of the Polish Ministry of Information went so far as to denounce the Nazi "tribal theory" of the Polish population, which categorized it according to sub-Slavic groups and Jews in colonial divide-and-rule style: that theory "is one of the many attempts to disintegrate, diminish and destroy the Polish nation."[23] Conceding the WJC request would also grant space to a nonstate actor without international legal personality – the WJC – that could open the door for other groups with disruptive consequences. Besides, these states did not think Jewish citizens were neglected: the Inter-Allied Information Committee in New York and official Polish and Czechoslovak organs published reports about the German occupation that featured the persecutions of Jews among other citizens.[24] This tension continued until Nuremberg, when the indictments of crimes against peace, war crimes, and crimes against humanity criminalized the invasion of Germany's neighbors and the destruction of their civilian populations, including the Holocaust.

These notions were being developed in the early 1940s in a transnational discussion between London, where the exiled government representatives rubbed shoulders with British lawyers and diplomats; New York and Washington, DC, where the WJC was developing its notion of war crimes in the teeth of State Department resistance; and Moscow, where Soviet scholars were conceptualizing the notion of aggressive warfare. At the same time, isolated at Duke University in North Carolina, Lemkin began to fashion his genocide notion. Like the inter-allied states and WJC, he was acutely conscious

---

[22] Stephen S. Wise and Nahum Goldman cable to Władysław Sikorski, Prime Minister of Poland, January 28, 1942. American Jewish Archive, World Jewish Congress Collection (AJA/WJC) C174–06 Nazi War Crimes, Reports and Correspondence, 1942–1944. On the tension between Polish and Jewish nationalisms, see David Engel, 'On Reconciling the Histories of Two Chosen Peoples', *American Historical Review* 114, no.4 (2009), 914–29.

[23] "The Work of Germanization in the General Gouvenement," *Polish Fortnightly Review*, no. 63 (March 1, 1943): 2.

[24] Inter-Allied Information Committee, *Persecution of the Jews*, Pamphlet 6 (London: HMSO, 1942); Polish Ministry of Information, *Bestiality ... Unknown in any Previous Record of History* (London: St. Clements Press, 1942); Henry Z. Lynn, "Biological Extermination of the Polish People," *Polish Review* 3, no. 38 (October 18, 1943): 3–5; Czechoslovak Ministry of Foreign Affairs, *Two Years of German Oppression in Czechoslovakia*, ch. 5, "Persecution of the Jews." On the churches, see H. E. Cardinal Hlond, *The Persecution of the Catholic Church in German-Occupied Poland: Reports Presented by H. E. Cardinal Hlond, Primate of Poland, to Pope Pius XII, Vatican Broadcasts, and Other Reliable Evidence*, pref. H. E. A. Cardinal Hinsley (London: Burn Oates, 1941).

that the Nazis were violating the Hague Conventions; the Germans and their allies were unquestionably guilty of multiple war crimes, he pointed out in *Axis Rule*. Lemkin similarly thought it necessary to transcend the Hague regime, because it was "silent regarding the preservation of the integrity of a people."[25] As he put it to a member of the US War Department in 1941, the Germans "do not recognize the principle accepted by other countries and inherent in the Hague Conventions, that wars are directed against sovereigns and armies. In their opinion, wars should be directed against subjects and civilians – in other words, against peoples."[26] Intuiting the Nazi permanent security project, he observed that it "intends to change the whole population structure of Europe for a thousand years. ... Certain nations and races will disappear completely or be crippled indefinitely." Consequently, he concluded, the current situation differed from World War I and the response of the Commission on Responsibility, namely "preventing isolated and wanton atrocities even on a large scale, as occurred in Belgium and France in 1914."[27]

The inability of Hague law to protect the principal targets of Nazi policy – nations as such – was anomalous, Lemkin implied, because of the minority protection treaties after World War I. Since "nations are essential elements of the world community," the law should be changed to protect them from the likes of the revolutionary German occupation.[28] His book was intended both to document and reconceptualize Axis crimes for postwar prosecution and to reform international law. In the meantime, he invoked the famous Martens Clause of the Hague Convention throughout *Axis Rule* to proscribe Nazi attacks on occupied civilians not covered by the Convention's specific articles.[29] Indeed, he had focused on the clause in his address to the North Carolina Bar Association in May 1942, underlining the status of "conscience" as a marker of "civilization," from which the Turks had distanced themselves by their "Armenian massacres" during World War I, and that Germans had consistently violated by subordinating law to "the idea of domination of the

---

[25] For example, it did not cover underlying Nazi aims embedded in policies like preventing marriages and subsidizing children fathered by occupation soldiers. Lemkin, *Axis Rule*, 32–3, 90, 92. Ramsay Moran, review of Raphael Lemkin, *Axis Rule in Occupied Europe*, in *Virginia Law Review* 31, no. 3 (1945): 730–3.

[26] Raphael Lemkin, *Totally Unofficial: The Autobiography of Raphael Lemkin*, ed. Donna-Lea Frieze (New Haven: Yale University Press, 2013), 108.

[27] Ibid., 109.   [28] Lemkin, *Axis Rule in Occupied Europe*, 90–1.

[29] Ibid., ix, x, 12–3, 23, 24, 30–1, 73, 74. "The treatment of the Jews in the occupied countries is one of the most flagrant violations of international law, not only of the specific articles of the Hague Regulations, but also of the principles of the laws of nations as they have emerged from the established usage among civilized nations, from the laws of humanity, and from the dictates of public conscience – laws that the occupant is equally bound to respect" (77).

world."[30] As we will see below, the meaning of the Martens Clause became the bone of contention between the small nations of the Inter-Allied Commission and WJC on the one side, and the British and Americans on the other.

In arguing for amendments of the Hague Conventions, Lemkin was seeking to deal with the "problem of genocide ... as a whole," whether in war- or peacetime, not by expanding the definition of war crimes but by inventing a "generic notion."[31] Some historians think that in doing so Lemkin illegitimately conflated distinctions in policies toward Jews and non-Jews because he did not fully understand Nazi antisemitic ambitions.[32] In fact, he was well aware of the distinctive Jewish experience; eliding this distinction was the point of his new concept. Despite fleeing his native Poland in 1939, he was broadly informed about subsequent Nazi rule, devoting a separate chapter (eight) to the Nazi treatment of Jews in *Axis Rule* that outlined the "special status" for them in every conquered country; they were "one of the main objects of German genocide policy," indeed, they were "to be destroyed completely" in extermination camps and by other means.[33] And yet he formulated an extraordinarily broad definition of genocide in recommending changes to the Hague Regulations:

> in the first should be included every action infringing upon the life, liberty, health, corporal integrity, economic existence, and the honor of the inhabitants when committed because they belong to a national, religious, or racial group; and in the second, every policy aiming at the destruction or the aggrandizement of one such group to the prejudice or detriment of another.[34]

When the immediate context of the writing of *Axis Rule* is understood, it is apparent that Lemkin had little choice but to proceed in this generalizing manner. Likewise, he resorted to the classic rhetoric of the language of transgression, echoing phrases from the Commission on Responsibility report, to make his case legible to contemporaries:

> ... [the Nazi] techniques of genocide represent an elaborate, almost scientific, system developed to an extent never before achieved by any nation. Hence the significance of genocide and the need to review

---

[30] Lemkin, "Law and Lawyers in the European Subjugated Countries," 109–12. As an authority on German political and intellectual history, he cited William M. McGovern, *From Luther to Hitler: The History of Fascist-Nazi Political Philosophy* (Boston: Houghton Mifflin Co., 1941).

[31] Lemkin, *Axis Rule in Occupied Europe*, 80, 92–3.

[32] Yehuda Bauer, "The Place of the Holocaust in History," *Holocaust and Genocide Studies* 2, no. 2 (1987):215; Steven T. Katz, *Holocaust in Historical Context*, Vol. 1 (Oxford: Oxford University Press, 1994), 1230n15; John Cooper, *Raphael Lemkin and the Struggle for the Genocide Convention* (Basingstoke: Palgrave Macmillan, 2008), 10, 23, 58–9.

[33] Lemkin, *Axis Rule in Occupied Europe*, 89, 81; cf. 21–2, 77, 249–50.   [34] Ibid., 93.

international law in the light of the German practices of the present war. These practices have surpassed in their unscrupulous character any procedures or methods imagined a few decades ago by the framers of the Hague Regulations. Nobody at that time could conceive that an occupant would resort to the destruction of nations by barbarous practices reminiscent of the darkest pages of history.[35]

As this chapter details, these claims were unoriginal: they were commonplace at the time. Lemkin's innovation was to market a grand simplification of points others were making, thereby inaugurating the problems of genocide.

Mitigated Knowledge

The timing of Lemkin's writing gives us a clue to his choice to subsume the fate of Jews and non-Jews under a generic concept. Until the US War Rescue Board published its report, *German Extermination Camps*, in November 1944 – the same month as *Axis Rule* – journalists and the US public, jaded by World War I atrocity propaganda, were largely skeptical about their systematic nature and the extent of Jewish mortality. Just because the Allies and press reported Nazi persecution and atrocities did not mean the public believed them. Moreover, such reports were rarely front-page news.[36]

Widespread antisemitism, among other factors, led to US opposition to accepting Jewish refugees or aiding Jews in Europe, whether by sending food or bombing Auschwitz. As in Great Britain, authorities worried about Nazi propaganda that claimed the war was waged on behalf of Jewish interests.[37] The British followed the exiled governments of occupied states in not naming Jews as a distinct nationality, and did not want to provide propaganda material for Zionist claims to independent statehood in Palestine. Until December

---

[35] Ibid., 90.

[36] Critical of the press coverage for underplaying Nazi persecution is Deborah E. Lipstadt, *Beyond Belief: The American Press and the Coming of the Holocaust, 1933–1945* (New York: Simon and Schuster, 1993), and Laurel Leff, *Buried by the Times: The Holocaust and America's Most Important Newspaper* (Cambridge: Cambridge University Press, 2005). On World War I propaganda, see Paul Morrow, "A Theory of Atrocity Propaganda," *Humanity: An International Journal of Human Rights, Humanitarianism, and Development* 9, no. 1 (2018): 45–62. Lemkin reports incredulity about "atrocity stories" in the Board of Economic Warfare: Lemkin, *Totally Unofficial*, 113.

[37] Saul S. Friedman, *No Haven for the Oppressed: United States Policy toward Jewish Refugees, 1938–1945* (Detroit, MI: Wayne State University Press, 2017); Deborah E. Lipstadt, "America and the Holocaust," *Modern Judaism* 10, no. 3 (1990): 283–96; Joseph W. Bendersky, "Dissension in the Face of the Holocaust: The 1941 American Debate over Antisemitism," *Holocaust and Genocide Studies* 24, no 1 (2010): 85–116; Tony Kushner, *The Persistence of Prejudice: Antisemitism in British Society during the Second World War* (Manchester: Manchester University Press, 1989).

1942, the British and US foreign policy establishments also doubted the extent of the Nazi campaign against Jews, discounting the August 1942 telegram from Gerhart Riegner (1911–2001), from the WJC Geneva office, about Nazi aims, although it was based on reliable German sources. Where the WJC saw a systematic extermination campaign, they perceived piecemeal ghettoization and starvation. The US State Department even withheld reports about mass murder of Jews.[38]

Even so, a great deal of information was on the public record. The St James Declaration from January 1942 has already been mentioned. The US left-wing magazine, *The Nation*, had been publishing critical exposés of the Nazi regime, speaking of "Mass Murder in Poland" already in 1940.[39] In March 1942, the *New York Times* carried an article titled "Extinction Feared by Jews in Poland" based on reports from the Polish underground. This fear was founded on observed mortality in the ghettos in which the Nazis had confined Jewish Poles. Before the full functioning of extermination camps, a Polish informant reported the Nazis' exterminatory intent with a formulation that would be repeated in part by Article II(c) of the Genocide Convention in 1948: the Germans had "deliberately managed to create such a condition in the ghettos as to annihilate the inhabitants in the shortest possible time."[40]

By the end of 1942, the specific targeting of Jews was gaining press attention. In early December, the London *Times* carried two articles on the "Nazi war on Jews" and its "deliberate plan for extermination," quoting from German publications about transportation of Jews "eastward in cattle trucks to an unknown destination, or killed where they stood." Polish underground sources spoke of the "complete extermination of Jews." The second article even mentioned a "final solution," and linked events in different occupied countries to a continental plan of extermination. Although it did not mention camps, the *Times* spoke of murderous intention: "a twin policy of murder on a mass scale and transference of whole communities to the bare eastern territories under conditions which even at their best, show that the German authorities care nothing whether the people survive or die."[41]

---

[38] John P. Fox, "The Jewish Factor in British War Crimes Policy in 1942," *English Historical Review* 92 (1977): 82–106; Breitman, *Official Secrets*, 100–1, 139–46; David S. Wyman, *The Abandonment of the Jews* (New York: Pantheon Books, 1984), 44–5, 65, 73–4, 81, 113–17, 179, 186.

[39] Freda Kirchwey, "The Jews in Hitler's Poland," *The Nation,* January 20, 1940; Howard Daniel, "Mass Murder in Poland," *The Nation,* January 27, 1940; Sara Alpern, *Freda Kirchwey: A Woman of The Nation* (Cambridge, MA: Harvard University Press, 1987).

[40] "Extinction Feared by Jews in Poland," *New York Times*, March 1, 1942. Article II(c) of the Genocide Convention is "(c) Deliberately inflicting on the group conditions of life calculated to bring about its physical destruction in whole or in part."

[41] "Nazi War of Jews: Deliberate Plan for Extermination," *The Times*, December 4, 1942, 3; "Terror Against Jews: European Pogrom," *The Times*, December 7, 1942, 3.

A few days later, the newspaper's sources were revealed as the Polish Ministry of Foreign Affairs' pamphlet, *The Mass Extermination of Jews in German Occupied Poland*, based on the eyewitness report of Polish agent, Jan Karski (1914–2000).[42] As its title indicated, the pamphlet exposed the Nazi aim as "Total extermination of the Jewish population of Poland." The Polish government wanted to inform "civilized governments" about "new methods of extermination," namely ghettoization, starvation, the transportation of German Jews, massacres, the use of poison gas (in Chelm) and electrocution (in Belzec). "Extermination camps" had been established in "Tremblinka [sic.], Belzec, and Sobibor" (there was no mention of Auschwitz) as destinations for deportation trains that were "deliberately calculated to cause the largest possible number of casualties among the condemned Jews." This report also availed itself of the standard tropes of the language of transgression. The "liquidation" of the Warsaw Ghetto entailed "horrors of which surpass anything known in the annals of history."[43]

In response a week later, the Allies issued a Joint Declaration by Members of the United Nations that condemned "in the strongest possible terms" the German "bestial policy of cold-blooded extermination" of Jews by ghettoization, starvation, and labor exploitation, though again not mentioning extermination camps.[44] British Foreign Secretary Anthony Eden then read the statement in the House of Commons, adding "that those responsible for these crimes shall not escape retribution," although, as we will see, neither he nor the Foreign Office were interested in running postwar trials.[45]

These declarations were both stimulated and registered by anxious Jewish Americans who staged public demonstrations in New York, and whose

---

[42] Polish Ministry of Foreign Affairs, *The Mass Extermination of Jews in German Occupied Poland: Note Addressed to the Governments of the United Nations on December 10, 1942* (New York: Hutchinson and Co., 1942); Jan Karski, *Story Of A Secret State: My Report To The World* (New York: Penguin Hardback Classics, 1999); David Engel, "An Early Account of Polish Jewry under Nazi and Soviet Occupation Presented to the Polish Government-in-Exile, February 1940," *Jewish Social Studies* 45, no. 1 (1983): 1–16; Martin Winstone, *The Dark Heart of Hitler's Europe: Nazi Rule in Poland under the General Government* (London: I. B. Tauris, 2015).

[43] Polish Ministry of Foreign Affairs, *The Mass Extermination of Jews in German Occupied Poland*, 6, 9. On the train deportations as an experience and mode of destruction, see Simone Gigliotti, *The Train Journey: Transit, Captivity, and Witnessing in the Holocaust* (New York and Oxford: Berghahn Books, 2009).

[44] "11 Allies Condemn Nazi War on Jews: United Nations Issue Joint Declaration of Protest on 'Cold-Blooded Extermination,'" *New York Times*, December 18, 1942. Lemkin quoted this declaration in *Axis Rule in Occupied Europe*, 89n45.

[45] United Nations Declaration, House of Commons Debates, December 17, 1942, Vol. 385, cc2082, http://hansard.millbanksystems.com/commons/1942/dec/17/united-nations-declaration.

representatives published accounts of Nazi policies toward Jews.[46] As late as April 1943, the WJC's magazine, *Congress Weekly*, emphasized starvation as the principle cause of mortality. "Should the war last much longer, gas chambers, suffocation in railroad cars and outright mass massacres of Jews will become superfluous; the bulk of the Jewish people will die of starvation."[47]

Lemkin absorbed this atmosphere when he arrived in the US and made his way to an externally (and poorly) funded two-year appointment at Duke University School of Law in April 1941.[48] He was shocked by the silence that greeted Karski's revelations between late 1942 and late 1943, when he finished his book (it was published a year later due to a contractual dispute), and dismayed by the lack of government reaction to these reports, even if he was too diplomatic to say so outright. Instead, he decried what he called the "tremendous conspiracy of silence" about the Nazi "execution of races." Without mentioning Jews by name, he made it clear what he meant: "No acknowledgement was made of the death of a nation that had given the world the belief in God, whose Bible was read every Sunday in the Allies' churches."[49] To be sure, joint declarations by US Christian and Jewish groups were issued and reprinted in *Congress Weekly*.[50] Roosevelt's sympathies were likewise reprinted there: on December 8, 1942, the president related that he was "profoundly shocked" to learn of the murder of two million Jews, adding in familiar terms that "The American people more than ever will feel, he thought, that the conscience of the United Nations and of free men everywhere was revolted by those deeds of savagery and attempted extermination."[51]

Lemkin shared Jewish Americans' sense of anguish and powerlessness to affect events in far-off Europe. He himself recalled later how his spirits plummeted after hearing about the German invasion of Soviet-occupied eastern Poland, where his parents lived; he could imagine what lay in store

[46] Editorial, "Challenge to Humanity," *Congress Weekly,* February 26, 1943, 1; Declaration and Resolution from March 1, published in *Congress Weekly*, March 5, 1943, 2; "The Tragedy of European Jewry," *Congress Weekly* 1, no. 4 (January 1943): 1–3.

[47] "Death by Starvation," *Congress* Weekly, April 1, 1943; "Accelerated Murder: The Further Record of Hitler's Extermination Program," *Congress Weekly*, February 26, 1943, 4–7.

[48] On his time at Duke, see Ernerst Zitser, "A White Crow: Raphael Lemkin's Intellectual Interlude at Duke University, 1941–1942," *North Carolina Historical Review* 96 (2019): 34–66. On US public opinion regarding Jews, see Susan Welch, "American Opinion Toward Jews During the Nazi Era: Results from Quota Sample Polling during the 1930s and 1940s," *Social Science Quarterly* 95, no. 3 (2014): 615–35.

[49] Lemkin, *Totally Unofficial*, 117.

[50] One example is "To Demand Action to Save Hitler's Victims," *Congress Weekly*, February 26, 1943, 2.

[51] "Statement of President Roosevelt to Representatives of Jewish Organizations, Dec. 8, 1942," *Congress Weekly*, December 24, 1942, 10.

for them.[52] The Joint Committee of Polish Jewish Organizations likely expressed his feelings when, "In the hour of unspeakable grief and travail," it declared December 2, 1942 as a day of mourning for Europe's Jews:

> The greatest calamity of Jewish history since the destruction of the Temple has befallen all Jewish communities in the European lands occupied by the enemy. His deliberate and Satanic purpose to destroy Jewish life wherever his power reaches has now been exposed to the world. Nearly two million Jews have already cruelly been done to death and the remaining millions live in the shadows of impending doom.[53]

Like American-Jewish leaders, Lemkin wanted more than sympathy. He demanded action. Ever hopeful, he sent Roosevelt a short memorandum about a genocide treaty (or so he claims in his autobiography) – to outlaw the "crime of crimes" – which he hoped the president could promote to help save the remaining Jews of Europe. Disappointed by the tepid response, Lemkin resolved to influence public opinion rather than appeal to political leaders.[54]

The War Rescue Board (WRB) report was a breakthrough in this respect. Based on two eyewitnesses of Auschwitz and Birkenau, the report was lent authority by the WRB, which Roosevelt had established in January 1944 to coordinate relief for European refugees after a domestic campaign by Jewish groups and Henry Morgenthau at the Treasury Department. Two months later, in March, Roosevelt then prepared the way for the Board's report by delivering a speech denouncing German and Japanese "systematic torture and murder of civilians" and "campaign of savagery." In adding that "the wholesale systematic murder of the Jews of Europe" constituted "one of the blackest crimes of all history," he mentioned yet another term to name Nazi criminality: the Nazis were committing "crimes against humanity in the name of the German people."[55] Articles by American journalists about their tour of the Majdanek extermination camp in Poland in August after its capture by the Red Army also drove home the scale of Nazi criminality.[56] Newspaper editorials assured readers of the WRB report's authenticity. A week after its release, 76 percent of the surveyed Americans believed the existence of concentration camps even if most could not imagine the staggering numbers murdered in

[52] Lemkin, *Totally Unofficial*, 110–11.
[53] "Text of Proclamation Issued by American Jewish Organizations Setting Wednesday December 2, 1942 as a Day or Mourning," *Congress Weekly*, December 24, 1942, 9.
[54] Lemkin, *Totally Unofficial*, 114–15. We are taking Lemkin at his word here; no record of this memo has been found.
[55] Statement by President Roosevelt, March 24, 1944, Foreign Relations of the United States: Diplomatic Papers, 1944, General, Vol. I, 740.00116 European War 1939/1368, 11, https://history.state.gov/historicaldocuments/frus1944v01/d771.
[56] Arieh J. Kochavi, *Prelude to Nuremberg: Allied War Crimes Policy and the Question of Punishment* (Chapel Hill and London: University of North Carolina Press, 1998), 158.

them.[57] The report concluded in the familiar terms of the language of transgression, equating the experiences of Jews and Christians: "It is a fact beyond denial that the Germans have deliberately and systematically murdered millions of innocent civilians – Jews and Christians alike – all over Europe. This campaign of terror and brutality, which is unprecedented in all history and which even now continues unabated, is part of the German plan to subjugate the free peoples of the world."[58] The report's conclusion expressed the domestic US consensus, reflected in the 1941 pamphlet, *Nazi Poison: How We Can Destroy Hitler's Propaganda against the Jews*, that antisemitism was a foreign import, antithetical to Christian American values.[59]

This notion was reflected by Roosevelt a year later when he announced the intention to punish "the ringleaders responsible for the organized murder of thousands of innocent persons and the commission of atrocities which have violated every tenet of the Christian faith."[60] Observing the Christianization of Nazi oppression, Lemkin concluded that appealing to the Christian majority was essential for helping European Jews. A broad, generic conception of group destruction would simultaneously unite Jewish and non-Jewish experiences as well as reflect the cultural sensibilities of small nations for which there were many types of destruction.

The Many Types of Destruction

Lemkin was not alone in expressing small nation experiences of group vulnerability. A cast of exile Polish and Czech contemporaries – virtually all Lemkin's age – wrote about their occupied homelands for English-speaking audiences. They shared a basic, and accurate, understanding of Nazism as radical Pan-Germanism that, in name of *Lebensraum* (living space), colonized and exploited their nations by deporting millions of Slavs and replacing them with German settlers who would rule over an enslaved class of helot-workers.

---

[57] Rebecca Erbelding, *Rescue Board: The Untold Story of America's Efforts to Save the Jews of Europe* (New York: Doubleday, 2018), 257–8.

[58] Executive Office of the President, War Refugee Board, "German Extermination Camps – Auschwitz and Birkenau," November 26, 1944, available at: www.fdrlibrary.marist.edu/_resources/images/hol/hol00088.pdf; "War Refugee Board Releases Report on Extermination of Millions of Jews in Nazi Camps," *Jewish Telegraphic Agency*, November 26, 1944, www.jta.org/1944/11/26/archive/war-refugee-board-releases-report-on-extermination-of-millions-of-jews-in-nazi-camps.

[59] *Nazi Poison: How We Can Destroy Hitler's Propaganda against the Jews* (New York: Council for Democracy, 1941); Bendersky, "Dissension in the Face of the Holocaust."

[60] White House News Release, *Department of State Bulletin*, October 10, 1942, 797. Quoted in Charles Cheney Hyde and Edwin D. Dickinson, "Punishment of War Criminals," *Proceedings of the American Society of International Law at Its Annual Meeting (1921–1969)* 37 (April 30–May 1, 1943): 39.

Nazism was thus a "racial imperialism" that imported extra-European colonial techniques into Europe while completely eliminating the Jewish population.[61] In the main, these authors were better known and better published than Lemkin but, although he repeated their ideas, they are now forgotten. Unlike Lemkin, they availed themselves of the inherited vocabulary of transgression – mentioning terror, destruction, and extermination – while generally distinguishing between Jewish and non-Jewish fates as they saw them. By contrast, Lemkin coined a new term that deliberately fudged this distinction, and that in its grand simplicity appealed to the nonexpert fascination with the Nazis' supposedly mysterious intentions.

Jewish and non-Jewish refugee commentators highlighted the Nazis' policies to financially benefit German settlers in their countries, whether by expropriation, exploitation, enslavement, or extermination. Paul Einzig (1897–1973), a Jewish-Hungarian economist who migrated to England in 1919, wrote extensively on Nazi economic policies. In *Hitler's "New Order" in Europe* (1941), he related that the German aim was "the complete enslavement and extermination of the vanquished by the victor."[62] Josef Hanč (1895–1977), the Czechoslovak consul-general in New York and later faculty member at Tufts College, wrote *Tornado Across Eastern Europe: The Path of Nazi Destruction From Poland to Greece* (1942), which self-consciously adopted the perspective of the small nations between Germany and Russia in highlighting their fate under Nazi domination.[63] Relying on source material from these countries' exiled embassies, consulates, and legations in London, René Kraus (1902–1947), an Austrian journalist and former press secretary of the German foreign minister, Gustav Stresemann, likewise outlined the Nazi policies to expropriate, enslave, and exterminate subject nations, like the Poles and Czechoslovaks, by means of plunder, terror, expulsion, and settlement of Germans.[64] Lemkin did not cite their work.

---

[61] Current scholarship: Isabel Heinemann, *Rasse, Siedlung, deutsches Blut: Das Rasse- und Siedlungshauptamt der SS und die rassenpolitische Neuordnung Europas* (Göttingen: Wallstein, 2003); Gerhard Wolf, *Ideologie und Herrschaftsrationalität: nationalsozialistische Germanisierungspolitik in Polen* (Hamburg: Hamburger Edition, 2012); Wolf Gruner and Jörg Osterloh, eds., *The Greater German Reich and the Jews Nazi Persecution Policies in the Annexed Territories 1935–1945* (New York and Oxford: Berghahn Books, 2015).

[62] Paul Einzig, *Hitler's "New Order" in Europe* (New York: Macmillan, 1941), 144; Einzig, *Europe in Chains* (New York: Penguin, 1940); Einzig, *Germany's Default: The Economics of Hitlerism* (London: Macmillan, 1934). Also see Maxine Y. Sweezy, *The Structure of the Nazi Economy* (Cambridge, MA: Harvard University Press, 1941).

[63] Josef Hanč, *Tornado Across Eastern Europe: The Path of Nazi Destruction from Poland to Greece* (New York: Greystone Press, 1942); Hanč, *Eastern Europe and the United States* (Boston: World Peace Foundation, 1942).

[64] René Kraus, *Europe in Revolt* (London: Jarrolds, 1942).

Neither did Lemkin consult the Austrian jurist and political scientist, Hans (later John) Ernest Fried (1905–1990), who migrated to the US in 1938 and worked as a research assistant at the Institute for Social Research, transplanted from Frankfurt to New York. His *The Guilt of the German Army* (1942) discerned a qualitatively new phase of German militarism in the Nazi regime and its style of warfare: "a concentration-camp warfare and extermination-militarism," he called it. Its essential features would be widely noted by writers at the time: "the waging of total war, the destruction of 'civilian' civilization, the dismemberment of other nations, the domination by military and party officials."[65]

Lemkin also overlooked Frank Munk (1901–1999), a Czechoslovak political economist who worked at various US universities and for the United Nations Relief and Rehabilitation Administration. In *The Legacy of Nazism: The Economic and Social Consequences of Totalitarianism* (1943), Munk discerned in German "space-politics" (*Raumpolitik*) an expansionism that manifested itself in multifaceted attacks on "persecuted minority groups," indeed in the "[w]holesale destruction of racial or national groups." His listing of how this destruction was effected is worth quoting in full because Lemkin's is so similar:

> They are deported to bleak and unprepared areas in pursuance of grandi-ose schemes of population redistribution; they are subject to discrimin-ation in the distribution of food, confiscation of capital, to exclusion from employment; the sexes are often separated; there are wholesale mass executions. By all methods a systematic campaign of extinction is being waged against them with a cold-blooded and premeditated cruelty that many people in more fortunate countries cannot conceive.[66]

In view of this multipronged attack on nationality, Munk fittingly devoted a chapter to "Banking and Germanization," and a section to the "Destruction of the Jewish entrepreneur," also asking "are small nations doomed?" Relying on English historian Lewis Namier, he reported the "End of European Jewry."[67] A source for the chapter on "Removal and Destruction of Populations" was Simon Segal's *New Order in Poland* (1942), in which Munk distinguished

---

[65] Hans Ernest Fried, *The Guilt of the German Army* (New York: MacMillan, 1942), 2, 348; Ernst C. Stiefel and Frank Mecklenburg, *Deutsche Juristen im amerikanischen Exil (1933-1950)* (Tübingen: J. C. B. Mohr, 1991), 91–3; Kim Christian Priemel, *The Betrayal: The Nuremberg Trials and German Divergence* (Oxford: Oxford University Press, 2016), 50–1.

[66] Frank Munk, *The Legacy of Nazism: The Economic and Social Consequences of Totalitarianism* (New York: Macmillan, 1943). 49. He is quoting John B. Condliffe, *Agenda for a Postwar World* (New York: Norton, 1942). Generally, see Alan E. Steinweis, "German Cultural Imperialism in Czechoslovakia and Poland, 1938–1945," *International History Review* 13, no. 3 (1991): 466–80.

[67] Munk, *The Legacy of Nazism*, 60–3, 72–6, 132–5.

between "transplantation" for non-Jews and "extinction" for Jews.[68] Like Lemkin, a Jewish Pole born in 1900, Segal (d. 1972) worked for the American Jewish Committee after migrating to the US in 1935. His book also informed Munk about Nazi plans to expel Czechs "somewhere in Russia or Siberia" and to replace them with German settlers.[69]

The reason for the resemblance between Munk's *The Legacy of Nazism* and Lemkin's famous book may lie in the fact that the latter reviewed Segal's *New Order in Poland* in 1943, although he did not cite it in *Axis Rule*.[70] The review praised Segal's findings about various dimensions of Polish national life: "population, religious life, cultural life, economics, labor, food, Jewish ghettos and underground movement." Lemkin noted the common pattern in analyses of Nazi policy at the time: that the German administration confiscated Jewish property to allocate to German settlers who were granted tax exemptions as a colonizing incentive; that, in turn, Poles were deported to Germany to work in agriculture and industry; and that the intelligentsia, "which in Poland has always been the bearer of Polish national ideas," was a particular Nazi target. Lemkin's only criticism was the lack of detail about eastern Poland that Germany occupied after its invasion of Soviet-annexed territory in June 1941. Here "every trace of Polish culture and Polish property" was being liquidated, and the "greatest atrocities against the Jews" were taking place by deportation to other countries "to be liquidated by a special regime of starvation and direct killings."[71]

Even Segal's analysis was hardly original. He was updating the approach of Oscar Janowsky (d. 1993), another Jewish Pole born in 1900 who made his way to the US. With Melvin M. Fagen, and under the auspices of the American Jewish Committee, Janowsky published *International Aspects of German Racial Policies* in 1937 to advance the case for League of Nations intervention on behalf of German Jews. The book detailed discriminatory racial legislation, denationalization policies, forced emigration measures, and the intent to drive non-Aryans from Germany. Like *Axis Rule*, about half the book reprints relevant documents, above all German legislation and decrees.[72]

---

[68] Simon Segal, *New Order in Poland* (New York: Alfred A. Knopf, 1942). See also Segal, "Eastern Poland," *American Jewish Year Book* 46 (September 18, 1944–September 7, 1945): 240–6; Munk, *The Legacy of Nazism*, 50.

[69] Munk, *The Legacy of Nazism*, 58.

[70] Reviewed by Raphael Lemkin, review of Simon Segal, *New Order in Poland*, in *The Annals of the American Academy of Political and Social Science* 299 (1943): 183–4.

[71] Ibid.

[72] Oscar I. Janowsky and Melvin M. Fagen, *International Aspects of German Racial Policies*, pref. James Brown Scott (New York: Oxford University Press, 1937). Janowsky came to the US in 1910 and taught history at City College in New York. James B. Loeffler, "Between Zionism and Liberalism: Oscar Janowsky and Diaspora Nationalism," *AJS Review* 34, no. 2 (2010): 289–308.

Lemkin learned the same lessons from those who he did choose to cite, such as the extensive reports of exiled governments and diaspora organizations in the late 1930s and early 1940s that documented their homeland's experience of Nazi occupation.[73] The Inter-Allied Information Committee in London issued a steady stream of pamphlets on all aspects of Nazi rule, as did the Polish Information Center in New York.[74] Like the Belgian, Bulgarian, and Armenian memoranda to the Commission on Responsibility in 1919, these World War II publications highlighted the multidimensional nature of Axis rule: the Germans took over the economy, banned local languages, engaged in deportations, transferred to German families children considered "racially valuable," arrested and murdered cultural elites, plundered forests, and so forth. Their nations were being destroyed in a variety of ways. Massacres were but one element of the ordeal.[75]

Czech writer Eugene V. Erdely (1890–1969) took the same approach in his study of German rule in Czechoslovakia, which he called *Germany's First European Protectorate*, also used by Lemkin.[76] The German advance "denotes degradation, impoverishment, enslavement and forced emigration," wrote Erdely, effected by "fraud, terrorism, disintegration and robbery."[77] Like other writers, he highlighted the degradation of some Slavs and the deportation of others to make way for Germans, also noting that Nazi guards, Gestapo, and military famers predominated among the settlers. This practice continued a

---

[73] Edvard Beneš, *Nazi Barbarism in Czechoslovakia* (London: Allen and Unwin, 1940). A brochure based on a speech delivered before the Press Club in London on March 29, 1940.

[74] Inter-Allied Information Committee, *The Axis System of Hostages* (London: HMSO, 1942); Polish Information Centre in New York pamphlet series, *Documents Relating to the Administration of Occupied Countries in Eastern Europe*; no. 1: *German Exploitation of Polish Forests;* no. 2: *German Destruction of Cultural Life in Poland*; no. 4: *German Persecution of Religious Life in Poland*; no. 8: *Extermination of the Polish People and Colonization by German Nationals* (New York: Polish Information Center, 1941). See Mateusz Gniazdowski, "Losses Inflicted on Poland by Germany during World War II: Assessments and Estimates – An Outline," *Polish Quarterly of International Affairs*, no. 1 (2007): 98–9. James Loeffler, *Rooted Cosmopolitans: Jews and Human Rights in the Twentieth Century* (New Haven: Yale University Press, 2018), 125–6.

[75] Polish Ministry of Information, *German Occupation of Poland* (*Polish White Book*) (New York: Greystone Press, 1941); Lithuanian Legation, "Current News on the Lithuanian Situation" (Washington, DC, June 1943); Czechoslovak Ministry of Foreign Affairs, *Czechoslovakia Fights Back*, intro. Jan Masaryk (Washington: American Council on Public Affairs, 1943); Serbian Eastern Orthodox Diocese for the United States of America and Canada, *Martyrdom of the Serbs* (Chicago, 1943); Polish Labor Group, *Poland Fights* (New York: May 16, 1942); United Nations Information Organisation, *Conditions in Occupied Territories: A Series of Reports*, Vols. 1–9 (London: HMSO, 1942–1945). Lemkin, *Axis Rule in Occupied Europe*, 84n23.

[76] Eugene V. Erdely, *Germany's First European Protectorate: The Fate of the Czechs and Slovaks* (London: Robert Hale, 1942). Lemkin, *Axis Rule in Occupied Europe*, 53.

[77] Erdely, *Germany's First European Protectorate*, 9.

pattern of German military colonization he discerned since the nineteenth century. Indeed, Imperial Germany's extra-European colonies furnished a model for German rule, amounting to colonial rule over Europeans: "No nation belonging to the white race has ever before had such conditions forced upon it." In fact, the protectorate "constituted the first German colonial statute in modern history for a white and civilized nation." In a telling statement about the logic of colonial conquest, he gestured to permanent security in referring to "Teutonic attempts to subjugate other nations permanently."[78] Lemkin would borrow this insight.

Lemkin was likely also inspired by his own Polish government in London, whose many publications he read. Already in December 1940 it issued a public statement about "German Crimes in Poland" that detailed infractions of the Hague Conventions. Significantly, the statement interpreted nonviolent violations, like cancelling the Polish citizenship of Poles in German-annexed Poland and forcing Poles to vitiate their oath of loyalty to the Polish state, as part of "*one long chain* of physical and moral violence directed towards the destruction of the Polish nation."[79] This style of reasoning linked comparatively anodyne government regulations to mass atrocities by virtue of their shared intention: national destruction. The intensity of anxiety about national survival and the loyalty of occupied Poles led the exiled Polish government to conclude that the "Violation of conscience ... is even worse than physical terror."[80] This statement followed the first volume of two so-called Black Books ("the black record of German barbarism"): *The German Invasion of Poland* appeared that year, a collection of documents with commentary on the atrocities of the German invasion in 1939.[81] Then a diplomatic note presented to the governments of the Allied and Neutral Powers by the Polish government on May 3, 1941 detailed multiple infractions of the Fourth Hague Convention in the German "acts of violence against the population," and in offences against religion, cultural heritage, and property, as its table of contents articulated the occupation modalities.[82] Throughout the war, the Ministry of Information also published the *Polish Fortnightly Review*, which Lemkin cited in his footnotes.[83]

---

[78] Ibid., 13, 34–41, 241, 249–50.

[79] "German Crimes in Poland," *The Times*, December 21, 1940, 3. Emphasis added.

[80] Ibid.

[81] Republic of Poland, Ministry of Foreign Affairs, *The German Invasion of Poland: Polish Black Book Containing Documents, Authenticated Reports and Photographs*, pref. Archbishop of York (London: Hutchinson and Co., 1940).

[82] The published note, which was an extract, ran to 187 pages with 189 documents quoted in its appendix: Republic of Poland, Ministry of Foreign Affairs, *The German Occupation of Poland; Extract of Note Addressed to the Governments of the Allied and Neutral power on May 3, 1941* (London: Cornwall Press, 1941).

[83] A typical example is the issue devoted to "The Work of Germanization in the General Gouvenement," *Polish Fortnightly Review*, no. 63 (March 1, 1943): 1–8.

To coincide with the St James meeting, the Polish Ministry of Information issued the second Black Book, *The German New Order in Poland* in January 1942, a 586-page analysis of the German occupation.[84] It prefigured *Axis Rule* in many ways. The book was organized under four general heading, nine sections, and 44 chapters, whose themes preempt Lemkin's eight "techniques of genocide" (political, social, cultural, economic, biological, physical, religious, and moral):

Persecutions, Murders, Expulsions
Part 1: Massacres and Tortures
Part 2: The Expulsion of the Polish Population from its Lands
Part 3: The Persecution of the Jews and the Ghettoes

Pillage and Economic Exploitation
Part 4: The Robbery of Public and Private Property
Part 5: The Economic Exploitation of Polish Territories Under German Occupation

Struggle Against the Polish Spirit
Part 6: Religious Persecutions
Part 7: Humiliation and Degradation of the Polish Nation
Part 8: The Destruction of Polish Culture

German Lawlessness
Part 9: The Violation by the Reich of International Law

Classical tropes of the language of transgression recur throughout the text, indicating that its authors understood the idiom with which to appeal to readers: "The robbery of public and private property ... has reached proportions unknown in modern history"; "the German authorities resort to terrorism"; "This book provides a basis for bringing the most serious indictment of a nation that has ever been made during the history of humanity." The Martens Clause was also cited and the Allies informed that it "must be interpreted in favour of the population of the occupied territory."[85]

As we will see below, particular phrases and concepts made their way into *Axis Rule*, for example, referring to Hitler's aim to "Germanize the soil" by first replacing the Polish population with German settlers; or unmasking the

---

[84] Polish Ministry of Information, *The German New Order in Poland* [Black Book, Vol. 2] (London: Hutchinson and Co., 1942).
[85] Ibid., 251, 512, 565, 526.

"German policy ... to destroy the Polish nation as an independent political and cultural unit, and even more, to destroy its biological force."[86] This mode of analysis was so common at the time that a relatively minor academic could publish a short article based on these sources in early 1944 called "Axis Domination in Central and Eastern Europe" that is a virtual anticipatory summary of *Axis Rule*.[87] American Jewish leaders also highlighted that group destruction could be effected in many ways.[88]

The Institute of Jewish Affairs and the Definition of War Crimes

Another major source for Lemkin was the Institute for Jewish Affairs, a research unit founded by the World Jewish Congress in February 1941 and directed by Jacob Robinson. Its original purpose was postwar planning, but the disastrous news from Europe demanded drastic revision of the assumption about the Jewish population available for migration to Palestine or requiring minority protection in Europe after Germany's defeat. The Institute's focus consequently moved to establishing wartime facts about the treatment of Jews in the lands between the Baltic states and Greece – the "European 'Middle East'" as Namier called this belt of small nations – in particular regarding individual and minority rights, modern economic nationalism, Nazi antisemitism, and refugees. Robinson's report on the Institute's activities in February 1944 listed some of its significant publications, among them *Hitler's Ten-Year War on the Jews* (1943) and *Racial State: German Nationalities Policy in the Protectorate of Bohemia-Moravia* (1944).[89] *Hitler's Ten-Year War* was based in part on law gazettes of all Axis countries, a practice Lemkin followed, while its listing of the various means of destruction – "planned starvation, forced labor, deportation, pogrom and methodical murder in the German-run extermination centers of Eastern Europe" – also appeared in *Axis Rule*.[90] The thesis of another Institute publication, *Starvation*

---

[86] Ibid., 144, 565. Cf. Lemkin, *Axis Rule in Occupied Europe*, 80, 81.

[87] Floyd A. Cave, "Axis Domination in Central and Eastern Europe," *Annals of the American Academy of Political and Social Science* 232 (March 1944): 116–25. Cave taught government at San Francisco State University. He also was the coauthor of Floyd A. Cave et al, *The Origins and Consequences of World War II* (New York: Dryden Press, 1948).

[88] Steven Wise, "Stop Hitler Now," *Congress Weekly*, March 5, 1943, 3–4.

[89] Institute for Jewish Affairs, "Planning a Postwar Program," February 28, 1944. AJA/WJC, C97–17 Postwar Planning, Rehabilitation and Relief, 1944; Boris Shub, ed., *Hitler's Ten-Year War on the Jews* (New York: Institute of Jewish Affairs of the American Jewish Congress, World Jewish Congress, 1943); Gerhard Jacoby, *Racial State: German Nationalities Policy in the Protectorate of Bohemia-Moravia* (New York: Institute for Jewish Affairs of the American Jewish Congress and World Jewish Congress, 1944).

[90] Shub, *Hitler's Ten-Year War on the Jews*, 300; Lemkin, *Axis Rule in Occupied Europe*, 88n44.

over Europe (1943), that the Nazis used food supply to destroy occupied peoples, likewise featured in Lemkin's book, again raising the issue of his originality.[91]

Lemkin himself gave a hint in a short note to Robinson in August 1946, in which he wrote that the latter had been "the great inspiration for genocide."[92] Indeed, along with the contemporary scholarship and commentary described above, the Institute was instrumental in forming Lemkin's analytical perspective. It is no accident that even though *Racial State* was published too late to integrate into *Axis Rule*, their analyses are virtually identical. Like Lemkin, and the Institute more generally, its author, Jewish-German lawyer Gerhard Jacoby (1891–1960), was interested in the legal measures by which Nazi occupation incrementally achieved its aim of extending *Lebensraum* – like the "one-long-chain-argument" also deployed by the Polish government – namely supplanting Czechoslovaks with Germans, particularly in the economy and institutions of cultural transmission, thereby turning the locals into "helots" and the colonists into "masters."[93] Chapter 12 "Depopulation and Resettlement" approximates to Chapter 9 on genocide in *Axis Rule*. It delineates the "techniques for inducing depopulation among the non-Germans" in various ways: "isolating men from women by calling them up separately for forced labor duties, or by deportation; cutting down the birth rate by oppression; and direct and indirect slaughter." Again there is the gesture to permanent security: the "plans for changing the composition of the population in their favor" were "to assure *permanent* German hold on the Protectorate area."[94] Characteristic of the contemporary view, Jacoby concluded that the Nazis were treating Europeans like colonial inferiors; the Protectorate was "the complete colonial subjection of an independent, highly civilized European people to the political, economic, and cultural domination of another European people."[95]

Unlike Erdely, but like Lemkin, Jacoby included a separate chapter on Jews, tellingly called "The Extinction of the Jews." While Christians would be enslaved or deported, Jews were to be eliminated entirely in a "series of successive stages ... forced emigration, local segregation, forced labor, and finally deportation" to labor camps or "the ghettos and extermination centers of Poland and the occupied Soviet territory."[96] The major theme of the

---

[91]   *Starvation over Europe (Made in Germany): A Documented Record* (New York: Institute of Jewish Affairs, 1943); Lemkin, *Axis Rule in Occupied Europe*, 87n35 where Lemkin states that he obtained permission from the Institute to use the data. This book and its grim findings were also reported in the *Congress Weekly* in February 1943. Mark Lewis pointed out to me the common use of gazettes. *Hitler's Ten-Year War on the Jews* is cited on 89n46.

[92]   Raphael Lemkin to Jacob Robinson, August 21, 1946. AJA/WJC, C14–21 Meeting Minutes, Speeches, Correspondence, London, Oct. 1945.

[93]   Jacoby, *Racial State*, 5–6, 43, 110, 126, 199.   [94]   Ibid., 221. Emphasis added.

[95]   Ibid., 267.   [96]   Ibid., 235, 240.

chapter, however, was less mass murder than the expropriation of Jewish property by legal measures tantamount to "civil death." Plundering Jews was the main goal of Nazi policy, he implied, and other goals also indicated a pragmatic, indeed political, logic for the elimination of the Jewish population.

> It paved the way for German resettlement. It was a pretext for extending Nazi control over Czech property. It was a Nazi test of Czech collabor-ation. And, it was a weapon in the psychological arsenal of Nazi rule; by their anti-Semitic policy, the Nazis planned to deflect Czech antagonism from themselves to another quarter; and, at the same time, to point a moral and post a warning of the consequences which opposition might entail.[97]

Such analysis was prefigured by Jewish experiences of discrimination against them by the small nations that gained independence after World War I. Writing in 1929, Robinson, for example, observed that these new countries decided to use the state apparatus to favor national majorities at the expense of minorities. Their systematic economic disadvantaging of Jews amounted to "some methods of colonial exploitation in the praxis of central Europe."[98]

This colonial paradigm reflected the conclusion of Jewish-German political scientist Franz Neumann (1900–1954), who left Germany for Britain and eventually the US after the Nazis seized power. Like Fried, he worked with the Institute for Social Research at Columbia University in New York, eventu-ally taking up position at the US Office of Strategic Services (the wartime espionage agency) in 1942.[99] His book on the Nazi regime published that year, *Behemoth: The Structure and Practice of National Socialism*, understood these policies as manifestations of the broader Nazi strategy, which he called a "racial imperialism" that sought to integrate the population into the authori-tarian state by promising it the spoils of "world conquest." In practice, this conquest entailed "reducing the vanquished states and their satellites to the level of colonial peoples."[100] By casting the Nazi occupation as intrinsically colonial, characterized by slavery, exploitation, settlement, and destruction, this common analysis was speaking the language of transgression.

---

[97] Ibid., 244, 246.

[98] Jacob Robinson, "Staatsbürgerliche und wirtschaftliche Gleichberechtigung!" *Süddeutsche Monatshefte* 26, no. 10 (1929): 711.

[99] Martin Jay, *The Dialectical Imagination: A History of the Frankfurt School and the Institute of Social Research 1923–1950* (Boston: Little Brown, 1973), 144; Jack Jacobs, *The Frankfurt School, Jewish Lives, and Antisemitism* (New York: Cambridge University Press, 2014)

[100] Franz Neumann, *Behemoth: The Structure and Practice of National Socialism* (New York: Ivan Dee, [1942] 2009), 150, 193. An analysis of Nazi plunder to maintain domestic consensus is Götz Aly, *Hitler's Beneficiaries: Plunder, Racial War, and the Nazi Welfare State*, trans. Jefferson Chase (London: Verso, 2007).

Controversially, Neumann criticized the popular "scapegoat theory" by which Jews were blamed for society's ills. As an alternative, he advanced the "spearhead" theory that postulated antisemitism as a means to political ends, namely the expropriation and incarceration of all regime opponents, ranging from pacifists to "members of the occupied peoples." The attack on Jews, then, marked the beginning rather than the endpoint of a political process whose telos was "the destruction of free institutions, beliefs, and groups." Jews were "guinea pigs in testing the method of repression," with antisemitism acting as "the spearhead of terror." Despite its instrumental view of antisemitism, this argument appeared in *Hitler's Ten-Year War*, which postulated that "Jewish forced labor in Germany, on the eve of war, provided the laboratory for the coming system of Nazi slave labor for all the subjugated peoples of Europe."[101] This notion was common. Erdely had written that "Anti-Semitism provides not only an important psychological stimulant but also valuable experience for future use against other races."[102]

As might be expected, the echoes of Neumann in Jacoby's invocation of political logics in Nazi antisemitism were not shared by other Institute members and contributors, like Kiev-born Jacob Lestchinsky (1876–1967). A demographer and founding member of the Institute for Jewish Research (YIVO) in Vilnius who fled to the US in 1938, he worked on *Hitler's Ten-Year War* but also submitted his own report on "The Effects of Three Years of War on the Jews in Europe" in September 1942. While he followed the general Institute line in highlighting the multifaceted attack on Jewish existence, especially in the economic domain, he differed in his explanation of antisemitism's meaning. Unlike Polish, Yugoslav, and French civilians who were killed "because of their resistance to Nazi enslavement or as hostages for the rebellion of their compatriots," Jews were executed for nonpolitical reasons: "for an unforgettable sin thousands of years old – for their having stood before Mount Sinai and having received the Ten Commandments there."[103]

---

[101] Neumann, *Behemoth*, 550–1. These quotations are taken from the appendix added in the 1944 edition. It cites statistics from Shub, *Hitler's Ten-Year War on the Jews*, indicating that Neumann was reading Institute publications. See also Neumann, "Anti-Semitism: Spearhead of Universal Terror," in *Secret Reports on Nazi Germany: The Frankfurt School Contribution to the War Effort*, ed. Raffaele Laudani (Princeton University Press, 2013), 27–30. Neumann has been criticized for underplaying the autotelic logic of antisemitism. See Jay, *Dialectical Imagination*, 34, 162; Bendersky, "Dissension in the Face of the Holocaust." Shub, *Hitler's Ten-Year War on the Jews*, 24.

[102] Erdely, *Germany's First European Protectorate*, 139.

[103] Jacob Lestchinsky, "Summary of the Effects of Three Years of War on the Jews in Europe," September 23, 1943, AJA/WJC, C174–6 Nazi War Crimes, Reports, and Correspondence, 1942–1944; Gur Alroey, "Demographers in the Service of the Nation: Liebmann Hersch, Jacob Lestchinsky, and the Early Study of Jewish Migration," *Jewish History* 20, nos. 3–4 (2006): 265–282. Lestchinsky's mention of biblical roots continued after the war: Uriel Tal, "On the Study of the Holocaust and Genocide," *Yad Vashem*

The differences within the Institute about the causal status of antisemitism reflected confusion about the logic of permanent security. The more secular the analysis – like Jacoby's – the better it understood the Nazis' political rationality. As we will see below, Institute authors were driven in this direction by the legal requirements of demonstrating German violations of the Hague Conventions. The alternative was to resort to biblical motifs, like Lestchinsky, in which Jews were murdered simply for being Jewish. Certainly, the latter interpretation was instinctual among Institute members and Jewish leaders, who were convinced that Jews were subject to distinct targeting compared to other peoples occupied by the Nazis. Robinson was concerned that Allied leaders understand this distinction, and other WJC personalities argued for a special Jewish indictment and representation in the unfolding Allied debate about war crimes trials.

Reports and declarations by the WJC are littered with versions of this conviction. A statement by WJC founders Nahum Goldman (1895–1982) and Steven S. Wise (1874–1949) in July 1942 on the "Nazi Massacres of Jews in Europe" averred the primacy of Jewish suffering thus: "The whole long history of man's inhumanity to man holds no record of persecutions more charged with brutality and horror. In the hierarchy of suffering which Nazi brutality has created they have the melancholy of occupying the first place."[104] In January 1943, Robinson presented Goldman and Wise with a commentary on the unfolding war crimes debate in which he underlined the particular character of the crimes against Jews. Whereas non-Jews could escape extermination by complying with the occupiers, Jews were killed simply for being Jews: "by the very fact of their birth, designated for extermination."[105] A few months later, on July 22, he itemized the particularity of the Jewish experience in four elements that, together, constituted a "specific crime," namely the "avowed sin of wholesale destruction of the Jewish people":

1. The "wholesale systematic murder of the Jews of Europe" – "one of the blackest crimes of all history";
2. The crime is being committed all over Europe;

Studies 13 (1979): 24–46. On the religious dimension of Nazi antisemitism, see also Alon Confino, *A World Without Jews: The Nazi Imagination from Persecution to Genocide* (New Haven, CT: Yale University Press, 2014).

[104] Nahum Goldman and Steven S. Wise, "Statement of World Jewish Congress on Nazi Massacre of Jews in Europe," AJA/WJC, C174-07 Extermination of Jews and Punishment of War Criminals Correspondence 1942–1944.

[105] Jacob Robinson, "Comments on 'Memorandum on the Necessity of a Jewish Representative on the International Committee for Penal Reconstruction and Development," January 8, 1943. AJA/WJC, C174-07 Extermination of Jews and Punishment of War Criminals Correspondence 1942–1944.

3. This crime has been going on at even increasing rate and scope since the advent of the Nazis to power;
4. This crime is a deliberate carrying into effect of Hitler's oft-repeated intention to exterminate the Jewish people in Europe.[106]

Two days before, a WJC delegation had visited Sir Cecil Hurst (1870–1963), Chairman of the United Nations War Crimes Commission (UNWCC), in London to put the case for "a body to investigate the special aspects of the Jewish war crimes." In addition to crimes against Jews as nationals of occupied states, it said, "there are special crimes against Jews which are crimes sui generis." Herewith the WJC also distinguished between Jews and non-Jews with the nonpolitical/political binary:

(a) All other crimes have some reason behind them (even crimes committed against hostages), but in the case of crimes against Jews, the only reason is the fact that they are Jews.
(b) Crimes against Jews are committed as part of a war of extermination against a whole people and there is no precedent in history of such a war against any other people.[107]

The WJC underlined that "membership of the Jewish race" was the only criterion for extermination, while "the degree of cruelty involved in its execution distinguishes those war crimes from those perpetrated upon other peoples and races." Its case for official Jewish involvement in the coming war crimes trials was thus also based on the style as well as the goal of Nazi policy: "the special and unique measures of racial humiliation and segregation [of Jews], of systematic destruction of religious, cultural and communal institutions, of differentiation in treatment in respect of food rations and otherwise, or access to means of transport, of deprivation of office and employment, and of wholesale confirmation of property which preceded the slaughter." The WJC's entreaty concluded by invoking classic tropes from the language of transgression. There could be "no true comparison between this slow torture of extermination accompanied by a denial, the most savage of all time, of the dignity of man, and the mass massacres in the past which have soiled the pages of history."[108]

---

[106] Jacob Robinson, "Memorandum on Definition of War Crimes," July 22, 1943. AJA/WJC, C174–07 Extermination of Jews and Punishment of War Criminals Correspondence 1942–1944.
[107] "Note of Conversation between Sir Cecil Hurst and a Delegation of the World Jewish Congress, 20/7/1944." AJA/WJC, C174–07 Extermination of Jews and Punishment of War Criminals Correspondence 1942–1944.
[108] World Jewish Congress to Cecil Hurst, July 20, 1944. AJA/WJC, C174–07 Extermination of Jews and Punishment of War Criminals Correspondence 1942–1944.

Herewith, the WJC encapsulated the case for the uniqueness of the Holocaust long before it became a subject of intense academic debate.[109] Against Hurst's reply that the Allied states could not grant special representation to Jews or allow a special indictment on their extermination, a WJC representative objected: "It is not merely a matter of Jewish citizens of this or that Government having had crimes committed against them but of crimes against Jews, qua Jews, irrespective of citizenship."[110] As Robinson put it looking back on these discussions, "It was a fight for our identity, a fight for the recognition that the victims were Jews, and not some anonymous allied nations, and that the chosen victim of Hitler was the Jewish People, the first target of his aggression."[111] He had a point. Although the Germans often had to compromise with puppet and collaborationist governments that were prepared to yield up foreign Jews on their soil but not their own Jewish citizens, Nazis conceived of Jews as a single people and aimed, ultimately, to exterminate them all. Germans were thus committing a "united crime," insisted Robinson, that should be "branded as such."[112]

The Allied states eventually understood this aspect of Nazi policy but were reluctant to adopt it to reconceptualize war crimes because, as mentioned above, it meant buying into the Nazi racism and the division of their own citizens. Robinson and WJC representatives persisted in trying to communicate their understanding of bigger stakes by reminding all that Jews "are an historical people":

> The Jewish people consist of all those dead and those who live. We consist of the hundreds of millions who have been living for three thousand years, and the eleven millions now alive. The six million Hitler victims take their place in this total picture, and it is therefore no miscalculation on our part to devote much of our energies to our fight for our concept of war crimes.[113]

---

[109] Ibid.; Alan S. Rosenbaum, *Is the Holocaust Unique? Perspectives on Comparative Genocide*, 3rd ed. (New York and London: Routledge, 2009). An early statement of the thesis is Jacob Lestchinsky, *Crisis, Catastrophe, and Survival: A Jewish Balance Sheet, 1914–1948* (New York: Institute of Jewish Affairs, 1948).

[110] "Note of Conference Between Representatives of the United Nations' Commission for the Investigation of War Crimes and the World Jewish Congress in London on 2nd August 1944 at the Law Courts, London." AJA/WJC, C174-07 Extermination of Jews and Punishment of War Criminals Correspondence 1942–1944.

[111] Address given by Dr Jacob Robison (Director of the Institute of Jewish Affairs in New York) on "The Jewish International Political Agenda," at the Conference held on October 10, 1945, at Friends House, Euston Road, London. AJA/WJC, C14–21 Meeting Minutes, Speeches, Correspondence, London, October 1945.

[112] Ibid.

[113] Address given by Jacob Robinson on the "Jewish International Political Agenda," at the Conference held on October 10, 1945 at Friends House, London. AJA/WJC, C176–09 War Crimes 1945.

This concept of war crimes, the collectivist approach, would also reveal "the 'grandeur' of the crime."[114] The WJC tried to stretch the category of war crimes to cover this united crime until "crimes against humanity" entered discussion. In the meantime, Lemkin branded that united crime as the "generic notion" of genocide but in an expansive way: by conjoining it to the persecution and crippling of Europe's Christian nations.[115]

For all its efforts, the WJC struggled to assert the significance of what its leaders called the "historic drama" of "a great crime against a great people" in relation to the "legal niceties" that Hurst consistently mentioned.[116] These niceties were significant, and they preoccupied Robinson. As Lemkin also argued in his story about discussing the Armenian massacres with his teacher in the late 1920s, Robinson related that one's "conscience is revolted at the idea" that it is illegal to murder individuals but not an entire people.[117] But the remit of the UNWCC was limited to crimes stipulated in the Hague Conventions committed during war. On these terms, the pre-1939 persecution of German Jews would be omitted, as well as that of stateless Jews – a major hiatus in international law.

The WJC was internally divided on the way forward. In London, the WJC and British chemist and Zionist leader Chaim Weizmann (1874–1952) tried to convince the Allies to include a separate indictment for exterminating Jews. By contrast, Robinson and Maurice Perlzweig (1895–1985), an English Rabbi and Zionist leader who moved to the US to head the WJC's Department of International Affairs, opposed a "separate Jewish treatment of anti-Jewish war crimes" for the same reasons that Lemkin was advocating a generic notion: because "we are having the most desperate difficulty to get any public acknowledgment in any form of the very existence of a specific aspect of the problem." Indeed, writing as late as August 1944, Perlzweig was concerned that even "intelligent people" in "positions of influence" still did "not believe the extermination accounts which we know to be true."[118] In their case, the

---

[114] Anonymous one-page briefing note recapitulating "the essentials of the 'collectivistic' approach to Nazi 'War Crimes' as distinct from the Individualistic' or 'Atomistic,'" October 15, 1945. AJA/WJC, C14–21 Meeting Minutes, Speeches, Correspondence, London, October 1945.

[115] Lemkin, *Axis Rule in Occupied Europe*, 92, 80.

[116] "Note of Conference Between Representatives of the United Nations' Commission for the Investigation of War Crimes and the World Jewish Congress in London on 2nd August 1944 at the Law Courts, London."

[117] Jacob Robinson, "War Crimes – Specific Crimes against the Jews," July 22, 1943. AJA/WJC, C176-7 Outline, Book, "Conspiracy vs Jewish People," 1945.

[118] Maurice Perlzweig to Office Committee, August 23, 1944. AJA/WJC, C174–07 Extermination of Jews and Punishment of War Criminals, Correspondence, 1942–1944. Maurice Perlzweig, *Perlzweig: Champion of British Zionism*, ed. David Caute (London: Vallentine Mitchell, 2018); "The Soviet Union and the Jews during

strategy was to stretch the category of war crimes rather than to invent a new one. He and Robinson reasoned that pre-1939 anti-Jewish persecution could be classed as a war crime in terms of the Hague Conventions if shown to be integrally related to German military preparations. This interpretation was "a radical development of international law," they confessed. He and Robinson were pleading for "quite a new principle, viz. that the civilized word is entitled to punish a government for acts of persecution against its own subjects on its own soil." Even if not currently a war crime, "we have our own reasons for insisting on their inclusion in the category of war crimes." Rather than seek a special Jewish indictment, then, it was "immensely more important" to secure input to and representation at any war crimes trials.[119]

The Institute in New York thus began preparing a "Book on War Crimes" that outlined its intentionalist view of the Nazi policy, namely as a premeditated and preconceived plan to exterminate European Jewry, irrespective of national differences among them, carried out in stages.[120] The collective focus aimed to avoid the dissipation of a focus on Jewish citizens of other small nations, while narrating the stages of persecution in an escalatory trajectory that culminated in mass murder. In this way, the confiscation of property, political disenfranchisement, deportations, ghettoization, enslavement, and starvation would be part of the same crime, an approach that bears striking resemblance to the Polish government's "one-long-chain" argument. The Institute's outline for a book on the "Conspiracy Against the Jewish People" put the case most succinctly, detailing "one continuous and indivisible criminal process":

> Specific feature of biological warfare against Jews: In case of other peoples, intent to weaken culturally, physically, and numerically; In case of Jews, intent to wipe out completely: Conspiracy aimed at total extermination. Destruction carried out by scientifically established method: First, disenfranchisement, humiliation, degradation, then uprooting, spoliation, ruthless exploitation of manpower, finally, wholesale annihilation. Undertaking embraces *one continuous and indivisible criminal process* the inception of which goes back to the birth of the Nazi party and the

World War II: British Foreign Office Documents Exchange of Letters between M. L. Perlzweig and Lord Halifax," *Soviet Jewish Affairs* 3, no. 2 (1973): 75–8.

[119] Ibid.

[120] Mark A. Lewis, "The World Jewish Congress and the Institute for International Affairs at Nuremberg: Ideas, Strategies, and Political Goals, 1942–1946," *Yad Vashem Studies* 36, no. 1 (2008): 181–210; Michael R. Marrus, "The Three Jewish Émigrés at Nuremberg: Jacob Robinson, Hersch Lauterpacht, and Raphael Lemkin," in *Against the Grain: Jewish Intellectuals in Hard Times*, ed. Ezra Mendelsohn, Stefani Hoffman, and Richard I. Cohen (New York and Oxford: Berghahn Books, 2014), 240–54.

execution of which starts with the advent of the Nazi regime, and the spread throughout Europe of the launching of the "red war."[121]

Like the Polish government, the Institute and WJC fixated on the notion of a continuous crime that began in peacetime. Robinson was under no illusion that he was thereby proposing a radical innovation to the accepted conception of war crimes. Current international law was inadequate for the Nazis' revolutionary form of warfare against civilians because they could prevail in the long-term demographic struggle even if they lost the war, he wrote in 1943: to win the peace, not just the war, as Lemkin also argued in *Axis Rule*.[122]

While Robinson realized the British and Americans would stick to the Hague regime, he understood that other instruments of international law could broaden its scope. Germany had signed the Kellog-Briand Pact against wars of aggression: if its rearmament before 1939 thereby violated the pact, the persecution of Jews could be covered when interpreted as effectively a mode of war preparation. This argument was also advanced by the Czech representative to the UNWCC, as the next chapter details.

A consequence of this framing was to render the persecution as political: Jews were targeted for strategic reasons of permanent security:

> German unity was the first prerequisite on the home front for waging war. Hitler, the man who is credited with the famous legend of the knife in the back, was obsessed by the idea that a second war might be lost for lack of national unity; and therefore all disturbing and heterodox elements in the country had to be eliminated. In the Nazi view these elements included the Jews, Socialists, so-called political Catholicism, and the fighting Protestant Church.

Jews, Robinson continued, "were a disturbing element for such German unity," which is "why their elimination was a measure of war."[123] Encouraged by various Allied declarations that announced the "wholesale and systematic" nature of the Nazi campaign against Jews, which he frequently noted that Roosevelt had denounced as the "blackest crimes of all history," Robinson pressed the argument to the limit. Like Neumann, he maintained

---

[121] A. A. Goldstein, H. Sindler, and Z. Warhaftig, "Outline of the Book on War Crimes by the Committee of Three, General Title: *Conspiracy against the Jewish People*," n.d. 4. AJA/WJC, C176–7 Outline, Book, "Conspiracy vs Jewish People," 1945. Emphasis added.

[122] Robinson, "War Crimes – Specific Crimes against the Jews"; Jacob Robinson, "War Crimes – Some Basic Ideas," July 22, 1942. AJA/WJC, C174–6 Nazi War Crimes, Reports and Correspondence, 1942–1944; Lemkin, *Axis Rule in Occupied Europe*, 81.

[123] Jacob Robinson, "Comments on the 'Memorandum on the Necessity of a Jewish Representative on the International Committee for Penal Reconstruction and Development," December 29, 1942, 2–3, AJA/WJC, C174–7 Extermination of the Jews and Punishment of War Criminals, Correspondence, 1942–1944.

that the persecution of Jews was preparation for other persecutions. They were crimes "committed in the course of and incidental of preparatory to the war by the Axis."[124] He understood the Nazis' permanent security aims in observing that its two crimes – "destruction or debilitation of the civil population" and "a program of systematic looting" – will "make Germany the dominant power in Europe for decades to come" irrespective of the war's outcome.[125] Targeting Jews thus had several pragmatic functions. In the Nazis' "new concept of war," Jews played a role by "disturbing the so-called unity of an aggressive nation, and so they had to be removed" by waging "an actual war against the Jews." They were "the Nazis' guinea pig" to test the resistance and reactions of the "outside world." Encouraging antisemitism in neighboring countries also made them easier to conquer by dividing their populations.[126]

Conclusion

Politicizing the Nazi persecution of Jews was inconsistent with the intuitions of the Institute and WJC. Like Lestschinsky, most of their members felt Jews were attacked solely because of their ethnicity or religion. The Allied conception of war crimes (analyzed in the next chapter) forced them to identify strategic and rational – political – reasons for Nazi policy; that is, to accurately capture the spirit of permanent security animating the German attacks. After the war, however, when genocide was conceived as a nonpolitical hate crime, the notion of the Holocaust as similarly nonpolitical could prevail. Until then, these émigré social scientists shared the analysis of their Christian émigré counterparts in emphasizing traditional themes in the language of transgression: state excesses resulting from savage imperialism that expropriated, enslaved, and exterminated native peoples whose resistance was ruthlessly suppressed. The difference with customary imperial settings was that colonial rule was now taking place in Europe.

Moreover, victims were neither passive, nor helpless. Praise of their patriotic underground resistance movements saturates the wartime propaganda of small nation leaders. Copying this style, Lemkin extolled Poles' "stubborn resistance," their "romantic and spiritual values," and "willingness to sacrifice everything for national liberty and national honor." As always, he linked Jewish and non-Jewish fates while briefly noting the specificity of the Jewish case.[127] Somewhat more romantically, René Kraus, writing in 1942, depicted Europe as occupied but unbowed, with Soviet partisans leading the resistance.

---

[124] [Jacob Robinson], "Memorandum on the Definition of War Crimes," July 22, 1943. AJA/ WJC, C174–7 Extermination of the Jews and Punishment of War Criminals, Correspondence, 1942–1944.

[125] Ibid.   [126] Robinson, "War Crimes – Specific Crimes against the Jews."

[127] Lemkin review of Segal, *New Order in Poland*, 184.

His book, *Europe in Revolt*, called for an Anglo-British invasion of the German "new order" where "two hundred million slaves are prepared to take up arms." Although – or perhaps because – many Europeans were collaborating with the Germans and volunteering for their military, Kraus emphasized their resistance qualities. "Europe's battered but unbeaten and unbroken nations wait, in desperate anxiety, for the signal across the seas."[128] In the meantime, representatives of these nations were pressing the British and Americans to expand the definition of war crimes to prosecute Germans after the war.

[128] Kraus, *Europe in Revolt*, 176. The Polish exiled government worried about the loyalty of its citizens: "German Crimes in Poland," *The Times*, December 21, 1940, 3. On this theme, see Mark Mazower, *Dark Continent: Europe's Twentieth Century* (London: Penguin, 1998).

5

Inventing Genocide in the 1940s

During World War II, a coalition of the World Jewish Congress (WJC) and "smaller nations" occupied by Germany (Lemkin called them "captive nations") pushed to criminalize the destruction of nations. As discussed in the previous chapter, the Martens Clause of the 1899 Hague Convention that governed military occupations of conquered territory was the legal vehicle of their endeavors. Famously, we recall, the contracting parties had deferred determination of further stipulations to protect civilians by agreeing to the Martens Clause in the convention's preamble as a general principle: "populations and belligerents remain under the protection and empire of the principles of international law, as they result from the usages established between civilized nations, from the laws of humanity and the requirements of the public conscience."[1] The bone of contention among the Allies in the first half of the 1940s was whether and how to codify these lofty precepts.

Far from supporting the campaign of small nations and the WJC, the great powers fighting the Nazis – the British, Americans, and Soviets – opposed innovations in international law that criminalized the prewar and the domestic policies of enemy states, and that obligated them to mount postwar trials: what states did to their own citizens was their own business, and they should prosecute violations of the "laws and customs of war" committed on their soil. The great powers all had sensitive domestic issues that they preferred to keep out of international forums, whether colonial rule in the British Empire, racial oppression in the American South, or mass incarceration and mortality in Soviet gulags. As public expectations to prosecute Nazis intensified in light of the growing awareness of their mass crimes in 1943 and 1944, however, the Allies settled on an ad hoc international military tribunal to sit in the German city of Nuremberg. The Nazis would be indicted for new legal notions of "crimes against peace," "war crimes," and "crimes against humanity." These rhetorically powerful legal categories transformed the lexical landscape. While crimes against humanity had debuted in international relations with the

---

[1] Theodore Meron, "The Martens Clause, Principles of Humanity and Dictates of Public Conscience," *American Journal of International Law* 94, no. 1 (2000): 78–89.

Entente note to the Ottoman leadership in 1915 about its treatment of Armenian civilians, it was not included in the postwar treaties and enjoyed no legal status. Now the concept was given official seal and a precise legal definition as one of the three indictments in the Charter of the International Military Tribunal in August 1945.

To Lemkin's grave disappointment, genocide was not one of the indictments, and it featured only marginally in proceedings. Published in November 1944, *Axis Rule in Occupied Europe* had entered the race to codify the Martens Clause too late to materially influence the American military thinkers planning the prosecutions.[2] Yet, just over a month after the conclusion of the trial of the major war criminals on October 1, 1946, the General Assembly of the United Nations (UNGA) passed a resolution calling for a convention on the prevention and punishment of genocide. While international lawyers did not take this curious new term seriously as a qualitatively new crime, journalists and religious leaders were beguiled by its humanitarian aura. The outsider, Lemkin cultivated them to publicize his neologism, and they obliged by lobbying their governments to support the UN Convention on the Punishment and Prevention of Genocide, which the UNGA passed in December 1948.

The lexical landscape changed dramatically again. There was little public enthusiasm for the work of the International Law Commission in formalizing the "Nuremberg Principles" when the UNGA entrusted it with the task. The main Nuremberg indictment – crimes against peace, meaning planning and waging a war of aggression – disappeared from international law until the Rome Statute in 1998.[3] And, although a draft code on crimes against humanity was adopted by the new International Criminal Court in 1998, after its use in the international criminal tribunals for Rwanda and the former Yugoslavia, no convention on them exists.[4] In the meantime, genocide became the "crime of crimes," the maximal attention-seeking claim. It had rhetorically vanquished its Nuremberg rivals.

---

[2] "Charter of the International Military Tribunal," *American Bar Association Journal* 31, no. 9 (1945): 454–7. See Alexa Stiller, "The Mass Murder of the European Jews and the Concept of 'Genocide' in the Nuremberg Trials: Reassessing Raphaël Lemkin's Impact," *Genocide Studies and Prevention* 13, no. 1 (2019): 144–72.

[3] Mauro Politi, "The ICC and the Crime of Aggression: A Dream that Came Through and the Reality Ahead," *Journal of International Criminal Justice* 10, no. 1 (2012): 267–88; Carrie McDougall, *The Crime of Aggression Under the Rome Statute of the International Criminal Court* (Cambridge: Cambridge University Press, 2013).

[4] In 2017, the International Law Commission presented draft articles on crimes against humanity for a future convention. Hugo A. Relva, "Three Propositions for a Future Convention on Crimes against Humanity: The Prohibition of Amnesties, Military Courts, and Reservations," *Journal of International Criminal Justice* 16, no. 4 (2018): 857–75.

Contingency rather than coherence governed this development. Had Lemkin published his book as planned in late 1943 instead of late 1944, it may have influenced the Nuremberg Charter negotiations, although it is hard to see that his ideas about criminalizing peacetime persecution of enemy civilians could have been accepted by the great powers. To limit the scope of crimes against humanity, they insisted on a connection with the German war effort. For that reason, the Nuremberg judges ultimately ruled that the persecution of Jewish Germans before 1939 was *not* a crime against humanity. Nor were any suspects indicted for crimes against humanity at the International Military Tribunal for the Far East (the Tokyo Trials). The status of crimes against humanity at Nuremberg did not meet the expectations of small nations and the WJC, thereby opening a moral and conceptual gap that genocide could fill.

Ingeniously opportunistic, Lemkin enabled the joint mobilization of hitherto rivals by linking the fate of Jewish and non-Jewish victims of Nazi occupation under the rubric of "genocide." They all feared national destruction and were dissatisfied by the legalistic and conservative Anglo-American approach to international law, even as they differed over how to prioritize their victim status.[5] In late 1946, after the unsatisfactory Nuremberg judgment, this coalition of small nations, along with many Latin American states, prevailed against the British, Americans, and French in convincing the UNGA to develop a convention against genocide. Were it not for the initial restrictive interpretation of crimes against humanity, then, the genocide concept would likely have died soon after birth in 1944.[6] We now know why Lemkin decided to invent his complex bridging concept and how he derived it from the debate on German criminality in the early 1940s. But his wager could succeed only when the rival categories of the crime of aggression, war crimes, and crimes against humanity lost their attraction. Genocide's breakthrough as a politically viable legal concept in the 1940s was dependent less on his well-known energetic advocacy than on its repositioning in a field of conceptual options over which he had no control.

Lemkin's achievement was not to invent a "new word ... to denote an old practice in its modern development" that supposedly reflected historical and current reality, as commonly supposed.[7] It was to contrive a conceptual artifice that enabled a politically effective coalition to create a new reality by

---

[5] Donald Bloxham, *Genocide on Trial: War Crimes Trials and the Formation of Holocaust History and Memory* (Oxford: Oxford University Press, 2001), 80. Raphael Lemkin, *Axis Rule in Occupied Europe: Laws of Occupation, Analysis of Government, Proposals for Redress* (Washington, DC: Carnegie Endowment for International Peace, 1944), 80.

[6] Lemkin himself admitted as much at the time. See his letter, "For Punishment of Genocide," in the *New York Times*, June 27, 1947, 24. See also William A. Schabas, "Origins of the Genocide Convention: From Nuremberg to Paris," *Case Western Reserve Journal of International Law* 40, nos. 1–2 (2008): 35–55.

[7] Lemkin, *Axis Rule in Occupied Europe*, 79.

combining the "crippling" and "extermination" of nations in a "generic notion."[8] Far from unthinkingly eliding the differences between Jewish and non-Jewish victims, as charged by his critics, uniting them was the point of the concept.[9] Even if some within the WJC bristled at this joining of Jewish and non-Jewish experiences, its leadership eventually supported "genocide" as a means of protecting Jewish minorities after World War II. By then, they understood the slim chances of convincing the Allies to accede to a specifically Jewish indictment in postwar trials.

Genocide's unexpected breakthrough in 1946 presented the great powers – the US, the Soviet Union, Britain, and France – with a dilemma. While they opposed or were ambivalent about the genocide concept, they did not want to be seen to thwart the UNGA consensus embodying "international conscience." So, they led the debates to ensure that its definition in the 1948 Convention would not inhibit their ability to wage war and to repress dissent at home or in their colonies. To that extent, the same issue of internal sovereignty that mitigated the definition of crimes against humanity at Nuremberg affected the legal definition of genocide: permanent security measures like population transfer, cultural genocide, and the liquidation of political groups and political motivations of destruction were excluded. At this moment, in 1948, the coalition of small nations and the WJC split as the latter and the new State of Israel joined the great powers in depoliticizing genocide so it would resemble the Holocaust-as-massive-hate-crime as closely as possible. In this way, the WJC position ultimately prevailed as "genocide" surpassed "crimes against humanity" in rhetorical force, but now understood in terms of its archetype, the Holocaust, increasingly understood as a unique, depoliticized hate crime.

Before "Genocide"

Exiled representatives of the occupied small nations, the WJC, and international lawyers discussed how to categorize and prosecute Axis criminality after the German conquests.[10] Four issues were on their agenda. Was violation

---

[8] Ibid., 84, 80.

[9] E.g., Dan Michman, "The Jewish Dimension of the Holocaust in Dire Straits? Current Challenges of Interpretation and Scope," in *Jewish Histories of the Holocaust: New Transnational Approaches*, ed. Norman J. W. Goda (New York and Oxford: Berghahn Books, 2014), 17–38.

[10] Kerstin von Lingen refers to the "London hub" in "Legal Flows: Contributions of Exiled Lawyers to the Concept of 'Crimes against Humanity' during the Second World War," *Modern Intellectual History* 17, no. 2 (2020): 507–25. Julia Eichenberg refers to a "London Moment" in her project: https://exilegov.hypotheses.org/about. Generally, see Daniel Marc Segesser, *Recht durch Rache oder Rache durch Recht? Die Ahndung von Kriegsverbrechen in der internationalen wissenschaftlichen Debatte 1872-1945* (Paderborn: Ferdinand Schöningh, 2010).

of the 1928 General Treaty for Renunciation of War as an Instrument of National Policy (the Kellogg-Briand Pact) an international crime? Did extant law cover Nazi persecution of German-Jewish citizens and stateless persons? Did extant law cover Nazi persecution of German citizens or foreign citizens before the outbreak of hostilities? Which courts – national or international – should hear proceedings against perpetrators, and which laws should they apply? Contrary agendas marked the debate from the outset.

The St James Declaration of January 1942 set the tone. Driven by small nations, it called for an expansive approach to international law to reflect the unprecedented nature of the Nazi project and mode of warfare. In the lead-up to the Declaration, Cambridge University hosted lawyers and representatives of nine European countries at an academic conference. Entitled "Rules and Procedures to Govern the Case of Crimes against International Public Order," it aimed to begin discussions about the salient legal issues. At subsequent meetings in the first half of 1942, participants determined that their domestic jurisdictions could cover war crimes committed on their territory but not against stateless people, nor against their nationals abroad. The concluding memorandum, written by Hersh Lauterpacht, spoke about war crimes and the possibility of an international court, though not about crimes against humanity or prewar persecutions of Axis citizens. However, his memorandum invoked the Martens Clause to argue that German Jews brought to other countries "in pursuance of a proclaimed policy of racial extermination – and against stateless persons" could be covered by national jurisdictions because they were international crimes. He himself advocated prosecuting German leaders for the "crime of war" for violating the Kellog-Briand Pact.[11]

Some months earlier, in September 1941, a larger and more diplomatically oriented advisory body was established under the auspices of the League of Nations: the London International Assembly (LIA), so named because this was the city in which exiled continental governments resided and could meet. The LIA was also dominated by lawyers and representatives of the small nations. In its deliberations over the next two years, the LIA also focused on whether the notion of war crimes should be expanded to include the Martens Clause and cover the gamut of Nazi policies. One of the Czechoslovak representatives, Bohuslav Ečer (1893–1954), also argued that aggressive warfare was a crime, echoing prominent Soviet jurist Aron Trainin (1883–1957), who maintained that "crimes against peace" was the primary infraction from which German

---

[11] Hersch Lauterpacht, "The Law of Nations and the Punishment of War Crimes," *British Yearbook of International Law* 21 (1944): 58–95. The text was written in 1942. Kirsten Sellars, *"Crimes against Peace" and International Law* (Cambridge: Cambridge University Press, 2013), 50; Oona Hathaway and Scott Shapiro, *The Internationalists: And Their Plan to Outlaw War* (New York: Allen Lane, 2017).

atrocities flowed.[12] In this way, the war's planners in Germany could be prosecuted, rather than solely lower-level criminals in the field who were covered by Hague law. This comity was no accident, as lawyers from "captive nations" communicated with their Soviet counterparts in the campaign to convince the reluctant Americans and British about the necessity of international postwar trials.[13]

Because continental states had been invaded and occupied, their representatives were concerned foremost with the crime of aggression, which was neither Lemkin's, nor the WJC's priority.[14] They also rejected the WJC's argument about the uniqueness of Jewish persecution. Even so, the LIA's long final report, "Punishment for War Crimes," issued in December 1943, advocated moving beyond the list of violations used by the Commission on the Responsibility in 1919 ("war crimes proper" or *stricto sensu*) to include waging aggressive warfare, and to expand war crimes to racial and political extermination committed beyond state borders. In this respect, the small nations and WJC were of one mind.[15]

Moving in the opposite direction, the "big three" of the Soviet Union, US, and Great Britain issued their own restrictive "Declaration on War Atrocities in Moscow" on October 30, 1943. They stuck to the orthodox interpretation of war crimes and eschewed an international tribunal. German officers were to be placed on trial in the countries in which they had perpetrated "atrocities, massacres and executions," while "major criminals whose offences have no particular geographical location" would be "punished by a joint decision of the Governments of the Allies," in other words, by political rather than legal means. The big three remained within the paradigm of the 1919 Commission on Responsibilities that the small nations and Lemkin sought to transcend. The latter argued that attacks on nationality could not be reduced to individual violations, and needed to be understood in their systematic totality.[16]

---

[12] Kerstin von Lingen, "Setting the Path for the UNWCC: The Representation of European Exile Governments on the London International Assembly and the Commission for Penal Reconstruction and Development, 1941–1944," *Criminal Law Forum* 24 (2014): 52–5.

[13] Regarding the Soviet contribution, see Kerstin von Lingen, *"Crimes against Humanity": Eine Ideengeschichte der Zivilisierung von Gewalt 1864–1945* (Paderborn: Ferdinand Schöningh, 2019), 233–5. Other aspects are highlighted by Francine Hirsch, *Soviet Judgment at Nuremberg: A New History of the International Military Tribunal after World War II* (Oxford: Oxford University Press, 2020).

[14] Sellars, *"Crimes against Peace" and International Law,* 50–3; Michelle Penn, "'Genocide is Fascism in Action': Aron Trainin and Soviet Portrayals of Genocide," *Journal of Genocide Research* 22, no. 1 (2020): 1–18.

[15] United Nations War Crimes Commission (UNWCC), *History of the United Nations War Crimes Commission and the Development of the Laws of War* (London: HMSO, 1948), 100–1.

[16] "Statement on Atrocities of Moscow Declaration of 30 October 1943," *ICC Legal Tools Dataset,* www.legal-tools.org/doc/3c6e23/; Arieh J. Kochavi, *Prelude to Nuremberg: Allied*

The confrontation between these approaches was staged in the next organ to consider the matter, the United Nations War Crimes Commission (UNWCC). It was established in October 1943, pursuant to the St James Declaration, to document Axis violations of the laws of war. The Americans and British approved of this intergovernmental commission, which might act as a deterrent to German behavior, and to ensure the accuracy of war crimes allegations. However, they did not invest it with investigative or judicial mandates, and its small secretariat was never capable of pooling the information that flowed in from the 17 Allied states. Nor did they wish to consider the prewar persecution of Axis Jewish citizens, because the council's remit was limited to collecting information about Axis violations of the Fourth Hague Convention: that is, breaches of the laws and customs of war (i.e., war crimes *stricto sensu*), like the 1919 Commission on Responsibilities.[17]

Meeting throughout 1944, the UNWCC members wrangled about these terms of reference: whether the category of war crimes could be extended to the German declaration of war and to the Axis treatment of its own citizens (above all German Jews). Ečer advanced the argument that a radical mode of warfare demanded a commensurate revision of the laws of war. In doing so, he invoked the rhetoric of the Martens Clause ("public conscience") as a source of law, as well as Trainin's case that German atrocities flowed from its primary crime, namely invasion.[18] He was also influenced by the German-Jewish émigré jurist, Georg Schwarzenberg (1908–1991), who taught at University College, London, where he moved in Czechoslovak circles. Like Trainin, Schwarzenberg argued that the Nazis were "gangsters" who should not benefit from the protections of international law.[19] The British representative, Arnold McNair (1885–1975), resisted this suggested innovation by stressing that states could not be criminally liable and thus could not be outlaws that were exempt from Hague Conventions stipulations regarding belligerent occupation. Launching an aggressive war was a political rather than legal question, he

---

War Crimes Policy and the Question of Punishment (Chapel Hill: University of North Carolina Press, 2000), 107–10.

[17] Narrelle Morris and Aden Knaap, "When Institutional Design Is Flawed: Problems of Cooperation at the United Nations War Crimes Commission, 1943–1948," *European Journal of International Law* 28, no. 2 (2017): 513–34.

[18] Kerstin von Lingen, "Fulfilling the Martens Clause: Debating 'Crimes against Humanity, 1899–1945,'" in *Humanity: A History of European Concepts in Practice from the Sixteenth Century to the Present*, ed. Fabian Klose and Mirjam Thulin (Göttingen: Vandenhoeck and Ruprecht, 2016), 194–200.

[19] Georg Schwarzenberger, *International Law and Totalitarian Lawlessness* (London: Jonathan Cape, 1943). Ečer quotes this book in "U.N. War Crimes Comm'n, Supplement to the Minority represented by Dr. B. Ečer on the question whether the preparation and launching of the present war should be considered as crimes being within the scope of the United Nations War Crimes Commission, Doc. C.56a, 6 October 1944," www.legal-tools.org/uploads/tx_ltpdb/File_3287-3302.pdf.

said, reflecting the view of the British Foreign Office. The issue remained unresolved until the end of the year.[20]

At the same time, the UNWCC was presented with another innovative augmentation of the laws and customs of war, namely "crimes against humanity" as the fulfilment of the Martens Clause's aspiration to codify the "laws of humanity."[21] The notion of crimes against humanity was not new of course. Famously, the French, British, and Russian joint declaration in May 1915 stated that they would hold Turkish leaders "personally responsible" for "new crimes of Turkey against humanity and civilization," namely massacres of Ottoman Armenian subjects.[22] It was taken up again in 1943 when two American legal academics, one of them a special assistant to the US Attorney General, argued that German officials who ordered or permitted "the perpetration of an act of wanton cruelty or violation of civilized methods of warfare" should be prosecuted for "a crime against the laws of humanity and of civilization."[23] In March 1944, US President Roosevelt, having just authorized the establishment of the War Refugee Board, denounced "the wholesale systematic murder of the Jews" as "one of the blackest crimes of all history" and as "crimes against humanity in the name of the German people."[24] In the same month, the US representative to the UNWCC, Henry Pell (1884–1961), appointed by Roosevelt against the wishes of his conservative State Department, asked whether "war crimes" could be expanded or "analogous crimes" introduced. For the latter, he suggested "crimes against humanity" to "refer, among others, to crimes committed against stateless persons or against any persons because of their race or religion."[25] Ečer was

---

[20] E.g., Bohuslav Ečer (Rapporteur), "Scope of the Retributive Action of the United Nations According to Their Official Declarations. The Problem of "War Crimes" in Connection with the Second World War, United Nations War Crimes Commission, Committee III, 27 April 1944," www.legal-tools.org/en/browse/record/274d1e/. Sellars, *"Crimes Against Peace" and International Law*, 59–64.

[21] Egon Schwelb, "Crimes against Humanity," *British Yearbook of International Law* 23 (1946): 181–2.

[22] France, Great Britain and Russia Joint Declaration, May 24, 1915: www.armenian-genocide.org/Affirmation.160/current_category.7/affirmation_detail.html.

[23] Charles Cheney Hyde and Edwin D. Dickinson, "Punishment of War Criminals," *Proceedings of the American Society of International Law at Its Annual Meeting (1921–1969)* 37 (April 30–May 1, 1943): 53.

[24] Franklin Delano Roosevelt Administration: Statement on Holocaust Victims and Justice (March 24, 1944), Jewish Virtual Library, www.jewishvirtuallibrary.org/roosevelt-state ment-on-holocaust-victims-and-justice.

[25] Dan Plesch, *Human Rights after Hitler: The Lost History of Prosecuting Axis War Crimes* (Washington, DC: Georgetown University Press, 2017), 161. Pell was close to American Jewish leaders. Michael S. Blayney, "Herbert Pell, War Crimes, and the Jews," *American Jewish Historical Quarterly* 65, no. 4 (1976): 335–52; Graham Cox, "Seeking Justice for the Holocaust: Herbert C. Pell versus the US State Department," *Criminal Law Forum* 25, nos. 1–2 (2014): 77–110. Pell was also influenced by the Polish-born Harvard

naturally supportive, as he wanted to use the concept to cover the prewar German persecution of Czechoslovaks.[26] By the end of the year, however, he and Pell had been outmaneuvered as their propositions met stiff resistance from the British in the UNWCC. The State Department removed Pell, while Ečer and others resigned in protest that the major war criminals would not be indicted. As a vehicle for small nations, the UNWCC would not be permitted to determine the direction of international criminal prosecutions. Lemkin's new concept could have attracted these figures in 1944, but his book was not published until November.

By the middle the year, the impending victory over Germany concentrated the minds of Allied military officials about the prospects of prosecuting Germans in their military courts. Politicians also felt pressured by intense public interest in such trials, including of those responsible for persecuting German-Jewish civilians before the war. Within the American administration, the Treasury Secretary, Henry Morgenthau (1891–1967), was making noises about victims who "met death because of his nationality, race, color, creed, or political conviction."[27] Expectations had been raised by the regular denunciations of German atrocities by Roosevelt, although he had not committed himself to an international trial. By September 1944, the British authorities contacted their American counterparts to raise the problem of how to handle the major war criminals, although they still opposed trials. For them, the war criminals presented a political rather than legal problem.[28] For its part, the WJC wanted a separate trial for conspiracy against the Jewish people as "the greatest sufferer of this war" as well as independent Jewish legal representation. Like the small nations that met at the St James Palace, American and British officials blocked such representations, while insisting that prewar persecutions were impossible to categorize as war crimes.[29]

The same arguments that beset the UNWCC now preoccupied American officials in the second half of 1944 and early 1945. Caught between legal scruples and public opinion, they decided on a compromise: first, by adopting

criminologist, Sheldon Glueck (1896–1980), who was in touch with the Institute for Jewish Affairs. Glueck was the author of numerous influential publications, including *War Criminals: Their Prosecution and Punishment* (New York: Alfred A. Knopf, 1944).

[26] Bohuslav Ečer, "The Scope of Retributive Action of the United Nations According to the Official Declarations (The Problem of "War Crimes" in Connection with the Second World War), Explanatory and Additional Note by Dr. Ečer to his Report (Doc. III/v)," III/4(a). UNWCC, Committee III, May 12, 1944; von Lingen, "Setting the Path for the UNWCC," 70.

[27] Bradley F. Smith, *The American Road to Nuremberg: The Documentary Record, 1944–1945* (Palo Alto: Hoover Institution Press, 1982), 28.

[28] Ibid., 31–2.

[29] Michael Marrus, "A Jewish Lobby at Nuremberg: Jacob Robinson and the Institute of Jewish Affairs, 1945–46," *Cardozo Law Review* 27, no. 4 (2006): 1651–65.

Trainin's notion of aggressive warfare in terms of a conspiracy in order to cover the German leadership that were difficult to prosecute under Hague law; and, second, by augmenting extant law with a mitigated notion of crimes against humanity to cover those prewar persecutions of Axis minorities linked to war preparations. In this way, the ideal of noninterference in the domestic affairs of other states could be maintained, and no foreign court would scrutinize the US's own dubious racial record, about which American officials were acutely conscious.[30]

The US Secretary of War, Henry L. Stimson (1867–1950), was candid about his government's concerns in a memorandum in September 1944. While he supported trials to avert Morgenthau's alternative of executing Germans, which Roosevelt momentarily supported, Stimson had to ensure they did not create mischievous precedents:

> While we appreciate the abhorrence of those crimes against civilization, I have yet to see any way by which we can treat them as a crime against ourselves or as a crime in the punishment of which we can participate. I don't see any more reason in law or in justice why we should intervene in the matter to punish the Germans who had been guilty of killing the Jews than Germany would have the right to intervene in our country to punish the people who are lynching the Negroes.[31]

After the trials, Robert Jackson (1892–1954), the American supreme court justice appointed as chief prosecutor, was willing to place this reasoning on the record: "Unless we have a war connection as a basis for reaching them, I would think we have no basis for dealing with atrocities," he wrote in his trial report, elaborating thus:

> We have some regrettable circumstances at times in our own country in which minorities are unfairly treated. We think it is justifiable that we interfere or attempt to bring retribution to individuals or to states only because the concentration camps and the deportations were in pursuance of a common plan or enterprise of making an unjust or illegal war in which we became involved. We see no other basis on which we are justified in reaching the atrocities which were committed inside Germany, under German law, or even in violation of German law, by authorities of the German state.[32]

So "crimes against humanity" would become an indictment that could cover prewar Nazi persecution of its own citizens only if it could be categorized as a

[30] Smith, *The American Road to Nuremberg*.

[31] Graham Cox, *Seeking Justice for the Holocaust: Herbert C. Pell, Franklin D. Roosevelt, and the Limits of International Law* (Norman: University of Oklahoma Press, 2019), 150–1.

[32] Robert H. Jackson, *Report of Robert H. Jackson, United States Representative to the International Conference on Military Trials, London, 1945* (Washington, DC: US Government Printing Office, 1949), 331, 333.

preparation to wage an illegal war. Underlying the determination to make as few changes to international law as possible, the major war criminals would not be tried before a new permanent international criminal court but by an ad hoc military tribunal constituted by the big three plus France. The small nations and WJC that had driven the war crimes debate throughout the war would play no formal role.[33]

Lemkin's Invention

As this debate unfolded in the early to mid-1940s, Lemkin was lecturing on military law at Duke. These lectures sparked the interest of the Judge Advocate General Office in Washington, DC, which sent Colonel Archibald King (1882–1971) to hear them. King, who was chief of the War Plans Division, helped oversee codification of military legislation and provided legal advice to the US government on the laws of war. His acquaintance with Lemkin likely led to the American Bar Association's invitation to address its meeting in Indianapolis in October 1941 on "Totalitarian Control Over Foreign Economies."[34] King also facilitated Lemkin's three lectures on military government in Europe in June 1942 at the War Department's newly opened School of Military Government in Charlottesville, Virginia.[35] This appearance and the intervention of Lemkin's host at Duke led to interest by George A. Finch (1884–1957) from the Division of International Affairs of the Carnegie Endowment and editor of the *American Journal of International Law*. Finch was looking for experts on military government and learned in May 1942 that Lemkin was working "on the government of countries occupied by enemies in the war of 1914–18," that he had collected German decrees from the current war, and that he planned "to publish two volumes on the general subject."[36] These studies and teaching flowed into Lemkin's *Axis Rule*, which he worked on in 1942 and 1943 after its commission by the Carnegie

---

[33] Smith, *The American Road to Nuremberg*; William A. Schabas, "Nuremberg and Aggressive War," in *Seeking Accountability for the Unlawful Use of Force*, ed. Leila Nadya Sadat (Cambridge: Cambridge University Press, 2018), 58–79.

[34] Ernest Zitser, "A White Crow: Raphael Lemkin's Intellectual Interlude at Duke University, 1941–1942," *North Carolina Historical Review* 96 (2019): 34–66.

[35] "Reading on Military Government in Europe," compiled by Raphael Lemkin, School of Military Government, Raphael Lemkin Papers, MS-60, Box 6, Folder 1, AJA.; Robert R. Wilson to Phillip G. Jessup, May 9, 1942, Robert R. Wilson Papers, Duke University Archives, Box 1, Correspondence February 1942–August 1942. American Jewish Archives, Box 6, Folder 1. *Readings on Military Government in Europe*; John Cooper, *Raphael Lemkin and the Struggle for the Genocide Convention* (Basingstoke: Palgrave Macmillan, 2008), 47; Raphael Lemkin, *Totally Unofficial: The Autobiography of Raphael Lemkin, ed. Donna-Lea Frieze* (New Haven: Yale University Press, 2013), 112.

[36] Robert W. Wilson to George A. Finch, May 23, 1942, Robert R. Wilson Papers, Duke University Archives, Box 1, Correspondence February 1942–August 1942.

Foundation. He completed it in late 1943, although publication was delayed a year due to a contractual dispute.[37]

The book analyzes and reproduces Axis occupation decrees that, Lemkin concluded, licensed the conquest, exploitation, looting, and ultimately destruction of occupied peoples by various means. He proposed a legal realization of the Martens Clause with his "generic notion" of genocide: to denote the "destruction of nations" by joining the ancient Greek word of *genos* (i.e. tribe, nation, or race) and the Latin *caedere* (to kill).[38] He did so by combining the Zionist conception of national cultures with the small nations ideology that the Entente Powers had mobilized against German expansionism in World War I.

> Among the basic features which have marked progress in civilization are respect for and appreciation of the national characteristics and qualities contributed to world culture by different nations – characteristics and qualities which, as illustrated in the contributions made by nations weak in defense and poor in economic resources, are not to be measured in terms of national power and wealth.[39]

In doing so, Lemkin was simultaneously invoking the Fourth Hague Convention (1907) to show how the Nazis violated international law while arguing that this law was inadequate.[40] Genocide had not been foreseen by the convention's formulators, he wrote: it covered individuals rather than peoples. Thus, while Hague law pertained to many Nazi policies and practices, it did not anticipate the Nazis' "various ingenious measures for weakening or destroying political, social, and cultural elements in national groups." Lemkin intended to intervene in the Allied debate about prosecuting Axis war criminals by dealing with "The entire problem of genocide ... as a whole."[41]

Axis Rule, then, aimed to supplement rather than replace existing law: that is why the book is generally about Axis violations of the laws of occupation: each chapter analyzes a domain of occupation that violated Hague law.[42] And that is why it contains a *single chapter* introducing his proposed innovation to this law: genocide as a "new technique of occupation." He stressed that it was a new crime only by criminalizing practices of national destruction that were partially covered by current international law. The legal innovation he proposed combined relevant dimensions of the Hague Regulations with new ones Lemkin identified – like "subsidizing children begotten by members of the

---

[37] Cooper, *Raphael Lemkin and the Struggle for the Genocide Convention*, 53.
[38] Lemkin, *Axis Rule in Occupied Europe*, 79.   [39] Ibid., 91.
[40] Not for nothing does *Axis Rule* abound with references to the Hague Regulations and the Martens Clause. Referring to the SS, for example, Lemkin wrote that "Such crimes are directed not only against municipal law of the occupied countries, but also against international law and the laws of humanity": Lemkin, *Axis Rule in Occupied Europe*, 23.
[41] Ibid., 92.   [42] E.g., ibid., 12–14, 77.

armed forces of the occupant and born of women nationals of the occupied area." Genocide was thus "a composite of different acts of persecution or destruction."[43]

Specifically, he suggested three changes to international law. To begin with, the Hague Convention should be amended by adding the following kinds of measures:

> every action infringing upon the life, liberty, health, corporal integrity, economic existence, and the honor of the inhabitants when committed because they belong to a national, religious, or racial group; and in the second, every policy aiming at the destruction or the aggrandizement of one such group to the prejudice or detriment of another.[44]

Second, because genocide could occur during peacetime, he suggested internationalizing the League's minority protection treaties: "An international multilateral treaty should provide for the introduction, not only in the constitution but also in the criminal code of each country, of provisions protecting minority groups from oppression because of their nationhood, religion, or race."[45] This was not yet the convention that the UN General Assembly called for in late 1946: each country's criminal code should prosecute perpetrators on the basis of "universal repression."[46]

In effect, Lemkin was repeating themes from the interwar debate, not only about terrorism, but about submarine warfare. Responding to Italian and German submarine attacks on Spanish vessels during the Spanish Civil War, Britain and France drove the Treaty of Nyon (1937), which declared that submarine attacks against neutral merchant shipping constituted "acts contrary to the most elementary dictates of humanity," thereby invoking the Martens Clause and echoing Woodrow Wilson's statement that German submarine warfare in World War I was "a warfare against mankind." Controversially, the treaty's preamble stated that such attacks "should be justly treated as piracy," thus proposing universal repression of submarine crews as criminals rather than as rights-bearing agents of sovereign states. Two years later, Hersch Lauterpacht elaborated the treaty by advocating the proposition that submarine crews were "enemies of mankind" subject to "universal jurisdiction": they should be prosecuted by any state. He was seeking to extend the remit of international law over a new military technology.[47] Lemkin's call for "universal repression" was not conceptually new.

Innovative was his third suggestion: establishing a mechanism to oversee international law. As the Hague Convention and the minorities treaties were

---

[43] Ibid., 92.   [44] Ibid., 93.   [45] Ibid.   [46] Ibid., 92.

[47] Daniel Heller-Roazen, *The Enemy of All: Piracy and the Law of Nations* (New York: Zone Books, 2009); Walter Rech, "Rightless Enemies: Schmitt and Lauterpacht on Political Piracy," *Oxford Journal of Legal Studies* 32, no. 2 (2012): 235–63.

no deterrent to the Germans, he urged "an international controlling agency vested with specific powers" to inspect "the occupied countries and mak[e] inquiries as to the manner in which the occupant treats nations in prison."[48] This notion eventually became partially realized by the International Commission of the Red Cross and the Geneva Conventions that it oversees. Taken together, genocide fulfilled the Martens Clause: "Genocide as described above presents one of the most complete and glaring illustrations of the violation of international law and the laws of humanity."[49]

In the immediate context of the war, we know that Lemkin intended genocide to refer to the Axis destruction of Christian and Jewish nations.[50] To this extent, his book was no different from the earlier Czechoslovak and Polish ones that likewise included the persecution of their Jewish citizens. Unlike those governments' books, though, he distinguished between the Nazis' persecution of Jews and Roma on the one hand and Christian majority on the other by arguing that the former was driven by ideological-racial hatred and the latter by political logics of repression and exploitation. This distinction imported instability into the genocide concept, rendering it confusing to his contemporaries, and controversial to the present day. For "the destruction of nations" is as intrinsically vague a notion as "nations" itself. Are they primarily "spiritual" or "biological" entities? If a combination of the two, when do attacks on the former reach a genocidal threshold? In other words, at what point in the "one long chain," analyzed in the previous chapter, does the violation of "honor" become "destruction"?

Certainly, nationalists agreed that attacks on culture alone destroyed their nations. The Polish government-in-exile, for example, declared that the German violation of Poles' "conscience" in forcing them to relinquish their citizenship "is even worse than physical terror."[51] Lemkin did not agree. He had to reconcile the differences between occupied Christian nations and the WJC, namely the tension between a conception of nation as cultural as well as biological, between incremental partial destruction ("crippling") and total destruction, between deportation-for-displacement and deportation-for-murder. So, while he referred to the persecution of various nations throughout *Axis Rule* and proposed an expansive notion of genocide, it contained an irreducible biological dimension, signalled here by the word "annihilation."[52]

> Generally speaking, genocide does not necessarily mean the immediate destruction of a nation, except when accomplished by mass killings of all members of a nation. It is intended rather to signify a coordinated plan of different actions aiming at the destruction of essential foundations of the

---

[48] Lemkin, *Axis Rule in Occupied Europe*, 93–4.   [49] Ibid., 94.   [50] Ibid., 92, 80.
[51] "German Crimes in Poland," *The Times*, December 21, 1940, 3.
[52] Lemkin, *Axis Rule in Occupied Europe*, 77, 89, 137–9 152.

life of national groups, with the aim of annihilating the groups themselves.[53]

Lemkin thus included biological destruction as the last or most extreme example of genocidal policy:

> The objectives of such a plan would be disintegration of the political and social institutions, of culture, language, national feelings, religion, and the economic existence of national groups, and the destruction of the personal security, liberty, health, dignity, and *even the lives of the individuals belonging to such groups*. Genocide is directed against the national group as an entity, and the actions involved are directed against individuals, not in their individual capacity, but as members of the national group.[54]

In an article in April 1945, he underlined the physical dimension of genocide by declaring that the minority protection treaties were unsatisfactory because they protected "political and civil rights, rather than the biological structure of the groups involved."[55]

Lemkin attempted to reconcile the WJC and small Christian nations imperatives by drawing on both Jewish and non-Jewish émigré sources. He adumbrated eight "techniques" of destruction, each of them a link in the chain[56]:

Political techniques refer to the cessation of self-government and local rule, and their replacement by that of the occupier. "Every reminder of former national character was obliterated."

Social techniques entail attacking the intelligentsia, "because this group largely provides the national leadership and organizes resistance against Nazification." The point of such attacks is to "weaken the national, spiritual resources."

Cultural techniques ban the use of native language in education, and inculcate youth with propaganda.

Economic techniques shift economic resources from the occupied to the occupier. Peoples the Germans regarded as of "related blood," like those of Luxembourg and Alsace-Lorraine, were given incentives to recognize this kinship.

Biological techniques decrease the birth rate of the occupied. "Thus in incorporated Poland marriages between Poles are forbidden without special permission of the Governor ... of the district; the latter, as a matter of principle, does not permit marriages between Poles."

[53] Ibid., 79.   [54] Ibid.

[55] Raphael Lemkin, "Genocide: A Modern Crime," *Free World* 4 (April 1945): 43.

[56] This discussion of the eight techniques is taken from Lemkin, *Axis Rule in Occupied Europe*, 82–90.

Physical techniques mean the rationing of food, endangering of health, and mass killing in order to accomplish the "physical debilitation and even annihilation of national groups in occupied countries."

Religious techniques try to disrupt the national and religious influences of the occupied people.

Moral techniques are policies "to weaken the spiritual resistance of the national group." This technique of moral debasement entails diverting the "mental energy of the group" from "moral and national thinking" to "base instincts."

Genocidal techniques thus covered the gamut of occupation policies, ranging from "aggrandizement of one such group to the prejudice or detriment of another" to mass murder. Lemkin's follow-up definition seemed ambiguous about the purpose of deportation: to expel or to destroy a population. "Genocide has two phases," he wrote: "one, destruction of the national pattern of the oppressed group: the other, the imposition of the national pattern of the oppressor. This imposition, in turn, may be made upon the oppressed population which is allowed to remain, or upon the territory alone, after removal of the population and the colonization of the area by the oppressor's own nationals."[57] However, although biological survival was implied by this definition, it was undercut by his insistence that terms like "denationalization" or "Germanization" – the imposition of the conqueror's "national pattern" on the conquered people – were unsatisfactory because "they treat mainly the cultural, economic, and social aspects of genocide, leaving out the biological aspects, such as causing the physical decline and even destruction of the population involved."[58]

The "biological essence of a nation" (or "national-biological power"[59]) was elemental, because "such a nation cannot rise again to resist an aggressor" if it is destroyed. Repeatedly, Lemkin stressed the demographic calculations of the Nazis: they "aimed at winning the peace even though the war itself is lost" by destroying, disintegrating, and weakening an "enemy nation." In this way, the occupier was "in a position to deal with ... other peoples from the vantage point of biological superiority."[60] Plainly, Lemkin thought biological attacks were an irreducible component of genocide, thereby combining the WJC and

---

[57] Ibid., 79.   [58] Ibid., 80.

[59] Raphael Lemkin, "Genocide as a Crime under International Law," *American Journal of International Law* 4, no. 1 (1947): 147.

[60] Lemkin, *Axis Rule in Occupied Europe*, 81, xi. "The Germans hoped to control permanently a depopulated Europe, and ultimately, in partnership with Japan... to dominate the world. Thus genocide became a basic element of geopolitics": Lemkin, "Genocide: A New International Crime – Punishment and Prevention," *Revue Internationale de Droit Pénal* 17 (1946): 364.

small nations perspectives. In this way, he could distinguish Nazi policies from Zionist and British discussions about partitioning Palestine and "transferring" parts of the Palestinian Arab population to make way for Zionist settlement.[61]

Individual occupied countries were treated in Part II of the book, in which the legal violations and combination of genocidal techniques could be observed. Here Lemkin treated Jews as citizens of those countries, as their exiled governments demanded. Their persecution and legalized mode of destruction predominated in the exposition. The genocide of Greeks in the Aegean region by Bulgarians, for example, was caused by closing Greek schools, imposing their language, expelling Greek refugees from Turkey, freezing bank accounts, instituting disadvantageous exchange rates, expropriating property and giving it to Bulgarian colonists, invalidating the licenses of Greek artisans and professionals so they could not support their families, and so on.[62] These policies thus affected the capacity of Greeks to reproduce themselves biologically. His subtle point is that seemingly nonlethal measures can be genocidal if they affect the biological viability of a people.

Could genocide occur without mass killing? Lemkin seemed to imply as much. In Luxembourg, for example, the religious technique of genocide entailed enrolling children in "pro-Nazi youth organizations" so as to loosen the grip of Roman Catholic culture. Alternatively, in Poland, where no such assimilation was possible, the Germans conducted "the systematic pillage and destruction of church property and persecution of the clergy" to "destroy the religious leadership of the Polish nation."[63] The genocide of Serbs also took place "mainly in political and cultural aspects," he continued. "Its national pattern is being destroyed by genocide legislation," mainly prohibiting Cyrillic. However, Lemkin concluded by mentioning "massacres and tortures" of "several hundred thousands" by the Croatian Ustasha, thereby introducing doubt about whether cultural repression could be genocidal without physical destruction.[64] The relationship between persecution and the cultural and biological in the destruction of nations was never clearly articulated.

This unstable synthesis was built into the structure of *Axis Rule*. The chapters in Part I cover successively the domains of Axis illegality: 1. Administration, 2. Police, 3. Law, 4. Courts, 5. Property, 6. Finance, 7. Labor, 8. The Legal Status of the Jews, 9. Genocide. Although Lemkin observed that Nazis attacked the nationality of virtually all European peoples they occupied, he also shared the WJC view about the distinctive Jewish experience, devoting Chapter 8 to the subject. It outlined the "special status" of Jews in each conquered country, and noted that they were "one of the main objects of German genocide policy" and were "to be destroyed completely." He knew

---

[61] On Zionist partition and transfer views, see Itzhak Galnoor, "The Zionist Debate on Partition (1919–1947)," *Israel Studies* 14, no. 2 (2009): 74–87.
[62] Lemkin, *Axis Rule in Occupied Europe*, 188–90.   [63] Ibid., 90.   [64] Ibid., 259–60.

about the extermination camps.[65] At the same time, Lemkin departed from the WJC view by coupling Jews and "Gypsies," much to Robinson's disgust, as targets of racial hatred, while other Europeans were deported and/or reduced in number to make way for German colonists.[66] For all that, genocide's conceptual incoherence was also its political genius; because it covered each link in the chain of destruction, genocide could operate as a bridging concept to attract both occupied Christian nation and WJC support. To break through, though, other concepts had to exhaust themselves.

The main rival was crimes against humanity. By all accounts, Lauterpacht, now the Whewell Chair of International Law at Cambridge University, had suggested it to Jackson, thereby passing on the notion that had been percolating in international discussions for at least two years. With this generic concept, he proposed to link the persecution of Jews with other groups without having to resort to an ethnically specific indictment that Jackson and the British opposed; he would have been aware of the failed WJC approaches to the Allies.[67] Juxtaposing Lauterpacht and Lemkin as avatars of fundamentally rival concepts – crimes against humanity defending individual and/or human rights and genocide defending group rights – misses the point that both notions were advanced to perform the same work. On the one hand, they were to cover the persecution of Jews before and during the war, and on the other to link it to non-Jewish experiences.[68] Like Lemkin, Lauterpacht had no doubts that Jews were especially targeted by the Nazi regime. His reasoning was the same as the WJC and Institute for Jewish Affairs: Jews were attacked for nonpolitical reasons, by virtue of their identity alone. It is worth quoting him at length:

> It is an unchallenged fact that numerically – both relatively and absolutely – the Jews have been the greatest victims of the war crimes committed by Germany in occupied territories. Moreover, as the avowed object of the war crimes committed against Jews has been the total extermination of the Jewish race on the continent of Europe, the resulting character of these crimes is such as to put them in a category of their own. . . . In the case of other races the reason given for deprivation of life has been an allegation of direct guilt or, in the case of hostages, of a kind of vicarious responsibility. In the case of Jews it has been membership of the Jewish race. . . . There is no true comparison between this slow torture of extermination

---

[65] Ibid., 89, 81. Cf. 21–2; 77; 249–50.

[66] Raphael Lemkin, "Hitler Case-Outline," AJA, Collection 60, Box 7, Folders 12 and 13. I have corrected spelling in this quotation.

[67] Bloxham, *Genocide on Trial*, 67; Hathaway and Shapiro, *The Internationalists*, 267; James Loeffler, *Rooted Cosmopolitans: Jews and Human Rights in the Twentieth Century* (New Haven: Yale University Press, 2018), 130–1.

[68] Symptomatic: Philippe Sands, *East-West Street: On the Origins of "Genocide" and "Crimes against Humanity"* (New York: Alfred A. Knopf, 2016).

accompanied by a denial, most savage of all time, of the dignity of man, and the mass massacres in the past which have soiled the pages of history.[69]

And yet, like Lemkin and eventually Robinson, Lauterpacht understood that pressing the Allies to accede to a specific Jewish indictment in mooted postwar trials was a fruitless endeavor. It was necessary to devise a generic notion that would cover "racial" persecution and appeal to the Christian sensibilities of the Allies. Which one would prevail?

The Nuremberg Disappointment

Lemkin's book, *Axis Rule*, gained immediate attention with reviews in the US press when published in November 1944.[70] On the basis of contacts and the book's success, Lemkin was employed temporarily in the War Crimes Office of the Judge Advocate General in May 1945 to contribute to the data collection effort of the planned international military tribunal. He was not alone. Throughout proceedings, Jackson also relied on the Institute for Jewish Affairs for information and advice; Robinson, whose acumen impressed Jackson, was even bidden to Nuremberg to assist.[71] Unsatisfied with a minor support role, Lemkin used the opportunity to popularize his new notion, but to little effect; indeed, he alienated many colleagues and was eventually frozen out of discussions.[72] His legal innovations were inconsistent with US and British visions of the trial. They did not want to establish a permanent mechanism to supervise occupations, still less enable the prosecution of genocide in peacetime and within their own borders. An outsider, Lemkin gained little traction against established academics like Glueck, Lauterpacht, and Trainin, still less the team at the Institute for Jewish Affairs.

The charter of the International Military Tribunal, signed in London in August 1945 ("The London Charter"), did not include genocide as a separate indictment, of which there were three: a common plan or conspiracy to commit crimes against peace, war crimes, and crimes against humanity. Genocide was listed, but under war crimes (Article 6a) as "deliberate and

---

[69] Loeffler, *Rooted Cosmopolitans*, 128. Jews were victims of human rights violations, not genocide, he thought: Hersh Lauterpacht, *An International Bill of the Rights of Man* (New York: Columbia University Press, 1945), vii.

[70] Editorial, "Genocide," *Washington Post*, December 3, 1944. Otto D. Tolischus, "Twentieth-Century Moloch: The Nazi-Inspired Totalitarian State, Devourer of Progress-and of Itself," *New York Times Book Review*, January 21, 1945. Book reviews in scholarly journals appeared in the same year.

[71] See Jackson's letter of thanks to the Institute of November 1, 1946, AJA/WJC, Box H157, File 17, Germany, War Crimes, Trials, Nuremberg, 1946–1947. See also Box C106, File 16, Nuremberg Trials, Contacts with Jackson, Robert H. 1945.

[72] Stiller, "The Mass Murder of the European Jews and the Concept of 'Genocide' in the Nuremberg Trials."

systematic genocide, viz., the extermination of racial and national groups, against the civilian populations of certain occupied territories in order to destroy particular races and classes of people and national, racial, or religious groups, particularly Jews, Poles, and Gypsies and others."[73] The accusation of genocide subsequently peppered the trials of the 23 major war criminals, and also the subsequent Nuremberg Military Tribunals of 185 lesser Nazis run by the US military from October 1946 to January 1949. Far from signaling the concept's breakthrough, its usage was intended to amplify the indictments of war crimes and crimes against humanity. Neither the prosecutors nor the judges recognized genocide as an independent crime – despite Lemkin's best efforts. Although occasionally used in the broad manner of *Axis Rule*, especially by the British prosecutor, Sir Hartley Shawcross (1902–2003), trial references to genocide increasingly took it as a synonym for physical destruction of national groups.[74]

Lemkin was crestfallen by the IMT judgment on October 1, 1946. He had failed to get his concept legally recognized. The judgment did not mention genocide and did not deem the prewar persecution of German Jews as a crime against humanity.[75] Anticipating this outcome months before, he had written an article advocating an "international treaty which would formulate genocide as an international crime, providing for its prevention and punishment in time of peace and war."[76] Now he set out to lobby for such a treaty within the nascent United Nations organization that was meeting for the first regular session in New York. Lemkin approached diplomats from small nations – naturally Czechoslovak leaders – and newer states from outside Europe that did not feel beholden to the great powers, Great Britain and France, which had set about consolidating and recovering their colonial territories immediately after the war. He also worked with US Jewish-Christian advocacy groups to

---

[73] Article 6 (a), War crimes, indictment, Nuremberg Trial proceedings Vol. 1, Avalon Project, available at: http://avalon.law.yale.edu/imt/count3.asp. Suggestions that Lemkin influenced elements of the indictments, like the conspiracy approach, are speculative.

[74] Office of the US Chief of Counsel, Public Relations Office, Special Release, July 27, 1946, in Raphael Lemkin Collection, Columbia University School of Law, Box 4, Folder 8, IMT-OCCW-PRO-Special Release No. 1, Introduction "Genocide," July 27, 1946; Alexa Stiller, "Semantics of Extermination: The Use of the New Term of Genocide in the Nuremberg Trials and the Genesis of a Master Narrative," in *The Nuremberg Trials Revisited: New Analyses and Interpretations*, ed. Kim Priemel and Alexa Stiller (New York and Oxford: Berghahn Books, 2012), 165–214; Hilary Earl, "Prosecuting Genocide before the Genocide Convention: Raphael Lemkin and the Nuremberg Trials, 1945-1949," *Journal of Genocide Research* 15, no. 3 (2013): 317–37.

[75] Anson Rabinbach, "The Challenge of the Unprecedented: Raphael Lemkin and the Concept of Genocide," *Simon Dubnow Institute Yearbook* 4 (2005): 409–10; Irvin-Erickson, *Raphaël Lemkin and the Concept of Genocide*, ch. 4.

[76] Raphael Lemkin, "Genocide," *American Scholar* 15, no. 2 (April 1946): 230.

convince the US delegation.[77] Already by November 2, Cuba, India, and Panama had asked the Secretary General to place a resolution on the punishment and prevention of genocide on the General Assembly agenda. At the Assembly's meeting on November 22, the Panamanian delegate explicitly referenced Nuremberg's limitations.[78]

In the lead-up to the meeting, Lemkin tried to remove impediments to the resolution's support by placing a letter in the *New York Times* that set out his new pragmatic approach to the question. While affirming his view that nations could be destroyed by policies "ranging from mass killings to the disintegration of its spiritual resources," he understood that the definition of genocide for "international legislation" needed to be "limited to more basic elements, such as killings, mayhem, and biological devises, as, for example, sterilization." Only "such acts which are serious enough to be of international concern" would be included, and they must be "undertaken habitually and systematically and deriving from an organized plan or conspiracy."[79] The day before, on December 7, 1946, he wrote to a colleague to explain his reasoning. "The resolution excludes rightly political groups or political parties, or similar groups," because international law could not contain "the differences existing now in political ideologies." Those ideologies were "political dynamite" that would scuttle a treaty, as they torpedoed the League of Nations terrorism convention in 1937. Consequently, "the restrained character of the resolution" should be praised. In any event, genocidal policies principally targeted national groups, he added in line with his lifelong commitment to that category of human identity.[80] This approach effectively depoliticized genocide, and also defined it as physical destruction as the WJC was advocating.[81]

The approach also reflected the meaning of genocide in the Nuremberg war crimes indictment and the increasingly widespread interpretation of genocide as a synonym for the Nazi persecution of Jews understood as mass murder. By late 1946, shocking imagery of Nazi death camps and surviving inmates was widespread in newsreels and photographs.[82] Having failed in their campaign

---

[77] Irvin-Erickson, *Raphaël Lemkin and the Concept of Genocide*, 152–7.

[78] R. Jimenez, "The Crime of Genocide: Request from the Delegations of Cuba, India, and Panama for the Inclusion of an Additional Agenda Item (document A/Bur/50)," 22nd Meeting of the General Assembly (A/C.6/84), 110.

[79] Raphael Lemkin, "Genocide before the UN: Importance of Resolution Declaring Crime International Is Stressed," *New York Times*, November 8, 1946, 22.

[80] Raphael Lemkin to Maynard Gertler, December 7, 1946, American Jewish Historical Society, Raphael Lemkin Collection, Box 1, Folder 18.

[81] AJA, WJC Papers, Box B84, File 6, Genocide 1947.

[82] Raymond Daniell, "War-Crimes Court Sees Horror Films," *New York Times*, November 30, 1945; Dan Stone, *The Liberation of the Camps: The End of the Holocaust and Its Aftermath* (New Haven: Yale University Press, 2015); Sharon Sliwinski, *Human Rights in Camera* (Chicago: University of Chicago Press, 2011), ch. 4.

for a Jewish indictment and separate trial at Nuremberg, and feeling dissatisfied with the trial's rendering of crimes against humanity, the WJC supported
"genocide" as a vehicle of minority protection after the war. Concerned about
the safety of Jewish communities in North Africa, the Middle East, and
Pakistan in light of the conflict in Palestine in late 1947 and 1948, the WJC
and other Jewish organizations also advocated for the Universal Declaration of
Human Rights.[83]

Resolution 96 "The Crime of Genocide" passed unanimously and without
debate on December 11, 1946. It expressed the language of transgression as it
had developed since the sixteenth century, though reflecting Lemkin's preoccupation with nationality as the building block of civilization.

> Genocide is a denial of the right of existence of entire human groups, as
> homicide is the denial of the right to live of individual human beings; such
> denial of the right of existence shocks the conscience of mankind, results
> in great losses to humanity in the form of cultural and other contributions
> represented by these human groups, and is contrary to moral law and to
> the spirit and aims of the United Nations.[84]

That it was on the agenda at all was his great achievement: his concept
appealed to the new General Assembly whose members – small and new
states – could no longer be marginalized by the big three; while the
Americans were cautiously supportive of the genocide proposition, the
British and Soviets opposed it. By the contingencies of the restricted application of crimes against humanity at Nuremberg and the refoundation of the UN
immediately thereafter, an improbable coalition of states and religious groups
could agree to criminalize genocide. This new concept was a peculiar artefact
of the war and early postwar years, created for a particular purpose and given
institutional life by particular circumstances. That it would develop was now
assured by the existence of a convention that meant other contingencies could
attach to it as a vehicle of political mobilization. But before it could become a
trope during the Cold War and decolonization struggles, the great powers set
about reimposing their Nuremberg discipline on international law. Nor did
they want the UN interfering in their attempts to assimilate ethnic minorities
in the manner of the interwar minority treaties.[85] They saw themselves as

---

[83] Loeffler, *Rooted Cosmopolitans*, 139–40; Loeffler, "'The Conscience of America': Human
Rights, Jewish Politics, and American Foreign Policy at the 1945 United Nations San
Francisco Conference," *Journal of American History* 100, no. 2 (2013): 401–28; Nathan
Kurz, *Human Rights and Jewish Internationalism after the Holocaust* (Cambridge:
Cambridge University Press, 2020).

[84] UNGA Resolution 96(1), "The Crime of Genocide," UN Documents, https://undocs.org/
en/A/RES/96/(I).

[85] Adam Weiss-Wendt, *The Soviet Union and the Gutting of the UN Genocide Convention*
(Madison: University of Wisconsin Press, 2017). Israel's ambivalence about the

speaking for civilized values. The 13 Nuremberg Trials between 1945 and 1949 and the UN debates showed that Germany was seen as the archetypal genocidal society that had diverged from the healthy Western, and international, norm.[86]

Excluding Permanent Security from the Genocide Convention

Genocide's meaning was not settled with success in the General Assembly. For one, Lemkin was wrong about the exclusion of political groups and political motivations from Resolution 96. It referred to "racial, religious, *political* and other groups" targeted "on religious, racial, *political* or any other grounds."[87] Adding to the uncertainty, only a year before, in April 1945, Lemkin had declared that genocide intended to "destroy or *degrade* an entire national, religious or racial group by attacking the individual members of that group."[88] These elements were included in a draft convention, commissioned by the UN Secretariat, which Lemkin coauthored with Vespasian V. Pella and Henri Donnedieu de Vabres as members of a "committee of experts." The idea was, as de Vabres put it, that they prepare "a text comprising all the possible solutions; all the future legislator would have to do was to draw upon it at will."[89] Lemkin's old mentors insisted on the inclusion of political groups to reflect the General Assembly resolution, while Lemkin now again insisted on each chain of destruction, which he previously called crippling, degrading, and dishonoring a nationality. As a compromise, the committee settled on a tripartite categorization of genocidal policies as "physical," "biological," and "cultural genocide." This was the structure of the Secretariat Draft of June 1947.[90]

Representatives of UN member states then spent the next 18 months wrangling about this and the next draft convention, the Ad Hoc Committee Draft of 1948. Broad as they were, these drafts already prefigured the debate by

Convention was characteristic of states generally. See Rotem Giladi, "Not Our Salvation. Israel, the Genocide Convention, and the World Court 1950–1951," *Diplomacy & Statecraft* 26, no. 3 (2015): 473–93.

[86] Kim Christian Priemel, *The Betrayal: The Nuremberg Trials and German Divergence* (Oxford: Oxford University Press, 2016); David Mayers, *America and the Postwar World: Remaking International Society, 1945–1956* (Abingdon: Routledge, 2018).

[87] The Crime of Genocide [1946] UNGA 66; A/RES/96 (I) (December 11, 1946), www .worldlii.org/int/other/UNGA/1946/. Emphasis added.

[88] Lemkin, "Genocide: A Modern Crime," 43. Emphasis added.

[89] Draft Convention on the Crime of Genocide, E/447, June 26, 1947. The UN deliberations are collected in Hirad Abtahi and Philippa Webb, eds., *The Genocide Convention: The Travaux Préparatoires*, 2 vols. (Leiden: Brill, 2009), 167, 230.

[90] Ibid., 235–6. Lemkin preferred more complex formulations and argued that all kinds of policies were genocidal if they affected the capacity of a group to biologically reproduce itself.

excluding some elements of permanent security from the outset. The Secretariat Draft stated that acts that "may result in the total or partial destruction of a group of human beings" are excluded if not intended to destroy "a group of human beings." Consequently, much Allied policy and practice in the recent war and postwar period were conveniently omitted: "international or civil war, isolated acts of violence not aimed at the destruction of a group of human beings, the policy of compulsory assimilation of a national element, mass displacements of population."[91] The experts' commentary of their draft readily admitted that civilian populations were affected in modern warfare with "more or less severe losses," but distinguished between such circumstances and genocide by arguing that in the latter "one of the belligerents aims at exterminating the population of enemy territory and systematically destroys what are not genuine military objectives." Military objectives, by contrast, aimed at imposing the victor's will on the loser, whose existence was not imperilled. In other words, killing masses of civilians was not illegal if motivated by military goals: victory, not destruction.[92] In this argument, collateral damage caused by war was legitimate even if as extensive as genocidal violence. This reasoning echoed that of prosecutors in the *Einsatzgruppen* Trial underway at the time (discussed below) and has been repeated in debates about genocide and civilian destruction to the present day. As we see in Chapters 10, 11, and 12, these arguments could be used by apologists for military violence because genocide had been distinguished from permanent security as military neccesity.

Excluding Population Expulsion and Cultural Genocide

The Secretariat Draft also took "mass displacements of populations" off the table. The Secretariat were motivated less by the impending partitions of India and Palestine, whose massive population expulsions began in the second half of 1947, than by the expulsion of millions of Germans from Central and Eastern Europe that the Allies had countenanced toward the end of war. Real-time events inevitably impinged on the debate. Responding to the refugee crisis occasioned by the flight and expulsion of Palestinians from their towns and villages by Zionist forces in 1948, the Syrian representative moved an amendment to include "Imposing measures intended to oblige members of a group to abandon their homes in order to escape the threat of subsequent ill-treatment." Yugoslavia supported the move by referring to German colonialism in the spirit of Lemkin and the wartime analysts covered in Chapter 4: "the Nazis had dispersed a Slav majority from a certain part of Yugoslavia in order to establish a German majority there. That action was tantamount to the

[91] Ibid., 231.   [92] Ibid.

deliberate destruction of a group. Genocide could be committed by forcing members of a group to abandon their homes." This argument did not carry the day. Led by the Soviet representative, who was not motivated to draw attention to his state's expulsion of Germans, most members of the Sixth Committee voted down the amendment. "Transfers of population did not necessarily mean the physical destruction of a group," declared the Belgian representative, stating the emerging consensus.[93]

The partition of India made its way into the debate in connection to "cultural genocide," which had been included on Lemkin's insistence and immediately raised hackles. The British were vehemently opposed to the 1946 General Assembly resolution and the Secretariat Draft, which they tried to side-track and thwart at every turn. An internal memo condemned the Secretariat Draft as a "highly political and provocative document" that confused minority protection (despite the draft's own distinction between cultural genocide and minority protection as well as forced assimilation) and covering the kinds of persecution included in the one-long-chain argument used by authors from small nations, including Lemkin in *Axis Rule*: "subjection of individuals to conditions of life likely to result in debilitation; confiscation of property; prohibition of the use of a national language, and destruction of books or historical and religious monuments."[94] Such measures were extraneous to genocide properly understood, and could threaten British interests: "Were it adapted, it might well serve to re-open recent political issues solutions of which have been condoned on grounds of expediency as for instance the expulsion of Germans from Poland." Regarding cultural genocide, the memo continued, "it might quite plausibly be argued that, were the Convention in force, His Majesty's Government would be guilty of genocide in several cases, against e.g. Germans in the British Zone, the Jews in Palestine, or even perhaps certain colonial peoples."[95] The Americans did not seek to block the Convention negotiations, as they feared "a loss of moral leadership on this question."[96] Instead, they sought to restrict its definition as much as possible. Cultural genocide could not be included because, they argued, genocide was "the heinous crime" of "mass extermination," namely the "physical elimination of the group." It should not be confused with the protection of

[93] A/C.6/SR.81, in ibid., 1479, 1490, 1492, 1495.
[94] UK National Archives, Draft Cabinet Office brief for UK Delegation to the Sixth Session of the Economic and Social Council on Genocide (January 7, 1948 for Cabinet on January 12), 3.
[95] Ibid., 4–5.
[96] National Archives Records Administration (NARA), Department of State telegram to John Maktos, April 13, 1948, RG 59, Box 2186.

minorities.[97] So confident were Department of State officials of the Convention's restricted application that they were "not particularly concerned about the question of lynchings."[98]

Other countries saw it differently. Pakistan was worried about the remaining Muslim population in India who far-right Hindus denounced as a "fifth column": "In India, thirty-five million Muslims were currently living under conditions of terror. Their existence as a separate cultural group was threatened. Although the use of Urdu, a language of Muslim origin, had not been prohibited by law, it was under heavy attack. Muslim cultural and religous [sic] monuments had been burned down or destroyed."[99] The extensive debate on cultural genocide played out according to the same logic as that about population expulsion: it was not genocide if not physical destruction akin to the Holocaust. The notion was struck from the final convention text and is not a legal concept, although protections of heritage and other aspects of culture made their way into other legal instructions.[100]

A Nonpolitical Crime

Genocide was depoliticized in three ways. In the first place, state representatives followed their interwar predecessors, discussed in Chapter 3, in determining that terrorism was not a political offense: suspects could only be extraditable from another country if the crime was nonpolitical. This reasoning was now transferred to genocide.[101] Second, after intense lobbying and debate, political groups were removed from the Convention. Third, political motivations suffered the same fate. Ultimately, genocide was defined narrowly to exclude the possibility that states could repress domestic political opposition with impunity: anticommunists for communist states, and communists for most Latin American states in particular.

---

[97] NARA, RG 59, Box 2186, "US Commentary of the Secretariat Draft Convention on Genocide," September 10, 1947, 2; "Position on Genocide Convention in ECSOC Drafting Committee," April 10, 1948, 2, in ibid; Durwald V. Sandifer memo to Ernest Gross, "Trip to New York on Genocide," April 14, 1948, 2, in ibid.

[98] NARA, RG 59, Box 2189, Durwald V. Sandifer memo to Ernest Gross, "Cultural Genocide," April 22, 1948, 1.

[99] A/C.6/SR.63, in Abtahi and Philippa Webb, The Genocide Convention, 1298.

[100] See generally Elisa Novic, The Concept of Cultural Genocide An International Law Perspective (Oxford: Oxford University Press, 2016).

[101] Article VII of the Convention on the Punishment and Prevention of Genocide holds that "Genocide and the other acts enumerated in article III shall not be considered as political crimes for the purpose of extradition." For one of several US memos assenting to this proposition, see National Records Administration, Maryland, RG 353, Box 100, Committee on International Social Policy, "Draft Convention for the Punishment and Prevention of Genocide, Commentary by the Government of the United States," September 8, 1947, 9.

The question of political groups revealed the incipient cleavages of the Cold War and imperatives of state security that concerned all states. The inclusion of political groups in two draft conventions threatened to derail negotiations and the Convention itself. The Soviets were stung by accusations of genocide leveled by emigre Baltic organizations who complained about the takeover of their countries after the war.[102] Their proposition closely mirrored that of Lemkin and the WJC, namely that genocide "is organically bound up with fascism-nazism and other similar race theories which preach national and racial hatred, the domination of the so-called higher races and the extermination of the so-called lower races." This was what the Soviet representative called the "scientific definition of genocide."[103] Conveniently, the Soviet attack on social groups, like kulaks in the 1930s, would thereby not be classifiable as genocide. But not for love of the Soviet Union did the Uruguayan representative support it when he agreed that "The concept of genocide was, indeed, the outcome of the Nazi theories of race superiority which were at the basis of the Hitlerian ideology."[104] The exclusion of political groups from the list of protected groups would make it easier for unstable states to put down domestic dissent, as some of them plainly admitted. Venezuela said that states would not ratify a convention that included political groups:

> fearing the possibility of being called before an international tribunal to answer charges made against them, even if those charges were without foundation. Subversive elements might make use of the convention to weaken attempts of their own Government to suppress them. He realized that certain countries where civic spirit was highly developed and the political struggle fought through electoral laws, would favour the inclusion of political groups. But there were countries where the population was still developing and where political struggle was very violent.[105]

This was the "political dynamite" about which Lemkin wrote. The Dominican Republic and Egypt agreed that the inclusion of political groups "would bring the UN into the domestic political struggle of every country and would make it difficult for many countries to adhere to the convention."[106] Brazil advanced the most self-serving argument, asserting that genocide:

---

[102] Beth Van Schaack, "The Crime of Political Genocide: Repairing the Genocide Convention's Blind Spot," *Yale Law Journal* 106 (1997): 2259–91; Weiss-Wendt, *The Soviet Union and the Gutting of the UN Genocide Convention*, 58.

[103] A/C.6/215/Rev.1, in Abtahi and Webb, *The Genocide Convention*, 1969; A/C.6/SR.74 in ibid., 1399.

[104] A/C.6/SR.74, in Abtahi and Webb, *The Genocide Convention*, 1401.

[105] A/C.6/SR.69, in ibid., 1356.   [106] Ibid., 1356, 1358.

was unknown in the countries of Latin America, since in those countries there did not exist that deep-rooted hatred which in due course led to genocide. .... In those countries political movements were always short-lived whereas the crime of genocide was by its very nature dependent on a profound concentration of racial or religious hatred. Such hatred could never grow out of the political movements current in Latin America.[107]

Like the Iranian representative, the Brazilian one equated genocide with racial hatred in order to depoliticize it. Racial destruction, the Iranian said, echoing Lemkin, was "more heinous in the light of the conscience of humanity, since it was directed against human beings whom chance alone had grouped together." The Brazilian added that "A crime committed for political motives did not contain a moral element, it was free from the intention of destroying the opposing group. Today's enemies became the friends of tomorrow."[108] This counter-intuitive unanimity of communists and anticommunists was based on a shared desire to be able to destroy one another's domestic instances with impunity.

The WJC also sought to remove the reference to political groups, now rejecting Lemkin's broad ideas about genocide that were reflected in the Secretariat Draft. Sensing that the Convention was in danger, and hopeful that it would help protect Jewish communities in Pakistan, the Middle East, and Eastern Europe, the Congress wrote to the UN Economic and Social Council in July 1947 to urge the deletion of the political groups clause:

> Throughout history most attacks were directed against racial, religious and national groups. Genocide as a crime is connected intimately with these victim-groups. The inclusion of the political groups might be a useful addition to civilized international life. However it acts already as an undue burden and it might keep governments from entering into the Convention. Governments will never be sincere in admitting that the inclusion of political groups is the main reason for their reluctance and they might use escapism and delay. As a people who suffered unbelievable losses we appeal to the governments of the world that the Genocide Convention should not be used for political fights among nations but rather for establishing civilized standards of international life.[109]

Lemkin advanced the same argument in memos and telegrams to Department of State officials. In one of them, he was reported as arguing "that in the Latin American countries, there were many revolutions and that exter-mination of opposing groups was resorted to as a result thereof. The Latinos do not want to admit that publicly. However, they may vote against the Convention or attempt to prevent its approval by the General Assembly."[110]

---

[107] Ibid., 1353-4.   [108] Ibid., 1355.   [109] AJA/WJC, B84-06, Genocide 1947.
[110] NARA, RG 59, Box 2186, Department of State, Memorandum of Conversation, July 16, 1948, 1.

In the event, Latin American states did publicly admit their security concerns. Political expediency thus demanded jettisoning political groups. Exterminating "opposing groups" would not be genocide concluded Lemkin and the WJC.

In opposition, Ecuador and Bolivia supported the retention of political groups by the same logic, only reversing the signs in a prescient manner: "if the convention did not extend its protection to political groups," they said, "those who committed the crime of genocide might use the pretext of the political opinions of a racial or religious group to persecute and destroy it, without becoming liable to international sanctions."[111] The American Catholic Association for International Peace agreed in their representations to the US Department of State. "Practically all persecutions in the past had some, if not a total, political basis," they argued.[112] The American diplomats tended to agree, if only to squeeze the Soviets for its domestic repression. With the British, they observed that the Nazis and Spanish fascists had also tried to destroy social and political groups and that the Cold War temperature would increase ideological rather than racial tension.[113] But these counterarguments did not carry the day: the Sixth Committee voted to exclude political groups.

The dispute was as heated regarding the question of listing specific motives in addition to the basic intention to destroy groups "on grounds of national or racial origin, religious belief or political opinion of its members," as the Ad Hoc Committee Draft put it. Again, the Soviet Union led the opposition:

> Crimes committed for political motives belonged to a special type of crime and had nothing in common with crimes of genocide, the very name of which, derived as it was from the word *genus* – race, tribe, referred to the destruction of nations or races as such for reasons of racial or national persecution, and not for political opinions of those groups.[114]

The Soviet Union and its supporters were happy to list motives but to omit political ones for the obvious reasons. This view was apparently compatible with freedom of speech. As the Salvadorian representative put it, "If the rebellious group were destroyed, it would be because of its activities, and not because of its political views."[115]

---

[111] A/C.6/SR.74, in Abtahi and Webb, *The Genocide Convention*, 1393.

[112] NARA, RG 59, Box 2186, Statement of the Ethics and Juridical Institutions Committee, Catholic Association for International Peace, "The Genocide Convention," August 2, 1948.

[113] Cf. Kurt Glaser and Stefan T. Possony, *Victims of Politics: The State of Human Rights* (New York: Columbia University Press, 1979), 8–9: "Through the dropping of political groups from the victim list, the most severe form of discrimination currently practiced is, in effect, tolerated and, in a sense, 'legalized' by omission."

[114] E/AC.25/SR.24, in Abtahi and Webb, *The Genocide Convention*, 1016.

[115] A/C.6/SR.77, in ibid., 1435.

The debate became mired in question of extradition, because the custom was that those accused of political crimes were not liable to extradition. Thus Article 8 of the Secretariat Draft stated that "genocide cannot be considered as a political crime and shall give cause for extradition."[116] The Soviet representative expressed the emerging postwar consensus that depoliticized genocide by pointing to victims' lack of agency: "genocide was the mass destruction of innocent groups and could never ... be considered as a political crime." In response, the British recognized that it "was inherently political in that its commission could usually be traced to political motives." For that reason, the convention text should "state that, for purposes of extradition, it should be considered as nonpolitical."[117]

The British also noted that listing motives would allow perpetrators "to claim that they had not committed that crime 'on grounds of' one of the motives listed in the article," an option that suited many countries. New Zealand's representative ended the debate when he pointed out that without listed motives "bombing may be called a crime of genocide," because "Modern war was total, and there might be bombing which might destroy whole groups."[118]

The British were quickly convinced and the deadlock was broken by Venezuela's compromise suggestion to replace a list of motives with the simple phrase "as such." It was intended, and widely interpreted to include, motives without listing any in particular. Since political groups had been excluded from the definition, destroying groups "as such" meant destroying its members simply by virtue of membership of them, in other words, because of their identity.[119] As the Professor of International Law at the University of Edinburgh, J. L. Brierly (1881–1955), told readers of a weekly BBC magazine in 1949, the intended destruction of the listed groups "as such" had a "limiting effect": this qualification meant excluding "many, probably most, of the famous massacres and persecutions of history." In historical reality, the facts of perpetrator motives "have been more obscure [than the Nazis'] and more mixed." To qualify as genocide, the victim population would have to be targeted "because they were Jews or Slavs, or members of some particular group of human beings whose elimination had been resolved on" — and not "enemies in war or rebels against a government." Accordingly, "putting a whole enemy population, men, women, and children, to the sword" would not necessarily be genocide. The Convention, he concluded pessimistically, promised more than it delivered: "nothing

---

[116] A/AC.10/42, in ibid., 118.   [117] A/C.6/SR.94, in ibid., 1630–1.
[118] A/C.6/SR.75, in ibid., 1415, 1418.
[119] Ibid., 1416–7, A/C.6/SR.76 in ibid., 1425–7, A/C.6/SR.77 in ibid., 1435. See, generally, A. W. Brian Simpson, "Britain and the Genocide Convention," *British Yearbook of International Law* 73, no. 1 (2002): 4–64.

important has happened at all" with its passing by the UN.[120] In fact, repressing political opposition and destroying entire peoples in warfare was now all the easier because the genocide threshold increasingly functioned to screen out military necessity and permanent security practices pertaining to state security.

Otto Ohlendorf, Aerial Bombing, and the Rescue of Military Necessity

A month after the Nuremberg Charter was issued, Justice Robert Jackson explained its rationale in a *New York Times Magazine* article. Titled "The Worst Crime of All," he justified why aggressive wars were the supreme crime because all other wartime crimes derived from the act of invasion. From the terrible ravages of the war that he witnessed as he toured defeated Germany and learned of its crimes, he drew a further conclusion: "If there are to be future wars we have got to win them" by "being better killers, by killing more and killing more quickly than the enemy, by killing with less risk to ourselves."[121] In making this declaration, he then proceeded – remarkably for a lawyer – to advocate violating the principle of distinction between combatants and noncombatants by casting warfare as conflict between peoples and not solely military forces. Reasoning like the strategic bombing planners of the 1920s and 1930s, he was subtly justifying civilian destruction, although he did not mention the Allies' bombing of German and Japanese cities that killed hundreds of thousands of civilians: he was thinking of the possible future war with the Soviet Union: "For the fact is obvious that modern war has become more and more a struggle between whole populations, not between armies alone. The issue is which shall be subjugated and which will survive."[122] Herewith Jackson, the avatar of Nuremberg justice, averred a military policy of liberal permanent security with destructive implications for civilians. Killing the enemy's civilians until they surrendered was the strategy.[123] The Nazis, by contrast, had killed people "for no military

---

[120] J. L. Brierly, "The Genocide Convention," *The Listener*, March 10, 1949. He was previously Chichele Professor of Private International Law at Oxford and the author of well-known works like *The Law of Nations* (Oxford: Oxford University Press, 1928), and *The Outlook for International Law* (Oxford; Clarendon, 1944).

[121] Robert Jackson, "The Worst Crime of All," *New York Times Magazine*, September 9, 1945, 89.

[122] Ibid. For a classic critique of such thinking, see Robert A. Pape, *Bombing to Win: Air Power and Coercion in War* (Ithaca, NY: Cornell University Press, 1996).

[123] Benjamin Valentino, Paul Huth, and Sarah Croco, "Covenants without the Sword: International Law and the Protection of Civilians in Times of War," *World Politics* 58, no. 3 (2006): 339–77.

purpose."[124] As we see in Chapter 10, this argument was taken up by apologists for US policy in Vietnam 30 years later.

In the meantime, Jackson's Nuremberg confidante and advocate of crimes against humanity and an International Bill of Rights, Hersh Lauterpacht, was doing the same.[125] Writing in the *British Yearbook of International Law* in 1952, while a member of the United Nations International Law Commission, he lent his enormous prestige to Jackson's line of reasoning. Recognizing that the distinction between civilians and combatants had effectively disappeared in the Allies' aerial bombing of Germany, he did not think it made sense to assess its legality, because doing so would undermine the legitimate war effort. There was no "absolute protection of the civilian population," he concluded, "in an age of total warfare and the perfection both of aircraft and of ground and other defences against aerial attack."[126] This was a convenient argument for the West when it enjoyed aerial and atomic superiority in the early years of the Cold War, and when the US was pounding North Korea.

This conclusion was the outcome of the successor Nuremberg Trials run by the US military, known as the National Military Tribunal. The notion that antisemitism – racial hatred – rather than military necessity or other political reasons drove the Holocaust animated the Nuremberg Trials, especially the *Einsatzgruppen* trial that ran between October 1946 and April 1949.[127] The prosecution's case, especially in the statements of Telford Taylor (1908–1988), bear the stamp of this mode of thinking. Jews had been deported and killed simply because they were Jews and not for anything they had done. Rather than attacking Jews because they prevented German war preparations, as argued in the earlier trials to establish the necessary nexus between persecution of Jews and the war, Taylor now maintained that they were the victims of Nazi racial doctrine about superior and inferior races. "In this primitive theory, derived in part from Nietzsche's teaching of the Germanic superman," he declared, "the Nazis found the justification for Germany's domination of the world."[128]

The chief defendant was Otto Ohlendorf, a committed intellectual Nazi who led *Einsatzgruppen D,* which murdered 90,000 Jews under his command. The

---

[124] Jackson, *Report of Robert H. Jackson,* 50. N. C. H. Dunbar, "Military Necessity in War Crimes Trials," *British Yearbook of International Law* 29 (1952): 442–52.

[125] Lauterpacht, *An International Bill of the Rights of Man.*

[126] Lauterpacht, "The Problem of the Revision of the Law of War," *British Yearbook of International Law* 29 (1952): 365–6. He expressed more scruples in Lassa Oppenheim, *International Law, A Treatise,* 2 Vols. *Disputes, War and Neutrality,* by Lassa Oppenheim, 7th ed. by Hersh Lauterpacht (Longmans, Green & Co, 1952), 525–30.

[127] *Trials of the War Criminals before the Nuremberg Military Tribunals,* Vol. 4, The "Einsatzgruppen Case." October 1946–April 1949 (Washington DC: US Government Printing Office, 1949). United States of America vs. Otto Ohlendorf, et al. (Case No. 9).

[128] Ibid., 31–2.

young American prosecutor, Benjamin Ferencz, remembered him as an "intelligent, well-educated man, who had made some good legal arguments, trying to show he had no criminal intent. He did his duty as he saw it, without questioning Hitler who had said that Germany was about to be attacked by the Russians."[129] Ohlendorf's unit's activities were described to the court in the following terms:

> Einsatz units entering a town or city ordered all Jews to be registered. They were forced to wear the Star of David under threat of death. All were then assembled with their families to be "re-settled" under Nazi supervision. At the outskirts of each town was a ditch, where a squad of Einsatz men waited for their victims. Whole families were arrayed, kneeling or standing near the pit to face a deadly hail of fire. Into the prisoner-of-war camps went the Einsatz units, selecting men for extermination, denying them the right to live. Helpless civilians were conveniently labeled "Partisans" or "Partisan-sympathizers" and then executed.[130]

After his capture, Ohlendorf had been initially happy to cooperate with British authorities because he did not believe he had committed any crimes. Indeed, he regarded the murders as militarily defensible in the name of security; they were certainly not motivated by racial hatred. He said that the German goal aimed at "an immediate and *permanent security* of our own realm against that realm with which the belligerent conflict is taking place."[131] What did this mean? He was asked whether executing civilians served this goal, to which he replied with the familiar Judeo-Bolshevik mantra of the Nazis and antisemites generally: "For us it was obvious that Jewry in Bolshevist Russia actually played a disproportionately important role," and, further:

> That the Communist functionaries and the active leaders of the Communists in the occupied area of Russia posed an actual continuous danger for the German occupation the documents of the prosecution have shown. It was absolutely certain that by these persons the call of Stalin for ruthless partisan warfare would be followed without any reservation.[132]

For Ohlendorf, executing Jews and Bolsheviks was a legitimate antipartisan policy.

As might be expected, the prosecution cross-examined him about killing those who could not pose a military threat: Jewish children. Here is the exchange:

Q. Will you agree that there was absolutely no rational basis for killing children except genocide and the killing of races?

---

[129] Heikelina Verrijn Stuart and Marlise Simons, *The Prosecutor and the Judge: Benjamin Ferencz and Antonio Cassese Interviews and Writings*, ed. Heikelina Verrijn Stuart Marlise Simons (Amsterdam: Amsterdam University Press, 2009), 22.

[130] The "Einsatzgruppen Case," 30–1.   [131] Ibid., 247. Emphasis added.   [132] Ibid.

A. I believe that it is very simple to explain if one starts from the fact that this order did not only try to achieve security, but also permanent security because the children would grow up and surely, being the children of parents who had been killed, they would constitute a danger no smaller than that of the parents.[133]

Rather than press Ohlendorf on the notion of permanent security, however, the cross-examiner allowed himself to be tied up by Ohlendorf's equation between Allied bombing of German civilians with his troops' mass execution of Jewish children.

Q. That is the master race exactly, is it not, the decimation of whole races in order to remove a real or fancied threat to the German people?
A. Mr Prosecutor, I did not see the execution of children myself although I attended three mass executions.

Q. Are you saying they didn't kill children now?
A. I did not say that. May I finish? I attended three mass executions and did not see any children and no command ever searched for children, but I have seen very many children killed in this war through air attacks, for the security of other nations and orders were carried out to bomb, no matter whether many children were killed or not.

Q. Now, I think we are getting somewhere, Mr. Ohlendorf. You saw German children killed by Allied bombers and that is what you are referring to?
A. Yes, I have seen it.

Q. Do you attempt to draw a moral comparison between the bomber who drops bombs hoping that it will not kill children and yourself who shot children deliberately? Is that a fair moral comparison?
A. I cannot imagine that those planes which systematically covered a city that was a fortified city, square meter for square meter, with incendiaries and explosive bombs and again with phosphorus bombs, and this done from block to block, and then as I have seen it in Dresden likewise the squares where the civilian population had fled to – that these men could possibly hope not to kill any civilian population, and no children. And when you then read the announcements of the Allied leaders on this – and we are quite willing to submit them as document – you will read that these killings were accepted quite knowingly because one believed that only through this terror, as it was described, the people could be demoralized and under such blows the military power of the Germans would then also break down.

---

[133] Ibid., 356.

Q. Very well, let's concede – I think there is truth in what you say, though I never saw it. Does it occur to you that when the German Wehrmacht drove into Poland without provocation, and when you drove into Norway, and when you drove into the Low Countries, and when you crushed France, and when you destroyed Belgrade, Yugoslavia, Greece, when you put Rumania, Bulgaria under your heel, and then attempted to destroy the Russian State, does it occur to you that people resisting your tyranny stand on a higher moral level when they resort to the same horrible cruelties which you initiated in order to destroy your tyranny? Answer that, please.

A. You will understand that I look at the events of the war which you referred to in a different way than you do.[134]

Here the prosecution justified killing German civilians because of its "higher moral level," as Jackson had implied as the rationale for the US way of war in his *New York Times Magazine* article: the point was to win because the Americans were automatically in the right.

The presiding Judge Musmanno abruptly ended this "illuminating" conversation, as he put it, because it "went beyond all bounds of normal discussion on a question of murder."[135] It was left to Telford Taylor to try to dispose of Ohlendorf's political defense of his unit's actions through his analogy with Allied aerial bombing.[136] Whatever their security imperative, Taylor said, the facts indicated that:

> These crimes were committed in execution of deliberate plans laid months earlier. And the crime itself is of staggering enormity – the annihilation of entire racial and national groups – such as Jews and gypsies – and all leading government and party officials. Questions of guilt or innocence of the victims played absolutely no part; *this was massacre for its own sake* and the intended victims numbered in the millions.[137]

Noteworthy here is Taylor's statement that the Einsatzgruppen committed "massacre for its own sake," a nonpolitical reasoning for genocide. He was rebutting the Nazi Judeo-Bolshevik thesis that all the Einsatzgruppen defendants repeated to the effect that Jews were agents of the Bolshevik regime and therefore represented an objective threat to German security. If Jews "feared the coming of the Germans," as Taylor put it, that could not be attributed to innate Jewish hostility to the Wehrmacht but to long-standing Nazi threats to Jews. What is more, the security argument was insincere, because it was likely that the murder of Jews would have continued after German victory.

> In short the crimes of the Einsatzgruppen were not, fundamentally, military crimes at all. They were not committed in order to make military victory possible. On the contrary, military victory was sought in order to

---

[134] Ibid., 356–7.   [135] Ibid., 358.   [136] Ibid., 370.   [137] Ibid., 378. Emphasis added.

put the victors in a position where these crimes could be committed. These crimes were a war objective, not a military means.[138]

Taylor and the prosecution did not address Ohlendorf's chilling point about permanent security and its rationale for child murder. They remained at the level of conventional military necessity, pointing out that killing Jews had no bearing on the German campaign. The German point, however, was about future threats.[139] Nor did Taylor challenge the assertion of Jewish-Bolshevik affiliation; in fact, he seemed to imply it was understandable in view of preexisting Nazi threats. Instead, he introduced the distinction between geno-cide as a nonpolitical hate crime and military necessity as a legitimate practice. Why he did so was related to the Nazi defense's point about Allied bombing of German civilians and imperative to rescue the concept of military necessity for Allied use. Even though the Nuremberg Charter proscribed the "wanton destruction of cities, towns or villages, or devastation not justified by military necessity," the German bombing of civilians was not prosecuted at Nuremberg so that Allied bombing could be justified by military necessity. The British, for one, found a military pretext for their bombing of German cities, which continued until the last month of the war, in the proposition that morale of the enemy population was a legitimate military target.[140] The 1923 Hague Convention on aerial bombing, we recall, was not ratified and its guidelines were ignored by all belligerents. The judges in the Einsatzgruppen Case repeated this Jacksonian reasoning in justifying aerial bombing by suggesting that German cities were filled with combatants who contributed to "military resistance":

> It was argued in behalf of the defendants that there was no normal distinction between shooting civilians with rifles and killing them by means of atomic bombs. There is no doubt that the invention of the atomic bomb, when used, was not aimed at noncombatants. Like any other aerial bomb employed during the war, it was dropped to overcome military resistance.[141]

The court concluded that Allied bombing was justified because it ceased when the enemy surrendered, whereas the German pursuit of Jews would have persisted after the end of hostilities.[142] The case hinged on the temporal

---

[138] Ibid., 382.   [139] Ibid., 467.

[140] Kevin Jon Heller, *The Nuremberg Military Tribunals and the Origins of International Criminal Law* (Oxford: Oxford University Press, 2011), 310, and D. H. N. Johnson, *Rights in Air Space* (Manchester: Manchester University Press, 1965), 48.

[141] The "Einsatzgruppen Case," 467.

[142] Robert Wolfe, "Putative Threat to National Security as a Nuremberg Defense for Genocide," *Annals of the American Academy of Political and Social Science* 450 (1980): 46–67; Hilary Earl, *The Nuremberg SS-Einsatzgruppen Trial, 1945–1958: Atrocity, Law,*

distinction between current and future threats rather than civilian destruction: killing hundreds of thousands of civilians was legitimate in the course of military operations, but not to avert a future threat. The Allies and Nazis were operating with different conceptions of warfare. This was one difference between liberal and illiberal permanent security.

Conclusion

This distinction was necessary for the developing US security strategy in the incipient Cold War: its aerial superiority and command of atomic weapons could not be criminalizable. Military necessity needed to be rescued, even if it let some Nazi generals off the hook. In the "Hostages Case," the tribunal, following the Hague Regulations of 1907, held that "[m]ilitary necessity permits a belligerent ... to apply any amount and kind of force to compel the complete submission of the enemy with the least possible expenditure of time, life, and money."[143] Thus, General von Leeb's siege of Leningrad, which lasted more than two years and caused hundreds of thousands of civilian deaths, was excused on the grounds of military necessity because starvation was not prohibited by the Hague Regulations. Likewise, the execution of partisans was widely excused if they did not meet the combatant requirements of the Hague Regulations. The tribunal even excused the German execution of civilian hostages as reprisals for partisan attacks because customary international law permitted it.[144]

But what if military necessity and genocide had been joined instead? What if the recourse to military necessity in which civilians are murdered, their villages destroyed, and remnant population expelled, were considered genocide as well, because it was driven not by racial hatred but by the quest for what Ohlendorf called permanent security? Why is murder on apparent racial grounds the "worst of all possible motives," as Taylor put it?[145] Such a possibility was stopped dead in its tracks at Nuremberg and during the UN debates on the Genocide Convention.

The contemporary understanding of what later became known as the Holocaust underwrote this legal conclusion. Already during the UN genocide debates, as we have seen, delegates referred to the Nazi treatment of Jews for the transgression effect in order to rescue permanent security. So did lawyers

and History (Cambridge: Cambridge University Press, 2009); Annette Weinke, *Law, History, and Justice: Debating German State Crimes in the Long Twentieth Century* (New York and Oxford: Berghahn Books, 2019), 128.

[143] United States v. Wilhelm List et al. ("The Hostage Case") (1948), XI TWC1253–54, 259.

[144] Heller, *The Nuremberg Military Tribunals and the Origins of International Criminal Law*, 207–11.

[145] The "Einsatzgruppen Case," 383.

during the Nuremberg trials. The Holocaust functioned as genocide's arche-type. Its special status was highlighted by the WJC during the war and by Jewish advocacy groups ever since. Most historians rightly understand the distinctive features the Nazis' anti-Jewish persecution even if they are uneasy with the language of uniqueness. Now this interpretation is a global norm, but it is unlikely that its consequences for civilian destruction are understood.[146]

The costs of this integrated legal and memory regime are the problems of genocide. To begin with is genocide's inherent conceptual instability. Lemkin's broad conception of genocide in *Axis Rule* contrasts with the narrow defin-ition of the UN Genocide Convention, but by denoting genocidal intention as "destruction" the convention imported some of his deliberate ambiguity. Recall his differentiation within the concept itself to reflect the empirical distinctions between Jewish and Christian European experiences: on the one hand, he wrote, Jews (and Roma) were attacked on racial grounds alone, that is, for nonpolitical reasons of identity. Genocide of the other "small nations" of Christian Poles, Serbs, and so forth, on the other hand, was driven by Nazi security imperatives, namely for political reasons. The UN effectively adopted the WJC approach of making genocide resemble the Holocaust by reducing genocide to intended physical destruction, thereby establishing a de facto hierarchy of criminality, atop which sits a "crime of crimes" against identity driven by nonpolitical imperatives. The effect is to lessen the significance of other catastrophic forms of mass violence like war crime, crimes against humanity, and the "collateral damage" of aerial bombing.

As we see in Section III, a consequence of this "global Holocaust culture" is that genocide claimants also feel compelled to depict mass violence as Holocaustal to gain attention. Henceforth, all that counts for those seeking international attention, intervention, and prosecutions are two questions: is a transgression an international crime, and – above all – is it genocide by somehow resembling the Holocaust? Whereas Lemkin designed the concept so Jewish suffering would be recognized by fusion with Christian suffering, now the reverse obtains. By institutionalizing genocide in this way, the Genocide Convention of 1948 was a turning point in the language of trans-gression. In lending such an impoverished view of genocide such weight, the rich pluralism of the language was diminished and the workings of permanent security concealed, indeed effectively licensed.

Some of these problems were anticipated by Haiti's representative in the Genocide Convention debates. Like the American Catholic Association for International Peace, he thought genocide was a political offense: "all the crimes

---

[146] Claudio Fogu, Wulf Kansteiner and Todd Presner, eds., *Probing the Ethics of Holocaust Culture* (Cambridge, MA: Harvard University Press, 2016); Sara Buttsworth and Maartje Abbenhuis, eds., *Monsters in the Mirror: Representations of Nazism in Post-war Popular Culture* (Santa Barbara, CA: Praeger, 2010).

envisaged were in reality committed for political reasons, whatever motive might be alleged." States "would always seek to describe as political any activities and organizations it might wish to suppress," he continued, concluding with the most succinct insight into the workings of permanent security: even "attempts made during the recent war to eliminate certain national groups were undertaken for reasons of state, in other words, for political motives."[147]

Unfortunately, Haiti's views did not carry the day. We are still living with the conceptual and legal consequences, and that is why the well-intentioned phrase of "never again" began to ring so hollow so soon after the Holocaust.

---

[147] A/C.6/SR.74, in Abtahi and Webb, *The Genocide Convention*, 1396. These points are the subject of Chapters 6 and 7.

PART II

Permanent Security

6

Permanent Security in History

Empire and Settler Colonialism

Imperial formations of one kind or another have been the political form in which most humans have lived for thousands of years: from the Nuba in North Africa, Assyrians in the Middle East, Manchus in China, Zulus in Africa, to the tribute systems of Meso-America, Mongols of Central Asia, Mughals in India, Safavids in Iran, and multinational land empires of the Ottomans, Habsburgs and Romanovs.[1] The European blue water empires were relative newcomers to the great game. Despite ideologies justifying imperial power in the name of peace, stability, or civilization, violence marked its expansion and consolidation. Throughout the long nineteenth century and into the interwar years, many Europeans equated the progress of human civilization with Western expansion, often ignoring the concomitant destruction of non-European societies. Frederick Kirkpatrick (1861–1953) of Cambridge University, for instance, told his audience in 1906 that "Down to the fifteenth century our ancestors were confined to this little Europe, and knew nothing of empty or half-empty countries inviting their occupation beyond the seas. Modern colonization and empire means the spread of Europe over the world."[2]

At other times, Europeans and European settler-colonists were brutally candid about the human costs of this expansion. Writing in 1839, Charles Darwin (1809–1882) observed this human interaction in terms of survival of the fittest: "The varieties of man seem to act on each other; in the same way as different species of animals the stronger always extirpating the weaker."[3] In the same year, ethnologist James Prichard sounded the tocsin about what he called "the extinction of human races" due to European settlement abroad:

---

[1] Anthony Pagden, *Peoples and Empires: Europeans and the Rest of the World from Antiquity to the Present* (London: Penguin, 2001), 8–10; Jane Burbank and Frederick Cooper, *Empires in World History: Power and the Politics of Difference* (Princeton: Princeton University Press, 2010).

[2] F. A. Kirkpatrick, *Lectures on British Colonization and Empire* (London: J. Murray, 1906), 1.

[3] F. W. Nicholas and J. M. Nicholas, *Charles Darwin in Australia* (Cambridge: Cambridge University Press, 1989), 30–1.

"their arrival has been the harbinger of extermination to the native tribes." Fearful that a further century of colonization would mean "the aboriginal nations of most parts of the world will have ceased to exist," he asked "whether any thing [sic.] can be done effectually to prevent the extermination of the aboriginal tribes."[4] Not much, suggested Darwin, because sustained contact entailed extinction: "Wherever the European has trod, death seems to pursue the aboriginal."[5]

Put in scholarly terms, the nineteenth century was the age of "settlerism," when millions of Europeans economically and demographically revolutionized host societies around the world.[6] One geographer likened this astonishing population substitution to a "demographic takeover," a phenomenon particularly prevalent in settler colonies – North America, South America, Australia, and New Zealand – that were less densely populated than Asia and Africa, and where disease threatened local inhabitants rather than the incoming Europeans.[7]

Europeans usually ascribed the apparent inevitability of extinction to the perceived weakness of people they called "natives," especially to disease and fertility decline. They were also certain that the value of their own civilization was sufficiently great to justify the destruction of the non-European ones, howsoever caused. Their extinction was the price of civilization as Andrew Jackson (1767–1845) explained in his US presidential address in 1830: "true philanthropy reconciles the mind to these vicissitudes [of Indian extinction] as it does to the extinction of one generation to make room for another."[8] There was also little sense of regret half a century later when the future US president, Theodore Roosevelt (1858–1919), distinguished the English Teuton from the Spanish and French by the nature of his ruthless nation building. "The English had exterminated or assimilated the Celts of Britain, and they substantially repeated the process with the Indians of America."[9] As late as 1927, the English soldier, collector, and archaeologist, George Augustus Henry Lane Pitt-Rivers (1890–1966), echoed these sentiments when he wrote that when a "superior race" overwhelmed an inferior one, "there should be no reason for members of a superior race to regret the gradual extinction of an inferior race

[4] James C. Pritchard, "On the Extinction of Human Races," *Edinburgh New Philosophical Journal* 28 (October 1839–April 1840): 169–70.
[5] Nicholas and Nicholas, *Charles Darwin in Australia*, 30–1.
[6] James Belich, *Replenishing the Earth: The Settler Revolution and the Rise of the Anglo-World, 1783–1939* (Oxford: Oxford: Oxford University Press, 2009).
[7] Alfred Crosby, *Germs, Seeds, and Animals: Studies in Ecological History* (London and New York: Routledge, 1994), 29–30.
[8] Patrick Brantlinger, *Dark Vanishings: Discourse on the Extinction of Primitive Races, 1800–1930* (Ithaca: Cornell University Press, 2003), 59.
[9] Theodore Roosevelt, *The Winning of the West*, 4 vols. (New York and London: Putnam's Sons, 1889), 1: 6, 11–12.

if only the future enrichment and welfare of the world is considered."[10] These were hard-hearted responses to humanitarians who complained about imperial depredations on the colonized, but to little avail.

The link between human catastrophes and the metanarrative of human progress was thus on the minds of European and naturally non-European intellectuals who were less enamoured by these developments. French anthropologist Georges Balandier noted somberly in 1951 that "the expansion throughout the entire world of most European peoples … has brought about the subjugation and, in some instances, the disappearance of virtually every people regarded as backward, archaic, or primitive."[11] His colleague, Claude Levi-Strauss, concurred, regretting that Western civilization had "committed a kind of unpardonable sin," in his "opinion the greatest sin ever committed in the history of humanity, which is to have destroyed or attempted to destroy half of the richness of humankind."[12]

At a very basic level, permanent security practices enabled imperial expansion and consolidation through the ages. To tease out their significance since the Spanish and Portuguese conquests of the Americas in the sixteenth century, it is necessary to consider an alternative distinction in imperial history, namely between empires of exploitation and settler colonies. This distinction was common in the nineteenth century. Kirkpatrick, for instance, highlighted it when he wrote that "The story of empire, of dominion over rich and populous cultures, apart from any considerable European emigration, deals chiefly with the commercial and political conquest of India and other Asiatic lands by Europeans; the study of colonization deals mainly with the migration of Europeans into the New World."[13] The French politician and thinker, Alexis de Tocqueville (1805–1859), had come to the same conclusion. "There are two ways to conquer a country," he wrote, "the first is to subordinate the inhabitants and govern them directly or indirectly. That is the English system in India."[14] "The second [way]," he continued, "is to replace the former inhabitants with the conquering race. This is what Europeans have almost always done."[15]

---

[10] George Henry Lane-Fox Pitt-Rivers, *The Clash of Culture and the Contact of Races* (London: George Routledge, 1927), 17.

[11] Georges Balandier, "The Colonial Situation: A Theoretical Approach (1951)," in *Social Change: The Colonial Situation*, ed. Immanuel Wallerstein (New York: John Wiley & Sons, 1966), 34.

[12] Marcello Massenzio, "An Interview with Claude Levi-Strauss," *Current Anthropology* 42, no. 3 (2001): 419.

[13] Kirkpatrick, *Lectures on British Colonization and Empire*, 5–6.

[14] Alexis de Tocqueville, *Writings on Empire and Slavery*, ed. Jennifer Pitts (Baltimore, MD, and London: The Johns Hopkins University Press, 2001), 61; William Gallois, *A History of Violence in the Early Algerian Colony* (Basingstoke: Palgrave Macmillan, 2013).

[15] de Tocqueville, *Writings on Empire and Slavery*, 65.

Roman historian Sallust (86 BCE–35 BCE) is apparently the first to refer to the Roman state as *imperium*. Over time, empire came to mean the domination of one society by another, usually backed by military force; imperial expansion entailed dominion, whether by annexation or through less formal means: but it did not necessitate colonization.[16] Indeed, empire can exist without colonization or colonialism. Thus, Ottoman rule in Egypt was not colonial because of the large measure of local self-administration and absence of permanent settlers. Alternatively, empires often engaged in settlement and resettlement, colonizing frontier regions with loyal subjects. The Romans referred to its settlements of soldiers on territory it conquered as *colonia*. Russian monarchs encouraged Germans to settle in the Lower Volga in the eighteenth century because their serfs were immobile. By 1914, 1.7 million ethnic Germans lived in east-central Europe, vulnerable to Russian paranoia about their loyalties in the looming war with Germany.[17]

These two modalities of conquest could be combined, added de Tocqueville: "The Romans, in general, did both. They seized the country's government, and in several parts of it they founded colonies that were nothing other than far-flung little Roman societies." Combined with colonization, imperial occupation robs societies of their "historical line of development" and transforms them "according to the needs and interests of the colonial rulers" as the historian Jürgen Osterhammel observes.[18] This is what de Tocqueville advised French authorities in subduing Algeria after 1830: domination of the interior so the coastal regions could be settled.[19] Colonial rule can thus radically alter the structure of, even dismember, indigenous societies. The greater the intensity of colonial rule, the greater its destructive impact.

Imperial Germany's colonialism in Africa is of particular interest in this regard because its relative lateness – effectively since the 1890s – meant that state power was intimately involved in creating highly authoritarian and racially segregated societies. In German Southwest Africa (Namibia today) and German East Africa (Tanzania today), Germans established a settler

---

[16] See the lucid discussion in Ronald Grigor Suny, "The Empire Strikes Out: Imperial Russia, 'National' Identity, and Theories of Empire," in *A State of Nations: Empire and Nation-Making in the Age of Lenin and Stalin*, ed. Ronald Grigor Suny and Terry Martin (Oxford: Oxford University Press, 2001), 23–66.

[17] James W. Long, *From Privileged to Dispossessed: The Volga Germans, 1860–1917* (Lincoln, NB, and London: University of Nebraska Press, 1988); Eric Lohr, *Nationalizing the Russian Empire: The Campaign against Enemy Aliens during World War I* (Cambridge, MA: Harvard University Press, 2003).

[18] Jürgen Osterhammel, *Colonialism: A Theoretical Introduction*, trans. Shelley L. Frisch (Princeton, NJ: Markus Wiener, 1997), 15. D. K. Fieldhouse, who is far less critical of European colonial rule, comes close to this definition: Fieldhouse, *Colonialism 1870–1945: An Introduction* (London: Weidenfeld and Nicolson, 1983), 12–15.

[19] de Tocqueville, Writings on Empire and Slavery, 61, 65.

colony and plantation colony of exploitation respectively. In the former, German immigrants and managers ruled over Africans whose political, cultural, and economic independence had been smashed in order to render them largely superfluous, or to transform them into a helot class of workers for agriculture in the latter.[20]

This intensification of colonial rule over the course of the nineteenth century points to a significant transition in the history of empire and of permanent security: from the land and continental empires that have organized humanity for millennia with economies of tribute and taxation on the one hand, to the blue water European empires since early modernity that inaugurated global capitalism and centralizing bureaucratic-military states on the other. As Kirkpatrick and de Tocqueville noted, both forms of foreign rule marked European expansion, beginning with the Spanish conquest of the Americas in the late fifteenth century. This was also part of what Karl Marx (1818–1883) called "so-called originary [*ursprüngliche*, often translated as "primitive"] accumulation," the process by which English commons and Church lands were privatized and agricultural producers were separated from their means of production to become wage laborers, whose surplus the capitalist kept in accumulating further capital. Marx focused on the expropriation and proletarianization of the English peasantry – what he called "the classic form" of originary accumulation – because he wanted to account for the birth of industrial capitalism in England.[21] But he also observed that this English transformation was dependent on earlier imperial developments. "In actual history," declared Marx, "it is notorious that conquest, enslavement, robbery, murder, briefly force, play the great part" in originary accumulation.[22] He adumbrated the violent expropriations of European empire beginning with the Spanish in the Americas:

> The discovery of gold and silver in America, the extirpation, enslavement and entombment in mines of the aboriginal population, the beginning of the conquest and looting of the East Indies, the turning of Africa into a warren for the commercial hunting of black-skins, signalised the rosy dawn of the era of capitalist production.[23]

This list suggests originary accumulation outside Europe consisted mainly of violent plunder: "The treasures captured outside Europe by undisguised looting, enslavement, and murder, floated back to the mother-country and were there turned into capital."[24] Marx followed his contemporaries in

---

[20] Jürgen Zimmerer, *Deutsche Herrschaft über Afrikaner: staatlicher Machtanspruch und Wirklichkeit im kolonialen Namibia* (Münster: Litt Verlag, 2001).

[21] Karl Marx, *Capital: A Critique of Political Economy*, ed. Friedrich Engels, trans. Samuel More and Edward Aveling (New York: Modern Library, 1906), 787.

[22] Ibid., 785.   [23] Ibid., 823.   [24] Ibid., 826.

distinguishing between colonies of exploitation and settler colonialism. The latter were "real Colonies, virgin soils, colonised by free immigrants" and "colonies properly called."[25] But he was less interested in the fate of their indigenous peoples than in the capitalist exploitation of settlers.[26] For that reason, he regarded colonies of exploitation as more brutal: "The treatment of the aborigines was, naturally, most frightful in plantation-colonies destined for export trade only, such as the West Indies, and in rich and well-populated countries, such as Mexico and India, that were given over to plunder."[27] Missing was a sustained analysis of the principal form of originary accumulation in settler colonies, namely the expropriation of the land after the removal of its indigenous owners.[28] Dispossession rather than proletarianization is the salient mode of accumulation in the settler colonies, amounting to a distinctive mode of "settler accumulation."[29]

This mode of accumulation has been analyzed most acutely by the Australian historian, Patrick Wolfe, who defined settler colonialism as a structure rather than event. Indigenous labor is not the main source of accumulation; land is. Labor – whether free or enslaved – is imported and is fed by the ceaseless expansion of agriculture that displaces the indigenous population. In this way, the international slave trade was premised on settler-colonial elimination of indigenous control of land.[30] Eliminating indigenous people could take various forms: "Indigenous people are either rendered dependent on the introduced economy or reduced to the stock-raids that provide the classic pretext for colonial death-squads."[31] Either way, their collective ownership of land needs to be smashed to enable the labor exploitation that more interested Marx. That is the deep structure of settler accumulation.

[25] Ibid., 838n1.
[26] Symptomatic is Philip McMichael, "Settlers and Primitive Accumulation: Foundations of Capitalism in Australia," *Review* 4, no. 2 (1980): 307–334. For an excellent analysis, see Gabriel Piterberg and Lorenzo Veracini, "Wakefield, Marx, and the World Turned Inside Out," *Journal of Global History* 10, no. 3 (2015): 457–78.
[27] Marx, *Capital*, 825.
[28] Glen Coulthard, *Red Skin, White Masks Rejecting the Colonial Politics of Recognition* (Minneapolis: University of Minnesota Press, 2014), 19–20.
[29] Nicholas A. Brown, "The Logic of Settler Accumulation in a Landscape of Perpetual Vanishing," *Settler Colonial Studies* 4, no. 1 (2014): 7.
[30] Patrick Wolfe, "Settler Colonialism and the Elimination of the Native," *Journal of Genocide Research* 8, no. 4 (2006): 387–409; Mohamed Adhikari, ed., *Genocide on Settler Frontiers: When Hunter-Gatherers and Commercial Stock Farmers Clash* (New York and Oxford: Berghahn Books, 2015); Michael Grewcock, "Settler-Colonial Violence, Primitive Accumulation and Australia's Genocide," *State Crime Journal* 7, no. 2 (2018): 222–50.
[31] Wolfe, "Settler Colonialism and the Elimination of the Native," 395.

For his part, Marx noted settler-colonial violence only briefly in his *Capital*, reporting how settlers in New England set premiums on "every Indian scalp and every captured red skin."[32] His mention that this practice occurred when "a certain tribe" was proclaimed "rebels," points to the logic of permanent security in colonialism and Western state-building: namely defending original accumulation from indigenous resistance. It is no accident that, in both German African colonies, the authorities perpetrated mass violence in suppressing indigenous uprisings against hyper-exploitation.[33]

The language of transgression traced in the first and second chapters criminalizes the most egregious manifestations of permanent security that I call illiberal. Las Casas's memorable excoriation of Spanish atrocities in the Americas meant that their violent extractive practices stood for abusive empire, at least for their Protestant rivals. The British settler colonies, by contrast, represented liberal permanent security in which putting down indigenous resistance was seen as legitimate because their empire was a vehicle for civilizational progress via agriculture and commerce. Accordingly, the violence of settler accumulation was screened out in the language of transgression: apart from isolated voices, contemporaries did not see their security measures as excessive or transgressive. For this reason, the social scientist Mark Neocleous observes that the wars of law as they developed in the early-modern period justified the crushing of indigenous resistance as legal: "In the bourgeois mind, *the global war of primitive accumulation was the archetypal just war.*" In other words, "the class war was historically a just war. International law was a key weapon used in the global class war."[34]

German jurist Carl Schmitt (1888–1985) made this point already in 1950, though from the opposite political perspective. A proponent of European empire and for a time an apologist for the Nazi state, Schmitt well understood the violence of what he called "land appropriation" (*Landnahme*). It is the

---

[32] Marx, *Capital*, 825–6.

[33] Dominik Schaller, "From Conquest to Genocide: Colonial Rule in German Southwest Africa and German East Africa," in *Empire, Colony, Genocide: Conquest, Occupation and Subaltern Resistance in World History* (New York and Oxford: Berghahn Books, 2008), 296–324; Jürgen Zimmerer and Joachim Zeller, eds., *Genocide in German South-West Africa: The Colonial War of 1904–1908 and Its Aftermath* (Monmouth: Merlin Press, 2008); Matthias Häussler, *Der Genozid an den Herero: Krieg, Emotion und extreme Gewalt in "Deutsch-Südwestafrika"* (Weilerswist: Velbrück, 2018).

[34] Mark Neocleous, "International Law as Primitive Accumulation; Or, the Secret of Systematic Colonization," *European Journal of International Law* 23 no. 4 (2012): 957. Original emphasis. See also A. Dirk Moses, "Empire, Resistance, and Security: International Law and the Transformative Occupation of Palestine," *Humanity: An International Journal of Human Rights, Humanitarianism, and Development* 8, no. 2 (2017): 379–409.

process of territorial conquest and annexation that he saw as the basis not only of European expansion but of statehood itself. The establishment of European states could be traced to what he termed "the so-called *Völkerwanderung*," mass migrations of peoples tantamount to "a series of great land appropriations." The same process obtained in empire: "The history of colonialism in its entirety is as well a history of spatially determined processes of settlement in which order and orientation are combined." The legal order of European empires was predicated on control of territory that was wrested from "'wild' peoples" in colonial wars of annihilation. These wars disregarded the constraints of competition and warfare among European states, which were displaced to the far-off non-European lands, thereby stabilizing Europe.[35] Combined with his influential theory of statehood as consisting in the sovereign's ability to proclaim states of emergency and violently impose order, Schmitt's notion of land appropriation effectively made imperial conquest and settler colonialism the secret driver of Western state development.

The language of transgression developed to allow this process of state formation and originary accumulation to reproduce itself. It enabled the unleashing of European imperial violence against non-Europeans who resisted them in two ways: first by justifying settler-colonial warfare against indigenous resistance, and second by condemning the illiberal permanent security practices of imperial rivals, whether the Iberian powers in the early-modern period or the fascist and communist ones in the twentieth century. Liberal permanent security thereby normalized its modality of settlement, state-formation, and originary accumulation as a theodicy, a story of civilizational progress that benefitted humanity.[36] Few were the commentators like Roosevelt who looked the human costs in the face and affirmed, indeed revelled, in them. Counterintuitively, the greater destructive potential inheres in liberal permanent security because it does not face the dilemma of its illiberal variant, namely having to limit reprisal killing because empires of exploitation depend on conquered populations for tribute and labor. Settler colonial formations, by contrast, tend to replace conquered populations as they seek the land and not the labor of those they conquer. What is more, because they tend to expansion rather than autarky, the ambition of permanent liberal security is global.[37]

---

[35] Carl Schmitt, *The* Nomos *of the Earth in the International Law of the* Jus Publicum Europaeum, trans. G. L. Ulmen (New York: Telos, 2003), 80–2, 132, 142. In *Search for Sovereignty Law and Geography in European Empires, 1400–1900* (Cambridge: Cambridge University Press, 2010), ch. 6, Lauren Benton observes that Schmitt's sharp distinction about the application of nascent laws of war between European and non-European space is too sharply drawn.

[36] Onur Ulas Ince, *Colonial Capitalism and the Dilemmas of Liberalism* (Oxford: Oxford University Press, 2018), follows Marx in contending that liberalism and the British Empire were at once dependent on colonial exploitation and its disavowal.

[37] Thanks to Lorenzo Veracini for discussions on this topic.

Illiberal Permanent Security I: Imperial Conquest and Exploitation

The founding of empires can be linked to the experience of a society of having been colonized and subject to imperial conquest and rule. The empire is created to ensure permanent security: that never again will it be dominated by another. The impulse for empire – the desire for invulnerability – emanates from previous feelings of abjection. Empire is both a security and a compensation for past humiliations. This process can also be seen as a chain in the continuity of conquest, reconquest, and yet more conquest that has marked human group interaction for thousands of years. A famous example is the beginning of the Spanish Empire in the Americas in the late fifteenth century that came in the wake of the *reconquista*, the Christian reconquest, conducted under Papal aegis, of the Iberian peninsula from the Moors who had populated the area since the eighth century. Christians settled in reconquered land.[38] A contemporaneous example is Imperial Russia. The Mongol invasions of the thirteenth century were overthrown by the Muscovite princes in the later fifteenth century in a Russian *reconquista*.[39] Within 100 years, the Tsars, who were centralizing control of their lands, began to conquer the Mongol successor states of Kazan, Astrakhan and Sibir (later Siberia) on the south-eastern boundary. Expansion into the Caucasus and Central Asia ensued in the eighteenth and nineteenth centuries.[40]

Wars were not intended to be exterminatory from the conqueror's perspective. They sought to use only as much force as necessary to achieve their aims. Even so, imperial conquest and warfare were governed by the logic of permanent security in various ways. In the first place, the aim of the colonizer was

---

[38] Elena Lourie, "A Society Organised for War: Medieval Spain," in Lourie, *Crusade and Colonisation: Muslims, Christians, and Jews in Medieval Aragon* (Aldershot: Variorum Brookfield Gower, 1990), 54–76; Anthony Pagden, *Lords of All the World: Ideologies of Empire in Spain, Britain and France c. 1500–c. 1800* (New Haven, CT: Yale University Press, 1995), 74.

[39] Mark Ferro, *Colonization: A Global History* (London: Routledge, 1997), 2.

[40] Michael Rywkin, ed., *Russian Colonial Expansion to 1917* (London: Mansell, 1988); Michael Khodarkovsky, *Russia's Steppe Frontier: The Making of a Colonial Empire, 1500–1800* (Bloomington and Indianapolis: Indiana University Press, 2005); Theodore R. Weeks, *Nation and State in late Imperial Russia: Nationalism and the Russification of the Western Frontier, 1863–1914* (Dekalb, IL: Northern Illinois University Press, 1996); Jeff Sahadeo, "Conquest, Colonialism, and Nomadism on the Eurasian Steppe," *Kritika: Explorations in Russian and Eurasian History* 4, no. 4 (2003): 942–54; Dominic Lieven, "Dilemmas of Empire, 1850–1918: Power, Territory, Identity," *Journal of Contemporary History* 34, no. 2 (1999): 163–200; Keziban Acar, "An Examination of Russian Imperialism: Russian Intellectual and Military Descriptions of the Caucasians during the Russo-Turkish War of 1877–1878," *Nationalities Papers* 32, no. 1 (2004): 7–21; John P. Ledonne, *The Russian Empire and the World, 1700–1917: The Geopolitics of Expansion and Containment* (New York: Oxford University Press, 1996); W. Bruce Lincoln, *The Conquest of a Continent: Siberia and the Russians* (New York: Random House, 1994).

not just to defeat military forces but also to annex territory and rule over a foreign people. War aims were not limited, as they customarily were in intra-European wars; they were absolute. "Colonial conquerors came to stay," entailing massive disruption to conquered communities. Second, the colonizer often ended up waging war against the entire population because it was difficult to distinguish between combatants and noncombatants, especially when guerrilla-style resistance ensued.[41] In the main, imperial troops prevailed over numerically superior opponents because they were regularly paid, well supplied, and trained. The ability to concentrate forces at one point was more decisive than technological superiority alone, especially if indigenous agents could be conscripted.[42] Colonial war could mean total war on a local scale.

The most fatal logic of permanent security is the violent escalation provoked by local resistance, which leads to reprisal and revenge killing to ensure that resistance is stamped out once and for all. Rome's armies occasionally exterminated entire cities that resisted its rule or rose up in rebellion.[43] Punishing and avenging treachery and betrayal, experienced as an insult and expression of contempt, was another motivation for destroying a people or city. Rome's attack on Carthage, which it accused of basic breaches of trust, is a classic example. Carthage's behavior meant that Rome withdrew the right of pity and limited warfare. Vengeance and indignation drove it to impose mass, collective capital punishment.[44] In 133 BCE, the Romans destroyed Numantia on the Iberian Peninsula for defying Roman rule, as they had Carthage 13 years earlier. The late sieges and subsequent destruction of Jerusalem between 70 and 136 BCE also can be seen in this light.

In the euphemistically termed "Harrying of the North," William I ("the Conqueror"), who invaded England in 1066, put down serious Saxon resistance around Yorkshire by destroying all villages and livestock between York and Durham, causing famine and the starvation of up to 100,000 people. The aim was to destroy the local society so that it could not provide sustenance to

---

[41] H. L. Wesseling, "Colonial Wars: An Introduction," in *Imperialism and War: Essays on Colonial Wars in Asia and Africa*, ed. Jaap A. de Moor and H. L. Wesseling (Leiden: Brill, 1988), 3; Peter Paret, "Colonial Experience and European Military Reform at the End of the Eighteenth Century," in *Warfare and Empires*, ed. Douglas M. Peters (Aldershot: Ashgate, 1997), 357–70.

[42] Michael Howard, "Colonial Wars and European Wars," in de Moor and Wesseling, *Imperialism and War*, 218–23; George Raudzens, "Why Did the Amerindian Defences Fail? Parallels in the European Invasions of Hispaniola, Virginia and Beyond," *War in History* 3, no. 3 (1996): 331–52; Luke Godwin, "The Fluid Frontier: Central Queensland, 1845-63," in *Colonial Frontiers: Indigenous-European Encounters in Settler Societies*, ed. Lynette Russell (Manchester: Manchester University Press, 2001), 112.

[43] Benjamin Isaac, *The Invention of Racism in Classical Antiquity* (Princeton: Princeton University Press, 2004), 216.

[44] David Konstan, "Anger, Hatred, and Genocide in Ancient Greece," *Common Knowledge* 13, no. 1 (2007): 170–87.

rebels, who hid in marshes and forests, and so that it could not serve as a base for future Danish attack. The land was largely uninhabited for a century thereafter.[45]

Betrayal was a common theme in Asian and Central Asian empires. The Mongols were acutely conscious of treachery by peoples they had absorbed into the multiethnic empires. Likely, no power surpassed them in the extent and violence of their reprisals. Peoples who broke alliances – and therefore an oath – by joining the enemy were sometimes destroyed years later by Mongol leaders who did not forget such betrayals.[46] Chinggis Khan was pitiless towards disloyalty, exterminating the Merkit in 1217 for attacks on his forces years before. Although they were more interested in booty than conquest, the Mongols were also prepared to wage war where sedentary peoples would not hand over their goods. Cities that resisted were razed, and devastated regions took generations to recover. Samarkand was reduced in population by 75 percent in the first decades of the thirteenth century. When Chinggis died in 1227, the mourning army slaughtered the entire population of Zhongxing city.[47]

Conquerors prevailed at length as the fate of the Karifuna in the Antilles demonstrates. The Spanish had smashed indigenous resistance by the middle of the seventeenth century and enslaved the inhabitants in agriculture and mining. On neighbouring islands, French and English colonists wanted the land and to continue the slave economy. Difficulties in subduing the Karifuna on Antigua resulted in dozens of English deaths in the 1620s and 1630s, which led to a joint French and English effort on St Kitts to kill and drive off as many of the natives as possible. Their survival and mingling with escaped African slaves led to calls in the 1670s for the extermination of the "Carib Indians." But the plantation owners' desire for labor and divisions between French and British authorities meant that such rhetoric remained unrealized. Only the eventual hegemony of the British by the late eighteenth century enabled the roundup and depositing of the survivors on an inhospitable island off Honduras, where a third of them starved within four months.[48]

---

[45] Peter Rex, *The English Resistance: The Underground War against the Normans* (Stroud: Amberly Books, 2004), 87–105.

[46] John Joseph Saunders, *The History of the Mongol Conquests* (Philadelphia, 2001), ch. 4.

[47] David Christian, *A History of Russia, Central Asia, and Mongolia*, vol. 1, *Inner Eurasia from Prehistory to the Mongol Empire* (Oxford: Wiley-Blackwell, 1998), 396–406.

[48] Hilary Beckles, "The Genocide Policy in English-Karifuna Relations in the Seventeenth Century," in *Empire and Others: British Encounters with Indigenous Peoples, 1600–1850*, ed. Martin Daunton and Rick Halpern (Philadelphia: University of Pennsylvania Press, 1999), 280–302. The Carib population of 8,000 fell to 630 by 1730, recovering to 900 by the mid-twentieth century. It comprised 1,136 in 1960 out of a total population of nearly 60,000, and nearly 2,000 in 1978.

Such permanent security imperative led to mass deaths in violent counterinsurgency. This pattern was repeated in the Anglo-Zulu war in 1879,
when British forces used scorched-earth tactics and massacred wounded
fighters and prisoners in their desperate efforts to put down Zulu resistance
to imperial rule.[49] The Italian subjugation of Cyrenaica in Libya resulted in
the deaths of over 6,000 local fighters and the internment in camps of some
76,000 people, about half the total population.[50] In 1952, British authorities
in colonial Kenya interned hundreds of thousands of supposed insurgents,
killed up to 20,000 in combat, hanged over 1,000, and tortured many
others. One historian claims up to 100,000 Mau Mau insurgents died in
the camps.[51]

Imperial and national elites were constantly worried about security on their
peripheries. In 1914, the Imperial Russian Army deported up to one million
Jews living in its western borderlands because they were suspected of disloyalty
and potential espionage for the Germans.[52] The common motivation for
deporting or destroying groups is the accusation that they are rebellious,
supporting rebellions, or cooperating with enemies across borders, like the
Ottoman Armenians in 1915.[53] Between 1935 and 1938, Soviet paranoia about
foreign infiltration in border regions led to the deportation of nine nationalities away from them. During World War II, in 1943, Soviet forces violently
deported Chechen and Ingush people from the North Caucasus, some of
whose number had allegedly collaborated with the invading Germans. In the
early 1930s, the famine in the Ukraine had been precipitated by anxieties that
it might secede from the Union.[54] Much of the murderous radicalization of the

[49] Michael Lieven, "'Butchering the Brutes All Over the Place': Total War and Massacre in
    Zululand in 1879," *History* 84 (1999): 614–32.
[50] John Gooch, "Re-Conquest and Suppression: Fascist Italy's Pacification of Libya and
    Ethiopia, 1922–39," *Journal of Strategic Studies* 28, no. 6 (2005): 1021; Nicola Labanca,
    "Colonial Rule, Colonial Repression and War Crimes in the Italian Colonies," *Journal of
    Modern Italian Studies* 9, no. 3 (2004): 300–13; Giuseppe Finaldi, "Fascism, Violence, and
    Italian Colonialism," *Journal of Holocaust Research* 33, no. 1 (2019): 22–42.
[51] David Anderson, *Histories of the Hanged: Britain's Dirty War in Kenya and the End of
    Empire* (London: W. W. Norton, 2004); Caroline Elkins, *Britain's Gulag: The Brutal End
    of Empire in Kenya* (London: Pimlico, 2004).
[52] Eric Lohr, "The Russian Army and the Jews: Mass Deportations, Hostages, and Violence
    during World War One," *Russian Review* 60, no. 2 (2001): 404–19.
[53] Donald Bloxham, *The Great Game of Genocide: Imperialism, Nationalism, and the
    Destruction of the Ottoman Armenians* (Oxford: Oxford University Press, 2005).
[54] Terry Martin, "The Origins of Soviet Ethnic Cleansing," *Journal of Modern History* 70
    (December 1998): 813–61; N. F. Bugai and A. M. Gonov, "The Forced Evacuations of the
    Chechens and Ingush," *Russian Studies in History*, 4:2 (2002), 43–61; Nick Baron,
    "Stalinist Planning as Political Practice: Control and Repression on the Soviet
    Periphery, 1935–1938," *Europe-Asia Studies* 56, no. 3 (2004), 439–62.

Pol Pot regime in mid-1978 was driven by regime paranoia about rebellious eastern border cadres and other Cambodians thought to be tainted by Vietnamese influence. The Cham nationality, which was targeted for destruction, was likewise considered "rebellious."[55]

If security anxieties have led to genocidal measures of military coercion, another policy option has been to colonize one's own borderlands. Imperial Germany's concerns about Polish population growth within its eastern border led to various schemes to counter "Polonization" with "Germanization," including the purchase of Polish-owned estates and their distribution to German peasant colonists. Sociologist Max Weber was one of many who advocated such measures.[56] The same applies to nation-states. The Sri Lankan government engaged in rural colonization schemes to displace Tamils.[57] The government of the Dominican Republic tried to counter the "pacific invasion" of Haitians by "colonizing" the border areas with Dominican peasants in the first decades of the twentieth century.[58]

In all these empires and nation-states, terror played an important role in conquest and governance. Massacring entire towns hastened the surrender of others when they heard the news.[59] The relentless pursuit of enemy peoples is also a recurring feature of permanent security through the ages. Sometimes the destruction was total, sometimes it was not. Enemies were pursued to the extent that they no longer represented a threat or that sufficient vengeance had been exacted. What these cases show is that real or imagined resistance to imperial or national rule can radicalize a policy of "pacification." Resistance leads to reprisals and counterinsurgency that can aim to keep destroying a presumed enemy to achieve permanent security: that never again would such resistance recur.[60]

[55] Ben Kiernan, *The Pol Pot Regime: Race, Power, and Genocide in Cambodia under the Khmer Rouge, 1975–79* (New Haven, CT: Yale University Press, 1996), 399, 428.

[56] William W. Hagen, *Germans, Poles, and Jews: The Nationality Conflict in the Prussian East, 1772–1914* (Chicago: University of Chicago Press, 1980), 134–5; Wolfgang J. Mommsen, *Max Weber and German Politics, 1890–1920* (Chicago: University of Chicago Press, 1974), 26–8.

[57] Chelvadurai Manogaran, "Space-Related Identity in Sri Lanka," in *Nested Identities: Nationalism, Territory and Scale*, ed. G. H. Herb and D. H. Kaplan (Lanham, MD, 1999), 199–216.

[58] Richard Lee Turtis, "A World Destroyed, A Nation Imposed: The 1937 Haitian Massacre in the Dominican Republic," *Hispanic American Historical Review* 82, no. 3 (2002): 589–635.

[59] Saunders, *The History of the Mongol Conquests*, 56; Isaac, *The Invention of Racism in Classical Antiquity*, 216.

[60] Benjamin A. Valentino, Paul Huth, and Dylan Balch-Lindsay, "'Draining the Sea': Mass Killing and Guerrilla Warfare," *International Organization* 58, no. 2 (2004): 375–407.

Illiberal Permanent Security II: Subaltern Genocide

That indigenous people would resist colonization did not always seem obvious to Europeans, who thought their gift of civilization would or should make them welcome. In the wake of Palestinian-Arab riots against the British fostering of Jewish colonization in 1920 and 1921, Vladimir Jabotinsky berated Labor Zionist leaders for believing their presence would be tolerated by the "natives," invoking the history of Western conquests and settlements:

> Every reader has some idea of the early history of other countries which have been settled. I suggest that he recall all known instances. If he should attempt to seek but one instance of a country settled with the consent of those born there he will not succeed. The inhabitants (no matter whether they are civilized or savages) have always put up a stubborn fight. Furthermore, how the settler acted had no effect whatsoever. The Spaniards who conquered Mexico and Peru, or our own ancestors in the days of Joshua ben Nun behaved, one might say, like plunderers. But those "great explorers," the English, Scots and Dutch who were the first real pioneers of North America were people possessed of a very high ethical standard; people who not only wished to leave the redskins at peace but could also pity a fly; people who in all sincerity and innocence believed that in those virgin forests and vast plains ample space was available for both the white and red man. But the native resisted both barbarian and civilized settler with the same degree of cruelty.[61]

However self-serving Jabotinsky's depiction of settler virtue and native savagery, it does acknowledge that colonialism was imposed on unwilling inhabitants, and that intense political emotions are generated in resisting it. Given his conviction that Jews were also indigenous to Palestine, he would understand: Revisionists experienced such emotions in attacking the British authorities. Two historians have referred to the resistance mechanism generated by colonialism as "subaltern genocide" when it leads to the destruction and not just expulsion of the settler-colonizer.[62]

Examples abound of anxieties that one's people will be extinguished or erased by demographic supplanting or mortally endangered by security threats. In 1937, Dominicans not only colonized border areas, as noted above, but slaughtered 15,000 Haitians there who they thought were endangering the nation.[63] Many Serbs (especially those in Bosnia and Kosovo), still traumatized by the

---

[61] Zev Jabotinsky, "An Iron Wall (We and the Arabs)," in *Zionism: Background Papers for an Evaluation*, vol. 4, ed. Eliezer Schwied et al. (Jerusalem, n.d.), 67.

[62] Nicholas A. Robins, *Native Insurgencies and the Genocidal Impulse in the Americas* (Bloomington and Indianapolis, IN, 2005); Nicholas A. Robins and Adam Jones, eds., *Genocides by the Oppressed: Subaltern Genocide in Theory and Practice* (Bloomington: Indiana University Press, 2009).

[63] Turtis, "A World Destroyed, A Nation Imposed. *Hispanic American Historical Review* 82, no. 3."

genocidal experience of World War II, felt demographically threatened in the early 1990s because 25 percent of Serbs lived outside of Serbia; they wanted a state to defend their ethnicity. The paranoia exhibited by the Khmer Rouge in their self-understanding as liberators of the homeland from foreign influence demonstrates this point in a gruesome manner.[64] The genocidal violence perpetrated against civilians in the Balkans was so grotesque because they were not held to be innocent, but dangerous bearers of a nationality that vitiated the identity of the other.[65] What is more, the subaltern "millenarian rebellions" against exploitative colonial rule were directed against perceived foreign elements that were threatening the survival of the indigenous people.[66]

The connection between permanent security fantasies and national liberation movements has been made by anti-imperial thinkers, not that they would have depicted subaltern resistance as necessarily genocidal. Writing of the so-called Indian Mutiny, Karl Marx thought the "infamous" conduct of the "sepoys" was "only the reflex, in a concentrated form, of England's own conduct in India, not only during the epoch of the foundation of her Eastern Empire, but even during the last ten years of a long-settled rule ... There is something in human history like retribution; and it is a rule of historical retribution that its instruments be forged not by the offended, but by the offender himself."[67] Writing in the same vein, Jean-Paul Sartre (1905–1980) noted that "In Algeria and Angola, Europeans are massacred at sight; it is the moment of the boomerang; it is the third stage of violence; it comes back on us, it strikes us, and we do not realize any more than we did the other times that it's we who have launched it."[68] Franz Fanon (1925–1961) agreed: "The violence of the colonial regime and the counterviolence of the native balance each other and respond to each other in an extraordinary

---

[64] Alexander Laban Hinton, *Why Did They Kill? Cambodia in the Shadow of Genocide* (Berkeley: University of California Press, 2004).

[65] Jacques Semelin, "Analysis of a Mass Crime: Ethnic Cleansing in the Former Yugoslavia, 1991–1999," in *The Specter of Genocide: Mass Murder in Historical Perspective*, ed. Robert Gellately and Ben Kiernan (Cambridge, 2003), 353–70; Bette Denich, "Dismembering Yugoslavia: Nationalist Ideologies and the Symbolic Revival of Genocide," *American Ethnologist* 21, no. 2 (1994): 367–90; Robert M. Hayden, "Imagined Communities and Real Victims: Self-Determination and Ethnic Cleansing in Yugoslavia," *American Ethnologist* 23, no. 4 (1996): 783–801; Damir Mirkovic, "The Historical Link between the Ustasha Genocide and the Croato-Serbian Civil War: 1991–1995," *Journal of Genocide Research* 2, no. 3 (2000): 363–73; Anthony Oberschall, "The Manipulation of Ethnicity: From Ethnic Co-operation to Violence and War in Yugoslavia," *Ethnic and Racial Studies* 23, no. 6 (2000): 982–1001.

[66] Mike Davis, *Late Victorian Holocausts: El Nino Famines and the Making of the Third World* (London: Verso, 2001), 177–210.

[67] Karl Marx, *Karl Marx on Colonialism and Modernization*, ed. and intro. Shlomo Avineri (New York: Doubleday, 1969), 224.

[68] Jean-Paul Sartre, "Preface," in Frantz Fanon, *Wretched of the Earth* trans. Constance Farrington (New York: Grove Weidenfeld, 1963), 20.

reciprocal homogeneity."[69] The Tunisian Jew Albert Memmi (1920–2020) was also attracted to the Marxist proposition that colonialism produced its own negation by bringing forth an utterly alienated colonized population whose only prospect of dignified life was the "complete liquidation of colonization."[70]

If an alienated "native" issued from colonialism, how was this alienation generated? These Francophone anticolonial thinkers in particular pointed out that the foundational binary between settler and native was a colonial product. In such a "Manichean world" (Fanon) of colonialism, in which the settler cast the native as the incarnation of absolute evil, the native had to invert this value hierarchy for his or her own self-respect. "Colonialism creates the patriotism of the colonized," wrote Sartre.[71] Memmi explained the source of this nativism in his famous book from 1957, *The Colonizer and the Colonized*. His basic message was also that "being considered and treated apart by colonialist racism, the colonized ends up accepting this Manichaean division of the colony and, by extension, of the whole world." Consequently, "in the eyes of the colonized, all Europeans in the colonies are *de facto* colonizers."[72]

What is more, the practical impossibility of assimilation – because of the colonizer's refusal and because of the self-denial entailed – meant that the native inevitably resorted to traditional values as a compensatory orientation. But these values, usually familial and religious, had become petrified by colonial pressure, and did not promote social progress. Nativism was reactionary. By ontologizing collectives in the same way as the settler, and "condemning each individual of that group," the colonized became "a xenophobe and racist."[73]

Sartre and Memmi did not applaud the chauvinism and racism of anticolonialist struggles, and Fanon's aversion to nativism is well known. Racism and "a legitimate desire for revenge" could not "sustain a war of liberation," Fanon thought. Memmi eventually left Tunis for Paris because, as a Jew, he found life impossible in postcolonial Muslim Tunisia.[74] As Marxists, they were

[69] Fanon, *Wretched of the Earth*, 88.
[70] Albert Memmi, *The Colonizer and the Colonized*, intro. Jean-Paul Sartre (Boston: Beacon Press, [1957] 1965), 151. Liah Greenfeld writes similarly of resentment – hate and envy – as the source of nationalism. See her *Nationalism: Five Roads to Modernity* (Cambridge, MA: Cambridge University Press, 1992), 16.
[71] Fanon, *Wretched of the Earth*, 93; Jean-Paul Sartre, "Introduction," in Memmi, *The Colonizer and the Colonized*, xxviii; Abdul R. JanMohamed, *Manichean Aesthetics: The Politics of Literature in Colonial Africa* (Amherst: University of Massachusetts Press, 1983), 4.
[72] Memmi, *The Colonizer and the Colonized*, 130–1.
[73] Ibid., 130, 139. Memmi's insight is very close to the theory of social regression advanced by Vamik Volkan. See his *Bloodlines: From Ethnic Pride to Ethnic Terrorism* (New York: Farrar, Straus and Giroux, 1997); Volkan, *Blind Trust: Large Groups and Their Leaders in Times of Crisis and Terror* (Charlottesville: University of Virginia Press, 2004).
[74] Fanon, *Wretched of the Earth*, 139; Albert Memmi, *Jews and Arabs* (Chicago: J Philip O'Hara, 1975).

cosmopolitan internationalists who preferred a popular front of anticolonialists. National liberation entailed transcending the terms of settler/native to create a new socialist nation of equal citizens. The colonial system needed to be transformed by expropriating the collaborating indigenous bourgeoisie, rather than simply expelling settlers.[75] They wished decolonization to be the assertion of freedom when the newly constituted people could gain political agency, enter history, and create its own authentic civilization, not just a variation of the colonizer's.

At the same time, these writers told their European reading publics that their expectation of a nonviolent and anticolonialist struggle was unrealistic.[76] Violent anticolonialism was a predictable phase through which colonized peoples had to pass, even if it entailed "tragic mishaps."[77] Fanon himself was ambivalent, famously praising this violence as a "cleansing force" through which "the native frees himself from his inferiority complex and from his despair and inaction; it makes him fearless and restores his self-respect." This redemptive nationalism was necessary to assert the new postcolonial national culture: "the most elementary, most savage, and the most undifferentiated nationalism is the most fervent and efficient means of defending national culture."[78] Sartre supported Fanon's rendition of the struggle with some stirring quotations: the struggle's "irrepressible violence is neither sound and fury, nor the resurrection of savage instincts, nor even the effect of resentment: it is man recreating himself."[79] For all the romanticization evident here, these thinkers both expressed and explained the revolutionary violence of the colonized as the moment of salvation. In certain circumstances, we see in the next chapter, it can be genocidal.

Even by the time he died prematurely in 1961, Fanon was aware that, far from being a transitional political emotion, racism was being used by the "national bourgeoisie" to secure its own position in the postcolonial order. Rather than constructing a new nation beyond race, these elites were allowing precolonial tribal rivalries to recur.[80] Moreover, the new state appeared to the liberated populations less as their own democratic creation than as a distant apparatus that was milked by a dominant, rival ethnic grouping for its own

---

[75] Fanon, *Wretched of the Earth*, 146, 158; Benita Parry, "Resistance Theory/Theorising Resistance or Two Cheers for Nativism," in *Colonial Discourse/Postcolonial Theory*, ed. Francis Barker, Peter Hulme, and Margaret Iversen (Manchester: University of Manchester Press, 1994), 172–91.

[76] Memmi, *The Colonizer and the Colonized*, 134–37; Sartre, "Preface," in Fanon, *Wretched of the Earth*, 18, 21.

[77] Fanon, *Wretched of the Earth*, 148.   [78] Ibid., 94, 24.

[79] Sartre, "Preface," in ibid., 22. "The native cures himself of colonial neurosis by thrusting out the settler through force of arms. When his rage boils over, he rediscovers his lost innocence and he comes to know himself in that he himself creates himself."

[80] Fanon, *Wretched of the Earth*, 156–9.

benefit. Their security and identity was therefore more likely to inhere in preindependence traditional ethnic attachments than in a chimerical supratribal national identity.[81] The political instability and ethnic violence of postcolonial African states has been blamed on this failure to transcend race during and after decolonization. Writing in the tradition of the Francophone intellectuals, historian Mahmood Mamdani attributed this failure on colonialism: "That greater crime was to politicize indigeneity, first as a settler libel against the native, and then as a native self-assertion."[82]

Liberal Permanent Security: Settler Colonialism

Settlement of territory need not entail destruction of locals. The conflict between "steppe and sown" was not a zero-sum game in medieval central Asia. Nomadic societies did not in fact seek to despoil sedentary ones, because they were needed for trade. The limitations of the nomadic economy, based on herds of stock, meant that luxury and other goods had to be extracted from agricultural societies – whether by "trade or raid" – with which they lived in tense symbiosis.[83] These relationships approximated what historian Richard White calls "middle ground" spaces in colonial America, in which peoples traded and negotiated with one another in mutually created forms of accommodation that were not reducible to the simple binary relationships of domination and subordination.[84] This delicate balance broke down in processes of "demographic takeover" when settlers and pastoralists destroyed indigenous peoples' livelihood, crushed resistance, and established their own societies in their stead.[85] Since the early-modern period, pastoral societies likewise displaced nomadic ones on the Eurasian continent.

---

[81] Clifford Geertz, "The Integrative Revolution: Primordial Sentiments and Civil Politics in the New States," in *Old Societies and New States: The Quest for Modernity in Asia and Africa*, ed. Clifford Geertz (New York: Free Press, 1963), 109–19; Anaïs Angelo, *Power and the Presidency in Kenya: The Jomo Kenyatta Years* (1958–1878) (Cambridge: Cambridge University Press, 2020).

[82] Mahmood Mamdani, "Beyond Settler and Native as Political Identities: Overcoming the Political Legacy of Colonialism," *Comparative Studies in Society and History* 43, no. 4 (2001): 651–4.

[83] Michael Adas, ed., *Agricultural and Pastoral Societies in Ancient and Classical History* (Philadelphia: Temple University Press, 2001); Peter B. Golden, "Nomads and Their Sedentary Neighbors in Pre-Cinggisid Eurasia," *Archivum Eurasiae Medii Aevi* 7 (1991): 41–81; Nicola Di Cosmo, "Ancient Inner Asian Nomads: Their Economic Basis and Its Significance in Chinese History," *Journal of Asian Studies* 52, no. 4 (1994): 1092–126.

[84] Richard White, *The Middle Ground: Indians, Empires, and Republics in the Great Lakes Region, 1650–1815* (Cambridge: Cambridge University Press, 1991).

[85] Donald Denoon, *Settler Capitalism: The Dynamics of Dependent Development in the Southern Hemisphere* (Oxford: Clarendon, 1983), 1.

The settlers' interest in the land rather than in the labor of the Indigenes means that a "logic of elimination" characterizes settler colonialism, as noted above: the nomads' connections to the land needed to be vitiated by their absorption into or expulsion from the new society.[86] If an Aboriginal presence made it difficult to hire shepherds, then it had to be eliminated. Settler colonialism cannot succeed unless it crushes indigenous resistance. "The coexistence of commercial farming and nomadism was impossible everywhere in the long run," observed Donald Denoon about the deep structure of settler colonialism.[87]

This pattern certainly holds true when a middle ground of rough parity became a colony. For instance, in British Columbia, approximately symmetrical relations of trade between British and Indians obtained until the 1850s, when it became a formal colony and land acquisition was the central determinant of interaction. The customary pattern of events unfolded. The British military tried to keep the peace, but imperatives for local rule and economizing in London meant that land policies were ultimately decided by settler politicians. They enclosed common land and legislated exclusive property rights over multiple usage so as to ensure that investments could be made good.[88] Indians could resist by moving, submitting petitions, and not cooperating with the new dispensation, but state and settler violence underwrote the eventual victory of the British social system.[89]

---

[86] Patrick Wolfe, "Structure and Event: Settler Colonialism, Time, and the Question of Genocide," in Moses, *Empire, Colony, Genocide*, 102–31, and A. Dirk Moses, ed., *Genocide and Settler Society: Frontier Violence and Stolen Indigenous Children in Australian History* (Oxford and New York: Berghahn Books, 2004). On settler colonialism: Lorenzo Veracini, *Settler Colonialism: A Theoretical Overview* (New York: Palgrave, 2010); Andrew Armitage, *Comparing the Policy of Aboriginal Assimilation: Australia, Canada, and New Zealand* (Vancouver: University of British Columbia Press, 1995); Lynette Russell, *Colonial Frontiers: Indigenous-European Encounters in Settler Societies* (Manchester: Manchester University Press, 2001); Ronald Weitzer, *Transforming Settler States: Communal Conflict and Internal Security in Northern Ireland and Zimbabwe* (Berkeley: University of California Press, 1990); Kate Darian-Smith, Liz Gunner, and Sarah Nuttall, eds., *Text, Theory, Space: Land, Literature and History in South Africa and Australia* (London and New York: Routledge, 1996); David Trigger and Gareth Griffiths, eds., *Disputed Territories: Land, Culture and Identity in Settler Societies* (Hong Kong: Hong Kong University Press, 2003); Tim Murray, *The Archaeology of Contact in Settler Societies* (Cambridge: Cambridge University Press, 2004).

[87] Denoon, *Settler Capitalism*, 26; Adhikari, *Genocide on Settler Frontiers*; Wolfe, "Structure and Event"; A. Dirk Moses, "Genocide and Settler Society in Australian History," in Moses, *Genocide and Settler Society*, 3–48.

[88] John C. Weaver, *The Great Land Rush and the Making of the Modern World, 1650–1900* (Montreal and Kingston: McGill-Queen's University Press, 2003).

[89] Cole Harris, "How Did Colonialism Dispossess Comments from an Edge of Empire," *Annals of the Association of American Geographers* 94, no. 1 (2004): 165–82. See also his *Making Native Space: Colonialism, Resistance, and Reserves in British Columbia* (Vancouver, 2002). On Canada, see Alexander Laban Hinton, Andrew Woolford, and Jeff Benvenuto, eds., *Colonial Genocide in Indigenous North America* (Durham, NC: Duke University Press, 2014), and Colin Samson, *A Way of Life That Does Not Exist: Canada*

The deployment of "terror" – a term common in early-modern sources – was a conscious policy of occupying powers, such as the English in Ireland.[90]

The Elizabethan conquest and colonization of Ireland, which was contemporaneous with significant contact of the English with Native Americans in the sixteenth century, saw the slaughter of men, women, and children when they resisted conquest. The women and children were considered fair game because they sustained the men, and because the Irish were regarded as pagan.[91] The violent Cromwellian quelling of Catholic uprisings in Ireland in the next century, such as the massacre of Drogheda in 1649, followed the same pattern, as did the Spanish counterinsurgency against the Yucatec Mayan uprising of 1761.[92]

Equally difficult to subdue were the Indians of the Argentine frontier in the nineteenth century. Well-armed and excellent horsemen, Indians prospered in the pampa, where their mobile lifeway rendered them less vulnerable to the disease that devastated those who attempted agriculture. Roaming Spanish patrols made little inroads into the region in the early eighteenth century, so the imperial authorities were forced to ally themselves with certain tribes against others. Tribute was paid to some of them for peace and information during this period of rough parity between different groups.

The Roman model of settling soldiers on the frontier failed in the face of resistance by ranchers and plutocratic governments loathe to give away land. Domestic Argentine imperatives in the 1830s led to the demand for more grazing land and a military solution, but 50 percent of the badly paid and trained soldiers and militia were casualties of frontier service. By the 1850s, alternative policies to propitiate Indians by granting them land allotments had also failed, with Indians driving off ranchers and settlers. Other efforts in the 1870s to integrate Indians into frontier society by winning them from their raiding/tribute economy also came to nought. Anxious about the interests of neighboring Chile in the region, a hard-line military solution was suggested in

and the Extinguishment of the Innu (London: Verso, 2003). On colonial enclosures, Lance van Sittert, "Holding the Line: The Rural Enclosure Movement in the Cape Colony, 1865–1910," *Journal of African History* 43, no. 1 (2002): 95–118.

[90] See the excellent discussion of the literature in Ronald Karr, "'Why Should You Be So Furious': The Violence of the Pequot War," *Journal of American History* 85, no. 3 (1998): 876–909.

[91] Nicholas P. Canny, "The Ideology of English Colonization: From Ireland to America," *William and Mary Quarterly*, 3rd series, 30, no. 4 (1973): 582–3; Susan Brigden, *New Worlds, Lost Worlds: The Rule of the Tudors 1485–1603* (London: Allen Lane, 2000).

[92] Katie Kane, "Nits Make Lice: Drogheda, Sand Creek, and the Poetics of Colonial Extermination," *Cultural Critique*, no. 42 (1999): 81–103; Robert Path, "Culture, Community, and 'Rebellion' in the Yucatec Maya Uprising of 1791," in *Native Resistance and the Pax Colonial in New Spain*, ed. Susan Schroeder (Lincoln and London: University of Nebraska Press, 1998), 67–83.

1875 by Julio A. Roca, chief of frontier forces. "In my judgment, the best system to finish the Indians, that is, exterminating them or removing them beyond the Rio Negro, is an offensive war," by which he meant lightning strikes by mobile forces. With the telegraph, railroad, and better-armed troops, his offensives in 1878 were successful. Thousands were killed, with survivors driven to Chile. Missions were built in the place of destroyed villages.[93]

A parallel story was unfolding further to the north. The US Army fought two wars at the same time; one, consistent with the Lieber Code, to defeat the Confederacy, and another, without the Code and with exterminationist dimensions, against the Apache and Plains Indians more generally. Consequently, when up to 200 members – mostly women and children – of the Cheyenne and Arapaho tribes were massacred by 700 federal militia at the Sand Creek, Colorado, in 1864, the code was not invoked in the subsequent investigation and no-one was prosecuted.[94] At the end of the century, such warfare would be waged against those resisting US occupation of the Philippines. The enforcement of the Lieber stipulations did the insurgents no good because they were categorized as irregulars and could be summarily executed. Indeed, in a telling linkage, President Roosevelt denounced these Filipinos as treacherous as "our Arizona Apache."[95] Tens of thousands of Filipinos died of starvation and disease in the US counterinsurgency operation in Batanguas between 1899 and 1902, when its forces laid waste to the countryside and forcibly separated the population into loyal and disloyal camps.[96]

Imperial thinkers devoted considerable thought to the problem of "small wars," with their pattern of conquest followed by resistance. Although they advised against exasperating the conquered population, the destruction of villages and crops was countenanced if necessary. Certainly, French and Russian authorities were happy to indulge in such scorched-earth tactics in

---

[93] Richard W. Slatta, "'Civilization' Battles 'Barbarism': The Limits of Argentine Indian Frontier Struggle," in *The Military and Conflict between Cultures: Soldiers at the Interface*, ed. James C. Bradford (College Station, TX: Texas A&M University Press, 1997), 131–46.

[94] John Fabian Witt, *Lincoln's Code: The Laws of War in American History* (New York: Free Press, 2012), 92–3, 96, 106, 337, 355–8; Karl Jacoby, "'The Broad Platform of Extermination': Nature and Violence in the Nineteenth Century North American Borderlands," *Journal of Genocide Research* 10, no. 2 (2008): 260. Helen M. Kinsella, *The Image before the Weapon: A Critical History of the Distinction between Combatant and Civilian* (Ithaca, NY: Cornell University Press, 2011), 98–101.

[95] Paul A. Kramer, *The Blood of Government: Race, Empire, and the United States and the Philippines* (Chapel Hill: University of North Carolina Press, 2006), 90, 101, 136–7; Stuart Creighton Miller, *Benevolent Assimilation: The American Conquest of the Philippines* (New Haven: Yale University Press, 1984), 88; Christopher J. Einolf, *America in the Philippines, 1899–1902: The First Torture Scandal* (Basingstoke: Palgrave Macmillan, 2014).

[96] Glenn A. May, "Filipino Resistance to American Occupation: Batanguas, 1899–1902," *Pacific Historical Review* 48, no. 4 (1979): 531–56.

their respective North African and Caucasian conquests during and after the
1830s.[97] Alexis de Tocqueville's liberal scruples were not shared by many
French in Algeria, as he reported in 1833. On one view:

> to subjugate the Arabs, we should fight them with the utmost violence and
> in the Turkish manner, that is to say, by killing everything we meet. I have
> heard this view supported by officers who took it to the point of bitterly
> regretting that we have started to take prisoners in some places, and many
> assured me that they encouraged their soldiers to spare no one. For my
> part, I returned from Africa with the distressing notion that we are now
> fighting far more barbarously than the Arabs themselves. For the present,
> it is on their side that one meets with civilization.

At the same time, he regarded burning harvests, emptying silos, and interning
civilians as "unfortunate necessities . . . to which any people that wants to wage
war on the Arabs is obliged to submit." The reason for such extreme measures
was that war was being waged on populations, not governments. Perceived
"necessity" could compel liberals like de Tocqueville to defend wars against
entire populations.[98]

The same pattern obtained in Australia where, in 1770, English explorer
James Cook claimed the whole east coast of the continent for the British
Crown on the grounds that it was ownerless wasteland.[99] The agriculturalist
argument animated settlers from the outset. One Hobart resident expressed it
when he wrote in 1874 of the indigenous peoples of Tasmania:

> The aboriginal's wants were, indeed, so few, and the country in which it
> had pleased the Almighty to place him supplied them all in such lavish

[97] C. E. Callwell, *Small Wars: A Tactical Textbook for Imperial Soldiers*, 3rd ed. (Lincoln,
NB, and London: University of Nebraska Press, [1906] 1990), 26–7, 45, 145; Peter
Holquist, "To Count, to Extract, and to Exterminate: Population Statistics and
Population Politics in Late Imperial and Soviet Russia," in *A State of Nations: Empire
and Nation-Making in the Age of Lenin and Soviet Russia*, ed. Ronald Grigor Suny and
Terry Martin (Oxford and New York: Oxford University Press, 2001), 111–44."

[98] De Tocqueville, *Writings on Empire and Slavery*, 70, 87; Jennifer Pitts, "Empire and
Democracy: Tocqueville and the Algeria Question," *Journal of Political Philosophy* 8, no.
3 (2000): 295–318; Cheryl B. Welch, "Colonial Violence and the Rhetoric of Evasion:
Tocqueville on Algeria," *Political Theory* 31, no. 2 (2003): 235–64. See most recently
Gallois, *A History of Violence in the Early Algerian Colony*.

[99] Alan Frost, "New South Wales as *Terra Nullius*: The British Denial of Aboriginal Land
Rights," *Australian Historical Studies* 19 (1981): 512–23. See also Pat Maloney,
"Colonisation, Civilisation and Cultivation: Early Victorians' Theories of Property
Rights and Sovereignty," in *Land and Freedom: Law, Property Right and the British
Diaspora*, ed. A. R. Buck, John McLaren, and Nancy E. Wright (Aldershot: Ashgate,
2001), 39–56. The Lockean tradition in Australia is best represented by Geoffrey Blainey,
A Land Half Won, rev. ed. (Melbourne: Sun Books, 1983); Blainey, *Triumph of the
Nomads*, rev. ed. (Melbourne: Sun Books 1983).

abundance, that he was not called on for the exercise of much skill or labour in satisfying his requirements. He had no inducement to work and (like all others who are so situated) he did not very greatly exert himself. Necessity, said to be the parent of invention, was known to him only in a limited degree; and in ingenuity was seldom brought into exercise. His faculties were dormant from the mere bounty of providence.[100]

On the basis of these assumptions, the British had argued that the "natives" had rights only to what they caught and gathered, while uncultivated land belonged to no-one, and was therefore available to Europeans to settle and exploit.[101] Judging by the furious reaction of British settlers to attacks on their property, the presumption that by their presence they were doing the Aborigines a favor fueled their indignation and proclivity to take savage reprisals.[102]

Governor Phillip of New South Wales, for instance, thought the collective punishment of random Aboriginal men by instilling "universal terror" would prevent "further mischief," like the spearing of his gamekeeper.[103] In 1828, Governor Arthur's executive council in Van Diemen's Land supported his measures against the local tribes by noting that "To inspire them with terror will be found the only effectual means of security for the future."[104] Security for the future is permanent security, for which terror was necessary.

Tactics of preventative counterinsurgency later characterized the Mounted Native Police in Queensland, leading to the decimation of indigenous peoples there. Fearing that "any large assemblage of blacks" entailed a conspiracy to massacre settlers, the Queensland government authorised their "dispersal" – which meant shooting – by the Native Police. This policy, too, was "justified by the extreme necessities of the case," as premier Arthur Palmer told Parliament in 1878.[105] For its indiscriminate slaughter of indigenous people – men,

---

[100] J. E. Calder, "Some Account of the Wars of Extirpation and Habits of the Native Tribes of Tasmania," *Journal of the Anthropological Institute of Great Britain and Ireland* 3 (1874): 19.

[101] On the English adaptation of this intellectual tradition, see Andrew Fitzmaurice, *Humanism and America: An Intellectual History of English Colonisation, 1500–1625* (Cambridge: Cambridge University Press, 2003), 140–1.

[102] Henry Reynolds, "The Written Record," in *Frontier Conflict: The Australian Experience*, ed. Bain Attwood and S. G. Foster (Canberra: National Museum of Australia, 2003), 79–87.

[103] Quoted in Shino Konishi, "The Father Governor: The British Administration of Aboriginal People at Port Jackson, 1788–1792", in *Public Men: Political Masculinities in Modern Britain*, ed. Matthew McCormack (London: Palgrave Macmillan, 2007), 66.

[104] Quoted in Henry Reynolds, "Genocide in Tasmania?" in Moses, *Genocide and Settler Society*, 135.

[105] Report of the Select Committee on the Native Police, "Instructions of Commandant to Officers and Camp Sergeants of Native Police." Appendix A, Queensland Votes and Proceedings, 1861, 152; W. Ross Johnston, *The Long Blue Line: A History of the Queensland Police Force* (Brisbane: Booralong, 1992), 92.

women, and children – this policy, rather than the notorious Tasmanian campaign, is the most obvious case of state-sanctioned, systematic genocide in Australian history.[106]

Not only was the spirit of revenge rife on the frontier, the justice of crushing indigenous resistance was as obvious to nineteenth-century commentators as it was to later Australian establishment historians in the 1930s.[107] Grenfell Price of the University of Adelaide, for instance, wrote in the *Cambridge History of the British Empire* that:

> So serious had been the troubles in the Murray area [in southeastern Australia] that settlement virtually ceased until troops were sent to the district, and at the "battle of Pinjarra" [in western Australia] in 1834 *half the males of the Murray tribe were destroyed.* This conflict enabled F.F. Armstrong and others to establish better relations with the natives, although the difficulty was not completely removed for many years.[108]

Two years later, in 1935, University of Sydney historian Stephen H. Roberts published an analysis of squatters in colonial Australia that betrayed the same Lockean assumptions. Such grievances as the natives had against the whites "were usually the result of their own ungovernable dispositions and their failure to see any sense in the white man's laws of property." While Roberts was prepared to concede that "Squatting life certainly impinged on native existence," the point was that "the interaction was as between landowner and raiders." Little wonder, he implied, that "Outrage, real or imaginary, was met by outrage, and Europeans killed natives on the slightest pretext."[109] His book on Nazi Germany, published in 1937 on the basis of his travels there, came too soon for him to be able to ponder connections between the British treatment of the natives with the German treatment of Slavs.[110]

Large-scale massacres were rare. Across the country, squatters, and the Native Police in Queensland, destroyed Aboriginal communities by shooting

---

[106] Alison Palmer, *Colonial Genocide* (Adelaide: Crawford House, 1999); A. Dirk Moses, "An Antipodean Genocide? The Origins of the Genocidal Moment in Australian History," *Journal of Genocide Research* 2, no. 1 (2000): 89–105.

[107] Anthony Trollope, *Australia*, ed. P. D. Edwards and R. B. Joyce (Brisbane: University of Queensland Press, [1872] 1967), 113.

[108] Grenfell Price, "Experiments in Colonisation," *Cambridge History of the British Empire*, Vol. VII, Part 1 (Cambridge: Cambridge University Press, 1933), 209–42. Emphasis added.

[109] Stephen H. Roberts, *The Squatting Age in Australia, 1835–1847* (Melbourne: Melbourne University Press, 1935), 408–11.

[110] Stephen H. Roberts, *The House That Hitler Built* (London: Methuen, 1937); Andrew G. Bonnell, "Stephen H. Roberts' *The House That Hitler Built* as a Source on Nazi Germany," *Australian Journal of Politics and History* 46 (2000): 1–20.

small groups in countless incidents.[111] This violence was a manifestation of the settler society's deep structure, because it is intrinsic to colonization conducted on the assumption of superior settler rights to the land. The agency of colonial actors was constrained by the nature of the society they were establishing, a settler colony, which was both a process and a structure. The constant reference to the "painful" or "unfortunate necessity" of destructive measures that were "forced upon" the settlers and authorities testifies to the existence of a colonization process they felt they could not control. The deep structure accounts for the pattern and extent of violence, which is not explicable by reference to individual intentions alone.

The statements of prominent Tasmanian settlers urging the expulsion or extermination of the Aborigines reveals how the eliminatory implications of settler colonialism became expressed through security anxieties. In March 1830, William Barnes wrote to the Governor about the conflict with Aborigines, noting that "the dreadful alternative only remains of a general extermination by some means or other." Another landowner, George Espie, told the government that he could see "no other remedy but their [the Aborigines'] speedy capture or extermination." Yet another leading settler, Temple Pearson, informed the Colonial Secretary that: "Total extermination however severe the measure, I much fear will be the only means left to the Government to protect the Whites." And the Director of the Van Diemen's Land Company, Edward Curr, expressed the zero-sum game of settlement project when he observed that "If they [the settlers] do not abandon the Island [and will not] submit to see the white inhabitants murdered one after another ... they must undertake a war of extermination on principles of which many will be disposed to question."[112]

Such statements did not originate in the evil intentions of random individuals. A historical rather than moralistic consideration of facts would see those settler intentions were formulated in response to a crisis that threatened the viability of the settlement project. The origin of such sentiments, then, is settler colonialism itself rather than the outrageous perfidy of specific men or tragic cultural misunderstandings between them and Aborigines. The formula that links colonialisms in terms of race and space needs to be revised to include the dynamism of the security imperative. The formula should be settler security in space.[113] In sum, land appropriation, which occurs via imperial incorporation and settler colonialism, lies at the basis of

[111] Raymond Evans, "'Plenty Shoot 'Em': The Destruction of Aboriginal Societies along the Queensland Frontier," in Moses, Genocide and Settler Society, 150–73.
[112] Quoted in Reynolds, "Genocide in Tasmania?" 141.
[113] For the formulation of race and space, see Jürgen Zimmerer, "Colonialism and the Holocaust: Towards an Archaeology of Genocide," in Moses, Genocide and Settler Society, 49–76.

all state-building. And at the basis of all state-building is permanent security. In its liberal mode, permanent security is expansive because capitalism is expansive. As a structure, originary accumulation in settler colonialism is not a precapitalist stage of development for capitalism proper, but is constitutive. It continues in various forms, whether in the hyper extraction of mining in the face of surviving indigenous land title or in the decimation of trade unions backed by state power.[114]

The Soviet Union

Born of revolution, Bolshevik elites were possessed by a political imaginary that divided the population into loyal and dangerous elements, an intensification of the Tsarist military mentality of distinguishing between reliable and unreliable national minorities, especially in border areas. The experience of the civil war substantially formed the Bolshevik habitus. Henceforth, not only was insurgency to be repressed, as it was with the "Decossackisation of the Don" in 1919, but it was to be prevented by actively removing (perceived) enemy elements, usually called "bandits" or "kulaks" (rich peasants).[115] During the Russian Civil war, both Red and White forces routinely "sifted" and "filtered" captured troops and populations for members of suspect groups they regarded as enemy groups. White forces, for instance, executed tens of thousands of Jews, Balts, Chinese and communists because they were seen as "incorrigible."[116] After victory, Soviet authorities executed some 25,000 people when they systematically "filtered" the population.

This state of hypervigilance was compounded by the Bolshevik perception that the Soviet Union was in a state of latent warfare with Western powers. The Soviet leadership felt encircled by enemies abroad and their agents within Soviet borders: peoples thought to be in league with these foreign enemies were necessarily "unreliable elements," "suspect nations," "nationalities of foreign governments."[117] In this context, leaders could make a statements like this one:

---

[114] David Harvey, *The New Imperialism* (Oxford: Oxford University Press, 2003); Lorenzo Veracini, *The Settler Colonial Present* (London: Routledge, 2015); Piterberg and Veracini, "Wakefield, Marx, and the World Turned Inside Out," 474.

[115] Peter Holquist, "'Conduct Merciless Mass Terror': Decossackization on the Don, 1919," *Cahiers due Monde russe*, 28, nos. 1–2 (1997), 127–62.

[116] Peter Holquist, "Violent Russia, Deadly Marxism? Russia in the Epoch of Violence, 1905–1921," *Kritika: Explorations in Russian and Eurasian History* 4, no. 3 (2003): 627–52.

[117] James Harris, "Encircled by Enemies: Stalin's Perceptions of the Capitalist World, 1918–1941," *Journal of Strategic Studies* 30, no. 3 (2008): 513–45.

We will annihilate every such enemy, even if he is an old Bolshevik, we will annihilate his entire clan, his family. We will mercilessly annihilate anyone who in actions or thoughts – yes, even in thoughts – who attempts [to undermine] the unity of the socialist state.[118]

Permanent security rather that racial imperatives governed the logic of this rhetoric and policy.

After abandoning the dream of world revolution in the 1920s, Soviet leaders, above all Stalin, determined to build "socialism in one country" and construct an autarkic economy that could hold out against the West. In this regard, modernizing the economy was of paramount importance. This aim entailed addressing the food supply, which had been a cause of crisis, including widespread famine accounting for millions of lives, during the civil war. Indeed, the Antonov rebellion in 1921 had been triggered by Bolshevik forced requisitioning of grain. In particular, the Bolsheviks, whose powerbase was in urban centres, distrusted the peasantry, which constituted the over-whelming proportion of the population that had benefitted from the subdivision of large private estates after 1918. It was a major security problem that this "reactionary" social class – especially "kulaks" – should control such a strategic asset, especially in view of their "backward" farming techniques. The solution was to rapidly industrialize and to "liquidate" the "kulak" control of agriculture.

The concept of enemy classes and people (*vrag narodo*) became a central element of the Soviet security paranoia. Stalin thought the kulaks an irredeemable enemy. Because of their large number and geographical dispersion, expulsion was no option. Starvation was a substitute policy, with genocidal consequences for Ukrainian and Caucasian peasants.[119] The aim of the first five-year plan, instituted in 1928, was rapid industrialization, financed by capital generated from exploitation of the farming sector. But artificially depressing prices sparked resistance among the peasantry, which withheld goods from the market, indicating the city's vulnerability to the countryside during the famines of the civil war. Stalin responded in late 1929 by ordering the sudden and coercive collectivization of agriculture. These measures also met with fierce resistance, and the secret police recorded almost 23,000 "terrorist acts" – attributed to kulak sabotage – for 1929 and 1930. Consequently, the Bolsheviks sentenced over 20,000 people to death in 1930 and deported 1.8 million kulaks in that year and the next, though many only within their own region. Their labor was to be exploited in forced

---

[118] Jeffrey Burds, "The Soviet War against 'Fifth Columnists': The Case of Chechnya, 1942–4," *Journal of Contemporary History* 42, no. 2 (2007): 283.

[119] Michael Ellman, "The Role of Leadership Perceptions and of Intent in the Soviet Famine of 1931–1934," *Europe-Asia Studies* 57, no. 6 (2005): 823–41.

industrialization while some were used for colonization of the Russian interior. As food production plummeted, forced confiscation of grain and other food-stuffs exacerbated the crisis in the countryside and led to widespread famine.

Worse still was the famine of 1931–1933, which some observers, particularly Ukrainian nationalists, consider a genocidal contrivance rather than the unintended consequence of a misguided policy – intense debate remains around the question. In Ukraine, as well as the North Caucasus grain-growing region, Stalin intensified the requisitions in the summer of 1932, and may have done so in part to break the back of secessionist movements among Ukrainian communists, incensed as he was by what he regarded as the "war of sabotage, a war to the death against Soviet power."[120] The military and police force were stationed to prevent Ukrainian and North Caucasian peasants leaving their areas, fating them to starvation. Around three million Ukrainians died from hunger – of the between five and six million Soviet famine fatalities over all – and nearly 100,000 were incarcerated for resisting the forced requisitions.[121]

If the main priority of Soviet repression until 1933 had been class warfare, namely eliminating kulaks (actually a synonym for any social refractory element), after 1933 national security concerns led the Bolsheviks to suspect national groups living in sensitive border areas of engaging in espionage and potential sabotage. The Ukrainian famine provides the transition, as Soviet policy was also driven by anxieties about cross-border influence from Poland, which contained a large Ukrainian population. Class and national criteria overlapped. 60,000 Kuban Cossacks were deported for failing to meet grain quotas.[122] Now the priority was "cleansing and making secure frontier regions."[123] As a multinational empire, the Soviet Union contained innumerable minority nations related to conationals on the other side of the border, especially Finns, Germans, Baltic peoples and Koreans, which, it was feared, would be instrumentalized by foreign powers against the Soviet Union.

The first of the "national operations" began in 1935 with the establishment of a 7.5 km "forbidden border zone" in the west in which no-one was permitted to live. German and Polish citizens of the Soviet Union were disproportionately resettled. Even though deportations entailed moving tens of thousands of people into interior territories like Kazakhstan, they were not

---

[120] Nicolas Werth, "The Crimes of the Stalin Regime: Outline for an Inventory and Classification," in *The Historiography of Genocide*, ed. Dan Stone (Basingstoke: Palgrave Macmillan, 2007), 407.

[121] Nicolas Werth, "Mass Deportations, Ethnic Cleansing, and Genocidal Politics in the Later Russian Empire and the USSR," in *The Oxford Handbook on Genocide Studies*, ed. Donald Bloxham and A. Dirk Moses (Oxford: Oxford University Press), 386–406.

[122] Martin, "The Origins of Soviet Ethnic Cleansing." See also Sarah Cameron, *The Hungry Steppe: Famine, Violence and the Making of Soviet Kazakhstan* (Ithaca, NY: Cornell University Press, 2018).

[123] Werth, "The Crimes of the Stalin Regime," 405.

total at this point, except for the Koreans, who were feared to be potential supporters of Japanese imperialism in the far east, and who were "administratively resettled" in 1937 into the interior.

These campaigns just preceded the "Great Terror" of 1937–1938, which cracked down on "counter-revolutionary" activities by a process of "social purification" of "foreign" (political refugees from abroad or anyone with a suspicious foreign link) or "socially-harmful" (class) elements like former Tsarist officials, white officers, clergy, and so forth. Of the 1.5 million people arrested then, 800,000 were executed but they should not be confused with the inner-communist purges that led to far fewer deaths than usually supposed.[124]

Suspicion of smaller, non-Russian nationalities in border areas increased dramatically after the invasion by the German Army in mid-1941. At least 750,000 ethnic Germans were summarily deported to the east. The small Muslim nations of the North Caucasus also bore the brunt of Soviet security concerns. Accused of collaborating with the retreating German Army in 1943, entire peoples were branded as "enemy nations" who were to be punished "in perpetuity" by banishment. Herded into cattle cars after their villages were raided by Soviet security and military forces in the winter of 1943–1944, a million people, comprising Chechens, Ingush, Kalmuks, Crimean Tatars, Karachais, and others, were sent off to far-flung corners of the Soviet empire. For their alleged betrayal of the Soviet Fatherland, the Chechens became a "bandit nation"; according to Beria, they were a nation of "active and almost universal participation in the terrorist movement directed against the Soviets and the Red Army."[125]

Certainly, the violence with which they were carried out – at points, NKVD troops who could not deliver their human cargo to the railway depots stuffed them in barns and burned them down – and the systematic and coordinated campaign marked a level of intensified brutality and ruthlessness, even by Soviet standards. Large numbers died under conditions of transit and some at particularly inhospitable destinations, which not all destinations were (some went to Siberia, many to central Asia). Finally, as political circumstances changed – the war ended and, most importantly, "de-Stalinization" arrived – deportations could be reversed, as was the case with most of the "punished peoples" in the 1950s, though notably not the Crimean Tatars, Meskhetian Turks, nor, less surprisingly, the Volga Germans.[126] All told, casualties of the Soviet regime amounted to between six and nine million.[127]

---

[124] Ibid., 402.   [125] Burds, "The Soviet War against 'Fifth Columnists,'" 270.
[126] Nicolas Werth, "The 'Chechen Problem': Handling an Awkward Legacy, 1918–1958," *Contemporary European History* 15, no. 3 (2006): 347–66.
[127] Timothy Snyder, *Bloodlands: Europe between Hitler and Stalin* (New York: Basic Books, 2010), 384.

Elements of Permanent Security

From this brief historical survey, four elements of permanent security can be distilled. First, groups are reified as the premise for accusations of *collective guilt*: minorities and social classes as internally homogeneous historical actors with collective agency and interchangeable parts. It is a group-based logic of vicarious responsibility, such that one can punish or kill members of a community in one locality to avenge crimes that some members or coreligionists (or conationals) in another community may have committed against one's own coreligionists/nationals elsewhere – even long ago: the logic operates in time as well as in space. As anthropologist Peter Loizos elaborates, this "totalizing doctrine of collective passive solidarity allows the nationalist to treat all members of an enemy group as dangerously active. If they are fertile women they will reproduce and nurture children who will grow into fighting men, or reproducers in turn. Older men and women are givers of advice and succour, and children are simply potential adults. To the reflective nationalist there can be neither non-combatants nor innocents."[128]

This conviction implies an implicit collective guilt claim by failing to distinguish between combatants and noncombatants. For example, European settlers racialized Apache Indians as enemies who were congenitally dangerous to their presence and should therefore be exterminated.[129] The tendency to group-based thinking of dangerous people was also evident in Imperial Russian elites in their conquest of the Caucasus between the 1830s and 1860s. Noting the French tactics in their pacification of Algeria, the Russians engaged in wholesale population expulsions with virtually genocidal consequences for nations like the Circassians.[130] Similar tactics were applied over a century later in Guatemala in the early 1980s, where the military regarded the entire Maya Ixil population as historically rebellious because they maintained the language, customs and independence from local elites, thereby representing the guerrillas' "base of support." Consequently, it must be destroyed.[131] In this way, "The civilian population was converted into the enemy, that which had to be fought," as an officer said: "I saw the young troops... firmly determined to fight and attack, they clearly saw the civilian population as an enemy. Because they were collaborating with the guerrilla they were against the army, against the country."[132] In this campaign between 1982 and 1983,

---

[128] Peter Loizos, "Intercommunal Killings in Cyprus," *Man* 23, no. 4 (1988): 650.
[129] Jacoby, "The Broad Platform of Extermination."
[130] Ramazan Traho, "Circassians," *Central Asian Survey* 10, nos. 1–2 (1991): 1–63.
[131] Jo-Marie Burt, "From Heaven to Hell in Ten Days: The Genocide Trial in Guatemala," *Journal of Genocide Research* 18, nos. 2–3 (2016): 149, 154.
[132] Manolo E. Vela Castañeda, "Perpetrators: Specialization, Willingness, Group Pressure and Incentives: Lessons from the Guatemalan Acts of Genocide," *Journal of Genocide Research* 18, nos. 2–3 (2016): 225–44.

the army's scorched-earth tactics resulted in over 600 massacres, the destruction of villages, farm animals, and crops, torture and forced sterilization, mass sexual violence against indigenous females of all ages, and displacement of over 30,000 people.[133]

The second element is *preemption*. Groups can be targeted not for what its members have done but for what some of them might do. Those sympathetic to state security imperatives will assert its strategic logic in such circumstances. Rounding up all members of a group because some of them collaborated with the enemy is routine in wartime emergencies, they will say. Liberal democracies have interned "enemy aliens" no less than authoritarian regimes just as they bomb built-up areas and kill many civilians as so-called collateral damage.[134] Punishing an entire group to prevent potential attacks by some of its members is a security crime. Seeking to destroy or cripple groups on this logic so they can never again represent a threat is a crime of permanent security. The Sudanese government was guilty of seeking permanent security in Darfur not due to a racist ideology of hate or Islamic supremacy, but because its forces – both official and proxy – were attacking civilians collectively and preemptively for the rebellious activity of a minority of men.[135] The question of preemption is central to permanent security because groups are criminalized without its members necessarily representing an objective threat; the fear, indeed paranoia, that they could represent a threat is held to justify the harshest measures.

The third element is thus *paranoia*. Permanent security is governed more by fantastical security imperatives – paranoid threat assessments – than by the aesthetic of racial purity as implied by the Holocaust archetype. We are blind to this insight because the conventional view suggests a hierarchy between types of human destruction. Nonpolitical violence is considered worse because it targets innocent victims of paranoid and ultimately inexplicable racial hysteria, while political violence is an explicable outcome of interethnic conflict, often in civil war, in which the victims are not passive and therefore not completely innocent. This distinction between political nongenocide on the one hand, and racial, ideological genocide on the one other conceals the combatant/civilian distinction *within* such groups. It ignores the fact that both categories of violence contain massacres of civilians who pose no objective

[133] Roddy Brett, "Peace without Social Reconciliation? Understanding the Trial of Generals Ríos Montt and Rodriguez Sánchez in the Wake of Guatemala's Genocide," *Journal of Genocide Research* 18, nos. 2–3 (2016): 287.

[134] Peter Irons, *Justice at War: The Story of the Japanese-American Internment Cases* (Berkeley: University of California Press, 1990).

[135] The International Criminal Court has issued an indictment for Sudanese president Bashir for genocide but continues the reasoning of the UN report, www.icc-cpi.int/en_menus/icc/situ ations%20and%20cases/situations/situation%20icc%200205/press%20releases/Pages/a.aspx.

threat to perpetrators in actual conflicts. After all, what kind of agency can we ascribe to such victims, like the women and children who were marched into the Mesopotamian desert by Ottoman authorities in April 1915?

The paranoia often emanates from traumatic and humiliating experience of loss and occupation; it is not forgotten, but nurtured, particularly in nationalist circles, as a motivating source for revenge and redemption. Indeed, the nature of traumatized consciousness means that past events are never really past: the past can repeat itself. Learning processes are catastrophized: never again will a group allow the disloyal national minority to undermine the survival of the state.[136] There are no limits in dealing with traitors in emergency circumstances. This dynamic indicates that distinction between violence based on (nonpolitical) hallucinatory threat perceptions and (political) real conflict is misleading. In fact, permanent security crimes are based on traumatic memories of past events in which "disloyal" peoples or perceived fifth column groups are held collectively guilty and then collectively deported or destroyed, preemptively to prevent the feared repetition of traumatic experiences. For the paranoid subject, the hallucinatory is all too real. Paradoxically, then, the policy prescriptions that follow from paranoid threat assessments seem all-too-rational. It was not hard for Hutu extremists to convince many Hutu Rwandans that they were involved in a "war of self-defense" against the invading Tutsi-dominated Rwandan Patriotic Front forces in 1994. The conclusions they drew were that "if we killed them all, they would not have the power to kill us."[137]

The popular image of the perpetrator needs to change accordingly. The distinction between evil men on the one hand, and frightened patriots on the other, underpins genocide studies and popular culture more broadly. The latter – the patriots – do not fit the conventional image of genocidal perpetrators as ideological fanatics driven by irrational hatred of minorities. Historians sympathetic to the Ottoman rulers during World War I, for example, do not regard Talaat Pasher, Enver Pasher, and their associates as cruel and savage dictators who ruthlessly exploited a long-sought opportunity for a much-desired genocide. Rather, they see them "as desperate, frightened, unsophisticated men struggling to keep their nation afloat in a crisis far graver than they had anticipated when they first entered the war ... reacting to events rather than creating them, and not fully realizing the extent of the horrors they had set in motion in 'Turkish Armenia' until they were too deeply committed to withdraw."[138]

---

[136] Mark Levene, *Genocide in the Age of the Nation State*, 2 Vols. (London: I. B. Tauris, 2007).

[137] Rhiannon Neilsen, "Toxification as a More Precise Early Warning Sign for Genocide than Dehumanization? An Emerging Research Agenda," *Genocide Studies and Prevention* 9 (2015): 83–95.

[138] Guenter Lewy, *The Armenian Massacres in Ottoman Turkey: A Disputed Genocide* (Lincoln: University of Nebraska Press, 2005), 221.

The closer one looks at how mass violence against civilians is instituted and justified, however, the more it appears committed in the name of security by frightened patriots and those indoctrinated in paranoia. That does not mean they do not hate the group they attacked; they do, often driven by revenge at perceived betrayals. It means that fear and paranoia rather than antipathy inaugurate the campaigns. A group is held *collectively guilty* and attacked *preemptively* for the actions of some of its members: the group as a whole is seen as a potential security risk – a potential fifth column – and can be interned, deported, or otherwise destroyed *in toto* for reasons of state.

Historian Taner Akçam has shown that the Young Turk elites governing the Ottoman Empire during World War I were determined to forever prevent the possibility of an Armenian state in Anatolia, which they feared would be carved out of the empire like the Christian states of the Balkans. The official documents use language like "comprehensive and absolute" for the intention to reduce Armenian population densities to between five and ten percent, an aim that could only be accomplished in a genocidal way.[139] Just because the Ottoman fear of partition was genuine, or based in an accurate determination, does not mean that its solution to prevent it cannot be criminal. The intimate relationship between *raison d'etat* – the justification of self-defense and self-preservation used by any state – and criminality is one of the disturbing lessons we can draw from these episodes. In other words, wicked, crazed, racist, and authoritarian leaders are unnecessary for the criminality of permanent security. It is largely fruitless to fixate on material interactions between victim and perpetrator as many Turkish historians do when claiming the Ottoman state was provoked by Armenian nationalists. The element of preemption means that groups are attacked *before* its members can subvert the state.

Permanent security is signalled by the language of final solutions, as in the Young Turk policies towards Armenians during World War I: they would be deported and destroyed so that *never again* could they betray the Ottoman Empire by acting as agents for foreign powers. That such beliefs, like the Nazis' fantastical prejudices about Jews, were wildly paranoid is obvious: Armenian and Jewish civilians did not threaten the Ottoman and Nazi empires respectively. The fatal logic of permanent security is the paranoid ascription of collective guilt and then preemptive action: groups are collectively liable for the actions of a few members and attacked before they can imperil the nation. In this sense, racial fantasies and security paranoia intersect with fatal consequences for victim groups.

---

[139] Taner Akçam, *The Young Turks' Crime against Humanity: The Armenian Genocide and Ethnic Cleansing in the Ottoman Empire* (Princeton: Princeton University Press, 2012); Akçam, *Killing Orders. Talat Pasha's Telegrams and the Armenian Genocide* (Basingstoke: Palgrave Macmillan, 2018).

For reasons of state, leaders of virtually any government, nation, and ethnic group can engage in mass violence against civilians to assure the security of their borders and their civilians – and of their foreign occupations. It happens often, whether it is called genocide, crimes against humanity, or war crimes.[140] What distinguishes such violence from regular security emergencies is the aspiration for permanent security: the end of politics, namely the rupture of negotiation and compromise with different actors. Permanent security means total domination.[141] The core assumption of the Holocaust and genocide studies fields – the victims' perspective that they are attacked because of their identity – leads to a misrecognition of genocides by equating them with mass hate crimes. They are thereby depoliticized, such that genocide cannot be conceived as political violence. For its part, the perpetrators' perspective is blind to its participation in collective guilt accusations and practices of pre-emption: they see only the legitimate security imperatives of a party to civil war. Observers confuse political violence with nonsymmetrical violence when they urge an "equidistance" that adjudges all parties as equally guilty or innocent.[142] The next chapter on permanent security and the Nazi empire demonstrates how German elites studied permanent security in history to formulate their own vision of a thousand-year empire. The tremendous destructive capacity of the Nazi empire was its combination of imperial and settler modalities of conquest and occupation.

---

[140] Mohammed Abed, "The Concept of Genocide Reconsidered," *Social Theory and Practice* 41, no. 2 (2015): 328–56.

[141] Neilsen, "Toxification as a More Precise Early Warning Sign for Genocide than Dehumanization?" This article makes a good case for the significance of security paranoias but adds other causal factors in its advocacy of "toxification" as the operative process in genocide.

[142] Daniele Conversi, "Moral Relativism and Equidistance in British Attitudes to the War in the Former Yugoslavia," in *This Time We Knew: Western Responses to the Genocide in Bosnia*, ed. Thomas Cushman and Stjepan Mestrovic (New York: NYU Press, 1996), 244–81.

7

The Nazi Empire as Illiberal Permanent Security

Introduction

The Nazi Empire and its notorious extermination policies mark the culmination of centuries of empire-building and destruction of domestic and foreign enemies, real and imagined: its goal was to make Germans great and safe again – for a thousand years. The policies that Adolf Hitler (1889–1945) and Nazi elites pursued were not the apogee of illiberal permanent security because of anonymous historical processes. They were the result of a conscious learning process in which Hitler sought to apply the perceived lessons of imperial history since antiquity reconstructed in the previous chapter. The terrible outcome of these lessons is well known: the most devastating military conflict in world history and the attempted destruction of many peoples. Such was the mass killing and cultural devastation wrought by Nazi Germany that illiberal permanent security was widely stigmatized by the Nuremberg Trials and then proscribed in the so-called "human rights revolution" of the late 1940s. In its stead, liberal permanent security policies and practices held sway in the West – at least until the unravelling of globalization after 2010 led to an illiberal reaction.

How and why did it come to Nazi excesses? One explanation highlights antisemitism as the driver of the Holocaust. If it does not account for other extermination policies, still less German expansion, that is because its proponents regard Nazism's essence as *The War against the Jews*, to invoke Lucy Dawidowicz's well-known book.[1] To capture the reasons for the Holocaust, Israeli historian Saul Friedländer coined the influential concept of "redemptive antisemitism." Fervently believed by the Nazi leadership and their followers, this pseudo-religious notion posited "the Jews" as the counterrace to "Aryans" who were locked in an apocalyptic struggle for humanity's future. By directing both Soviet Bolshevism and Western capitalism that undermined the purity and health of races, Jews were a corrosive force whose destruction would be a

[1] Lucy Dawidowicz, *The War against the Jews, 1933–1945* (New York: Holt, Rinehart and Winston, 1975).

redemptive act.[2] The Holocaust's uniqueness, so the argument continues, was not based solely on the total and absolute nature of Nazi antisemitism. It was also entailed by the particular status of the victims; Jews, the representatives of Western civilization. Their intended destruction was therefore not a regulation genocide, but rather a nihilistic attack on the monotheistic values that the Nazis sought to transvalue: "God, redemption, sin and revelation," as Israeli historian Uriel Tal put it.[3] Not for nothing does another historian refer to the Holocaust as a "profound civilizational break."[4]

This brand of antisemitism thus distinguished the Holocaust from banal racisms. Whereas "normal" ethnic/national conflict pertains to "real" issues, like land, resources, political power, and national security, no such conflict is said to be discernible in the Holocaust of European Jewry, whose victims were passive and agentless objects of the perpetrators' "hallucinatory" ideology.[5] The consequence is that the genocide of European Jewry should be distinguished from other genocides. It is a nonpolitical crime of racial hatred. Philosopher Philippe Lacoue-Labarthe expressed this idea in writing that "the extermination of the Jews ... is a phenomenon which follows *essentially* no logic (political, economic, social, military, etc.) other than a spiritual one, degraded as it may be."[6] Historian Martin Gilbert was referring to this distinction when he asserted that the Nazis killed Jews not "because they were soldiers or partisans, or constituted a threat to German rule, but because they had been characterized as beneath the dignity of human beings."[7] Jews were killed for who they were, not for what they had done. The French political scientist, Jacques Semelin, likewise separates destruction for the sake of

---

[2] Saul Friedländer, *Nazi Germany and the Jews, 1933–1939*, vol. 1, *The Years of Persecution* (New York: Harper Perennial, 1998). Other versions of the antisemitism argument include Daniel J. Goldhagen, *Hitler's Willing Executioners: Ordinary Germans and the Holocaust* (New York: Knopf, 1996); Gavin I. Langmuir, *Toward a Definition of Antisemitism* (Berkeley: University of California Press, 1996); Paul Lawrence Rose, *Revolutionary Anti-Semitism from Kant to Wagner* (Princeton: Princeton University Press, 1990); Jeffrey Herf, *The Jewish Enemy* (Cambridge, MA: Harvard University Press, 2006).

[3] Uriel Tal, "Forms of Pseudo-Religion in the German *Kulturbereich* Prior to the Holocaust," *Immanuel* 3 (1973–1974): 68–73.

[4] Dan Diner, *Beyond the Conceivable: Studies on Germany, Nazism, and the Holocaust* (Berkeley: University of California Press, 2000), 3.

[5] Goldhagen, *Hitler's Willing Executioners, passim*; Leo Kuper, *Genocide: Its Political Use in the Twentieth Century* (New Haven: Yale University Press, 1981), 91–4. For a symptomatic indication of this widespread belief, see Eric Ehrenreich's review of Donald Bloxham, *The Final Solution: A Genocide* (Oxford: Oxford University Press, 2009) in the *American Historical Review* 15, no. 4 (2010): 1244–5.

[6] Philippe Lacoue-Labarthe, *Heidegger, Arts and Politics*, trans. Chris Turner (Oxford: Blackwell, 1990), 37.

[7] Martin Gilbert, "Twentieth-Century Genocides," in *America and the Armenian Genocide*, ed. Jay Winter (Cambridge: Cambridge University Press, 2004), 25.

subjugation, which is political and partial, from destruction as total eradication, like the Holocaust, which is driven by delusional, paranoid, and non-political considerations of ethnic purity and aesthetics.[8] The former characterizes civil wars, the latter genocide. By disembedding genocide from the ubiquitous military contexts in which such violence against civilians takes place, this threshold effectively makes them massive hate crimes.[9] The argument of this book, by contrast, is that all Nazi extermination policies were expressions of permanent security.

An alternative to the antisemitism paradigm is that of imperialism or colonialism. For some 60 years, analysis of National Socialism has been advanced in terms of colonial and imperial expansion, not only by leftist and non-European thinkers. The Nuremberg prosecutors considered Nazi settlement policies to be intrinsic to its crimes.[10] Using German documentation, the US Army intelligence officer and historian, Robert Koehl (1922–2015), wrote a major monograph on Nazi demographic policies as well as a number of studies on German colonization of Eastern Europe before and during World War I.[11] At the same time, the German-born, US-raised Alexander Dallin (1924–2000), also a US Army intelligence officer and later university historian, presented an important book on the Nazi occupation of the Soviet Union, which he called "a vast new area for [German] colonial exploitation and settlement."[12]

Before them, as Jews were being murdered in death camps, scholars and commentators routinely took Nazism at its word as an imperial project of expansion and colonial domination over subject peoples that would exploit their lands while settling Germanic farmers in Eastern Europe. Already in 1939, the Austrian communist writer, Franz Borkenau (1900–1957), wrote a book called *Germany's New Empire*, predicting its ceaseless expansion, while we know that Karl Korsch and Franz Neumann echoed these views. This approach drew on Rosa Luxemburg's interpretation of World War I as an imperial conflict that introduced colonial methods and norms of warfare into

---

[8] Jacques Semelin, *Purify and Destroy: The Political Uses of Massacre and Genocide* (New York: Columbia University Press, 2007), 37–42, 332–42.

[9] Martin Shaw, *War and Genocide: Organized Killing in Modern Society* (Cambridge: Polity, 2003); Shaw, *What Is Genocide?* (Cambridge: Polity, 2007).

[10] Kim Priemel and Alexa Stiller, ed., *The Nuremberg Trials Revisited: New Analyses and Interpretations* (New York and Oxford: Berghahn Books, 2012).

[11] Robert Koehl, "Colonialism Inside Germany: 1886–1918," *Journal of Modern History* 25, no. 3 (1953): 255–72; Koehl, "A Prelude to Hitler's Greater Germany," *American Historical Review* 59, no. 1 (1953): 43–65; Koehl, "The Politics of Resettlement," *Western Political Quarterly* 6, no. 2 (1953): 231–42; Koehl, *RKFDV: German Resettlement and Population Policy 1939-1945: A History of the Reich Commission for the Strengthening of Germandom* (Cambridge, MA: Harvard University Press, 1957).

[12] Alexander Dallin, *German Rule in Russia, 1941-1945* (London: Macmillan [1957] 1981).

Europe: Europe imported into its midst the barbarism that constituted its colonial conquests and exploitation.

Influenced by them, the German-Jewish philosopher, Hannah Arendt (1906–1975), based her analysis on the concept of "race imperialism" before eventually opting for "totalitarianism" in her *The Origins of Totalitarianism* in 1951.[13] Her well-known, if often misunderstood, book has been pivotal in maintaining interest in the link between colonialism and Nazism. Rediscovered each decade by a new generation of historians, she is routinely invoked to authorize the proposition that German or European colonialism (somehow) prefigured Nazism and the Holocaust.[14]

Non-European intellectuals, like African-American commentators Ralph Bunche and W. E. B. Du Bois, also linked Nazism and imperialism, highlighting their common capitalist and racist dimensions.[15] Aimé Césaire (1913–2008), in his famous *Discourse on Colonialism* (1955), regarded Nazism as the apogee of European colonial exploitation of non-Europeans that had been imported into Europe. Writing 12 years later, Frantz Fanon (1925–1961) followed his lead: "Deportations, massacres, forced labor, and slavery have been the main methods used by capitalism to increase its wealth, its gold or diamond reserves, and to establish its power. Not long ago, Nazism transformed the whole of Europe into a veritable colony."[16]

For some time, the question about the origins or dimensions of National Socialism and the Holocaust turned on the question of continuities and transfers from German Southwest Africa. Leading the proponents of such links, German historian Jürgen Zimmerer made three basic points. First, he highlighted the "structural parallels" of "race and space" shared by the genocidal counterinsurgency against the Herero and Nama people in German Southwest Africa between 1904 and 1907 and the National Socialist conquest of Eastern Europe. As a result, he claimed, the Nazi campaign "against Poland and the USSR was without doubt the largest colonial war of conquest in history."[17] Second, the African case was also an "important precedent" of

---

[13] Roy T. Tsao, "The Three Phases of Arendt's Theory of Totalitarianism," *Social Research* 69, no. 2 (2002): 587.

[14] Hannah Arendt, *The Origins of Totalitarianism* (New York: Schocken, 1951). See Richard H. King and Dan Stone, eds., *Hannah Arendt and the Uses of History: Imperialism, Nation, Race, and Genocide* (New York and Oxford: Berghann Books, 2007). The apologetic as opposed to critical intent of Lemkin's approach is covered in Chapter 10 below.

[15] Ralph J. Bunche, "French and British Imperialism in West Africa," *Journal of Negro History* 21, no. 1 (1936): 45; W. E. B. Du Bois, *The World and Africa* (New York: International Publishers, [1947] 1976), 23.

[16] Frantz Fanon, *Wretched of the Earth* (New York: Grove, 1963), 101.

[17] Jürgen Zimmerer, "Colonialism and the Holocaust: Towards an Archaeology of Genocide," in *Genocide and Settler Society: Frontier Violence and Stolen Indigenous*

"race war" without which the Holocaust "would probably not have been thinkable": it broke the taboo against destroying entire peoples. Third, the Germany Army's lethal pursuit of the Herero was at once the "culmination of colonial genocide" generally, which hitherto groups of settlers had perpetrated in private actions, as well as the "first step toward the bureaucratised murder of the Third Reich." It linked the more or less unsystematic destruction of indigenous peoples in all European colonies to the Nazis' genocide conquest of Europe by containing elements of both.[18]

As might be expected, the proponents of the antisemitism paradigm reject the imperialism one. Some are anxious that the imperial contextualization "diminishes the Holocaust" by detracting from the independent variable of antisemitism.[19] The Marxist-inspired focus on capitalist imperialism virtually ignores antisemitism, they say, and cannot satisfactorily account for the genocidal campaign against Jews. Could Nazism be seen, first and foremost, as a form of "bourgeois dominance," as was common in East German historiography?[20] Was the Holocaust the inevitable result of nation-building and violent, racist expansionism? Does the formula racism-colonialism-fascism obscure as much as it reveals?[21]

Although Zimmerer was not advancing his case in these Marxist terms, proving significant *empirical* links between late nineteenth- and early twentieth-century colonialism and the Holocaust is difficult. Imperial Germany's colonial possessions and commensurate government infrastructure were small compared with its rivals, and the numbers of colonial officials, soldiers, and scientists who became Nazis were not large. Much has been made of the fact that Hermann Göring's father, Heinrich (1839–1913), had been a

Children in Australian History, ed. A. Dirk Moses (New York and Oxford: Berghahn Books, 2004), 49.

[18] Jürgen Zimmerer, "Annihilation in Africa: The 'Race War' in German Southwest Africa (1904–1908) and Its Significance for a Global History of Genocide," *German Historical Institute Bulletin*, no. 37 (2005): 56–7.

[19] Prominent in this regard are two Yad Vashem historians: Robert Rozett, "Diminishing the Holocaust: Scholarly Fodder for a Discourse of Distortion," *Israel Journal of Foreign Affairs* 6, no. 1 (2012): http://israelcfr.com/documents/6-1/6-1-5-Rozett.pdf; Dan Michman, "The Jewish Dimension of the Holocaust in Dire Straits? Current Challenges of Interpretation and Scope," in *Jewish Histories of the Holocaust: New Transnational Approaches*, ed. Norman J. W. Goda (New York and Oxford: Berghahn Books, 2014), 17–38.

[20] Peter Schmitt-Egner, "Wertgesetz und Rassismus: Zur begrifflichen Genesis kolonialer und faschistischer Bewußtseinsformen." *Gesellschaft*, nos. 8–9 (1976): 350–404.

[21] Henning Melber, "Kontinuitäten totaler Herrschaft: Völkermord und Apartheid in 'Deutsch-Südwestafrika,'" *Jahrbuch für Antisemitismusforschung* 1 (1992): 91–115; Alexandre Kum'a Ndumbe III, "Nationalsozialismus, Rassismus und Kolonialideologie," in *Rassendiskriminierung, Kolonialpolitik und ethnisch-nationale Identität*, ed. Wilfried Wagner et al. (Münster: Lit, 1992), 161–82.

colonial administrator in Southwest Africa, and that anthropologist Eugen Fischer (1874–1967) had studied racial mixing there and had subsequently advocated the sterilization of the so-called "Rhineland Bastards," the children of African troops and German women stationed in Germany from the early 1920s.[22] But they did not advocate, plan, or expedite the Holocaust. Terms like "continuity," "structural parallels," and "important precedents" are suggestive but lack causal precision.[23]

What is more, so the criticisms continue, the German experience in Southwest Africa was not exceptionally violent compared to the conquests and violent pacifications by the French, Spanish, and American colonial empires throughout the nineteenth century.[24] There could be no German taboo violation before 1914 because these other empires had already rendered such a taboo nonexistent in their own counterinsurgencies. France and Britain had longer-standing and equally violent empires, yet did not unleash a Holocaust. Germany did.[25] Moreover, Nazi rule cannot be deemed colonial because it differed so radically in its brutality and spurning of indigenous development that characterized the French and British empires in the interwar period. Hitler's admiring statements about British rule in India do not prove that Nazis sought to construct a colonial empire in Eastern Europe. To confuse colonial rhetoric with colonial practices is to be distracted from what the Nazis were actually doing in Eastern Europe, which cannot be read off their dispersed references to other empires. The differences between the Nazi and Western colonial empires are too great to bridge with Hitler's positive rhetoric about the latter.[26]

In reply, proponents of the imperial explanation can point to problems in the antisemitsm one. The latter is caught on the horns of a temporal dilemma.

---

[22] Annegret Ehmann, "From Colonial Racism to Nazi Population Policy," in *The Holocaust and History*, ed. Michael Berenbaum and Abraham J. Peck (Bloomington: Indiana University Press, 1998), 115–34.

[23] Birthe Kundrus, "Kontinuitäten, Parallelen, Rezeptionen: Überlegungen zur 'Kolonialisierung' des Nationalsozialismus," *Werkstattgeschichte*, no. 43 (2006): 45–62; Matthew P. Fitzpatrick, "The Pre-History of the Holocaust? The Sonderweg and Historikerstreit Debates and the Abject Colonial Past," *Central European History* 41, no. 3 (2008): 477–503.

[24] Robert Gerwarth and Stephan Malinowski, "Hannah Arendt's Ghosts: Reflections on the Disputable Path from Windhoek to Auschwitz," *Central European History* 42, no. 2 (2009): 279–300; Lorenzo Veracini, "Colonialism and Genocides: Notes for the Analysis of a Settler Archive" in *Empire, Colony, Genocide: Conquest, Occupation and Subaltern Resistance in World History*, ed. A. Dirk Moses (New York and Oxford: Berghan Books, 2008), 148–61; Zimmerer responds to Gerwarth and Malinowksi in his *Von Windhuk nach Auschwitz? Beiträge zum Verhältnis von Kolonialismus und Holocaust* (Münster: Lit Verlag, 2011).

[25] Gerwarth and Malinowski, "Hannah Arendt's Ghosts," 289.

[26] Ibid., 293; Kundrus, "Kontinuitäten, Parallelen, Rezeptionen."

How can one insist on the historical *novum* of the Holocaust while invoking the *tradition* of antisemitism, even in its most radical instantiation? Friedländer and his cohort substitute one continuity – antisemitism – for others such as imperialism. Invoking traditions of antisemitism thus embeds the Holocaust diachronically into a narrative of steadily intensifying anti-Jewish feeling with the Holocaust as its possible, if not logical, outcome. Leaving aside the fact that casting the Nazi project as an exclusively German-Jewish story omits other victims of the Nazis, we are confronted with a temporal *aporia* regarding its continuity and rupture with European traditions. That the historical mind reaches the limits of its temporal imagination with the Nazi project is indicated in the ambivalence of various terms used to describe the German right: conservative revolutionaries, reactionary modernism, redemptive antisemitism, and so forth. How can the tension between tradition and revolution be negotiated satisfactorily?

Despite these interpretive differences, the basic fact of Nazi Empire is no longer controversial.[27] The question is the status of its extermination policies, above all the Holocaust. Was the destroying of Jews its purpose or a by-product of Nazi expansion? What kind of empire did the Nazi leadership envision and how was it related to rival empires? Saul Friedländer posed the analytical task thus: how to explain why Nazis and many other Europeans regarded Jews "as an *active threat*, for all of Aryan humanity in the long run, and in the immediate future for a Reich embroiled in a world war," meaning that "the Jews had to be exterminated before they could harm 'Fortress Europe' from within or join forces with the enemy coalition they had themselves set against the Reich."[28] Friedländer recognized that Nazi antisemitism was a form of threat perception: Jews were not only hated but feared as actively threatening. Permanent security was the logical response. Antisemitism was a political project.

The historiographical dispute occludes the basic point that Germans waged World War II in the name of permanent security. Founding a self-sufficient empire and destroying internal and external empires was undertaken to this end. To account for Nazi permanent security, it is necessary to engage in what historian Kiran Klaus Patel calls the "transnational historicization" of National Socialism and the Holocaust. He has pleaded for synchronic and diachronic multiperspectival analyses of the regime, meaning, among other aspects,

---

[27] Wendy Lower, *Nazi Empire-Building and the Holocaust in Ukraine* (Chapel Hill, NC: University of North Carolina Press, 2005); Mark Mazower, *Hitler's Empire: Nazi Rule in Occupied Europe* (New York: Penguin, 2009); Shelley Baranowski, *Nazi Empire: German Colonialism and Imperialism from Bismarck to Hitler* (Cambridge: Cambridge University Press, 2011); Geoff Eley, *Nazism as Fascism: Violence, Ideology, and the Ground of Consent in Germany, 1930–1945* (New York: Routledge, 2013).

[28] Friedländer, *The Years of Extermination*, 557. Emphasis in original.

interactions between the elites, peoples and institutions of occupying and occupied societies in terms of mutual perceptions, transfers, adaptations, and translations of experiences, policies, and practices. Highlighting these dimensions of the Nazi imperial project shows that it is impossible to account for its features solely in terms of German history.[29] Hitler's writings, for example, force analysis out of the nation-state container. Just as Greek and Roman antiquity were salient for British political and intellectual circles as they imagined and invested meaning in their unparalleled domination of the globe, so they were for Hitler. Drawing analogies and making distinctions between ancient and modern empires came naturally to European elites, who were, of course, in the main, raised on a diet of classical Greek and Roman history and literature.[30] Processes of translation and adaption of images and models between the distant past and present are intrinsic to a diachronic multiperspectivity.

That does not mean because Hitler said Germans should rule Ukraine as the British governed India that we take him at his word and claim these two cases are in fact somehow the same. It means that to discount the self-understanding of historical actors is to overlook what they thought they were doing – which was also what they were doing. Can the ideal of Rome be omitted from a full account of the American and French revolutions? This ideal – or rather the revolutionaries' understanding of how to found and consolidate a republic in light of the Roman model – influenced their various projects at the end of the eighteenth century.[31] Like most of his contemporaries, Hitler's historical horizon was not just modern European colonialism since 1800. This autodidact studied the empires of antiquity, mainly land or continental empires – Rome held a special place because the Holy Roman Empire of the German People was the central feature of the German imaginary – as the historical sources that he thought provided models and countermodels for his purposes. The literature scholar, Julia Hell, uses the felicitous term of "genuine imperial mimesis" that aims at "creative renovation" rather than "mere

---

[29] Kiran Klaus Patel, "Analysen und Alternativen: Der Nationalsozialismus in transnationaler Perspektive," *Blätter für deutsche und internationale Politik* 49, no. 9 (2004): 1123–34; Patel, "In Search of a Transnational Historicization: National Socialism and its Place in History," in *Conflicted Memories: Europeanizing Contemporary History*, ed. Konrad H. Jarausch and Thomas Lindenberger (New York and Oxford: Berghahn Books, 2007), 96–116. Mazower's *Hitler's Empire* is very strong on these elements of Nazi rule, as is Donald Bloxham, *The Final Solution: A Genocide* (Oxford: Oxford University Press, 2011).

[30] Richard Jenkyns, *The Victorians and Ancient Greece* (Oxford: Blackwell, 1980); Duncan Bell, *The Idea of Greater Britain: Empire and the Future of World Order, 1860–1900* (Princeton: Princeton University Press, 2007).

[31] Hannah Arendt, *On Revolution* (New York: Viking Press, 1963).

repetition."[32] Nazi admiration of Britain was also genuine, though based on an understanding of the latter that was far removed from the British self-image as a humane imperial ruler. In fact, so sincere was the admiration for the brutality of British conquest that anti-British propaganda, which mocked its hypocrisy by pointing to the disparity between the image and reality of its rule, ceased once Germany's own conquests began in 1939; otherwise, the parallels would be uncomfortably close.[33]

Skeptics may respond that such political rhetoric distracts from the real issue, in this case, the enormous differences between the Roman and Nazi empires, and the distinctively modern sources of the Nazi extermination policies.[34] The differences were obvious to contemporaries, too; the modern state, industrialization, and technology rendered warfare qualitatively more extensive and violent. Striking, however, is the persistence with which contemporaries returned to the world history of empire – an imperial archive – to draw basic lessons about their circumstances. These "lessons of empire" were integral to the development and articulation of political projects, that is, ideology.[35] Metaphors of transfer, continuity, and even knowledge-exchange are too linear and mechanical to account for this ideology-making. They imply the circulation of discrete units of information or motivation but miss the mediating dimension of interpretation and application.

To reimagine the role of human agency in historical processes, to understand how and why Germans imagined the most radical vision of illiberal permanent security, this chapter proceeds as follows. First, it suggests that an alternative temporal concept, namely the "political imaginary," offers historians a more fruitful way to integrate human agency with historical processes. Second, it shows how an imperialist political imaginary functioned in sections of the German political class between the 1890s and 1930s. Then it examines how Adolf Hitler utilized this imaginary for his own purposes: his raiding of the imperial archive to construct permanent security for Germans. Fearing Germany's destruction due to its catastrophic territorial and biopolitical losses after World War I, he concluded that exploitation and extermination had

---

[32] Julia Hell, "*Kathechon*: Carl Schmitt's Imperial Theology and the Ruins of the Future." *Germanic Review* 84, no. 4 (2009): 295; Veracini, "Genocide and Colonialisms."

[33] Gerwin Grobl, *The Germani Isle: Nazi Perceptions of Britain* (Cambridge: Cambridge University Press, 2000), ch. 3. The same applied with Hitler's admiration for US colonization: it stopped as soon as the war started: Jens-Uwe Guettell "The US Frontier as Rationale for the Nazi East? Settler Colonialism and Genocide in Nazi-Occupied Eastern Europe and the American West," *Journal of Genocide Research* 15, no. 4 (2013): 401–19.

[34] Thomas Kühne, "Colonialism and the Holocaust: Continuities, Causations, and Complexities," *Journal of Genocide Research* 15, no. 3 (2013): 339–62.

[35] Craig Calhoun Frederick Cooper, and Kevin W. Moore, eds., *Lessons of Empire: Imperial Histories and American Power* (New York: New Press, 2006).

attended European imperial expansion over the centuries. Based on his idio-syncratic perspective on world history, and in view of Germany's desperate situation in the 1920s and 1930s, he resolved to consciously apply the "lessons of empire" as he saw them. The next section examines how Jews figured as the ultimate enemy in his and Nazi thinking. Because Hitler's views cannot be taken as the key for the functioning of the National Socialist system as a whole, we will also see that, as a project of imperial conquest, the Nazi Empire entailed a consciously radical combination of imperial conquest and settler colonialism that was in part copied from Fascist Italy. National Socialism was illiberal permanent security incarnate.

Imperial Imaginary

The central dimension of the European social and political imaginary in the 100 years after 1850 was imperial and colonial. Literature scholar Edward Said drew attention to the imperialist nature of the modern imaginary when he noted that empire depended on a "structure of attitude and reference."[36] Politics could not be conceived except in terms of binaries like colonizer and colonized, occupier and occupied; or as German economist Max Sering (1857–1939) put it at a procolonial policy discussion in 1907, "Here, the maxim counts that whoever does not want to be the hammer will become the anvil,"[37] closely echoing Thucydides' Athenian justification of empire: "[I]t was not we who set the example, for it has always been the law that the weaker should be subject to the stronger. Besides, we believe ourselves to be worthy of our position."[38] Hitler, we will see below, advanced this argument in fore-shadowing his version of German empire in Europe.

This harkening to antiquity should also make us question the postulated modernity of the imperialist imaginary. Customarily, the imperialist imagin-ary is thought to have originated in the period of intense European imperial and colonial expansion followed by intra-European wars characterized by genocide. In fact, it was suffused with medieval beliefs about violent relations among different peoples, beliefs based on the Old Testament and antique legends, such as the destruction of Carthage, Melos, and Troy. These myths showed that migration and settlement, the divine mission of particular people, and the merciless slaughter or dispersion of others accorded with destiny or

---

[36] Edward Said, *Culture and Imperialism* (London: Vintage Books, 1993), 10.
[37] Max Sering, in *Schmoller, Dernburg, Delbrück, Schäfer, Sering, Schillings, Brunner, Jastrow, Penck, Kahl über Reichstagsauflösung und Kolonialpolitik*, offizieller stenogra-phischer Bericht über die Versammlung in der Berliner Hochschule für Musik am 8. Januar 1907, ed. Kolonialpolitschen Aktionskomite (Berlin: Dr. Wedekind, 1907), 25.
[38] Thucydides, *Pelopennesian War*, trans. Richard Crawley, rev. and intro. T. E. Wick (New York: The Modern Library, 1982), 1.76.

divine will. They percolated into the heroic sagas of many European clans, tribes, and peoples – legends of indigenous pasts, safeguarded by warriors and endless violence.[39]

A modern social and economic imaginary of individualism and social contract replaced this early-modern imaginary based on "hierarchical division into types," natural domination, the priority of the communal and divine order.[40] But such images persisted "nonsynchronically," as German-Jewish philosopher Ernst Bloch (1885–1977) put it. They could be activated *against* the modern imaginary in destructive ways at moments of crisis. Classicist Moses Finley's observation of the Athenian empire of antiquity could apply to paranoid political leaders millennia later: "[A] reassertion of the universal ancient belief in the naturalness of domination."[41] Where Bloch attributed the persistence of such myths to the crises of declining premodern social classes, they were generally accessible and available cultural resources.[42]

Just as importantly, imaginaries framed how politics was conceived at all. European powers distinguished between their active historical agency, which spread civilization through colonialism on the one hand, and the passive objects of their endeavors, the colonized, waiting to be enlightened and modernized on the other. Such a worldview was necessarily racist because it presumed the inherent, indeed often biological, superiority of the European colonizers over non-Europeans, as well as their inherent right to dominate other peoples. At the very least, the Europeans were *Kulturvölker* (peoples of culture) and most non-Europeans were *Naturvölker* (people of nature).[43]

Nowhere was the imperialist imaginary more apparent than in the contemporary fascination with the global spread of European empires and settlers, and the consequent "disappearance" of the "natives." Commentators noted, and some even welcomed, this disappearance, and their observations were usually comparative in nature.[44] After his extensive travels around the British Empire, English radical and later politician Charles Dilke (1843–1911)

---

[39] Len Scales, "Bread, Cheese and Genocide: Imagining the Destruction of Peoples in Medieval Western Europe," *History* 92 (2007): 284–300.

[40] Charles Taylor, "Modern Social Imaginaries," *Public Culture* 14 (2002): 94–8.

[41] Moses I. Finley, "The Athenian Empire: A Balance Sheet," in *Imperialism and the Ancient World*, ed Peter D. A. Garnsey and Charles R. Whittaker (Cambridge: Cambridge University Press, 1978), 125.

[42] Ernst Bloch, "Nonsynchronism and the Obligation of Its Dialectics," *New German Critique* 11 (1977): 22–38. This article was originally published in 1932.

[43] Marcia Klotz, "Global Visions: From the Colonial to the National Socialist World," *European Studies Journal* 16 (1999): 37–68; Richard Grove. *Green Imperialism: Colonial Expansion, Tropical Island Edens and the Origins of Environmentalism, 1600–1860* (Cambridge: Cambridge University Press, 1995).

[44] For example, Georg Gerland, *Über das Aussterben der Naturvölker* (Leipzig: Friedrich Fleischer, 1868).

proclaimed with some satisfaction in his best-selling *Greater Britain* that: "The Saxon is the only extirpating race on earth. Up to the commencement of the now inevitable destruction of the Red Indians of Central North America, of the Maories [*sic*], and of the Australians by the English colonists, no numerous race had ever been blotted out by an invader."[45] Writing 20 years later, Theodore Roosevelt, the future US president, was equally entranced by the "spread of the English-speaking peoples." Having moved to North America, they were natural conquerors whose destiny was "to grasp literally world-wide power."[46] Part of this "race history," as he put it, was the superiority of their "race characteristics," which meant, as noted in the previous chapter, that the English conquered Britain by assimilating or desroying the Celts, and then continuing this pattern with Indians in North America.[47] Both Dilke and Roosevelt compared the British conquering and settling prowess favorably with the Iberian powers, whose colonists had disastrously intermarried with the Indians of the Americas and even been expelled by them on occasion. Writing much later, the American eugenicist Madison Grant (1865–1937) was equally blunt in his assessment of racial history: "No ethnic conquests can be complete," he wrote, "unless the natives are exterminated and the invaders bring their own women with them," lest they be racially absorbed.[48]

German colonialism, like that of other nations, was an expression of aspirations for power, prosperity, and status: for permanent security. Expansionism to these ends could aim just as well at contiguous as remote lands, providing a country was willing to pay the price in conflict. For this reason, applying the term "colonialism" only to maritime empires is misleading. *Weltpolitik* (the acquisitions of extra-European colonies with a strong navy) and *Ostpolitik* (Eastern Europe as Germany's imperial space) represented flipsides of the same coin.[49] The affinity between these notions accounts for the ease with which Hans Grimm's (1875–1959) book about German colonialism in Africa, *Volk ohne Raum* (People without Space), published in 1926, morphed in the public mind into a message about Germany's possibilities in Eastern Europe.[50] That region had been long regarded, in the words of General Erich Ludendorff (1865–1937), as "primal

---

[45] Charles Wentworth Dilke, *Greater Britain: A Record of Travel of English-Speaking Countries During 1866 and 1867* (London: Macmillan, 1868), 308–9.

[46] Theodore Roosevelt, *The Winning of the West*, Vol. 1. (New York: G. P. Putnam's Sons, 1889), 4.

[47] Ibid., 11–12.

[48] Madison Grant, *The Passing of the Great Race* (New York: Scribners, 1916), 65.

[49] Vejas G. Liulevicius, *War Land on the Eastern Front: Culture, National Identity and German Occupation in World War I* (Cambridge and New York: Cambridge University Press, 2000), 166–7.

[50] W. D. Smith, *The Ideological Origins of Nazi Imperialism* (New York and Oxford: Oxford University Press, 1986).

German settlement territory," because Germans had colonized it centuries earlier and in some places still constituted the leading social stratum.[51] Furthermore, Imperial Germany already was a continental land empire that, like its Russian and Austro-Hungarian counterparts, included national minorities – above all Poles, who composed more than 6 percent of the population, mainly in Prussian border regions, where they often constituted a majority. Attempts to drive these people out and replace them with German-speakers enjoyed considerable support. Indeed, Chancellor Otto von Bismarck (1815–1898) launched the Royal Prussian Colonization Commission in 1886 to acquire Polish-owned estates for German farmers as part of an effort to change the ethnic composition of Germany's eastern provinces. The Society for the Support of Germandom in the Eastern Marches was established in 1894 to advance similar aims. The latter group (nicknamed the H-K-T Society or *Hakatisten* after the initials of its founders) depicted Poles and Slavs as primitive people who deserved to be supplanted by Germans and modernity.[52]

Before as well as during the Nazi period, a versatile form of colonial rhetoric saturated political discourse. *Lebensraum* (living space), a term coined in the 1890s by political geographer Friedrich Ratzel (1844–1904), became the chief rationale of German overseas and continental expansion. Ratzel literally rooted success in the Darwinian struggle for collective survival in a people's possession of sufficient land to provide prosperity. *Lebensraum* became a slogan for the political right in the 1920s and a central concept of the new academic discipline of "geopolitics," which explained national foreign policies as responses to the location and resources of states. Via Rudolf Hess (1894–1987) and Alfred Rosenberg (1893–1946), such thinking influenced Hitler, who concluded that Germany's *Lebensraum* lay in Eastern Europe.[53]

German commentators felt they could learn from the Anglo-American experience, and possessed no illusions about the violence of conquest. Thus one author, in the pages of the German Colonial Society's journal, answered the question of what the authorities should do with the survivors of Herero genocide by looking to the US. He approvingly noted the earlier "policy of extermination" (*Politik der Vernichtung*) against the "Red Skins," followed by one of protective reservations.[54] Support of colonialism did not have to

---

[51] Koehl, "A Prelude to Hitler's Greater Germany," 56.
[52] Roger Chickering, *We Men Who Feel Most German: A Cultural Study of the Pan-German League, 1886–1914* (London and Sydney: Allen & Unwin, 1984).
[53] Smith, *The Ideological Origins of Nazi Imperialism*, 6.
[54] Rittmeister a. D. von Simon, "Wie wird sich die Zukunft der Eingeborenen in SW Afrika gestalten müssen?" *Zeitschrift für Kolonialpolitik, Kolonialrecht und Kolonialwirtschaft* 8 (1906): 855.

approve of extermination, but even "scientific" colonialism regarded the fate of "dying races" with equanimity.[55] Liberal Bernard Dernburg (1865–1937), the German-Jewish first state secretary of the Colonial Office from 1907 to 1910, was a reformer who opposed genocidal policies towards Germany's African subjects. However, he noted in similar terms that:

> It cannot be doubted that some aboriginal tribes, like some animals, will have to disappear in the civilization process ["*in der Zivilisation unterge-hen müssen*"] if they are not to degenerate and become wards of the state. We are fortunate in our German colonies that we are not too heavily burdened by such elements. But the history of colonization of the United States, surely the greatest colonial project that the world has ever seen, had as its first act, the virtually complete extermination ["*Vernichtung*"] of the aborigines.

He was happy to report that if destruction marked the old style of coloniza-tion, the new style relied on conserving the native population and exploiting the land's resources scientifically.[56] In this vein, 30 years later, the anthro-pologist Richard C. Thurnwald (1869–1954), Professor of Ethnology, Race Psychology, and Sociology at the University of Berlin, defended his plans for a "scientific" exploitation of future Nazi-governed African colonies by comparing them with previous colonialisms: "My proposal is, in any event, more humane than the practice of the Americans when they largely exterminated the Indians, and the Australians when they made sport of shooting the blacks, as well as the violent deportations of the Russian communists."[57]

The question that German academic elites were asking was: how do we compete, indeed, survive in an international system of states and empires in which we are such late starters? One consequent anxiety was biopolitical. British settler colonies – the US, Canada, and Australia – had become home to millions of German settlers who rapidly assimilated at the expense of global *Deutschtum*. Writing in 1905, Pan-German leader Ernst Hasse (1846–1908) commented explicitly on Dilke's and Roosevelt's celebration of the Anglo-Saxon expansion, warning of German vulnerability abroad.[58]

---

[55] On "dying races," see Patrick Brantlinger, *Dark Vanishings: Discourse on the Extinction of Primitive Races, 1800–1930* (Ithaca, NY: Cornell University Press, 2003).

[56] Dernberg in Kolonialpolitschen Aktionskomite, *Schmoller, Dernburg, Delbrück*, 8.

[57] Richard C. Thurnwald, "Die Kolonialfrage," *Jahrbuch für Nationalökonomie und Statistik*, no. 145 (1937): 83. On Thurnwald, see Kevin S. Amidon, "'Diesmal fehlt die Biologie!': Max Horkheimer, Richard Thurnwald, and the Biological Prehistory of German Sozialforschung," *New German Critique* 104 (2008), 103–37.

[58] Ernst Hasse, *Das Deutsche Reich als Nationalstaat* (Munich: J. S. Lehmann's Verlag, 1905), 132–3.

This anxiety about biopolitical security recurs consistently among liberals and conservatives.[59] German sociologist Max Weber (1864–1920) and, later, Carl Schmitt observed enviously that those Anglo-Saxons knew how to retain their national homogeneity. In Australia, "the immigration of Chinese is banned," wrote Weber, comparing them to "the Poles [who] are even more dangerous due to the possibility of mixing and of bringing down German culture."[60] The political imaginary of a zero-sum game struggle between peoples was virtually ubiquitous, framing the analysis of sophisticated intellectuals. Decades later, Hitler made challenging Anglo-Saxon world hegemony, coded as Jewish domination, the keystone of his political program.[61]

Another security anxiety was land and imperial competition. The competition among core states for resources and geopolitical advantage was registered by anyone with an interest in global affairs, such as Berlin historian Dietrich Schäfer (1845–1929) in 1907:

> Our colonial policy does not deal with the will or lack or will of individuals. We are standing amid a gigantic movement that has all nations in its grasp, and in which we must participate if we want to avoid being overrun. [...] The earth is being given away; we must seize land ["*Besitz ergreifen*"] that is still on offer and that is useful and necessary for us.[62]

Lessons were offered by rival powers. Geographer Friedrich Ratzel gained his interest in continental expansion and control from his visit to the US, where he met the famous historian, Frederick Jackson Turner (1861–1932). Likewise, Max Sering traveled in the US and Canada, where he too admired the American settlers. He drew specifically German conclusions in the book, *Die innere Kolonisation im östlichen Deutschland* (The Inner Colonization in Eastern Germany), in which he regarded Eastern Europe as a frontier equivalent for settlement, as did his colleague Gustav Schmoller (1838–1917) and many others.[63] Not for nothing did Pan-German leaders like Ernst Hasse come to see Eastern Europe rather than Africa as the destiny of the German

---

[59] Sebastian Conrad, "Globalization Effects, Mobility, and Nation in Imperial Germany, 1880–1914," *Journal of Global History* 3 (2008): 43–66.

[60] Quoted in ibid., 59; Carl Schmitt, *The Crisis of Parliamentary Democracy*, trans. Ellen Kennedy (Cambridge, MA: MIT Press, 1988), 90, fn. 6.

[61] Adam Tooze, *The Wages of Destruction: The Making and Breaking of the Nazi Economy* (London: Penguin, 2007), xxiv.

[62] Dietrich Schäfer in Kolonialpolitschen Aktionskomite, *Schmoller, Dernburg, Delbrück*, 20, 22; see also Erik Grimmer-Solem, "The Professors' Africa: Economists, the Elections of 1907, and the Legitimation of German Imperialism," *German History* 25, no. 3 (2007): 313–47.

[63] Max Sering, *Die innere Kolonisation im östlichen Deutschland* (Schriften des Vereins für Sozialpolitik, vol. 56, 1893). Robert Nelson, ed., *German, Poland, and Colonial Expansion to the East: 1850 Through the Present* (New York: Palgrave Macmillan, 2009).

Empire. The fascinating circulation of notions of continental expansion and German expansion eastwards occurred in a hyperimperialist context; that is what makes it meaningful.

This context determined the self-understanding of Germany in the international system. Paul Rohrbach (1869–1956) was typical in taking a consistent anti-British, anti-French, and anti-imperial line in the 1920s and 1930s, praising the nationalist movements of colonial peoples seeking independence from the established European powers. Rohrbach claimed to recognize equally the rights of all "oppressed" peoples, be they German, Indian, Arab, or African. According to this common view, Germany was a young nation that, like these non-European ones, had to cast off the yolk of Anglo-French world domination. For this reason, he defended Japan's occupation of China and Southeast Asia in the mid-1930s as a reaction to Anglo-Saxon imperialism and American economic warfare, though he thought Germany's allies had an obligation to respect the rights of sovereign nations.[64]

Later, in the Weimar Republic, eugenicists also felt the compulsion to "catch-up" with Western rivals. It was "absolutely necessary to create a scientific center for anthropology, human heredity, and eugenics in Germany," noted leaders of the Kaiser-Wilhelm Gesellschaft, "since Sweden, the United States, and England have gone ahead with work in this area, in particular because these inadequacies and dilettante efforts in this area have to be countered."[65] As we shall see below, Hitler, too, wanted both to counter Germany's enemies and perfect their imperial policies.

This is also the context for the truculent reaction of humiliated Germans to the Treaty of Versailles, which sliced territory off Germany's eastern and western borders and entrusted its African colonies to its colonial rivals. German complaints that world politics remained imperial and colonial, despite the postcolonial rhetoric of the League of Nations, were borne out by statements of British politicians who regarded their ex-German African trusts as de facto annexations unaccountable to any foreign body. Germany had been relegated to the second rung of European powers or worse, while Britain and France continued, in effect, to rule much of the world.[66]

The imperialist imaginary was also readily apparent in the mutual penetration of antisemitism and colonial racism at the end of the nineteenth century.

---

[64] Eric Kurlander, *Living with Hitler: Liberal Democrats in the Third Reich* (New Haven: Yale University Press, 2009).

[65] Peter Weingart, "German Eugenics between Science and Politics," *Osiris*, 2nd series, 5 (1989): 63.

[66] A. Edho Ekoko, "The British Attitudes towards Germany's Colonial Irredentism in Africa in the Inter-War Years," *Journal of Contemporary History* 14 (1979): 289; Marcia Klotz, "The Weimar Republic: A Postcolonial State in a Still-Colonial World," in *Germany's Colonial Pasts*, ed. Eric Ames, Marcia Klotz, and Lora Wildenthal (Lincoln and London: University of Nebraska Press, 2005), 135–47.

Contrary to the conventional view that these two racisms represent entirely distinct "continuities" to the Holocaust, they became rhetorically intertwined and impossible to disentangle entirely. The social location of this intersection between colonial racism and antisemitism is the right-wing milieu of the Pan-Germans.[67] Their understanding of a future German European Empire in the 20 years before World War I was influenced by contemporaneous discussions about German colonialism in Africa and the Pacific; and by the possibility of reverse colonization.[68] Upset by the success of Jewish integration into German society, they became obsessed with racial mixing, which they called "bastard-ization," a problem that they thought led to the destruction of the Roman Empire. Their ideal of a "tribal empire" (*Stammesreich*) in Europe posited a racially pure utopia of German rule over Slavs.[69] Radical *völkisch* ideology was the nexus that explains Pan-German imperialism, the drive for living space on the continent, ethnic cleansing, and a "progressive" belief in social engineer-ing/welfare, from Hasse – and Heinrich Class (1868–1953), president of the Pan-German League between 1908 and 1939 – to Hitler.[70]

German rule over Africans provided the model of racial subjugation, segre-gation, and oppression. For instance, in the 1890s, these antisemites demanded that Jews be placed under a special alien law at the same time as they advocated that Africans be subject to a separate "native law." They defended Carl Peters (1856–1918) – the German colonial adventurer whose brutal treatment of the locals in German East Africa scandalized sensibilities at home – by insisting that European norms of war could not apply to Africans, who effectively occupied another moral universe.[71] Above all, the understanding of the Jewish presence in Germany occurred in the context of a

---

[67] See the standard work of Geoff Eley, *Reshaping the German Right: Radical Nationalism and Political Change after Bismarck* (New Haven: Yale University Press, 1980).

[68] Dennis Sweeney, "The Racial Economy of *Weltpolitik*: Imperialist Expansion, Domestic Reform, and War in Pan-German Ideology, 1894–1918," in *German Modernities from Wilhelm to Weimar: A Contest of Futures*, ed. Geoff Eley, Jennifer L. Jenkins, and Tracie Matysik (London: Bloomsbury, 2016), 139–62. See also Dennis Sweeney, *Work, Race, and the Emergence of Radical Right Corporatism in Imperial Germany* (Ann Arbor: University of Michigan Press, 2009).

[69] Elisa von Joeden-Forgey, "Nobody's People: Colonial Subjects, Race Power and the German State, 1884–1945" (Ph.D. dissertation, University of Pennsylvania, 2005), 434–44; Elisa von Joeden-Forgey, "Race Power, Freedom, and the Democracy of Terror in German Racialist Thought," in King and Stone, *Hannah Arendt and the Uses of History*, 21–37.

[70] Eric Kurlander, *The Price of Exclusion: Ethnicity, National Identity, and the Decline of German Liberalism, 1898–1933* (New York and Oxford: Berghahn Books, 2006).

[71] Christian Stuart Davis, *Colonialism, Antisemitism, and Germans of Jewish Descent in Imperial Germany* (Ann Arbor: University of Michigan Press, 2012). For the German racial order in Southwest Africa, see Jürgen Zimmerer, *Deutsche Herrschaft über Afrikaner*, 3rd ed. (Münster: Lit, 2004).

race-conscious worldview in which conquest and colonization of foreign peoples, hierarchies of civilization, progress and decline, survival, and extinction were central elements.[72]

Hitler's Imperial History of Permanent Security

The loss of Germany's colonies in World War I occasioned a persistent effort to win them back, especially since the great powers remained unremittingly imperialist. Much was at stake. Article 22 of the Treaty of Versailles disqualified Germans from governing "natives" by highlighting, somewhat hypocritically, German colonial abuses. Driven by German colonial associations, the countercampaign used trade fairs, exhibitions, publications, and lobbying to raise consciousness in the German population, to restore national honor, and to advance the cause in the international community. Hitler was no enthusiast for this colonial revisionism, although he rhetorically supported the return of German colonies. He saw no point in challenging the British maritime empire. The ambition to do so after the 1890s had led to a disastrous war, and the German colonial possessions were not worth the sacrifice.

Surveying the wreck of German Empire in the 1920s, Hitler concluded, on the basis of his eclectic reading and exposure to the new discipline of geopolitics that Germany's future lay in a European empire. Here, too, he followed in the steps of the Pan-Germans, who had advocated annexation and ethnic cleansing in east-central Europe during World War I. Past empires – Greek, Persian, Mongol, Aztec, Inca, and Spanish – were part of Hitler's historical repertoire. Ancient and medieval history did not yield examples of peaceful economic expansion. On the contrary, he thought, they succeeded by violent conquest. He was especially interested in the Roman Empire, whose success he attributed to its absorption of Aryan blood by its ruling strata. The destruction of that empire was – here he followed the Pan-German view – caused by racial intermixing. Christianity, with its pernicious doctrine of racial equality, was to blame. A Jewish invention as well, Bolshevism performed the same corrosive, levelling function.[73]

Traumatized by Germany's loss in World War I and convinced that Germans faced extinction, Hitler consciously applied the perceived lessons of world history imagined imperialistically and without sentimentality. In his hands, he fantasized, Germany would never again be open to internal colonization by a foreign people (Jews), at the mercy of foreign powers, or vulnerable to the labor movement that he thought had stabbed the army in the back.[74] Germans required permanent security. Applying these lessons meant founding an autarkic

---

[72] von Joeden-Forgey, "Nobody's People," 12.   [73] Ibid., 78.

[74] Hitler blamed the labor movement in particular. Timothy W. Mason. "Die Erbschaft der Novemberrevolution für den Nationalsozialismus," in Mason, *Sozialpolitik im Dritten*

continental empire – "a great Germanic empire" – eradicating opposition, depopulating superfluous Slavs, and settling its border regions with "Aryan" colonists.[75] Hitler was not mechanically repeating historical patterns; he was radicalizing them.[76] Once the temporal frame is extended backward in time, it is possible to see in the Nazi project a conscious appropriation of imperial and colonial history combined with the coercive powers of a modern state and economy. Whether his views of imperial history were empirically tenable is not the point. That he and many other Germans believed them to be true and acted upon them is the salient consideration.

This German Empire would not be formed "in a fit of absence of mind," then, but deliberately in light of world history. Hitler drew on an ancient imperialist imaginary to make sense of Germany's place in the world. We know that that he thought world history was driven by ruthless expansion, including the British Empire: "no nation has more carefully prepared its economic conquest with the sword with greater brutality and defended it later on more ruthlessly than the British."[77] Its professed humanitarian ideals were a sham, indeed a fig leaf that masked the fact that British wealth stemmed from the "capitalist exploitation of 350 million slaves."[78] Of course, if Indians and Hitler concurred in decrying British hypocrisy, they differed in their assessment of European domination. Long rule in India had inculcated in the British a racial arrogance and born-to-rule mentality that Hitler wished Germans to emulate.[79] His imperial commissars in Ukraine should act like viceroys.[80] Ironically, then, Hitler shared Karl Marx's views about the violence of originary accumulation. Admirably, the British had taken on the mantle of the Romans, "based on its general national political attributes as well as its average political value."[81] They were the glory of the "white race":

Reich: Arbeiterklasse und Volksgemeinschaft (Opladen: Westdeutscher Verlag, 1977), 15–41.

[75] Lower, *Nazi Empire-Building and the Holocaust in Ukraine*.

[76] Ashis Nandy, "The Defiance of Defiance and Liberation for the Victims of History: Ashis Nandy in Conversation with Vinay Lal," in *Dissenting Knowledges, Open Futures: The Multiple Selves and Strange Destinations of Ashis Nandy*, ed. Vinay Lal (Delhi: Oxford University Press, 2000), 57.

[77] Adolf Hitler, *Mein Kampf* (Boston: Houghton Mifflin, 1971), 189.

[78] Adolf Hitler, *Hitler's Table-Talk, 1941–1945: His Private Conversations*, pref. and intro. H. R. Trevor-Roper (Oxford: Oxford University Press, 1953), 193. See also Johannes H. Voigt, "Hitler und Indien," *Vierteljahrshefte für Zeitgeschichte* 19 (1971): 33–63.

[79] Dan Stone, "Britannia Waives the Rules: British Imperialism and Holocaust Memory," in Dan Stone, *History, Memory and Mass Atrocity* (London: Mitchell Vallentine, 2006), 174–95.

[80] Dallin, *German Rule in Russia, 1941–1945*, 103.

[81] Adolf Hitler, *Hitler's Second Book: The Unpublished Sequel to Mein Kampf*, ed. Gerhard Weinberg (New York: Enigma, 2006), 161.

We have the so-called white race that, since the collapse of Antiquity, has over around 2,000 years taken on a leading position in the world. I could understand the economic dominance of the white race over the rest of the world unless I related it closely to a political dominance that the white race possesses naturally for hundreds of years and that it has projected outwards. Think of any area; consider India: England has not won India with justice and law but without regard for the desires, aspirations or laws of the natives, and it has when necessary maintained its dominance with the most brutal measures (*Rücksichtslosigkeit*): just like Cortez or Pizarro claimed Central America and the northern states of South America not on the grounds of some legal basis but out of the absolute, inherited feeling of dominance of the white race. The settlement of the north American continent succeeded just as little from some democratic or international conception of legal claims, but out of a sense of justice that is rooted only in the conviction of superiority and with that the right of the white race.[82]

The rise and fall of empire-states and the destiny of peoples thus formed the horizon against which Hitler imagined the role of Germany in human history.[83] "What are two thousand years in the life of people?" he asked. "To-day [sic], we're renewing that tradition."[84] "Roman history," declared Hitler, "will remain the best teacher, not only for our own time but also for the future." There were two aspects to its glory: "To have succeeded in completely ruling the world!" And to have done so on behalf of a superior civilization: "no empire has spread its civilization as Rome did."[85] This civilization was essentially Hellenic, and it "should be preserved for us in all its marvellous beauty." While Athenian architecture expressed the heroic greatness of ancient Greek culture and its racial pride, Sparta was also a signal example of a racially hierarchical city-state that "ruled three hundred and forty-five thousand helots."[86] It was a source of contemporary European civilization, he continued, "the product of thousands of years of historical

---

[82] Adolf Hitler, *Hitler Reden und Proklamationen, 1932–1945,* Vol. 1, *Triumph (1932–1938),* ed. Max Domarus (Würzburg: Süddeutscher Verlag, 1962), 74–5.

[83] Hitler's recourse to imperial history was not, as supposed by some historians, made only during the war with the Soviet Union to legitimize unlimited violence or generally to make history available for power assertion.

   Franz-Lothar Kroll, "Geschichte und Politik in Weltbild Hitlers." *Vierteljahrshefte für Zeitgeschichte* 44, no. 3 (1996): 347; Kroll, "Die Reichsidee im Nationalsozialismusm," in *Imperium, Empire, Reich: Ein Konzept Politischer Herrschaft im Deutsch-Britischen Vergleich,* ed. Christoph Kampmann, Franz Bosbach, and Hermann Hiery (Munich: Saur, 1999), 187; Kundrus, "Kontinuitäten, Parallelen, Rezeptionen," 60–1.

[84] Adolf Hitler, *Hitler's Table Talk,* intro. Hugh Trevor Roper (London: Weidenfeld and Nicholson, 1953), 116.

[85] Hitler, *Mein Kampf,* 237.

[86] Hitler, *Hitler's Table-Talk,* 116; cf. Alexander Scobie, *Hitler's State Architecture: The Impact of Classical Antiquity* (University Park: Penn State University Press, 1990), 14–16.

development."[87] Not for nothing did Hitler want to redesign Berlin as "Germania," inspired by antiquity.

The relationship between Rome and Germany, or *Germanentum*, was complicated by the fact that the Germanic hero, Arminus (or Hermann), had defeated the Roman Legions in the Battle of the Teutoburg Forest by uniting German tribes against the imperial forces. They were praised by Tacitus, among other things, for their pure bloodlines.[88] With typical inconsistency, Hitler lauded both the ruthless expansionism of Rome and the Germanic resistance.[89] At any rate, Hitler believed that, at its height, the Roman elites were racially German, which accounted for their state-building prowess. In fact, he elaborated, the powerful empires of history had been governed by "Germanic organizers and leaders" of an "inferior race," like the Russians.[90] But since Rome's demise, Western history had largely fallen into darkness, except briefly for its sometime successor, the Holy Roman Empire. Like most of his contemporaries, he thought that the fall of Rome represented a historical rupture and source of constant comparison between "then" and "now." Geopolitical conclusions could be drawn thus:

> At the former juncture we were a young people and we stormed a world which was made up of great States that were already in a decadent condition, of which the last giant was Rome, to whose overthrow we contributed. To-day [sic.] we find ourselves in a world of great and powerful States, among which the importance of our own Reich is constantly declining more and more.[91]

Racial lessons were equally important. Whereas once "the Roman protected himself sub-consciously against any racial adulteration," Christianity's universalist creed undermined his "racial integrity," thereby spreading Jewish ideas of racial equality. St Paul's "egalitarian theories had what was needed to win over a mass composed of innumerable uprooted people." If an influx of German blood had temporarily rescued the empire, it was ultimately doomed nevertheless. One conclusion he drew was to heighten racial consciousness as a form of hypervigilance: "We must do all we can to foster this racial awareness until it attains the same standard as obtained in Rome in the days of her glory." The other conclusion was to oppose the perceived Jewish-Bolshevik takeover of Russia because it represented the contemporary equivalent of the Christian-Jewish degeneration of Rome. The civilizational lesson was that

---

[87] Hitler, *Mein Kampf*, 237.
[88] Bernard Mees, "Hitler and Germanentum," *Journal of Contemporary History* 39, no. 2 (2004): 264.
[89] Hitler, *Hitler's Table Talk*, 486.   [90] Hitler, *Mein Kampf*, 361.   [91] Ibid., 355.

Germany would improve the east just as Rome had improved northern Europe.[92]

A lesson that Hitler does not explicitly mention but that he internalized was the Roman doctrine of preemption. Roman writers such as Cicero justified preemptive strikes against internal and external enemies, arguing that it made no sense to wait until a likely threat was imminent. The destruction of Carthage was justified in this way.[93] Finally, like both Rome and the ancient Germans, the new German Reich would save European civilization from Asiatic barbarism.[94] Asiatic barbarism – "this Central Asian flood" – represented above all by Genghis Khan and the Mongols, and contemporaneously by the Bolsheviks, was the "eternally latent danger to Europe." "For centuries," declared Hitler in 1943, "the old Reich was forced to wage its fight against Mongols and Turks alone, or with a few allies, in order to spare Europe a fate whose consequences would have been as unthinkable as realizing a Bolshevization would be today."[95]

Hitler was likely informed about Genghis from SS leader Heinrich Himmler (1900–1945) – the Mongol leader does not appear in *Mein Kampf* – who was enamored of the book *Tschingis Chan, der Sturm aus Asien* by a Russian émigré, Michael Prawdin (1894–1970). A revised and expanded version was published as *Tschingis Chan und seine Erbe* (Genghis Khan and his Legacy) in 1938, and Himmler had a copy sent to every SS officer and frequently made a gift of it. For the Nazi elite, the Jews were the latest ruling class of the enduring, external, Asiatic threat to Europe.[96] It was no accident that resort was made to such historical imagery when the war against the Bolsheviks floundered, but even in late 1941 Hitler had combined his Jewish-plot theory of history with one in which European civilization had withstood the "Asiatic invasion" (*asiatischem Ansturm*) over the millennia.

> First it was Greeks against the Persians, then the campaign of the Carthaginians against Rome, the Huns in the Battle of the Catalaunian Plains, the Turkish wars beginning with the Battle of Poitiers, finally the Mongol storm from which Europe was rescued without realizing that

---

[92] Hitler, *Hitler's Table Talk*, 563, 78–9, 110–11.

[93] See the discussion in Richard Tuck, *The Rights of War and Peace: Political Thought and the International Order from Grotius to Kant* (Oxford: Oxford University Press, 2001), 18–20.

[94] Houston Stewart Chamberlain's *Foundations of the Nineteenth Century*, which had influenced Hitler, featured this idea: Mees, "Hitler and Germanentum," 264.

[95] Adolf Hitler, *Hitler: Speeches and Proclamations, 1932-1945: The Chronicle of a Dictatorship*, 4 vols, ed. Max Domarus (Wauconda, Il: Bolchazy-Carducci, 1962), 4:4: 2773–4, 2967.

[96] Richard Breitman, "Hitler and Genghis Khan," *Journal of Contemporary History* 25, no. 2 (1990): 343.

something was wrong at home! Now the worst storm of all: the mobilization of Asia by Bolshevism.[97]

If the showdown with Bolshevism possessed the world-historical significance
with which Hitler and Nazi elites invested it, then there could be no limits to
the warfare Germany should wage to defend Europe. In this context, Genghis
Khan could also be an example to follow as well as to fear. Thus Hitler told his
senior officers about the plans to invade Poland in the following terms:

> Our strength lies in our quickness and in our brutality; Genghis Khan has
> sent millions of women and children into death knowingly and with a
> light heart. History sees in him only the great founder of States. As to
> what the weak Western European civilisation asserts about me, that is of
> no account. I have given the command and I shall shoot everyone who
> utters one word of criticism, for the goal to be obtained in the war is not
> that of reaching certain lines but of physically demolishing the opponent.
> And so, for the present only in the East, I have put my death-head
> formations in place with the command relentlessly and without compas-
> sion to send into death many women and children of Polish origin and
> language. Only thus we can gain the living space that we need. Who after
> all is today speaking about the destruction of the Armenians?
>
> For you, gentlemen, fame and honour are beginning as they have not since
> centuries. Be hard, be without mercy, act more quickly and brutally than the
> others. The citizens of Western Europe must tremble with horror. That is the
> most human way of conducting a war. For it scares the others off.[98]

These words show that Hitler had indeed internalized lessons from the
Mongol style of rule and warfare. The former entailed, *inter alia*, ruthlessly
exterminating enemy peoples, that is, those who betrayed the Mongols by
displaying disloyalty. Motivated by punishment, revenge, and security, the
Mongols relentlessly pursued them over generations; they became hereditary
enemies. The second was the use of extreme terror and exemplary, collective
punishment to intimidate other opponents and cow them into submission.[99]
These features of Mongolian conquest would have appealed to Hitler who,
already in *Mein Kampf*, wrote of Jews as "the hereditary enemy of our people,"
the "mortal," "bitterest," and "most deadly enemy."[100] By then, he conceived of

[97] Adolf Hitler, *Monologe im Führer-Hauptquartier, 1941–1945*, ed. Werner Jochmann
(Hamburg: Albrecht Knaus, 1980), 136. Cf. Adolf Hitler, *Hitler's Words: Two Decades of
National Socialism, 1923–1943*, ed. Gordon W. Prange, intro. Frederick Schuman
(Washington, DC: American Council on Public Affairs, 1944), 154, 270–2.

[98] Adolf Hitler, "The Obersalzberg Speech, August 22, 1939, https://sourcebooks.fordham
.edu/mod/hitler-obersalzberg.asp.

[99] J. J. Saunders, *The History of the Mongol Conquests* (Philadelphia: University
Pennsylvania Press, 2001), ch. 4.

[100] Hitler, *Mein Kampf*, 343, 349–50.

history in exterminatory terms, drawing analogies between the fate of Carthage, destroyed by the Romans as a security threat, and Weimar Germany: "The fall of Carthage is a terrible example of the slow agony of a people which ended in destruction and which was the fault of the people themselves."[101]

Hitler has been interpreted as being, in principle, against far-off colonies, but in fact he admired how the British could use many of their colonies for both settlement and resource exploitation. The problem with Imperial Germany's African colonies had been that their harsh climate and economy was ill-suited to North American- or Australian-style settler colonialism.[102] They were dominated by capitalists rather than settlers. A *völkische Boden- and Raumpolitik* (folkish ground- and space policy) for Germany must be based on contiguous territory in Eastern Europe. Germany needed to colonize this space as it had in the past, but now systematically via state planning and implementation.[103] Dismissing the Western colonial rhetoric of civilizational uplift and local autonomy as brazen hypocrisy – "indirect rule" was an excuse not to improve the natives, Hitler thought – he enjoined ruthless exploitation in the manner that he thought the West actually governed their colonial possessions.[104] In sum, he wanted an extractive empire like the British in India but also settler colonies, supplemented by outright plunder. Some think this vision has nothing to do with colonialism because, in the Anglophone settler colonies, the settlers preceded the state, whereas the reverse was the case with the Nazi colonization plans in the *Generalplan Ost*.[105] But this is to apply a limited standard of colonialism. In other cases, population expulsion and decimation preceded colonization by loyal settlers, as in the Russian conquest of the Caucasus in the nineteenth century.[106] What is more, the Nazis thought they were merely systematizing and steering the settlement processes that had unfolded haphazardly in North America and Australasia.

They did not need to improvise in this respect. The example of Italian fascist colonization of Libya and Japanese colonization of Manchuria in the 1930s furnished contemporary examples that bridged fantasy and practical realization. As the recent research of Patrick Bernhard shows, Nazi planners at the highest levels were particularly fascinated by the Italian settlement projects in their North African possessions, which transplanted 20,000 Italians into

---

[101] Ibid., 368.

[102] Adolf Hitler, *Hitlers zweites Buch: Ein Dokument aus dem Jahr 1928*, foreword Hans Rothfels, intro. Gerhard L. Weinberg (Stuttgard: Deutsche Verlags-Anstalt, 1961), 100.

[103] Hitler, *Hitler's Words*, 26–7.   [104] Ibid., 353.

[105] Gerwarth and Malinowski, "Hannah Arendt's Ghosts," 294; Ulrike Jureit, "Ordering Space: Intersections of Space, Racism, and Extermination," *Journal of Holocaust Research* 33, no. 1 (2019): 64–82.

[106] Robert Geraci, "Genocidal Impulses and Fantasies in Imperial Russia," in Moses, *Empire, Colony, Genocide*, 343–71.

40 new towns and hundreds of farms in 1938.[107] All told, they settled 100,000 colonists in five years, although they wanted to settle millions by mid-century. These efforts received considerable international attention and approval in the West as well.[108] For the Germans, they demonstrated what careful planning and state investment in the latest science and technology could achieve in a relatively short period of time. Seeking to learn from the Italian example, German officials established academic and diplomatic contacts, founded agricultural and planning institutes and publications that translated the Italian knowledge, established joint agricultural settlement training programs, and visited the colonies to behold the miracle first-hand. The Italians' design of villages and the legal regulation of racial segregation was of particular interest. Also attractive was the notion that the settled lands were not to be regarded as far-off colonies but as intrinsic parts of the homeland in which a new breed of "soldier-peasants" could be formed to defend its borders. Here was a modern model of empire-building to emulate.

Redemptive Imperialism

Nazi imperialism, then, was not intended to continue the *Weltpolitik* of Imperial Germany, which sought to coexist with other empires and was defeated in World War I. It was a project to take up where Rome and medieval German colonists had left off centuries before by going east to carve out its own zone as a base for final showdown of world-historical significance. This was a redemptive imperialism.

> We National Socialists consciously draw a line beneath the foreign policy of our prewar period. We take up where we broke off six hundred years ago. We stop the endless German movement to the south and west, and turn

---

[107] Patrick Bernhard, "Borrowing from Mussolini: Nazi Germany's Colonial Aspirations in the Shadow of Italian Expansionism," *Journal of Imperial and Commonwealth History* 41, no. 4 (2013): 617–43; Bernhard; "Hitler's Africa in the East," *Journal of Contemporary History* 51 (2016): 61–90; Bernhard, "Colonial Crossovers," *Journal of Global History* 12 (2017): 206–27. See also Jens Steffek and Francesca Antonini, "Toward Eurafrica! Fascism, Corporativism, and Italy's Colonial Expansion," in *Radicals and Reactionaries in Twentieth-Century International Thought*, ed. Ian Hall (Basingstoke: Palgrave Macmillan, 2015), 145–70.

[108] Roberta Pergher, *Mussolini's Nation-Empire: Sovereignty and Settlement in Italy's Borderlands, 1922–1943* (Cambridge: Cambridge University Press, 2018), 83, 96. The *Daily Telegraph* correspondent, Martin Moore, accompanied the Italian settlers and reported on the intense state efforts to implant them as a favorable example for the British Empire. See his *Fourth Shore: Italy's Mass Colonization of Libya* (London: George Routledge & Sons, 1940). For the interest in Jewish settlement in Ethiopia after the Italian conquest in 1935, see Richard Pankhurst, "Jewish Settlement in Ethiopia," *Centro Primo Levi Online Monthly*, October 3, 2014, https://primolevicenter.org/printed-matter/jewish-settlement-in-ethiopia/.

our gaze to the east. At long last we break off the colonial and commercial policy of the prewar period and shift to the soil policy of the future.[109]

In Hitler, the imperial models of centuries of human history congealed into a single, total, imperial fantasy of genocidal conquest, colonization, and exploitation. The Nazis turned the ubiquitous ideology of colonial rule into ruthless expansionism by emphasizing its exploitative dimension over any meliorative counterdiscourses. Nazism's *raison d'être* was imperial expansion.[110] The purpose was not just to challenge the "Judeo-Bolshevism" of the Soviet Union, but also to secure continental hegemony for the ultimate showdown with the US, whose awesome economic power Hitler had begun to appreciate only after writing *Mein Kampf*.[111]

To trivialize these fantasies as hapless groping for orientation or as post facto legitimations of conquest misses the point about the framing function of the imperialist imaginary.[112] The rise and fall of empires and concomitant extinction of peoples was constitutive of the global political gaze, as we saw with Dilke, Roosevelt, and Thurwald. These were not marginal figures but popular writers, national leaders, and intellectuals. This gaze meant that when senior bureaucrats, academics, and Nazis gathered in 1934 to plan the Nuremberg Laws they were inspired less by the intermarriage ban in the former German colonies than by such bans in North American states and, later, in the Italian colonies in Libya.[113]

The imperial, indeed, catastrophically illiberal history of humanity lay before Hitler, as for his contemporaries like Oswald Spengler (1880–1936), who also expounded on the rise and fall of civilizations, for interpretation and guidance. That much seems clear. But why the apocalyptic conclusions drawn by Hitler? Spengler's rigid historical philosophy is a case in point, with its pessimistic conclusion that Western culture was dying because it had reached the stage of overcultivated civilization. His cyclical theory was pessimistic because of its maudlin acceptance of long-term, inevitable developments that cultured men had to stoically bear.[114] By contrast, Hitler was a revolutionary who would not accept the cards that history and world events had dealt the German people. He wanted to assert his people's freedom against its destiny by

---

[109] Hitler, *Mein Kampf*, 656.
[110] Smith, *The Ideological Origins of Nazi Imperialism*, 231.
[111] Philipp Gassert, *Amerika im Dritten Reich* (Stuttgart: Steiner, 1997); Tooze, *Wages of Destruction*, 10.
[112] Kundrus, "Kontinuitäten, Parallelen, Rezeptionen," 60–1.
[113] Claudia Koonz, *The Nazi Conscience* (Cambridge, MA: Belknap Press of Harvard University Press, 2003), 172–6; James Q. Whitman, *Hitler's American Model: The United States and the Making of Nazi Race Law* (Princeton: Princeton University Press, 2017).
[114] Oswald Spengler, *Der Untergang des Abendlandes: Umrisse einer Morphologie der Weltgeschichte*, 2 vols. (Munich: Beck Verlag, 1918–22).

an act of radical imagination. World War I had ruptured received categories of political and historical interpretation, opening up the political and imaginative space for revolutionary activity in the name of rival projects of human freedom, whether Bolshevik or racist.

National Socialism was experienced as "national liberation" by many Germans, who wanted to rid the country of parliamentarism and "Jewish social democracy"; in other words, to replace modern political imaginary of the social contract and liberalism represented by "the Jew" with a premodern one of hierarchy and order embodied by National Socialism – though, of course, with ultramodern techniques. The natural order would be restored after the disorder of modern German politics. There would be a "rebirth of our racial life force," as the head of the Nazi Party's Department for Racial Matters, Walter Gross (1904–1945), put it. The Nazi psychologist, Max Wundt (1879–1963), too, wrote of "rebirth," linking it to his "unshakeable faith in the liberating mission of the Führer."[115] The question, then, is less about "continuities" than "caesura," the quasi-aesthetic attempt to "*fiction*" a new beginning in light of a disastrous past; as philosopher Lacoue-Labarthe put it, to effect a "violent *abortion* of [the old] Germany in its frenzied attempt to appropriate itself as such (to identify itself) and to step into the light of history."[116]

For the Nazis and their supporters, destroying the "Jewish spirit" and its bearers, "the Jews," was necessary for the birth of a new Germany, a Germany inhabited by now racially conscious citizens that had transcended the bitter class divisions of the Weimar years, an Imperial nation that would protect itself from inner and outer enemies. An imperial country that had been thwarted by the Jewish colonizer whose international system held Germany in its thrall, Germans could now embark on their destiny.[117] Only a radical gesture of political imagination and action could inaugurate and vouchsafe the national-racial German project by rupturing the temporal flow of events that had conspired to prevent German "becoming." Enduring for a thousand years, Germany would defeat its enemies – and time itself.[118] Redemptive antisemitism was a function of a broader project: redemptive imperialism.

Needless to say, Germany was not in fact being colonized by Jews. But, to explain the appeal of redemptive imperialism, the stories that the imperialists

---

[115] Both quotations in Uriel Tal, *Religion, Politics and Ideology in the Third Reich: Selected Essays*, foreword Saul Friedländer (London: Routledge, 2004), 94, 104.

[116] Lacoue-Labarthe, *Heidegger, Art, and Politics*, 75–6. Emphasis in the original. Contrast with Helmut Walser Smith, *The Continuities of German History: Nation, Religion, and Race across the Nineteenth Century* (New York: Cambridge University Press, 2008).

[117] There is further discussion in A. Dirk Moses, "Empire, Colony, Genocide: Keywords and the Philosophy of History," in Moses, *Empire, Colony, Genocide*, 34–40.

[118] See Neil Levi, *Modernist Form and the Myth of Jewification* (New York: Fordham University Press, 2013); Neil Levi, "'Judge for Yourselves!': The Degenerate Art Exhibition as Political Spectacle," *October* 85 (1998): 41–64.

tell themselves are centrally important – especially if they are paranoid.[119] For all the differences between the Nazis' antisemitism and anticolonial "nativist" violence, the tendency to hold members of the "occupying" group *collectively* guilty is striking. So is the totality of the ambition. Frantz Fanon wrote that "Liberation is the total destruction of the colonial system."[120] Hitler also aimed at the total destruction of the Jews who, in his view, ran the corrupt world and Weimar systems that were destroying the Germans.

Why the Jewish Enemy?

"International Jewry"

The Nazis' belief in the unified political agent, "international Jewry," reflected widespread belief in its existence and power among Europeans, Americans and many others at the time. So did Jews. Chaim Weizmann (1874–1952), president of the World Zionist Organization and a British citizen, invoked "the Jews" in his organization's declaration "that the Jews stand by Great Britain and will fight on the side of the democracies," in the coming war, thereby conveying what philosopher Berel Lang calls a "sense of a corporate decision or will like the stereotyped myths of Jewish power and conspiracy." Rather than express surprise that the Nazis took it seriously, Lang thinks it is hardly surprising: "How else to interpret this open declaration of war by Weizmann? And why *not* see it as another now public step in a progression that began earlier with others that were less overt but pointed in the same direction?"[121]

These impressions were common because geopolitics in the first half of the twentieth century was conducted generally on the assumption that "world Jewry" (or "international Jewry") existed as a political subject and that the differences of opinion lay in varying assessments of its power. By 1939, Weizmann's arrogation had been made for at least a century. When, in 1840, the English philanthropist and Jewish community leader, Moses Montefiore (1784–1885), led an international delegation to the ruler of Syria, Mehemet Ali (1769–1849), to protest the imprisonment of some Damascan Jews for alleged ritual murder, he noted that it represented "the Israelites of the

---

[119] Alon Confino, "Fantasies about Jews: Cultural Reflections on the Holocaust," *History and Memory* 17 (2005): 297, 317.

[120] Frantz Fanon, *Towards the African Revolution*, trans. Haakon Chevalier (London: Penguin, 1970), 105.

[121] Berel Lang, "The Jewish 'Declaration of War' against the Nazis," *Antioch Review* 64, no. 2 (2006): 370. Emphasis in original. Contrast Lang's view with Herf, *The Jewish Enemy*, 61, who notes that Weizmann "was in no position to speak for Jews in general" while expressing surprise how "that was how the Nazi propagandists viewed his statement."

whole world."[122] The infamous "Damascus affair" of that year had seen the unprecedented emergence of national and transnational Jewish public spheres in the wake of the scandalous accusations. Rather than engage only in the traditional tactic of *shtadlanut* – intercession by Jewish notables on behalf of oppressed Jews – Jews campaigned openly across Europe, with sympathetic gentile support, for the release of the captives.[123] The exhilarating construction of collective Jewish agency for an "overtly Jewish cause," notes the Israeli diplomatic historian, Aharon Klieman, meant that "it became possible for the first time in centuries to speak once again of 'world Jewry' as a political reality rather than a purely ethnic, religious or geographical abstraction."[124]

The material dimension of this achievement during the nineteenth century was the cooperation of Jews across the Ottoman Empire with British commercial interests, which in turn fed into British interest in Jewish welfare there. The Jews were for the British in the Ottoman Empire what Roman Catholic Arab Christians were for the French, and Orthodox and Armenian Christians were for the Russians. For his services to the empire, Montefiore became a British "imperial hero."[125] The humanitarian activism of Jewish organizations on behalf of oppressed Eastern European Jewry, especially but not only in Romania, was a feature of European diplomacy from the Congress of Berlin in 1878 until the Treaty of Versailles. Although Jewish organizations often worked against one another – Zionists favored migration to Palestine while non-Zionists urged equal rights in their current countries – the existence of "Jewish diplomacy" was widely acknowledged.[126]

---

[122] Jonathan Frankel, *The Damascus Affair: "Ritual Murder," Politics, and the Jews in 1840* (Cambridge: Cambridge University Press, 1997), 433. *Shtadlanut* was disliked by Zionists because it entailed dependence on gentile goodwill: Zvi Y. Gitelman, *The Emergence of Modern Jewish Politics: Bundism and Zionism in Eastern Europe* (Pittsburgh: University of Pittsburgh Press, 2003), 93.

[123] David Vital, *A People Apart: The Jews in Europe, 1789–1939* (Oxford: Oxford University Press, 1999), 2, 233–48; Ronald Florence, *Blood Libel: The Damascus Affair of 1840* (Madison: University of Wisconsin Press, 2004).

[124] Aharon Klieman, "*Shtadlanut* as Statecraft by the Stateless," *Israel Journal of Foreign Affairs* 2, no. 3 (2008): 109.

[125] Abigail Green, "Nationalism and the 'Jewish International': Religious Internationalism in Europe and the Middle East c.1840–c.1880," *Comparative Studies in Society and History* 50, no. 2 (2008): 535–58; Green, *Moses Montefiore: Jewish Liberator, Imperial Hero* (Cambridge, MA: Harvard University Press, 2010).

[126] Mark Levene, *War, Jews and the New Europe: The Diplomacy of Lucien Wolf, 1914–1919* (Oxford: Litman Library of Jewish Civilization and Oxford University Press, 1992); Carole Fink, *Defending the Rights of Others: The Great Powers, the Jews, and International Minority Protection, 1878–1938* (New York: Cambridge University Press, 2004), ch. 1; James Renton, *The Zionist Masquerade: The Birth of the Anglo-Zionist Alliance, 1914–1918* (Basingstoke: Palgrave Macmillan, 2007).

British elites, no less than others, were fascinated by this diplomacy and "international Jewish power." In thrall to this perception, they thought during World War I that Jews could deliver them Russian and American support against Germany, which they feared enjoyed Russian- and American-Jewish sympathy. Even philosemites like British politician Arthur Balfour thought Jews "undoubtedly constitute a most formidable power whose manifestations are not by any means always attractive."[127] Weizmann confirmed the prejudices of interlocutors in the British Foreign Office so as to assure them of Russian Jewish favor:

> If you give us a declaration in favour of Zionism, the declaration will make the Jews of the world understand that you are really friendly and the friendship of the Jews of the world is not a thing to be blown upon, it is a thing that matters a great deal, even for a mighty empire like the British.[128]

Whether Weizmann had any right to speak on behalf of world Jewry is not the point. The fact is that he did so, and his presumption – indeed the claim that it possessed great influence – was instrumental in the British government's Balfour Declaration in 1917. Named after the British Foreign Secretary who negotiated it, the declaration committed Great Britain to using "their best endeavours to facilitate the achievement" of "a national home for the Jewish people" should the Entente defeat the Ottomans and win the war.[129]

The Foreign Office and Winston Churchill (1874–1965), then Secretary of State for War, also thought that Zionism was an effective antidote to the perceived Jewish predilection for revolution and Bolshevism. In a February 1920 article in the *Illustrated Sunday Herald*, he argued that the "Zionist Jew" could tempt Jews from Bolshevism by constructing the Jewish homeland in Palestine for the benefit of both Jews and European civilization.[130] Weizmann likewise recommended Zionism to the British as an alternative to Russia as a pole of attraction for Jews.[131]

The British Foreign Office wanted to use Zionism as an asset for proxy imperialism because direct and continuing occupation of Palestine would

---

[127] David Vital, *Zionism: The Crucial Phase* (Oxford: Oxford University Press, 1987), 302. Balfour thought, however, that "the balance of wrong-doing" was "greatly on the Christian side."

[128] Cited in Mark Levene, "The Balfour Declaration: A Case of Mistaken Identity," *English Historical Review*, no. 107 (1992): 73.

[129] Fink, *Defending the Right of Others*, 88–89; Sharman Kadish, *Bolsheviks and British Jews: The Anglo-Jewish Community, Britain and the Russian Revolution* (London: Frank Cass, 1992), 137–44.

[130] Winston Churchill, "Zionism versus Bolshevism: A Struggle for the Soul of the Jewish People," *Illustrated Sunday Herald*, February 8, 1920; Kadish, *Bolsheviks*, 138–42. See generally Michael Makovsky, *Churchill's Promised Land: Zionism and Statecraft* (New Haven, CT: Yale University Press, 2007).

[131] Kadish, *Bolsheviks*, 156.

upset American Wilsonianism. In return, the British patronage of the Zionist movement yielded it official status as a diplomatic entity, the Jewish Agency, and official standing in the Mandate for Palestine. Palestine was now the internationally guaranteed prospective home for all Jews, from Sydney to Warsaw, not only Jewish residents of Palestine. There was no input from Palestinian Arabs in these negotiations, despite the fact they constituted about 90 percent of the population.[132]

It is immaterial that Zionists were in no position to deliver on their promise of Jewish support in the US and Russia. What is relevant is that they played on this fascination by exaggerating their influence and the significance of Jewish influence in those countries. Everyone played the game of the international Jewish simulacra. "The fact remains that the Jew is as susceptible to myths about the character of his own community as any Gentile," observed historian Sharman Kadish of Weizmann's efforts.[133] Weizmann admitted as much when he said in 1927 that:

> We Jews got the Balfour Declaration quite unexpectedly; or, in other words, we are the greatest war profiteers ... The Balfour Declaration of 1917 was built on air, and a foundation had to be laid for it through years of exacting work; every day and every hour of these last ten years, when opening the newspapers, I thought: Whence will the next blow come? I trembled lest the British Government would call me and ask: "Tell us, what is this Zionist Organisation? Where are they, your Zionists?" For these people think in terms different from ours. The Jews, they knew, were against us; we stood alone on a little island, a tiny group of Jews with a foreign past. This period has passed now. Now we have an address, a name and, above all, great moral credit. Now we can build and now we can make demands, now is the time.[134]

The realization in public law of a corporate, global Jewish entity guaranteed the highest-level access to British elites; indeed, Zionists were part of this elite. Thus, Weizmann and the Jewish Agency were granted (sympathetic) audiences with a special cabinet sub-committee after they vehemently opposed the Passfield White Paper in 1930, which gestured to Palestinian Arab grievances. Palestinian Arab leaders were not accorded such hospitality in London.

---

[132] John J. McTague, Jr, "Zionist-British Negotiations over the Draft Mandate for Palestine, 1920," *Jewish Social Studies* 42, nos. 2–3 (1980): 281–92. On Palestinian politics during the mandate, see Rashid Khalidi, *The Iron Cage: The Story of the Palestinian Struggle for Statehood* (Boston: Beacon Press, 2007), and Weldon C. Matthews, *Confronting an Empire, Constructing a Nation: Arab Nationalists and Popular Politics in Mandate Palestine* (London: I.B. Tauris, 2006).

[133] Kadish, *Bolsheviks*, 165.

[134] Chaim Weizmann, "Reminiscences: Address at a Banquet at Czernowitz, December 12th, 1927," in *Chaim Weizmann: A Tribute on His Seventieth Birthday*, ed. Paul Goodman (London: Victor Gollancz, 1945), 199.

Weizmann contacted the wife and son of Prime Minister Ramsay MacDonald (1866–1937) to put his case, curtly reminding the British leadership that there is "one thing that Jews will never forgive, and that is being fooled."[135] He threatened to resign and conservatives mobilized public opinion against the government. Conservatives were not the Zionists' only supporters. Within the Labor circles, influential figures like Harold Laski (1893–1950) supported Weizmann. He, too, blamed the Grand Mufti of Jerusalem for the riots of 1929 and refused to ascribe authentic nationalist feelings to the Palestinian Arabs, who he thought were manipulated and exploited by their feudal notable leaders like the Mufti. The Jewish settlers, by contrast, brought progress and socialism to Palestine that would benefit all.[136]

This kind of mobilization had proven successful in the past. When the first High Commissioner of Palestine, Herbert Samuel (1870–1963), not exactly hostile to Zionists, suggested that Jews abjure the goal of statehood in favor of a nonsovereign homeland, as laid out in the mandate, he too was met with "utter outrage" by Zionists who insisted that the British enable Jewish immigration to achieve a majority forthwith. Weizmann even contemplated having him removed.[137] So concerned were the prime minister and Lord Passfield (Sidney Webb, 1859–1947) about the economic power they feared American Jewry could wield against the depressed English economy that they reversed course and acceded to the Zionists' demands in the notorious "black letter" of 1931.[138] Historians, like Israeli Gabriel Sheffer, who decry the apparent belief that the Jewish Agency exerted an "overwhelming influence" on the British government still concede that "Zionist influence was inflated by certain Zionist leaders' vanity about the exercise of such influence and by the need for their political strategy."[139] That is the point: high politics on this terrain was a game of smoke and mirrors.[140]

---

[135] Chaim Weizmann, *Trial and Error* (New York, 1949), 321–25.

[136] Paul Keleman, "Zionism and the British Labour Party, 1917–1939," *Social History* 21, no. 1 (1996): 71–87.

[137] Bernard Wasserstein, "Herbert Samuel and the Palestine Problem," *English Historical Review*, no. 91 (1976): 768–9.

[138] Gabriel Sheffer, "Intentions and Results of British Policy in Palestine: Passfield's White Paper," *Middle East Studies* 9, no. 1 (1973): 47, 53–4; Kenneth W. Stein, *The Land Question in Palestine, 1917–1939* (Chapel Hill: University of North Carolina Press, 1984), 126–33; Norman A. Rose, *The Gentile Zionists: A Study in Anglo-Zionist Diplomacy, 1929–1939* (London: Routledge, 1973), ch. 1.

[139] Gabriel Sheffer, "British Colonial Policy-Making towards Palestine (1929–1939)," *Middle East Studies* 14, no. 3 (1978): 307–22. He gives no examples of historians who allege such influence.

[140] The same applied with terribly different stakes when Zionist agents negotiated with Eichmann in 1944 about exchanging Jews for trucks; both sides, though not the Allies, presumed the existence of world Jewry and its supposed power to influence the Allies:

The game continued into the 1930s. Zionists consistently invoked "the fundamental rights of the Jewish people" and threatened boycotts against Great Britain by "Zionists all over the world" whenever it announced policy changes favorable, or rather less unfavorable, to the Palestinian Arabs.[141] There was consistency in the Zionist reference to its global presence. David Ben Gurion (1886–1973) insisted that the British conceive of Jews and Arabs as global entities to convince the British that the latter had more than enough land while the largely homeless Jews only wanted, and desperately needed, a tiny portion of the Middle East.[142] It was this argument that led another British High Commissioner, John Chancellor, to note that "world Jewry possessed rights that the Arabs themselves did not possess in Palestine."[143] He was right. That is what Weizmann and Ben Gurion wanted.

Even though the British and Zionists later clashed about Jewish immigration levels to Palestine and even rethought the terms of the mandate in the 1939 White Paper, the game of positing world Jewry as a politically articulated global entity had allowed Zionists to gain a firm foothold from which it could not be dislodged, as Churchill and Weizmann had intended. But it could also expose them when their lack of actual power was revealed.[144] What if an imperial power thought that "the Jews" were not its friend, a useful tool in its geopolitical calculations as they had been for the British, but an implacable enemy? This potential was the losing, fatal side of the equation of positing collective agents like "the Jews." It leads to the "Judeo-Bolshevik" myth, the central, mythical actor in the Nazi imagination.

Jews in Germany

Although antisemitism figured in the minority of the Nazi propaganda campaigns, it lay at the core of the German destruction anxiety.[145] Of the more than 2,100 daily editions of the Nazi newspaper, Der Völkische Beobachter, during the war, only 84 of its headline stories were inspired by antisemitism. The rest were denunciations of conventional state enemies.[146] However, because the Nazis posited "international Jewry" as a unified political subject – indeed as a belligerent via its puppets, the British, Americans, and Soviets – they coded the

Yehuda Bauer, Jews for Sale? Nazi-Jewish Negotiations, 1933–1945 (New Haven, CT: Yale University Press, 1994), 170–1.

[141] Yehodaya Haim, "Zionist Policies and Attitudes towards the Arabs on the Eve of the Arab Revolt, 1936," Middle East Studies 14, no. 2 (1978): 212–4.

[142] Michael J. Cohen, "Secret Diplomacy and Rebellion in Palestine, 1936–1939," International Journal of Middle East Studies 8, no. 3 (1977): 381.

[143] Stein, The Land Question in Palestine, 1917–1939, 130.   [144] Vital, Zionism, 360.

[145] Cf. Aristotle A. Kallis, Nazi Propaganda and the Second World War (Basingstoke: Palgrave Macmillan, 2005). 74.

[146] Herf, The Jewish Enemy, 26.

war as an existential military contest between Germans and all Jews.[147] The murder of innocents becomes militarily justifiable in this way. The Nazis made this pitch by arguing that if Germans did not prevail then "international Jewry" would destroy them: they perpetrated genocide against European Jewry preemptively – and as "retaliation" for Allies' attacks – to forestall a feared destruction.

Paranoia explains why the Nazis radicalized their anti-Jewish measures after 1939. Since Ernst Gombrich in the late 1960s, scholars attuned to social psychology have invoked the paranoia concept.[148] By 1939, when Germany launched the war, antisemitism had become the Nazis' principle framework for understanding global politics. Until 1939, Nazi persecution of German Jews was not dissimilar to discriminatory regimes elsewhere in the world. The war altered the stakes of Germany's confrontation with its neighbors in which the Jews, both civilians and combatants, were cast as responsible for Germany's woes.[149]

The Nazis reasoned inferentially, at least in their propaganda. For example, in trying to understand the apparent paradox of American concern about the German violation of Czech sovereignty, Goebbels wrote: "There must be an anonymous power that is standing behind everything ... It is the same power that confronted us National Socialists at the time of the battles (*die Kampfzeit*) in Weimar Germany ... The Jews are guilty!"[150] Because Jews were not an autonomous belligerent and were present in the populations of all enemy countries, Goebbels had to convince Germans that "international Jewry" was in fact pulling the levers behind the scenes. He and his colleagues went to great lengths to prove the accusation, producing posters depicting the specific Jews in the American and Soviet governments that supposedly ran the show. Their antisemitic faith, then, was buttressed positivistically with "evidence," however specious. The distinction between xenophobic and chimerical antisemitism – the former based on a "kernel of truth," the latter totally divorced from reality – does not reflect how the Nazis constructed their propaganda.[151] They appealed to "facts" to put their case about a world Jewish conspiracy to the German public, though it goes without saying that the leap from "facts" to fantasy was enabled by preexisting, Christian-infused prejudices about Jews. If Goebbels did not invent all his "facts," thereby making the propaganda superficially plausible for much of the population, they were refracted through paranoid,

---

[147] Cf. Norman Cohn, Warrant for Genocide: The Myth of the Jewish World-Conspiracy and the *Protocols of the Elders of Zion*, 3rd ed. (Chico, CA: Scholars, 1981), 12–13.

[148] E. H. Gombrich, *Myth and Reality in German War-Time Broadcasts* (London: Athlone, 1970). Friedländer, *The Years of Persecution*, 99; Dominick LaCapra, *History and Memory after Auschwitz* (Ithaca, NY: Cornell University Press, 1998), 52.

[149] Herf, *The Jewish Enemy*, viii.   [150] Ibid., 54–5.

[151] Langmuir, *Toward a Definition of Antisemitism*, 311–52.

antisemitic lenses.[152] For example, the Nazis' anti-imperial and anti-British rhetoric was based on how German elites experienced the evisceration of their military power and strategic reach in the 1920s and 1930s. The consignment to seemingly permanent second- or third-rate status entailed the inability to forge one's own destiny, indeed it meant the prospect of lying at the mercy of avaricious neighbors. The sudden loss of great power status was unbearable – probably not unlike how the British thought about the prospect of German naval parity since the turn of the century. The Nazis' often-expressed fear of destruction – which repeated right-wing political rhetoric from the 1920s – did not have to mean mass murder. The language of destruction was routinely invoked to name the fear of permanent subordination. This fear, which was not entirely baseless in the interwar period, was widespread in the German population. Promising to reverse German power-lessness was a source of Nazi popularity.[153]

An important distinction between colonial racism and antisemitism was the fact that Jews were *in* Germany and doing well. This spatial difference inverted the framing dichotomy of colonizer-colonized in Germany. Especially during World War I, antisemites coded events in terms of Jewish success and non-Jewish German suffering, indeed, as Jewish domination over non-Jewish Germans. Already during the 1912 national elections, right-wing Germans had decried supposed Jewish control of the "red" and "gold" internationals. In Austria, they complained that Jews owned more than 50 percent of banks and held 80 percent of the key positions in that sector. The development of capitalism was regarded as a Jewish imposition, a "control system" over gentiles.[154] During the war, the military, in particular, complained about shirking and profiteering by Jews. Ludendorff leveled an accusation that would be common during the Weimar Republic:

> They acquired a dominant influence in the "war corporations" [...] which gave them the occasion to enrich themselves at the expense of the German people and to take possession of the German economy, in order to achieve one of the power goals of the German people.[155]

In other words, many Germans regarded themselves as an "indigenous" people who were being slowly colonized by foreigners, namely Jews. The cult of indigeneity was signaled by the *völkisch* obsession with "ancient German tribes" whose virtues of simplicity and honesty were contrasted with the decadent

---

[152] Herf, *The Jewish Enemy*, 82.   [153] Ibid., 66, 71, 78.

[154] George L. Mosse, *The Crisis of the German Ideology* (London: Weidenfeld and Nicolson, 1964), 142.

[155] Friedländer, *The Years of Persecution*, 74–82. In fact, Jews were overrepresented in the German armed forces: Werner Angress, "The German Army's 'Judenzählung' of 1916," *Leo Baeck Institute Yearbook* 23 (1978): 117–35.

civilization of the French and British. The trend to identify with "Aryans" participated in this cultural phenomenon, eventually locating their origin not in India but in northern Europe.[156] This ideology culminated in the "blood and soil" rhetoric of the Nazis, who idealized the peasant rooted in the land. Nomadic peoples like Arabs and Jews were parasites, whereas settlers, such as "Nordic" colonists in North America, spread civilization and advanced humanity.[157] If settlers were mobile as well, they eventually became agriculturalists and rooted in the soil. Ironically, the environmentalist racialism prevalent in Germany speculated that Jews could not be part of the *Volkskörper* because their racial characteristics had been formed by another geographical environment.[158] Applying the North American term of "nativism," Jeremy Cohen identifies this reaction already in the medieval period in Christian Germany.[159] It is a nativism that justifies colonial expansion by coding its movement as productive and that of "nomads" – and sedentary Slavic peasants – as parasitic.

The anxiety about "colonization" by Jews was compounded after World War I when the Rhineland was occupied by French troops from Africa. Not only had Germany been forcibly decolonized by its imperial rivals (and recolonized by its rivals under the mandate system), they had imposed "inferior" Black troops on the country. Germany was now the colonized, not the colonizer.[160] Right-wing Germans launched a massive propaganda campaign against the "black disgrace" of the occupation, replete with lurid tales of rapes and violence against local women. In thrall to conspiracy theories, they believed the occupation was an international plot to contaminate Germans with "inferior blood." Foreign Minister Adolf Köster spoke for many when he complained that "the German *Volkskörper* was facing permanent annihilation on his western front."[161] In effect, the occupation was a policy of destruction, as Hitler believed in *Mein Kampf*:

---

[156] Klaus von See, "Kulturkritik und Germanenforschung zwischen den Weltkriegen," *Historische Zeitschrift* 245 (1987): 343–62; Klaus von See, "Der Arier-Mythos," in Klaus von See, *Ideologie und Philologie: Aufsätz zur Kultur- und Wissenschaftsgeschichte* (Heidelberg: Universitätsverlag, 2006), 9–53.

[157] Mosse, *The Crisis of the German Ideology*, 67–71; Clifford R. Lovin, "Blut und Boden: The Ideological Basis of the Nazi Agricultural Program," *Journal of the History of Ideas* 28 (1967): 283–4.

[158] David T. Murphy, "Familiar Aliens: German Antisemitism and European Geopolitics in the Inter-War Era," *Leo Baeck Institute Yearbook* 43 (1998): 181.

[159] Jeremy Cohen, *The Friars and the Jews: The Evolution of Medieval Anti-Judaism* (Ithaca, NY: Cornell University Press, 1982), 260–1.

[160] Jared Poley, *Decolonization in Germany: Weimar Narratives of Colonial Loss and Foreign Occupation* (Bern: Peter Lang, 2005).

[161] Christian Koller, "Enemy Images: Race and Gender Stereotypes in the Discussion on Colonial Troops," in *Home/Front: The Military, War and Gender in Twentieth-Century Germany*, ed. Karen Hagemann and Stefanie Schüler-Springorum (Oxford and New York: Berg, 2002), 145–7.

It was and is the Jews who bring the negro to the Rhine with the same concealed thought and clear goal of destroying, by the bastardisation which would necessarily set in, the white race which they hate, to throw it down from its cultural and political height and in turn to rise personally to the position of master.[162]

His sense of panic about Jewish rule was palpable. Jews, as a "foreign people," had erected a "tyranny" over Germany, and now enslaved, through the stock exchange and media, but also via cultural life and the state, the Weimar Republic.[163] His arguments that Jews had infiltrated the ruling strata by intermarriage were echoed by other writers, like *Sippenforscher* Heinrich Banniza von Bazan (1904-1950), who deplored Jewish emancipation and the "flood" of immigration from Poland. "It looks like a planned dividing up of all German cultural areas. Four sons enter the four university faculties, another becomes an artist, while the daughter disports herself as the wife of the pastor." This integration did not bode well for Germany. "Since the collapse of the German people after the world war, [Jewish] domination over the political fate of the nation became totally naked. A racially alien strata developed that arrogated to itself the power to codetermine the welfare and direction of the German people." As a result, by the Nazi seizure of power in 1933, "some 2.5 million residents had Jewish blood coursing through their veins."[164]

The solution to the perceived problem needed to be permanent, declared Nazi official Achim Gercke (1902-1997) in a Nazi journal. In 1933, he and others thought in terms of emigration.

> All proposals that include a permanent presence, a permanent regulation of the Jews in Germany, do not solve the Jewish Question, for they do not eliminate the Jews from Germany (*denn sie lösen die Juden nicht von Deutschland*). And that is what we want to do. If the Jews are able to exploit their host peoples forever, they will remain a constant source of the open, destructive flame of Bolshevism, making it easy to repeatedly kindle it again, not to mention the political uncertainties resulting from disunity within the people and the danger to racial unity. Let us swear off such thinking forever, whether it results from poor thinking or evil intentions. To summarize, the state can and must focus on systematical elimination, on emigration.[165]

In fact, Nazi officials shared the views of British officials about the suitability of Palestine as a site of emigration. Thus, Gercke echoed Churchill in supporting

---

[162] Hitler, *Mein Kampf*, 448-9.   [163] Ibid., 426-33.

[164] Heinrich Banniza von Bazan, *Das deutsche Blut im deutschen Raum: Sippenkundliche Grundzüge des deutschen Bevölkerungswandels in der Neuzeit* (Berlin: Alfred Meßner Verlag. 1937), 92-3.

[165] Achim Gercke, "Die Lösung der Judenfrage," *Nationalsozialistische Monatshefte*, no. 38 (May 1933): 195-7, https://research.calvin.edu/german-propaganda-archive/gercke.htm.

Zionism as an alternative to Bolshevism: "If we support Zionist plans and attempt an international solution by establishing a homeland for the Jews, we will be able to solve the Jewish Question not only in Germany, but in Europe and the entire world. The entire world has an interest in such a solution, on eliminating this source of disorder, which constantly proceeds from Bolshevism."[166]

His colleague, Johann von Leers (1902–1965), agreed in the emigration option, because it did not entail "extermination."

> Only a barbarian standing outside of the last great divine manifestation of world history would propose a general antisemitic battle aimed at the extermination of this people. The goal of the highly developed peoples is not to promote hatred where there is a decent way to solve the problem.[167]

Here was an expression of antisemitism that consciously rejected the apocalypticism of its redemptive version, and that shared many assumptions with mainstream thinking in the West. Like British officials, Nazi ones were divided about Palestine, however. Von Leers, for instance, did not think Palestine was sufficiently large for the world's Jews, so he speculated that they could find a home in the colonies of the Western imperial powers, where they could toil productively to mutual benefit:

> Those major Western European colonial powers, who are always worked up about the Jewish Question and its effects in Eastern and Central Europe, without however really seeing the connections, would perform a work not only of humanity, but also statesmanlike wisdom that would bring peace to the world and the solution of one of its most serious problems were they to make such a settlement area available. That would not only relieve Europe of the Jewish problem, but also enable Jewry to become a people.[168]

This view lay behind the short-lived Nazi-Zionist collaboration to facilitate Jewish emigration to Palestine. It would fall foul of Hitler's own hardline views about Zionism, which opposed a Jewish state anywhere as a potential danger for a German empire and eventual global domination.[169] Not unlike the Pan-German leader, Heinrich von Class (1868–1953), Hitler's "nativist" response at this perceived colonization and foreign rule was to expel the colonists and

---

[166] Ibid.
[167] Johann von Leers, "Das Ende der jüdischen Wanderung," *Nationalsozialistische Monatshefte*, no. 38 (May 1933): 229–31.
[168] Ibid.
[169] Frank Nicosia, *Nazi Germany and the Arab World* (Cambridge: Cambridge University Press, 2014); Nicosia, *Zionism and Anti-Semitism in Nazi Germany* (Cambridge: Cambridge University Press, 2008).

establish an autarkic economy: to preserve its "national character" by removing it from "international finance control," that is, from Jewish hands.[170] Otherwise, the fate that met other peoples in the past awaited Germany: "Carthage's fall is the horrible picture of such a slow self-earned execution of a nation."[171] Time was short. The perceived Jewish colonizer was pressing its rule over the world: "The British Empire is slowly becoming a colony of the American Jews!"[172]

"Judeo-Bolshevism" and Political Paranoia

How to explain the extraordinary self-perception of the Nazis that they were attacking Jews in self-defense?[173] A skeptical tradition attributes "no kernel of truth" (Gavin I. Langmuir) to the myth, which is based solely on "chimerical hostility."[174] An alternative approach recognizes that the myth is based on "fiction *and* reality," for Jews were undeniably prominent in revolutionary and Bolshevik movements before and after World War I. Socio-historical analysis investigates why some Jews were attracted to revolutionary politics and how the surrounding Christian populations depicted this phenomenon. It unpacks how prejudice is generated and functions.[175]

The key moment for the myth's crystallization was, of course, the Bolshevik revolution and its interpretation by White Russian anti-Bolsheviks, although the link between Jews and progressive and socialist-Marxist thinking predates

---

[170] On Class, see Mosse, *The Crisis of the German Ideology*, 220–5; Smith, *The Continuities of German History*, 206–10, 222.

[171] Hitler, *Mein Kampf*, 380, 969.

[172] Hitler, *Monologe im Führer-Hauptquartier, 1941–1945*, 305.

[173] André Gerrits, *The Myth of Jewish Communism: A Historical Interpretation* (Brussels: Peter Lang, 2009). Earlier and specialist literature includes Zvi Y. Gitelman, *Jewish Nationality and Soviet Politics: The Jewish Sections of the CPSU, 1917–1930* (Princeton, NJ: Princeton University Press, 1972); Erich E. Haberer, *Jews and Revolution in Nineteenth-Century Russia* (Cambridge: Cambridge University Press, 1995); Agnieszka Pufelska, *Die "Judäo-Kommune": Ein Feindbild in Polen. Das polnische Selbstverständnis im Schatten des Antisemitismus 1939–1948* (Paderborn: Ferdinand Schöningh Verlag, 2007); Jaff Schatz, "Jews and the Communist Movement in Interwar Poland," in *Studies in Contemporary Jewry*, ed. Jonathan Frankel, vol. 20 (2004), 3–37. There is of course an extensive literature on the related question of the world Jewish conspiracy and the "Protocols of the Elders of Zion," e.g., Richard S. Levy, *A Lie and a Libel: The History of the Protocols of the Elders of Zion* (Lincoln: University of Nebraska Press, 1995); Sonja Margolina, *Das Ende der Lügen: Rußland und die Juden im 20. Jahrhundert* (Berlin: Siedler Verlag, 1992); Wolfram Meyer zu Uptrup, *Kampf gegen die "jüdische Weltverschwörung": Propaganda und Antisemitismus der Nationalsozialisten 1919 bis 1945* (Berlin: Metropol Verlag, 2003).

[174] André Gerrits, "Antisemitism and Anti-Communism: The Myth of 'Judeo-Communism' in Eastern Europe," *East European Jewish Affairs* 25, no. 1 (1995): 51–2.

[175] Ibid.

the Bolshevik revolution. In the years immediately preceding and following emancipation, Jews (or formerly Jewish individuals or persons perceived as Jews) found opportunities for *visible* political activism and leadership only on the left.[176] Their conviction that socialism was a Jewish project responsible for countless atrocities, indeed that the Bolshevik regime was a Jewish tyranny over the Russian masses, made a great impression on many in the West, such as Churchill, who supported the White forces in the Russian civil war. The myth was most fervently believed in Poland, Hungary and Romania because of the relative size of their Jewish populations, the general culture of antisemitism, and the "real experience of Communism and 'Jewish' participation in it."[177] These countries suffered Bolshevik invasions, which were interpreted as Russian-Jewish violations. Hungary had a short-lived Bolshevik government with conspicuous Jewish leadership during which the country lost territory and prestige. Russian-Jewish rule, so to speak, was linked to foreign domination and fear of national annihilation.[178] The antisemitic interpretation of this participation is the conviction that Jews by nature aim to subvert Christian society via secret societies and violence. It is a paranoid and self-referential interpretative circle: all revolutionary politics is Jewish and Jews tend to revolution.[179]

Contrary to the myth, Russian Jews did not start revolutionary movements in the late nineteenth century, although they energetically participated in them in growing numbers. These young Jews rebelled both against the illiberalism of Russian society and the traditionalism of their parents: theirs was a double revolution. Joining left-wing movements based on universal human values offered an identity politics that transcended caste constrictions. They were "the most revolutionary (along with the Latvians) group in the Russian Empire. They were also the best at being revolutionaries."[180] If their membership of the Bolshevik Party during the civil war was small – under 6 percent – their superior literacy catapulted them into leadership positions of conspicuous visibility. Thus, Jews constituted a quarter of the Party's central

---

[176] Moreover, Jewish support for the Masonic movement (in its anticlerical phase) as well as support for the political changes that led to emancipation in various European countries branded Jews for many Christians as people who naturally thought "left" and "internationalist" undermined both nation and religion. My thanks to Peter Black for discussions on this material.

[177] Gerrits, "Antisemitism and Anti-Communism," 63; Michael Makoskvy, *Churchill's Promised Land: Zionism and Statecraft* (New Haven, CT: Yale University Press, 2008), 82–6.

[178] Gerrits, "Antisemitism and Anti-Communism," 65; Paul Hanebrink, "Transnational Culture War: Christianity, Nation, and the Judeo-Bolshevik Myth in Hungary, 1890–1920," *Journal of Modern History* 80 (2008): 76.

[179] Gerrits, "Antisemitism and Anti-Communism," 55.

[180] Yuri Slezkine, *The Jewish Century* (Princeton, NJ: Princeton University Press, 2004), 154.

community between 1919 and 1921, half of the office for combating counter-revolution, and so forth.[181]

Many in the Christian Russian population, accustomed to socially subordinate Jews, thought them "too prominent" in leftist politics, and found them guilty of forming the "backbone and core" of the Bolshevik movement.[182] The rhetoric was no different in Hungary where conservatives charged that "a significant and lively part of Jewry took part actively" in the short-lived Béla Kun (1886–1938) regime in 1919. The slippage from "facts" to myth is evident when they concluded that "This revolution is a Jewish revolution." The visibility of Jews in these movements and regimes furnished "objective proof" for the Judeo-Bolshevik myth for these Hungarians, but the salient factor here is their preexisting prejudices about Jews as cursed and unusually powerful. The myth was prepared discursively during the war when such leaders interpreted the increasing secularization of the Hungarian state as a Jewish "takeover." The situation was much the same in Poland.[183]

These were not experienced as ordinary political developments, then; rather, they heralded an apocalyptic challenge to Christian Europe by a pan-European enemy, "Judeo-Bolshevism," a paranoid fear that combined terror at the prospect of the revolutionary remaking of the social order with resentment that it was (supposedly) led by Jews. The feared annihilation of the state was virtually realized in Hungary when the Béla Kun government was unable to prevent the partition of the country: the rule of Jews, so to speak, coincided with, even caused, national destruction. Jews, the antisemites determined, represented a grave security threat to the state.[184] The German right drew the same kind of conclusions, accusing leftists and Jews of stabbing the army in the back in 1917 and 1918 with domestic labor unrest, for consenting to the debilitating Treaty of Versailles, leading the Bolshevik uprisings and republics in Munich and Berlin, and then for imposing the weak Weimar Republic on the hapless German population for the benefit of the Allies. The Jews, they said, had proven themselves to be a disloyal enemy people that never again could be permitted to imperil the German nation.[185]

What does this political dynamic tell us about how paranoia works? All too often, minority groups are held collectively guilty and are collectively punished for the actions for some of its members. The group as a whole is seen as a

---

[181] Ibid., 175–7.   [182] Ibid., 181.

[183] Hanebrink, "Transnational Culture War," 75; Joanna Michlic, "The Soviet Occupation of Poland, 1939–41, and the Stereotype of the Anti-Polish and Pro-Soviet Jew," *Jewish Social Studies* 13, no. 3 (2007): 135–76.

[184] Paul Hanebrink, *A Specter Haunting Europe: The Myth of Judeo-Bolshevism* (Cambridge, MA: Harvard University Press, 2018).

[185] Mark Levene, "The 'Jewish Question' in International Affairs, 1919–1939," in *The Origins of the Second World War: 70 Years On*, ed. Frank McDonough (London: Continuum, 2011), 342–59.

potential security risk, and so it can be interned, deported, or otherwise destroyed *in toto* for reasons of state. Thus, the Polish government in early 1946 held the Lemko ethnic group collectively responsible for a Ukrainian nationalist assassination of a Polish military war hero: 18,000 communist troops expelled some 200,000 people from southeast Poland. No distinction was made between those who had been loyal to the communist regime or not.[186] That was a government decision, but the logic of pogroms works in the same way. During World War I in England, for instance, hysteria about the presence of people with German ancestry – they might be spies and agents, the so-called "hidden hand" of German influence in the country – led to violent riots comprising 5–6,000 people. After the German sinking of the *Lusitania* in 1915, some in the press condemned Germans as a "branded race" with the "attributes of devils." Right-wing agitation went further. Horatio Bottomly called for the extermination of all "Germhuns" in Great Britain. The targets of the violence sometimes included Russian Jews with German-sounding names.[187] But what did the German state really have to do with naturalized Britons of German descent? The "logic" at work here is the notion of "ethnic guilt" based on the proposition that members of an ascribed "group" (in this case, all people of German descent irrespective of citizenship) are vicariously liable for the actions of other members.

The link between domestic minority and foreign threat seems an enduring feature of genocidal violence. Conventional studies of prejudice that omit the geopolitics of ethnic loyalty and security cannot account for why ethnic differences become dangerously politicized at particular points. Take the case of Jews in Syria in the 1920s and 1930s. The Balfour Declaration and subsequent European rule in the region sparked intense fears that the terms of the former would be fulfilled, indeed that the Islamic world would be destroyed or at least dominated by infidels and *dhimmi* populations. Local Jews were thereby tied to a despised alien power and their loyalty was impugned. Earlier, in Ottoman Turkey, the same dynamic was played out between Christians and the majority Muslim population as the socially mobile Christians were sponsored by the European powers which it was feared, would place them in charge after Ottoman defeat. The operating fear is "about 'foreigners' attempting to destroy the empire" by "becoming a collaborator

---

[186] Chris M. Hann, "Ethnic Cleansing in Eastern Europe: Poles and Ukrainians beside the Curzon Line," *Nations and Nationalism* 2, no. 3 (1996): 389–406; Krystyna Kersten, "Forced Migration and the Transformation of Polish Society in the Postwar Period," in *Redrawing Nations: Ethnic Cleansing in East-Central Europe, 1944–1948*, ed. Philipp Ther and Ana Siljak (Lanham, MD: Rowman and Littlefield, 2001), 80.

[187] Panikos Panayi, "Anti-German Riots in London during the First World War," *German History* 7, no. 2 (1989): 184–203; Peter Edgerly Firchow, *The Death of the German Cousin: Variations on a Literary Stereotype, 1890–1920* (London: Bucknell University Press, 1986), 164.

with a foreigner." Because Jews were not implicated in this dynamic, they were not attacked like the Armenians and other Ottoman Christians.[188] Where Jews were caught up in loyalty dilemmas, as in Soviet-occupied Poland in 1939 – they were accused of welcoming Soviet tanks with flowers and kisses – Jews were subject to terrible retributive violence by the local Poles, as were other non-Polish minorities seen to be disloyal.[189]

Nazi propaganda made constant reference to Jewish-Zionist collaboration with British and American imperial designs in the Middle East, and exhorted Egyptians to kill them for planning to aid the British should their rule be threatened. Noteworthy here is that this exhortation is posited as an act of self-defense: "You must kill the Jews, before they open fire on you." It is cast less as a race war than as a security emergency. Indeed, the Nazi radio broadcast accused Jews of "plotting against your security" by "planning to violate your women, to kill your children and to destroy you." Arabs should "annihilate" Jews because, ultimately, they were "base supporters of British imperialism."[190] Sudden changes in ethnic status hierarchies, which typically accompany for-eign occupations, cause intense fear and resentment among the previously dominant population, which exacts violent revenge after the occupiers leave.[191] In "double occupations," especially in the borderlands of east-central Europe, status loss and fear of extinction led to affects like rage and vengeance with accusations of collective, ethnic guilt.[192]

---

[188] Aaron Rodrigue, "The Mass Destruction of Armenians and Jews in Twentieth-Century Perspective," in *Der Völkermord an den Armeniern und die Shoah*, ed. Hans-Lukas Kieser and Dominick J. Schaller (Zürich: Chronos Verlag, 2002), 305–8. Important work on these fatal dynamics is Mark Levene, "Creating a Modern 'Zone of Genocide': The Impact of Nation and State Formation on Eastern Anatolia 1878–1923," *Holocaust and Genocide Studies* 12, no. 3 (1998): 393–433, and "Is the Holocaust Simply Another Example of Genocide?," *Patterns of Prejudice* 28 (1994): 3–26.

[189] Jan T. Gross, *Revolution from Abroad: The Soviet Conquest of Poland's Western Ukraine and Western Belorussia* (Princeton: Princeton University Press, 1988), 29–37. What those Poles did not recognize was that the Jews had every reason to welcome the Soviets: they would save them from the Germans.

[190] "Despatch No. 502 from the American Legation at Cairo, Egypt, Axis Broadcasts in Arabic for the Period July 3 to 9, 1942, Cairo, July 21, 1942," 14. National Archives and Record Administration, Maryland, US, RG 84: Records of the Foreign Service Posts of the Department of State, US Embassy and Legation, Cairo, Classifed and Unclassified General Records, 1936–1955, 815.4–820.02, Box 77.

[191] Roger Petersen, *Understanding Ethnic Violence: Fear, Hatred, and Resentment in Twentieth-Century Eastern Europe* (Cambridge: Cambridge University Press, 2002).

[192] "Desperation is a theme that runs through a great deal of ethnic violence. A good many groups are convinced that they are or soon will be swamped, dominated, and dispos-sessed by their neighbors, perhaps even rendered extinct": David L. Horowitz, *The Deadly Ethnic Riot* (Berkeley: University of California Press, 2001), 393. Gross, *Revolution from Abroad*; Kate Brown, *Biography of No Place: From Ethnic Borderland*

Such collective emotions can issue in paranoid politics. The traumatic and humiliating experience of loss and occupation is not forgotten but nurtured, particularly in nationalist circles, as a motivating source for revenge and redemption.[193] In fact, the nature of traumatized consciousness means that past events are never really past: they are all too present or, at least, the past can repeat itself all too readily. Such learning processes are catastrophized: "never again" will a group allow the disloyal national minority to undermine the survival of "its" state. There are no limits in dealing with traitors in emergency circumstances.[194] What this dynamic reveals about the distinction between violence based on "hallucinatory" and "real" conflict is that both are based on traumatic memories of past events in which "disloyal" peoples are held collectively guilty and then collectively punished or deported or destroyed, often *preemptively*, to prevent the feared repetition of the previous traumatic experience. For the paranoid subject, the "hallucinatory" is all too real.

The customary distinction, as Leo Kuper classically framed it, "between massacres of a weak defenseless hostage group used as a scapegoat, and massacres arising in the course of a conflict in which there is some realistic threat or challenge to the interests of the dominant group in the host society"[195] does not distinguish between the loyal and disloyal within such groups. Accordingly, it is largely fruitless to search for "real" interactions between victim and perpetrator. The element of preemption means that groups are attacked before its members can subvert the state. And, as noted above, preemption is based on a temporal slippage, that is, on particular memories of past interactions, however fantastically interpreted.

Preemption indicates paranoia; attacking groups because of what some or many of its members might do. Permanent security imperatives rather than the imperative of racial purity drive policies of destruction. The stark dichotomy of ideology on the one hand and political rationality on the other should be replaced with a spectrum that recognizes how paranoid threat assessment leading to preemptive strikes against collectives is present generally. To that extent, destructive policies can be placed on this spectrum with the Holocaust rather be separated into a distinct category.

It might be said, rightly, that the Nazi-Jewish political dynamic was based on a distorted interpretation of the past: after all, the few Jewish Bolsheviks

---

to *Soviet Heartland* (Cambridge, MA: Harvard University Press, 2004); Alexander Prusin, *Nationalizing a Borderland* (Tuscaloosa: University of Alabama Press, 2005).

[193] Dan Stone, "Genocide and Memory," in *The Oxford Handbook on Genocide Studies*, ed. Donald Bloxham and A. Dirk Moses (Oxford: Oxford University Press, 2010), 102–21.

[194] Mark Levene, *Genocide in the Age of the Nation State*, vol. 2, *The Rise of the West and the Coming of Genocide* (London: I. B. Tauris, 2005), 54, 58, 77, 128, 158.

[195] Kuper, *Genocide*, 91–4.

and capitalists were not acting as Jewish nationalists in the same way as, say, Armenian nationalists in the 1890s and afterwards who so exercised Ottoman elites. There were not explicitly Jewish political parties to stab the German Army in the back or ferment revolution in 1918. Indeed, the Jewish case is remarkable for the mediation or displacement of some "Jewish" politics (leaving aside explicitly Jewish political movements like Bundism and Zionism) in essentially non-Jewish social forces like capitalism and Bolshevism. The conspiracy accusation functioned to place "the Jews" as the hidden power behind them both. For that reason, the cultural history of these images and processes is important.[196] But, if we are to understand how and why such pervasive racism could be mobilized in a destructive direction in specific instances, it is important to understand the interaction between it and the economic and political activity of its victims.

In doing so, it is necessary to avoid, on the one hand, "blaming the victim" like the Nazis and those who empathize with them; and pretending, on the other, that there is no interaction at all between different kinds of Jews and their enemies. Scholarship needs to move beyond the "kernel of truth" argument, as if any truth can be discerned in Nazi antisemitism. The Nazis did refer to "real" events in the past – the point of their policies in Germany was to forestall the kind of domestic collapse they think crippled Germany at the end of World War I – but their view of reality was always through an extremely distorted lens. The fact is that a minority of Jews were Bolsheviks and a minority of Bolsheviks were Jews, and Jews eventually became victims of Bolshevism. But, for paranoid antisemites, the behavior of a small minority of Jews converted all Jewish civilians into potential deadly enemies who could be dealt with accordingly.[197]

Two other dimensions of political paranoia are also noteworthy. First, it *produces* the truth the perpetrators want to prevent. If "world Jewry" came to oppose the Nazi state in the 1930s – with international boycotts, demonstrations against Germany, and Weizmann's "war declaration" – that was not because "world Jewry" set out to destroy Germany, as the Nazis claimed, but because Jews were reacting to Nazi persecution in Germany.[198] Second,

---

[196] Alon Confino, *A World without Jews: The Nazi Imagination from Persecution to Genocide* (New Haven: Yale University Press, 2014).

[197] Cf. Semelin, *Purify and Destroy*, 21; Jan Gross, *Fear: Anti-Semitism in Poland after Auschwitz* (Princeton, NJ: Princeton University Press, 2006) shows the persecution suffered by Jews in Poland.

[198] Dan Stone, *Responses to Nazism in Britain, 1933–1939* (Basingstoke: Palgrave Macmillan, 2003); Richard A. Hawkins, "'Hitler's Bitterest Foe': Samuel Untermyer and the Boycott of Nazi Germany, 1933–1938," *American Jewish History* 93, no. 1 (2007): 21–50; Moshe Gottlieb, "The Anti-Nazi Boycott Movement in the United States: An Ideological and Sociological Appreciation," *Jewish Social Studies* 35, nos. 3–4 (1973): 198–227.

political paranoia then leads to excessive reactions to the very opposition that the paranoid subject conjured. The exaggerated fear that one is about to be destroyed by the enemy licences "final solutions" to perceived security risks.[199]

Political paranoia is a form of projective identification in which the subject displaces intolerable, negative feelings onto others who thence incarnate the disavowed, persecutory self. By externalizing internally experienced feelings of worthlessness, they are rendered manageable, and a positive self-image is maintained – though at considerable cost: the construction of a delusional reality. The subject is always the victim and the other the persecutor.[200] Political paranoia is at once a psychological regression to a child-like "paranoid-schizoid position" and an interpretative disorder constituted by hysterical threat assessments.[201]

Victims are not selected randomly. Because they represent the abject attributes disowned by the paranoid perpetrator, empathy with the victims is all the more threatening: for to imaginatively occupy their subject position would entail introjecting the intolerable feelings that were split off in the first place. This empathetic disconnection means that enemies are represented as absolutely evil, thereby licensing their destruction in self-defense and with a clean conscience.[202] The interaction with "enemy" is thus "real" to a certain, if limited, extent: "For most political paranoids the delusion is likely to involve exaggeration and distortion of genuine events and rational beliefs rather than pure psychotic invention."[203] Fatally, if the victim responds to their role in the paranoid's externalization, "what began as fantasy is transformed into

---

[199] Robert S. Robins and Jerrod M. Post, *Political Paranoia: The Psychopolitics of Hatred* (New Haven: Yale University Press, 1997). There is much more to consult, of course: Jeffrey M. Bale, "Political Paranoia v. Political Realism: On Distinguishing between Bogus Conspiracy Theories and Genuine Conspiratorial Politics," *Patterns of Prejudice* 41, no. 1 (2007): 45–60; Thomas C. Ellington, "Won't Get Fooled Again: The Paranoid Style in the National Security State," *Government and Opposition* 38, no. 4 (2003): 436–55; Stanley Schneider, "Fundamentalism and Paranoia in Groups and Society," *Group* 26, no. 1 (2002): 17–27; Angela L. Apple and Beth A. Messner, "Paranoia and Paradox: The Apocalyptic Rhetoric of Christian Identity," *Western Journal of Communication* 65, no. 2 (2001): 206–27; Roderick M Kramer, "Political Paranoia in Organizations: Antecedents and Consequences," *Research in the Sociology of Organizations* 17 (2000): 47–88; Stanley Schneider, "Peace and Paranoia," in *Even Paranoids Have Enemies: New Perspectives on Paranoia and Persecution*, ed. Joseph H. Berke (New York: Routledge, 1998), 203–18; John Mirowsky and Katherine E. Ross, "Paranoia and the Structure of Powerlessness," *American Sociological Review* 48 (1983): 228–39; Stephane J. Baele, "Conspiratorial Narratives in Violent Political Actors' Language," *Journal of Language and Social Psychology* (2019), 1–29, DOI: 10.1177/ 0261927X1986849.
[200] Semelin, *Purify and Destroy*, 46.
[201] See generally Timothy Melley, *Empire of Conspiracy: The Culture of Paranoia in Postwar America* (Ithaca, NY: Cornell University Press, 2000).
[202] Robins and Post, *Political Paranoia*, 104.   [203] Ibid., 49, 19.

reality" – the self-fulfilling prophecy mentioned above.[204] That is the fatal, productive power of paranoia. Fifty years ago, Gombrich pointed out this self-confirming dynamic thus:

> Once you are entrapped in this illusionary universe it will become reality, for if you fight everybody, everybody will fight you, and the less mercy you show, the more you commit your side to a fight to the finish. When you have been caught in this truly vicious circle there really is no escape.[205]

The material condition of political paranoia is collective trauma, whether in foreign occupations or national defeat. Both can be experienced as collective disintegration that produce apocalyptic, compensatory visions of redemption.[206] Redemptive imperialism and antisemitism do not mean, however, that the strategic and military operations to realise them are irrational. On the contrary, the ultraviolent anticipatory suppression of resistance made good sense to planners of a country with limited resources that needed to win the war quickly before the Soviet Union could mobilize its vastly greater resources. However illegal it was to deport and starve Russian and Polish civilians, it seemed rational if the aim was to replace them with German settlers in conditions of limited food supply. Moreover, Germans understood that Poles and Soviet citizens would not accept their countries becoming German *Lebensraum*; resistance was inevitable.

As for the Holocaust, security was also the aim: as Otto Ohlendorf, leader of *Einsatzgruppe D* that murdered 90,000 Jews told the Nuremberg court, the German goal aimed at "an immediate and permanent security of our own realm against that realm with which the belligerent conflict is taking place."[207] That ambition entailed executing Jewish civilians because, he told the Nuremberg court, "it was obvious that Jewry in Bolshevist Russia actually played a disproportionately important role." In linking Jews to Bolsheivsm, he was expressing the Judeo-Bolshevik myth, which led him to collapse the mass murder of Jews into general partisan warfare.

> That the Communist functionaries and the active leaders of the Communists in the occupied area of Russia posed an actual continuous danger for the German occupation the documents of the prosecution have

---

[204] Ibid., 94.   [205] Gombrich, *Myth and Reality in German War-Time Broadcasts*, 23.

[206] Robins and Post, *Political Paranoia*, 13; Cristina Jayme Montiel, "Political Trauma and Recovery in a Protracted Conflict: Understanding Contextual Effects," *Peace and Conflict: Journal of Peace Psychology* 6, no. 2 (2000): 93–111; Y. Y. I. Vertzberger, "The Antinomies of Collective Political Trauma: A Pre-Theory," *Political Psychology* 18 (1997): 863–76.

[207] United States of America vs. Otto Ohlendorf, et al. (Case No. 9), *Trials of the War Criminals before the Nuremberg Military Tribunals*, Vol. 4, The *"Einsatzgruppen Case." October 1946 – April 1949* (Washington, DC: US Government Printing Office, 1949), 247.

shown. It was absolutely certain that by these persons the call of Stalin for
ruthless partisan warfare would be followed without any reservation.[208]

When asked whether there was a "rational basis for killing children except
genocide and the killing of races," Ohlendorf articulated the term that I argue
is the hidden truth of state power at its foundation and crisis moments: "I
believe that it is very simple to explain if one starts from the fact that this order
did not only try to achieve security, but also permanent security because the
children would grow up and surely, being the children of parents who had
been killed, they would constitute a danger no smaller than that of the
parents."[209] For him, as for many Germans engaged in military security,
preemptive killing of enemy children was rational after the determination that
their parents were potential partisans and communist leaders. What their
reasoning discounts is that their securitization of Jews created the potential
security threat they now had to confront. Paranoia and rationality became
fatally entwined in Nazi Empire and permanent security.

Nazi Empire and Illiberal Permanent Security

Nazi occupation policy in Eastern Europe had three central and incompatible
agendas – economic exploitation (which included slave labor), population
resettlement, and security. In practice, even in occupied Poland, which was
the object of more sustained occupation and planning than the Soviet Union,
reconciling these competing agendas was impossible because ruthless exploitation and forced resettlement gave Slavs no incentive to harvest their crops
and drove them into the hands of partisans.[210] Hitler's imperialism was
internally incoherent.

German plans for the racial restructuring of Polish and later Soviet territory
were certainly colonial in style and form.[211] Whether in the prewar Polish
territories annexed to Germany or in those grouped into the General
Government or captured from the Soviet Union in 1941, the German

---

[208] Ibid.   [209] Ibid., 356.
[210] Christian Gerlach, *The Extermination of the European Jews* (Cambridge: Cambridge
University Press, 2016); Gerhard Wolf, *Ideologie und Herrschaftsrationalität: nationalsozialistische Germanisierungspolitik in Polen* (Hamburg: Hamburger Edition, 2012);
Devan Pendas, Mark Roseman and Richard Wetzell, eds., *Beyond the Racial State
Rethinking Nazi Germany* (Cambridge: Cambridge University Press, 2017). Mazower,
Hitler's Empire, ch. 8, shows that regime insiders debated styles of imperial rule, some
among them enjoining moderation and co-option rather than the plunder and exploit-
ation so as not to alienate occupied peoples who may otherwise collaborate with the
Germans. But they, like Werner Best, did not carry the day.
[211] Rolf Dieter Müller, "From Economic Alliance to a War of Colonial Exploitation," in
Germany and the Second World War, vol. 4, *The Attack on the Soviet Union*, ed. Horst
Boog et al. (Oxford: Clarendon, 1998), 118–224.

occupiers consistently referred to the land and their mission in colonial terms, depicting the Poles and Jews as backward and uncivilized and the land as undeveloped.[212] Demographic planners set out to make room for German settlers by removing Poles and Jews. The authors of the *Generalplan Ost* and later the *General-Siedlungsplan*, the long-term Nazi plans for the German East, envisaged not only the largest genocide in history – the anticipated deportation and starvation of tens of millions of Slavs to "modernize" the economic structure – but also the permanent rule of German colonists who would occupy fortified settlements where they would rule over a "helot" population of denationalized "slaves."[213] In other parts of Eastern Europe, "native non-Bolshevik governments" would govern on behalf of Germans, and the Slavic population would be mobilized against Jews in the manner of colonial divide-and-rule tactics.[214]

Jews were barely mentioned in the *Generalplan Ost* because they had no long-term future within occupied Poland's General Government, even though – against the will of its governor, Hans Frank (1900–1946) – Jews from elsewhere in German-occupied Europe were temporarily ghettoized there. Still, the fact that the systematic mass killing of Jews did not begin until the invasion of the Soviet Union in mid-1941 indicates that settlement policy alone cannot account for the Holocaust. Moreover, *Reichsführer* of the SS, Heinrich Himmler (1900–1945), who was in charge of German settlement, largely abandoned those demographic plans after the defeat at Stalingrad in 1943.[215] Henceforth ready to compromise about population policies toward Slavs, the extermination of Jews became a priority when expulsion was no longer possible and Hitler denounced "world Jewry" for the war.

[212] Götz Aly and Susanne Heim, *Architects of Annihilation: Auschwitz and the Logic of Destruction* (London: Phoenix, 2002).

[213] Alexa Stiller, *Völkische Politik: Praktiken der Exklusion und Inklusion in polnischen, französischen und slowenischen Annexionsgebieten 1939–1945* (Göttingen: Wallstein, 2020); Gerhard Wolf, *Ideology and the Rationality of Domination: Nazi Germanization Policies in Poland* (Bloomington: Indiana University Press, 2020); Wolf Gruner and Jörg Osterloh, eds., *The Greater German Reich and the Jews Nazi Persecution Policies in the Annexed Territories 1935–1945* (New York and Oxford: Berghahn Books, 2015); Alex J. Kay, *Exploitation, Resettlement, Mass Murder: Political and Economic Planning for German Occupation Policy in the Soviet Union, 1940–1941* (New York and Oxford: Berghahn Books, 2006); Alex Kay, Jeff Rutherford, and David Stahel, eds., *Nazi Policy on the Eastern Front, 1941: Total War, Genocide, and Radicalization* (Rochester, NY: University of Rochester Press, 2012); Alex Kay and David Stahel, eds., *Mass Violence in Nazi-Occupied Europe* (Bloomington: Indiana University Press, 2018).

[214] Jürgen Förster, "Operation Barbarossa as a War of Conquest and Annihilation," in Boog et al., *Germany and the Second World War*, 481.

[215] Czeslaw Madajczyk, "Besteht ein Synchonismus zwischen dem 'Generalplan Ost' und der Endlösung der Judenfrage?" in *Der Zweite Weltkrieg: Analysen, Grundzüge, Forschungsbilanz*, ed. Wolfgang Michalka (Munich and Zürich: Piper, 1989), 849.

The Nazis targeted all Jews collectively and preemptively as a security threat because they thought Jews represented mortal danger to the Nazi project. As discussed above, the Nazis had convinced themselves that Jews were responsible for the traumatic collapse of the German home front and military morale in 1917 and 1918, as well as the short-lived postwar socialist government in Munich.[216] As the supposed bearers of Bolshevism, Jews were linked by Nazis to both insurrection at home and the terrorist regime in the Soviet Union that had exterminated classes and peoples in an "Asiatic" manner. There could be no place for such a dangerous people in the German Empire. This was of course a wildly paranoid reaction to the German trauma of 1918–1920 and the Weimar Republic, significantly radicalizing prewar antisemitism.

Soviet Jews in particular were targeted as security threats in the conquest of the east. Of course, they were not in fact such a threat. They were murdered *preemptively* so they would not present a threat. Himmler articulated the link between the mass murder of Jews and anticipatory counterinsurgency in December 1941 in conveying Hitler's decision to all SS and police agencies:

> The task entrusted to us is to guarantee security, law and order in the territories allocated to us, especially in the rear of the German front. This task demands of us that we eliminate ruthlessly every center of resistance and impose in the most drastic way the just death penalty upon the enemies of the German people.[217]

In his notorious Posen speech in October 1943, he expressed the Nazis' traumatic sensibility in permanent security terms: the killing aimed to prevent the repetition of the domestic collapse that crippled Germany at the end of World War I:

> In our history this is an unwritten and never-to-be-written page of glory, for we know how difficult we would have made it for ourselves if today – amid the bombing raids, the hardships and the deprivations of war – we still had the Jews in every city *as secret saboteurs, agitators, and demagogues. If the Jews were still ensconced in the body of the German nation, we probably would have reached the 1916–17 stage by now.*[218]

The role of security thinking thus proved to be decisive in shaping policy toward the Jews. Head of the Reich Main Security Office, Reinhard Heydrich

---

[216] Hitler, *Hitler's Words*, 246; Förster, "Operation Barbarossa as a War of Conquest and Annihilation,'" 498.

[217] Wolfgang Benz, Konrad Kwiet, and Jürgen Matthäus, eds., *Einsatz im "Reichskommissariat Ostland": Dokumente zum Völkermord im Baltikum und in Weissrussland 1941–1944* (Berlin: Metropol Verlag, 1998), 28. Thanks to Konrad Kwiet for drawing my attention to this document.

[218] Dawidowicz, *The War against the Jews*, 133. Emphasis added.

(1904–1942), summarized the connection in his remark that "political pacification is the first prerequisite for economic pacification."[219] Political pacification meant the elimination of actual or even potential resistance to German rule. The Nazis were convinced that Communist Party functionaries and Red Army officers would form the nucleus of organized resistance after German military victory, a belief intensified by Stalin's call for a "partisan war to be unleashed" behind the German lines.[220] Potential insurgents were to be hunted down in rear areas and liquidated.[221] Passive resistance would lead to collective punishment, and "suspicious elements" should be handed to security forces even if they had not (yet) committed an offence. Such potential insurgents were to be hunted down in rear areas and liquidated.[222]

Soviet Jewish men, and eventually women and children, were murdered by *Einsatzgruppen* acting according to the formula "Jew equalled Bolshevik equalled partisan."[223] Meanwhile, in orders and reports, German military officials routinely associated Jews with other security threats: "It is ultimately of the utmost importance to eradicate the influence of the Jews and deploy the most radical measures to eliminate these elements, because they in particular ... maintain contacts with the Red Army and the bandits we are fighting"; "The Jewish class, which forms the largest section of the population in the towns, is the driving force behind the growing resistance movement in some areas."[224] By the end of the war, the logic of pacification meant that in parts of the Soviet Union everyone except active collaborators was considered a criminal resister. On October 23, 1942, the commissioner for "anti-bandit warfare" in central Russia, General Curt von Gottberg (1896–1945), criminalized the entire civilian population with the following order: "bandits, a population of bandit suspects and bandit sympathizers, Jews, Gypsies, horse-riders and juveniles to be considered spies."[225] Hitler approved of such methods. To crush the resistance, he insisted, "barbaric methods" were justified, especially

---

[219] Robert Gerwarth, *Hitler's Hangman: The Life of Heydrich* (New Haven: Yale University Press, 2011), 189; Kay, *Exploitation, Resettlement*, 105.

[220] Hannes Heer, "The Logic of the War of Extermination: The Wehrmacht and the Anti-Partisan War," in *The War of Extermination: The German Military and World War II, 1941-1944*, ed. Hannes Heer and Klaus Naumann (New York and Oxford: Berghahn Books, 2000), 103-4, 95.

[221] Förster, "Operation Barbarossa as a War of Conquest and Annihilation," 491–492; Förster, "Securing 'Living Space,'" in Boog et al., *Germany and the Second World War*, 1189; Förster, "Hitler's Decision in Favour of War against the Soviet Union," in Boog et al., *Germany and the Second World War*, 48; Ben Shepherd, *War in the Wild East: The German Army and Soviet Partisans* (Cambridge, MA: Harvard University Press, 2004), 75.

[222] Heer, "The Logic of the War of Extermination," 101.

[223] Shepherd, *War in the Wild East*, 88.

[224] Quoted in Heer, "The Logic of the War of Extermination," 104.   [225] Ibid., 103-14.

as the death of so many fine German soldiers tipped the demographic balance in favor of criminal elements at home who might support Bolshevism and insurrection, his greatest fear since the leftist uprising in 1919.[226]

This worldview had much to do with colonialism and, in particular, colonial-style warfare, in which the laws of war withheld legitimate combatant status to insurgents. By criminalizing Soviet and Jewish enemies, the German state authorized its military to conduct the eastern campaign as a colonial conflict in which the laws of war regarding treatment of combatants and civilians did not apply. All resistance was regarded as illegitimate, and civilians were targeted *preemptively* and often *collectively* to forestall future resistance, just as in colonial wars of "pacification" against unruly tribes. Hitler rejected the application of the laws of war in the Soviet campaign with the infamous "commissar order" of June 6, 1941, which permitted the summary execution of Bolshevik functionaries.

The Nazis shelved *Generalplan Ost* because they never managed to pacify Eastern Europe. The partisan war, which resembled colonial counterinsurgency in many respects, persisted throughout, tying down vast German resources.[227] The "conventional" war was colonial in nature as well, or contained colonial dimensions, because of the notorious Nazi decision not to apply the laws of war to Soviet troops. Arguing like international lawyers had for centuries, the Nazis reasoned that, because "Asiatics" and "Judeo-Bolsheviks" did not respect these laws, they should not be accorded their protection. The Soviets were to be treated like non-European belligerents, summarily executing or starving POWs and not distinguishing between combatants and civilians.[228] The Nazi aim was to conquer and impose order on Eastern Europe (as elsewhere in Europe) so they could erect their thousand-year empire. By the war's end, they had allowed over three million Soviet POWs to perish in rudimentary camps and had killed many million Soviet citizens, mainly in reprisal actions and through starvation caused by blockade and plunder.[229]

It goes without saying that the Nazi regime was more radically violent and exploitative in its imperial rule than the British from which Hitler drew historical inspiration. But just because Nazi Germany permanent security

[226] Hitler, *Monologe im Führer-Hauptquartier, 1941–1945*, 348.

[227] Alexander Hill, *The War behind the Eastern Front: The Soviet Partisan Movement in North-West Russia, 1941–1944* (London and New York: Frank Cass, 2005).

[228] Alfred Streim, "International Law and Soviet Prisoners of War," in *From Peace to War: Germany, Soviet Russia, and the World, 1939–1941*, ed. Bernd Wegner (Providence and Oxford: Berghan Books, 1997), 293–308.

[229] Christian Streit, *Keine Kameraden: Die Wehrmacht und die Sowjetischen Kriegsgefangenen, 1941–1945* (Bonn: Dietz, 1978), 244–50.

was illiberal compared to its Western competitors does not make it a non-imperial project. It was indeed a new type of political regime in many respects, but one inspired by many examples of imperial expansion past and present, a process that constitutes an immensely significant intellectual transfer, or better: appropriation. The Nazis' extensive recourse to the "imperial archive" and the Italian fascist example invites an analysis that lays bare how they nurtured and articulated their terrible ambitions. Britain and France may have had larger and longer-standing empires, but, unlike Germany, they increased their imperial prowess after World War I, even if the US and Soviet Union were beginning to dwarf them. They did not experience the same racial anxieties nor economic and political crises of the forcibly decolonized Weimar Republic: anxieties and crises that fueled the traumatic and compensatory fantasies of many Germans who hoped a new empire, colonies, and the expulsion and later elimination of "enemy peoples" would make them invulnerable forever.

The Holocaust was less the ineluctable consequence of scientific racism or even a millennia of antisemitism than of frustrated and paranoid imperial elites lashing out at a perceived enemy that it thought was intent on destroying it – however outlandish that belief.[230] Conventional images of the Holocaust as a megahate crime do not capture this dimension. It issued from an obsession with security rather than solely with race, an obsession intrinsic to the empire-states of Eurasia that for centuries had preemptively targeted supposedly enemy cities, religions, and peoples for deportation or extermination. Harmless noncombatant members of these groups were held to be as objectively guilty as combatants because groups as a whole were considered objectively guilty. Racial typologies identified the enemies, but did not cause the genocides. Much more conventional perceptions of inner and outer threats based on imperial security, ranging from preemption to the relentless pursuit of hereditary enemies, need to be considered.

The Holocaust was not a classical case of "colonial genocide," that is, of a colonizer destroying the colonized. The function of Jews – or rather "the Jew" – in Nazi thought and as objects of genocidal practice was so ubiquitous and varied that it cannot be captured by such a simple formula. But that does not mean imperial modalities were irrelevant. On the contrary, they were central in a number of ways. German Jews were killed as perceived *colonizers* who had – in the Nazi imagination – dominated Germany and led it to the brink of extinction. Integrating the Holocaust into this picture has been challenging because Jews, especially assimilated ones, do not fit conventional

---

[230] For the Nazi belief and propaganda about the supposedly genocidal intention of Jews towards Germany, see Herf, *The Jewish Enemy*.

images of a colonized people. But the key fact is that many Germans believed that *they* were being colonized *by* Jews. German antisemitism radicalized during and after World War I primarily because many Germans convinced themselves that Jews not only profited from the conflict, but also used it to take control of the Weimar Republic.

Such beliefs, as real as they were paranoid, need to be reconstructed, explained, and contextualized in a world of empires in which one either colonized or was colonized and condemned to slavery or extinction. In this apocalyptic scenario, a Holocaust could be conceived and perpetrated. The Holocaust was rooted in a Nazi imperial vision that sought to correct the mistakes of Wilhelmine colonialism by forging an empire in which inner enemies were exterminated and foreign regimes were powerless to interfere. Eastern European Jews had to be expelled and then murdered because they provided the "breeding ground" for those colonists: they, too, were murdered as colonists.[231] The colonial modality of this genocide was subaltern: the indigene destroying the colonizer in a murderous act of decolonization

The fact that Hitler had no sympathy for indigenous liberation movements abroad, except where they suited geopolitical strategy, however, indicates that he regarded Germans also as a colonizing people. German administrators and soldiers often thought of Eastern European Jews in terms of colonial stereotypes: as uncivilized, dirty, lazy, and so forth. For that reason, population planners could not envisage a place for them in the General Government's future.[232] Germans and collaborators murdered these Jews like colonized people everywhere where their labor was not coveted: they were killed as security threats or they were worked to death. Soviet Jews were labeled as security threats to the conquest of the east and therefore murdered *preemptively*. The Holocaust, then, arose out of the union of different imperial impulses. It was born of a frustrated imperial nation struggling against a perceived colonizer, and it fed on the compensatory fantasies of many Germans during the interwar period: of achieving permanent security through a new empire, colonies, and the expulsion and later elimination of "enemy peoples."

Conclusion

Lemkin understood this project very well. In *Axis Rule in Occupied Europe*, he catalogued Nazi occupation policies in great detail. He knew that their purpose was permanent security: to change for Germany "the balance of

---

[231] David Furber and Wendy Lower, "Colonialism and Genocide in Nazi-Occupied Poland and Ukraine," in Moses, *Empire, Colony, Genocide*, 372–400.
[232] Ibid.

biological forces between it and the captive nations for many years to come."[233] This was an explicable geopolitical project: it was not driven by racial hatred as such but to benefit one people at the expense of others. However, like other proponents of liberal security, he refused to accord it formal political character, because the aim was carried out by criminal means: by violating the Hague Convention and international norms that marked out "civilized society." He thus effectively likened Nazis to pirates, as Lauterpacht had argued in his elaboration of the 1937 Treaty of Nyon: "If . . . a sovereign seeks office with a program of crimes against humanity, then his office and functions become a danger to international life and preclude them from enjoying the privileges granted by the comity of nations. International courtesy cannot go so far as to permit freely the murder of other nations."[234] His legal point was to undermine the defense of superior orders that Germans pleaded at the Nuremberg Trials, namely by criminalizing the state they served. That entailed also depoliticizing them, as he also argued about terrorism a decade before: "if a criminal acting from political motives, commits a crime of an especially heinous character, he cannot claim the privilege of being a political criminal. Hitler must be considered a common criminal."[235] Lemkin could not seriously entertain the proposition that "civilized states," the vehicles of international law and liberal permanent security, could also engage in organized criminality by sanctioning crimes. In a telling admission, he concluded that "No civilized order can admit this principle without destroying the very basis of organized society."[236]

---

[233] Raphael Lemkin, *Axis Rule in Occupied Europe: Laws of Occupation, Analysis of Government, Proposals for Redress* (Washington, DC: Carnegie Endowment for International Peace, 1944), 81, xi. "The Germans hoped to control permanently a depopulated Europe, and ultimately, in partnership with Japan. . . to dominate the world. Thus genocide became a basic element of geopolitics": Raphael Lemkin, "Genocide: A New International Crime – Punishment and Prevention," *Revue Internationale de Droit Pénal* 17 (1946): 364.

[234] Raphael Lemkin, "The Legal Case against Hitler," *The Nation*, February 24, 1945, 205; Lemkin, *Axis Rule in Occupied* Europe, 24; Walter Rech, "Rightless Enemies: Schmitt and Lauterpacht on Political Piracy," *Oxford Journal of Legal Studies* 32, no. 2 (2012): 235–63.

[235] Lemkin, "The Legal Case against Hitler," 206.   [236] Ibid., 207.

8

Human Rights, Population "Transfer," and the Foundation of the Postwar Order

Some of the United Nations' constituent states were either complicit in or products of partition and/or subsequent population expulsions in the second half of the 1940s: the partitions of Germany, India, and Palestine between 1945 and 1950. About 12 million ethnic Germans were forced out of Central and Eastern Europe. Over 14 million refugees crossed the new borders between Pakistan and India in 1947 and 1948, mostly in Punjab. And about 700,000 Palestinian Arabs fled fighting or were expelled from their towns and villages by Zionist forces and then prevented from returning. These demographic transformations were and remain foundational for the postwar order. Any reversal of this foundational violence was inconceivable for the new order's architects – and remains so today. Despite the ethnic cleansings and massacres, these states regarded themselves as liberal from the outset: constitutional democracies committed to modernity and progress. India, Pakistan, and Israel supported the "human rights revolution." Indeed, they participated in and sometimes drove the UN deliberations about human rights and genocide. The imperative to omit their foundational violence from legal proscription and moral purview informed the negotiation and ultimate formulation of each constituent element of the human rights revolution. These states set the threshold of what "shocks the conscience of mankind" to exclude liberal permanent security from legal proscriptions and moral condemnation. The language of transgression we use today narrowed and crystallized at this moment in global history.

This chapter and the next examine these dramatic and traumatic demographic transformations in Europe, the Levant and South Asia as modalities of liberal permanent security: conducted in the name of the liberal values of human rights and genocide prevention. I examine these modalities not by reconstructing the local mechanisms of mobilization and interaction but by tracing the intersecting and divergent imaginings of national belonging, state borders, and minority loyalty.[1] Our context is the convergence of

---

[1] Recent local studies include Subhasish Ray, "Intra-Group Interactions and Inter-Group Violence: Sikh Mobilization during the Partition of India in a Comparative Perspective," *Journal of Genocide Research* 19, no. 3 (2017): 382–403; Ranabir Samaddar, "Policing a

decolonization struggles in India and Palestine against the horizon of imperial dissolutions and expansions in Europe from the 1920s to the 1940s: the breakup of the continental land empires after World War I and foundation of new states, including the Greek–Turkish population exchange of 1923; Nazi Germany's extensive border changes of allied and enemy nation-states; and its defeat, resulting in massive expulsions of ethnic Germans from Central and Eastern Europe. I am less interested in the details of these well-studied events and processes than in the arguments advanced to justify the permanent security of nations–in–the–making in the form of new states, their ethno-religious substances, and the question of minorities.[2]

The 1920s to the 1940s were not only the decades of authoritarian and fascist revisionism, but also saw the intensification of human rights and atrocity prevention language among members of the League of Nations. Progressive politicians and intellectuals linked these ideals to ethnically homogeneous nation-states. To this end, they proposed population "transfers" and partitions as "humane" solutions to seemingly intractable nationality conflicts and as a precondition for social and economic development. Far from being somehow in tension with partition and transfer, as supposed by international lawyers today, human rights and the repertoire of civilization norms for which the concept stood, justified them. The commitment to human rights and genocide prevention, as understood then, as well as population transfer, was a consistent and coherent position in the 1940s.[3] The euphoric rhetoric about the human rights revolution obscures its intrinsic role in the liberal permanent security of the postwar order.[4] After the war, human rights and genocide prevention rhetorics became the language of the "standard of civilization" that is intrinsic to liberal permanent security formations. But they were not only

Riot-Torn City: Kolkata, 16–18 August 1946," *Journal of Genocide Research* 19, no. 1 (2017): 39–60; Samir Kumar Das, ed., *Minorities in South Asia and in Europe: A New Agenda* (Kolkota: Samya, 2010).

[2] Inis L. Claude, *National Minorities: An International Problem* (Cambridge, MA: Harvard University Press, 1955); Mark Mazower, "Strange Triumph of Human Rights, 1933–1950," *Historical Journal* 47, no. 2 (2004): 379–98; Mazower, *No Enchanted Palace: The End of Empire and the Ideological Origins of the United Nations* (Princeton: Princeton University Press, 2009); Eric D. Weitz, "From the Vienna to the Paris System: International Politics and the Entangled Histories of Human Rights, Forced Deportations, and Civilizing Missions," *American Historical Review* 113, no. 4. (2004): 1313–43.

[3] Cf. Jack Donnelly, "Human Rights: A New Standard of Civilization?" *International Affairs* 74, no. 1 (1998): 1–23; Marco Duranti, "'A Blessed Act of Oblivion': Human Rights, European Unity and Postwar Reconciliation," in *Reconciliation, Civil Society, and the Politics of Memory: Transnational Initiatives in the 20th Century*, ed. Marco Duranti and Birgit Schwelling (Bielefeld: Transcript Verlag, 2012), 1–25.

[4] Cf. Mark Levene, *The Crisis of Genocide*, Vol. 2, *Annihilation. The European Rimlands 1939–1953* (Oxford: Oxford University Press, 2014), which discusses the sacrifice of minorities and diversity for the postwar order of nation-states.

providing rhetorical cover or post facto justification for population expulsions. The human rights revolution codified the modalities of liberal permanent security that founded the postwar liberal order.

These two chapters undertake a "conjunctural" analysis of this codification by focusing on the temporal coincidence of debates about partitions, population exchanges, human rights, and atrocity prevention.[5] In particular, I trace the relationship between them to the interwar discussion on population "transfers" and a slightly earlier partition debate, namely the partition of Palestine recommended by a British commission in 1937. This discussion was characterized by a Janus-faced reference system: on the one hand, the commission defended its population transfer recommendation in terms of the Greek-Turkish population exchange of 1923 and, on the other, important commentators thereafter linked the partitions of Germany, British India, and Palestine with population transfer and human rights ideals. Transfer was to be carried out not in contravention of human rights but in the name of establishing a new order based on the "rights of man" and what now is called genocide prevention; to use the contemporary terminology, the transfers were to be expedited in the name of "humanity" and in a "humane" manner. The violence would be temporary and, so the reasoning went, would be redeemed by creating a future in which genocidal violence of this order would never recur. This is the pacification logic of liberal permanent security.

In this chapter, I unfold the argument in four stages. First, I briefly overview liberal permanent security modalities of population management in the first half of the twentieth century. Then I account for the enabling relationship between human rights language and transfer in these decades. In the third section, I analyze the discussion about the morality and efficacy of population "transfer" in the 1930s, because at the time "transfer" became ineluctably associated with partition, and was justified in terms of modernity and preventing ethnic civil wars. In the fourth section, I show how it became related to the question of human rights in the early 1940s. In the main, my subjects are academic or quasi-academic policy analysts and advocates who advised major organizations and/or states rather than the familiar actors, Churchill, Stalin, Roosevelt, and other political elites, whose support for transferring German civilians is well known. Anything but isolated academic scribblers, these half-forgotten figures not only delivered the justifications employed by governments as they negotiated a distinctive phase of decolonization and its relationship to evolving human rights norms: the end of the Nazi Empire in Europe

---

[5] A well-known non-conjunctural analysis is T. G. Fraser, *Partition in Ireland, India, and Palestine: Theory and Practice* (London: Palgrave Macmillan, 1984). A defense of the human rights revolution teleology is Akira Iriye et al., eds., *The Human Rights Revolution: An International History* (New York: Oxford University Press, 2012).

and dissolution of British imperial control in the Middle East and South Asia.[6] They also made the case for the foundational violence of the new order in which we live today. As we will see, the consensus linking partition, population "transfer," and human rights emerged in a highly Eurocentric, and historically specific, context: that of debate around the fate of German minorities in Central and Eastern Europe, and Zionist aspirations in Palestine.

Partitions, Minorities, Expulsions as Liberal Permanent Security

Partitions, empires, federations, and commonwealths were liberal modes of permanent security in the first half of the twentieth century.[7] Imperial governors often advanced federalism as a form of minority protection. Federations could restrain refractory white settlers, as in the case of the (ultimately unsuccessful) "closer union" proposals in the late 1920s to extend the native protection provisions of Britain's Tanganyikan League of Nations mandate to Kenya and Uganda. If the settlers would not submit to incorporation, they could be subject to "administrative separation," the functional equivalent of partition.[8] For the most part, however, "native" majorities were distrusted to justly govern those less numerous minority population groups on whose collaboration empires had long depended in their divide-and-rule tactics. Such was the aim of the Cabinet Mission option the British presented to the All India Congress and All India Muslim League in 1946: a united India of grouped Hindu- and Muslim-majority provinces with a weak center to ensure that the majority Hindus could not dominate the minority Muslims. Similarly, the Anglo-American Committee of British and American delegates who toured Palestine in the same year concluded diplomatically that any political solution had to be based on three principles: "I. That Jew shall not dominate Arab and Arab shall not dominate Jew in Palestine. II. That Palestine shall be neither a Jewish state nor an Arab state. III. That the form of government ultimately to be established, shall, under international guarantees, fully protect and preserve the interests in the Holy Land of Christendom and of the Moslem and Jewish faiths."[9] Its recommendations led to the Morrison-Grady plan of Arab and Jewish provincial self-rule under federal

---

[6] A recent student on prominent Jewish figures engaged in human rights and Zionist activity is James Loeffler, *Rooted Cosmopolitans Jews and Human Rights in the Twentieth Century* (New Haven, CT: Yale University Press, 2016).

[7] A notable exception is Laura Robson, *States of Separation: Transfer, Partition, and the Making of the Modern Middle East* (Berkeley: University of California Press, 2017).

[8] Michael D. Callahan, "The Failure of 'Closer Union' in British East Africa, 1929–31," *Journal of Imperial and Commonwealth History* 25, no. 2 (1997): 267–93.

[9] Anglo-American Committee of Inquiry, Chapter I, Avalon Project: Documents in Law, History, and Diplomacy, Yale Law School, http://avalon.law.yale.edu/20th_century/angch01.asp.

UN-British trusteeship that bore some resemblance to the Cabinet Mission plan in India. Like the Indian parties, Zionists and Arabs rejected this option – accurately discerning the continuing imperial logic of external enforcement and intervention – as did US President Harry Truman, who inclined toward it but was under electoral pressure to lean to the Zionist viewpoint.[10]

In general, the metropole preferred to bundle territory and societies in empire-lite or postimperial arrangements, like federations and common-wealths, if they could be managed with local elites who they often created and empowered with new positions and governance structures.[11] Partition made sense if this could not be done, or only with difficulty. Britain's partition of Bengal in 1905 was a divide-and-rule measure to that end, although it was reversed only six years later after vehement protest.[12] It is no accident that federative arrangements were canvassed in the British, French, and Dutch empires after World War II: the Malay Federation (predecessor of Malaysia and Singapore) between 1948 and 1963, the Central African Federation of 1953–1963, the West Indies Federation between 1958 and 1962, the Federation of South Arabia (forerunner of South Yemen) of 1962–1967, French West African federative ideas, the United States of Indonesia (preferred by the Netherlands to a unified state), and the Dutch-Indonesian Union.[13] To be sure, federal ideas were also attractive to some African leaders of national movements who saw the political benefit of strength in numbers and eco-nomic advantage of continued relationships with a metropole.[14] On the whole, though, the drive for sovereignty in a unitary state predominated as decolo-nization's political model. The UN's imposed federation of Eritrea and

---

[10] H. Levenberg, "Bevin's Disillusionment: The London Conference, Autumn 1946," *Middle Eastern Studies* 27, no. 4 (1991): 615–30; John B. Jurdis, "Seeds of Doubt: Harry Truman's Concerns about Israel and Palestine Were Prescient – and Forgotten," *New Republic*, January 15, 2014.

[11] Mahmood Mamdani, *Citizen and Subject: Contemporary Africa and the Legacy of Late Colonialism* (Princeton, NJ: Princeton University Press, 1996).

[12] Penny Sinanoglou, "The Peel Commission and Partition, 1936–1938," in *Britain, Palestine and the Empire: The Mandate Years*, ed. Rory Miller (Aldershot: Ashgate, 2010), 119–40. Penny Sinanoglou, *Partitioning Palestine: British Policymaking at the End of Empire* (Chicago: University of Chicago Press, 2019).

[13] Michael Collins, "Decolonization and the 'Federal Moment,'" *Diplomacy and Statecraft* 24, no. 1 (2013): 21–40; Jennifer Foray, "A Unified Empire of Equal Parts: The Dutch Commonwealth Schemes of the 1920s–40s," *Journal of Imperial and Commonwealth History* 41, no. 2 (2013): 259–84; Spencer Mawby, *Ordering Independence: The End of Empire in the Anglophone Caribbean, 1947–69* (Basingstoke: Palgrave Macmillan, 2012); James C. Parker, *Brother's Keeper: The United States, Race, and Empire in the British Caribbean, 1937–1962* (Oxford: Oxford University Press, 2008).

[14] Frederick Cooper, *Citizenship between Empire and Nation: Remaking France and French Africa, 1945–1960* (Princeton, NJ: Princeton University Press, 2014); Gary Wilder, *Freedom Time: Negritude, Decolonization, and the Future of the World* (Durham, NC: Duke University Press, 2015).

Ethiopia in 1952 lasted only until 1962, when the latter annexed the former, precipitating decades of war and ultimately two nation-states.[15]

If the British Empire's motivations in considering partition were to control the outcome of the Irish and later partitions, then the context of continental European imperial breakup after World War I is relevant, in part because the British codesigned the postwar architecture, in part because Indian leaders in particular studied these developments for possible lessons. Partition and minority protection dramas were not just British questions, they affected millions of Europeans. To understand the partitions of the 1940s, we need to explore their various linkages and bundle them as an international conjuncture of nation- and people-construction in the name of liberal permanent security.

The creation of new states in Europe after World War I pressed territorial disputes with partition potential onto the agenda, creating minority "problems" and thereby questions of protection and population transfer. Within Europe, the redrawing of borders to reward the Entente's allies and punish the war's losers resulted in the creation of large national minorities in the new states of Poland and Czechoslovakia. Hungarians decried the partition of their country in the Treaty of Trianon (1920) because of its drastic territorial losses and because ethnic Hungarians became minorities in neighboring states, especially Romania. To ensure stability, the League imposed minority protection treaties on these newcomers, thereby delineating hierarchies of sovereignty that those newcomers found humiliating.[16] Having been created from the territory of empires, these states then squabbled among themselves. In 1919, Poland and Czechoslovakia fought and negotiated over the Teschen/ Cieszyn province of Silesia, which was eventually split between them without consulting the local population.[17] Next door, the League of Nations insisted on a plebiscite in Upper Silesia in 1920 in the dispute between Poland and Germany. To ensure that the respective minorities were well treated, they signed a convention that included the portentous phrase "equitable reciprocity," based on the League's recommendation: mutual observation of the convention would guarantee the welfare of German and Polish conationals across the border.[18] Then, most dramatically, the League condoned the

[15] Tekeste Negash, *Eritrea and Ethiopia: The Federal Experience* (Uppsala: Nordiska Afrikainstitutet, 1997).

[16] Carol Fink, *Defending the Rights of Others: The Great Powers, the Jews, and International Minority Protection, 1878–1938* (Cambridge: Cambridge University Press, 2006); Weitz, "From the Vienna to the Paris System."

[17] Kevin Hannan, *Borders of Language and Identity in Teschen Silesia* (New York: Peter Lang, 1996).

[18] Geneva Convention Concerning Upper Silesia, Signed May 15, 1922, Annex 1, Part 3, Rights of Minorities in Upper Silesia (Minority Schools) (in French), www.icj-cij.org/files/permanent-court-of-international-justice/serie_A/A_15/52_Droits_de_minorites_en_Haute_Silesie_Ecoles_minoritaires_Annexe_1.pdf; Julius Stone, *Regional Guarantees*

Turkish-Greek population exchange in the Treaty of Lausanne (1923) after the brutal warfare between Turkish and Greek forces following the latter's invasion in 1919, hoping thereby to bring peace on the basis of religious homogeneity.[19]

These interwar settlements, largely conducted at the expense of World War I's losers, were eventually overturned by revisionist powers. Beginning with Germany's annexation of the Czechoslovak Sudetenland, with its preponderance of irredentist ethnic Germans, Czechoslovakia was effectively partitioned in 1938 with the reluctant consent of the very Western powers that had confected it after World War I. Poland took little time in opportunistically swallowing Czechoslovak Teschen/Cieszyn, thereby recovering what it regarded as previously partitioned Polish territory. A year later, the secret protocols of the Molotov–Ribbentrop Pact between the Soviet Union and Nazi Germany partitioned Poland between them and assigned parts of Romania to the Soviets. During the war, Germany further partitioned Romania by returning to its Hungarian and Bulgarian allies those lands they lost in the Trianon palace at Versailles. The German vision was of a minority-free Europe, especially of German ones, which should be (re)patriated *heim ins Reich*.[20]

Given the role of Sudeten Germans in destabilizing Czechoslovakia, the war's victors thought European minorities should be transferred where possible. Referring to the 1923 Lausanne agreement on the Turkish-Greek population exchange, British Prime Minister Winston Churchill called for a clean sweep of Germans from Poland in late 1944, and the British Foreign Office insisted that all ethnic Germans, not just the "guilty" ones, be expelled from Czechoslovakia. They agreed with Edvard Beneš (1884–1948), the leader of the Czechoslovak government in exile, who wanted to drive out the three million Germans and exchange ethnic Hungarians with Slovaks living in Hungary. All told, about 12 million ethnic Germans were expelled from Eastern and Central Europe. The rump of Germany was divided into the four occupation zones that, after the commencement of the Cold War, congealed into partitioned East and West Germany. In this way, the Nazi ideal of a minority-free Europe underlay the postwar order.[21]

---

of Minority Rights: A Study of Minorities Procedure in Upper Silesia (New York: Macmillan, 1933), 3, 6, 223. Generally, see Brendan J. Karch, *Nation and Loyalty in a German-Polish Borderland: Upper Silesia, 1848–1965* (Cambridge: Cambridge University Press, 2018).

[19] Volker Prott, *The Politics of Self-Determination: Remaking Territories and National Identities in Europe, 1917–1923* (Oxford: Oxford University Press, 2016).

[20] Roger Moorhouse, *The Devil's Alliance* (New York: Basic Books, 2014); Anthony Read and David Fisher, *The Deadly Embrace: Hitler, Stalin and the Nazi-Soviet Pact, 1939–1941* (New York: W. W. Norton, 1989).

[21] R. M. Douglas, *Orderly and Humane: The Expulsion of the Germans after the Second World War* (New Haven, CT: Yale University Press, 2013). Ethnic Hungarians were to be

Human Rights, Partition, and "Transfer"

That contemporaries could link human rights to population transfer in such a counterintuitive manner is explicable when we realize that most of them were not thinking of *international* human rights, as we do today.[22] Figures like Frenchman René Cassin (1887–1976), who was instrumental in drafting the human rights declaration, understood the concept as translating the French *les droits de l'homme* – "the rights of man" – thereby linking them to the venerable revolutionary tradition of the national self-determination of sufficiently developed peoples rather than the new and abstract notion of international human rights *against* the state.[23] "Human rights" did not possess a stable meaning or serve uniform purposes from the interwar years to the present day.[24] Beneš himself referred to the "rights of man," which he interpreted as intrinsic to the "democratic way of life in which Anglo-Saxons have been pioneers," and he wanted them to "be applicable to the people of all countries."[25] Americans, too, thought in these terms. Thus, James Brown Scott (1886–1943), editor of the *American Journal of International Law*, wrote in 1937 that the "conception of human rights, subsequently embodied in the Constitution of the United States, became ... the conception of all of the Republics of the American Continent." To be sure, they could be "stated in terms of international law," but, as Beneš was to argue as well, they referred

---

expelled from Czechoslovakia for the same reason, but the Hungarian state would not accept them. Josef Kalvoda, "National Minorities under Communism: The Case of Czechoslovakia," *Nationalities Papers* 16, no. 1 (1988): 1–21.

[22] Samuel Moyn, *The Last Utopia: Human Rights in History* (Cambridge, MA: Harvard University Press, 2010).

[23] Glenda Sluga, "René Cassin, *Les droits de l'homme* and the Universality of Human Rights, 1945–1966," in *Human Rights in the Twentieth Century*, ed. Stefan-Ludwig Hoffman (New York: Cambridge University Press, 2011), 29–44, 108. This distinction is a core analytical point in Moyn, *Human Rights in History*. On Cassin, Jay Winter, *René Cassin and Human Rights: From the Great War to the Universal Declaration* (Cambridge: Cambridge University Press, 2013).

[24] A. W. Brian Simpson, *Human Rights and the End of Empire: Britain and the Genesis of the European Convention* (Oxford: Oxford University Press, 2004), 161, 325; Alfred de Zayas, *Nemesis at Potsdam: The Anglo-Americans and the Expulsion of the Germans: Background, Execution, Consequences* (London: Routledge and Kegan Paul, 1977). Most recently in *Orderly and Humane*, R. M. Douglas observes the human rights violations endured by *Volkdeutsche* in their expulsion that the Allies accepted as a necessary price. Latest scholarship includes Hugo Service, "Reinterpreting the Expulsion of Germans from Poland, 1945–9," *Journal of Contemporary History* 47, no. 3 (2012): 528–50.

[25] Eduard Beneš, "Speech to the Liberal Social Council, London, May 12, 1942," in *War and Peace Aims of the United Nations, September 1, 1939–December 31, 1942*, ed. Louise W. Holborn, intro. Hajo Holborn (Boston: World Peace Foundation, 1943), 430.

ultimately to the obligations of national governments.[26] They, rather than imperial or international authorities, would be vehicles of human rights by enacting progressive policies for the benefit of a democratic people. The transformation he and others envisaged was cast in terms of a starkly drawn binary: human rights characterized modern, democratic, ethnically homogenous societies; they did not obtain in feudal/premodern, undemocratic ones whose mixed populations demanded colonial supervision and/or minority protection. That is why Beneš said that the second priority for which the Allies were fighting was "a new social and economic order" – the first was the rights of man. His technocratic modernization agenda was dependent on demographic homogeneity.[27] Other contemporaries likewise nestled human rights in an ensemble of the Western civilizational attributes that qualified a people for independence: fundamental freedoms and democracy, the rule of law, economic progress and modernity, often linked to settler colonial projects.[28]

The correlate of the nation-state's embodiment of human rights was its independence, meaning self-determination, which crowned the Allied ideals declared in the Atlantic Charter of 1941. As Hannah Arendt later wrote about the Nazi occupation in Europe, "Not only did loss of national rights in all instances entail the loss of human rights; the restoration of human rights, as the recent example of the State of Israel proves, has been achieved so far only through the restoration or the establishment of national rights."[29] The Allied wartime ideals required the total defeat of the Nazi occupier and the elimination of the causes of its temporary victory. Those obstacles to the progressive new order included German minorities in Eastern and Central Europe as well as Palestinian Arabs, who represented an obstacle for Zionists who closely observed the Czechoslovak plans to expel Germans. Of course, the Palestinian Arabs were no minority but a large majority in Mandate Palestine; that they would become a minority was the avowed Zionist goal. Because human rights became synonymous with civilization and modernity, namely the project of

[26] James Brown Scott, "Preface," in Oscar I. Janowsky and Melvin M. Fagen, *International Aspects of German-Racial Policies* (New York: Oxford University Press, 1937), vi–vii.

[27] Beneš, "Speech to the Liberal Social Council," 431. Philipp Ther's important book is strong on this point: Philipp Ther, *The Dark Side of the Nations State: Ethnic Cleansing in Modern Europe* (New York and Oxford: Berghahn Books, 2014).

[28] The evidence from the interwar period suggests that the link between civilization, modernity, and human rights can be located then rather than after World War II, as suggested by Mark Mazower, "The End of Civilization and the Rise of Human Rights: The Mid-Twentieth-Century Disjuncture," in Hoffman, *Human Rights in the Twentieth Century*, 29–44.

[29] Hannah Arendt, *The Origins of Totalitarianism*, new ed. and prefs. (San Diego: Harcourt Brace, [1951] 1973), 299.

democratic self-governance of occupied nations after the defeat of Nazi barbarism, postwar stability was elemental for their institutionalization.[30]

There thus was no revolution in sovereignty despite hopes for human rights revolution. Resurgent nation-states and imperial powers scotched the revolutionary dreams of federations and world government that were so intensively discussed by academics and civil society in the interwar period and during the war. These dreams were designed to counter the integral nationalism held responsible for the instability of interwar Europe and the Nazi project, but the surviving and new nation-states naturally wished to govern without UN interference. They were the ones to ensure that the human rights instruments would not impinge on their sovereignty or question the circumstances of their foundation.

The Interwar Debate on the "Humanity" of Transfer

Let us consider the interwar debate on population transfer and partitions in relation to the question of "humane" and "inhuman" policies, as the language of the time put it. It has become a commonplace to highlight the 1923 population exchange convention between Turkey and Greece, blessed and supported by the League of Nations, as a precedent for later commentators, policy makers, and politicians, and so it was. It also bears recalling that it was highly controversial at the time, with leading British figures expressing their unease with its compulsory dimension and the suffering of the over one million Greek Orthodox civilians who were driven from western Turkey and the roughly 350,000 Muslims who were then compelled to leave Greece for Turkey.[31] For the post-World War I norm was not population exchange but minority protection, which entailed leaving minorities *in situ* and guaranteeing them legally articulated rights. What is more, Western policy-makers felt the exchange was effectively forced upon them by precipitate Turkish expulsions of Greeks well before 1923, though it cannot be denied that some of them were complicit in the Greek invasion of Anatolia and were well aware that Greek action had provoked the Turkish response. A major refugee problem needed

---

[30] Jay Winter, "From War Talk to Rights Talk: Exile Politics, Human Rights and the Two World Wars," in *European Identity and the Second World War*, ed. Menno Spiering and Michael Wintle (Basingstoke: Palgrave Macmillan, 2011), 55–74.

[31] Mark Mazower, "Minorities and the League of Nations in Interwar Europe," *Daedalus* 126, no. 2 (1997): 49; Christa Meindersma, "Population Exchanges: International Law and State Practice–Part 1," *International Journal of Refugee Law* 9, no. 3 (1997): 341; Weitz, "From Vienna to the Paris System," 1136. Despite evidence to the contrary, Howard Adelman and Elazar Barkan come to the opposite conclusion: Adelman and Barkan, *No Return, No Refuge: Rites and Rights in Minority Repatriation* (New York: Columbia University Press, 2011), ch. 2.

to be solved, and the exchange convention bestowed largely retrospective blessing and logistical support for the rehabilitation of refugees, at least concerning the Greeks.

Ever since, commentators who were partial to population transfers and exchanges have pointed to the peace and stability the Lausanne convention brought to the eastern Mediterranean. The compulsory nature of the exchange was a small price to pay, it was reasoned, in what was ultimately a "humane" policy because future genocidal warfare had effectively been abolished: population transfer as a form of preventing ethnic civil wars. Commentators who argued in these terms were on the margins in the 1920s but found their arguments in the mainstream of even liberal internationalism a decade later, echoing earlier discourses about the removal of indigenous peoples to protect them from frontier violence.[32]

These points are well covered in the scholarly literature.[33] What has not been registered sufficiently about Lausanne and population transfers, nor connected with the Palestine problematic, is how the commentary on these phenomena embedded them in a discourse about modernity and the role of settler projects in its development, so typical of permanent liberal security discourses. Eduard Beneš, the Czechoslovak leader who urged the expulsion of the Sudeten Germans, for example, complained that they were settlers and colonists in Slavic territory, of a lower cultural level, whereas the Western European states had sent settlers around the world and "opened up new regions, and played a civilizing role."[34] While he was expressing the perspective of a superior indigenous people, the Czechs and Slovaks, his frame of reference was the benefits that settlers brought to extra-European countries. He was merely reflecting the contemporary norm.[35]

The advantages conveyed to Greece by the refugees it received from Turkey are a case in point about the connection between population transfers, humane policies, and modernization. Zionist commentary in the 1930s in particular was fascinated by the agricultural development that the refugees brought to Macedonia, coupled with land reform, modern farming techniques, and

---

[32] On the European context, see Matthew Frank, "Fantasies of Ethnic Unmixing: Population 'Transfer' and the End of Empire in Europe," in *Refugees and the End of Empire: Imperial Collapse and Forced Migration in the Twentieth Century*, ed. Panikos Panayi and Pippa Virdee (Basingstoke: Palgrave Macmillan, 2011), 81–101. Thanks to Lorenzo Veracini for pointing out the indigenous parallel.

[33] Matthew Frank, *Making Minorities History Population Transfer in Twentieth-Century Europe* (Oxford: Oxford University Press, 2017).

[34] Eduard Beneš, "The Organization of Postwar Europe," *Foreign Affairs* 20, nos. 1–4 (1941–1942): 235.

[35] On settler colonialism, see Lorenzo Veracini, *Settler Colonialism: A Theoretical Overview* (Basingstoke: Palgrave Macmillan, 2010) and the journal he has coestablished, *Settler Colonial Studies*.

general economic progress. What is more, the country's ethnic homogeneity made it more peaceful and modern. Norman Bentwich (1883–1971), the first Attorney-General of Mandate Palestine, ardent Zionist and later professor of international relations at the Hebrew University, wrote already in 1926 about "Macedonia, which was formerly the most desperate welter of nationalities and the traditional breeding ground of feuds and wars, has now obtained an almost homogeneous Greek population. The productivity of the land has been doubled, and in some cases, trebled by the settlers." He concluded by extolling the virtues of the population change's effects on Greece: "This enormous enterprise of settlement has been executed by a sustained national effort which is a lesson for the whole of Europe."[36] In this discourse, the refugee becomes the settler colonist: the bearer of modernity and its democratic social system.

The Jewish Agency dispatched missions to study and report on this Greek miracle just as the British mandate authorities were considering the fate of Palestine in the wake of the Arab rebellion, which began in 1936. Infamously, the Peel Commission, as it was unofficially called, recommended the partition of the mandate after determining the irreconcilable nature of the Jewish settlers' European civilization and that of the Palestinian Arabs. What is more, because of the impossibility of drawing borders to create a viable Jewish state, it recommended the transfer of Arabs eastwards into less fertile territory, allocating the more fertile areas to the minority Jewish population, which it regarded as the better agriculturalists. The interior was to be made habitable for the Palestinian Arabs by irrigation projects and other forms of capital investment. It is for this reason that the report devotes so many of its pages to the question of agriculture and the ability of the country to sustain particular population densities.

For the Zionist leaders making representations to the commission, the success of Greek settlers/refugees after 1923 was evidence that population transfers were progressive acts that benefited all sides. The problem of landless Arab peasants could be solved this way, for example, while bringing prosperity to the underpopulated regions of Transjordan, Syria and Iraq. Ben Gurion himself declared at a Zionist congress in 1937 that it was a "humane and Zionist ideal, to shift part of a people [Arabs] to their own country and to

---

[36] Norman Bentwich, "The New Ionian Migration," *Contemporary Review*, no. 130 (July/December 1926): 323, 325. The modernization theme is central to Umut Özsu, "Fabricating Fidelity: Nation-Building, International Law, and the Greek-Turkish Population Exchange," *Leiden Journal of International Law* 24 (2011): 823–47; Elisabeth Kontogiorgi, *Population Exchange in Greek Macedonia: The Rural Settlement of Refugees 1922–1930* (Oxford: Clarendon Press, 2006). Contemporary commentary is John Hope Simpson, "The Work of the Greek Refugee Settlement Commission," *Journal of the Royal Institute of International Affairs* 8, no. 6 (1929): 583–604.

settle empty lands," by which he meant transferring Palestinian Arabs eastwards to other countries.[37]

The Commission agreed. Its report was largely written by Oxford historian
Reginald Coupland (1884–1952), who sympathized with the Zionists' modernizing project.[38] The report tackled the thorny moral question of compulsion in the following way:

> ... so vigorously and effectively was the task accomplished that within
> about eighteen months from the spring of 1923 the whole exchange was
> completed. Dr. Nansen was sharply criticized at the time for the
> inhumanity of his proposal, and the operation manifestly imposed the
> gravest hardships on multitudes of people. But the courage of the Greek
> and Turkish statesmen concerned has been justified by the result. Before
> the operation the Greek and Turkish minorities had been a constant
> irritant. Now the ulcer has been clean cut out, and Greco-Turkish rela-
> tions, we understand, are friendlier than they have ever been before.[39]

Again, population transfer was seen as an anti-atrocity measure, or a "question
of humanity" as the report put it. Reasoning analogically, the Commission
applied these lessons to Palestine:

> We are not questioning the sincerity or the humanity of the Mufti's
> intentions and those of his colleagues; but we cannot forget what recently
> happened, despite treaty provisions and explicit assurances, to the
> Assyrian minority in Iraq; nor can we forget that the hatred of the Arab
> politician for the National Home has never been concealed and that it has
> now permeated the Arab population as a whole.
>
> ...
>
> There are 400,000 Jews in Palestine. They have come there not only
> with our permission but with our encouragement. We are answerable,
> within reason, for their welfare. We cannot, in the present state of affairs,
> abandon them to the good intentions of an Arab government.[40]

In other words, the Commission did not trust the backward Arab majority to
rule over the progressive Jewish minority. Partitions and transfer participated
in the same logic as minority protection: the prevention of ethnic warfare.[41]
Modernization also played a key role in the option for partition:

---

[37] Quoted in Benny Morris, "Refabricating 1948," *Journal of Palestine Studies* 27, no. 2
(1998): 86. Also see Patrick Wolfe, "Purchase by Other Means: The Palestine *Nakba* and
Zionism's Conquest of Economics," *Settler Colonial Studies* 2, no. 1 (2012): 133–71.

[38] Sinanoglou, "The Peel Commission and Partition, 1936–1938."

[39] *Palestine Royal Commission Report 1937* (London: HM Stationary Office, 1937), 390.
Laila Parsons, "The Secret Testimony of the Peel Commission (Part I): Underbelly of
Empire," *Journal of Palestine Studies* 49, no. 1 (2019): 7–24.

[40] *Palestine Royal Commission Report 1937*, 141.

[41] Cf. Benny Morris, "Explaining Transfer: Zionist Thinking and the Creation of the
Palestinian Refugee Problem," in *Removing People: Forced Removal in the Modern*

Nor is it only a question of humanity. We have tried to show that the National Home is essentially a European institution, essentially modern, and, on its economic side especially, intimately linked with the outer world. We mean to imply no reflection on the natural ability of Arab leaders if we say that the National Home, with its peculiar and delicate economic constitution cannot prosper under a government which has had little experience of modern capitalism and is not fully acquainted with financial and commercial problems on a worldwide scale.[42]

The Commission had also been influenced by events in Europe and India: "The 'Minority Problem' has become only too familiar in recent years, whether in Europe or in Asia," it wrote. "It is one of the most troublesome and intractable products of post-war nationalism." For this reason, it concluded that "If ... the settlement is to be clean and final, this question of the minorities must be boldly faced and firmly dealt with. It calls for the highest statesmanship on the part of all concerned" – like the leaders of the Lausanne settlement, the report implied.[43]

As might be expected, many Zionists were excited by the transfer aspect of the report, as was the Polish government, which saw it as an opportunity for Jews to migrate from Poland.[44] The future prime minister of Israel, Levi Eshkol (1885–1969) – then called Shkolnik – had traveled to Greece in 1926 to study the exchange, writing at the time that it was "an enormous and interesting project" with lessons for the Zionist movement.[45] Also typical was scientist Kurt Mendelsohn of the Jewish Agency, who made his way to Greece to inspect the results of the exchange so as to urge its analogous benefits for the Palestine case. Writing in 1938 in a pamphlet called *The Balance of Resettlements: A Precedent for Palestine*, he took pains to counter the moral scruples about compulsory transfer. "The circumstances accompanying their realization or execution may indeed tend to obliterate the idea, or may even bear the stamp of inhumanity," he wrote, "but this is by no means

---

World, ed. Richard Bessel and Claudia Haake (Oxford University Press, Oxford, 2009), 349–60. The murderous attack on Jews in Hebron in 1929 shocked the Zionist leadership in Palestine, which commenced self-defense measures and pressed the mandate authorities for greater protection.

[42] *Palestine Royal Commission Report 1937*, 141. Victor Kattan, "The Empire Departs: The Partitions of British India, Mandate Palestine, and the Dawn of Self-Determination in the Third World," *Asian Journal of Middle Eastern and Islamic Studies* 12, no. 3 (2018): 304–27.

[43] Ibid., 390.

[44] Yossi Katz, "Transfer of Population as a Solution to International Disputes," *Political Geography* 11, no. 1 (1992): 55–72. On the Polish government's position, see Susan Pedersen, "The Impact of League Oversight on British Policy in Palestine," in Miller, *Britain, Palestine and Empire*, 57.

[45] Tom Segev, "The June 1967 War and the Palestinian Refugee Problem," *Journal of Palestine Studies* 36, no. 3 (2007): 9.

an inherent element." However strong the "impression of injustice, suffering and cruelty" associated with what he euphemistically called "the withdrawal of the Greeks from Anatolia," Mendelsohn stressed the "constructive and progressive features even in these difficult circumstances."[46] They were the familiar trinity of economic development, social reform, and international peace. Population transfer was linked to the end of reactionary social relations and to the onset of modernity. Of Lausanne, Mendelsohn wrote "Not until the unmixing of population and the creation of homogeneous States and territories, was the way cleared for the economic development of these countries, for the victory over feudalism, and for the social liberation of the peasants. Only with the exchange of population, and under the pressure of the exigencies of resettlement was this incubus of the past washed away."[47] He continued that the situation resembled the British settler colonies a century earlier, namely the combination of unused population reserves and empty land – all to the benefit of the indigenous Arab population of course.

Mendelsohn dealt with the compulsion question by acknowledging the suffering it caused: "Even if a resettling process is carried out as humanely as possible, with the greatest consideration for the individual and the group, the separation from what had hitherto been home will always be very painful to many and there are undoubtedly indications that a part of the old generation are not yet reconciled to their forced transfer," he conceded. Then comes the "but": "But it is as certain that the growing generation have taken firm root in their new country and have completely adapted themselves to the new conditions of life."[48] In making such arguments, these Zionists thinkers were hardly alone. They were only echoing Lord Curzon's (1859–1925) statement in 1923 that "the suffering entailed, great as it must be, would be repaid by the advantages which would ultimately accrue to both countries from a great homogeneity of population and from the removal of old and deep-rooted causes of quarrel."[49]

Now, for all that, few statesmen at the time were willing to publicly endorse the thorny issue of *compulsory* transfer; indeed, Curzon himself famously had huge misgivings about the Lausanne Convention. After all, the Greek-Turkish case had been a fait accompli thanks to Turkish expulsions. *Initiating* transfers to affect a partition was quite another matter, one that bore on the question of

---

[46] Kurt Mendelsohn, *The Balance of Resettlements: A Precedent for Palestine* (Leiden: A. W. Sijthoff's Uitgeversmaatschappij, N. V., 1939), 3.

[47] Ibid., 19.   [48] Mendelsohn, *The Balance of Resettlements*, 28.

[49] Lord Curzon, January 27, 1923, Lausanne Conference on Near Eastern Affairs, quoted in Michael Barutciski, "Lausanne Revisited: Population Exchanges in International Law and Policy," in *Crossing the Aegean: An Appraisal of the 1923 Compulsory Population Exchange between Greece and Turkey*, ed. Renée Hirschon (New York and Oxford: Berghahn Books, 2003), 29. A more balanced assessment can be found in J. R., "The Exchange of Minorities and Transfers of Population in Europe since 1919-I," *Bulletin of International News* 21, no. 15 (June 22, 1944): 579–88.

what we today call human rights. Even so, Reginald Coupland and Jewish Agency operatives were prepared to entertain this proposition because of the perceived long-term benefits to both parties, as the Greek-Turkish case had shown. Others, like Yosef Weitz (1890–1972), head of the Jewish National Fund's Land Department, preferred to devise incentives for Arabs to abandon their land, because he could not envisage any power to forcibly transfer the Arabs.[50] And, sure enough, the Foreign Office and Anthony Eden (1897–1977) rejected Coupland's plan as unfeasible, as they could not foresee imposing it upon the majority Arab population whose leaders made it clear that they were not going to be enticed to abandon their villages and fertile land for arid areas in the east on the promise of irrigation and development.[51]

The question of compulsion and repatriation as great power policy was placed on the table by Hitler and Nazi Germany's agreements with the Soviet Union and other European states to bring Germans "home into the Empire" (*heim ins Reich*). Europe could be stabilized by ending its minority problems.

> ... the whole of East and South-east Europe is interspersed with untenable splinters of the German nation. In this lies the reason for the continued disturbances between States. In this age of the nationality principle and the racial idea it is utopian to believe that members of superior race can simply be assimilated. It is therefore one of the tasks of a far-seeing regulation of European life to carry out resettlements in order thus to remove at least part of the causes of conflict in Europe.[52]

What was good for Europe could benefit the Middle East. The revisionist Zionist leader, Ze'ev Jabotinsky (1880–1940), who had opposed the partition and transfer recommendation of the Peel Commission because it entailed relinquishing significant parts of Palestine to the Arabs, softened his opposition to population exchanges in light of Germany and Italy's agreement about populations in South Tirol in 1939.[53] Likewise, as we will see, Hitler's

---

[50] Katz, "Transfer of Population as a Solution to International Disputes," 64–5.

[51] Roza I. M. El-Eini, *Mandated Landscapes: British Imperial Rule in Palestine, 1929–1948* (New York: Routledge, 2006), 367–8.

[52] Quotation in Wenzel Jaksch, "Mass Transfer of Minorities," *Socialist Commentary* (October 1944), 1–4. A different translation appears in J. R., "The Exchange of Minorities and Transfer of Population in Europe since 1919-II," *Bulletin of International News* 21, no. 17 (August 19, 1944): 658, and in Matthew Frank, *Expelling the Germans: British Opinion and Post-1945 Population Transfer in Context* (Oxford: Oxford University Press, 2007), 40.

[53] Joseph B. Schechtman's biography of Jabotinsky, *Fighter and Prophet: The Vladimir Jabotinsky Story, The Last Years* (New York and London, 1961), 325–6. Discussions of the vigorous Zionist debate on partition include Aaron S. Kleiman, "The Resolution of Conflicts through Territorial Partition: The Palestine Experience," *Comparative Studies in Society and History* 22, no. 2 (1980): 281–300, and Itzhak Galnoor, "The Zionist Debate on Partition (1919–1947)," *Israel Studies* 14, no. 2 (2009): 74–87.

reasoning was taken up by Beneš and the British Labour Party international relations expert and politician, Hugh Dalton (1887–1962), in the 1940s. Beneš and Dalton knew one another in London, as Dalton moved in exile circles, the Vansittartist convictions of which he shared.[54] A closer inspection of Beneš's views shows that he provided the template for reasoning about forced population expulsions, democracy, and human rights.

Human Rights and Transfer

What, then, was the relationship between human rights language and population transfer? In the early 1940s, Beneš was publishing in English-language journals to advocate "the transfer of populations" in view of the failed minority protection regime and the success of the Greek-Turkish exchange nearly 20 years before; it had prevented "a systematic mass murder of millions of people." Not only was it an exercise in atrocity prevention, and therefore humane, the praxis could also be humanized: "If the problem is carefully considered and wide measures are adopted in good time, the transfer can be made amicably under decent human conditions, under international control and with international support."[55] He elaborated his case in a well-known essay, "The Organization of Postwar Europe," published in that venerable journal, *Foreign Affairs*, whose editor was sympathetic to Beneš's views. A future democratic and federal Europe could no longer allow Germany to use its minorities in other countries as a fifth column to tyrannize their democratic majorities. What is more, Nazi crimes deserved punishment, and the German people as a whole were responsible for them as any people were responsible for its state's actions. Indeed, German minorities had become what he called an "international menace," and they should be transferred, though he disavowed "any method which involves brutality or violence." Presumably, this scruple was consistent with his reference to Hitler's precedent: "Hitler himself has transferred German minorities from the Baltic and from Bessarabia. Germany, therefore, cannot *a priori* regard it as an injury to her if other states adopt the same methods with regard to German minorities."[56] All these measures also entailed the modernization of the country, he added.

Dalton proposed Beneš's ideas as Labour Party policy, also invoking Hitler. "The German 'national minorities' were one of the plagues of Europe in the inter-war period," he wrote in a draft party report in 1943. "This time, the frontiers having been drawn, having regard to geographical and economic convenience, all minorities should be encouraged to join the national States to

---

[54] Frank, *Expelling the Germans*, 63–64.
[55] Eduard Beneš, "The New Order in Europe," *The Nineteenth Century*, no. 130 (September 1941): 154.
[56] Beneš, "The Organization of Postwar Europe," 227–8.

which they belong. In particular, all Germans left outside the post-war frontiers of Germany should be encouraged to 'go home to the Reich'": here he
consciously invoked Hitler's terminology, turning the Nazi logic against the
Germans.[57] Again, Lausanne was referred to as a successful precedent. Rather
than adjust borders to people, one should adjust populations to borders.
Consistently, the Labour Party and Dalton also supported transfer in
Palestine, although that did not become British government policy after the
war.[58]

How could these arguments be justified in terms of human rights? The
question is relevant because Beneš was a member of the *Institut du Droit
International* that in 1929 issued a declaration on the "international rights of
man," and in 1942 he himself wrote an article on "The Rights of Man and
International Law" that made a case for an international regime to promote
democracy as the postwar norm.[59] Democratic rights were human rights for
Beneš: "The protection of minorities in the future should consist primarily in
the defense of human democratic rights and not of national rights," he wrote.
The resulting stability, he was arguing, was the precondition to federal blocs of
democratic countries with progressive social policy dedicated to development.
"Human Rights must be constitutionally established throughout the world," he
declared, although they should not become an excuse to intervene capriciously
or opportunistically in the affairs of other countries.[60]

There is no contradiction between human rights and population expulsion,
as commonly supposed, because at this point human rights were to be
guaranteed primarily by the state and by an international organization like
the UN only as a last resort. The first priority was to establish the modern,
democratic, and homogeneous nation-state dedicated to human rights. The
expelled minorities' temporary suffering was for the greater good, and besides
they were collectively guilty. The UN can then host a human rights regime that
applies to all countries, rather than selectively like the interwar minorities
treaties; it can condemn the persecution of individuals as necessary, but
minorities as such would enjoy no collective rights. Beneš assured the international public that the "protection of the democratic and human rights of

---

[57] Frank, *Expelling the Germans*, 66.
[58] On British policy, see Wm. Roger Louis, *Ends of British Imperialism: The Scramble for
Empire, Suez and Decolonization* (London: I. B. Tauris, 2007).
[59] It is translated with a commentary by George A. Finch as "Declaration of the
International Rights of Man," *American Journal International Law* 35, no. 4 (1944):
662–5; Edward Beneš, "The Rights of Man and International Law," *Czechoslovak
Yearbook of International Law* (1942): 1–6. Background to the 1929 declaration can be
found in Jan Herman Burgers, "The Road to San Francisco: The Revival of the Human
Rights Idea in the Twentieth Century," *Human Rights Quarterly* 14 (1992): 447–77.
[60] Beneš, "The Organization of Postwar Europe," 237; Beneš, "Czechoslovakia's Struggle for
Freedom," *Dalhousie Review* 21 (October 1941): 259–72, esp. 269.

every citizen are guaranteed in Czechoslovakia forever," but retained a loophole for his expulsion program. Only those citizens could stay who had "remained faithful to the Republic, kept its laws and helped defend its independence" during the Nazi occupation, meaning that only those few Germans who joined the anti-Nazi resistance were safe. What is more, those who threatened what he called "Czechoslovak national tradition of humanitarian democracy" with the prospect of "a most serious civil war," namely the German and Hungarian minorities, could not be allowed to remain.[61] Individual human rights were selectively applied for the greater good of a new human rights order. At a material level, the redistribution of expellee property in Czechoslovakia promoted this modernization and democratization agenda.[62]

This was common reasoning at the time. Beneš's colleague, the Czechoslovak foreign minister in exile, Jan Masaryk, also saw no place for the German minority in the state when Nazi tyranny ended. The majority of ethnic Germans had welcomed the annexation of the "Sudetenland" and took on German citizenship. There would be a reckoning with them, he implied in 1943, when comparing the "liberation" of the country from Austro-Hungarian rule in 1918 with the coming liberation: whereas there was no "retribution" against the German oppressors, who had come as "settlers" hundreds of years earlier and taken over, after World War I, there would be retribution after World War II. The "minority problem shall be settled radically and with finality," he declared to his Jewish audience in London, for interests of economic, political, and religious "security."[63]

It was also no accident that other celebrated members of the *Institut du Droit International* advanced such arguments: Nicolas Politis, the Greek-French jurist and politician, and René Cassin, the French lawyer instrumental in the formulation of the UN's Universal Declaration of Human Rights. Politis

[61] Eduard Beneš, "Czechoslovakia Plans for Peace," *Foreign Affairs* 23, nos. 1–4 (1944–1945): 33, 35–6. Cf. Bruce R. Berglund, "'All Germans Are the Same': Czech and Sudeten German Exiles in Britain and the Transfer Plans," *National Identities* 2, no. 3 (2000): 225–44. Cf. Benjamin Frommer, *National Cleansing: Retribution against Nazi Collaborators in Postwar Czechoslovakia* (New York: Cambridge University Press, 2005); Tara Zahra, *Kidnapped Souls: National Indifference and the Battle for Children in the Bohemian Lands, 1900–1948* (Cambridge, MA: Harvard University Press, 2011), ch. 8.

[62] Paul J. Edwards, "The Trends of Law in Czechoslovakia," *Wisconsin Law Review*, no. 4 (1947): 671–2.

[63] Jan Masaryk, *Minorities and the Democratic State*, Lucien Wolf memorial lecture (Jewish Historical Society of England, 1943), 19–20. On the Jewish question in Czechoslovakia, see Jan Láníček, *Czechs, Slovaks and the Jews, 1938–48: Beyond Idealisation and Condemnation* (Basingstoke: Palgrave Macmillan, 2012); Livia Rothkirchen, *The Jews of Bohemia and Moravia: Facing the Holocaust* (Lincoln: University of Nebraska Press, 2012).

also incarnated the easy reconciliation of liberalism, internationalism, and population transfers. A highly regarded proponent of "international morality," the "juridical conscience," collective security and arbitration, Politis was at the vanguard of the League's mission to convert diplomacy from force to law. Reform, whether at home or abroad, required stability, and because minorities led to instability, he shared the policy of liberal Greek governments to homogenize the non-Greek populations gained with northern territory won in the Balkan Wars of 1912–1913. He drafted the treaty with Bulgaria after World War I to voluntarily exchange populations and the compulsory population exchange with Turkey soon thereafter, which he regarded as a raging success for reducing the minority population, increasing the overall population and cereal production. Writing in 1940 soon after Nazi Germany had commenced extensive population exchanges with neighboring states, he commended the policy with striking candor to his French audience. Minority agitation had destabilized Europe, he declared, agreeing with Hitler. He was equally candid that compulsory exchange was inconsistent with "humanity" but, like other transfer proponents, stressed the long-term benefits. Significant was his invocation of human rights. "International human rights," he assured, "will one day be a valid rule for all States, without any exception." But not yet. First national and international "health" had to be achieved, by which he meant national homogeneity to guarantee stability. "Surgery" was required to effect continental recovery. "It is a painful operation, but it is true of all operations," he conceded; the gain, however, should not be "arrested by false feelings," a distorted sentimentalism.[64]

Cassin argued in similar terms in relation to Zionism and Palestine. At the same time as he advocated human rights at the UN in 1947, he led the French *Alliance Israélite Universelle* campaign for the UN's partition of Palestine in 1947, a marked change from its French republican prewar hostility to a Jewish state or nation. Jewish national rights trumped Palestinian ones – Arabs were not mentioned by name in the memo he wrote, "On the Palestine Problem." Again there was no contradiction in his mind between his agendas because the benefits of the new order would justify the means of its establishment, in this case Jewish settlers acting as the vehicle of democracy in the darkness of the orient: "the democratic hope in the Near East can only progress under the influence of the Jewish ambition in Palestine," he wrote. The establishment

---

[64] Nicolas Politis, "Le transfert des populations," *Politique étrangère* 5, no. 2 (1940): 93–4; Robert Kolb, "Politis and Sociological Jurisprudence of Inter-War International Law," *European Journal of International Law* 23 no. (2012): 239; Marilena Papadaki, "The 'Government Intellectuals': Nicolas Politis – An Intellectual Portrait," *European Journal of International Law* 23 no. (2012), 221–31; Umut Özsu, "Politis and the Limits of Legal Form," *European Journal of International Law* 23 no. (2012): 243–53.

of Israel, Cassin was suggesting, would at once alleviate the Jewish refugee crisis in Europe and inaugurate a human rights order in a part of the world run by what he called the "thieving and bloody indigenous masters" of Jewish minorities in the Middle East, namely the Arabs who he saw as oppressors of Jewish minorities in North Africa.[65]

Arab human rights were entirely consistent with their denationalization. As Chaim Weizmann had argued a few years before, despite the fact that Jews "will control their own immigration" in their future state, and cease "to be a minority dependent on the will and pleasure of other nations," all citizens will enjoy "complete civil and political equality of rights ... without distinction of race or religion, and, in addition, the Arabs will enjoy full autonomy of their own internal affairs."[66] In this mode, human rights did not trump minority rights; here they trumped Arab *majority* rights. In the worldview making human rights a marker of democracy, dangerous and/or backward peoples like German minorities and Arab majorities had to make way for the progressive and modern nation-state led by civilized titular minorities or majorities. The right to self-determination did not belong to defeated Axis powers and their supporters. The Palestinians, Weizmann said, were after all supporters of the Axis Powers. And as the Peel Commission had determined, they were most definitely not modern. These assumptions also underlay the Programme for Peace produced by the Committee on Peace Aims of the New Zealand League of Nations Union in 1942. Chaired by Professor Julius Stone (1907–1985) of the University of Sydney, it advocated "large-scale settlement" of the persecuted "Jewish people in central and eastern Europe" to Palestine and elsewhere "in conformity with the dictates of humanity," although Stone opposed Beneš's transfer notions because it implied a mono-national state. His main target was Britain's 1939 White Paper that restricted Jewish migration to Palestine.[67]

---

[65] René Cassin, "Mémorandum de l'AIU sur le problème palestinien," June 9, 1947, 3, Alliance Israélite Universelle Archive, Paris, AM Présidence 030. The second quotation is taken from Jay Winter, "René Cassin and the Alliance Israélite Universelle," *Modern Judaism* 32, no. 1 (2012): 16.

[66] Chaim Weizmann, "Palestine's Role in the Solution of the Jewish Problem," *Foreign Affairs* 20, nos. 1–4 (1941/42): 337. He immediately added that "if any Arabs do not wish to remain in a Jewish state, every facility will be given to them to transfer to one of the many and vast Arab countries."

[67] Julius Stone, *The Atlantic Charter: New Worlds for Old* (Sydney and London: Angus and Robertson, 1943), 134, 78–9. Like many of his generation, Stone was a proponent of the minorities treaties before becoming a partisan of Israel: Stone, *International Guarantees of Minority Rights: Procedure of the Council of the League of Nations in Theory and Practice* (London: Oxford University Press, 1932); Stone, "Behind the Cease-Fire Lines: Israel's Administration in Gaza and the West Bank," in *Of Law and Men: Essays in Honor of Haim M. Cohn*, ed. Shlomo Shoham (New York: Sabra Books, 1971), 79–110; Stone,

The discursive link between Europe, Palestine, and India was also provided by the Lithuanian Jewish jurist, Jacob Robinson, who we encountered in Chapters 3 and 4. That he was a major Jewish thinker of the global order and the place of Jews in it was evident in his various positions. Until 1948, he acted as a special consultant for Jewish affairs to the US chief of counsel at the Nuremberg Trials, and as a consultant to the UN Secretariat in the establishment of the Human Rights Commission.[68] The Jewish Agency appointed him a legal advisor when the Palestine question came before the UN, and in 1948 he entered the service of the new State of Israel. Later, he was the author of a bitter polemic against Hannah Arendt's *Eichmann in Jerusalem*.[69]

Like many European Jewish lawyers of his generation, he was a proponent of the minority protection treaty regime that sought to safeguard Jewish and other minorities after World War I. His eventual embrace of population expulsion as well as human rights and, if we may use the term anachronistically, Holocaust consciousness, combines in one person the fundaments of the postwar international order and its memory regime. By 1943, he had largely abandoned his faith in the minority protection regime and saw the future of the surviving European Jews in the mass colonization of Palestine.[70] Debates within the World Jewish Congress show that most Jewish leaders disagreed with his Palestine exclusivism and advocated continuing protection for Jewish rights in the diaspora. There was some alarm at Beneš's transfer and anti-minority position at a time when German authorities were deporting Jewish minorities to "the east," so assurances were sought from him that he did not mean to expel Jews from Czechoslovakia.[71] They were less consequential than Jabotinsky, who by 1939 concluded that deporting Palestinian Arabs was the only solution to Jewish demographic challenges, now supporting the terms of the Peel Commission and the precedent of the Turkish-Greek population exchange.[72] Robinson split the difference between the Congress and Jabotinsky with an ingenious argument. In an article about "Minorities in a

---

Israel and Palestine: Assault on the Law of Nations (Baltimore: Johns Hopkins University Press, 1981).

[68] Omry K. Feuerstein, "Geschichterfahrung und Völkerrecht: Jacob Robinson und die Gründung des Institute of Jewish Affairs," *Leipziger Beiträge* 2 (2004): 307–30; Mark A. Lewis, "The World Jewish Congress and the Institute for International Affairs at Nuremberg: Ideas, Strategies, and Political Goals, 1942–1946," *Yad Vashem Studies* 36, no. 1 (2008): 181–210.

[69] Jacob Robinson, *And the Crooked Shall Be Made Straight* (Philadelphia: Jewish Publication Society of America, 1965).

[70] Jacob Robinson, "Uprooted Jews in the Immediate Postwar World," *International Conciliation* 21 (1942–1943): 291–310.

[71] Gil S. Rubin, "The End of Minority Rights: Jacob Robinson and the Minority Question in World War II," *Jahrbuch des Simon-Dubnow-Instituts* 11 (2012): 55–72.

[72] Gil S. Rubin, "Vladimir Jabotinsky and the Population Transfers," *The Historical Journal* 62, no. 2 (2019): 495–517.

New World" in 1943, he criticized the tendency to condemn all minorities as "vicious fifth columns who contributed to the downfall and ruin of their states." Adopting the tone of moderation and reasonableness, he argued that distinctions needed to be made between irredentist minorities and those that reconciled themselves to their minority status, as he did not think the League of Nations minorities rights system had abjectly failed. If it had weaknesses, that was due to *"Those groups which permitted themselves to be used as tools for the disruptive plans of their powerful co-nationals."*[73] German minorities were the worst of irredentist minorities, while Jewish minorities were a model minority who did not cause problems for their host state. They could stay.

Now, he continued, the need was to look at what he called "specific danger zones where this problem is of special importance, regions like Central-Eastern Europe, India, and others." The post-World War I period offered two solutions to the problem, namely transfer and minority protection. And now some new special provisions included "guarantees of human rights."[74] But he doubted the efficacy of any human and minority rights; after all, the minority protection treaties had not saved the Jews, and nor likely would human rights declarations. He drew the following conclusion: "Realistically, therefore, we must envisage ... the transfer of populations" in these danger zones.

Regarding the coercion question, he admitted that "Of course, the humanitarian aspect cannot be neglected, and hardship must certainly be avoided, or at least reduced. Moreover, it is certainly undemocratic to force a person to emigrate against his will." Like commentators since Lausanne 20 years earlier, he immediately qualified this humanitarian sensibility and theodicy of the future pay-off with a sentence beginning with "but":

> But after all, the peace of Europe and the world is of greater importance than adherence to certain procedures for the protection of minorities ....
> If it is well established that both the state and the minority will otherwise remain dissatisfied, why not – with all necessary safeguards against hardships and with guarantees for the property of transferred – remove the reasons for the perpetuation of hatred and dissension?[75]

By 1947, Robinson had embraced the coming human rights regime because it meant that what he called "militant Fascist minorities" could not appeal as collectives to an international body against the democratic majority, an

---

[73] Jacob Robinson, et al., *Were the Minorities Treaties a Failure?* (New York: Institute of Jewish Affairs, 1943), 260. Emphasis in original.
[74] Jacob Robinson, "Minorities in a Free World," *Free World* 5, no. 5 (May 1943): 450–4.
[75] Ibid., 453.

argument made by Beneš before him.[76] Indeed, he cited Beneš as the "prophet" of population homogeneity and progress, noting that population transfer enabled the "liberated peoples to destroy the last vestiges of Nazism and Fascism and to create democratic institutions of their own choice. This is the principle of the Atlantic Charter," he added, "the right of all peoples to choose the form of government under which they live – the restoration of sovereign right and self-government to those people who had been forcibly deprived of them by the aggressor nations." Henceforth, they could "form interim governmental authorities broadly representative of all democratic elements in the population." Human rights, then, depended on the ability to create what "conditions of stability and well-being which are necessary for peaceful and friendly relations among nations." And such conditions entailed mobilizing what he called "all democratic elements in the population" against the irredentist, fascist ones.[77] That is why Churchill had said the Atlantic Charter norms did not apply to the Axis Powers, and why the Allies were able to ignore the minorities protection treaties when agreeing to expel the Germans at their Potsdam meeting in August 1945.[78] For all his modifications, Robinson followed Beneš in making human rights a license to expel. Writing that year, Hans Morgenthau declared the stabilizing formula to be "partition and repatriation."[79]

Robinson apparently did not write much about Palestine until he was appointed by the Jewish Agency to represent its case in the UN in 1947. The figure who connected the dots between partition, transfer, and human rights in the Middle East was Joseph Schechtman (1891–1970), long cited as the authority on population exchanges. Recent scholarship has reminded us that he was a Russian-born revisionist Zionist, indeed a biographer of Jabotinsky, with a personal investment in the subject.[80] Early in the 1940s, he was employed by Robinson at the Institute for Jewish Affairs to write about the German expulsions and colonization in Europe.[81] Subsequently, in 1949, he

---

[76] Cf. Joseph B. Schechtman, "Decline of International Minority Protection," *Western Political Quarterly* 4, no. 1 (1951): 2.

[77] Jacob Robinson, "From Protection of Minorities to Promotion of Human Rights," *Jewish Yearbook of International Law* 1 (1949): 137–41. This article was likely written in 1947.

[78] E/CN.4/367, Commission on Human Rights, sixth session, 7 April 1950, "Study of the Legal Validity of the Undertaking Concerning Minorities Treaties," 60.

[79] Hans Morgenthau, *Germany Our Problem* (New York: Harper & Brothers Publishers, 1945), 160.

[80] Nur Masalha, "From Propaganda to Scholarship: Dr. Joseph Schechtman and the Origins of the Israeli Polemics on the Palestinian Refugees," *Holy Land Studies* 2 (2002): 188–97; Mazower, *No Enchanted Palace*, 117–23; Antonio Ferrara, "Eugene Kulischer, Joseph Schechtman and the Historiography of European Forced Migrations," *Journal of Contemporary History* 46, no. 4 (2011): 715–40.

[81] Ferrara, "Eugene Kulischer, Joseph Schechtman and the Historiography of European Forced Migrations."

was engaged by the State of Israel to justify the expulsion of Palestinian Arabs and the refusal to allow their return.[82]

Impressively industrious, Schechtman published his book *Population Transfers in Asia* in 1949, covering South Asia and the Middle East. Of the former, he wrote that "Both Pakistan and Indian leaders . . . stubbornly refused to accept the exchange of population as a bitter but inevitable necessity and to conduct it in a constructive way" and, in the last section of the book, he made a case for an exchange of Jewish and Arab populations in the Middle East: Jews in Arab countries going to Israel and Arabs in Palestine replacing them in other parts of the Middle East. Partition by itself was insufficient there, he argued. For "The minority problem, which is a question of life and death for the success of any constructive scheme for Palestine," he wrote, "cannot be solved without resorting to what Beneš called 'the grim necessity of transfer'."[83] Using the same arguments as Robinson, Schechtman was effectively saying that the Arabs were an irredentist minority – or rather majority – for their inexplicably stubborn refusal to be reduced to minority status in a majority Jewish Palestine.[84]

Norman Bentwich, now at the Hebrew University, agreed. Also writing in 1949 in the wake of the Palestine refugee crisis, he regarded the massive population transfers in India's partition as a successful precedent. Referring to the Palestinian refugees, he insisted that "Some large transfer of population was inevitable, and it offered the most humane as well as the most realistic solution," as well as ending what he termed "stagnation in that part of the world" by enabling the foundation of Israel in terms reminiscent of Cassin's memo two years before. They should be resettled, he concluded, like the refugees of Indian partition, and thereby halt the "enmities in what has been for thirty years one of the danger spots of the world." In a few sentences, he repeated the well-worn arguments for transfer since Lausanne: atrocity prevention and material progress. And like Cassin and Weizmann, he asserted that the self-determination of Jews in their ancestral homeland would benefit all. The Arabs could not return, he added, now that their houses had been occupied by Jewish refugees from Europe; again resorting to analogy, he

---

[82] Rafael Medoff, *Militant Zionism in America: The Rise and Impact of the Jabotinsky Movement in the United States, 1926-1948* (Tuscaloosa: University of Alabama Press, 2002), 214–5.

[83] Joseph B. Schechtman, *Population Transfers in Asia* (New York: Hallsby Press, 1949), 86. There is no footnote for this quotation, but we know he was quoting Beneš, "Speech at the Foreign Press Association, London, 28 April 1942," in Holborn, *War and Peace Aims of the United Nations*, 427–28. Cf. Masalha, "From Propaganda to Scholarship"; Ferrara, "Eugene Kulischer, Joseph Schechtman and the Historiography of European Forced Migrations."

[84] Morris makes the point that in the 1930s Zionist leaders had adjudged a future Palestinian minority to be irredentist: Morris, "Explaining Transfer," 353.

observed that their position resembled those of the Orthodox Greeks driven from Turkey into Macedonia in 1922.[85]

The 1948 conflict between Zionist and Arab forces provided the opportunity for forced transfer that was missing after the Peel Commission a decade earlier. Presciently, a year before, in 1947, in an unpublished memo, Robinson had warned Zionists that India's planned partition offered no model for Palestine because South Asia was what he called "static" whereas Palestine was still a "dynamic" situation.[86] The message of his guarded prose is not difficult to decipher. "Dynamic" was the term that Zionists like Mendelsohn used to depict Palestine's malleable demography: "not only to consider mechanically the present relative strength in the number of the two populations but the differences in their economic quality and in their potentialities," by which he meant "not only the actual but probable number of immigrants, the country's absorptive capacity and the scarcity of settlers in the neighbouring countries."[87] The problem with the Indian case – Robinson was writing before the population expulsions in the second half of 1947 – was that it left large minorities in India and Pakistan; no population exchanges were envisaged by the Muslim League and Congress leaders, and nor were provisions made for their protection – that is why it was a static situation. In view of his earlier advocacy of transfer in "danger zones," it is fair to suppose that he was implying that transfer was still on the cards in Palestine, and he was right.

These mainstream Zionist views were likely shared by Lemkin who, as we know from Chapter 3, advocated for Jewish migration and state formation in Palestine. Like Lauterpacht and other political Zionists covered in this chapter, he was well disposed to the British Empire as a vehicle for civilizational development, meaning the rule of law and protection of small nations, above all Jews. Such protection did not extend to granting independence to groups like Palestinian Arabs who were not considered sufficiently developed to qualify as "nations." Settler colonialism under the aegis of liberal empire was the vehicle of civilizational progress. The reading Lemkin undertook after the war equipped him with a scientific theory of cultural change to accompany the hierarchies that international lawyers deployed in categorizing societies. Drawing on fellow Pole, anthropologist Bronislaw Malinowski (1884–1942) in particular, Lemkin favored what he called "cultural diffusion" via intercultural exchange: more powerful societies induced weaker societies to adopt their institutions because they better fulfill basic needs. "Diffusion is gradual and relatively spontaneous," he wrote, "although it may lead to the eventual

[85] Norman Bentwich, "The Arab Refugees," *Contemporary Review*, no. 176 (1949): 81–2.
[86] Jacob Robinson, "Partition of India: Implications for Palestine," Confidential Memo #24, 1947, Central Zionist Archive, S25\9029.
[87] Mendelsohn, *Balance of Resettlements*, 30.

disintegration of a weak culture."[88] The governing technique of an empire that promoted diffusion was "indirect rule," Malinowski argued, because it supposedly enabled the autonomous indigenous acquisition of European institutions.[89] Accordingly, Lemkin concluded that "The rise and fall of civilizations have been explained on this general basis."[90] Consistent with these assumptions, he approved of indirect rule in which each people were embedded in its historical homeland, following Malinowki's arguments, which were themselves influenced by Lugard's famous book, *The Dual Mandate in British Tropical Africa*, the manifesto of indirect rule discussed in Chapter 2.[91] When indigenous people were massacred or exploited in British colonies, Lemkin did not hold responsible British authorities and the empire they served: unruly settlers were to blame.[92] It is no accident that he pointed to elite rather than to peasant culture when describing the contributions of nations to the human cosmos. He was more disturbed by occupations in anti-British empires governed by Muslims and Germans.[93]

Conclusion

What then of the relationship between these partitions, transfer, minorities, and the question of refugees? A common misunderstanding is that the British imposed partition on India and Palestine with a perfidious imperial policy of "divide and quit." In fact, they referred the Palestine mandate to the UN in part because they were unwilling to impose partition on the Palestinian majority, and because the Zionists had commenced a violent uprising against

[88] Raphael Lemkin, "The Concept of Genocide in Anthropology," New York Public Library, Lemkin Collection, Box 2, Folder 2.

[89] Paul T. Cocks, "The King and I: Bronislaw Malinowski, King Sobhuza II of Swaziland and the Vision of Culture Change in Africa," *History of the Human Sciences* 13, no. 4 (2000): 25–47.

[90] Lemkin, "The Concept of Genocide in Anthropology." He cited Bronislaw Malinowski, *A Scientific Theory of Culture and Other Essays* (Chapel Hill: University of North Carolina Press, 1944); Arthur Toynbee, *A Study of History* (London: Oxford University Press, 1947); Ruth Benedict, *Patterns of Culture* (London: George Routledge, 1935); Leo Louis Snyder, *Race: A History of Modern Ethnic Theories* (New York: Longmans, Green and Co., 1939); and Herbert J. Seligmann, *Race against Man* (New York: G. P. Putnam's Sons, 1939).

[91] Frederick D. Lugard, *The Dual Mandate in British Tropical Africa* (Edinburgh and London: William Blackwood and Sons, 1922), 223; George W. Stocking, "Maclay, Kubary, Malinowski," in *Colonial Situations: Essays on the Contextualization of Ethnographic Knowledge*, ed. George W. Stocking (Madison: University of Wisconsin Press, 1991), 53.

[92] Raphael Lemkin, "Tasmanian" *Patterns of Prejudice* 39, no. 2 (2005): 170–96.

[93] Raphael Lemkin, "The Germans in Africa," American Jewish Archives, Collection 60, Box 6, Folder 9.

its plan to hand over the state to that majority as set out in the White Paper of 1939. The British only reluctantly resorted to partition in India when they could not convince the contending parties to sign off on the Cabinet Mission's federal solution in 1946. Leo Amery (1883–1955), the Secretary of State for India, asked Reginald Coupland, the English architect of the abandoned 1937 Palestine partition proposal, in late 1940 to write a study of the problem.[94] This time he opposed partition because he did not think population exchanges were viable in the Indian case; the numbers were far too large for the "clean cut" envisaged by such a policy (in the next chapter, we will see that Indian actors disagreed).[95] In the end, only the partition of Germany's 1937 borders and population transfers were supported by the British, and even then they were taken aback by the extent and vehemence of the expulsions. Given the wild cleansings and Soviet annexation of eastern Poland, the British and Americans were presented with a fait accompli, as were the Greeks and League of Nations in 1922 and 1923 when the Turks expelled its Orthodox population. It was far from the "orderly and humane" procedure that the Potsdam Agreement had licensed.

In effect, the UN Palestine partition plan and the partition of India were closer to the League of Nations model of statehood: new states with large minorities and no population exchanges, though now without minority protection. While the British favored national homogeneity in Central and Eastern Europe, they entreated heterogeneous federations in South Asia and the Middle East that would allow them to retain the residual imperial presence they deemed essential to their global security strategy. This time, however, in India and Palestine, nationalists on each side prevailed on the ground, or rather the civil war broke out that the British had feared all along, and in which they did not wish to become embroiled. The 1923-style refugee exchange fait accompli occurred in India as well, sanctioned after the fact by the two new states in 1950. That it has not been so sanctioned in Palestine – namely, that the Palestinian refugee issue remains on the international table – vexes those today who, like Schechtman and Bentwich in 1949, assert that a Lausanne-style retrospective blessing of transfer should occur.[96]

---

[94] On Coupland, see Arie Dubnov, "The Architect of Two Partitions or a Federalist Daydreamer? The Curious Case of Reginald Coupland," in *Partitions: A Transnational History of 20th Century Territorial Separatism*, ed. Arie M. Dubnov and Laura Robson (Stanford, CA: Stanford University Press, 2019), 56–84.

[95] Reginald Coupland, *India: A Re-Statement* (London: Oxford University Press, 1945), 263; T. G. Fraser, "Sir Reginald Coupland, the Round Table and the Problem of Divided Societies," in *The Round Table, the Empire/Commonwealth, and British Foreign Policy*, ed. Andrew Bosco and Alex May (London: Lothian Foundation Press, 1997), 413–4.

[96] Adelman and Barkan, *No Return, No Refuge.* They ignore the minimum requirements for consensus identified by Dimitri Pentzopoulos, *The Balkan Exchange of Minorities and Its Impact upon Greece* (Paris and The Hague: Mouton & Co, 1962), 248–52. First, the

Why it has not occurred is part of the later story of human rights as well as of self-determination and its roots in the assumption of the new world order that all peoples should be housed in their national homeland. The logic of homeland belonging and self-determination claimed by Zionists could be easily utilized by Palestinians as well, after all. As time passed, Palestinians and their supporters dislodged human rights from its nesting in the nation-state and claimed it as an abstract norm to protest their treatment – or to make self-determination a human right. Thus in 1961, in his debate with the Israeli foreign minister, historian Arnold Toynbee said "I submit that the human rights of the native inhabitants of a country have an absolute priority over all other claims upon that country, and that these overriding rights are not forfeited if the native inhabitants are dispossessed of their homes and property." By paying the price for Germany's genocide of the Jews – that is, expulsion from their country – he concluded, "The Palestinian Arabs have, in fact, been treated as if they did not have human rights."[97]

The roots of this abstraction can be found much earlier, however – before and during the expulsions. In 1944, the Sudeten German Social Democrat leader Wenzel Jaksch (1896–1966) had warned that the "transfer can only be effected if the victorious Powers are resolved to disregard human rights."[98] Contemporaries linked these measures to the illiberal permanent security measures of the defeated and disgraced Nazis. Based at Harvard University, Italian leftist Gaetano Salvemini (1873–1957), deplored the spread of what he called the "Nazi mentality ... thanks to the moral degradation brought about by war." He argued for a supranational board to protect minorities; indeed, he urged that a supranational police force occupy the kind of danger zones identified by Robinson.[99] The Johns Hopkins University political geographer, sometime State Department advisor, and antisemite, Isaiah Bowman (1878–1950) tried to dissuade Eleanor Roosevelt (1884–1962) from her Zionism by noting similar parallels. It would not be in the US's interest if it were perceived "by enemies of the Jews that they have drawn us into a distinct

---

affected countries should both accept the exchange; second, the exchange must be carried out under international supervision; third, economic compensation must be provided for the refugees; and fourth, there must be an effective management to accommodate, feed, and integrate the refugees into the new society. Thanks to Volker Prott for this reference. See his *The Politics of Self-Determination*.

[97] Arnold Toynbee, "Jewish Rights in Palestine," *Jewish Quarterly Review*, n.s., 52, no. 1 (1961): 1–11.

[98] Jaksch, "Mass Transfer of Minorities," 4.

[99] Gaetano Salvemini, "The Frontiers of Italy," *Foreign Affairs* 23, nos. 1–4 (1944–1945): 58; Salvemini, "Wanted: A Policy for Europe's 'Cooling Period'," *Antioch Review* 2, no. 4 (1942): 511–35. Generally: Matthew Frank, "The New Morality: Victor Gollancz, 'Save Europe Now' and the German Refugee Crisis, 1945–46," *Twentieth Century British History* 17, no. 2 (2006): 230–56.

quarrel on a basis that is difficult to distinguish from Hitler's *Lebensraum*. This may seem like a harsh characterization. But is it not true? Is it not putting power behind a nationalist program in such a way as to take away land occupied by one people and give it to another."[100] At the same time, however, he told the State Department's Political Subcommittee in 1942 that one could deport the Germans: "people were getting used to the idea of moving minorities because Hitler had carried the process so far."[101] Writer George Orwell (1903–1950), publisher Victor Gollancz (1893–1967), and other prominent commentators like the Lord Bishop of Chichester (1883–1958) similarly deplored the deportation of Germans on the grounds that Nazis had used such methods. The latter summed up the position when he declared in the House of Lords in January 1946 that the deportation "involves a denial of human rights and it is extremely difficult to see how to distinguish it in principle from the mass deportations of civilian populations for which the National Socialist leaders are now on trial as a war crime at Nuremburg."[102]

Like the bishop, Bertrand Russell (1872–1970) connected the trials of Germans for wartime deportations with the contemporary Allies' policy towards the Germans, even accusing them all of "extermination." He asked: "Are mass expulsions crimes when committed by our enemies and justifiable measures of social adjustment when carried out by our allies in times of peace?"[103] The answer was that such liberal permanent security measures were indeed justifiable for the Allies because they were necessary to institutionalize the ideals for which they were fighting the Nazis.[104] As the émigré

---

[100] Neil Smith, *American Empire: Roosevelt's Geographer and the Prelude to Globalization* (Berkeley and Los Angeles: University of California Press, 2003), 306. Bowman's anti-semitism is discussed in James Loeffler, "'The Conscience of America': Human Rights, Jewish Politics, and American Foreign Policy at the 1945 United Nations San Francisco Conference," *Journal of American History* 100, no. 2 (2013): 419–20.

[101] Political Subcommittee Chronological Minutes, Meeting 2, March 14, 1942, Box 55, 17. Harley Notter Files, Record Group 59, NARA. Thanks to Stephen Wertheim for sharing this material.

[102] House of Lords Debates on "Mass Transfer of Germans," January 30, 1946, vol. 139, cc68–90. This was a common critique at the time from many quarters, such as the New York academic, Oscar I. Janowsky, *Nationalities and National Minorities* (New York: MacMillan, 1945), xii: "Moreover, while population transfers, if humanely administered, might prove expedient in limited areas, so drastic a remedy cannot be applied to the millions of minorities without resorting to some of the savage ways of the Nazis."

[103] Bertrand Russell, letter to the editor, "Mass Deportations," *The Times*, October 23, 1945, 5.

[104] This is the answer to the hypocrisy argument advanced by Alfred M. de Zayas, "International Law and Mass Population Transfers," *Harvard International Law Journal* 16, no. 2 (1975): 207–58, and Timothy William Waters, "Remembering Sudetenland: On the Legal Construction of Ethnic Cleansing," *Vanderbildt Journal of International Law* 47, no. 1 (2006): 63–145. Authors who criticize the Allies for violating the laws of belligerent occupation ignore the point that the Allies did not regard

Harvard historian, Fritz T. Epstein (1898–1979), noted, "The transfer solution, in spite of its utter disregard for human rights, is regarded more and more as the only possible way out."[105]

The "human rights revolution" was ultimately a mixed-blessing for the Palestinians. For while Arab governments successfully insisted that the right to "return to his country" be included in Article 13 during of the UN Declaration of Human Rights,[106] and the Fourth Geneva Convention prohibited "individual or mass forcible transfer ... regardless of their motive,"[107] it came a year too late for Palestinians. Moreover, the Refugee Convention of 1951 gestured primarily to the plight of European refugees whose imperative was the granting of asylum elsewhere rather than right of return, though Arab governments were able to water down Cassin's attempt to enshrine the right to asylum with a lesser right to "seek and enjoy" it.[108] German advocates of those expelled from Central and Eastern Europe argued in similar terms, invoking a right of return and of homeland, though without legal effect.[109] Likewise, the UN General Assembly's resolution 194 of December 11, 1948, for the return of Palestinian refugees has no standing in international law and has proven impotent even though it was hardly an unqualified approval of mass repatriation: it made any return contingent upon the refugees' acceptance of the new State of Israel (i.e., no longer constitute an irredentist entity).[110]

Arab commentators, like the Secretary of the Arab League, Edward Atiyah (1903–1964), had conceded that Jewish displaced persons (DPs) possessed "a human and moral right against the whole civilised world," but not a right to asylum in Palestine where they would come as settlers to overwhelm or displace the indigenous Arabs – as Weizman, Bentwich, and Cassin always intended. Accordingly, he argued that the DPs should be granted asylum "on an international basis, by all the countries of the UN opening their

themselves as occupying sovereign territory but of enjoying all the attributes of sovereignty in their occupation because Nazi Germany was an illegitimate regime. That is why ignoring minority protection treaties and norms was legally possible.

[105] Fritz T. Epstein, "Recent Literature on Minorities," New Europe 4 (July–August 1944): 29.

[106] Mary Ann Glendon, A World Made New: Eleanor Roosevelt and the Universal Declaration of Human Rights (New York: Random House, 2001), 153.

[107] International Committee of the Red Cross, Convention (IV), Protection of Civilian Persons in Time of War, August 12, 1949, http://www.icrc.org/ihl.nsf/WebART/380-600056.

[108] G. Daniel Cohen, In War's Wake: Europe's Displaced Persons in the Postwar Order (Oxford: Oxford University Press, 2012), 21.

[109] Lora Wildenthal, "Rudolf Laun and the Human Rights of Germans in Occupied and Early West Germany," in Hoffman, Human Rights in the Twentieth Century, 125–44.

[110] UNGA Resolution 194 (III), December 11, 1948.

doors to them in proportion to their resources and absorptive capacities."[111] Atiyah's main point, though, was to contest the UN's decision to partition Palestine, a decision in which the plight of the DPs had played a large role. The right of indigenous people to resist the settler would not prevail for the reasons Coupland had set out in his shelved report of 1937. Zionist advocates had supplied it to the UN delegates, but it is difficult to say whether Coupland's arguments swayed them; certainly, however, Coupland thought that the UN partition recommendation endorsed his ideas.[112] We do know that, in June 1948, Moshe Sharett (1894–1965), Israel's future foreign minister and prime minister, told an interim government meeting that the flight of Palestinian Arabs resembled the expulsion of Germans from Czechoslovakia as well as the earlier, omnipresent Lausanne precedent. He concluded with a statement that summarized the basis of the postwar order: "they are not coming back . . . they need to get used to the idea that this [a possible return] is a lost cause and this is a change that cannot be undone."[113] Indeed, the process continued. Israeli politicians and officials concocted many plans to induce Palestinians in newly occupied territory – whether Gaza or the West Bank – to leave. In 1967, flush with victory in the Six Day War, David Ben-Gurion and Levi Eshkol told the Israeli Cabinet that Lausanne was a model for the dilemma of new Palestinian refugees now under their control, as did many Israeli citizens who wrote to Eshkol urging expulsion to Arab countries in the spirit of a population exchange.[114] Liberal permanent security measures could not be reversed without unravelling the postwar order and its vaunted human rights revolution..

---

[111] Edward Atiyah, "Palestine," *Contemporary Review*, no. 174 (1948): 7.

[112] Fraser, "Sir Reginald Coupland, the Round Table and the Problem of Divided Societies," 417. Abba Eban reports thus on his meeting with Coupland whom he visited in Oxford; Eban, *An Autobiography* (London: Weidenfeld and Nicolson, 1978), 85.

[113] Eban cited in Alon Confino, "Miracles and Snow in Palestine and Israel: Tantura, a History of 1948," *Israel Studies* 17, no. 2 (2012): 42–3. Cf. Abba Eban, *How to Solve the Arab Refugee Problem* (New York: Israel Office of Information, 1957).

[114] Segev, "The June 1967 War and the Palestinian Refugee Problem," 7, 9.

9

Imagining Nation-Security in South Asia and Palestine

Partition, Population Exchange, and Communal Hostages

Imperial elites were not the only ones to imagine geopolitical security after World War II. As we saw in the last chapter, Zionist and Czechoslovak ones hitched their carts to Western – and, in the Czechoslovak case, also Soviet – designs for the postwar order. Needless to say, South Asian and Palestinian leaders and thinkers also planned for a post-imperial future. They too tried to forge national self-determination by constructing ethnic homogeneity or guaranteeing ethnic dominance over minorities: these were the only guarantee of permanent security. We know that the modalities for such security were partition and population exchanges. As imagined by national rather than imperial elites, however, another modality of liberal permanent security was considered: "communal hostage taking." All of them were designed to avoid the scenario where sectarian militias and even highly motivated individuals took matters into their own hands: calculated murders, massacres, and expulsions carried out from below based on cycles of revenge and retaliation.[1]

Driving these imaginings was – and remains – the construction of primordial consciousness of emplacement, group belonging, and collective fate that Lemkin bought into with his Zionist conception of nationally constituted world society. As anthropologist Liisa Malkki has observed, homeland is invested with ontological significance, as in phrases like "the land rose in rebellion" or in the belief about the sacredness of "national soil," thereby naturalizing the relationship between people and land. Botanical metaphors commonly express the link, suggested by the language of "uprooting" from native lands in which people live. Nationality thus constructs refugees as "displaced" from their indigenous settings.[2] Ubiquitous familial terms also gesture to the tribal imaginary of nationalists. The image of a "family of nations," so central to the liberal nationalism of Giuseppe Mazzini in the

---

[1] Cf. Allen D. Grimshaw, "Genocide and Democide," in *Encyclopedia of Violence, Peace, and Conflict*, 3 vols. (San Diego: Academic Press, 1999), 2:58; Paul R. Brass, "The Partition of India and Retributive Genocide in the Punjab, 1946–47: Means, Methods and Purposes," *Journal of Genocide Research* 5, no. 1 (2003): 71–101.

[2] Liisa Malkki, "National Geographic: The Rooting of Peoples and the Territorialization of National Identity," *Current Anthropology* 7, no. 1 (1992): 24–44.

nineteenth century, echoes this notion.[3] Together, they posit "divine carto-graphies" that neatly map peoples as naturally emplaced in their homelands, dangerously effacing the heterogeneity and overlapping borders that obtain in the real world.[4] The drama of the "geo-body" can thus endure for millennia.[5] Consequently, fantasized conationals are imagined as "stranded" in historic-ally indigenous territories temporarily occupied by aliens. On the basis of these assumptions, the "occupier" can also imagine them as potential hostages, objects of possible reprisal for perceived mistreatment of their own nationals likewise "stranded" across the border. Permanent security entailed a nation being housed in "its" state; the consonance of the cultural and political nations.

These assumptions gain popularity during communal crises. Historian Taylor Sherman observes a "moral economy" of retribution in Indian partition violence, whereby a symmetry of suffering was required for communal justice. This economy was based on the assumption of subcontinental, indeed global, Muslim homogeneity: Muslims had more in common with Muslims in other parts of India, even the world, than with their non-Muslim neighbors. Because of the confessionalization and nationalization of Indian politics over preceding decades, this balancing was now a subcontinental calculation, meaning that innocent Muslims could be made to atone for violence that Muslim militants had perpetrated against innocent Hindus elsewhere.[6] Fatally, this assumption was also shared by Muslim communalists like the All India Muslim League in its "two-nations theory" that South Asian Muslims constituted a nation in every respect like the Hindu nation, rather than a religious minority submerged within a Hindu-dominated India.[7] As we see in this chapter, the same assumptions were applied to Jews living in Arab and Muslim countries, making them potential hostages. As noted in the previous chapter, the assumption of Arab homogeneity enabled fantasies of "transferring" Palestinians to neighboring countries to make room for Jewish settlers.

These mental operations were necessarily global in projection and meta-reflective in practice, as leaders of states-in-waiting not only studied political

---

[3] Malkki calls this mode of thinking the heroization or romanticization of the indigenous, which she regards suspiciously as a sedentarism that "directly enables a vision of territorial displacement as pathological." Malkki, "National Geographic," 31.

[4] Sankaran Krishna, *Postcolonial Insecurities: India, Sri Lanka and the Question of Nationalism* (Minneapolis: University of Minnesota Press, 1999).

[5] Thongchai Winichakul, *Siam Mapped: A History of the Geo-Body of a Nation* (Honolulu: University of Hawaii Press, 1994).

[6] Taylor C. Sherman, *Muslim Belonging in Secular India: Negotiating Citizenship in Postcolonial Hyderabad* (Cambridge: Cambridge University Press, 2015), 21–2, 35–6.

[7] Cemil Aydin, *The Idea of the Muslim World: A Global Intellectual History* (Cambridge, MA: Harvard University Press, 2017); Reece Jones, "The False Premise of Partition," *Space and Polity* 18, no. 3 (2014): 285–300. On South Asian Islam, see Ayesha Jalal, *Self and Sovereignty: Individual and Community in South Asian Islam Since 1850* (London: Routledge, 2000).

dramas in other parts of the world, but also scrutinized the lessons that their rivals drew from them. A political history of ideas can show how national security thinking was embedded in practices of analogy making. Historians of empire have long noted what they call a "competitive politics of comparison that accelerated circuits of knowledge production and imperial exchange," practices of mutual observation and borrowing in relation to governance and security.[8] More recently, a global intellectual history posits circulation, diffusion, and adaptation in the study of ideas and texts "across geographical parameters far larger than usual."[9] Whether a global entanglement or global conjuncture, a ubiquitous practice from the 1920s to the 1940s was the mutual observation, analogizing, comparison, and distinguishing of subject positions not only by imperial elites, but by those they governed waiting impatiently to found their own states.[10]

India and Interwar Europe

European affairs served as a screen for various analogical appropriations as Indians imagined post-British security. Because of Zionism and Britain's Palestine Mandate, the continent was coimagined with the Middle East and British Empire, offering still more objects for identification and distinction. The German-Czechoslovak confrontation in 1938 in particular was a rich mine for projection possibilities. On one side, a Hindu journalist could write that the creation of an independent Pakistan in the northwest "would place the rest of India at the mercy of an aggressor even more decisively than the loss of the Sudetenland put Czech territory at the mercy of the Nazis."[11] On the other, two Aligarh Muslim University academics drew a different conclusion: "the Muslims of India are a nation by themselves – they have a distinct national entity wholly different from the Hindus and other non-Muslim groups; indeed, they are more different from the Hindus than the Sudeten Germans were from the Czechs."[12] Given the prominence of the German-Czechoslovak conflict in India, this was a statement about the intensity of feeling there.

---

[8] Ann Laura Stoler and Carole McGranahan, "Imperial Formations," in *Imperial Formations*, ed. Ann Laura Stoler, Carole McGranahan, and Peter C. Perdue (Santa Fe, NM: SAR, 2007), 4.

[9] Samuel Moyn and Andrew Sartori, "Approaches to Global Intellectual History," in *Global Intellectual History*, ed. Samuel Moyn and Andrew Sartori (New York: Columbia University Press, 2013), 4.

[10] Arie M. Dubnov, "Notes on the Zionist Passage to India, or: The Analogical Imagination and Its Boundaries," *Journal of Israeli History* 35, no. 2 (2016): 177–214.

[11] B. Shiva Rao, "A Vicious Circle in India," *Foreign Affairs* 19 (July 1941): 846.

[12] Syed Zafarul Hasan and Mohamad Afzal Husain Qadri, "The Problem of Indian Muslims and Its Solutions," February 2, 1939, in *The Paradoxes of Partition, 1937–1947*, ed. S. A. I. Tirmizi (New Delhi: Manak, 1998), 612.

Vinayak Damodar Savarkar (1883–1966), leader of the ultranationalist Hindu Mahasabha revivalist movement in the 1930s and 1940s, readily agreed that Muslims were utterly distinct from Indians. His *Hindutva: Who Is a Hindu?* (1923) articulated "Hindu-ness" as the authentically indigenous Indian identity that coded Muslims in South Asia as alien conquerors and cultural usurpers; their mass conversion of Hindus should be reversed as part of the Hindu renaissance. He consequently opposed the secular Indian National Congress, founded in 1885, which comprised Indians of all confessions. His notions of national purity and regeneration intersected with foreign national dramas in rigorously consistent ways. In *Hindutva*, he welcomed "Zionist dreams" in Palestine, observing that only Jews approached Hindus in possessing the "conditions under which a nation can attain perfect solidarity and cohesion," namely "people who inhabit the land they adore, the land of whose forefathers is also the land of their Gods and Angels, of Seers and Prophets" – that is, "if ever the Jews can succeed in founding their state there [in Palestine]."[13]

The intensive identification with Jewish nationalism also came from a perception of virtually simultaneous destructive Muslim invasions of their respective homelands: "The Arabian Moslems invaded Palestine only a few decades before they invaded our Sindh and just as their fanatical fury exterminated the ancient Egyptians or Persians, they attempted to wipe out with fire and sword the Jewish people too."[14] Savarkar thus applauded the UN's decision in November 1947 to partition Palestine and create a Jewish state: "After centuries of sufferings, sacrifices and struggle the Jews will soon recover their national Home in Palestine which has undoubtedly been their Fatherland and Holyland."[15] Opposed to British partitions of the sacred Indian motherlands until the last minute when it meant saving Hindu-majority areas from Pakistan, he regretted that Jews were not granted the entirety of the Palestine Mandate.[16]

---

[13] Vinayak Damodar Savarkar, *Hindutva: Who Is a Hindu?*, 5th ed. (Bombay: S. S. Savarkar, 1969), 136–7. The affinity between Zionism and this Hindu nationalism continues to this day in the intimacy between Israel president Benjamin Netanyahu and Indian Prime Minister Narendra Modi. See Sumantra Bose, "Why India's Hindu Nationalists Worship Israel's Nation-State Model," *The Conversation*, February 14, 2019, http://theconversation .com/why-indias-hindu-nationalists-worship-israels-nation-state-model-111450.

[14] Marzia Casolari, "Hindutva's Foreign Tie-up in the 1930s: Archival Evidence," *Economic and Political Weekly*, January 22, 2000, 224.

[15] V. D. Savarkar, "Glad to Note That Independent Jewish State Is Established," December 19, 1947, *Historic Statements by Savarkar*, ed. S. S. Savarkar (Bombay: G. P. Parchure, 1967), 135.

[16] I cannot determine whether Savarkar was aware of the European Enlightenment debates about Jewish assimilation and citizenship that resulted in the Jews' construction as a minority and that Aamir R. Mufti argues provided the paradigm for minoritization processes in the imperial possessions like India; Aamir R. Mufti, *Enlightenment in the*

With brutal consistency, Savarkar supported Germany's right to follow National Socialism and to expel Jews. Germans could legitimately choose Nazism because nations were constituted by ethnic homogeneities. After all, Jews and Muslims, he said in 1939, identified more with coreligionists abroad than with fellow citizens of the majority population.[17] Such policies were a model for India in relation to the minority Muslim population. He also supported Nazi Germany's policy toward the German minority in the Sudeten region of neighboring Czechoslovakia on the grounds of ethnic democratic self-determination, an argument that Hindu nationalists would later make about princely states ruled by Muslims whose majority population was Hindu:

> [A]s far as the Czechoslovakia question was concerned the Hindu Sanghatanists [Mahasabhaits] in India hold that Germany was perfectly justified in uniting the Austrian and Sudeten Germans under the German flag. Democracy itself demanded that the will of the people must prevail in choosing their own government. Germany demanded plebiscite, the Germans under the Czechs wanted to join their kith and kin in Germany. It was the Czechs who were acting against the principle of democracy in holding the Germans under a foreign sway against their will . . . . Now that Germany is strong why should she not strike to unite all Germans and consolidate them into a Pan-German state and realise the political dream which generations of German people cherished.[18]

Identifying now with Germans rather than Jews, Savarkar hoped that India was so strong as to politically unify Hindus spread across multiple polities on the Indian subcontinent.

Ironically, the Muslim League reasoned in similar terms even if with different signs. The Sindh League leader, Abdullah Haroon (1872–1942), praised Hitler for liberating ethnic Germans from Czechoslovak domination in the same way that League-dominated areas should come to the aid of endangered Muslims if persecuted by Hindus. Muhammad Ali Jinnah (1876–1948) even invoked British practices of humanitarian intervention: "if Britain in Gladstone's time could intervene in Armenia in the name of protection of minorities, why should it not be right for us to do so in the case of our minorities in Hindustan – if they are oppressed."[19] In his address to the Sindh Muslim League conference in October 1938, he elaborated the identification:

Colony: The Jewish Question and the Crisis of Postcolonial Culture (Princeton, NJ: Princeton University Press, 2007).

[17] Casolari, "Hindutva's Foreign Tie-up," 224.   [18] Ibid., 223.

[19] Venkat Dhulipala, *Creating a New Medina: State Power, Islam, and the Quest for Pakistan in Late Colonial North India* (Delhi: Cambridge University Press, 2015), 19.

It was because the Sudeten Germans who were forced under the heel of the majority of Czechoslovakia who oppressed them, suppressed them, maltreated them and showed a brutal and callous disregard for their rights and interests for two decades, hence the inevitable result that the Republic of Czechoslovakia is now broken up and a new map will have to be drawn. Just as the Sudeten Germans were not defenceless and survived the oppression and persecution for two decades, so also the Mussalmans are not defenceless and cannot give you their national entity and aspirations in this great continent.[20]

Like their mortal enemies the Hindu Mahasabha, the Muslim League identified with the Germans, although with opposite intentions: the former regarded Germans as akin to Hindus striving to unite against a despotic ruler (the princely states, the British, and the Czechoslovak state as the villains), while the latter sought partition against a tyrannical majority (with Slavs and Hindus as villains). The Muslim League thereby sided with the British in its infamous Munich Agreement with Hitler to partition Czechoslovakia. If the lessons of new postwar states had taught the League anything, it was that minority status was untenable. Majorities could not be expected to treat minorities well and, unlike raw power, League of Nations treaties and constitutional protections counted for little.

As might be expected, Indian National Congress leaders rejected these analogies. Rajendra Prasad (1884–1963), a lawyer from Bihar who later became the county's first president, sounded a warning about false humanitarian interventions: "Since the authors [the Aligarh Muslim University academics] have compared Hindus and Muslims to Czechs and Sudeten Germans ... one can only hope that it is not intended that history should repeat itself and India see a war for the conquest of the Czechs (the Hindus) and of Hindustan (Czecho Slovakia) on the pretext of the Indian Czechs' – the Hindus' – ill-treatment of the Indian Sudetens – the Muslims."[21] His colleague, Jawaharlal Nehru (1889–1964), also sympathized with Czechoslovakia as a new, democratic, left-leaning, post-imperial, and multinational state, albeit with a fractious, indeed irredentist, German minority. With his daughter, he visited the country in 1938 as a mark of solidarity before the Munich Conference, declining an official invitation to Nazi Germany. An Indo-Czechoslovak Society in Bombay was founded in 1938 to the same end. The Indian national independence movement attracted great attention and sympathy in Czechoslovakia. Already in 1934, Czechoslovak-Indian commercial and cultural relations were institutionalized in university positions and an Oriental Institute in Prague.[22] After his tour of the country, which was

---

[20] Hector Bolitho, *Jinnah: Creator of Pakistan* (Karachi: Oxford University Press, 1954), 109.

[21] Rajendra Prasad, *India Divided*, 3rd ed. (Bombay: Hind Kitabs, 1947), 183.

[22] Stanislava Vavroušková, "Ways to Understand India: The Czech Experience," *Acta Orientalia Vilnensia* 9, no. 2 (2008): 125–32.

preceded by a visit to Republican forces in Spain's civil war, Nehru wrote a series of articles in the English and Indian press denouncing German aggression and Western acquiescence, which he saw as more sinister than appeasement:

> As events have shown they [the Czechoslovaks] are prepared to go to extraordinary lengths to satisfy every minority claim and preserve peace but everybody knows that the question at issue is not a minority one. If it was the love of minority rights that moved people why do we not hear of the German minority in Italy or the minority in Poland? The question is one of power politics and the Nazi desire to break up the Czecho-Soviet alliance, to put an end to the democratic state in central Europe, to reach the Rumanian oil fields and wheat, and thus to dominate Europe. British policy has encouraged this and tried to weaken that democratic state.[23]

Like European leftists and many anticolonial nationalists, he associated fascism and imperialism, placing Nazi Germany and the British Empire in the same camp as disavowed allies opposing the Soviet Union, with which he also sympathized, although he himself was not a communist. Unlike Savarkar and the Muslim League, he was dismayed, if not surprised, by the British and French betrayal of Czechoslovakia.

The Congress followed Nehru's line, passing a resolution in March 1939 that condemned British foreign policy toward Germany, Italy, and Spain, including Germany's persecution of its Jewish citizens, again in contrast to Savarkar: "International morality has sunk so low in Central and South-Western Europe that the world has witnessed with horror the organized terrorism of the Nazi Government against people of the Jewish race and the continuous bombing from the air by rebel forces of cities and civilian inhabitants and helpless refugees [in Spain]."[24] How German imperialism and Pan-Germanism – a cypher for pan-Islamism in Congress eyes – played out in Czechoslovakia confirmed its fears. Not only did the Sudeten-German leader, Konrad Henlein (1898–1947), claim parity with the Slav majority, but the Nazis detached Slovakia from the Bohemian lands when they occupied the country. The fragmentary implications of Pan-Islamic communalism in India for a united country seemed portended in Central Europe. "The entire course of events was fully reported and closely observed in India,"

---

[23] Jawaharlal Nehru, "The Betrayal of Czecho-Slovakia," *Manchester Guardian*, September 8, 1938, in *Unity of India: Collected Writings, 1937–1940* (New York: John Day, 1942), 286; Miloslav Krasa, "Jawaharlal Nehru and Czechoslovakia at the Time of the 1938 European Crisis," *India Quarterly* 45, no. 4 (1989): 333–66.

[24] Maulana Abul Kalam Azad, *India Wins Freedom: An Autobiographical Narrative* (Hyderabad: Orient Longman, 1988), 26.

noted the inaugural professor of politics at Allahabad University, Beni Prasad (1895–1945), in 1941.[25]

The Dalit lawyer, political thinker, and drafter of India's first independent constitution, B. R. Ambedkar (1891–1956), also used the Czechoslovak drama to draw lessons for India in *Thoughts on Pakistan* (1941), which he augmented in *Pakistan or the Partition of India* (1945).[26] Speaking as a member of a low-status minority, he was acutely conscious of the demographic preponderance of Hindus, whose caste hierarchies he wished to "annihilate" in a new social order, as he wrote in 1936. His distrust of majorities – and consequent favoring of national homogeneity – thus had two sources: caste and religion.[27] He noted the Muslim League's enthusiastic identification with Germany's intervention for their Sudeten conationals and did not dispute the power of the lesson. It was less the Sudeten Germans that interested him, however, than the Slovak nationalists, who used the Sudeten precedent to win constitutional and administrative autonomy within the state. No sooner had they extracted these concessions then they used the threat of German invasion to secede altogether and form a separate state. On the basis of this experience, and the breakup of the Ottoman Empire, Ambedkar instructed his readers on the power of nationalism: "Really speaking the destruction of Czechoslovakia was brought about by an enemy within her own borders. That enemy was the intransigent nationalism of the Slovaks who were out to break up the unity of the state and secure the independence of Slovakia."[28]

The poisoned fruit of such nationalism was terrible violence. In a remarkable section of *Pakistan or the Partition of India*, Ambedkar graphically detailed communal conflict between 1920 and 1940 based on official reports. They made "most painful and heart-rending reading" and indicated "twenty years of civil war between the Hindus and the Muslims in India, interrupted by brief intervals of armed peace." Violence against women in particular showed "the depth of the antagonism which divided the two communities." What is more, violent acts were not condemned by communal authorities "but were treated as legitimate acts of warfare for which no apology was necessary." In the circumstances, "Hindu-Muslim unity" was less a mirage than "out of sight and also out of mind."[29] The two could not be one nation irrespective of united government administrations. Contemporary European history and

[25] Beni Prasad, *The Hindu-Muslim Questions* (Allahabad: Kitabistan, 1941), 67–72.

[26] B. R. Ambedkar, *Thoughts on Pakistan* (Bombay: Thacker, 1941); Ambedkar, *Pakistan or the Partition of India* (Bombay: Thacker, 1945). The second book contains long passages taken verbatim from the first, including the material on Czechoslovakia. A recent study is Aishwary Kumar, *Radical Equality: Ambedkar, Gandhi, and the Risk of Democracy* (Stanford, CA: Stanford University Press, 2015).

[27] B. R. Ambedkar, *Annihilation of Caste*, ed. S. Anand (London: Verso, 2014).

[28] Ambedkar, *Pakistan or the Partition of India*, 203.   [29] Ibid., 175–8.

local experience also taught him this cold reality. Addressing Hindus, he asked them to ponder the viability of an independent India with such internal national conflict:

> This is a lesson which the Hindus will do well to grasp. They should ask themselves: if the Greek, Balkan and Arab nationalism has blown up the Turkish State and if Slovak nationalism has caused the dismantling of Czechoslovakia, what is there to prevent Muslim nationalism from disrupting the Indian State? If experience of other countries teaches that this is the inevitable consequence of pent-up nationalism, why not profit by their experience and avoid the catastrophe by agreeing to divide India into Pakistan and Hindustan?[30]

In view of irreconcilable nationality conflicts and consequent violence, Ambedkar concluded that states were left with no alternative but to strive for demographic homogeneity. To that end, he supported partition and an independent Pakistan already in 1941, only a year after the landmark Lahore Resolution of the Muslim League, writing, "It is obvious that if Pakistan has the demerit of cutting away parts of India it has also one merit namely of introducing homogeneity."[31]

Minorities: Hostages or Transfer?

The problem for Indian partitionists was that schemes devised in the 1930s and 1940s left large minorities in the new territories. Should they be protected, kept as hostages, or exchanged? The Muslim League's Lahore Resolution was an exercise in studied ambiguity in order to assuage Muslim-majority provinces that wanted to guard their autonomy from a strong central government. The resolution mentioned neither partition nor Pakistan, instead calling for "areas in which the Muslims are numerically in a majority, as in the North-Western and Eastern Zones of India" to constitute "autonomous and sovereign," indeed "Independent States" within a constitutional framework. It thus implied a decentralized Indian union of extant provinces, in which the issue of sovereignty was deferred.[32] As the resolution also implied that the Muslim-majority provinces of the northwest and Bengal would contain large non-Muslim minorities, they should be protected by "adequate, effective and mandatory safeguards," just as Muslim minorities in India should be similarly

---

[30] Ibid., 209.   [31] Ambedkar, *Thoughts on Pakistan*, 217.

[32] See the discussion in Ayesha Jalal, *The Sole Spokesman: Jinnah, the Muslim League, and the Demand for Pakistan* (Cambridge: Cambridge University Press, 1994), 54–8; Harshan Kumarasingham, *A Political Legacy of the British Empire: Power and the Parliamentary System in Post-Colonial India and Pakistan* (London: I. B. Tauris, 2013), ch. 4.

protected by constitutional provisions.[33] Commenting later on the resolution, Jinnah was characteristically vague, telling minority Muslims to demand safeguards "known to any civilized government" while reminding them that they would be no better off in a united India in which all Muslims, including the "Muslim homeland," remained a minority subject to the Hindu majority. "The division of India will throw a great responsibility upon the majority in its respective zones to create a real sense of security amongst the minorities and win their complete trust and confidence," he said hopefully.[34]

As Sikh leaders never tired of pointing out, why should Sikh collective security in their Punjab homeland not be guaranteed with *their* local sovereignty in the same way as Muslim security? They were not reassured by Muslim League arguments about effective Sikh influence in Punjab under Pakistan, which bore a striking resemblance to Congress arguments about effective Muslim influence in a united India. When partition finally became a reality in early 1947, Sikhs, the Hindu Mahasabha, and Congress insisted that non-Muslim areas of Punjab and Bengal become part of India in any partition demarcation; they could not become minorities in Pakistan. Ambedkar was also adamant on this point.[35]

This logic was shared by Muslim League leaders even from Muslim-minority areas like Uttar Pradesh: the main priority was self-government of Muslim-majority areas so they could not be intimidated by the national Hindu majority. How, then, could Muslim security in non-Muslim areas be guaranteed? Were Jinnah's and the Lahore Resolution's anodyne references to minority protection sufficient? They could be if backed by power. The well-known breakthrough to the notion of a separate Muslim polity was the speech of the lawyer, poet, and politician, Muhammad Iqbal (1877–1938), at a Muslim League meeting in 1930. There he demanded "the formation of a consolidated Muslim State in the best interests of India and Islam." The interests of both parties, he suggested obliquely, were served by a system of mutual deterrence: "For India, it means security and peace resulting from an *internal balance of power*."[36]

---

[33] Jalal, *The Sole Spokesman*, 241–2; Lahore Resolution (1940), HistoryPak.com, http://historypak.com/lahore-resolution-1940.

[34] Muhammad Ali Jinnah, "Statement on the Lahore Resolution," in *Some Recent Speeches and Writings of Mr. Jinnah*, ed. Jamil-ud-din Ahmad (Lahore: Sh. Muhammad Ashraf, 1942), 159.

[35] Sugata Bose, "A Doubtful Inheritance: The Partition of Bengal in 1947," in *The Political Inheritance of Pakistan*, ed. D. A. Low (London: Palgrave Macmillan, 1991), 130–43; Ambedkar, *Pakistan or the Partition of India*, 104.

[36] Muhammad Iqbal, "Presidential Address to the 25th Session of the All-India Muslim League Allahabad, 29 December 1930," in *Speeches, Writings, and Statements of Iqbal*, ed. Latif Ahmed Sherwani, 2nd rev. ed. (Lahore: Iqbal Academy, 1977), 15. Emphasis added. Amar Sohal, "Ideas of Parity: Muslims, Sikhs and the 1946 Cabinet Mission Plan," *South*

Muslim League figures made explicit what remained implicit in Iqbal's hint, namely, a "hostage theory" guarantee of communal peace based on a simple proposition: if you mistreat our minorities, we'll mistreat yours. For that reason, League politicians from Muslim-minority areas, like Choudhry Khaliquzzaman (1889–1973) of United Provinces, wanted all minorities to remain in situ to guarantee mutual deterrence, as he made clear in a letter to Jinnah in 1942: "one of the basic principles lying behind the Pakistan idea is that of keeping hostages in Muslim Provinces as against the Muslims in the Hindu Provinces. If we allow millions of Hindus to go out of our orbit of influence, the security of the Muslims in the minority Provinces will greatly be minimised."[37] There could be no equitable reciprocity if Pakistan was homogenous.

British leaders were well aware of the theory. Secretary to the governor of the Punjab, Penderel Moon (1905–1987), recalled hostage theory calculations among League leaders in the late 1930s: "there would be so many Muslims in Hindustan and so many Hindus in Pakistan that both sides would hesitate to harass their minorities for fear of reprisals."[38] Choudhry Khaliquzzaman shared these views with the British Cabinet Mission in April 1946 when asked how Muslims remaining in India would benefit from the establishment of Pakistan. "It was not so much that Muslims in Hindu-majority Provinces would be benefited directly," he was reported as saying, "but that the advantages would be indirect because the Government of Hindustan would not be so ready to ill-treat Muslims if they knew that the Government of Pakistan would retaliate. Some sort of balance of power was essential."[39] Hossain Imam, a Muslim League lawyer from Bihar, where Muslims were also a minority, likewise told the British secretary of state that "if there were a Pakistan in being, the Muslims in the minority Provinces would be assured that the Hindus could not treat them badly with impunity" because of the fear of reprisals, even if they were not enacted.[40]

Whether Imam really believed this scheme would work was indicated by his frank admission that minority Muslims would suffer for a redemptive purpose: they "were in effect prepared to sacrifice the interests of 25 million Muslims in Hindustan for the benefit of the rest of the community in Pakistan." Loyally following Jinnah's line, he continued: "The Muslims in

---

Asia 40, no. 4 (2017): 709–10. See Faisal Devj, "From Minority to Nation," in *Partitions: A Transnational History of Twentieth-Century Territorial Separatism*, ed. Arie Dubnov and Laura Robson (Stanford: Stanford University Press, 2019), 31–55.

[37] Quoted in Jalal, *The Sole Spokesman*, 59 n. 54, 182.

[38] Penderel Moon, *Divide and Quit* (London: Chatto and Windus, 1961), 20.

[39] *The Transfer of Power, 1942–7. The Cabinet Mission, 23 March – 29 June 1946*, vol. 7, ed. Nicholas Mansergh (London: Her Majesty's Stationary Office, 1977), 166.

[40] Ibid., 246.

the minority Provinces would rather face whatever was in store for them than allow the whole Muslim population to be maltreated."[41] The few, nonetheless tens of millions of Muslims, would suffer to secure Iqbal and Jinnah's vision of a Muslim homeland: as Jinnah put it, the "opportunity [for Muslims] to development their spiritual, cultural, economic, and political life in accordance with their own genius and shape their own future destiny."[42]

The British listeners were unconvinced by the hostage theory. One of them suggested, presciently, that the retaliatory logic, far from dampening violence, might result in "a crescendo of ill-treatment of minorities on both sides of the border."[43] A memo from a British administrator in United Provinces to the viceroy in January 1946 about a conversation with Choudhry Khaliquzzaman registered the skepticism: "He was very naïve about this [the hostage theory] and almost smacked his lips at the thought of the fun the Pakistan Government(s) would have in protecting – vicariously – the interests of their coreligionists in Hindustan!"[44] Choudhry Khaliquzzaman migrated to Pakistan at partition and succeeded Jinnah as leader of the Muslim League. He also knew that Muslims stranded in India were effectively left high and dry because the establishment of Pakistan would mean the absence of an effective Muslim voice at the center of Indian politics.[45]

Accordingly, Jinnah hoped that the League would inherit an unpartitioned Punjab and Bengal with its large Hindu (and in Punjab, also Sikh) minorities, as he made clear in the Cabinet Mission negotiations in 1946.[46] Until the catastrophic population exchanges from below of 1947 and 1948, Jinnah apparently continued to believe in the hostage theory, telling an English journalist that Muslims in India were "fortunate that there would be a corresponding minority of 25,000,000 Hindus in Pakistan." On partition, he was reported as saying, "The minorities are in effect hostages to the requirement of mutual cooperation and good neighbourliness between the Governments of Pakistan and the Indian Union."[47] However, while a sizable

---

[41] Ibid., 245–6; Dhulipala, *Creating a New Medina*, 172.

[42] Jinnah, "Statement on the Lahore Resolution," 158.

[43] *The Transfer of Power*, vol. 7, 166–7. Affirming this view is S. R. Sen, "Communal Riots: Anticipation, Containment and Prevention," *Economic and Political Weekly* 28, no. 15 (1993): 628.

[44] *The Transfer of Power, 1942–7. The Post-War Phase: New Moves by the Labour Government, 1 August 1945–22 March 1946*, vol. 6, ed. Nicholas Mansergh (London: Her Majesty's Stationary Office, 1976), 727.

[45] Choudhry Khaliquzzaman, *Pathway to Pakistan* (Lahore: Longmans, 1961).

[46] Hamsa Alavi, "Ethnicity, Muslim Society, and the Pakistan Ideology," in *Islamic Reassertion in Pakistan: The Application of Islamic Laws in a Modern State*, ed. Anita M. Weiss (New York: Syracuse University Press, 1986), 23.

[47] A. G. Noorani, "Jinnah & Muslims of India," *Criterion Quarterly* 3, no. 4, November 20, 2012, www.criterion-quarterly.com/jinnah-muslims-of-india; Weldon James interview with Jinnah, *Collier's*, August 25, 1947.

Muslim minority remained in India, very few Hindus, Sikhs, and other non-Muslims were left in Pakistan, leading to considerable handwringing there. There were even calls for Hindus to return.[48]

Hindu observers were registering this security logic of Muslim communal leaders already in 1931. Sanat Kumar Roy-Chaudhuri, mayor of Calcutta and senior member of the Hindu Mahasabha, predictably derided the hostage theory as yet another Muslim strategy to dominate Hindus because more non-Muslims would be under Muslim control than the reverse. Iqbal's speech the year before, he continued, implied a Pan-Muslim federation in the northwest to overawe India, a fear also shared by Ambedkar. On the eve of partition, Savarkar predictably vowed that any Muslim mistreatment of Hindus would be met in kind.[49]

By contrast, senior Congress figures were appalled by the hostage theory, which was catching on within their ranks. Maulana Abul Kalam Azad (1888–1958), a Muslim Congress leader, recalls that, during the partition decision, members reassured Hindu delegates from Sindh, where Hindus were a minority, by saying "the Hindus in Pakistan need have no fear as there would be 45 millions of Muslims in India and if there was any oppression of Hindus in Pakistan, the Muslims in India would have to bear the consequences." He felt that the notion of "retaliation as a method of assuring the rights of minorities seemed ... barbarous."[50] Rajendra Prasad agreed: "The very idea of ill-treating people who have done nothing wrong and may for all practical purposes be the best of citizens in their own State, because some other independent Government with which they have no concern has misbehaved, is so repugnant to our sense of natural justice that it is inconceivable that either Pakistan or Hindustan will resort to reprisal against its own subjects for the act of an independent Government."[51]

Ambedkar was also appalled by "a scheme of communal peace through a system of communal hostages."[52] He drew on his broad study of European affairs to come to startling conclusions based on arresting analogies. Hindus stuck in Pakistan would be in the "position of the Armenians under the Turks or of the Jews in Tsarist Russia or in Nazi Germany," in this case "as a helpless

[48] Vazira Fazila-Yacoobali Zamindar, *The Long Partition and the Making of Modern South Asia: Refugees, Boundaries, Histories* (New York: Columbia University Press, 2007), 71–6.

[49] Sanat Kumar Roy-Chaudhuri, "The Hostage Theory and Its Dangers in Constitution Framing," *Modern Review*, September 1931, 303–6; Ambedkar, *Pakistan or the Partition of India*, 374; Dhanajay Keer, *Veer Savarkar*, 2nd ed. (Bombay: Popular Prakashan, 1966), 381.

[50] Maulana Abul Kalam, *India Wins Freedom,* complete ed. (Madras: Orient Longman, 1988), 151, 216.

[51] Prasad, *India Divided*, 232, 328.   [52] Ambedkar, *Pakistan or the Partition of India*, 96.

prey to the fanaticism of a Muslim National State."[53] What is more, India's sovereignty would be threatened by the hostage theory. After all, were Muslims incorrect to observe that "Hitler's bullying tactics" in the German-Czechoslovakia confrontation were "better able to protect the Sudeten Germans in Czechoslovakia than the Sudetens were able to do themselves?"[54] For these reasons, Ambedkar urged a dramatic and drastic alternative: population exchange. The Balkans provided a precedent, in part because of their dreadful record of minority protection, in part because those states successfully transferred minorities. Anticipating skepticism about logistics, he noted the magnitude of the challenge they faced: "It involved the transfer of some 20 million people from one habitat to another. But undaunted, the three [Turkey, Greece, and Bulgaria] shouldered the task and carried it to a successful end because they felt that the considerations of communal peace must outweigh every other consideration." Sounding like the British Peel Commission's invocation of the Turkish-Greek population exchange, Ambedkar concluded that "there is no reason to suppose that what they did cannot be accomplished by Indians."[55] That was the only way to make Hindustan homogenous, he averred.

Ambedkar was not alone in this line of thinking. Syed Abdul Latif (1891–1971), an English literature university academic in Hyderabad, suggested the same from the Muslim perspective in *The Muslim Problem in India* in 1939. He, too, was well aware of the difficulties, indeed sacrifices, that a population exchange would entail, but he thought it was better that this generation made them for the peace of subsequent generations. He proposed that the League and Congress collaborate on a mutually agreeable scheme for which European history gave plenty of precedents, and that should commence with voluntary migration.[56] The idea comes up occasionally in Jinnah's speeches. Population exchange, he declared, "as far as practicable will have to be considered."[57]

While the Muslim League toyed with the hostage theory and population exchange, the Congress rejected them for minority protection, although this commitment was tested by communal violence. Rajendra Prasad criticized population exchange as utterly impractical because it would be too costly, the suffering caused too immense, and the affected populations in India too intermingled, too far from likely borders, and vastly larger than in the Turkish-Greek case. He was, in any event, against the proposition of

---

[53] Ibid., 98.   [54] Ibid., 103.   [55] Ibid., 102.

[56] Syed Abdul Latif, *Muslim Problem in India together with an Alternative Constitution for India*, foreword by Sir Abdulla Haroon (Bombay: Times of India Press, 1939), 35–8.

[57] Jinnah, "Statement on the Lahore Resolution," 158. More quotations in *Jinnah on World Affairs: Select Documents, 1908–1948*, ed. Mehrunnisa Ali (Karachi: Pakistan Study Centre, University of Karachi, 2007).

homogeneous states; states always had minorities.[58] But, by the time he signed off on the third edition of *India Divided* in July 1947, after the failed Cabinet Mission and ensuing communal violence in and after August 1946, he had changed his mind. He amended the addendum that supplemented the second edition, now supporting the idea: "The wisest course might therefore be to bring about an exchange of populations and squares between Muslims and non-Muslims, all the Muslims going over to the districts which may be assigned to the Muslim zone, all non-Muslims from those districts being transferred to a district assigned to the non-Muslim zone."[59] The scheme would have to focus on Punjab, the Sikh homeland, transferring Sikhs into a non-Muslim zone.

In the event, the partition plan agreed to by all parties in June 1947 did not include population exchanges, in contrast to the Peel Commission report in Palestine 10 years before. The "Radcliffe Line" sundered Punjab and Bengal to separate Muslims and non-Muslims in those majority-Muslim provinces without demographic transfers. When asked about the matter, Viceroy Louis Mountbatten said it was not a question for All-India deliberations: "There are many physical and practical difficulties involved. Some measure of transfer will come about in a natural way ... perhaps governments will transfer populations. Once more, this is a matter not so much for the main parties as for the local authorities living in the border areas to decide."[60] He had not given the matter much thought.

Indeed, local forces in the border areas ultimately determined events, but not the authorities Mountbatten invoked. Prasad's concerns about the Sikh factor in Punjab were well placed. Throughout their consultations with the Cabinet Mission, Sikh leaders had issued veiled threats that they would take matters into their own hands if partition sundered their lands and if many of them were to be stranded in Pakistan. In fact, they had called for population exchanges to concentrate Sikhs – and that is what occurred.[61] In large measure, the partition violence in that region was organized by Sikh militias that brutally expelled Muslims from areas that they settled with Sikhs who left – or who were likewise expelled from – the eastern Pakistan areas.[62] In total, up to 17.9 million people left or were driven from their homes during the next four years, mainly in the Punjab and in Bengal, more than three million going

---

[58] Prasad, *India Divided*, 27, 188–93, 324–7.   [59] Ibid., 400.
[60] Yasmin Khan, *The Great Partition: The Making of India and Pakistan*, new ed. (New Haven, CT: Yale University Press, 2017), 100.
[61] Ibid., 122.
[62] Subhasish Ray, "Intra-Group Interactions and Inter-Group Violence: Sikh Mobilization During the Partition of India in a Comparative Perspective," *Journal of Genocide Research* 19, no. 3 (2017): 382–403; Brass, "The Partition of India"; Swarna Aiyar, "August Anarchy: The Partition Massacres in Punjab, 1947," *South Asia* 18 (1995): 13–36.

missing or dying in the process, and hundreds of thousands of girls and women suffering rape and abduction.[63] This was not the orderly population exchange envisaged by some, and certainly not in the numbers required to homogenize India, although Pakistan came close to the ideal.

Certainly, the hostage theory was disproved by this wrenching process; indeed, it was a mechanism of escalation as the British Cabinet Mission had predicted. No government had been able to protect the welfare of its respective communities despite the existence of hostages. State retaliation, as opposed to communal violence, was politically untenable, despite covert support for, or wilful blindness to, their pogroms. Instead, now, "many of the original protagonists of Pakistan found themselves a hated minority in an even more completely Hindu polity," as an American observer noted at the time.[64] Ultranationalist retributive violence was destructively creative by homogenizing national demography and political culture so that reality would more closely accord to the abstraction of the imagined collective. Hossain Imam, the Bihar Muslim League representative who told the British that he "would rather face whatever was in store for them [Muslims] than allow the whole Muslim population to be maltreated," now complained that he expected to be treated as a citizen of India and not as a hostage.[65]

Muslim Zion?

Were the projections of identity between India, Europe, and the Middle East so intense as to make Pakistan a "Muslim Zion"?[66] Certainly, the two movements shared the notions of a cultural homeland and elaboration of a nation that, though posited as an abstraction of imagined homogeneity, did not yet exist, and indeed was supposed to be made in and by the future state. If British authorities hesitated to equate the partitions of India and of Palestine, that was because they could not analogize between largely European Jewish settlers whom they regarded as civilizationally superior to the indigenous Arabs, and Indian Muslims whom they orientalized like Arabs. They would have agreed with Maulana Abul Kalam Azad, who rejected the "analogy of the Jewish demand for a national home" in April 1946:

---

[63] Prashant Bharadwaj, Asim Khwaja, and Atif Mian, "The Big March: Migratory Flows After the Partition of India," *Economic and Political Weekly* 43, no. 35 (2008): 39–49; Prashant Bharadwaj, Asim Khwaja, and Atif Mian, "Population Exchange and Its Impact on Literacy, Occupation and Gender – Evidence from the Partition of India," *International Migration* 53, no. 4 (2014): 90–106.

[64] Phillips Talbot, "The Rise of Pakistan," *Middle East Journal* 2, no. 4 (1948): 387.

[65] Papiya Ghosh, "Writing Ganga-Jamni: In the 1940s and *After*," *Social Scientist* 34, nos. 11–12 (2006): xi–xii.

[66] Faisal Devji, *Muslim Zion: Pakistan as a Political Idea* (London: Hurst, 2013).

One can sympathize with the aspiration of the Jews for such a national home, as they are scattered all over the world and cannot in any region have any effective voice in the administration. The condition of Indian Muslims is quite otherwise. Over 90 millions in number they are in quantity and quality a sufficiently important element in Indian life to influence decisively all questions of administration and policy. Nature has further helped them by concentrating them in certain areas.[67]

Like the Muslim League, the Congress decried the Balfour Declaration and British imperialism in general. Unlike the League, the Congress perceived Zionism since the 1930s as a secessionist movement akin to the Muslim League, both collaborating illegitimately with the British, and so found it easy to reject Palestine's partition. The League's opposition was predictable: it supported the majority-Muslim Palestinian Arabs in their quest for self-determination and would not equate itself with Zionists. A League resolution in 1938 went so far as to warn the British that its "pro-Jewish policy in Palestine" would make them appear as an "enemy of Islam."[68] The Congress also identified with an independent and united Palestine. As the Zionist demographer and historian Joseph Schechtman lamented, it was Mohandas Gandhi (1869–1948) who set the Congress against Zionism by declaring Palestine an Arab country.[69]

Although both parties agreed to partition in South Asia – Congress most reluctantly – both Pakistan and India opposed it for Palestine. India was a member of the UN Special Committee on Palestine (UNSCOP) and, with Iran and Yugoslavia, submitted the minority report supporting a federalization of Palestine. This was the very solution that the Congress had rejected for India because it wanted a strong central state. Pakistan, which led the UN subcommittee to study the Arab proposal for a united Palestine, joined other Islamic countries in contesting partition and, failing that, seeking to limit Jewish control to the small amount of Jewish-owned land (6 percent). When the Arab unitary state proposal was rejected, both Pakistan and India supported the federal idea, which foresaw a binational state. In his memoirs, Pakistan UN representative Sir Chaudhry Zafarullah Khan (1893–1985) – himself a member of the Ahmadi minority – said he had been attracted to the binational idea of Judah Magnus, president of the Hebrew University of Jerusalem, whom

[67] Azad, *India Wins Freedom*, 150.
[68] Presidential Address of Mr M. A. Jinnah Read on 8th October 1938, 5–6, Internet Archive, https://archive.org/stream/SpeechesOfPoliticalReligiousLeadersOfSindhGulhayatInstitute/ PresidentialAddressOfMrMaJinnahOctober1938ResolutionsAndDonations_djvu.txt; Fareed Ali Shamsi, "India and the Problem of Palestine" (Master's thesis, Aligarh Muslim University, 1968), chap. 1.
[69] Joseph B. Schechtman, "India and Israel," *Midstream* (August–September 1966): 48–61.

he had met in 1945. Magnus had impressed upon him the necessity of securing bipartisan support for any solution.[70]

How was one to avoid the implication of hypocrisy by denying Jews national sovereignty when the Muslim League had argued that Muslims constituted a distinct nationality and therefore deserved their own state? The difference, Khan said at the UN, was that both sides had consented to partition in India whereas in Palestine it was being imposed against the will of the majority; that Muslims were a part of India in a way that could not be said of Jews in Palestine, most of whom had arrived in recent years, thereby artificially creating a nationality conflict; and that Muslims in India claimed only majority population areas whereas in Palestine Jews were a minority in virtually all the land they were to be granted by the UN.[71] Besides, he added, would the Americans take Pakistan refugees just because they wanted to go to the US?[72] For India, partition violated the sacred principle of self-determination. After the failure of the federal plan, which was also dismissed by the Arab bloc, India supported the latter in opposing partition. From the Indian perspective, partition in South Asia was not a concession to secession but a recognition of its right to self-determination.[73] Distinguished in this way, India and Pakistan could oppose the partition of Palestine but reluctantly support the partitions of the Muslim majority provinces of Punjab and Bengal.[74]

Despite the scattered references to population exchange, there was no Pakistan expectation or commitment to an ingathering of all Muslims from India. The League and Pakistan leadership did not envisage the large-scale immigration of Indian Muslims to a historic homeland in the manner that Zionists hoped and anticipated Jews would eventually settle in Eretz Israel.[75]

---

[70] Muhammad Zafrullah Khan, *The Forgotten Years: Memoirs of Sir Muhammad Zafrullah Khan*, ed. A. H. Batalvi (Lahore: Vanguard, 1991), 184–5.

[71] S. M. Burke, *Pakistan's Foreign Policy: An Historical Analysis* (London: Oxford University Press, 1973), 138; T. G. Fraser, *Partition in Ireland, India and Palestine: Theory and Practice* (London: Palgrave Macmillan, 1984), 176; P. R. Kumaraswamy, "Beyond the Veil: Israel-Pakistan Relations," *Memorandum* no. 55 (Tel Aviv: Jaffee Center for Strategic Studies, Tel Aviv University, March 2000), http://institutobrasilisrael.org/cms/assets/uploads/_BIBLIOTECA/_PDF/democracia-e-sociedade-israelense/4766c3f1ea0a333fdf43b17de01ade0f.pdf.

[72] Ad Hoc Committee on the Palestinian Question: Report of Sub-Committee 2, A/AC.14/32, November 11, 1947, http://unispal.un.org/pdfs/AAC1432.pdf.

[73] Leonard A. Gordon, "Indian Nationalist Ideas About Palestine and Israel," *Jewish Social Studies* 37, nos. 3–4 (1975): 221–34.

[74] Umbreen Javaid and Malik Tauqir Ahmad Khan, "Pakistan and the Question of Recognising Israel: Historical Issues and Future Prospects," *South Asian Studies* 29, no. 2 (2014): 61–71.

[75] Tahir Hasnain Naqvi, "The Politics of Commensuration: The Violence of Partition and the Making of the Pakistani State," in *Beyond Crisis: Re-Evaluating Pakistan*, ed. Naveeda Khan (New Delhi: Routledge, 2010), 77–8.

In fact, amid partition violence in October 1947, Jinnah told Pakistan armed forces offices that the flight of Hindus from Sindh in particular harmed the economy and the state; the exodus "was part of a well-organized plan to cripple Pakistan."[76] These are hardly the sorts of sentiments one would have heard from David Ben-Gurion regarding Palestinian Arabs. Nor, later, did Jinnah think that Indian Muslims had an a priori right to settle in Pakistan; the state had no Law of Return like Israel's. He advised Muslims in India to swear "unflinching loyalty to the State."[77] Treating minorities well was the policy as stated in the Lahore Resolution. There was no talk of hostages.

However, because some in India were "bent upon the eviction and extermination of Muslims in India by brutal and inhuman means," Jinnah placed population exchange on the agenda: "If the ultimate solution to the minority problem is to be mass exchanges of population, let it be taken up at the Governmental palace" rather than "sorted out by bloodthirsty elements."[78] Such a scheme was never seriously considered; neither state had the capacity to cope with more refugees or the willpower to exchange minorities for the reasons Rajendra Prasad had given in *India Divided*. India resisted pressure from the far-right Hindus for population exchange and war for more territory to settle migrants. Talk of population exchange was an expression of desperation and hopelessness in the face of seemingly intractable violence from below. Latif seems to have recanted his views as impractical already by 1946.[79]

Instead, Jinnah took rhetorical responsibility for Muslims in India, who thereby became what Willem van Schendel calls "proxy citizens."[80] This was not a new idea in South Asian discourse, as the Lahore Resolution indicated. If the two-nations theory was to be taken seriously, Indian Muslims were in fact culturally Pakistani. To that extent, partition had sedimented into the new states the minority question that was on the table in the All-India discussions. The practice of dealing with the 197 remnant enclaves in one another's countries exemplified this approach. Both sides behaved as if they were responsible for coreligionists/conationals in enclaves across the border. The issue was pressing because majority militias demanded enclave loyalty to the surrounding state, which they attacked when it was not forthcoming.[81] In the interests of stemming further refugee flows – in opposite fashion to the situation in Israel and its neighbors at the same time – the states started

---

[76] Muhammad Ali Jinnah, "Address to Civil, Naval, Military & Air Force Offices of the Pakistan Government at Khaliqdina Hall, Karachi, October 11, 1947," in *Speeches and Writings of Mr. Jinnah*, ed. Jamil-ud-din Ahmad, Vol. 2 (Lahore: Sh. Muhammad Ashraf, 1947), 418.

[77] Ibid., 420.   [78] Ibid.   [79] Khan, *The Great Partition*, 122.

[80] Willem van Schendel, "Stateless in South Asia: The Making of the India-Bangladesh Enclaves," *Journal of Asian Studies* 61, no. 1 (2002): 127.

[81] Ibid., 123, 131.

meeting at interdominion conferences in January 1948 to manage the situation.

It took until 1950 for the two new states to stabilize the situation. Like the League of Nations minority protection regime, the "Agreement Between the Governments of India and Pakistan Regarding Security and Rights of Minorities" (the Nehru–Liaquat Agreement) provided minority protection as an alternative to population expulsion and/or exchange, though without the supervisory oversight of an international organization: "The Governments of India and Pakistan solemnly agree that each shall ensure, to the minorities throughout its territory, complete equality of citizenship, irrespective of religion, a full sense of security in respect of life, culture, property and personal honour, freedom of movement within each country and freedom of occupation, speech and worship, subject to law and morality."[82]

Joint minority commissions were established for Assam and East and West Bengal, where Hindus remained, to oversee minority rights. Each state's incentive to act against the egregious persecution of minorities at the local level was to forestall the other state becoming the minority's "protector."[83] Likely without realizing the precedent, the India and Pakistan agreement partially replicated the 1930 Greek-Turkish treaty that made each country responsible for the compensation of those who arrived as part of the Lausanne agreement, ending the mixed commissions supervised by the League.[84] For all the theorizing about hostages and population exchanges, the parties settled on the minority protection option they had disparaged in the lead-up to partition because of its failure in Europe. The League seemed to share a Zionist sense of proprietary interest in proxy citizens abroad, but as a transitional rather than a permanent arrangement. Indian Muslims were to stay put; Pakistan was not their home irrespective of what the Hindu Mahasabha thought. And yet, as we will see, the Muslim-Zion connection was apparent in another, more fatal way.

Palestine, Israel, and Minorities

In the British Mandate of Palestine, leaders from Jewish and Arab sides appealed to the ruling British to guarantee their security. Leaders of the large Arab majority urged the authorities to limit, if not cease, Jewish immigration

---

[82] Agreement Between the Governments of India and Pakistan Regarding Security and Rights of Minorities (Nehru–Liaquat Agreement), April 8, 1950, LII of India, Indian Treaty Series, www.commonlii.org/in/other/treaties/INTSer/1950/9.html.

[83] Pallavi Raghavan, "The Making of South Asia's Minorities: A Diplomatic History, 1947–52," *Economic and Politics Weekly*, May 21, 2016, 45–52.

[84] Nicolas Doumanis, *Before the Nation: Muslim-Christian Coexistence and Its Destruction in Late-Ottoman Anatolia* (Oxford: Oxford University Press, 2013), 170.

from the outset. For their part, Zionists, who could not foresee an independent Jewish state in the 1920s and 1930s, sought to build up the Jewish national home by having the British enable a Jewish majority over time via immigration. Already in 1937, Jewish leaders reluctantly accepted the Peel Commission's partition recommendation, which included Arab population transfers, because a truncated state with a demographic majority was preferable to long-term struggle with a hostile Arab population with no guarantee of eventual sovereignty. As might be expected, Arab leaders resisted the partition recommendation. Throughout the mandate, they insisted that Palestine be granted independence according to the strictures of Class A Mandates – like Iraq, for instance – as a democratic polity in which Jewish minority rights were respected. As noted above, the idea that non-European majorities could not be trusted to protect the rights of a "minority," particularly a white European one, long predated the British mandate. However, the massacre of Assyrians after Iraqi independence in 1933 and violence between Jews and Arabs in Palestine in 1929 gave the British a convenient pretext not to entrust the state to the Arab majority; that is why they considered partition and transferring Arabs from the Jewish territory.[85] Both parties advocated minority rights in the state they wanted to govern. Unlike India, there was no official discussion of equitable reciprocity or hostages, although that did not preclude retributive violence at the local level. Even so, as we will see below, hostage and population logics were discernible in regional perspective.

In 1947, UNSCOP determined to partition the British mandate after the British had referred the matter to the UN. The committee's majority report, which awarded most of the mandate to the Zionists, who constituted a third of Palestine's population, was supported by the General Assembly after considerable arm-twisting of allies by the US, and in the face of vehement opposition by the majority Arab population.[86] The generous award was designed for future population growth, whose immediate sources were Jewish displaced persons languishing in camps in Germany, although the aim to demographically prevail in Palestine long preceded the Holocaust and was reflected in the Peel Commission's dramatic redistribution of territory to the Zionists, coupled with population transfer, 10 years before. Refugee pressures that Europe, the

---

[85] Benny Morris does not probe the British pretext: Morris, "Explaining Transfer: Zionist Thinking and the Creation of the Palestinian Refugee Problem," in *Removing Peoples: Forced Removal in the Modern World*, ed. Richard Bessell and Claudia B. Haake (Oxford: Oxford University Press, 2009), 349–60.

[86] Benny Morris, *1948: A History of the First Arab-Israeli War* (New Haven, CT: Yale University Press, 2008), 52–60. For details of the internal and external pressures on the US position, see John B. Jurdis, *Genesis: Truman, American Jews, and the Origins of the Arab/Israeli Conflict* (New York: Farrar, Straus and Giroux, 2014).

US, Canada, or Australia were unwilling to accommodate in their own countries were transferred to the Middle East.

The Arab states supported Palestinian leaders in rejecting both the federal state
and partition plans of the minority UNSCOP report and majority reports.[87] They
sought the termination of the mandate and establishment of an independent
Palestinian state; Jewish minority rights would be safeguarded "in accordance with
international law and the United Nations Charter."[88] This was an enduring Arab
demand, made recently by Arab representatives to the Anglo-American
Committee of Inquiry of 1946. The most articulate representative was the
British-Lebanese civil servant and historian, Albert Hourani (1915–1993), then
working for the Arab Office in Jerusalem.[89] The question of minorities and
violence underlay his presentation. Arabs did not want to be converted into a
minority via Jewish immigration; if Jews supported partition to avoid ruling over
Arabs, the problem was not solved by a Jewish state because it, too, would
inevitably contain a large Arab minority, an argument advanced by Sikhs in India.

Partition was not a solution, Hourani declared. A Jewish neighbor-state in a
partitioned Palestine would lead to instability, because it would seek to
expand: "I can imagine [that] the pressures of population in the Jewish State
would be so great [that] it would turn the thoughts of the governing body to
expansion, either in order to settle Jewish immigrants outside the Jewish State,
or else in order to evacuate their Arab minority." Arabs, he reminded the
committee, had been listening to the Jewish talk of an "evacuation" of Arabs,
although he thought, incorrectly as it turned out, that in practice "this Arab
minority could not be transferred forcibly because you can't transfer peasants
forcibly."[90] Indeed, an intense Zionist discussion about "transferring"
Palestinians had been under way for a decade. While it did not constitute
official policy, the preferences of the Zionist high command were readily
apparent by 1947.[91] Golda Myerson (Meir) (1898–1978), as acting head of
the Jewish Agency Political Department, declared that "we are interested in

---

[87] UNSCOP Minority Report of 1947: A Federated State, www.pa-il.com/2011/09/unscop-
minority-report-of-1947.html.

[88] Nabil Elaraby, "Some Legal Implications of the 1947 Partition Resolution and the
1949 Armistice Agreements," *Law and Contemporary Problems* 33, no. 1 (1968): 99.
Elaraby was an Egyptian diplomat and First Secretary, Mission of the United Arab
Republic to the United Nations.

[89] Walid Khalidi, "On Albert Hourani, the Arab Office, and the Anglo-American
Committee of 1946," *Journal of Palestine Studies* 35, no. 1 (2005): 60–79.

[90] Albert Hourani, "The Case against a Jewish State in Palestine: Albert Hourani's Statement
to the Anglo-American Committee of Enquiry of 1946," *Journal of Palestine Studies* 35,
no. 1 (2005): 82, 86.

[91] Nur Masalha, *Expulsion of the Palestinians: The Concept of "Transfer" in Zionist Political
Thought* (Washington, DC: Institute for Palestine Studies, 1992); Nur Masalha, *A Land
Without a People: Israel, Transfer and the Palestinians, 1949–96* (London: Faber and Faber,
1997).

less Arabs who will be citizens of the Jewish state." Yitzhak Gruenbaum (1879–1970) of the Jewish Agency Executive said that Arabs remaining in the post-partition Jewish state who were citizens of its Arab neighbor would represent "a permanent irredenta" – that is, a security threat. Irrespective of citizenship status, such Arabs, Ben-Gurion maintained, would become a "Fifth Column" in time of war. He feared Arabs would take citizenship in the Jewish state, meaning that they could not be legally expelled.[92]

Even so, continued Hourani, Arabs were willing to share citizenship with Jews who had arrived legally and wanted to be "full members of the political unity," adding ironically, "to try the dangerous experiment of people of different races and ideals living together." He thought the offer generous.[93] Addressing the minority question in a united state, he struck the pose of Indian Congress leaders:

> ... what the Jews could expect would be full civil and political rights, control of their own communal affairs, municipal autonomy in districts in which they are mainly concentrated, the use of Hebrew as an additional official language in those districts, and an adequate share in the adminis-tration. It should be clear from this that there is no question of the Jews being under Arab rule in the bad sense of being thrust into a ghetto, or being cut off from the main stream of life of the community, always shunned and sometimes oppressed. The Arabs are offering not this ghetto status in the bad sense, but membership of the Palestinian community. If that community has an Arab character, if the Palestinian state is to be an Arab state, that is not because of racial prejudice or fanaticism but because of two inescapable facts: the first that Palestine has an Arab indigenous population, and the second that Palestine by geography and history is an essential part of the Arab world.[94]

The question for the Arab leadership, he continued, was between "goodwill and force": Were Jews "to live in Palestine with the goodwill of the Arabs," or were they "to rely on force, their own or [that of] others"?[95]

These are the terms that the Muslim League rejected from the Congress because of the fear that permanent minority status could not guarantee security and national development. Similarly, Jews did not want to live in an Arab country, however defined, nor share equal citizenship with Palestinians – again, long before the Holocaust. They felt they were in Palestine by right, not by Arab sufferance, and the British agreed. Hourani was naïve. He did not understand that Zionists could stand firm for three reasons. First, they understood their overwhelming military superiority to the Palestinians after the revolt between 1936 and 1939 had been brutally quashed and the Palestinian leadership imprisoned or exiled.

---

[92] Morris, *1948*, 52.   [93] Hourani, "The Case against a Jewish State in Palestine," 82.
[94] Ibid., 87.   [95] Ibid.

Second, the British and Zionist leadership shared the belief of the Yishuv's essential civilizational superiority to the Arabs, one also held by the majority of League and UN officials and delegates. Arab leaders failed to recognize that the political rights of liberal internationalism were not meant to apply to them, meaning that they continued to send petitions and deputations despite the fact that they had little chance of a hearing.[96] Tellingly, it was obdurate Palestinian resistance, as in the revolt, that led to policy changes in their favor, like the White Paper of 1939. Third, no nationalist movement like Zionism or the Muslim League would rely on its adversary's goodwill. Ambedkar had highlighted 20 years of violence to underline the lack of goodwill in India. In the Palestine case, it was similarly difficult to imagine goodwill in light of the violent Palestinian resistance of the 1930s and Zionist terror campaign in the mid-1940s.[97]

The Anglo-American Committee of Inquiry doubted some of Hourani's propositions as well. Its report struck an artful balance between the sides, including the American pressure to allow in 100,000 Jewish refugees. Palestine was neither purely Arab, nor Jewish. Neither side should control the other; minority protection declarations and provisions inevitably would prove inadequate. Consequently, to avoid the inevitable "civil strife" that would ensue from "the determination of each to achieve domination" and to establish an independent state, an international mandate should continue, with local self-government to be worked out.[98] The British historian who largely drafted the Peel Commission report, Reginald Coupland, wrote to the *London Times* to criticize the Anglo-American Committee report and to readvocate his partition plan. Jews had been ripe for proper self-government for a long time, he insisted. His intervention was anything but prescient, assuring readers – contra Hourani – that "it was impossible to suppose that the Jewish State … would be so mad as to violate it [the frontier] and to seek to occupy Arab land beyond it."[99] Coupland could not know that Zionists would assure UNSCOP that they would accept partition on the condition of future expansion.[100]

[96] Natasha Wheatley, "Mandatory Interpretation: Legal Hermeneutics and the New International Order in Arab and Jewish Petitions to the League of Nations," *Past and Present*, no. 227 (2015): 205–48.

[97] Ami Pedahzur and Arie Perliger, *Jewish Terrorism in Israel* (New York: Columbia University Press, 2011).

[98] *Anglo-American Committee of Inquiry Report*. The Final Report by the Anglo-American Committee of Inquiry on Palestine (April 30, 1946), The Avalon Project: Documents in Law, History, and Diplomacy, Yale Law School, https://avalon.law.yale.edu/subject_menus/angtoc.asp.

[99] Reginald Coupland, "The Jew and the Arab. Conditions of Settlement in Palestine: The Case for Partition Restated," *Times* (London), July 13, 1946, 5.

[100] Eldad Ben-Dror, "The Success of the Zionist Strategy vis-à-vis UNSCOP," *Israel Affairs* 20, no. 1 (2014): 19–39.

Hourani's reply in the *Times* rightly pointed out that Coupland was pre-pared to consign Arabs to minority status in a Jewish state, but not the reverse. But his vague statement that it was dangerous for minorities to rely on foreign powers for protection for "refusing to accept the duties of citizenship" ignored the fact that Zionists had been able to rely on great power backing for much of the mandate, even if they had felt betrayed by the 1939 White Paper that rejected partition and restricted Jewish migration. The fact remained that a British military presence enabled the development of the Yishuv whatever the latter felt about the former. Nor did Hourani foresee that Israelis could rely on military hardware and support from European states until 1967 and especially the Americans thereafter.[101] Power, not justice and the avoidance of violence, mattered in the end.

Like the British partition plan in India a few months earlier, the UNSCOP plan did not foresee population exchanges but minority protection. And, as in India, force prevailed on the ground. Security concerns about the loyalty of remnant enclaves governed the expulsion (and prevention of the return of) Palestinian Arabs by Israeli forces in 1948 and 1949 and territorial expansion well beyond the borders of the 1947 UN partition plan. Take the case of the expulsion of Palestinians from Lydda in July 1948, which Israeli historian Anita Shapira describes in terms of Hourani's predictions:

> A brief uprising by the residents of Lydda (Lod) exposed the danger inherent in leaving a large bloc containing a hostile population behind the advancing army, midway between Tel Aviv and Jerusalem. The commanders Allon and Yitzhak Rabin, who were considering a large-scale population evacuation, went to consult with [Prime Minister] Ben-Gurion. Ben-Gurion listened to them and did not react; he had an uncanny ability to keep silent when he needed to. It was only at the end of the discussion, as the commanders were about to leave for the battle-field, that, according to Rabin, Ben-Gurion waved his hand and said: "Expel them." ... [L]ike most of his ministers, he saw the Arabs' exodus as a great miracle, one of the most important in that year of miracles, since the presence of a hostile population constituting some forty percent of the new state's total populace did not augur well for the future.[102]

This operation, which included a massacre of about 250 townspeople, was the outcome of plans to secure territory by destroying Palestinian Arab militias and the villages from which they operated. The outcome, writes historian Benny Morris, was a "war of conquest," even if it unfolded in piecemeal fashion, with local commanders often taking the initiative to expel

---

[101] Albert Hourani, "Jew and Arab," letter to the *Times* (London), July 30, 1946.
[102] Anita Shapira, *Ben-Gurion: Father of Modern Israel*, trans. Anthony Berris (New Haven, CT: Yale University Press, 2014), 170–1.

Palestinians from towns and villages.[103] There was retaliatory violence on both sides. The massacre of the villagers of Deir Yassin in April 1948 by Irgun auxiliaries was avenged by the murder of Jewish academic and medical personnel in a 10-vehicle convoy in Jerusalem by Arab militias.[104]

After the guns fell silent, approximately 700,000 Palestinians had fled or been expelled, while 160,000 Palestinian Arabs were left behind Israeli lines as internal refugees or, if they were lucky, in their own homes. They were then subject to a military occupation until 1966, during which they suffered extensive land expropriation and mobility restrictions and were generally closely monitored. The possibility of expulsion lay open in the case of further conflict with Arab states.[105] The state appealed to "the Arab inhabitants of the State of Israel ... on the basis of full and equal citizenship," much like Hourani's offer.[106] The Israeli Proclamation of Independence from May 1948 mentioned "complete equality of social and political rights to all its inhabitants irrespective of religion, race or sex." A minorities ministry headed by the first Israeli government's only Sephardic minister, who had liberal views toward the Arab minority, was quickly shut down by Prime Minister Ben-Gurion in 1949. He was effectively replaced by Yehoshua Palmon (1913–1995), advisor to the prime minister on Arab affairs, to oversee Muslim religious institutions with a ministry of religious affairs, thereby casting Palestinians as a religious rather than a national minority. A security hawk who coordinated the martial law regime governing Palestinians, Palmon did not believe in democratic Arab self-administration and "personified the quest for control of the minority and the suspicion of its inherent disloyalty to the state," as one scholar puts it.[107]

At the same time, Jews from Arab countries began arriving in Israel. Now there was talk of an informal population exchange. We know from the previous chapter that Joseph Schechtman wrote about the European, Indian, and Middle Eastern cases in real time, and that in 1949 the State of Israel engaged him to provide

---

[103] Morris, *1948*, 290, 119.   [104] Ibid., 125–8.

[105] Arnon Degani, "The Decline and Fall of the Israeli Military Government, 1948–1966: A Case of Settler-Colonial Consolidation?" *Settler Colonial Studies* 5, no. 1 (2014): 84–99; Shira Robinson, *Citizen Strangers: Palestinians and the Birth of Israel's Liberal Settler State* (Stanford, CA: Stanford University Press, 2013).

[106] Provisional Government of Israel, "Proclamation of Independence," The Knesset, www .knesset.gov.il/docs/eng/megilat_eng.htm; Michael M. Karayanni, "The Separate Nature of the Religious Accommodations for the Palestinian-Arab Minority in Israel," *Northwestern Journal of International Human Rights* 5, no. 1 (2006): 41–71; Amal Jamal, *Arab Minority Nationalism in Israel: The Politics of Indigeneity* (Abingdon: Routledge, 2011).

[107] Alisa Rubin Peled, *Debating Islam in the Jewish State: The Development of Policy Toward Islamic Institutions in Israel* (Albany: State University of New York Press, 2001), 150–1; Don Peretz, "Early State Policy towards the Arab Population," in *New Perspectives on Israeli History: The Early Years of the State*, ed. Laurence J. Silberstein (New York: New York University Press, 1991), 98.

academic justification for the expulsion of Palestinian Arabs and its refusal to allow their return.[108] Observing that Pakistani and Indian leaders did not follow the Zionist viewpoint regarding expulsion, he regretted their "stubbornly refusal to accept the exchange of population as a bitter but inevitable necessity and to conduct it in a constructive way."[109]

In fact, we also know that Indian and Pakistan elites did consider population exchange, but that it was inconsistent with the hostage theory that possessed a higher status in Muslim League calculations in particular. Schechtman did note the hostage theory in his short book *Population Transfers in Asia*, published in 1949, but, as might be expected, he came to the opposite conclusion.[110] Although he did not say so directly, the hostage logic could not work in the Middle East because of the scale of the Palestinian expulsion in 1948 and of course because of the Israeli intention not to allow the refugees to return. How could deterrence function if the conditions of equitable reciprocity no longer existed? Far from guaranteeing Jewish security in Arab countries, then, hostage status brought no leverage for Arab leaders. In the event, he made his pitch in terms of Arab hostility to Jews: "As a result of the growing anti-Zionist policy on the part of the Arab and Moslem states," he concluded, "the situation of the Jewish minorities in those countries is unbearable. They are considered and treated as hostages." To make his point, he quoted Arab leaders who linked the establishment of Israel to the fate of Jews in their countries. They threatened retaliation. These communities now faced a "very real threat of physical extermination," and so their "speedy evacuation" was "a matter of utmost urgency."[111]

Reflecting Israeli government policy, Schectman then advanced the argument for a de facto population exchange. Transferring Jews from Arab countries to Israel would represent the "fundamentally essential counterpart to the movement of Arabs from Palestine."[112] The Arab-Jewish migration was part of a grand demographic bargain: the mistreatment of Jews resulting from hostage thinking would impel their evacuation and balance out the inexplicable flight (as he conceived it) of Palestinian Arabs. Surely not coincidentally, he was also giving voice to Ben-Gurion's public position that reversed the retaliatory logic, making the expelled Palestinian Arabs extraterritorial hostages. They could not return if Jews in Arab countries were mistreated: "the ultimate position of

---

[108] See 356 above. On preventing refugee return, see Benny Morris, "The Crystallization of Israeli Policy against a Return of the Arab Refugees: April-December, 1948," *Studies in Zionism* 6, no. 1 (1985): 85–118.

[109] Joseph B. Schechtman, *Population Transfers in Asia* (New York: Hallsby, 1949), 86.

[110] Ibid., 10.

[111] Ibid., 115. An analysis of this grand bargain is Itamar Mann, "Disentangling Displacements: Historical Justice for Mizrahim and Palestinians in Israel," *Theoretical Inquiries in Law* 21, no. 2 (2020). DOI: https://doi.org/10.1515/til-2020-0020.

[112] Ibid.

the 300,000-odd Arab refugees from Palestine," the new state leader was reported as stating, "would depend on the treatment meted out to Jewish populations in the Arab lands."[113] In reality, he had no intention of permitting their return and worked to encourage the immigration of Jews in general.

Such notions of equitable reciprocity had been voiced before, notably at the World Jewish Congress meeting in 1937 when "population exchange" was the term to refer to Arab Jews while "transfer" applied to Palestinian Arabs, though the idea gained no traction until the realization dawned that the Holocaust had robbed Zionism of its favored migration source. By 1942, Arab Jews were recognized as necessary to populate a future Jewish state, and by the early 1950s the Israeli state realized that their mass migration to Israel could be used as a diplomatic weight to offset the Palestinian refugee problem. This campaign continues to this day.[114] The terms of this migration are thus fraught and contested. The position of the state and advocacy groups for Jews from Arab countries paints a picture of enduring and intense anti-semitic discrimination that culminated in riots and other measures that drove Jews from their millennia-long homes to Israel; they do not compare this experience to the military occupation endured by Palestinian Arab citizens of Israel between 1948 and 1966, which was more severe.[115] Arab ultranational-ists, by contrast, paint these communities as economically exploitative and Zionist, disloyally supporting the enemy Israel with whom many Arab states were at war in 1948; this argument evinces a retaliatory logic.

Scholarship on the question depicts an uneven process of push and pull factors that resulted in the punctual departure of Arab Jews to many countries. These factors include intense Zionist activism to provoke migration, ranging from competition with communists to win the hearts and minds of Iraqi Jews from the early 1940s – mostly unsuccessfully – to the terrorist plot Operation Susannah in Egypt in 1954.[116] In class terms, Jews were associated with cosmopolitan commercial elites who had close ties to colonial powers, though few to Zionism. Well integrated into these societies, Jews had little incentive to migrate; even impoverished Yemeni Jews, more than 40,000 of whom were

---

[113] C. L. Sulzberger, "Ben Gurion Bans Immigration Curb," *New York Times*, July 22, 1948, 16; Schechtman, *Population Transfers in Asia*, 130.

[114] Yehouda Shenhav, "Arab Jews, Population Exchange, and the Palestinian Right of Return," in *Exile and Return: Predicaments of Palestinians and Jews*, ed. Ann M. Lesch and Ian S. Lustick (Philadelphia: University of Pennsylvania, 2005), 225–45.

[115] Justice for Jews from Arab Countries, www.justiceforjews.com/narrative.html. A useful corrective in the press is David Cesarani, "A Different Kind of Catastrophe: The Suffering of Jewish Communities in Arab Countries Shouldn't Be Played Off against the Plight of the Palestinians," *The Guardian*, June 23, 2008.

[116] Esther Meir-Glitzstein, *Zionism in an Arab Country: Jews in Iraq in the 1940s* (London: Routledge, 2004); Joel Beinin, *The Dispersion of Egyptian Jewry: Culture, Politics, and the Formation of a Modern Diaspora* (Berkeley: University of California Press, 1998), 19–20.

induced to leave for Israel under the auspices of a deal cut between Israeli authorities, Jewish organizations, and the rulers of Aden and Yemen.[117]

At the same time, other geopolitical forces were impinging on these communities from the interwar period onward, with the simultaneous rise of Zionism in Palestine, which was reliant on British power, and Arab nationalism, which was anti-imperial in orientation. The notorious Farhud riot in Baghdad in June 1941, during which Arabs murdered between 150 and 180 Jews and destroyed their property, was the result of collaboration charges with the British who defeated a short-lived pro-Axis, independent Iraqi regime and reoccupied the country. In fact, these communities were loyal and saw their futures in Arab states.[118] Israel's defeat of these states' armies in 1948 discredited their elitist, pro-Western, and conservative regimes with which Jewish communities were associated. In response, these regimes licensed retaliatory violence against Jewish communities to shore up their crumbling position. As a consequence, some 123,000 Iraqi Jews left for Israel between 1949 and 1950.

But, even with the replacement of these regimes by nationalist revolutionaries in coups during the 1950s, most Jews remained in Egypt, for example, and those who left did not choose Israel as their destination. It was further military defeat to Israel, in 1956 and 1967, that entrenched ultranationalist conceptions of Arab nationhood and intensified legal and economic pressure on Jews to leave. Upon Algerian independence in 1962, most Algerian Jews, who had held French citizenship since 1870, migrated to France. Joel Beinin's summary of the Egyptian pattern could be generalized: "Between 1919 and 1956, the entire Egyptian Jewish community ... was transformed from a national asset to a fifth column."[119] Postcolonial Arab nationalism had no place for Jews in its conception of the Arab polity and its permanent security. These regrettable outcomes flowed from Lemkin's ontology of humanity as first and foremost comprising ethnic nations.

---

[117] Esther Meir-Glitzstein, *The Magic Carpet: Exodus of Yemenite Jewry: An Israeli Formative Myth* (Eastbourne: Sussex Academic Press, 2014). The Imam of Yemen apparently profited from the Jewish property, and more than 800 of them died en route because of logistical bungling.

[118] Orit Bashkin, *New Babylonians: A History of Jews in Modern Iraq* (Stanford, CA: Stanford University Press, 2012); Aline Schlaepfer, "When Anticolonialism Meets Antifascism: Modern Jewish Intellectuals in Baghdad," in *Minorities and the Modern Arab World*, ed. Laura Robson (Syracuse, NY: Syracuse University Press, 2016), 93–106.

[119] Beinin, *The Dispersion of Egyptian Jewry*, 22; Norman Stillman, "Frenchmen, Jews, or Arabs? The Jews of the Arab World between European Colonialism, Zionism, and Arab Nationalism" in *Judaism and Islam: Boundaries, Communication, and Interaction*, ed. Benjamin H. Hary, John L. Hayes, and Fred Astren (Leiden: Brill, 2000), 123–38; Rachel Simon, "Zionism," in *The Jews of the Middle East and North Africa in Modern Times*, ed. Reeva Spector Simon, Michael Menachem Laskier, and Sara Reguer (New York: Columbia University Press, 2002), 176–8; Abdelwahab Meddeb and Benjamin Stora, eds., *A History of Jewish-Muslim Relations: From the Origins to the Present Day*, trans. Jane Marie Todd and Michael B. Smith (Princeton, NJ: Princeton University Press, 2013).

PART III

The Language of Transgression, Permanent
Security, and Holocaust Memory

10

Lemkin, Arendt, Vietnam, and Liberal
Permanent Security

The struggle to define genocide began during its canonization in international law in 1948: with India and Pakistan's mutual accusations during partition massacres, in Arab and Jewish complaints about the violent aftermath of the British Mandate in Palestine, and in complaints by Eastern European exiles that the Soviet Union was destroying their nations. Thereafter, leaders of national liberation and secessionist movements, activists, intellectuals, and journalists routinely invoked genocide to draw attention to their cause, to denounce their opponents, or simply to express horror at massacres they had witnessed. The Algerian National Front claimed the French committed genocide in suppressing its independence struggle in the 1950s, contemporaries denounced Hutu massacres of Tutsi in Rwanda in 1964 as genocide, philosopher Jean-Paul Sartre (1905–1980) excoriated the US war in Vietnam in the same terms, while the unsuccessful Biafran secession struggle from Nigeria in the late 1960s was marketed as forging a safe haven from genocide. Bengalis seeking to carve out Bangladesh from Pakistan in 1971 said the government's repression was genocidal, while scholars thought they saw "selective genocide" in Burundi a year later, and in attacks on Paraguayan Indians soon thereafter.[1] None of these cases became generally recognized as genocide; they rarely appear in university syllabi and textbooks on the subject. The reason is that their anticolonial and civil war contexts cannot be registered as genocide in its dominant interpretation without making it conform to its Holocaust archetype. How and why this frame was effected is the subject of this chapter.

---

[1] Shiromani Gurdwara Parbandhak Committee, *Muslim League Attack on Sikhs and Hindus in the Punjab 1947* (Allahabad: Allahabad Law Journal Press, 1949); "Rwanda Policy of Genocide Alleged," *The Times*, February 3, 1964; Mohammed Harbi and Gilbert Meynier, eds., *Le FLN: Documents et Histoire 1954–1962* (Paris: Fayard, 2004); Auberon Waugh, *Britain and Biafra: The Case for Genocide* (London: Britain-Biafra Association, 1969); Jean-Paul Sartre, "On Genocide," *New Left Review*, no. 48 (March–April 1968): 12–25; Kaylan Chaudhuri, *Genocide in Bangladesh* (Bombay: Orient Longman, 1972); René Lemarchand and David Martin, *Selective Genocide in Burundi* (London: Minority Rights Group, 1974); Richard Arens, *Genocide in Paraguay* (Philadelphia: Temple University Press, 1976).

After World War II, Nehemiah Robinson (1898–1964) and his brother Jacob directed the Institute for Jewish Affairs in New York. Nehemiah's early commentaries on the postwar international agreements on human rights, refugees, stateless people, and genocide are well known. Largely forgotten is his little book on *The United Nations and the World Jewish Congress*, a study of the Congress's (WJC) diplomacy during the negotiations of these agreements. On the WJC's categorization of genocide, Robinson reported in 1955 that it:

> consistently held that Genocide was a non-political crime, i.e., one which was not necessarily connected with struggles of States for predominance or influence. It involved inhuman acts against groups which the other, stronger, groups sought to eliminate not for political but for racial, religious, or similar reasons.[2]

This conceptualization of genocide reflected the evolving view at the time and persists to this day. The consensus lies with the nonpolitical understanding of genocide, namely as violence driven by racial hatred. Genocide is thus a species of hate crime, in which the victim is attacked for who they are – for their identity – rather than for their actions. Thus defined, genocide cannot occur in suppressing an insurgency – whether in a domestic or colonial context – because the political agency entailed by insurgent action implies politics and even collective guilt.[3] Separating genocide from acts of state or para-state violence more generally isolates it as a peculiar form of violence, presenting genocide as exceptional rather than as a manifestation of permanent security.

The instalment of genocide as the "crime of crimes" marked a turning point in the centuries-old language of transgression: now only mass criminality motivated by race-hatred that resembled its archetype, the Holocaust, shocked the conscience of mankind. This depoliticization had momentous consequences for the visibility of permanent security. Now only illiberal permanent security – embodied by the Axis Powers that disgraced themselves in World War II – counted as seriously criminal. Practices of liberal permanent security

---

[2] Nehemiah Robinson, *The United Nations and the World Jewish Congress* (New York: Institute for Jewish Affairs, 1955), 21. Robinson, *Universal Declaration of Human Rights: Its Origins, Significance, and Interpretation* (New York, Institute of Jewish Affairs, World Jewish Congress, 1950); Robinson, *Convention Relating to the Status of Refugees: its History, Significance and Contents* (New York: Institute of Jewish Affairs, 1952); Robinson, *Convention Relating to the Status of Stateless Persons* (New York: Institute for Jewish Affairs, 1955); Robinson, *The Genocide Convention: A Commentary* (New York: Institute for Jewish Affairs, 1960).

[3] Maurice T. Vambe and Abebe Zegeye, "Racializing Ethnicity and Ethnicizing Racism: Rethinking the Epistemic Conditions of Genocide in Africa," *Social Identities* 14, no. 6 (2008): 776.

were not so shocking, notwithstanding the postwar peace movement's attempt to link Auschwitz and Hiroshima.[4] The war's victors embodied liberal permanent security in different ways: both Western liberalism and Soviet communism purported to represent "humanity." While they mobilized the reconfigured language of transgression against one another in the Cold War, the academic field of Genocide Studies developed in the West, which came to dominate the term's definition.[5]

The most dramatic decades are the mid-1960s to the early 1980s, when scholars and activists who excoriated the US bombing and counterinsurgency strategy in Vietnam, and its nuclear weapons program, coined new terms: "ecocide" and "omnicide." They conceptualized liberal permanent security with the legal categories inherited from the Nuremberg Trials – aggressive warfare, war crimes, crimes against humanity. They even invoked the Martens Clause like representatives of small nations before them, this time opposing American empire. Some of them also said the Americans were committing genocide, because modern warfare against a popular national liberation movement necessarily targets the entire population. At issue were the notions of "national security" and "military necessity," the watchwords of the juggernaut they called the US "national security state." These notions could not rationalize killing millions of Vietnamese civilians, insisted these scholars and activists.

In reply, conservatives and some liberals provided legal cover for US action in Vietnam: the Allied bombing of German and Japanese cities was not proscribed at Nuremberg, they pointed out; indeed, it had helped win the war. Bombing the enemy in Vietnam now would vanquish the communist threat.[6] What is more, they continued, there could be no question of genocide, which was modelled on the Holocaust. So successful was the institution of the Holocaust archetype of genocide, and so powerful was the moral aura of victory in World War II, that even Marxist philosophers like Sartre felt compelled to analogize between the American and German motivations. As we see in the next chapter, those who later sought to affix the genocide label to the Armenian and Darfur cases analogized likewise, distorting their cases in the process.

---

[4] Ran Zwigenberg, *Hiroshima: The Origins of Global Memory Culture* (Cambridge: Cambridge University Press, 2016).

[5] For the Cold War context, see Anton Weiss-Wendt, *A Rhetorical Crime: Genocide in the Geopolitical Discourse of the Cold War* (New Brunswick, NJ: Rutgers University Press, 2017).

[6] Symptomatic is the cavalier defense of the "incineration of people in cities" in World War II by Dan Plesch, *Human Rights after Hitler: The Lost History of Prosecuting Axis War Crimes* (Washington, DC: Georgetown University Press, 2017), 143.

Raphael Lemkin: Affixing the Holocaust Archetype

After the US voted for the UN Genocide Convention in 1948, President Truman transmitted it to the Senate for advice and consent to ratification. The Senate Foreign Relations Committee held hearings on the Convention in 1950. Members of the State Department and leaders of communal organizations were invited to make submissions to the committee, which amount to over 500 pages of text. The elephant in the room was the same one that concerned State Department officials in 1944 and 1945: could new international instruments be used to embarrass the US during the Cold War? Senators and the American Bar Association expressed intense anxiety that local racial discrimination would expose the country to international law and humiliation.[7]

They had good reason to worry that public discussion of genocide would shed light on inconvenient facts. Religious and ethnic community leaders, who represented small nations consciousness, sought ratification and did not think that admitting past genocidal episodes in US history should present an obstacle. Dorothy Madders Robinson of the Methodist Church declared that "every American school child knows the tragic story of the crime of genocide as it affected the Acadians of the Gaspe peninsula a little more than 200 years ago, and is still better acquainted with genocide as practiced so tragically on many tribes of American Indians."[8] The Armenian National Council of America agreed with her criticism of the American Bar Association's opposition to the convention's ratification. "It seems hard to believe that any document with such highly laudable purposes should encounter any opposition in a country like the United States, where there have never been any incidents of genocide (excepting perhaps in the cases of the American Indian and of some of the worst abuses of the slaves before the Civil 'War')."[9] Harry S. Barger from the National Economic Council wondered if the Convention had teeth because it was unlikely to cover those who were committing it now, such as when "the Zionists

---

[7] Lawrence J. LeBlanc, *The United States and the Genocide Convention* (Durham, NC: Duke University Press, 1991); Richard F. McFarland, "The United States and the United Nations Convention on the Punishment and Prevention of Genocide" (PhD diss., American University 1971).

[8] Committee on Foreign Relations, Genocide Convention: Hearings Before a Subcommittee of the Committee on Foreign Relations, United States Senate, 81st Congress, 2nd Sess., On Executive O, The International Convention on the Prevention and Punishment of Genocide, January 23, 24, 25, February 9, 1950 (Washington, DC: US Government Printing Office, 1950), 281; Binoy Kampmark, "Shaping the Holocaust: The Final Solution in US Political Discourses on the Genocide Convention, 1948–1956," *Journal of Genocide Research* 7, no. 1 (2005): 85–100.

[9] Committee on Foreign Relations, Genocide Convention, 503.

exterminated every man, woman, and child" in the Palestinian village of "Deir Yazin" or in the Soviet Union.[10]

James Finucane from the National Council for the Prevention of War excoriated the US for its support of the expulsion of Germans in Central and Eastern Europe, claiming that "our earlier attitude toward the Germans is an example of the genocide possible under the Potsdam convention." Invoking the Nuremberg Trials, which he considered victor's justice because they did not prosecute Allied war crimes, he pointed out that "In all the wars since 1945 – Palestine, Indochina, Indonesia, Indo-Pakistan – the Nuremburg trials have not received the compliment of a single imitation.[11] He concluded by repeating the arguments made during the UN Convention debates and by the American Bar Association that the omission of political rationales from the Convention enabled authorities to avoid its clutches by claiming to persecute racial minorities on political grounds. "What could this convention have done to Hitler? Would it have saved the Jews? Not likely. Rather, Hitler might have exploited it to persecute the Jews, because he charged the Jews were plotting to destroy the German nation."[12] Such statements were politely ignored by senators and State Department officials but made apparent the geopolitical mischief that the genocide concept and Convention would cause if they were broadly construed.

In the meantime, the State Department determined that discrimination against, and segregation of, Native Americans represented "a 50 percent chance" of "international intervention."[13] Even so, it persisted with ratification efforts because of the nation's moral leadership in global affairs. As US Solicitor General Philip B. Perlman (1890–1960) put it, "the United States, as a leading protagonist for world peace and order under law, is committed to cooperative efforts to prevent and stamp out the devastating lawlessness represented in genocide."[14] The US stood for the international law, and that was why the Convention should be ratified. But then the genocide definition should be safely contained.

The Deputy Undersecretary of State, Dean Rusk (1903–1994), who later became Secretary of State during the Vietnam War, represented the department. While he began with the Lemkian observation that genocide was "as old as the history of man," he immediately yoked it to the Holocaust archetype: its unique character, which so shocked civilized conscience, contained genocide's meaning.

---

[10] Ibid., 303.   [11] Ibid., 313–5.   [12] Ibid., 317. Cf. the Bar Association, 214.
[13] Adam Weiss-Wendt, *The Soviet Union and the Gutting of the UN Genocide Convention* (Madison: University of Wisconsin Press, 2017), 117.
[14] Committee on Foreign Relations, Genocide Convention, 28.

But the worst atrocities of Nero against the Christians failed to reach the level of those perpetrated by Hitler against the Jews. No one can yet have forgotten the organized butchery of racial groups by the Nazis, our enemies in World War II, which has resulted in the extermination of some 6,000,000 Jews. Decent men everywhere were outraged and revolted by the barbaric and bestial conduct of the rulers of Germany at that time. These events so shocked the conscience of civilized men that after World War II it had come to be accepted that such conduct could no longer be tolerated in civilized society, and that it should be prohibited by the international community.[15]

He urged the Convention's ratification because it could be used to advance the cause of freedom, that is, to turn the spotlight onto the Soviet Union:

It is a familiar role, therefore, for the United States to take the lead in raising moral standards of international society. And, prevailing international conditions make it imperative that the United States continue to play this role. We all know too well that millions of human beings are still subjected to the domination of ruthless totalitarian regimes, and that the specter of genocide still haunts mankind. It should be made clear to such governments that the United States and other civilized countries do not condone such conduct now any more than in the past.[16]

Despite their own anticommunism, senators were unconvinced whether Rusk's analogical link between the Holocaust and the Soviet crimes held. While the former was clearly genocide due to Hitler's repeated statements "that they were going to kill all the Jews, exterminate them," one of them said, "millions of people" could be exterminated in Russia "simply because they may grumble a little about the existing government": that is, political repression was not racially motivated. Rusk could only reply by admitting that the Convention was limited to "a national, ethnical, racial, or religious group." In other words, it did not apply to the Soviets after all.[17]

There was no equivocation about the utility of the Convention's depoliticization in other contexts. The debate thus turned on the term "in part" in Article 2 of the Convention: the intent to destroy a group "in whole or in part." Dean Rusk insisted that the wording meant that the intention to destroy the whole group, even if only part was ultimately destroyed. Following this line of reasoning, one senator, relying on advice from the Solicitor General and the State Department, opined that localized lynchings in US states would not constitute genocide because they did not evince a general intent to exterminate: "the intention has to be to continue on from Illinois to Indiana and then down to Georgia to wipe them all out, you see."[18] Neither the "violent expression of prejudice which is directed against individual members of

---

[15] Ibid., 10–11.   [16] Ibid., 20.   [17] Ibid., 21.   [18] Ibid., 304.

groups" – i.e., anti-Black violence – nor, by implication, the fate of Native Americans, could be considered genocide. "It can thus be readily seen that genocide, as defined in this convention," concluded Rusk, "has never occurred in the United States and is not likely to occur here in the future." Genocide happened elsewhere, justifying humanitarian interventions, such as the US intervention in Cuba in 1898, he continued.[19] US imperial expansion was cast as moral leadership. For the State Department, ratifying the Convention would not threaten US interests, as feared by the American Bar Association: on the contrary, the Convention would help prosecute the US's agenda in the Cold War.

Raphael Lemkin was understandably anxious that the senators would not support US ratification of the Convention. He thus wrote to the committee to argue that "in part" meant a substantial part. And he insisted on a narrow definition of genocide to exclude US racial violence, beginning his letter thus: "A thorough analysis of the Genocide Convention proves conclusively the Convention does not apply either to lynching or to rights." Genocide does not apply to individuals he said, but to groups. "Certainly," he continued, "a casual lynching is not of this nature. It does not destroy the Negro race as such." Lynching and race riots were acts "of local terrorism." Their logic was to maintain racial hierarchy rather than group destruction. He thus concluded that "Genocide is a crime that does not happen in the U.S.A," adding tactlessly: "It is like African leprosy." He shared Rusk's evocation of the US's world-historical mission: "This country is called upon to cooperate in fighting this disease for humanitarian and defensive reasons only."[20]

Only a year later, this conviction was challenged directly by a controversial petition directed to the General Assembly of the UN by the communist-backed Civil Rights Congress, founded in 1946 and led by African-American lawyer William Patterson (1891–1980).[21] Less a petition than a 239-page closely reasoned and exhaustively documented indictment of racial violence and discrimination in the US, *We Charge Genocide* accused the US of genocide against African Americans.[22] Using statistics from the National Association for the Advancement of Colored People, its empirical claims were not challenged. It was the genocide frame that was consciously controversial. Because

[19] Ibid., 12–13, 20.   [20] Ibid., 370.

[21] William Patterson, *The Man Who Cried Genocide: An Autobiography* (New York: International Publishers, 1971); Gerald Horne, *Black Revolutionary: William Patterson and the Globalization of the African American Freedom Struggle* (Champaign: University of Illinois Press, 2013).

[22] William Patterson, ed., *We Charge Genocide: The Historic Petition to the United Nations for Relief from a Crime of the United States Government Against the Negro People* (New York: Civil Rights Congress, 1951). It was signed by luminaries like singer Paul Robson (1898–1976) and scholar and writer W. E. B. Du Bois (1868–1963). "Robeson Says Uncle Sam Is 'Mass Killer,'" *New York Amsterdam News*, December 22, 1951, 6.

Patterson was a lawyer and wanted to provoke international legal proceedings, he cleaved closely to the UN definition, organising the text under the headings of Article 2(b) of the Convention with its five modes of destruction. Lynching featured centrally, as did economic disadvantaging of African Americans, which he claimed reduced their life expectancy by eight years compared to whites.[23]

The book both reflected the Soviet view during the Convention debates that genocide was the product of "nazism-fascism" and anticipated the New Left critique of American foreign and domestic policy during the Vietnam War 15 years later. The aim of segregating African-American ghettos with poor housing, education, and medical care, wrote Patterson and his comrades, was "the perpetuation of economic and political power by the few through the destruction of political protest by the many." By the few, they meant "a reactionary clique" that seeks "to increase ... profits and unchallenged control."[24] They also invoked the language of transgression, comparing Nazi Germany and the US, urging the Nuremberg precedent, and mingling of racial and political categories, which indicated the pull exerted by the Holocaust. "Shocked by the Nazis' barbaric murder of millions of Jews and millions of Poles, Russians, Czechs and other nationals on the sole basis of 'race' under Hitler's law – just as Negroes are murdered on the basis of 'race' in the United States under Mississippi, Virginia, and Georgia law." The petition then cited Justice Jackson's statement at Nuremberg that the persecution of a domestic minority could be a sign of war preparations in order to impugn US foreign policy in the early years of the Cold War.[25]

As might be expected, *We Charge Genocide* was denounced as communist propaganda in the press and by the State Department. The latter prevented Patterson from delivering it to the UN in Paris and attempted to confiscate his passport. To a large extent, it succeeded in burying the petition.[26] Again, Lemkin lent his support to the department, criticizing the petitioners for diverting "attention from the crimes of genocide committed against Estonians, Latvians, Lithuanians, Poles and other Soviet-subjugated peoples."[27] He did not mention that their diasporic communities in the US were paying him to write about their cases at the time. In various press pieces, he said that genocide could not be taking place when African Americans were

---

[23] Patterson, *We Charge Genocide*, 31–2.   [24] Ibid., 5.   [25] Ibid., 31–2.

[26] A minor article is "US Accused in UN of Negro Genocide," *New York Times*, December 18, 1951, 13.

[27] "UN Asked To Act against Genocide In United States," *Afro-American*, December 29, 1951, 19; Carol Anderson, *Eyes off the Prize: The United Nations and the African American Struggle for Human Rights, 1944–1955* (Cambridge: Cambridge University Press, 2003); Erik Gellman, *Death Blow to Jim Crow: The National Negro Congress and the Rise of Militant Civil Rights* (Chapel Hill: University of North Carolina Press, 2012).

enjoying improved living conditions. The "fright" occasioned by lynching was not tantamount to the "serious mental harm" stipulated in the Convention. What is more, genocide was a rare crime of great magnitude, which he defined narrowly as "annihilation" by divorcing it from the Nazi policies of discrimination that he had included in his earlier work.[28] "The tragically dramatic nature of genocide should not be permitted to be deflated," he wrote, sounding like the WJC. "By confusing genocide with discrimination injustice is done not only to existing international law but also to the good name of some democratic societies which might be unjustly slandered for genocide." In again defending his adopted home by so closely joining the Holocaust and genocide, he sealed his abandonment of the "one long chain" argument about genocide he had advanced during World War II when, we recall from Chapter 5, he wrote that under genocide:

> in the first should be included every action infringing upon the life, liberty, health, corporal integrity, economic existence, and the honor of the inhabitants when committed because they belong to a national, religious, or racial group; and in the second, every policy aiming at the destruction or the aggrandizement of one such group to the prejudice or detriment of another.[29]

It went without saying that he ignored African-American communist author and contributor to *We Charge Genocide*, Oakley C. Johnson (1890–1976), who effectively repeated Lemkin's wartime argument back to him: far from Klan actions frightening individuals, they terrorized an entire community; just as millions of Jews survived the war, so surviving African Americans did not entail the absence of genocidal intent; and discrimination could not be counterposed to genocide but was "*a factor in genocide*."[30] But to no avail. Lemkin did not need such allies in his quest to have the US ratify the Genocide Convention. Accordingly, he argued like the WJC during the war when it distinguished between the fates of European Jews and Christian nations under Nazi occupation: "Genocide implies destruction, death, annihilation, while discrimination is a regrettable denial of certain opportunities of life. To be

---

[28] "Charge of U.S. Genocide Called Red Smoke Screen" *Washington Post*, December 16, 1951, M6; Editorial, "The Genocide Trap," *Chicago Daily Tribune*, December 22, 1951, 8; "Lemkin Calls Soviet Guilty of Genocide," *New York Times*, January 18, 1953, 13; Raphael Lemkin, "Nature of Genocide: Confusion With Discrimination against Individuals Seen," *New York Times*, June 14, 1953, E10.

[29] Raphael Lemkin, *Axis Rule in Occupied Europe: Laws of Occupation, Analysis of Government, Proposals for Redress* (Washington, DC: Carnegie Endowment for International Peace, 1944), 93.

[30] Oakley C. Johnson to Raphael Lemkin, June 24, 1953, American Jewish Historical Society, Raphael Lemkin Collection, Box 1, Folder 10. Emphasis in original.

unequal is not the same as to be dead."[31] This turn in his thinking is fitting given his enduring Zionism and partisan attachment to the new state of Israel.

That Lemkin ended up advancing these arguments was unsurprising. Now that he lived in the world's most dominant global power, the anticommunist Lemkin identified the US as the vehicle for the civilizing mission that his nineteenth-century international lawyer predecessors had ascribed to European imperial power. Indeed, he invoked these lawyers – who I mention in Chapter 1 – as inspiration, and even cited US President Theodore Roosevelt's 1904 justification for muscular US interventionism: "Brutal wrongdoing, or impotence, which results in the general loosening of ties of civilized society, may finally require intervention by some civilized nation, and in the Western Hemisphere, the United States cannot ignore its duty."[32] Genocide, he stated in the introduction to his unpublished world history of genocide, was the culmination of the language of transgression since the early-modern period, and this language justified humanitarian intervention:

> The history of genocide provides examples of the awakening of humanitarian feelings which gradually have been crystalized in formulae of international law. The awakening of the world conscience is traced to the times when the world community took an affirmative stand to protect human groups from extinction. Bartolome de las Casas, Vitoria, and humanitarian interventions, are all links in one chain leading to the proclamation of genocide as an international crime by the United Nations.[33]

The world conscience resided in New York in the 1950s, also the new home of another Jewish émigré, the famous German-Jewish political thinker, Hannah Arendt (1906–1975). Lemkin lent his prestige to the installation of the Holocaust as genocide's archetype, and he invested the US with a world-historical interventionist task. That archetype depoliticized the language of transgression in its capacity as the "crime of crimes." Arendt completed the process by depoliticizing the Holocaust and articulating the arguments to insulate the West from its contamination. As we see further below, these

---

[31] Tanya Elder, "What You See Before Your Eyes: Documenting Raphael Lemkin's Life by Exploring his Archival Papers, 1900–1959," *Journal of Genocide Research* 7, no. 4 (2005): 469–99.

[32] Raphael Lemkin, "Pyschol. Scars/Int'l Law, etc.," Raphael Lemkin Papers, New York Public Library, Box 2, Folder 4.

[33] Raphael Lemkin, "Introduction to the Study of the Genocide," in *Lemkin on Genocide*, ed. Stephen Leonard Jacobs (Lanham, MD: Lexington Books, 2012), 10–11; "Proposal for Introduction to the Study of Genocide," Raphael Lemkin Papers, New York Public Library, Box 2, Folder 1.

themes and postures were taken up by Comparative Genocide Studies in the 1980s and 1990s.

Hannah Arendt: Depoliticizing the Holocaust and Defending the West

Hannah Arendt's significance in the conceptual history of genocide has two dimensions: her historico-philosophical justification of the thesis, long advanced by the WJC, that the Holocaust is distinct from genocide by virtue of this nonutilitarian, nonpolitical motivation; and her argument that Western traditions are not to blame for the Holocaust. Here was the claim for the Holocaust as a "civilizational rupture" (*Zivilisationsbruch*) decades before German-Israeli historian Dan Diner popularized the notion.[34] Far from proposing a continuity or "boomerang" thesis regarding colonialism and the metropole, as commonly supposed, Arendt intended to show discontinuity between what she called "the Western tradition" and totalitarian crimes. Rendered this way, the political logics that she perceived in genocide – including Western colonial violence – but not in the Holocaust, were forgotten as the latter became the archetype for the former. In this way, the Holocaust functioned as a screen memory that blocked from view the violence and civilizational, indeed racial, hierarchies on which the liberal permanent security of the West is founded.

If Arendt's vaunted cosmopolitanism was less universalist than commonly supposed, her Eurocentrism was also revealed by her intuitively emotional reaction to the first news of Auschwitz. "Decisive" was not "1933" but "1943," as she put it upon hearing credible information about the death camps. "Something happened there to which we cannot reconcile ourselves," she said. "[T]he method, the fabrication of corpses, and so on," was radically new. "Personally, I could accept everything else."[35] To confront the historical realm of "real evil" led to "speechless horror, when all you can say is: This should never have happened."[36] What occurred in the decade after 1933 was explicable, even acceptable, she implied.

Arendt was not alone in her reaction. Critic George Steiner (1929–2020) wrote that his "own consciousness is possessed by the eruption of barbarism in

---

[34] Dan Diner, "Den Zivilisationsbruch erinnern: Über Entstehung und Geltung eines Begriffs," in *Zivilisationsbruch und Gedächtniskultur des beginnenden 21. Jahrhunderts*, ed. Heidemarie Uhl (Innsbruck: Studien Verlag, 2003), 17–34.

[35] Hannah Arendt, "'What Remains? The Language Remains': A Conversation with Günter Gaus," in Arendt, *Essays in Understanding, 1930–1954*, ed. Jerome Kohn (New York: Schocken, 1994), 13.

[36] Arendt, "Some Questions of Moral Philosophy," *Social Research* 61, no. 4 (1994): 761, 763.

Europe," which "did not spring up in the Gobi desert or the rain forests of the Amazon," although, somewhat disingenuously, he disclaimed "for this hideousness any singular privilege."[37] The issue is the coding of the Holocaust as "the eruption of barbarism in Europe," that traditional civilizational category enabling the extermination of native peoples and imperial wars over millennia. Arendt, Steiner, and others were not shocked by barbarism outside Europe, whether ascribable to Europeans or non-Europeans: this was the historical norm that constituted European and, generally, Western hegemony.[38] Shocking was the genocide of Europeans by Europeans, and above all of their own persons, family, and friends.

It was not always so: Arendt's own experience of flight and exile as a German–Jewish refugee in the 1930s and during World War II inclined her to antifascist analyses of National Socialism. She was enamored of Rosa Luxemburg's view of imperialism, and she associated Jewish national liberation – Zionism – with the anticolonial arc of history. Even if she understandably regarded the British Empire and US as "the last bulwark against the new barbarism" of Nazism, these decentralized entities in her mind portended a "commonwealth of European nations with a parliament of its own" after the war. Inspired by Bundism, she also admired the Soviet Union as a federative alternative to the assimilation of the interwar nation-state that had discriminated against Jews.[39] In 1945, she declared fascism to be the "arch-evil of our time" and its roots to be "antisemitism, racism, imperialism."[40] She was developing a sustained analysis of permanent security in all its modes.

By 1951, when she published *The Origins of Totalitarianism*, Arendt had changed her tune. Her anxiety about the Soviet threat to "the West," a term she used to connote a political tradition and community of values, led her to couple the illiberal permanent security of the Soviet Union with Nazism in the composite concept of "totalitarianism," while defending Western imperial powers and the liberal permanent security agenda of the US.[41] She was not

---

[37] George Steiner, *Language and Silence* (New York: Atheneum, 1977), viii.

[38] Theodor W. Adorno, *Minima Moralia* (Frankfurt: Suhrkamp, 1951/1986), 288–9.

[39] Hannah Arendt, "The Minority Question," in Arendt, *The Jewish Writings*, ed. Jerome Kohn and Ron H. Feldman (New York: Schocken, 2007), 130. Hannah Arendt, review of Oscar I. Janowsky, *Nationalities and National Minorities* (New York: Macmillan, 1945) in *Jewish Social Studies* 8, no. 3 (1946): 204. On that question of Zionism and anticolonialism, see Mark Levene, "Jews, Britons, Empire: And How Things Might Be Very Different," *Jewish Culture and History* 12, nos. 1–2 (2010): 61–74.

[40] Hannah Arendt, "The Seeds of the Fascist International," in Arendt, *Essays in Understanding*, 150.

[41] Hannah Arendt, *The Origins of Totalitarianism* (New York: Andre Deutsch, 1986); Roy T. Tsao, "Three Phases of Arendt's Theory of Totalitarianism," *Social Research* 69, no. 2 (2002): 579–619. On the Cold War context of "Western civilization," see Patrick Thaddeus Jackson, *Civilizing the Enemy: German Reconstruction and the Invention of the West* (Ann Arbor: University of Michigan Press, 2006).

alone. Fellow Central European émigré scholar, Hans Kohn (1891–1971), also advocated a "New West" as an alternative to communism.[42] So did her friend, Dwight Macdonald (1906–1982), who ran the influential leftist *Politics* journal in which many New York intellectuals published. After appraising Soviet society, he "chose the West" to combat its "evil," thereby setting the tone for disillusioned leftists and the "end of ideology" atmosphere of the 1950s.[43] "Western civilization," a term with a nineteenth-century pedigree, became the glue of the anticommunist alliance.

This glue, Arendt argued, was rooted in the Roman republic that incarnated her ideal of incorporating diverse peoples into a federated international order. Rome's mythic foundation in colonial conquest and settlement and its spread of civilization by violent expansion was, she thought, an acceptable, indeed necessary, theodicy that could be distinguished from modern imperialism. Her fierce criticism of the latter and hypothesis that it was one of the "origins of totalitarianism" could have captured liberal permanent security's operation. Instead, she went to great lengths to distinguish what she called "the more respectable imperialism of the Western nations" from the continental imperialism of Pan-Germanism and Pan-Slavism that she thought led to Hitler and Stalin respectively.[44] Legitimate empire building – establishing settler colonial societies and spreading Western civilization – was distinct from the illegitimate imperialism of the late nineteenth century.

> Imperialism is not empire-building and expansion is not conquest. The imperial passion, old as history, time and again, has spread culture and law to the four corners of the world. The conqueror wanted nothing but spoils and would leave the country after the looting; or he wanted to stay permanently and would then incorporate the conquered territory into the body politic and gradually assimilate the conquered population to the standard of the mother country. This type of conquest has led to all kinds of political structures – to empires in the more distant and to nations in

---

[42] Adi Gordon, "The Need for West: Hans Kohn and the North Atlantic Community," *Journal of Contemporary History* 46, no. 1 (2011): 33–57.

[43] Dwight Macdonald, "The Root Is Man: Part I," *Politics* 3, no. 4 (1946): 97–115; Macdonald, "The Root Is Man: Part Two," *Politics* 3, no. 6 (1946): 194–214; Macdonald, "USA v. USSR," *Politics* 5, no. 2 (1948): 75–7; Hannah Arendt, "He's All Dwight," *New York Review of Books*, August 1, 1968; Gregory D. Sumner, *Dwight Macdonald and the Politics Circle: The Challenge of Cosmopolitan Democracy* (Ithaca, NY: Cornell University Press, 1996).

[44] Arendt, *The Origins of Totalitarianism*, 222–4. George Steinmetz, "Decolonizing German Theory: An Introduction," *Postcolonial Studies* 9, no. 1 (2006): 3–13, and the essays in Richard H. King and Dan Stone, eds., *Hannah Arendt and the Uses of History: Imperialism, Nation, Race and Genocide* (New York and Oxford: Berghahn Books, 2007).

the more recent past. At any rate, conquest was but the first step towards preparing a more permanent political structure.[45]

Consequently, while Arendt was well aware that European colonists eliminated the indigenous peoples who stood in their way, she did not invest this violence with any significance: that was the cost of liberal permanent security, which she justified with Roman traditions of just war and reasons of state.[46]

The relevance of her invocation of British colonialism in Africa in her *Origins of Totalitarianism* was not to demonstrate their infection of Germany, let alone Russia. It was to redeem British colonial rule, which she admired. The German colonialism and imperialism relevant to Nazism and the Holocaust was not to be found in Africa, as commonly supposed, but in the Pan-Germanism and Pan-Slavism of Central Europe. "Continental imperialism," as she called Pan-Germanism and Pan-Slavism, fed into totalitarianism and its unique crimes. She was explicit that the roots of Nazism did *not* lie in African colonialism or imperialism.[47]

The point of her British example is to show how that Western empire resisted the temptation to crush native resistance with "administrative massacres" and eventually relinquished "government over subject races." Its parliament and public opinion ensured that minimum human rights were respected in the colonies, violent pacification and oppression notwithstanding. "It is to the salutary restraining of these institutions that we owe those benefits which, after all and despite everything, the non-European peoples have been able to derive from Western domination."[48] The French, far from being driven out of North Africa, had "*dared* to give up Algeria."[49] The success of European decolonization was a major story for her. "It is one of the *glories* of Europe,

[45] Hannah Arendt, "Imperialism, Nationalism, Chauvinism," *Review of Politics* 7, no. 4 (1945): 444; Arendt, *The Origins of Totalitarianism*, 130. This view was not uncommon at the time: Benjamin Gerig, et al., "Colonial Aspects of the Postwar Settlement," *International Conciliation* 21 (1942–1943): 196–7.

[46] For analyses of Arendt on race and empire, see Jimmy Casas Klausen, "Hannah Arendt's Primitivism," *Political Theory* 38, no. 3 (2010): 394–423; Kathryn T. Gines, "Race Thinking and Racism in Hannah Arendt's *The Origins of Totalitarianism*," in King and Stone, *Hannah Arendt and the Uses of History*, 38–53, and Robert Bernasconi, "When the Real Crime Began: Hannah Arendt's *The Origins of Totalitarianism* and the Dignity of the Western Philosophical Tradition," in King and Stone, *Hannah Arendt and the Uses of History*, 54–67.

[47] Hannah Arendt, "Totalitarian Imperialism: Reflections on the Hungarian Revolution," *Journal of Politics* 20, no. 1 (1958): 37–8.

[48] Arendt, "Imperialism, Nationalism, Chauvinism," 447.

[49] Arendt, *The Origins of Totalitarianism*, xvii. Emphasis added. Cf. Yehouda Shenhav, "Beyond 'Instrumental Rationality': Lord Cromer and the Imperial Roots of Eichmann's Bureaucracy," *Journal of Genocide Research* 15, no. 4 (2013): 379–99.

and especially of Great Britain, that she preferred to liquidate the empire."[50] For Arendt, this development marked the victory of the nation-state over the transnational movements of racism and imperialism that overwhelmed Germany and Russia. The Western empire-states – the principal drivers of liberal permanent security – represented the survival of the Western political tradition that she wished to redeem. This tradition also inhibited genocide. She praised the Italian reluctance to join in the Nazi persecution of Jews by ascribing it to "the almost automatic general humanity of an old and civilized people," although she was also aware that Italian troops at the time were butchering citizens of Ethiopia by aerial bombing.[51]

The cost of isolating positive Western imperial history from negative continental imperialism was to tolerate, even justify, the violent excesses of the former.

> There have almost always been wars of aggression; the massacre of hostile populations after a victory went unchecked until the Romans mitigated it by introducing *parcere subjectis*; through centuries the extermination of native peoples went hand in hand with the colonization of the Americas, Australia and Africa; slavery is one of the oldest institutions of mankind and all empires of antiquity were based on the labor of state-owned slaves who erected their public buildings.[52]

Her admission that treaties were not signed with indigenous peoples, who were so often exterminated, undermines her case about the emollient effects of the Roman way of war. In fact, such extermination was built into its assumptions, as she effectively conceded when she wrote of "those isolated tribes who were vegetating their lives away when first discovered on new continents by European explorers, tribes that the Europeans then either drew into the human world or eradicated without ever being aware that they too were human beings."[53] Arendt was able to entertain such notions about empire by consigning to a footnote the apparently atypical case of the Belgian Congo, whose conquest she knew had cost tens of millions of lives, and excusing the large-scale massacres as instrumentally limited actions.[54] She was opposed, not

---

[50] Arendt, "Totalitarian Imperialism," 35, emphasis is mine; Arendt, *The Origins of Totalitarianism*, xviii.

[51] Hannah Arendt, *Eichmann in Jerusalem: A Report on the Banality of Evil*, rev. enl. ed. (New York: Viking Press, 1964), 179; Arendt, "Between Silence and Speechlessness: Articles from *Aufbau*," in Hannah Arendt, *The Jewish Writings*, ed. Jerome Kohn and Ron Feldman (New York: Schocken, 2007), 168.

[52] Arendt, *The Origins of Totalitarianism*, 440. The "colonization of America and Australia," for example, "was accompanied by comparatively short periods of cruel liquidation because of the natives' numerical weakness": ibid., 187n4.

[53] Hannah Arendt, *The Promise of Politics*, ed. and intro. Jerome Kohn (New York: Schocken, 2007), 176.

[54] Arendt, *The Origins of Totalitarianism*, 444n8, 185.

to civilizational progress, but only to "the nineteenth century belief of *unlimited* progress."[55]

Ultimately, she did not think that the Romans and, later, the Europeans, were aggressors. Her reliance on Theodor Mommsen's famous *History of Rome* (1854–1856) suggests she was influenced by the theory of "defensive imperialism" – the accretive acquisition of empire by confronting perceived external threats rather than by premeditated aggression – which was popular among the ancient Roman apologists as well as in her day.[56] This view was consistent with her subscription to the *Aeneid* myth that, since Vitoria, had justified European expansion by reference to posited norms of hospitality and commerce that coded indigenous resistance as aggression and European violence as self-defense.[57]

The Uniqueness of the Holocaust

How, then, does the Holocaust fit into her schema? The analytical task was to separate previous imperial violence from Nazi genocidal imperialism. Nazism, Arendt declared, "owed nothing to any part of the Western tradition, be it German or not, Catholic or Protestant, Christian, Greek or Roman."[58] The Roman Empire had certainly committed excesses, she conceded, often referring to its destruction of Carthage. Sometimes, she even hinted at a connection between Roman and Nazi campaigns. The "practical abolition" of "wars of annihilation" over the last 100 years, she thought, echoing Lemkin, meant that their reappearance with totalitarianism was the "reversion of warfare to the days when the Romans wiped Carthage off the face of the earth."[59] On the whole, though, she lauded the Romans for replacing the Greek mode of

---

[55] Hannah Arendt, "On Violence," in Hannah Arendt, *Crises of the Republic: Lying in Politics, Civil Disobedience, On Violence, Thoughts on Politics and Revolution* (New York: Houghton Mifflin Harcourt, 1972), 131. Emphasis in the original. On this point, see the lucid discussion in Tony Barta, "Mr. Darwin's Shooters: On Natural Selection and the Naturalizing of Genocide," *Patterns of Prejudice* 39, no. 2 (2005): 116–37; and Barta, "On Pain of Extinction: Laws of Nature and History in Darwin, Marx and Arendt," in King and Stone, *Hannah Arendt and the Uses of History*, 87–108.

[56] Jerzy Linderski, "*Si vis pacem, para bellum*: Concepts of Defensive Imperialism," in *The Imperialism of Mid-Republican Rome*, ed. William V. Harris (Rome: Papers and Monographs of the American Academy, 1984), 133–52; Eric Adler, "Late Victorian and Edwardian Views of Rome and the Nature of 'Defensive Imperialism,'" *International Journal of the Classical Tradition* 15, no. 2 (2008): 187–216.

[57] See Chapter 6.

[58] Hannah Arendt, "Approaches to the German Problem," in Arendt, *Essays in Understanding*, 109; Arendt, "Totalitarian Imperialism"; Arendt, "Imperialism, Nationalism, Chauvinism"; Bernasconi, "When the Real Crime Began."

[59] Hannah Arendt, *On Revolution* (New York, The Viking Press, 1963), 5; Arendt, *The Human Condition* (Chicago: University of Chicago Press, 1958), 228.

unlimited warfare with a political modality that ended hostilities with a treaty and alliance, "inventing a new outcome for war's conflagration."[60]

The Rome–Carthage confrontation clinches Arendt's defense of liberal permanent security. Peace was impossible with Carthage because its leaders were untrustworthy, thereby embodying "an anti-Roman political principle against which Roman statesmanship was powerless and which would have destroyed Rome had not Rome destroyed it first." Carthage was also equally powerful and hardly likely to yield on Roman terms.[61] Her analysis of the reasoning for Rome's policy of destruction in the Third Punic War shows that it mirrored the logic of colonial and imperial wars of expansion that so often ended in genocidal counterinsurgency and indigenous destruction – namely, the conqueror cannot accept parity with a rival. Roman political virtues were predicated on submission to its rule. Those that declined these terms would be destroyed. Such were the limits of Rome's vaunted toleration and pluralism. Cicero and Augustine may have concurred with this reasoning because of their partiality for Rome, but even they evinced greater unease at Carthage's fate than did Arendt. It was accordingly understandable that she inclined toward Cato the Elder, the model citizen whose aphorisms she often quoted, who was the instigator of Carthage's destruction.[62] This is the view of apologists for American empire today, as we see in the last chapter.

Arendt's emphasis on the historical rupture of the Holocaust led her to follow Lemkin's subtle distinction within the genocide concept discussed in Chapters 3 and 4. Her only extensive discussion of this question appears in *Eichmann in Jerusalem*. She criticized the indictment of Eichmann by the Jerusalem court for interpreting the Holocaust as "not much more than the most horrible pogrom in Jewish history," instead of recognizing its unprecedented nature. Unprecedented was the Nazi regime's determination that "the entire Jewish people disappear from the face of the earth." This was a "new crime," a crime "against the human status." "Expulsion" (by which she seemingly meant forced emigration, deportation, and what today is often called "ethnic cleansing"), by contrast, was "an offense against fellow-nations." Genocide, she continued, was "an attack on human diversity as such," a statement that echoed the United Nations Declaration on Genocide in 1946, which was heavily influenced by Lemkin's Zionist philosophy that the "human

[60] Arendt, *The Promise of Politics*, 178.
[61] Ibid., 176, 184–6. Cf. David W. Bates, "Enemies and Friends: Arendt and the Imperial Republic at War," *History of European Ideas* 36, no. 1 (2010): 112–24.
[62] Augustine, *The City of God against the Pagans*, ed. and trans. R. W. Dyson (Cambridge: Cambridge University Press, 1998), book 2, chs. 18 and 21, where he discusses Sallust and Cicero in relation to Carthage. Cf. J. Warren Smith, "Augustine and the Limits of Preemptive and Preventive War," *Journal of Religious Ethics* 35, no. 1 (2007): 141–62.

cosmos" was violated by the destruction of its constituent nations.[63] But why did she insist that genocide was unprecedented when elsewhere she suggested it was not? Even if she qualified this statement by confining it to the modern era, was she suggesting that no genocides took place, for instance, in the colonial world since 1500?

The answer is that she distinguished the Holocaust from (other) genocides. The former was purely ideological (nonpolitical) while the latter were pragmatic (political). Whereas genocides were limited by utilitarian aims, such as pacification or domination, and were to that extent rational, the extermination of Jews was unlimited, running counter to the war effort by the diversion of resources; it was therefore irrational.[64] The posited homology was the limitless expansionism of imperialism with the limitless, ideologically motivated intention to exterminate all Jews. The Holocaust, she explained, "could not be explained by any utilitarian purpose; Jews had been murdered all over Europe, not only in the East, and their annihilation was not due to any desire to gain territory that 'could be used for colonization by Germans.'" This distinction has become a commonplace among proponents of the uniqueness thesis, who similarly set off the Holocaust from other mass crimes.[65]

What Arendt meant by "utilitarian purpose" was apparent from her references to territorial gain and colonization, and also from her praise of the Jerusalem court for making an important distinction. On the one hand, states could suppress opposition, which resulted in "war crimes, such as shooting of partisans and killing of hostages" and even ethnic cleansing and destruction "of native populations to permit colonization by an invader." These were a "known, though criminal, purpose," a telling slippage about the transgressive nature of imperial expansion through the ages on which she did not elaborate. Indeed, she had noted that "massacres of whole peoples are not unprecedented. They were the order of the day in antiquity, and the centuries of colonization and imperialism provide plenty of examples of more or less successful attempts of that sort."[66]

On the other hand, the extermination of the Jews was a "'crime against humanity', whose intent and purpose were unprecedented." For Arendt, "the unprecedented crime of genocide *in the midst of Occidental civilization*"

---

[63] Arendt, *Eichmann in Jerusalem*, 267–69.

[64] Arendt, *The Origins of Totalitarianism*, 445.

[65] Arendt, *Eichmann in Jerusalem*, 275. See Yehuda Bauer, *Rethinking the Holocaust* (New Haven: Yale University Press, 2001), ch. Alan Milchman and Alan Rosenberg observe that for Arendt it is the nonutility of the Holocaust rather than its ideology that is new and distinctive, but the two issues are linked. See their "Two Kinds of Uniqueness: The Universal Aspects of the Holocaust," in *New Perspectives on the Holocaust: A Guide for Teachers and Scholars*, ed. Rochelle L. Millen (New York: New York University Press, 1996), 6–18.

[66] Arendt, *Eichmann in Jerusalem*, 275, 288.

applied only to the Holocaust.[67] Genocide outside Occidental civilization – the West – was not so shocking. Consequently, she objected in particular to the penchant of historians to "draw analogies" between Hitler and other notorious figures in history. "The point is that Hitler was not like Jenghiz Khan and not worse than some other great criminal but entirely different. The unprecedented is neither the murder itself nor the numbers of victims and not even 'the number of persons who united to perpetrate them.' It is much rather the ideological nonsense which causes them, the mechanization of their execution, and the careful and calculated establishment of a world of the dying in which nothing any longer made sense."[68] Totalitarianism was a wholly new phenomenon and should not be confused with previous regime forms and their crimes:

> For the moral point of this matter is never reached by calling what happened by the name of "genocide" or by counting the many millions of victims: extermination of whole peoples had happened in antiquity, as well as in modern colonization. It is reached only when we realize that this happened within the frame of a legal order and that the cornerstone of this "new law" consisted of the command "Thou shalt kill," not thy enemy but innocent people who were not even potentially dangerous, and not for any reason of necessity but, on the contrary, even against all military and other utilitarian considerations.[69]

To make her point, Arendt tested Eichmann's claim that German actions could be understood in terms of a *realpolitische* state of emergency, the rule of *raison d'état* that originated with Roman thinkers like Cicero and Tacitus.[70] She may have known that Hitler also availed himself of reason of state (*Staatsraison*), and German historian Friedrich Meinecke linked it to the Nazis as well.[71] Arendt's immersion in the tradition provided her with the tools she needed to make the necessary distinctions. Two sorts of reasons of

---

[67] Arendt, *The Origins of Totalitarianism*, xiv. Emphasis added.

[68] Hannah Arendt, "Social Science Techniques and the Study of Concentration Camps," in Arendt, *Essays in Understanding, 1933–1954*, 243; Arendt, *The Origins of Totalitarianism*, viii, 444.

[69] Hannah Arendt, "Personal Responsibility under Dictatorship," in Arendt, *Responsibility and Judgment*, ed. and intro Jerome Kohn (New York: Schocken, 2003), 42. See also Arendt, "The Destruction of Six Million" in Arendt, *Jewish Writings*, 491–2.

[70] Cf. Richard Tuck, *Rights of War and Peace: Political Thought and the International Order from Grotius to Kant* (Oxford: Oxford University Press, 1999).

[71] Lothar Gruchmann, "Hitler über die Justiz: Das Tischgespräch vom 20. August 1942," *Vierteljahrshefte für Zeitgeschichte* 12 (1964): 99; Friedrich Meinecke, *The German Catastrophe: Contemplations and Recollections,* trans. Sidney B. Fay (Cambridge, MA: Harvard University Press, 1950). See also Meinecke, *Machiavellism: The Doctrine of Raison d'État and Its Place in Modern History,* trans. Douglas Scott (New Haven: Yale University Press, 1957).

state could be distinguished: a ruthless one that would break treaties and commit excesses when expeditious, commonly identified with Tacitus and later with Machiavelli (illiberal permanent security),[72] and a milder version, sourced in Cicero, that was taken up by later thinkers whom Arendt admired, like Augustine and, later, Edmund Burke (liberal permanent security). Here, the operative principle was necessity rather than expediency. The reasons for action needed to be universally recognizable, could not become a regular principle of government, and needed to eschew "infamy."[73]

In keeping with this tradition, she noted that "concessions [can be] made to the stringencies of *Realpolitik*, in order to preserve power and thus assure the continuance of the existing legal order as a whole." Such crimes, she conceded, were exempt from legal redress, "because the existence of the state itself is at stake, and no outside political entity has the right to deny a state its existence or prescribe how it is to preserve it."[74] This argument did not apply to Eichmann, she hastened to explain, when a state like the Nazi regime "is founded on criminal principles." Here she was also applying the test of exiled Germans, like jurist Georg Schwarzenberg (1908–1991) and Gustav Radbruch (1878–1949), who argued, following Cicero and Augustine, that laws that were intolerably and deliberately unjust could not be regarded as legal.[75]

This defense of the softer version of *Staatsraison* meant the legitimizing of destruction of indigenous peoples who were usually legally classified as rebels and therefore not protected by the laws of war. Arendt was not especially interested in this aspect of settler societies, the form of colonialism she praised consistently in her writings, because the English colonists, in particular, established political societies to her liking.[76] It is for this reason, perhaps, that she does not mention Rome's laying waste of the rebellious Numantia on the Iberian peninsula in 133 BC or the destruction of Jerusalem in 70 AD, which

---

[72] Peter Burke, "Tacitism, Scepticisim, and Reason of State," in *The Cambridge History of Political Thought, 1450–1700*, ed. J. H. Burns (Cambridge: Cambridge University Press, 1991), 479–98. Arendt, *The Human Condition*, 35; Arendt, "What Is Authority?" in Arendt, *Between Past and Future: Eight Exercises in Political Thought* (London: Penguin, 1961), 138.

[73] David Armitage, "Edmund Burke and Reason of State," *Journal of the History of Ideas* 61, no. 4 (2000): 617–34; Richard Bourke, "Edmund Burke and the Politics of Conquest," *Modern Intellectual History* 4, no. 3 (2007): 403–32. See the discussion in Chapter 6.

[74] Arendt, *Eichmann in Jerusalem*, 291–2.

[75] Georg Schwarzenberger, *International Law and Totalitarian Lawlessness* (London: Jonathan Cape, 1943); Frank Haldemann, "Gustav Radbruch vs. Hans Kelsen: A Debate on Nazi Law," *Ratio Juris* 18, no. 2 (2005): 162–78.

[76] The Mayflower compact of Puritan settlers, for instance, received lavish praise in *On Revolution*, and positive references to North America and Australia abound throughout her work: Arendt, *On Revolution*, 167–8; Arendt, "Imperialism, Nationalism, Chauvinism," 452.

Lemkin cited as a case of genocide.[77] Arendt limited the Roman way of warfare to interstate conflicts, occluding colonial and civil wars and thereby licensing reason of state for permanent security.[78]

Arendt's loyalty to the West meant that she was a latecomer in denouncing the Vietnam War's corrupting effects on the North American polity in terms of the "boomerang effect": the war was undermining the polity's precious foundation that she had celebrated in *On Revolution*. As we see in the next section, others had been mounting withering analyses for the country's Vietnam adventure, which included millions of civilian deaths, for several years by the time she published her interventions in the first half of the 1970s.[79] As might be expected, she was then equally hard on such critics. When German writer Hans Magnus Enzensberger (b. 1929) assailed the Cold War arms race and possible nuclear Armageddon – that is, of permanent security regimes on both sides in 1965 – Arendt objected.[80] She naturally rejected his claim that Auschwitz had discredited the Western political tradition, which he held accountable for the possibility of future "Holocausts" by producing the technological capacity for global nuclear annihilation. Such a generalization of Auschwitz's meaning, she complained, was "a highly cultivated form of escapism," because it diluted German national responsibility for the crime. She was invoking the Germans' responsibility for the Holocaust against his brand of critique.[81]

Enzensberger replied that his future-oriented construction was in fact necessary to prevent further catastrophes. While assuring Arendt that he had never sought to diminish Germany's culpability, the real escapism, he retorted, was to consign the Holocaust solely to the German context and to the past, and fail to draw pressing, more general, conclusions about the present. Such a conclusion highlighted the destructive trajectory of a technologically driven Western civilization, of which Auschwitz was hitherto its most extreme instance, an argument he derived from other German-Jewish émigrés, Max Horkheimer (1895–1973) and Theodor W. Adorno (1903–1969), who moved to West Germany after the war.[82]

---

[77] Lemkin, *Axis Rule in Occupied Europe*, 80n3. On Arendt and Lemkin, see Seyla Benhabib, *Politics in Dark Times: Encounters with Hannah Arendt* (Cambridge: Cambridge University Press, 2010), 219–46.

[78] Arendt, *The Promise of Politics*, 190.

[79] See, among other texts, Arendt, "Lying in Politics: Reflections on the Pentagon Papers [1971]," in Arendt, *Crises of the Republic*, 9–42, and "Home to Roost [1975]," in Arendt, *Responsibility and Judgment*, 257–75. There is an excellent discussion of Arendt's critique of US empire in Bates, "Enemies and Friends," 120–4.

[80] Hans Magnus Enzensberger, *Politik und Verbrechen* (Frankfurt: Suhrkamp, 1964).

[81] Hannah Arendt "*Politik und Verbrechen*: ein Briefwechsel," *Merkur*, no. 205 (1965), 380–1.

[82] Formative was Max Horkheimer and Theodor W. Adorno, *Dialectic of Enlightenment*, trans. John Cumming. (New York: Continuum [1947], 1998). See Martin Jay, *The*

Arendt, who disliked Horkheimer and Adorno and their pessimistic philosophy of history, remained unconvinced. While not disagreeing with the
imperative to avoid future disasters, the question remained regarding the
correct lessons the Holocaust taught. The "equation" of Auschwitz and the
"megadeath" of nuclear war, she insisted, obscured the anti-Jewish specificity
of the former, and this distinction resulted in very different political implications than those urged by Enzensberger. "The fatal dimension of Auschwitz
[ADM: unlike nuclear war], of course, is that a repetition is possible without
catastrophic consequences for all participants." She concluded by warning
against an "apparent radicalism" that subsumed particular cases under general
categories, and she urged commentators to forsake abstractions and constructions in favour of the "concrete."[83] The debate about what was later called
"omnicide" would recur decades later. While Arendt was excoriating
Enzensberger, Americans were debating the question of genocide and permanent security in Vietnam.

Vietnam, Genocide, and the Critique of Liberal Permanent Security

The US military intervention in Indochina – principally in Vietnam, but also
its bombing of Viet Cong supply routes in Cambodia and Laos – from 1955 to
1973 was designed to stop the spread of communism in Southeast Asia.
Instigating anticommunist coups in Iran in 1953 and in Guatemala in
1954 set precedents, as did the carving out of South Korea in a brutal war
with communist forces between 1950 and 1953.[84] In the paranoid Cold War
logic driving US national security elites, nothing less than the fate of the West
was at stake. Liberal permanent security confronted its illiberal sibling with the
consequent civilian destruction.

The initial US strategy was to assist the French in retaining their imperial
hold on Indochina, but the victory of communist-led Viet Minh forces in the
Battle of Dien Bien Phu in 1954 forced them out. The ensuing diplomatic

---

Dialectical Imagination: A History of the Frankfurt School and the Institute of Social
Research, 1923–1950, 2nd ed. (Berkeley: University of California Press, 1996); John
Abromeit, Max Horkheimer and the Foundations of the Frankfurt School (Cambridge:
Cambridge University Press, 2011).

[83] Arendt, "Politik und Verbrechen," 384.

[84] Greg Grandin, Empire's Workshop: Latin America, The United States and the Rise of the
New Imperialism (New York: Metropolitan Books, 2006). Paul Chamberlin, The Cold
War's Killing Fields: Rethinking the Long Peace (New York: HarperCollins, 2018); Wen-
Qing Ngoei, Arc of Containment: Britain, the United States, and Anticommunism in
Southeast Asia (Ithaca, NY: Cornell University Press, 2019); Vincent Bevins, The Jakarta
Method: Washington's Anticommunist Crusade and the Mass Murder Program that
Shaped Our World (New York: Public Affairs Books, 2020).

agreement partitioned the country between a communist Democratic Republic of Vietnam in the north and anticommunist State of Vietnam in the south until unification after free elections. When South Vietnam refused those elections with US blessing, the North resolved to unify the country by supporting a "people's" or "protracted popular" war in the South to overthrow the US-backed regime. This mode of warfare was the Maoist strategy of drawing the stronger enemy into the countryside, where it would be worn down over time by low-intensity conflict, while maintaining peasant support. In this case, the South-based Viet Cong insurgents would be covertly supported by the Northern Army. The strategy was encapsulated in a much-quoted statement by Northern General Võ Nguyên Giáp (1911–2013): "The form of combat adopted was guerrilla warfare ... each inhabitant a soldier; each village a fortress .... The entire population participates in the armed struggle, fighting, according to the principles of guerrilla warfare, in small units."[85] Conflating the distinction between combatants and noncombatants was part of the Northern strategy of popular warfare.

The US became drawn into ever-greater military engagement. The Kennedy administration (1961–1963) supported South Vietnam with materiel, advisors, and limited personnel. After continuing Southern political instability and military incompetence, the Johnson administration (1963–1969) escalated US intervention to counter the successful Viet Cong insurgency, first with aerial bombing, then combined with large ground troop commitments. In addition to bombing targets in North Vietnam and Laos, the US and its allies, South Vietnam and Australia, tried to separate the population from insurgents in "search and destroy" missions conducted by conventional forces, by destroying arable land and forest cover, and by terrorizing the population to flee in order to create "free-fire zones" in which remaining Vietnamese, presumably Viet Cong, could be bombarded. These and other practices, like tallying "body counts" as a marker of mission success, caused immense civilian casualties and a major refugee crisis. In the words of Secretary of Defense Robert McNamara (1916–2009), in a note to President Johnson, "the picture of the world's greatest superpower killing or seriously injuring 1,000 noncombatants a week, while trying to pound a tiny backward nation into submission on an issue whose merits are hotly disputed, is not a pretty one."[86] If minor sections of the American public were scandalized by this mode of warfare that they saw on their televisions, there was general, indeed

---

[85] Telford Taylor, *Nuremberg and Vietnam: An American Tragedy* (Chicago: Quadrangle Books, 1971), 135; Hammond Rolph, "Vietnamese Communism and the Protracted War," *Asian Survey* 12, no. 9 (1972): 783–92.

[86] Max Friedman, *Rethinking Anti-Americanism: The History of an Exceptional Concept in American Foreign Relations* (Cambridge: Cambridge University Press, 2012), 203.

global, indignation at the massacre of over 500 Vietnamese villagers at My Lai by US soldiers when it was exposed in 1969.[87]

An articulate global antiwar movement developed to oppose the military campaign, combining mass demonstrations with a stream of publications that conservatives denounced as antiwar propaganda. Some publications were based on self-appointed, nongovernmental commissions of inquiry, modeled in part on the International Military Tribunal at Nuremberg.[88] In condemning American policy, antiwar critics stretched the revamped language of transgression to breaking point. Was the Nuremberg triumvirate of aggressive warfare, war crimes, and crimes against humanity, supplemented by the UN Genocide Convention, adequate to grasp this extreme manifestation of liberal permanent security?[89] The genocide accusation leveled by leftists, pacifists, and some liberal politicians failed to gain adherents in view of its Holocaust archetype: to that extent, genocide's restrictive definition succeeded in its purpose of screening out Western imperial violence. Other critics, who tended to be non-Marxist leftist academics with a legal training, adapted the Nuremberg legacy to challenge the Vietnam campaign, thereby inaugurating a creative and lively critique of what they called the US "national security state" that they hoped to tame with law. Countering them, conservatives and some liberals excused US action by referring to the laws of war defended at Nuremberg; as we saw in Chapter 5, the ancient right of "military necessity" was also one of its legacies. These apologists for US empire justified the civilian destruction allowed by these laws as the price worth paying to defeat totalitarianism. Combined with the subsequent breakthrough of Genocide Studies in the 1990s and 2000s, when US

---

[87] Marilyn B. Young, "Bombing Civilians: From the Twentieth- to the Twenty-First Centuries," in *Bombing Civilians A Twentieth-Century History*, ed. Yuki Tanaka and Marilyn B. Young (New York: Free Press, 2010), 157; John Tirman, *The Deaths of Others: The Fate of Civilians in America's Wars* (Oxford: Oxford University Press, 2011), ch. 5; Lewis M. Simmons, "Free Fire Zones," in *Crimes of War: What the Public Should Know*, ed. Roy Gutman (New York: W. W. Norton, 1999), 151–2. My Lai was not the only massacre: Gary D. Solis, *Son Thang: An American War Crime* (Annapolis: Bantom, 1997).

[88] See the many books on the subject reviewed by Neil Sheehan, "Should We Have War Crimes Trials?" *New York Review of Books*, March 28, 1971. Scholarship on the aerial bombing: Earl H. Tilford, Jr. *Crosswinds: The Air Force's Setup in Vietnam* (College Station: Texas A&M University Press, 1993); Mark Clodfelter, *Limits of Air Power: The American Bombing of North Vietnam* (Lincoln: University of Nebraska Press, 2006).

[89] "Human rights" was not the term of choice for antiwar activists. Barbara Keys, *Reclaiming American Virtue: The Human Rights Revolution of the 1970s* (Cambridge, MA: Harvard University Press, 2014), 9; Jan Eckel, "The International League for the Rights of Man, Amnesty International, and the Changing Fate of Human Rights Activism from the 1940s through the 1970s," *Humanity* 4 (2013): 183–214.

military interventions increased in frequency and scale, these arguments have held the field to this day.[90]

Genocide in Vietnam?

The extent of US military violence shocked liberals and leftists, leading some to accuse the US of genocide. In his best-selling book, *The Pursuit of Loneliness* (1970), sociologist Philip Slater (1927–2013) discerned "genocidal patterns of thought" in the Vietnam War.

> Official policy was expressed in more restrained language, but the euphemisms could not entirely hide the same genocidal assumptions. "Rooting out the infrastructure," for example, meant that you no longer killed only soldiers carrying weapons but every civilian who might be related to or sympathetic to these soldiers. Since there is no way of telling this at a glance in a civil war, it simply meant killing every civilian around.[91]

In the same year, the Democratic Senator, Don Edwards (1915–2015), who promoted civil and voter rights, and later led efforts to reign in state security agencies, declared that the US was committing the genocide in Vietnam for which it had condemned Germany and Japan after World War II.[92] Democratic senator George McGovern (1922–2012) sounded the same note in his presidential campaign in 1972 when he called the war "the most barbaric action any country has committed since Hitler's effort to exterminate Jews in Germany." Such rhetoric branding the US as "immoral and genocidal" sealed his electoral fate, confessed a party aide after McGovern's landslide loss to Richard Nixon.[93]

Leftist intellectuals tended to draw less on outraged liberal morality than on long-standing critiques of capitalist imperialism, while invoking outright parallels between the Holocaust and the American war in Vietnam. Their main vehicle was the unofficial "International War Crimes Tribunal" that met in two sessions in Sweden and Denmark in 1967.[94] Organized by English

---

[90] Kenneth J. Campbell, *Tale of Two Quagmires: Iraq, Vietnam, and the Hard Lessons of War*, foreword Richard A. Falk (London and New York: Routledge, 2017).

[91] Philip Slater, *The Pursuit of Loneliness: American Culture at the Breaking Point* (Boston: Beacon Press, 1970), 32.

[92] "Congressman Says U.S. Is Practicing Genocide," *Los Angeles Times*, February 21, 1970, 8. Thanks to Barbara Keys for a copy of this article.

[93] Keys, *Reclaiming American Virtue*, 71–2.

[94] Much of the proceedings are collected in John Duffett, ed., *Against the Crime of Silence: Proceedings of the International War Crimes Tribunal* (New York and London: O'Hare, 1968). By then, Russell had already published *War Crimes in Vietnam* (London: George, Allen, and Unwin, 1967). An excellent analysis is Berthold Molden, "Vietnam, the New Left and the Holocaust: How the Cold War Changed Discourse on Genocide," in *Memory*

philosopher Bertrand Russell (1872–1970) and featuring well-known pacifists and leftists like African-American writer Stokely Carmichael (1941–1998), the Russell Tribunal, as it was commonly called, utilized the continuing prestige of the Nuremberg indictment as a normative standard with which to condemn the US. The tribunal duly invoked the laws of war, listing its first complaint as aggressive warfare and its final, fifth one, as genocide: "Have forced labour camps been created, has there been deportation of the population or other acts tending to the extermination of the population and which can be characterised juridically as acts of genocide?"[95] The publicity surrounding the tribunal fixated on the genocide charge, in part because the French Marxist philosopher, Jean-Paul Sartre, addressed it in his address "On Genocide."[96]

Sartre made many telling points about liberal permanent security. Sounding like the interwar air-war theorists, he observed that industrial society blurred the combatant–noncombatant distinction because disabling the enemy's economic capacity necessitated total war, namely attacking its factories and their workers. The same dilemma applied in the wars of national liberation at this stage of capitalism, when the US replaced conventional occupiers. Whereas the violent repression of, say, the French in Indochina, had been limited by the need to retain native labor to serve their settlers, the US was not thus constrained. It did not seek to exploit the population but to stop socialist revolutions. Because such revolutions in peasant nations were the product of people's wars with their guerrilla tactics, exterminating an insurgent people was a neoimperial imperative: "In effect, genocide presents itself as the only possible reaction to the insurrection of a whole people against its oppressors." What is more, the American strategy was intended to warn national liberation movements in Latin America in particular, and the Third Word in general, about the consequences of challenging Western-backed regimes: "submit or face extermination" – at least partially.[97] Many commentators agreed that these points were borne out by the evidence that journalists and witnesses assembled in the 1960s, and by the secret Pentagon Papers about the US's Vietnam policy when they were leaked in 1971.[98]

---

in a Global Age: Discourses, Practices, and Trajectories, ed. Aleida Assmann and Sebastian Conrad (Basingstoke and New York: Palgrave Macmillan, 2010), 79–96.

[95] "Aims and Objectives of the International War Crimes Tribunal," in Duffet, *Against the Crime of Silence*, 15.

[96] Jean-Paul Sartre, "On Genocide," in Duffett, *Against the Crime of Silence*, 612–26, and *New Left Review*, no. 48 (1968): 11–21. On Sartre in this mode, see Paige Arthur, *Unfinished Projects: Decolonization and the Philosophy of Jean-Paul Sartre* (London: Verso, 2010).

[97] Sartre, "On Genocide," in Duffet, *Against the Crime of Silence*, 625, 619.

[98] The point had been made already by Bernard Fall, *Last Reflections on a War*, ed. Dorothy Fall (New York: Doubleday, 1964), 229. On US global strategy, see Paul Chamberlin, *The*

On this telling, liberal permanent security entailed exterminatory violence against civilians until insurgents submitted to US-backed governments. But did "genocide" capture this logic? Only a few agreed. One of them was the Swedish politician and lawyer, Hans Göran Frank (1925–1998), who advanced a similar argument in his role as General Secretary of the Citizens Commission of Inquiry on US War Crimes in Vietnam, which succeeded the Russell Tribunal.[99] The question turned on genocidal intent: did the US intend genocide in Vietnam? Frank and Sartre argued in the affirmative because thwarting Vietnamese self-determination was tantamount to national destruction, whether by destroying the socialist project or by enclosing the population in "strategic hamlets" whose conditions were akin to concentration camps. Moreover, being national in nature, the killing met the stipulations of the Genocide Convention.[100] The Vietnamese were attacked simply for being Vietnamese just as a Jew was attacked *"because he was a Jew,"* declared Sartre, i.e., "not for having been caught carrying a weapon or for having joined a resistance movement."[101] He and Frank tried to obscure the obvious factual difference between the cases – Jews were not engaged in an insurgency against Germans – by pointing to American soldiers' racism and the logical tendency of US policy to keep killing until victory was achieved.

It was not difficult for reviewers to point out the argumentative flaws: the Americans had not escalated the war to total destruction, desisting from nuclear weapons and saturation bombing of the North, restrained as they were by the prospect of Chinese and Soviet intervention. Neither did Sartre hold the Soviets to the same standard: the Russell Tribunal and Citizens Committee participants tended to be partisans for the Viet Cong and the North.[102] By adhering to the Holocaust archetype, Sartre and Frank made it easy for critics to distinguish the cases. Philosopher Hugo Adam Bedau's

Global Offensive: The United States, the Palestine Liberation Organization, and the Making of the Post-Cold War Order (Oxford: Oxford University Press, 2012).

[99] Keys, *Reclaiming American Virtue*, 59; Weiss-Wendt, *A Rhetorical Crime*, 105; Patrick William Kelly, *Sovereign Emergencies: Latin America and the Making of Global Human Rights* (Cambridge: Cambridge University Press, 2018), 120–1. US veterans participated in the commission. See Michael Uhl, *Vietnam Awakening: My Journey from Combat to the Citizens' Commission of Inquiry on US War Crimes in Vietnam* (Jefferson, NC, and London: McFarland, 2007).

[100] Hans Göran Frank, "International Law and the US War in Indochina," in *The Wasted Nations*, ed. Frank Browning and Dorothy Forman (New York: Harper and Row, 1972), 302, 307.

[101] Sartre, "On Genocide," in Duffett, *Against the Crime of Silence*, 612. Emphasis in the original.

[102] Anthony A. D'Amato, review of *Against the Crime of Silence: Proceedings of the International War Crimes Tribunal*, ed. John Duffett (London and New York: O'Hare, 1968), and *On Genocide*, by Jean-Paul Sartre (Boston: Beacon Press, 1968), in *California Law Review* 57, no. 4 (1969): 1037.

detailed assessment of Sartre's address in 1973 began by reminding readers of the Holocaust archetype:

> Genocide is not just another crime, not even another "war crime" or "crime against humanity." For many, it is the ultimate offense. Moreover, accusations of genocide in our time are colored by the paradigm case still very much within living memory, the treatment of European Jews and other "undesirables" by the Nazi government until its defeat in 1945. The very term "genocide" entered our language as the designation of that holocaust.

As a consequence, he continued, "there is a strong temptation to assert that injuries that fail to measure up to the fury of 'the final solution' the Nazis designed for the Jews do not fit under the genocidal rubric."[103] The inevitable, and familiar, conclusion was that Jews were killed "not as a means to some further end but simply for its own sake," as Arendt had argued before him. So while American tactics "tended towards genocide results," the requisite intent was missing.[104]

A hostile critic, the German-born political scientist at the University of Massachusetts Amherst, Guenter Lewy (b. 1929), also commenced his reply in this manner: "The prototype of genocide which inspired the convention was, of course, Hitler's attempted extermination of the Jews of Europe, designed to bring about the 'final solution' of the Jewish question."[105] The American campaign did not resemble this prototype. There could be no question of genocide. What is more, the Vietnamese population was increasing.[106] Nonpartisan international lawyers also quibbled whether taking sides in the Vietnamese civil war counted as a genocidal situation.[107] The genocide argument did not stick.

To strike a partisan political blow by equating the US with Nazi Germany and its campaign in Vietnam with the Holocaust, Sartre and Frank became mired in hair-splitting about genocidal intent that distracted from their disturbing points about liberal permanent security. This distraction, of course,

---

[103] Hugo Adam Bedau, "Genocide in Vietnam?" *Boston University Law Review* 53, no. 2 (1973): 577.
[104] Ibid., 602.
[105] Guenter Lewy, *America in Vietnam* (New York: Oxford University Press, 1978), 300. Lewy built a career by denying the applicability of genocide to cases other than the Holocaust. Lewy, *The Nazi Persecution of the Gypsies* (New York and Oxford: Oxford University Press. 2000); Lewy, *The Armenian Massacres in Ottoman Turkey: A Disputed Genocide* (Salt Lake City: University of Utah Press, 2005).
[106] Lewy, *America in Vietnam*, 302–3; Norman Podhoretz, *Why We Were in Vietnam* (New York: Simon and Schuster, 1982).
[107] M. Cherif Bassiouni, "International Law and the Holocaust," *California Western International Law Journal* 9 (1979): 274–5.

was the function of the genocide concept informed by the Holocaust archetype: that which did not meet its lofty threshold was partially obscured despite
the Russell Tribunal's claim that "The conscience of mankind is profoundly
disturbed by the war being waged in Vietnam."[108] In proceeding in the
conventional manner, Sartre and Frank fell into the trap of tying genocide to
its Holocaust archetype rather than conceptually stretching or challenging
international law.

The Nuremberg Legacy and Liberal Permanent Security

Another approach was taken by left-liberal academics who agreed with much
of Sartre's case but rejected his overstated argument about genocide. Many of
them gathered at the Congressional Conference on War and National
Responsibility, sponsored by ten House of Representative Democrats, in
February 1970. Besides politicians, its participants featured liberal academics
and journalists with links to power and prestigious institutions: like the former
Nuremberg prosecutor and Columbia law professor, Telford Taylor
(1908–1998), the Yale psychiatry professor, Robert Jay Lifton (b. 1926), the
University of Pennsylvania historian of American foreign policy, Gabriel
Kolko (1932–2014), the Princeton law professor, Richard Falk (b. 1930), the
former government advisor and now critic, Marcus Raskin (1934–2017), the
University of Chicago international relations expert, Hans J. Morgenthau
(1904–1980), and the *New Yorker* journalist and author of books on US
atrocities in Vietnam, Jonathan Schell (1943–2014). Taylor initially supported
American involvement in Vietnam, and Morgenthau had acted as a foreign
policy consultant to the Kennedy administration, leaving government service
when he dissented from the Johnson administration's military escalation. Even
so, their concern mirrored that of Sartre and the unofficial tribunals: "We are
not fighting an army," Morgenthau told the meeting. "We are not even
fighting a group of partisans, as the Germans did in Yugoslavia. We are
fighting an entire people. And since everyone in the countryside of Vietnam
is to a lesser or greater degree our potential enemy, it is perfectly logical to kill
everyone in sight."[109]

---

[108] "Aims and Objectives of the International War Crimes Tribunal," 14.

[109] Erwin Knoll, *War Crimes and the American Conscience* (New York: Henry Holt, 1970),
15. More generally, see Hans Morgenthau *Truth and Power: Essays of a Decade,
1950–1960* (New York: Praeger, 1970). Also see Richard A. Falk, Gabriel Kolko, and
Robert Jay Lifton, eds., *Crimes of War: A Legal, Political-Documentary, and Psychological
Inquiry into the Responsibility of Leaders, Citizens, and Soldiers for Criminal Acts in War*
(New York: Random House, 1971). On Morgenthaus and Vietnam, see Udi Greenberg,
The Weimar Century: German Émigrés and the Ideological (Princeton: Princeton
University Press, 2014), ch. 4.

Unlike the nongovernment tribunals and citizens commissions that invoked the laws of war for rhetorical purposes, this heterogeneous group truly believed in them. Accordingly, they were faithful to Nuremberg's hierarchy of crimes, with aggressive warfare as the supreme crime. It was not only *how* the US waged war that violated international law, but also *that* it waged war at all. Although Falk thought that the American way of war tended in the genocidal direction that Sartre and Morgenthau indicated – the entire population as a military target – clinching the legal case for genocide was not his aim. He and Taylor were interested in applying the Nuremberg legacy to the current war. In his much-discussed *Nuremberg and Vietnam*, Taylor stuck closely to the original judgments to convict the American campaign of war crimes in its population displacement policies and use of disproportionate force.

> [T]he by now voluminous reportorial literature on the Vietnamese war leaves little doubt that air strikes are routinely directed against hamlets and even single habitations ... in reliance on information of varying reliability. Obviously, these tactics are a response to the nature of guerrilla warfare, and the difficulty of sifting out the "enemy" in a society where there are many shades of inimical activity.[110]

Certainly, then, the Viet Cong tactics were legally dubious, but that did not excuse the American response, Taylor thought. Fidelity to Nuremberg meant that not only soldiers on the spot should be convicted, but also those who formulated strategy and gave the orders. Regarding massacres by US soldiers, he went so far as to suggest that American leaders could find themselves in the same situation as Japanese General Yamashita, who the Allies hanged after the war for crimes committed by his troops despite his lack of knowledge or approval of them.[111] At the same time, fidelity to Nuremberg also meant that Taylor did not object to the aerial bombing campaign because it was not indicted at Nuremberg.[112]

For his part, Falk did not think that liberals like Taylor went far enough, in part because they wished to retain proximity to power, in part because of their static view of Nuremberg, which did not take account of geopolitical developments and forgot that the Tribunal charter was itself contested by legal literalists at the time. Rather than see Nuremberg as a fixed template, Falk urged contemporaries to take it as a flawed breakthrough in taming Leviathan. In other words, this legacy needed to be regarded dynamically as embodying possibilities that transcended its own compromised findings. "Nuremberg has reached beyond itself when applied to Vietnam, and this moral growth, so to

---

[110] Taylor, *Nuremberg and Vietnam*, 143, 144–5.   [111] Ibid., 52, 174, 188.
[112] Ibid., 142, 181–91.

speak, was implicit within its initial historical dimension."[113] Accordingly, it was shortsighted to cleave literally to the Nuremberg judgment, which was silent about bombing civilians because the Allies had also bombed civilians: clearly, that practice violated the spirit if not the letter of international law.

This was an approach that Falk adapted from his mentor at Yale, Myres S. McDougal (1906–1998), who taught that law was not about applying neutral rules (as Taylor was) but a vehicle of policy and social change.[114] The promise of Nuremberg thus needed to be seen in the context of geopolitical challenges since the trials and formulation of the UN Charter in the 1940s: nuclear warfare and postcolonial civil wars that involved powerful outside states – like in Vietnam. The international system was defective by leaving military security in the hands of insecure states that regularly committed crimes "if measured by Nuremberg standards," concluded Falk: the French colonial wars, the British and French in Suez, and the Soviets in Hungary. Unlike the self-appointed tribunals that lacked what he called "lawyer-like restraint," Falk was advancing a general critique of permanent security that did not pit one form against the other.[115]

The antiwar movement, he believed hopefully, signaled a transition in the international system between the "Westphalian statism" that invested the right of war and peace in sovereign states on the one hand, and the "UN Charter communitarianism" that qualified it "through rules of restraint and creation of international institutions of review," on the other.[116] He thus urged the development of supranational institutions, the renewal of international law, and the education of national elites. Although he was pessimistic about the prospect of such institutional change, he hoped international law could prevent the worst by holding national leaders to account for aggressive warfare, as at Nuremberg. Because the US was not in fact like Nazi Germany, a peace movement could press the case for accountability. "The question before all of us, at this time," he wrote in 1971, "is whether we who originally lit the Nuremberg torch can keep it aflicker in these times of barbarism."[117]

The genocide accusation was unhelpful in meeting this challenge unless it was interpreted metaphorically, Falk continued, rather than as a strictly legal undertaking that was unlikely to satisfy a court. By contrast, using the adjective "genocidal" was appropriate as a tool of political mobilization if based on accurate information regarding "massive indiscriminate destruction of civilian

---

[113] Richard A. Falk, "Nuremberg: Past, Present and Future," *Yale Law Journal* 80, no. 5 (1971): 1510.

[114] Richard A. Falk, "Some Thoughts on the Jurisprudence of Myres S. McDougal," in Richard A. Falk, *The Status of Law in International Society* (Princeton, NJ: Princeton University Press, 1970), 642–59. Falk leavened McDougal's legal activism by also insisting on law's autonomy, a point he took from Hans Kelsen.

[115] Falk, "Nuremberg," 1524, 1501.   [116] Ibid., 1508–9.   [117] Ibid., 1528.

populations as a central feature of war strategy designed to defeat a popularly based revolutionary movement." In that case, US citizens were confronted with a stark choice: "pacifism or genocide."[118] Although Falk did not see realistic prospects for prosecutions of the war's architects, Dean Rusk or Richard Nixon, he thought their possibility could be a valuable regulative norm for policy makers in the future. If citizens of countries elsewhere held their leaders to account on the Nuremberg principles of individual responsibility, they could, together, develop a "global populism" and "build a new world order based on curtailed role of government bureaucracies and other corporate actors with wealth and power at their disposal." The "international conscience," he declared in the language of transgression, resided in these popular forces rather than with states.[119] Falk thus opposed a "neo-Wilsonian" that invested the US with "a unilateral responsibility and prerogative to establish ideologically self-serving global rules of order as part of its mission to bring into being a peaceful world."[120] Interventionism smacked of aggression, Nuremberg's supreme crime. As we will see below, this conviction distinguished Falk and his colleagues from the field of Genocide Studies that would develop a decade later.

Falk's imperative was to encourage state restraint: this was Nuremberg's core principle. If his utopianism was articulated as a negative – preventing the worst rather than effecting a utopia – he joined others in appealing to the Martens Clause to extend international law to protect new objects, namely the environment. The extraordinary damage inflicted on the Vietnamese countryside and agriculture by chemicals and bulldozers inspired commentators to call for a new crime of "ecocide." There was no gainsaying the urgency: "Surely it is no exaggeration to consider the forests and plantations treated by Agent Orange as an Auschwitz for environmental values."[121] The Genocide Convention needed to be supplemented by an Ecocide Convention, he declared, along with a new Hague Convention as part of a general renewal of international law.

---

[118] Richard A. Falk, "Ecocide, Genocide, and the Nuremberg Tradition of Individual Responsibility," in *Philosophy, Morality, and International Affairs*, ed. Virginia Held, Sidney Morgenbesser, and Thomas Nagel (New York: Oxford University Press, 1974), 127–9.

[119] Ibid., 132.

[120] Richard A. Falk, *Legal Order in a Violent World* (Princeton, NJ: Princeton University Press, 1968), 257.

[121] Richard A. Falk, "Environmental Warfare and Ecocide: Facts, Appraisal, and Proposals," *Bulletin of Peace Proposals* 4, no. 1 (1973): 84; Falk, *The Endangered Planet: Prospects and Proposals for Human Survival* (New York: Random House, 1971); David Zierler, *The Invention of Ecocide: Agent Orange, Vietnam, and the Scientists Who Changed the Way We Think about the Environment* (Athens: University of Georgia Press, 2011).

Reflecting on the war in 1974, Falk was less optimistic, because international law seemed helpless in the face of the realities on the ground in Vietnam. There was no question that the Northern strategy violated the laws of war by intermingling fighters with the civilian population. To that extent, communist permanent security risked massive civilian destruction, as conservative defenders of the US military never tired of pointing out.[122] Yet they missed the bigger point, he continued, which was that the radical asymmetry of the firepower and the fact that the population clearly supported, indeed protected, the Viet Cong made a nonsense of a legalistic approach. In such conditions, the US military's strategy was necessarily indiscriminate and thus illegal. Moreover, it was stood on the wrong side of a just cause, because supporting South Vietnam entailed entrenching a regime based on an exploitative land-lord class. A new Hague Convention was required to criminalize externally orchestrated insurgencies and counterinsurgencies that plagued the global system. But because other countries faced such insurgencies, Falk predicted that they would not press to legal reform to hold military strategists account-able for the consequences of their policies, still less to insist on the principles of proportionality in domestic conflict.[123]

As it happened, the year in which Falk wrote this essay, 1974, saw the beginning of the international negotiations that led to the two Protocols Additional to the Geneva Conventions in 1977. National liberation move-ments participated in their formulation and successfully demanded that "people's wars" be recognized as international conflicts, with the consequent subjection of guerrilla fighters to the protections of international law. The International Committee of the Red Cross and many Western states, however, would not accept the elision of the combatant/noncombatant distinction, nor was a supervisory mechanism established. To this extent, the Protocols did not materially change the requirement that insurgents distinguish themselves from civilians. Even so, the US and Israel did not sign the Protocols.[124] What is

---

[122] Richard A. Falk, "Law and Responsibility in Warfare," *Instant Research on Peace and Violence* 4, no. 1 (1974): 8; Falk, "Six Legal Dimensions of the United States Involvement in the Vietnam War," in *The Vietnam War and International Law*, ed. Richard A. Falk, 4 vols. (Princeton, NJ: Princeton University Press, 1969), 2: 215–59.

[123] Falk, "Law and Responsibility in Warfare," 10.

[124] Eleanor Davey, "Decolonizing the Geneva Conventions: National Liberation and the Development of Humanitarian Law," in *Decolonization, Self-Determination, and the Rise of Global Human Rights Politics*, ed. A. Dirk Moses, Marco Duranti, and Roland Burke (Cambridge: Cambridge University Press, 2020), 375–96; Jessica Whyte, "The 'Dangerous Concept of the Just War': Decolonization, Wars of National Liberation, and the Additional Protocols to the Geneva Conventions," *Humanity* 9, no. 3 (2018): 313–41; Helen Kinsella, *The Image Before the Weapon: A Critical History of the Distinction between Combatant and Civilian* (Ithaca, NY: Cornell University Press, 2011), ch. 7; Antonio Cassese, "The Status of Rebels under the 1977 Geneva Protocol

more, this legal innovation did not address a main concern of the peace movement: nuclear weapons and the security paranoia of the states that manufactured them, namely the US and Soviet Union.

Among Falk's generational cohort, Marcus Raskin and Richard J. Barnet (1929–2004) were most prominent pacifist intellectuals. The three had been connected at least since an ad hoc Congressional Conference on Vietnam in January 1966, when they appeared along with Bernard Fall (1926–1967), the Austrian-born Jewish-French war correspondent and political scientist at Howard University who was killed by a landmine in Vietnam a year later.[125] In March 1969, Falk, Raskin, and Barnet again met with Senate and House of Representative members who hosted a Congressional Conference on the Military Budget and National Priorities. These Congressmen, among them J. William Fulbright (1905–1995), who chaired the Senate Foreign Relations Committee, also invited liberal academics like Harvard economist John K. Galbraith (1908–2006) and Hans Morgenthau to discuss the war, the militarization of US foreign policy, and the inability of Congress to exercise oversight over the executive. Their concerns were urgent: "Our country is in danger of becoming a national security state," declared the editors of the volume that records the meeting's deliberations. "No other country has extended its military influence around the world in the way we have, and yet we continue to feel insecure – but now this insecurity reflects deep concern for the internal fabric of our own country."[126]

Participants did not blame the military alone for the Vietnam disaster and domestic unrest: civilian leaders and faulty institutions were the problem. They had become "militarized" by incorporation into the military apparatus just as military leaders had become "civilianized" by advising about ever-more-complex military technologies. Most worryingly, no "counterbalancing forces in our society" existed to restrain this intimidating "apparatus," which was now threatening domestic freedoms by quashing opposition in the name of national security.[127] In the discussion, Raskin resorted to the traditional analytical tools to unmask liberal permanent security, declaring "We are a great empire. And we are imperialists."[128] He and Barnet opposed President Johnson's declaration the year before that the US is "the *Number One Nation*,"

on Non-International Armed Conflicts," *International and Comparative Law Quarterly* 30, no. 2 (1981): 416–39.

[125] *Congressional Record: Proceedings and Debates of the 89th Congress*, Vol. 112, Part 24 (Washington, DC: United States Government, Printing Office, 1966), A782.

[126] Erwin Knoll and Judith Neiss, eds., *American Militarism, 1970: A Dialogue on the Distortion of our National Priorities and the Need to Reassert Control Over the Defense Establishment* (New York: Viking, 1969), 11–12.

[127] Ibid., 14.   [128] Ibid., 23.

and would remain "the *Number One Nation*."[129] This ambition was the problem: "Do we intend to be top dog in the world?" asked Raskin. "Are we prepared to intervene all over the world? And are we prepared to pay that price?" By which he meant domestic freedom.

In these debates, Raskin coined the memorial phrase "national security state." Controlling it became his and Barnet's ambition.[130] These were the concerns central to a new thinktank they established in 1963, the Institute for Policy Studies, when they both left government service, disillusioned with the direction of foreign policy. Soon after the Congressional Conference in 1969, they published a controversial book based on the Pentagon Papers, *Washington Plans an Aggressive War*, that decried executive irresponsibility and its "imperial war making."[131] Barnet also wrote book after book excoriating what he called the "bureaucratic homicide" committed by "national security managers" that allowed them to kill impersonally with high-tech weapons from afar. Engaging in "permanent war" in the guise of making the "world safe for democracy," the national security bureaucracy comprised about 400 bureaucrats, rooted in industrialist, banker, and corporate lawyer circles, whose ability to identify economic opportunities abroad as the national interest was enabled by a manipulatable public. No Marxist, however, he also saw interventionist imperatives in the national security bureaucracies of communist states. Such bureaucrats on both sides operated according to their own power interests that, in the US case, could contradict the internationalist orientation of multinational corporations.[132] The *New York Times* review of Barnet's *Roots of War* (1972) elaborated darkly on the book's conclusions about permanent war: "Security through terror, peace through war, truth through lies. This has been the model for United States foreign policy for nearly two generations."[133]

In their emphasis on an unaccountable elite, with its interwoven military, corporate, and political networks, Barnet and Raskin were developing themes of the prematurely deceased Columbia University sociologist, C. Wright Mills

---

[129] Lyndon B. Johnson, *Containing the Public Messages, Speeches, and Statements of the President, 1968–1969*, 2 vols. (Washington, DC: United States Government Printing Office, 1970), 1: 144.

[130] Knoll and Neiss, *American Militarism, 1970*, 24.

[131] Ralph Stavins, Richard J. Barnet, and Marcus G. Raskin, *Washington Plans an Aggressive War* (New York: Random House, 1971). Barnet had been an official at the State Department Control and Disarmament Agency, while Raskin had worked at the National Security Council, among other government roles.

[132] Richard J. Barnet, *Intervention and Revolution: America's Confrontation with Insurgent Movements Around the World* (New York: World Publications, 1968); Barnet, *Roots of War* (New York: Atheneum, 1972), 5, 13.

[133] Ronald Steel, review of Richard Barnet, *Roots of War* (New York: Atheneum, 1972) in the *New York Times*, June 11, 1972.

(1916–1962). Unlike other leftists who celebrated the victory over fascism in World War II, Mills was concerned by the increase of executive power and rearrangement of the economy to seemingly permanent military readiness, which the Cold War entrenched.[134] His books set the terms for their analysis. *The Power Elite* (1956) disaggregated the US political class into three group-ings of national power: the "corporate rich," the "war lords," and the "political directorate." Access to these elites had become ever more restrictive and self-selective, as the upper strata of each group shut out the lower strata, making the former a "status group" rather than a class. Based on familiarity, members of each group were increasingly interchangeable, leading to a remarkable degree of autonomy for the power elite in pursuing its own interests. Mills was dismayed by this reduction of political pluralism in the US polity, whose system of checks and balances on power had been undermined.[135]

This was the analytical framework for his subsequent polemic, *The Causes of World War Three* (1958).[136] The antiwar framework came from intellectuals like critic Bertrand Russell and Lewis Mumford (1895–1990), who assailed atomic weapons immediately after their use on the Japanese cities of Hiroshima and Nagasaki. "Madmen govern our affairs in the name of order and security," warned Mumford in 1946. "What they call continued progress in atomic warfare means universal extermination, and what they call national security is organized suicide."[137] Later, he went so far as to call their use "the Nazi's firmest victory and democracy's most servile surrender."[138] While the Genocide Convention was being negotiated in 1948, he proclaimed the danger of "militant genocide" – meaning atomic warfare – that could "turn the planet

---

[134] Daniel Geary, *Radical Ambition: C. Wright Mills, the Left, and American Social Thought* (Berkeley: University of California Press, 2009). On US security calculations at the time, which planned a global network of bases, see Melvyn P. Leffler, "The American Conception of National Security and the Beginnings of the Cold War, 1945–48," *American Historical Review* 89, no. 2 (1984): 346–81; Leffler, "The Emergence of an American Grand Strategy, 1945–1952," *Cambridge History of the Cold War*, ed. Melvyn P. Leffler and Odd Arne Westad (Cambridge: Cambridge University Press, 2010), 1: 67–89.

[135] C. Wright Mills, *The Power Elite* (Oxford: Oxford University Press, 1956). He took the status group approach from Max Weber. Mills was the coeditor of a very popular anthology of Weber's writings. Hans H. Gerth and C. Wright Mills, *From Max Weber: Essays in Sociology* (New York: Oxford University Press, 1946).

[136] C. Wright Mills, *The Causes of World War Three* (New York: Ballantine Books, 1958).

[137] Lewis Mumford, "Gentlemen: You Are Mad!" *Saturday Review of Literature*, March 2, 1946, 5–6. See generally, Rens van Munster and Casper Sylvest, *Nuclear Realism: Global Political Thought during the Thermonuclear Revolution* (London and New York: Routledge, 2016).

[138] Lewis Mumford, "The Morals of Extermination," *Atlantic Review Monthly*, no. 204 (October 1959), 39.

into an extermination camp."[139] In Mumford's creative analogizing, Nazi death camps became the symbol, not of the Holocaust, but of the atomic destruction of civilians. The bomb and the attack on civilians generally, then, not Auschwitz, was the war's lesson. Here was a full-throated critique of permanent security as an irrational cult that threatened a war in which there could be no winners.

Mumford was not alone in voicing concerns about nuclear weapons. Before him, in August 1945, Bertrand Russell condemned the bombing of Hiroshima and raised a new "sombre" prospect: "Mankind are faced with a clear-cut alternative: either we shall all perish, or we shall have to acquire some slight degree of common sense. A great deal of new political thinking will be necessary if utter disaster is to be averted."[140] In 1956, philosopher G. E. M Anscombe (1919–2001) protested Oxford University's awarding Harry Truman an honorary doctorate because, as US president, he had ordered the use of the atomic bomb. She was a vehement opponent of arguments that made combatants of entire populations because they allegedly aided the war effort. "I am not sure how children and the aged fitted into this story," she observed bitingly, "probably they cheered the soldiers and munitions workers up."[141] Always a minority, these antibomb intellectuals confronted an establishment that believed "the delicate balance of terror" guaranteed the Cold War peace, and which doubted that limited use of nuclear weapons entailed mutual annihilation. If the Russians had recovered from their loss of 20 million souls in World War II, they could so if the Americans wiped out a few of their cities. Tactical nuclear warfare was indeed viable.[142]

Such calculations terrified Mill, who thought nuclear weapons vitiated the alternatives of their tactical and strategic usage. "The distinction between military and civilian is obsolete," he complained: "World populations are the bemused combatants."[143] Since war was now total, it had become absurd. But, alarmingly, the political establishment was preparing for World War III on the mistaken assumption that peaceful coexistence with the Soviet Union was impossible. The invidious options it posited were "Capitulation or Extermination."[144] He was appalled by this truncated political imagination and acceptance of mass violence in US foreign policy. He was likewise dismayed by the psychological anxieties that drove its permanent security

---

[139] Lewis Mumford, "Atom Bomb: 'Miracle' or Catastrophe?" *Air Affairs*, July 1948, 329.
[140] Bertrand Russell, "The Bomb and Civilization," *Forward* [Glasgow] 39, no. 3 (August 18, 1945): 1.
[141] G. E. M. Anscombe, *Mr. Truman's Degree* (Oxford, 1956), 2.
[142] Albert Wohlstetter, "The Delicate Balance of Terror," *Foreign Affairs* 37, no. 2 (1959): 211–34. This essay could be seen as a response to Mills. The best recent analysis of such thinkers is Daniel Bessner, *Democracy in Exile: Hans Speier and the Rise of the Defense Intellectual* (Ithaca, NY: Cornell University Press, 2018) and Greenberg, *The Weimar Century*, ch. 3.
[143] Mills, *The Causes of World War Three*, 10.   [144] Ibid., 13.

strivings: "What one side considers a defence the other considers a threat. In the vortex of the struggle, each is trapped by his own fearful outlook and by his fear of the other; each moves and is moved within a circle both vicious and lethal."[145] On the basis of this paranoia, the political class, including many intellectuals, were busily preparing for the next war. So pervasive was this "ethos of war" that Mills observed war was "no longer an interruption of peace." Rather "peace itself had become an uneasy interlude between wars; peace has become a perilous balance of mutual terror and mutual fright." For this reason, he prioritized the Nuremberg hierarchy of crimes: "Surely war and peace are now the most important issues men anywhere can reason about."[146]

How did this disastrous situation come about? Mills leveraged his analysis in *The Power Elite* to argue that the course of modernization had not only centralized state power and military violence in the hands of "small ruling circles in both superstates," but also bureaucratized their decision making. As a consequence, "political struggles tend to be replaced by administrative decisions." The vaunted practical realism of these elites, which he called "a permanent war establishment," masked what Mumford had called the madness of their violent calculations.[147]

Mills was unmasking the logics of permanent security. Both the Soviet Union and US were "imperialistic" by using their militaries to solve their problem of political security externally and due to the internal interplay of "economic, political and military institutions." Whereas the Soviets engaged in colonial exploitation of Eastern Europe, the Americans were drawn to Middle Eastern oil, leading to inventions when considered necessary. At the same time, he continued, the Soviets were developing a noncapitalist industrial economy that challenged the US conceit to embody progress and modernity. They were leading the way in the colonial and developing world, he believed. The US determination to defend the status quo by seeking to quash the Soviet alternative was a cause of the coming war.[148]

Unfortunately, Wright continued, "the great American public" could not be relied upon to resist this war. It was fragmented and largely absorbed into the state, meaning no public as such existed to scrutinize the power elite.[149] Earlier, he had studied trade union leaders and concluded they no longer

---

[145] Ibid., 11. He was effectively invoking the notion of the "security dilemma" first articulated shortly before by John H. Herz, "Idealist Internationalism and the Security Dilemma," *World Politics* 2, no, 2 (1950): 157–80.

[146] Mills, *The Causes of World War Three*, 14.

[147] Ibid., 27, 29, 31. Mumford is quoted at 54.   [148] Ibid., 69–78.

[149] Ibid., 39. In explaining how the US was "far removed from the eighteenth-century idea of the public of public opinion," Mills was advancing the argument about the corruption of the public space before the German thinker Jürgen Habermas made it famous. Habermas, *The Structural Transformation of the Public Sphere: An Inquiry into a Category of Bourgeois Society*, trans. Thomas Bürger (Cambridge, MA: MIT Press,

represented an oppositional force to the developing militarized capitalist economy. For its part, the middle class, as white collar employees, was a creature of the market economy that colonized individual subjectivities in the form of alienated yet tame "marketing personalities."[150] More drastically, the entire population had become morally insensitive by accepting without "shock" the atrocities of both world wars. World War II, in particular, had accustomed the public to saturation bombing and the two atomic bombs on Hiroshima and Nagasaki. He saw important links with the Holocaust: "That Hiroshima was more sudden and more impersonal than Auschwitz, whatever other moral differences may be discerned, makes it none the less immoral." The bombing of Korea in the 1950s showed that "the principle of obliteration had become totally accepted as part of the moral universe of mass society."[151] The ordinary citizen also felt they could not affect such policies in any event. Anticipating Hannah Arendt's notion of the "banality of evil" and Robert Jay Lifton's theories of moral desensitization, Mill thought that functionaries of the "social machine" depersonalized and split their consciousnesses to avoid relating their action and their terrible effects. This was a sensibility he thought Nazis dramatized, but likewise the US fighter pilots who flattened Korean towns and cities "with their petroleum-jelly broiling of children and women and men." This was the mechanism that enabled the participation of "brisk generals and gentle scientists" in developing weapons of mass destruction for the next war. Mills thought this situation represented the new "barbarism."[152] He was adapting the language of transgression to the antiwar cause: to sensitize readers to the shocking implications of the arms race. Genocide, let alone the Holocaust, was not his priority.

To confront the "military metaphysic," meaning the "accumulation of military power" as "an ascendant end in itself," meant imagining alternatives. Central to this metaphysic was "military necessity," which we recall Justice Jackson had defended at Nuremberg.[153] Whereas liberalism and Marxism

---

[1962] 1989). Mills was likely drawing on John Dewey, *Public and Its Problems* (New York: Henry Holt and Co., 1927), about whom he wrote his masters thesis in 1939.

[150] C. Wright Mills, *The New Men of Power: America's Labor Leaders* (Urbana: University of Illinois Press, 1948); Mills, *White Collar: The American Middle Classes* (New York: Oxford University Press, 1951).

[151] Mills, *The Causes of World War Three*, 82. An overwhelming majority of Americans supported the dropping of the atomic bombs on Hiroshima and Nagasaki: Elliot Aronson, Timothy D. Wilson, and Robin M. Akert, *Social Psychology: The Heart and the Mind* (New York: HarperCollins, 1994), 483; Conrad C. Crane, *Bombs, Cities, and Civilians: American Airpower Strategy in World War II* (Lawrence: University of Kansas Press, 1993), 29–30.

[152] Mills, *The Causes of World War Three*, 83–4. Lifton's ideas are discussed in the next chapter.

[153] Ibid., 53–6, 101.

were concerned with freedom and rationality, the new reality was the rise of "the power elite ... [as] a token of the centralization of the means of history-making itself." This novelty required an ideological alternative that opened the way for "new formations of power" or, at the very least, to promote the "the idea of political responsibility" to challenge the elite's cant about "tragic responsibility" and the "historical inevitability" of war.[154] Disillusioned with the power elite and the manipulated "people in general," Mills addressed his book to a readership that shared his unease and that could be provoked into "bolder reflection." Hope lay in the critical role of "intellectuals, scientists, and ministers" in confronting what the majority regarded as the inevitable drift to war.[155]

This conclusion lay in his critique of American pragmatist philosopher John Dewey and Marx about the role of intellectuals. Just as consciousness does not determine material existence, neither does the reverse hold true. Between them is the symbolic world of communication, the "cultural apparatus," the "lens of mankind through which men see ... the semi-organized source of their very identities and of their aspirations."[156] "Political intellectuals," among whom he included scientists and clergymen, could take control of the cultural apparatus and the "science machine" that produced deadly weapons. They could challenge the power elite's definition of geopolitical reality and effect what he called "rehabilitation of political life."[157] Ironically, President Dwight Eisenhower came to similar conclusions about the danger of the "military-industrial complex" in his farewell address two years later, although he had earlier threatened a nuclear attack during the Korean War, authorized the coups in Iran and Guatemala, and supported the French in Vietnam and then South Vietnam.[158]

When Mills wrote this manifesto in 1958, he had not appreciated the early development of the New Left, still less incorporated the African-American civil rights struggle.[159] Only two years later, after spending time in Europe and

---

[154] Ibid., 42–6.   [155] Ibid., 16.

[156] C. Wright Mills, *Power, Politics, and the People*, ed. and intro Irving Louis Horowitz (New York: Oxford University Press, 1963), 407.

[157] Mills, *The Causes of World War Three*, 121; Stanley Aronowitz, *Taking It Big: C. Wright Mills and the Making of Political Intellectuals* (New York: Columbia University Press, 2012). Theologians struggled to reconcile their anticommunism and opposition to the killing of civilians: William Nagle, ed., *Morality and Modern Warfare: The State of the Question* (Baltimore: Helicon Press, 1960).

[158] William D. Hartung, "Eisenhower's Warning the Military-Industrial Complex Forty Years Later," *World Policy Journal* 18, no. 1 (2001): 39–44. On the militarization of national security in this period, see Norman A. Graebner, ed., *The National Security: Its Theory and Practice, 1945–1960* (New York and Oxford: Oxford University Press, 1986).

[159] C. Wright Mills, *Listen Yankee: The Revolution in Cuba* (New York McGraw-Hill, 1960). If he was blind to questions of race that was not because he was insensate to racist suffering: he consistently pointed to the violence of US military interventions in the

Cuba, whose revolutionary regime he initially lauded, a global New Left had come onto his radar. He welcomed the youthful rebellions in Asia and Latin America. In his "Letter to the New Left," addressed to British comrades, in particular the authors of *Out of Apathy*, edited by the historian and antinuclear activist, E. P. Thompson (1924–1993), he encouraged them to challenge the pessimism of former leftists like Dwight Macdonald and the liberals of the Congress of Cultural Freedom, who coined the phrase "the end of ideology" in 1955.[160] Such a nonpolitics reflected the position of intellectuals in rich countries, but that could change. But if reideologization was imperative, it could not be done with the "Victorian" Marxist romanticization of the working class that he discerned in the English New Left.[161] Orthodox Marxists rejected his message that the intellectual rather than the working class could "prevent catastrophe," but it was perfectly suited to New Left university students, who devoured Mills' books. His evocation of their social role was faithfully reflected in the Port Huron Statement of Students for a Democratic Society (SDS) in 1962, a few weeks before he died.[162]

The Vietnam War was not the students' or Mills's horizon at the time, as the US escalation followed three years later. After the SDS and other sections of the New Left moved into actionist directions, Barnet and Raskin, as codirectors of the Institute for Policy Studies, took up Mills's baton by focusing on national security officials among the power elite and their imperial ambitions as a means to resolve economic problems and class conflict. Law graduates – Raskin had been an assistant to Quincy Wright at the University of Chicago – they combined legal and sociological approaches. If anything, the Vietnam War exemplified many of Mills's predictions, they thought, though less regarding the use of nuclear weapons than with the smashing of national liberation movements with indiscriminate counterinsurgency tactics. They could also observe violent suppression of opposition to racism at home and imperialism abroad, as well as further interventions, like the US-backed coup against Salvador Allende in Chile in 1973. Now that the civil rights, peace, and

---

Global South. It was likely that his focus on geopolitics – the question of war and peace – kept his eyes on the power elites.

[160] Giles Scott-Smith, "The Congress for Cultural Freedom, the End of Ideology and the 1955 Milan Conference: 'Defining the Parameters of Discourse,'" *Journal of Contemporary History* 37, no. 3 (2002): 437–55.

[161] C. Wright Mills, "Letter to the New Left," *New Left Review*, no. 5 (September–October 1960): 18–23; E. P. Thompson, ed., *Out of Apathy* (London: New Left Books, 1960); Daniel Bell, *The End of Ideology: On the Exhaustion of Political Ideas in the Fifties* (New York: Free Press, 1960).

[162] George Novack, "The World of C. Wright Mills," *International Socialist Review* 2, no. 3 (1960): 84–90; Daniel Geary, "'Becoming International Again': C. Wright Mills and the Emergence of a Global New Left," 1956–1962," *Journal of American History* 95, no. 3 (2008): 710–36.

student movements had demonstrated some popular mobilization and broken the power elite's "cultural hegemony," Raskin could propose that not only intellectuals, but democracy itself, confront the national security state that had developed since 1933 and had metastasized since 1947. By democracy, he meant the rule of law and checks and balances on arbitrary power that he observed in CIA operations against domestic opposition and in foreign interventions. Similarly, the Joint Chiefs of Staff "operates according to its own rules and regulations, taking little or no account of public law and asserting its own definition of national security and national interest – a definition which is invariably ruling class oriented." Like Mills, Raskin was seeking to utilize the language of transgression to unmask liberal permanent security by encouraging civil disobedience in the name of higher principles "against laws or governmental acts which shock the conscience of the society."[163]

Fittingly, in view of this rhetorical flourish, Raskin invoked the Nuremberg legacy of personal accountability for government officials. He was acutely conscious of this legacy from his association with Telford Taylor, who had successfully defended him in the celebrated Boston Five case, in which Raskin and others were indicted for encouraging draft evasion. Reviewing Taylor's *Nuremberg and Vietnam* in 1971, Raskin adopted Nuremberg for his cause: "The banner of the Nuremberg judgments has been carried by upholders of the United Nations, pacifists, individuals against bureaucratic and executive frolics, the New Left and draft resisters." Sharing Falk's faith in international law, he thought that "small nations" could apply pressure to the US's aggressive warfare in the international arena.[164] He continued the argument five years later in entreating the Nuremberg and Asian War Crimes Trials as setting standards that should be applied to American officials. "These standards can reach the entire issue of the national security apparatus because they are based not on values which are imperial in nature but on a recognition that governments must be controlled if civilization is not to be lost."[165]

Taylor, Raskin, Barnet, Falk, and other critics who spoke in the legal idiom of Nuremberg were heartened by a resurgent Congress that began to cut funding for the Vietnam War. At the same time, however, Richard Nixon easily won his reelection in 1972. The majority may have wearied of the war, but they did not oppose American empire as such. Appealing to democracy

---

[163] Among many publications: Marcus G. Raskin, "Democracy versus the National Security State," *Law and Contemporary Problems* 40, no. 3 (1976): 205, 203, 207; Raskin, *The Politics of National Security* (New Brunswick, NJ: Transaction, 1979); Brian S. Mueller, "Confronting America's National Security State: The Institute for Policy Studies and the Vietnam War," *Diplomatic History* 41, no. 4 (2017): 694–718.

[164] Marcus G. Raskin, Review of *Nuremberg and Vietnam: An American Tragedy* by Telford Taylor, *Yale Review of Law and Social Action* 1, no. 4 (1971): 93, 96.

[165] Raskin, "Democracy versus the National Security State," 216.

while, like Mills, doubting the critical capacities of the population isolated the Institute for Policy Studies in the absence of an assertive social movement.[166] As might be expected, they met intellectual resistance from the spokespeople of American empire who were convinced that the law supported liberal permanent security.

Liberal Permanent Security Fights Back

The legal defenders of the American war effort cleaved closely to international law because it supported their case. Contra Falk, they did not regard the Nuremberg legacy as a dynamic precedent that pointed to a reformation of the international system by setting new standards of accountability. Rather, as Justice Jackson and his team in Nuremberg intended, the trials ensured that the notion of military necessity, embodied in the Hague Conventions and military handbooks, was rehabilitated for use by the US in making the world safe for democracy. The American neoconservative intellectual and long-time editor of *Commentary* magazine, Norman Podhoretz (b. 1930), made plain the political stakes. In *Why We Were in Vietnam* (1982), he drew on Hannah Arendt's *Origins of Totalitarianism* to argue that the struggle against Nazism needed to be continued in the "moral crusade against Communism" as they were effectively the same enemy. This meant that containing communism in Vietnam "was therefore on the same moral plane as going to war against Nazism had been."[167] Given the greater cause and imperative to save American lives, he continued like Jackson in his 1946 article in the *New York Times Magazine* discussed in Chapter 5: causing Vietnamese civilian casualties by applying disproportionate power was entirely legitimate. That was the American way of war.[168] Guenter Lewy concurred, also reasoning like Jackson: "For all but the pacifist, the decision as to whether any particular military conflict is justified therefore has to be made not on the basis of

---

[166] In quasi-anarchist fashion, Raskin thought the population needed to engage in "social reconstruction" to transform its consciousness by replacing dependence on corrupt institutions with autonomy organization. His manifesto, in part inspired by David Riesman's *Lonely Crowd: A Study of the Changing American Character* (New Haven: Yale University Press, 1950), is *Being and Doing* (New York: Random House, 1971). It is no accident that the famous sociologist, Riesman (1909–2002), was a member of the Institute for Policy Studies. See Brian S. Mueller, "An Alternative to Revolution: Marcus Raskin's Theory of Social Reconstruction," *Journal for the Study of Radicalism* 13, no. 1 (2019): 43–74.

[167] Podhoretz, *Why We Were in Vietnam* in *The Norman Podhoretz Reader: A Selection of His Writings from the 1950s through the 1990s*, ed. Thomas L. Jeffers, intro Paul Johnson (New York: Free Press, 2004), 177–8.

[168] Ibid., 176; Robert Jackson, "The Worst Crime of All," *New York Times Magazine*, September 9, 1945, 89.

whether innocent civilians are likely to be killed but in terms of a country's national interest."[169]

Podhoretz otherwise repeated the legal case of lawyers and political scientists who had taken on Taylor, Falk, and Sartre in the 1970s. The war critics' arguments had cut to the bone, leading to complaints about a "war crimes industry" and "left-wing McCarthyism"[170] Even so sober a figure as Waldemar A. Solf (1913–1987) from the Judge Advocate General Department of the US Army quoted a sympathetic academic to the effect that "antimilitarism has become the anti-Semitism of the intellectual community."[171] Despite such rhetorical exaggerations, he and others got down to the business of a black-letter legal exculpation of the military. This was not difficult. Even liberals like Nuremberg prosecutor Benjamin Ferencz, noted – and seemed to approve – the legal probity of the US bombing of North Vietnam despite his own misgivings about the war in general.[172] Lewy, though not a lawyer, proceeded in a legalistic fashion with help from military attorneys whose arguments he repeated.[173] He saw no legal problem with collective punishment because the North Vietnamese strategy explicitly militarized the civilian population:

> If guerrillas live and operate among the people like fish in water, then, legally the entire school of fish may become a legitimate military target. In such a case, the moral blame, too, would appear to fall on those who have enlarged the potential area of civilian death and damage.[174]

Besides, he continued, claims about the American violence was exaggerated. The bombing was no worse than in Korea where it had "leveled practically all major population centers."[175] What is more, citing Hersch Lauterpacht's commentary on international law and the Hostages Case at Nuremberg, the Hague Convention allowed "general devastation" on an area in "exceptional cases," although he did not ask whether the 1949 Geneva Conventions superseded this concession to military necessity.[176] No doubt, some of the

---

[169] Lewy, *America in Vietnam*, 304.   [170] Podhoretz, *Why We Were in Vietnam*, 168.

[171] Waldemar A. Solf, "A Response to Telford Taylor's *Nuremberg and Vietnam: An American Tragedy*," *Akron Law Review* 5, no. 1 (1972:) 43. He quoted Charles G. Moskos from the Department of Sociology at Northwestern University.

[172] Benjamin B. Ferencz, review of *Nuremberg and Vietnam: An American Tragedy* by Telford Taylor, in *American Journal of International Law* 65 (1971): 640–3.

[173] See the devastating review by Kevin Buckley, "Vietnam: The Defence's Case," *New York Review of Books*, December 7, 1978.

[174] Lewy, *America in Vietnam*, 299.   [175] Ibid., 304.

[176] Ibid., 228–9. Hersch Lauterpacht referred to Article 23G of the 1907 Hague Convention in *International Law, A Treatise*, 2 Vols. *Disputes, War and Neutrality*, by Lassa Oppenheim, 7th ed. by Hersh Lauterpacht (London: Longmans, Green & Co, 1952), 2: 415–6.

shelling was "lavish," he conceded, but civilian casualties were "an inevitable part of modern war and modern military technology."[177] Solf made the same noises: "Unquestionably there have been cases when air power or artillery fire was deliberately misused. Such incidents inevitably occur in war."[178]

True, concluded Lewy, regrettable incidents had occurred even if they were not illegal: "There was much in the American military effort in Vietnam that was legal but should probably not have happened."[179] But the apologists' case was clear: civilian casualties were unfortunate but predictable, though not criminal; excesses were accidents and could be prosecuted on an ad hoc basis. Lewy encapsulated the logic of permanent liberal security in a single sentence: "While the American way of war undoubtedly took the life of many non-combatants, these casualties were never inflicted as a matter of policy."[180]

Solf mounted the most rigorous defense of military necessity by using the Nuremberg Trials to his advantage. The doctrine, he accurately explained, extended "only rudimentary protection to civilians who get caught in the cross fire of military operations on the battle field."[181] Its application was limited by the rules of proportionality, meaning that noncombatants could not be deliberately targeted. But it was up to field commanders on the spot to assess the relationship between the value of a military target and the likely civilian casualties; and that allowed them a large leeway. Moreover, as others also pointed out, the Viet Cong did not regard itself as bound by the Geneva Conventions, and its mode of warfare violated the distinction between combatants and noncombatants. Those who fought without markings violated the laws of war and could be punished with death.[182] That said, Solf also saw that the Viet Cong mode of warfare required the Americans to innovate if they were to respect the law's "basic principles."[183] The innovation was the creation of "free-fire zones" by evacuating civilians from battle areas, a policy that Taylor regarded as violating the Geneva Convention's prohibition of transferring populations. That prohibition applied only in conditions of belligerent occupation, however, so the Americans had a free hand, argued Solf, echoing arguments that had long been made about the inadequacy of insisting on the principle of distinction in modern warfare.[184]

That Solf led the defense of the military campaign and military necessity is significant because he worked closely with the International Committee of

---

[177] Lewy, *America in Vietnam*, 230.
[178] Solf, "A Response to Telford Taylor's *Nuremberg and Vietnam*," 54.
[179] Lewy, *America in Vietnam*, 306.   [180] Ibid., 301.
[181] Solf, "A Response to Telford Taylor's *Nuremberg and Vietnam*," 45–6.   [182] Ibid., 51.
[183] Ibid., 54.
[184] See Julius Stone's review of Lauterpacht's *International* Law, noted above, in the Sydney *Law Review* 17 (1954): 270–5. Here Stone argued for the creation of civilian "sanctuaries" so that factories and their workers, who he regarded as combatants because they participated in the war effort, could be bombed.

the Red Cross and advocated for international humanitarian law within the army. He defended the 1977 Additional Protocols against the Reagan Administration's criticisms. For him, law and the ability of the military to fulfill its mission were compatible. When he died in 1987, academic colleagues remembered him as a champion of "the principle of humanity."[185] The Institute for Policy Studies could not then predict how Solf's position would portend the US and UN interventions of the 1990s and beyond, justified as they were in terms of "humanity" and legitimated by lawyers who cleared missile and drone strikes so that the inevitable collateral killing of civilians was legal.[186] Even so, Mills and then Raskin, Barnet, and Falk, had sounded the tocsin about permanent war long before. The combination of "forever" wars with the legal killing of civilians in the name of humanity represented the victory of liberal permanent security in the 1990s and 2000s. This was a disaster from Raskin's perspective. In 1976, he warned that "It does not seem likely to me that those who struggled in the sixties to develop a new meaning of democracy will settle for bureaucratic or corporate fascism."[187] By the time he died in 2014, he could see that he was wrong.

[185] Robert Kogod Goldman, "Waldemar A. Solf: An Appreciation," *American University International Law Review* 2, no. 2 (1987): 403–4.

[186] David Kennedy, *The Dark Side of Virtue: Reassessing International Humanitarianism* (Princeton: Princeton University Press, 2004); Kennedy, *Of War and Law* (Princeton, NJ: Princeton University Press 2006); Jens David Ohlin, ed., *Theoretical Boundaries of Armed Conflict and Human Rights* (Cambridge: Cambridge University Press, 2016).

[187] Raskin, "Democracy versus the National Security State," 220.

11

Genocide Studies and the Repression of the Political

The North American and Israeli scholars who founded Comparative Genocide Studies in the 1980s and 1990s also insisted on genocide's Holocaust archetype, following Lemkin, who had done so in the 1950s when he opportunistically limited his concept to win the support of skeptical American politicians. These scholars successfully resisted the "conceptual stretching" of genocide to include political criteria in its definition.[1] In doing so, they repeated foundational arguments by the German-Jewish political thinker, Hannah Arendt, that severed connections between the West and the Holocaust. Domestically, they advocated an apolitical "toleration" pedagogy as genocide's antidote.

The US victory in the Cold War in 1991 sidelined the lively critique of the US national security state and gave rise to a new age of interventions. Vietnam-induced doubts were left behind as "the indispensable nation" became the world's hyperpower. Although they were liberals who opposed the Vietnam War, the founders of Comparative Genocide Studies eagerly filled the space as the academic handmaiden of US global aspirations: the field anointed its military power as the benign force to police the non-West in the form of humanitarian interventions to prevent genocide, other "atrocity crimes," and to wage "war on terror."[2] In this mode, the analytical and scholarly outcome of the disastrous Vietnam and Nigeria-Biafra wars was not the institution of exacting analyses of permanent security in its various forms, most urgently of the US and Soviet empires that sponsored dirty proxy wars and envisaged killing hundreds of millions of people in nuclear warfare. Instead, the aura of the Holocaust and victory in World War II was captured by liberal permanent security in the form of Comparative Genocide Studies, which followed the new Human Rights field in "reclaiming American virtue."[3]

---

[1] On conceptual stretching, see Giovanni Sartori, "Concept Misformation in Comparative Politics," *American Political Science Review* 64, no. 4 (1970): 1033–53; David Collier and James E. Mahon, Jr., "Conceptual 'Stretching' Revisited: Adapting Categories in Comparative Analysis," *American Political Science Review* 87, no. 4 (1993): 845–55.

[2] These assumptions and this pedagogy are examined in the next chapter.

[3] Barbara Keys, *Reclaiming American Virtue: The Human Rights Revolution of the 1970s* (Cambridge, MA: Harvard University Press, 2014). The journal *Human Rights Quarterly*

The field of Genocide Studies did not exist during the Nigeria-Biafra war, 1967–1970, and Vietnam War with which it overlapped. It started to crystallize only in the early 1980s, and consolidated and developed in the 2000s, spurred by the wars of Yugoslav secession and the Rwandan genocide in 1994. The field's effective founders were academics and graduate students at the time of Vietnam and the Biafra conflict, however, and reflected on it in the 1980s as they debated definitions of genocide for social scientific research rather than for strictly legal purposes. In many ways, they were rowing against the tide, as these were also the decades when the Holocaust assumed public and academic prominence as a supposedly singular or unique event. Engaging in Comparative Genocide Studies, as the emerging field called itself, could be seen as heretical. Sociologist Helen Fein (b. 1934) recalls that her presentation about different national responses to Jewish persecution during the Holocaust, which included a comparison with the Armenian genocide, at the First International Scholars' Conference on the Holocaust in 1975, was regarded as "radical" because "the dominant position was that the Holocaust was unique, noncomparable and to some, non-explicable as a historical event – viewed as a mystifying or transcendent event": this was a position that sober sociologist Fein could not share, despite her personal commitment to Holocaust research.[4] As late as 1992, Robert Melson (b. 1937) felt compelled to preface his *Revolution and Genocide* with the statement that the book's pairing of the Holocaust and Armenian genocide "does not spring from a desire to trivialize the Holocaust by spuriously universalizing human suffering and denying its unique and perhaps unfathomable characteristics."[5] In the event, it was not the Armenian genocide but the Biafran case had profound implications for the field and study of postcolonial genocides generally. As we will see, the Holocaust-as-archetype-of-genocide came to shape these scholars' moral and political imaginations.

---

was founded in 1982. On the 1970s as the breakthrough for human rights as an apolitical utopia, see the paradigm shifting book by Sam Moyn, *The Last Utopia: Human Right in History* (Cambridge, MA, and London: The Belnap Press of Harvard University Press, 2010), and Jan Eckel and Sam Moyn, eds., *The Breakthrough: Human Rights in the 1970s* (Philadelphia: University of Pennsylvania, 2015). Now called Genocide Studies, the field began life as Comparative Genocide Studies. To be sure, critical alternatives like Peace and Conflict Studies flourished, but they could not invoke the Holocaust in the same way. Foundational was Johan Galtung, "A Structural Theory of Imperialism," *Journal of Peace Research* 13, no. 2 (1971): 81–117.

[4] Helen Fein, "From Social Action to Social Theory and Back: Paths and Circles," in *Pioneers of Genocide Studies: Confronting Mass Death in the Century of Genocide*, ed. Samuel Totten and Steven L. Jacobs (New Brunswick, NJ: Greenwood, 2002), 223.

[5] Robert Melson, *Revolution and Genocide: On the Origins of the Armenian Genocide and the Holocaust* (Chicago: University of Chicago Press, 1992), xviii.

Biafra

The secessionist Nigeria-Biafra war raged between 1967 and 1970, making headlines around the world, above all for the major famine caused by the Nigerian state's (Federal Military Government, FMG) blockade of the self-proclaimed separatist region of Biafra in the country's east. The crisis drove prominent academics and journalists to mobilize public opinion around stopping genocide, and prompted a major international relief operation to bring supplies to starving civilians. For many who believed Biafran propaganda, the Igbo – the majority people in the self-proclaimed republic – were the Jews of Africa, and they were suffering a Holocaust.[6] These claims placed immense pressure on the British government, which supported the FMG. Public opinion in Britain was firmly on the Biafran side; government rhetoric about Nigerian unity and its long-standing military relationship was no match for images of starving babies circulated by the Biafran public relations campaign and sympathetic Western journalists. The FMG and British ultimately won the propaganda war, however, by sponsoring an international observer team to visit Nigeria and report on the genocide issue. The FMG played along, although it forbade the team entry to Biafran territory where the famine and aerial bombing of eastern Nigerians were actually occurring. The team determined that genocide was not taking place, and international public opinion largely concurred.[7] Critics of Biafran strategy and its international supporters pointed out that prolonging Biafran resistance and the war exacerbated civilian casualties: the conflict was a civil war rather than a genocide.[8]

Robert Melson's intellectual journey about Biafra is particularly important, because he was a leading and symptomatic figure of Comparative Genocide

[6] Auberon Waugh and Susan Cronje, *Biafra: Britain's Shame* (London: Joseph, 1969); Frederick Forsyth, *The Biafra Story* (Harmondsworth: Penguin, 1969); Conor Cruise O'Brien, "A Condemned People," *New York Review of Books*, December 21, 1967; O'Brien, "Biafra Revisited," *New York Review of Books*, May 22, 1969; Stanley Diamond, "Who Killed Biafra?" *New York Review of Books*, February 26, 1970.

[7] Douglas Anthony, "Irreconcilable Narratives: Biafra, Nigeria and arguments about genocide, 1966–70," Roy Doron, "Marketing Genocide: Biafran Propaganda Strategies during the Nigerian Civil War, 1967–1970," and Karen E. Smith, "The UK and 'Genocide' in Biafra," in *Postcolonial Conflict and the Question of Genocide: The Nigeria-Biafra War, 1967–1970*, ed. A. Dirk Moses and Lasse Heerten (London and New York: Routledge, 2018), 47–71, 72–94, 137–55; S. Elizabeth Bird and Fraser Ottanelli, *The Asaba Massacre: Trauma, Memory, and the Nigerian Civil War* (New York: Cambridge University Press, 2017).

[8] William Shawcross, *The Quality of Mercy: Cambodia, Holocaust and Modern Conscience* (New York: Fontana and Collins, 1985), 424–7, and Ian Smillie, *The Alms Bazaar: Altruism under Fire: Non-Profit Organizations and International Development* (London: Intermediate Technology Publications, 1995), 104–5.

Studies; and revealing because he was a *bona fide* Nigeria expert, having spent 1964 and 1965 in the country for his doctoral research on its labor movement. News of a Biafran friend's murder brought back traumatic memories of the Holocaust, which he had barely survived as a child in Poland. "I could not help but make the connection between their experience and my own." Biafrans were being killed purely for their identity: it was "as if the twenty-some years after the Second World War had been compressed into a few minutes. The Holocaust monster was on the prowl again, and it was no use trying to escape its implications in Africa or elsewhere."[9] He consequently supported their secessionist campaign. This initial moment of empathetic recognition soon passed, though, when he saw that the FMG did not intend to exterminate all Biafrans after its victory in 1970, and indeed apparently sought to integrate them into the state: "The Nigerians were not Nazis, and the Ibos were not Jews."[10] This could not be genocide because its messy script did not resemble the tidy dramaturgy of the Holocaust of utterly innocent victims and monstrous perpetrators bent on their total extermination.

Genocide, Melson concluded like many before him, needed to entail the attempt to destroy a group in its entirety. Accordingly, he criticized the UN genocide definition's criminalization of group destruction "in whole or in part" for conflating what he called "total" and "partial genocides" (or "genocides in part"). Unlike the Holocaust, Armenian and Cambodian genocides, which were cases of attempted total destruction by revolutionary regimes driven by redemptive ideologies, the Biafran and other cases were partial, meaning the aim was to "coerce and alter" a group's identity and social status rather than to eliminate it, even though it exceeded massacres in scale and effect.[11] Thus, although he acknowledged that "over a million Biafrans starved to death as a result of the deliberate Nigerian policy of blockade and disruption of agricultural life," the policy could not be called genocidal because the FMG policies "did not include extermination of the Ibos."[12] Melson also implied another feature intrinsic to genocide. Igbos were not being killed for ideological reasons and purely for their identity but because they were a party to a secessionist civil war. Not the product of a global ideology of racism, the Nigerian violence was rather a territorially contained conflict of self-determination resulting from the tensions of postcolonial state-building and modern nationalist ideology.

---

[9] Robert Melson, "My Journey in the Study of Genocide," in Totten and Jacobs, *Pioneers of Genocide Studies*, 142.

[10] Melson, *Revolution and Genocide*, xviii.   [11] Ibid., xvix, 23–8.

[12] Robert Melson, "Paradigms of Genocide: The Holocaust, the Armenian Genocide, and Contemporary Mass Destructions," *Annals of the American Academy of Political and Social Science*, no. 548 (1996): 158, 163.

As an expert on African politics and, later, genocide, Melson would have been aware of Leo Kuper (1908–1994), a South African lawyer and sociologist who also moved from African Studies to Genocide Studies. In his field-defining book from 1981, *Genocide: Its Political Use in the Twentieth Century*, Kuper briefly mentioned the Biafran conflict, particularly the 1966 massacres in the north before the civil war and famine, as a case of "genocidal massacre," a new concept he introduced to the field; it performed the same qualifying function as Melson's distinction between total and partial genocide. He thought Biafran propaganda about genocide to be excessive and also noted that no attempt was made to exterminate the Igbo after their military defeat.[13]

Kuper drew two conclusions from conflicts like Biafra. First, postcolonial political instability was caused by these states' internal ethnic pluralism, one close to Melson's own approach to ethnic communalism, which he thought was intensified by modernization processes. Genocide within states was "particularly a phenomenon of the plural or divided society, in which division persists between peoples of different race or ethnic group or religion, who have been brought together in the same political unit."[14] Second, these genocides needed to be contrasted with ones produced by what he calls "totalitarian political ideologies, of absolute commitment to the remaking of society in conformity with radical specifications, and a rooting out of dissent."[15] The salient point of this distinction is that "between situations in which there is some threat, however slight, to the interests of those who perpetrate or plan or incite massacres, and situations devoid of such threat." He insisted that "one can distinguish between massacres of a weak defenceless hostage group used as a scapegoat, and massacres arising in the course of a conflict in which there is some realistic threat or challenge to the interests of the dominant group in the host society."[16] In the latter, political considerations are salient, but not in the former, which are purely ideological. And the Holocaust was the most striking example of it, as Hannah Arendt had insisted years earlier.[17]

This political/nonpolitical distinction ensured the exclusion of the Nigeria-Biafra war from Genocide Studies. Thus, the first anthology on genocide,

---

[13] Leo Kuper, *Genocide: Its Political Use in the Twentieth Century* (New Haven: Yale University Press, 1981), 73–6. He based his account on Anthony H. M. Kirk-Greene, *The Genesis of the Nigerian Civil War and the Theory of Fear* (Uppsala: Scandinavian Institute of African Studies, 1975), and John de St. Jorre, *The Nigerian Civil War* (London: Hodder and Stoughton, 1972).

[14] Kuper, *Genocide*, 17. Kuper, "Plural Societies: Perspectives and Problems," in *Pluralism in Africa*, ed. Kuper and M. G. Smith (Berkeley: University of California Press, 1969), 7–26; Kuper, *The Pity of it All: Polarisation of Ethnic and Racial Relations* (Minneapolis: University of Minnesota Press, 1977); Robert Melson and Howard Wolpe, "Modernization and the Politics of Communalism," *American Political Science Review* 64, no. 4 (1970): 1112–30.

[15] Kuper, *Genocide*, 17.   [16] Ibid., 92–3.   [17] Ibid., 143–4.

published by Jack Nusan Porter (b. 1944) in 1982, contained a section on the Hutu-Tutsi in Burundi, the Ache of Paraguay, the Buddhists of Tibet, East Timor, Cambodia, and East Pakistan, but not the Igbos of Nigeria.[18] In a much-cited article in 1988, Ted Gurr and Barbara Harff did not count the 1966 massacre of Igbos in the north because "there was no deliberate, sustained policy of extermination dictated and organized by ruling groups," but then also excluded the subsequent state-induced famine.[19] Helen Fein was prepared to refer very briefly to the "Ibos in Nigeria (preceding the Biafran secession in 1966)" in her well-known analysis, *Genocide: A Sociological Perspective* (1990), although she too omitted the deliberate famine.[20] The Biafran case was not covered in Frank Chalk and Kurt Jonassohn's influential anthology, *The History and Sociology of Genocide* (1990), but they included a bibliographical reference despite their stated misgivings.[21] Neither did Jonassohn's survey of "man-made famines" mention the million or more Biafran victims.[22] The paucity of research was evident when Israel W. Charny's pioneering *Encyclopedia of Genocide* (1999) contained a perfunctory paragraph-long entry on the Igbos based wholly on Kuper's own brief summary.[23] The Rutgers University sociologist, Irving Louis Horowitz (1929–2012), underlined this point when he distinguished "between those who are truly victims of genocidal massacre and those who are killed as an adjunct of a wartime effort, as the official Nigerian position holds."[24] This

---

[18] Jack Nusan Porter, ed., *Genocide and Human Rights: A Global Anthology* (Washington, DC: University Press of America, 1982).

[19] Barbara Harff and Ted Robert Gurr, "Toward Empirical Theory of Genocides and Politicides: Identification and Measurement of Cases since 1945," *International Studies Quarterly* 32, no. 3 (1988): 368. Several years later, however, she did include Igbos in the north in a chart on "Victims of Genocide and Politicides since WWII": Harff, "Recognizing Genocides and Politicides," in *Genocide Watch*, ed. Helen Fein (New Haven: Yale University Press, 1992), 32. This anthology includes cases on Iraqi Kurds, Burundi, the Ukrainian famine, and Bahai in Iran but not Nigeria/Biafra.

[20] Helen Fein, "Genocide: A Sociological Perspective," *Contemporary Sociology* 38, no. 1 (1990): 6.

[21] Frank Chalk and Kurt Jonassohn, *The History and Sociology of Genocide: Analyses and Case Studies* (New Haven: Yale University Press, 1990), 429, 455.

[22] Kurt Jonassohn, "Hunger as a Low Technology Weapon, with Special Reference to Genocide," in *Genocide Perspectives*, ed. Colin Tatz, Vol. 1 (Sydney: Centre for Comparative Genocide Studies, Macquarie University, 1997), 263–88.

[23] Torben Jørgensen and Eric Markusen, "Igbos, Genocide of (1966–1969)," in *Encyclopedia of Genocide*, 2 vols., ed. Israel W. Charny (London: Mansell, 1988), 1: 347. There is a more detailed discussion in Rhoda E. Howard-Hassmann, *Human Rights in Commonwealth Africa* (Lanham, MD: Rowman & Littlefield, 1986), 94–7. She also disqualifies the genocide categorization.

[24] Irving Louis Horowitz, *Taking Lives: Genocide and State Power*, 5th ed. (New Brunswick, NJ: Transaction, 2002), 33. Five pages later, he suggested that the Biafran case was an example of the transition between war and genocide.

argument persists to the present day. Writing in an anthology on the Nigeria-Biafra war in 2013, Paul Bartrop continued the insistence that "until it can be demonstrated that their [the FMG] goal was the *total destruction* of the Igbo as a people, and not forcing the surrender of Biafra and its reincorporation into the Nigerian Federal Republic, caution must be exercised in concluding the genocide occurred."[25]

Until the Bosnian and Rwandan cases of 1994, the canonical genocides were the Holocaust and Armenian genocide. The first comparative genocide studies conference, held in Israel in 1982, was limited to these cases. Why this was the case can perhaps be explained by the biographies of the founding generation of genocide scholars, who were in the main Holocaust survivors or their children, Israelis and Armenians. Yet, as Melson's journey indicates, the Holocaust was not the initial focus. It was too traumatic to write about the Holocaust early in his life, he reported later. The interest in postcolonial Africa functioned as a displacement. "As did so many of my generation growing up in the late 1950s and 1960s, I had hoped that Africa, the Third World, would avoid the recent horrors of Europe." Biafran spurred him less to explore contemporary Africa and similar contemporary cases, however, than to go back in time: "I knew I had to return to the Holocaust to try to make sense of it both at the level of personal emotion and in some broader comparative intellectual perspective."[26]

Europe's traumatic past, then, led to a commitment to postcolonial reconstruction, and then back to the Holocaust when these hopes for the new postcolonial nation-states were dashed.[27] After spending 1977 in Jerusalem, overlooking the occupied Judean desert and Dead Sea from the Hebrew University's elevated campus, Melson decided to work on the Holocaust and became a charter member of the Jewish Studies program at his home institution, Purdue University in Indiana, US. Seeking a case to compare to the Holocaust, Melson settled on Armenia rather than Biafra – or Cambodia – because it "most resembled [the Holocaust]."[28] Fein, too, had initially written about colonial violence after a period of anti-Vietnam war activism, before rediscovering her

---

[25] Paul R. Bartrop, "Getting the Terminology Right," in *The Nigeria-Biafra war: Genocide and the Politics of Memory*, ed. Chima J. Korieh (Amherst, MA: Cambria Press, 2012), 57. Emphasis added.

[26] Melson, *Revolution and Genocide*, xviii.

[27] Robert Melson, "Nigerian Politics and the General Strike of 1964," in *Protest and Power in Black Africa*, ed. Robert A. Rotberg and Ali A. Mazrui (New York: Oxford University Press, 1970), 171–87. He analyzes the Biafra question in Robert Melson and Howard Wolpe, eds., *Nigeria: Modernization and the Politics of Communalism* (East Lansing: Michigan State University Press, 1971). Later he would write about his Jewish family's survival during the Holocaust: Melson, *False Papers: Deception and Survival in the Holocaust* (Urbana and Chicago: University of Illinois Press, 2000).

[28] Melson, "My Journey in the Study of Genocide," 143.

Jewish identity while living in India in the early 1970s and resolving to work on the Holocaust, antisemitism, genocide, and refugees.[29]

In a very concrete sense, the canonization of the Holocaust and Armenian genocide came at the conceptual expense of Biafra and other so-called partial colonial and postcolonial genocides; rather than the political dimensions of postcolonial conflict into Genocide Studies, its Holocaust focus meant that only conflagrations somehow resembling this "maximal standard" (Martin Shaw) could be imaginable as genocide, that is, as the terrible outcome of redemptive ideologies whose victims were passive objects of revolutionary state violence.[30]

Founding Genocide Studies

Leaving aside Lemkin, who died in 1959, the postwar genocides listed above occurred in the adult lifetime of the founders of Genocide Studies. Predominantly of Jewish and Armenian backgrounds, they thematized the genocidal victimization of their own families as a motivation for their endeavors.[31] Jack Nusan Porter came to it from his work on Jewish radicalism. He claims to have taught the first course on genocide in 1978 "under the mentorship of a sociologist of the Armenian genocide, Levon Chorbajian."[32] Irving Horowitz exemplifies the trajectory of these founders in distinguishing themselves from their mentors' emphasis on nuclear warfare and

---

[29] Fein, "From Social Action to Social Theory and Back," 221; Helen Fein, *Imperial Crime and Punishment: The Massacre at Jallianwala Bagh and British Judgment, 1919–1920* (Honolulu: University Press of Hawaii, 1977); Fein, *Accounting for Genocide: National Responses and Jewish Victimization during the Holocaust* (New York: Free Press, 1979); Fein, ed., *The Persisting Question: Sociological Perspectives and Social Contexts of Modern Antisemitism* (Berlin and New York: de Gruyter, 1987). Her criticisms of the Indian caste system and valorization of Jewish-Western ethics of equality mirror those of American feminist Katherine Mayo in *Mother India* (1927). On this trope, see Mrinalini Sinha, *Spectres of Mother India: The Global Restructuring of Empire* (Durham, NC: Duke University Press, 2006).

[30] It is no coincidence that Melson resists the recent attempt to join the genocidal and colonial domains of inquiry: Robert Melson, "Critique of Current Genocide Studies," *Genocide Studies and Prevention* 6, no. 3 (2011): 279–86; Martin Shaw, *What is Genocide?* (Cambridge: Polity Press, 2007), ch. 3.

[31] See the autobiographical sketches in Totten and Jacobs, *Pioneers of Genocide Studies*. The affinity between Jews and genocide studies mirrors that between American Jews and liberalism. On the latter, see Geoffrey Brahm Levey, "The Liberalism of American Jews: Has It Been Explained?" *British Journal of Political Science* 26, no. 3 (1996): 369–401.

[32] Jack Nusan Porter, *Jewish Radicalism: A Selected Anthology* (New York: Grove Press, 1973); Porter, "Sociology and Genocide Studies," *Footnotes: A Publication of the American Sociological Association* 36, no. 5 (May–June 2008): www.asanet.org/foot notes/mayjun08/geno.html; Arthur Liebman, *Jews and the Left* (New York: John Wiley & Sons, 1979).

indiscriminate aerial bombing. A junior colleague of C. Wright Mills, Horowitz soon distanced himself from Mill's enthusiasm for the Cuban revolution and, above all, from his view of World War II as a conflict between rival imperialisms. Horowitz attributed Mills's relativism to his wrongheaded subscription to this understanding of the war propounded by the Fourth International (the anti-Stalinist international socialist organization established by Leon Trotsky in 1938). Horowitz came to have no truck with 1960s anti-imperialism, and even suggested that Mills exerted a sinister influence on the New Left.[33]

Horowitz's development mirrored that of Melson. In an autobiographical reflection, he relates that he followed the course of World War II as the young son of leftist Eastern European immigrants in New York for whom the antifascist struggle of the Soviet Union and in the US was paramount. As an adolescent, he developed "the sense of the Jewish people as a universal people" and appropriated its "special conditions" in the interwar years into his "intellectual arsenal."[34] Although now aware of the Holocaust, his earliest work in the 1950s reflected the contemporary concern with nuclear extinction, but by the 1960s he was researching leftist rationalizations of violence. A visiting professorship at the Hebrew University in Jerusalem accelerated his journey from Mills and his followers. In Israel, he internalized "the magnitude of the Holocaust" and met survivors from his parents' home region. As might be expected, these encounters led to an intense preoccupation with Israel as a place of Jewish rebirth and with Soviet Jews, whose persecution weighed on him, as on many others in the 1970s. He became their "fervent advocate" with Hannah Arendt and other luminaries in the Academic Committee on Soviet Jewry. Confronting terrorism and Soviet leftist antisemitism in the guise of anti-Zionism now occupied his academic and political attention. If the Nazi regime was disastrous for the Jewish, it had been defeated, while the genocidal potential of the Soviet Union remained a continuing danger. For this reason, Horowitz suggested that exaggerating the uniqueness of the Holocaust detracted from the communist threat, which was equally genocidal. The significant lesson to learn was that "anti-democratic states are the unique carriers of the poison of genocide."[35] From his youthful progressivism, he

---

[33] Irving Louis Horowitz, "The Stalinization of Fidel Castro," *New Politics* 4, no. 4 (1965): 61–9; Horowitz, *C. Wright Mills: An American Utopian* (New York: The Free Press, 1982). In the early 1960s, by contrast, he was still the loyal disciple. See his effusive introduction to C. Wright Mills, *Power, Politics, and People: The Collected Essays of C. Wright Mills*, ed. and intro Irving Louis Horowitz (New York: Oxford University Press, 1963).

[34] Horowitz, *Taking Lives*, 391; Horowitz, "From Pariah People to Pariah Nation: Jews, Israelis, and the Third World," in *Israel in the Third World*, ed. Michael Curtis and Susan Gitelson (New Brunswick, NJ: Transaction, 1976), 369–9.

[35] Horowitz, *Taking Lives*, 399; Horowitz, *Radicalism and the Revolt against Reason: The Social Theories of Georges Sores* (New York: Humanities Press, 1961); Horowitz, ed., *The*

had developed into a fervent neoconservative intellectual. The press he founded in 1962 to disseminate social science research, Transaction Publishers, became the major vehicle for Genocide Studies in the 1970s and 1980s.

Horowitz and other Genocide Studies scholars imagined the field as a derivation of totalitarianism theory, despite his fanciful claim that it lay at the "extreme end of the continuum involved in war and peace studies."[36] It is no coincidence that Horowitz was an enthusiastic disciple of Arendt, whom he praised as a "radical conservative."[37] This conceptualization made sense in the second half of the 1970s in light of the Khmer Rouge's murderous regime in Cambodia. It also effectively made space for the inclusion of the Ukrainian famine of 1932–1933 – the Holodomor – in Genocide Studies. James Mace (1952–2004), a postdoctoral fellow at the Harvard Ukrainian Research Institute, became a regular contributor to genocide conferences and anthologies in the 1980s.[38] Established by anticommunist émigré scholars in 1973, the institute was an important motor of genocide recognition. While working there, Mace assisted Robert Conquest (1917–2015), the author of well-known books on Stalinist terror, in his study, *The Harvest of Sorrow: Soviet Collectivisation and the Terror-Famine*. Fittingly, Mace directed the Congressional Commission on the Ukrainian Famine from 1985 to 1988, whose report concluded that the famine was genocidal.[39] Including this Soviet mass violence in Genocide Studies did not import conceptual confusion, because the Holocaust remained the ideal type of genocide: only Soviet terror that targeted nations and minorities was captured by the genocide optic, excluding other aspects of Soviet permanent security. The "Holocaust is not over and done with," declared Horowitz, "because there are other peoples victimized by the very model created by the Armenian and

---

Anarchists (New York: Dell, 1964); Horowitz, *Israeli Ecstasies and Jewish Agonies* (New York and Oxford: Oxford University Press, 1974).

[36] Horowitz, *Taking Lives*, 394, 399.

[37] Irving Louis Horowitz, *Hannah Arendt: Radical Conservative* (London and New York: Routledge, 2012).

[38] James Mace, "The Man-Made Famine of 1933 in the Soviet Ukraine: What Happened and Why?" in *Toward the Understanding and Prevention of Genocide: Proceedings of the International Conference on the Holocaust and Genocide*, ed. Israel W. Charny (Boulder, CO: Westview, 1984), 67–83; Mace, "Genocide in the USSR," in *Genocide: A Critical Bibliographical Review*, ed. Israel W. Charny (New York: Facts on File, 1988), 116–36. See also Frank Sysyn, "The Ukrainian Famine of 1932–3: The Role of the Ukrainian Diaspora in Research and Public Discussion," in *Studies in Comparative Genocide*, ed. Levon Chorbajian and George Shirinian (Basingstoke: Palgrave Macmillan, 1999), 182–215.

[39] Commission on the Ukraine Famine, *Report to Congress: Investigation of the Ukrainian Famine, 1932–1933* (Washington, DC: United States Government Printing Office, 1988), xii, xiii. Robert Conquest, *The Harvest of Sorrow: Soviet Collectivisation and the Terror-Famine* (New York and Oxford: Oxford University Press, 1986).

Nazi genocide."[40] That included Ukrainians – even though the Holocaust had not occurred by the time of the Holodomor.

For Horowitz, establishing a hierarchy of mass criminality with the destruction of identity at its apex was a means of establishing Genocide Studies as a serious social scientific discipline. Doing so meant countering the cacophony of the indiscriminate claim of genocide by political activists of every stripe.[41] Setting the agenda was his field-founding *Genocide, State Power and Mass Murder* (1976), which defined genocide "as a structural and systematic destruction of *innocent* people by a state bureaucratic apparatus." The state decided such people "represent symbolic evil," he elaborated, rather than a "real threat" – like Lemkin, Lauterpacht, and the WJC decades before.[42] This distinction between the innocent and the guilty became hegemonic within Comparative Genocide Studies in the 1980s and 1990s. Sociologist Helen Fein defined genocide as the destruction of "defenseless" and "non-violent collectivities," meaning she drew a strict line between them and victims of Allied bombing in World War II.[43] Israel W. Charny (b. 1931), an American family therapist who migrated to Israel in 1973 and became active in founding the field, exemplified this proposition in his definition of genocide: "the mass killing of substantial numbers of human beings, when not in the course of military action against the military forces of an avowed enemy, under conditions of the essential defenselessness and helplessness of the victims."[44] Political scientist Manus Midlarsky, Horowitz's successor at Rutgers, followed him in asserting that "Genocide is understood to be the state-sponsored systematic mass murder of innocent and helpless men, women, and children."[45] The philosopher, Berel Lang, likewise identified the particular evil of genocide as "the intent of genocide to destroy members of a group not because of any act they have been responsible for individually." He then added the ethnic, national, and racial element that is elemental to the Holocaust archetype: people were destroyed "solely because of their identification as members

---

[40] Horowitz, *Taking Lives*, 399, 39, 169–71.

[41] Porter, "Introduction," *Genocide and Human Rights*, 9–10.

[42] Irving Louis Horowitz, *Genocide, State Power and Mass Murder* (New Brunswick, NJ: Transaction Publishers, 1976), 16–8. Emphasis added. Later editions are called *Taking Lives: Genocide and State Power*. As examples, he referred to Jews in Poland, peasants in the Ukraine, Catholics in Northern Ireland, Indians in Uganda, blacks in South Africa. Horowitz, *Taking Lives*, 78.

[43] Helen Fein, "Genocide, Terror, Life Integrity, and War Crimes: The Case for Discrimination," in *Genocide: The Conceptual and Historical Dimensions of Genocide*, ed. George Andreopolous (Philadelphia: University of Pennsylvania Press, 1994), 95–107.

[44] Israel W. Charny, "Toward a Generic Definition of Genocide," in Andreopolous, *Genocide*, 75.

[45] Manus Midlarsky, *The Killing Trap: Genocide in the Twentieth Century* (Cambridge: Cambridge University Press, 2005), 10.

of that group."[46] Hatred of identity was the genocidal motivation, its destruction the intention. Legal scholar William Schabas reflected this view in noting that "the purpose of the [Genocide] Convention ... was to protect national minorities from crimes based on ethnic hatred."[47] The consensus was indicated by the Jewish Studies scholar, Alan L. Berger, in an essay tellingly entitled "The Holocaust: The Ultimate and Archetypal Genocide." The question of agency was central, echoing Kuper's distinction between political and nonpolitical genocides: "it was not *what* Jews did," propounded Berger in 1988, "but rather *that* they were Jews which constituted their 'crime.'"[48]

Genocide Studies expressed the moral impulse of mainly Jewish scholars to universalize the lessons of the Holocaust in light of postwar violence. Charny spoke for them when he stated that he was "committed to the ideal that understanding the processes which brought about the unbearable evil of the Holocaust be joined with the age-old Jewish tradition of contributing to the greater ethical development of human civilization, and that a unique memorial to the Holocaust be forged in the development of new concepts of prevention of genocide to all peoples."[49] Their cosmopolitan liberalism can be measured against the background of the debate in the 1970s in which some claimed that Holocaust and genocide should refer only to the Nazi destruction of Jews and could not be "shared" with others.[50] Genocide scholars (as they called themselves) opposed this proposition, though they regarded the Holocaust as the most extreme genocide, indeed, as its archetype. The German-born political scientist, Barbara Harff, exemplified the approach when she wrote that "The Jewish Holocaust ... is employed as the yardstick, the *ultimate criterion* for assessing the scope, methods, targets, and victims of [other] genocides."[51] The Holocaust was the exemplary genocide, just as Jews were the exemplary victim.[52] That is why the names of university centers and institutes they established generally refer to "Holocaust and Genocide Studies," and not solely to "Genocide Studies."

---

[46] Berel Lang, *Genocide: The Act as Idea* (Philadelphia: University of Pennsylvania Press, 2017), 33.

[47] William A. Schabas, *Genocide in International Law: The Crime of Crimes*, 1st ed. (Cambridge: Cambridge University Press, 2000), 119.

[48] Alan L. Berger, "The Holocaust: The Ultimate and Archetypal genocide," in Charny, *Encyclopedia of Genocide*, 1: 59. Emphasis in original.

[49] Israel W. Charny, "Narrative Biography," *Prevent Genocide*: http://preventgenocide.org/education/events/charnyCV2000.htm.

[50] Irving Louis Horowitz, "Many Genocides, One Holocaust? The Limits of the Rights of States and the Obligations of Individuals," *Modern Judaism* 1, no. 1 (1981): 74–89.

[51] Barbara Harff, "Genocide as State Terrorism," in *Government Violence and Repression*, ed. Michael Stohl and George A. López (New York: Greenwood Press, 1986), 165. Emphasis added.

[52] See Helen Fein's rejection of Steven T. Katz's arguments in The Holocaust in Historical Context in her *Genocide: A Sociological Perspective* (London: Sage, 1993), 53. The notion of exemplary victim is discussed in the next chapter.

No sooner had the fledgling field found its feet than it was subject to withering attack by the Jewish Studies scholar, Steven T. Katz, who did not like to share genocide in this way. Based on what he called the Holocaust's "phenomenological uniqueness," he thought that the field was incoherent by including too many cases. Armenians, Ukrainians, and Cambodians were victims of mass murder rather than genocide, because "the concept of genocide applies only where there is an actualized intention, however successfully carried out, to physically destroy an entire group," not just in part. Katz was heavily criticized by Genocide Studies scholars but his premise accurately reflected the field's founding assumptions: the Holocaust was indeed genocide's archetype. The point of contention between them was how seriously to take the destruction of a group "in part," as the Genocide Convention stipulated.[53]

For Armenians, genocide was well suited to associate their catastrophe of 1915 with the Holocaust and thereby gain academic respectability and attention.[54] Not surprisingly, the interest in comparative analyses was limited to the Holocaust and the Armenian genocide, the latter then a concern largely confined to the Armenian diaspora community. And, as might be expected, these scholars were also concerned with "genocide denial," especially as the Turkish state, in collusion with the Israeli state, attempted to silence them – attempts that they defied, often to their cost. A conference on both cases that Charny organized in Tel Aviv in 1982 was placed under immense pressure by the Israel authorities, including Yad Vashem, themselves responding to Turkish representations, leading to the withdrawal of conference patron Elie Wiesel (1928–2016). It went ahead anyway, but Charny paid the price within his university.[55]

---

[53] Steven T. Katz, *The Holocaust in Historical Context*, Vol. 1, *The Holocaust and Mass Death before the Modern Age* (Oxford: Oxford University Press, 1994), 129; Katz in his review of Frank Chalk and Kurt Jonassohn, *History and Sociology of Genocide* (New Haven: Yale University Press, 1990) concludes that most cases should not be included under the heading of genocide. The Holocaust alone merits the name of genocide: *Commentary* 91, no. 1 (1991): 52–7. Cf. Yves Ternon, "Reflections on Genocide," in *Minority Peoples in the Age of Nation-States*, ed. Gerard Chaliand (London: Pluto Press, 1989), 127.

[54] Vahakn N. Dadrian, "The Convergent Aspects of the Armenian and Jewish Cases of Genocide," *Holocaust and Genocide Studies* 3, no. 2 (1988): 151–69; Dadrian, "The Historical and Legal Interconnections between the Armenian Genocide and the Jewish Holocaust," *Yale Journal of International Law* 23, no. 2 (1998): 503–59; Richard Hovannisian, ed., *Looking Backward, Moving Forward: Confronting the Armenian Genocide* (New Brunswick, NJ: Transaction, 2003).

[55] "Armenians to Take Part in Tel Aviv Seminar," *New York Times*, June 16, 1982. This short article reports the efforts of the Turkish and Israeli states to shut down Charny's Genocide Studies conference. Charny notes that his defiance of the Tel Aviv University president likely cost him his tenure there: Charny, "A Passion for Life and Rage at the Wasting of Life," in Totten and Jacobs, *Pioneers of Genocide Studies*, 441–2. Israel W. Charny and Shamai Davidson, eds., *The Book of the International Conference on the Holocaust and Genocide. Book One, The Conference Program and Crisis* (Institute of the

With his new Institute on the Holocaust and Genocide in Jerusalem, Charny produced a newsletter forum for activists and researchers between 1985 and 1995 called *Internet on the Holocaust and Genocide*. At the same time, in 1982, Helen Fein founded the Institute for the Study of Genocide at the John Jay College of Criminal Justice of the City University of New York with a mission to "fill a gap in both the scholarly and the human rights communities which did not recognize the continued prevalence of genocide."[56] These scholars engaged in a whirlwind of activity, producing bibliographies, encyclopaedias, and other reference works.[57] In 1994, it crystallized into the Association of Genocide Scholars (later International Association of Genocide Scholars), running a biannual conference attended mainly by North American-based academics. They saw themselves as incarnating the humanitarian conscience that Lemkin identified with Las Casas half a millennium before. The editorial in the first newsletter of the Center for Comparative Genocide Studies at Macquarie University, Sydney, in 1994, exemplified this self-understanding in soliciting donations: "The Centre can and will *act as your conscience*. We have the experts. You have the ability to make possible the research and dissemination of this expertise. Please be with us."[58]

Such exorbitant claims reflected the field's precarious early status. In the lead-up to the aforementioned 1982 Tel Aviv conference, one of its organizers tried to lure a Robert Jay Lifton with the statement that "The Conference is a MUST for mankind as a whole and especially for those who have already suffered attempted genocide." After much back and forth with conference organizers, Lifton and Horowitz declined to participate because Charny could not guarantee the payment of their travel and accommodation. Unable to raise sufficient funds up front, he was planning to finance the undertaking by securing the participation of these academic stars in order to attract the necessary paid registrations. It was a high-risk venture that necessitated inflated claims about the importance of the nascent field for the sake of its business model.[59]

International Conference on the Holocaust and Genocide, 1983). Eldad Ben Aharon, "A Unique Denial: Israel's Foreign Policy and the Armenian Genocide," *British Journal of Middle Eastern Studies* 42, no. 4 (2015): 638–54. On the Israeli state and the Armenian Genocide, see Yair Auron, *The Banality of Denial: Israel and the Armenian Genocide* (New Brunswick, NJ: Transaction Publishers, 2003).

[56] Institute for the Study of Genocide, http://studyofgenocide.org/.

[57] Jack Nusan Porter, ed., *Genocide and Human Rights: A Global Anthology* (Washington, DC: University Press of America, 1982); Israel W. Charny, ed., *Genocide: A Critical Bibliographic Review*, 2 vols. (London: Mansell, 1988); Charny, ed., *The Encyclopedia of Genocide*, 2 vols. (Santa Barbara, CA: ABC-CLIO, 1999).

[58] Colin Tatz, "Editorial," *Newsletter for the Centre for Comparative Genocide Studies*, Macquarie University 1, no. 1 (August–September 1994): 1. Emphasis added.

[59] See the exasperated correspondence between Israel Charny and other organizers with Robert Jay Lifton and Irving Horowitz in Robert Jay Lifton Papers, New York Public

This model and the field's Holocaust optic were brutally exposed by the implosion of Yugoslavia in the first half of the 1990s and the Rwandan genocide of 1994. Angry letters to newspapers urging Western intervention fell on deaf ears. It was all too easy for policy makers to distinguish these events from genocide modeled on the Holocaust. US Secretary of State Warren Christopher (1925–2011) justified his reluctance to commit the Clinton administration to intervention in Bosnia by using the Holocaust archetype to his advantage: "It's somewhat different than the Holocaust," he determined. "It's been easy to analogize this to the Holocaust, but I never heard of any genocide by the Jews against the German people." There were, he continued damningly, "atrocities on all sides," suggesting that victim agency disqualified the genocide label.[60] Similarly, State Department officials declared Rwanda to be a civil war, and the academic who would briefly direct the US Holocaust Memorial Museum, Steven T. Katz, agreed that it was a case of "tribal domination, not genocidal purpose."[61] The presence of the political, which disqualified Biafra from inclusion in Genocide Studies, now came back to haunt the field. It had painted itself into a conceptual corner with its Holocaust-inspired definition of genocide. The Ponzi scheme was intellectual as well as financial.

Excluding Permanent Security

Devastated by the impotence of the international community in preventing genocide in Africa and the Balkans, this little community made preventing future genocides its priority.[62] The agenda of the Association for Genocide

---

Library, Box 128, Folder "Charny, Israel." The quotation is in a letter from Ephraim M. Howard to Robert Jay Lifton, December 29, 1980.

[60] Norman Kempster, "All Sides Share Guilt in Bosnia, Christopher Says," *Los Angeles Times*, May 19, 1993. Also see the trenchant analysis in Nick Cohen, "The Holocaust as Show Business," *New Statesman*, November 20, 2000, 22–3. Generally, see Alan Steinweis, "The Auschwitz Analogy: Holocaust Memory and American Debates Over Intervention in Bosnia and Kosovo in the 1990s," *Holocaust and Genocide Studies* 19, no. 2 (2005): 276–89. Warren was arguing that the conflict was "complex" rather than "intentional," to use the categories of Carrie Booth Walling, *All Necessary Measures: The United Nations and Humanitarian Intervention* (Philadelphia: University of Pennsylvania Press, 2013), 23–6. The standard discourse analysis is Lene Hansen, *Security as Practice: Discourse Analysis and the Bosnian War* (London and New York: Routledge, 2006).

[61] Gregory H. Stanton, "Could the Rwandan Genocide Have Been Prevented?" *Journal of Genocide Research* 6, no. 2 (2004): 211–28. Katz quoted in Liz McMillen, "The Uniqueness of the Holocaust," *Chronicle of Higher Education*, June 22, 1994.

[62] Charny had foreshadowed this priority with calls for "early warning systems" long before: Israel W. Charny, "A Pilot Project for a Genocide Early Warning System," *Reconstructionist* 45 (November 1979): 7–12; Charny, *How Can We Commit the*

Studies leadership was clear: the preoccupation with genocide prevention activism necessitated support of a powerful agent to effect humanitarian (i.e., military) intervention into ongoing mass violence. The "unipolar moment" of US geopolitical domination after the Cold War meant that the US was the only candidate in view of the UN's relative military impotence and its catastrophic failures in Rwanda and Bosnia.[63] This message was reflected in Samantha Power's Pulitzer prize-winning book, *"A Problem from Hell": America in the Age of Genocide* (2002), about the unwillingness of the US to prevent genocide during the twentieth century. She did not ask whether the US might have been complicit in genocide like, say, the mass murder of Indonesian communists in 1965. Including sins of commission as well as of omission would have disturbed the book's valorization of liberal permanent security. Fittingly, the Institute for the Study of Genocide awarded her book its Raphael Lemkin prize in 2003. Lemkin would have approved.[64]

Instead of exposing the function of permanent security, the Genocide Studies leadership now relentlessly excommunicated scholars who revived the Vietnam-era link of genocide and empire that jeopardized their favored view of the US as world sheriff. The Australian historian, Tony Barta, inspired by Sartre's notion of an objective genocidal situation, drew attention to "relations of genocide" in colonial cases where land-hungry settlers rather than the state were the primary actors in smashing indigenous resistance and taking their land.[65] In reply, Frank Chalk and Helen Fein rejected his insights for supposedly muddying the waters about state intention and genocidal ideology. Where Barta highlighted the moral ambiguity of settler colonialism, a phenomenon ignored by Genocide Studies at the time, his critics saw an unnecessary complication of a world they saw divided by the genocidal non-West and

Unthinkable? Genocide, the Human Cancer (Boulder, CO: Westview Press, 1982). See also Leo Kuper, *The Prevention of Genocide* (New Haven: Yale University Press, 1985), and Herbert Hirsch, *Anti-Genocide: Building an American Movement to Prevent Genocide* (Santa Barbara, CA: Praeger, 2002).

[63] Charles Krauthammer, "The Unipolar Moment," *Foreign Affairs* 70, no. 1 (1990–1991): 23–33. For historical contextualization, see Charles S. Maier, *Among Empires: American Ascendancy and Its Predecessors* (Cambridge, MA: Harvard University Press, 2006), and Paul A. Kramer, "Power and Connection: Imperial Histories of the United States in the World," *American Historical Review* 116, no. 5 (2011): 1348–92.

[64] Samantha Power, *"A Problem from Hell": America in the Age of Genocide* (New York: Harper, 2002); The Institute for the Study of Genocide Raphael Lemkin Award: http://studyofgenocide.org/lemkin/. On the US and genocide, see Jeffrey S. Bachman, *The United States and Genocide (Re)Defining the Relationship* (London and New York: Routeldge, 2019).

[65] Tony Barta, "Relations of Genocide: Land and Lives in the Colonization of Australia," in *Genocide and the Modern Age*, ed. Isidor Wallimann and Michael Dobkowski (Westport, CT: Greenwood Press, 1987), 237–52.

the antigenocidal West.[66] In the face of Barta's heresy, Chalk instructed readers that "we must never forget that the great genocides of the past have been committed by [state] perpetrators who acted in the name of absolutist or utopian ideologies aimed at cleansing and purifying their worlds."[67] Settler colonial violence against indigenous peoples was screened out by this ultimate criterion.

Other legacies of the Vietnam-era critique of permanent security were also marginalized, even if more politely because its most significant protagonist, Robert Jay Lifton, was a famous psychiatrist at Yale and then Harvard universities. Interested in state terror and its traumatic effects on survivors, he wrote books on Chinese and Westerners brainwashed in Communist China (1961) and Hiroshima bomb survivors (1968). He then joined Richard Falk in opposing the Vietnam War and writing about the traumatic impact of atrocities on US veterans.[68] Although Jewish and very much concerned with the Holocaust – he wrote an acclaimed book about Nazi doctors in 1986 – his overriding concern was the effect of nuclear weapons on human consciousness, in particular in relation to death and temporality. The bomb's potential for total destruction ruptured symbolic capacities to imagine a human future, leading to "psychic numbing" and desensitization, a point he likely took from Mumford's early polemics against "the bomb."[69] To that end, he and Falk coauthored a volume in 1982 fittingly called *Indefensible Weapons: The Political and Psychological Case against Nuclearism*. It defined nuclearism as a function of security thinking: "psychological, political, and military dependence on nuclear weapons, the embrace of weapons as a solution to a wide variety of human dilemmas, most ironically that of 'security.'"[70]

---

[66] Frank Chalk, "Definitions of Genocide and their Implications for Prediction and Prevention," *Holocaust and Genocide Studies* 4, no. 2 (1989): 155–7; Fein, *Genocide*, 15–16, 79–80. This book was first published as an extended essay in *Current Sociology* 38, no. 1 (1990): 1–126.

[67] Frank Chalk, "Redefining Genocide," in Andreopolous, *Genocide*, 58.

[68] Robert Jay Lifton, *Thought Reform and the Psychology of Totalism: A Study of "Brainwashing" in China* (New York: Norton, 1961); Lifton, *Death in Life: Survivors of Hiroshima* (New York: Random House, 1968); Lifton, *Home from the War: Vietnam Veterans – Neither Victims nor Executioners* (New York: Simon & Schuster, 1973); Richard A. Falk, Gabriel Kolko, and Robert Jay Lifton, eds., *Crimes of War: A Legal, Political-Documentary, and Psychological Inquiry into the Responsibility of Leaders, Citizens, and Soldiers for Criminal Acts in War* (New York: Random House, 1971).

[69] Lewis Mumford, "Atom Bomb: Social Effects," *Air Affairs*, March 1947, 370–82.

[70] Robert Jay Lifton and Eric Olson, *Living and Dying* (New York: Praeger, 1974), 137; Lifton, *History and Human Survival: Essays on the Young and Old Survivors and the Dead, Peace and War, and on Contemporary Psychohistory* (New York: Random House, 1970); Lifton, *The Nazi Doctors: Medical Killing and the Psychology of Genocide* (New York: Basic Books, 1986); Lifton and Richard A. Falk, *Indefensible Weapons: The Political and Psychological Case against Nuclearism* (New York: Basic Books, 1982), xi.

In identifying the problems of mass death at this level, Lifton was not denying the Holocaust its specific features. The "Holocaust" – with capital H – refers to "the uniqueness of the Nazi project of genocide," he wrote. But he was more interested in lower-case holocausts – mentioning the Greek origin of the word meaning "total consumption by fire" – that refer "with literal grotesqueness, to Auschwitz and Buchenwald, and also to Nagasaki and Hiroshima." His concern was with "total disaster: the physical, social, and spiritual obliteration of a human community."[71] The Holocaust was thus not the archetype that it was becoming in Comparative Genocide Studies at the time. Even so, members of that community were intrigued by Lifton and invited him to conferences and requested inclusion of his work in their anthologies. There was room for the idea of "nuclear Holocaust" on the margins of the nascent field.[72]

Ultimately, the differences between these circles proved greater than similarities. The early Comparative Genocide Studies scholar–activists were exercised by how and why genocides occurred in the past and could be prevented in the present and future, meaning that they followed ongoing ethnic conflict and refugee crises, as a study of Leo Kuper's correspondence indicates.[73] By contrast, Lifton's papers indicate a network around peace and antinuclear activism: he corresponded with and/or was a member of organizations like the Committee for US Veterans of Hiroshima and Nagasaki, Academic Liaison against Renewed Militarism, Mobilization for Survival, The New York Mobilizer: Zero Nuclear Weapons, Physicians for Social Responsibility, and the Citizens' Hearings for Radiation Victims. Lifton established a Center on Violence and Human Survival at City University of New York, which examined "fundamental issues of violence" based on the premise that violence "from individual to urban to national and international and, of course, ultimately nuclear – are somehow interconnected."[74] His concerns mirrored those of philosopher John Somerville (1905–1994), who coined the term

---

[71] Robert Jay Lifton, "Witnessing Survival," *Society* 15 (March–April 1978): 40.

[72] See the correspondence with Israel Charny and Jack Nusan Porter in the Robert Lifton Papers, New York Public Library, Box 28 and Box 128, Folder "Charny, Israel." Two short chapters on the subject were included in the volume of Charny's 1982 conference: Ronald E. Santoni, "Nuclear Insanity and Multiple Genocide," and Gerard A. Vanderhaar, "Genocidal Mentality: Nuclear Weapons on Civilian Populations," in Charny, *Toward the Understanding and Prevention of Genocide*, 147–53, and 175–82. Sociologist of nuclear weapons Eric Markusen wrote the entry on "Genocide, Total War, and Nuclear Omnicide," in Charny, *Genocide: A Critical Bibliographical Review*, 229–47.

[73] Leo Kuper Papers, Collection 1550, Department of Special Collections, University of California at Los Angeles Library,

[74] Robert Jay Lifton to John Darton of the *New York Times*, May 24, 1988, New York Public Library, Robert Jay Lifton Papers, Box 36 Correspondence, 1988, May–June.

"omnicide" in the early 1980s. For antinuclear peace scholars and activists, genocide was a subcategory of a broader problem: the threat of human extinction that the Cold War made a possibility, especially after the election of Ronald Reagan as US president in 1980. The English Marxist historian, E. P. Thompson, referred to this threat as "exterminism."[75] Earlier, we recall, Falk had invoked the Nuremberg principles of aggressive warfare as the supreme crime from which others like war crimes, crimes against humanity, and genocide ensued.[76]

Lifton was certainly aware that his approach was not to everyone's tastes. Writing to his Harvard colleague, sociologist David Riesman, in 1982, he hoped that Elie Wiesel's apparent conversion to an antinuclear position might help allay Jewish objections "to seek parallels in the European Holocaust and the present overall nuclear-weapons situation," adding that this "must be done carefully."[77] Such caution in drawing "lessons of the Holocaust for our nuclear weapons situation" meant striking the right balance:

> Generally speaking, my impression is that these comparisons come off best when developed carefully and in ways that include differences. Otherwise one risks not just great hostility (which will come from certain circles in any case) but considerable misunderstanding and vulnerability to accusations to oversimplification or worse.[78]

Lifton was right about such accusations. When he and the younger sociologist, Eric Markusen (1946–2007), wrote a book about the "Nazi Holocaust and Nuclear Threat" called *The Genocidal Mentality* in 1990, they were pilloried in the usual manner. Lifton and Markusen contended that, despite manifest differences between the two cases, they shared a "genocidal mentality" based on the fetishization of science and technology, the collaboration of professionals, and the psychic numbing that allowed them to disassociate their work from the inevitable terrible outcomes. "In the name of national security, we and they [the Soviets] threaten actions that could destroy the world."[79] Unconvinced about the book's comparison and implicit attack on the US

---

[75] John Somerville, "Einstein's Legacy and Nuclear Omnicide," *Peace Research* 18, no. 1 (1986): 20–5, 53–8. Cf. E. P. Thompson, *Exterminism and Cold War* (London: Verso, 1982), 1–34.

[76] A book ignored by the Genocide Studies field that reflects the Lifton-Falk program is Charles B. Strozier and Michael Flynn, ed., *Genocide, War, and Human Survival* (Lanham, MD: Rowman and Littlefield, 1996). An earlier book in this mode is Wallimann and Dobkowski, *Genocide and the Modern Age*.

[77] Robert Jay Lifton to David Riesman, August 27, 1982. New York Public Library, Robert Jay Lifton Papers, Box 47, Reisman, David, 1971–1979.

[78] Robert Jay Lifton to Henry T. Nash, June 6, 1988 New York Public Library, Robert Jay Lifton Papers, Box 36, Correspondence, 1988, May–June.

[79] Robert Jay Lifton and Eric Markusen, *The Genocidal Mentality: Nazi Holocaust and Nuclear Threat* (New York: Basic Books, 1990), 2.

security state, Dutch-Jewish writer Ian Buruma (b. 1951) mobilized the familiar Arendtian arguments about Nazi ideology and the Holocaust's nonutility
in the *New York Review of Books*. Despite Lifton patiently explaining his case
in a subsequent exchange, Buruma missed the book's point, namely that
killing millions of people in the name of security linked the two cases – and
remained a present possibility. As always, the critics focused on the intentions
of the perpetrators rather than the outcome of their deeds: civilian
destruction.[80]

To be sure, Leo Kuper was aware of the problem that Lifton and Markusen
were raising about civilian destruction and permanent security in interstate
conflicts, but he did not make it central to his model – or at least his essay on
the topic was not registered as emblematic in the field. Instead, his thesis about
the genocidal potential he saw in "plural societies" – which he called "domestic
genocide" – became paradigmatic.[81] Genocidal violence within sovereign
states was the salient issue rather than the civilian destruction caused by
armed conflict between them, he thought. Horowitz concurred in regarding
genocide as "essentially a stratagem to maintain and extend totalitarian control" over a society.[82] Their views set the tone for the field. Its gatekeepers
excluded books that coupled genocide and nuclear warfare, as well as
Markusen's provocative cowritten study comparing (though not equating)
the Holocaust to the Allies' bombing of German and Japanese cities in
World War II, *The Holocaust and Strategic Bombing*. Charny, who wrote the
foreword to the book, indignantly rejected the association, as did reviewers.[83]
The intolerance of alternative perspectives continued at the Association for
Genocide Studies conference in Minnesota in 2001, at which Helen Fein
attacked English historian Mark Levene. His paper, "A Dissenting Voice,"
was denounced as "ideological" because it evinced skepticism about US

---

[80] Ian Buruma, "The Devils of Hiroshima," *New York Review of Books*, October 25, 1990;
"The Nuclear Difference, Robert Jay Lifton reply by Ian Buruma," *New York Review of
Books*, January 17, 1991, www.nybooks.com/articles/1991/01/17/the-nuclear-difference/.

[81] Leo Kuper, "Theoretical Issues Relating to Genocide: Use and Abuse," in Andreopolous,
Genocide, 31–46.

[82] Horowitz, *Taking Lives*, xii.

[83] Kuper, *Genocide*, 14, 17; Strozier and Flynn, *Genocide, War, and Human Survival*; Eric
Markusen and David Kopf, *The Holocaust and Strategic Bombing: Genocide and Total
War in the Twentieth Century* (Boulder, CO: Westview Press, 1996). Particularly vehe-
ment reviews are David Cesarani in *Studies in Contemporary Jewry* 14 (1998): 271–3, and
Gerald Weinberg in the *American Historical Review* 102, no. 1 (1997): 89–90. Military
scholars also advanced the usual objections: Malham M. Wakin in *Armed Forces and
Society* 23, no. 2 (1996): 299–301, and Joe Ross in *Air Power History* 43, no. 4 (1996): 60.
Recent scholarship rejects the nuclear warfare equals genocide argument: Richard C.
Maguire, "Nuclear Weapons and Genocide: Lessons from 1940," in *The Routledge History
of Genocide*, ed. Cathie Carmichael and Richard C. Maguire (London and New York:
Routledge, 2015), 321–33.

humanitarian intervention by linking genocide to the global climate crisis.[84] Attempts to stretch the concept of genocide to other modes of permanent security have so far met with limited success despite the efforts of younger Genocide Studies scholars who followed in Levene's footsteps.[85]

In the wake of the genocidal crises of the 1990s, the field was able to harness the Holocaust's aura to sideline Lifton and Falk's human-survival paradigm. The collapse of the Soviet Union and end of the Cold War in 1991 removed the imminent threat of nuclear war and seemed to confirm Kuper's preferred focus on genocidal violence within states, even if the Rwandan genocide and post-Yugoslav wars were effectively also international armed conflicts.

Leaving the ambivalence of the Vietnam years behind them, humanitarians now looked to the diplomats, soldiers, and weapons of "the indispensable nation" to prevent genocide. The opening of the US Holocaust Memorial Museum on the National Mall in Washington, DC, in 1993 also underscored the relationship between Holocaust memory, genocide prevention, and power. Its "Committee on Conscience," whose board features Elliot Abrahams, the hawkish US diplomat involved in US sponsorship of terrorist regimes in Latin America during the 1980s, had a mandate "to alert the national conscience, influence policy makers, and stimulate worldwide action to confront and work to halt acts of genocide or related crimes against humanity."[86] Rather than expressing concern about the discourse of "rogue states" – which, in 2001, Secretary of State Madeline Albright called "states of concern" – that licensed on-demand interventionism, intervening in such states was an animating

---

[84] An extended version of the paper was published in two parts as "A Dissenting Voice; or How Current Assumptions of Deterring and Preventing Genocide May be Looking at the Problem Through the Wrong End of the Telescope," Parts 1 and II, *Journal of Genocide Research* 6, nos. 2 and 3 (2004): 153–66, 43–5.

[85] Mark Levene, "Is the Holocaust Simply Another Example of Genocide?" *Patterns of Prejudice* 28, no. 2 (1994): 3–26; Adam Jones, ed., *Genocide, War Crimes and the West: History and Complicity* (London: Zed Books, 2004); Dan Stone, ed., *The Historiography of Genocide* (Basingstoke: Palgrave Macmillan, 2008); Donald Bloxham and A. Dirk Moses, eds., *The Oxford Handbook on Genocide Research* (Oxford: Oxford University Press, 2010). A new literature on colonial genocide has developed but made no impact on popular consciousness or changed the field's coordinates: Dan Stone and A. Dirk Moses, eds., *Genocide and Colonialism* (London and New York: Routledge, 2007); A. Dirk Moses, ed., *Empire, Colony, Genocide: Conquest, Occupation, and Subaltern Resistance in World History* (New York and Oxford: Berghahn Books, 2008); Jeff Benvenuto, Andrew Woolford, and Alexander Laban Hinton, eds., *Colonial Genocide in Indigenous North America* (Durham, NC: Duke University Press, 2014).

[86] Governing Body: Committee on Conscience, www.ushmm.org/genocide-prevention/ simon-skjodt-center/committee-on-conscience. This mandate is now carried out by the museum's Simon-Skjodt Center for the Prevention of Genocide. On Guatemala, see Bachman, *The United States and Genocide (Re)Defining the Relationship*, ch. 5.

premise of Genocide Studies.[87] After briefly parting company in the 1970s and 1980s, when the humanitarian conscience challenged permanent security in all its modes, they again became one and the same entity – as they had been for much of the previous 500 years.

Civil War or Genocide?

Genocide Studies' installation of the Holocaust as the field's archetype distorted analyses of permanent security by corralling it into a fruitless debate about whether mass violence was civil war/counterinsurgency or genocide. Apologists for violence claim the former, thereby excusing excesses as less-than-shocking, while victim groups and their supporters assert the latter, attempting to make their particular circumstances appear Holocaust-like. The blinding effect of these operations can be seen by studying the reasoning of state leaders and their supporters in the ongoing debate about the Armenian genocide and in the UN's consideration of the conflict in Darfur, Sudan. The African Union (AU), Arab League, China, and Russia have invoked this reasoning to absolve Sudan's leader, Omar Bashir, of genocide, for example.[88] According to the AU chair, Nigerian president Olusegun Obasanjo (b. 1937), "What we know is that there was an uprising, rebellion, and the government armed another group of people to stop that rebellion," adding: "That does not amount to genocide from our own reckoning."[89] The stakes of "the politics of naming," as Ugandan anthropologist Mahmood Mamdani puts it, are thus clear: allies can legitimately put down rebellions with counterinsurgency, while enemies engage in genocide.[90] The core problem of genocide, then, is its separation of racial/national/ethnic violence (driven by "hate") from political violence, meaning that the gamut of permanent security polices are trivialized.

---

[87] Christopher Marquis, "U.S. Declares 'Rogue Nations' are Now 'States of Concern,'" *New York Times*, June 20, 2000.

[88] The International Criminal Court (ICC) issued an arrest warrant for Sudanese President Omar Bashir for crimes against humanity in 2009 and for genocide in 2010, but the reasoning follows the UN's 2007 report, discussed below, that genocide was not committed. See the ICC's documentation: www.icc-cpi.int/darfur/albashir.

[89] Quoted in Mahmood Mamdani, "The Politics of Naming: Genocide, Civil War, Insurgency," *London Review of Books*, March 8, 2007, 5; Vambe and Zegeye, "Racializing Ethnicity and Ethnicizing Racism."

[90] The conceptual challenge of marrying civil war and genocide is exemplified in Mamdani's own work, for he says the civil war was the context in which the genocide took place in the Rwandan case, but denies genocide is an appropriate label for what was essentially a counterinsurgency in the Sudanese one: Mahmood Mamdani, *When Victims Become Killers: Nativism, and the Genocide in Rwanda* (Princeton: Princeton University Press, 2001), 268, and "The Politics of Naming."

Armenian Rebellion or Armenian Genocide?

The official Turkish rejection of the genocide claim is that the Ottoman Empire faced an existential crisis in the simultaneous invasion and internal Armenian rebellion, leading the authorities to deport Christian civilians from conflict zones and repress the Armenian uprising. This framing of events dates from the war itself.[91] In these circumstances of emergency, so the narrative goes, it was regrettable that many Armenian civilians perished – but then so did many Muslims. Here was a neat and convenient symmetry of suffering: the civil war-rather-than-genocide argument in which two roughly equal sides were pitched against one another: "The totality of evidence thus far uncovered by historians tells a grim story of serious inter-communal conflict, perpetrated by both Christian and Muslim irregular forces, complicated by disease, famine, and many other of war's privations," declares the Turkish Ministry of Foreign Affairs. "The evidence does not, however, describe genocide." What is more, continues the diplomatic statement, "The Armenians took arms against their own government. Their violent political aims, not their race, ethnicity or religion, rendered them subject to relocation."[92] A Turkish diplomat in Israel told newspaper readers there that Holocaust could be distinguished from the "the events of 1915" by the fact of Armenian agency. "Armenian armed forces, gearing up for a nation state of their own in eastern Anatolia, where they constituted a minority of the population, were leading the Russian troops and attacking the supply lines of the Turkish Army. So the Ottoman Empire decided to apply relocation."[93] Although this reasoning vastly inflates Armenian military agency into fantastical proportions, it is an article of faith in Turkey.[94]

---

[91] David Gutman, "Ottoman Historiography and the End of the Genocide Taboo: Writing the Armenian Genocide into Late Ottoman History," *Journal of the Ottoman and Turkish Studies Association* 2, no. 1 (2015): 167–83; Vahakn N. Dadrian, "The Series of Major Trials and the Related Verdicts: The Falsification of the Arguments of 'Relocation,' 'Civil War' and 'Intercommunal Clashes,'" in *Judgement at Istanbul: The Armenian Genocide Trials*, ed. Vahakn N. Dadrian and Taner Akçam (Oxford and New York: Berghahn Books, 2011), 108–25.

[92] Turkish Ministry of Foreign Affairs, "The Armenian Allegation of Genocide: The Issue and the Facts," www.mfa.gov.tr/the-armenian-allegation-of-genocide-the-issue-and-the-facts.en.mfa.

[93] Doğan Işık, "The Events in Anatolia of 1915 are Incomparable to the Holocaust," *Ha'aretz*, May 7, 2015, www.haaretz.com/opinion/.premium-1.65533. Another Turkish diplomat provides the book length version in Yucel Güçlü, *Armenians and the Allies in Cilicia, 1914–1923* (Salt Lake City, UT: University of Utah Press, 2012).

[94] Ron Suny, *"They Can Live in the Desert but Nowhere Else": A History of the Armenian Genocide* (Princeton: Princeton University Press, 2015); Taner Akçam, *The Young Turks' Crime against Humanity: The Armenian Genocide and Ethnic Cleansing in the Ottoman Empire* (Princeton: Princeton University Press, 2012); Ugur Ümit Üngör and Mehmet Polatel, *Confiscation and Destruction: The Young Turk Seizure of Armenian Property*

This distinction permeates popular culture. Turkish writer Ayşe Kulin followed this line of argument when she rejected the genocide label for the Armenian case; for although liking "Armenians very much," the deportations had occurred "during the war," which meant they could not be genocidal.[95] Ottoman Christians operate with the same logic. The American Hellenic Council urged American Greeks to boycott the Turkish-produced film, *The Ottoman Lieutenant*, because it was perceived to posit the civil war symmetry: the film was "a blatant attempt to repudiate the upcoming movie, *The Promise*, and mislead impressionable youth into believing the Genocide was a 'two-sided' event."[96]

Kulin also introduced the other common element in this conceptual blockage: the slippage between genocide and the Holocaust. Thus, she sought to mitigate her frank admission of the killing by pointing to Armenian provocation, a political factor one did not find in the Holocaust: "We did not butcher the Armenians without a reason." Even then, there was no systematic extermination as in Auschwitz she implied: "They [Turks] didn't do anything to them like the Jews."[97] Similarly using the Holocaust as an archetype for genocide, Turkish journalist Mustafa Akyol opined that ethnic cleansing (*tehcir* = deportation) rather than genocide had occurred, because "the Ottoman government only pushed Armenians out of Anatolia, whereas the Nazis searched for Jews everywhere in order to exterminate them one by one," repeating Tusk's argument from 1950.[98] Historian Bernard Lewis (1916–2018) repeated this commonplace in agreeing that the German persecution was not regional and partial, but continental and aimed at "total annihilation." He added, using Arendtian reasoning, that the Holocaust "was a different matter" from the Armenian case, because "[t]here was no rebellion, armed or otherwise." German Jews, by contrast, were "intensely loyal," and were attacked "wholly and solely by their alleged racial identity."[99]

(London: Bloomsburgy, 2011); Donald Bloxham, "The Armenian Genocide of 1915–1916: Cumulative Radicalization and the Development of a Destruction Policy," *Past and Present*, no. 181 (2003): 141–91.

[95] "'We Didn't Butcher the Armenians Without Reason,' Says Turkish Writer," *Asbarez*, February 7, 2014, http://asbarez.com/119300/we-didnt-butcher-the-armenians-without-reason-says-turkish-writer.

[96] "The American Hellenic Council Calls for a Boycott of 'The Ottoman Lieutenant,'" *Armenian Weekly*, March 13, 2017, http://armenianweekly.com/2017/03/13/ahc-calls-for-a-boycott-of-the-ottoman-lieutenant.

[97] "'We Didn't Butcher the Armenians Without Reason,' Says Turkish Writer."

[98] Mustafa Akyol, "What Was Behind the Ethnic Cleansing of Armenians?," *Al-Monitor*, April 9, 2015, www.al-monitor.com/pulse/originals/2015/04/turkey-was-the-ethnic-cleansing-of-armenians-islamic.html#ixzz3i2moXLvp. This is also the reasoning of historian Steven T. Katz in "The Uniqueness of the Holocaust: The Historical Dimension," in *Is the Holocaust Unique? Perspectives of Comparative Genocide*, ed. Alan S. Rosenbaum, 3rd ed. (Boulder, CO: Westview Press, 2009), 69–70.

[99] Bernard Lewis, *Notes on a Century: Reflections of A Middle East Historian* (London: Wiedenfeld & Nicolson, 2009), 204.

This invocation of the Holocaust to discount the current Armenian campaign for genocide recognition pervades the discussion. It has roots in a broader Turkish endeavor to join the international club of so-called civilized states that promote Holocaust memory and research by burnishing the country's credentials for supposedly rescuing Jews during the Holocaust.[100] Far from increasing consciousness of genocide in its past, this diplomatic project revives an Ottoman legacy of multinational cohabitation. It thereby dismisses the Armenian and Kurdish positions for disrupting the harmonious empire a century ago with their noisy and disloyal particularism, just as they threaten Turkey today with mischievous genocide accusations to advance revisionist and secessionist agendas.

Because of the Holocaust's ascribed sacral aura, it is impossible for state leaders to conceive that genocide occurred in their history or was committed by their coreligionists. In 2007, Turkey's ambassador to the US suggested that the genocide accusation implied it was a precedent for Hitler and thus "is a very injurious move to the psyche of the Turkish people."[101] Two years later, Turkish president Recep Tayyip Erdoğan dismissed criticism for hosting the Sudanese president, Omar al-Bashir, who is indicted by the International Criminal Court, with the words that "no Muslim could perpetrate a genocide."[102] But Muslims could be its victims. Thus, Erdoğan proclaimed Rohingyas of Mynmar to be victims of genocide even though their treatment closely resembles the Ottoman genocide of Armenians.[103]

Turkey was as the forefront of genocide prevention insisted Mehmet Ali Şahin, speaker of the Turkish Grand National Assembly on the International Day of Commemoration in Memory of the Victims of the Holocaust in 2011. "Throughout the [sic.] history our nation has adopted a principled and peaceful approach which cares for the oppressed peoples, while sharply rejecting all kinds of persecution, injustice and oppression against humanity."[104] The accompanying Turkish Ministry of Foreign Affairs press statement

---

[100] Corry Guttstadt's research demonstrates that the Turkish state's claims are greatly exaggerated. See her *Turkey, the Jews, and the Holocaust* (Cambridge: Cambridge University Press, 2013). Turkey is an observer member of the International Holocaust Remembrance Alliance that is dedicated to the Stockholm International Forum on the Holocaust, www.holocaustremembrance.com/observer-countries. See Seyla Benhabib, "Of Jews, Turks and Armenians – Entangled Memories: A Personal Recollection," *Journal of Genocide Research* 17, no. 3 (2015): 363–72.

[101] "Unearthing the Past, Endangering the Future," *The Economist*, October 18, 2007, 34; Ayşe Zarakol, "Ontological (In)security and State Denial of Historical Crimes: Turkey and Japan," *International Relations* 24, no. 1 (2010): 3–23.

[102] Seth Freedman, "Erdogan's Blind Faith in Muslims," *The Guardian*, November 11, 2009.

[103] "Erdoğan Accuses Myanmar of 'Genocide' as Thousands of Rohingya Flee to Bangladesh," *The Guardian*, September 2, 2017.

[104] Message from Mehmet Ali Şahin, speaker of the Turkish Grand National Assembly to the Commemoration Event in Istanbul on the International Day of Commemoration in

declares the Holocaust the "gravest crime against humanity in history," and committed Turkey to the lessons of "protecting and promoting democracy and human rights" and "combating racism, xenophobia and anti-Semitism."[105] What else could measure up to the gravest crime in history? Plainly, genocide could not be part of this glorious past; it occurred elsewhere. Attacking Turkish Kurds, the military campaign in 2015 and 2016 was undertaken with a clean conscience.

The Turkish position mirrors Israeli foreign policy that also seeks to make the Holocaust the ultimate threshold of transgression, one that consciously excludes the Armenian genocide by conflating the Holocaust and genocide. Thus, the former Israeli foreign minister, Shimon Peres (1923–2016), stated that "We reject attempts to create a similarity between the Holocaust and the Armenian allegations. What the Armenians went through is a tragedy, but not genocide."[106] As if singing from the same song-sheet, the Turkish Ambassador to the US told readers of the *Washington Post* that calling the events of 1915 a genocide "dilutes the moral force that recollection of the Holocaust should generate for us all."[107]

This campaign has scored notable successes. In the trial of Turkish politician and lawyer Dogu Perinçek in Switzerland for denying the Armenian genocide, the European Court of Human Rights ruled that he was not guilty because, unlike the Holocaust, the Armenian case was not by broad consensus one of genocide.[108] Since the Armenian case does not resemble the Holocaust,

Memory of the Victims of the Holocaust, January 27. 2011, www.holocausttaskforce .org/images/itf_data/documents/12_observer_states/turkey-tbmm%20bakan%20sayn %20mehmet%20ali%20ahin%20mesaj%20ng%2027%20ocak%202011.pdf.

[105] Turkish Ministry of Foreign Affairs, Press Release Regarding the International Day of Commemoration in Memory of the Victims of the Holocaust, January 27, 2011, www .holocausttaskforce.org/images/itf_data/Turkey-27Ocak2011.pdf.

[106] "Peres: Armenian Allegations are Meaningless," *Turkish Daily News*, April 10, 2001. See Eldad Ben Aharon, "A Unique Denial: Israel's Foreign Policy and the Armenian Genocide," *British Journal of Middle Eastern Studies* 42, no. 4 (2015): 1–17.

[107] Sukru Elekdag, "Letters to the Editor: The Turkish Ambassador Replies" *Washington Post*, April 26, 1983. Thanks to Jennifer Dixon for this reference. See her "Defending the Nation? Maintaining Turkey's Narrative of the Armenian Genocide," *South European Society and Politics* 15, no. 3 (2010): 467–85. On the loaded function of the "dilution" metaphor in relation to the Holocaust, see Alexander Laban Hinton, "Critical Genocide Studies," *Genocide Studies and Prevention* 7, no. 1 (2011): 10–11.

[108] European Court of Human Rights, Second Section, Case of Perinçek vs. Switzerland, Judgement, Strasbourg, December 17, 2013, 3.4.1: "In its case-law... the Federal Court has held that Holocaust denial objectively constitutes the factual element of the offence... since it concerns a historical fact that is generally acknowledged as established..., although the judgment in question makes no reference to the historical intention of the legislature..." The Grand Chamber of the European Court of Human Rights did not dispute this determination when it ruled on the case almost two years later: https:// anca.org/wp-content/uploads/2015/10/ECHR_PerincekRuling_101515.pdf.

ergo it cannot be genocide. The victorious appellant, Perinçek, tweeted that "This is not a historical debate or legal dispute. This is a defence of the country. A fight for independence!"[109]

Another consequence of investing the Holocaust and genocide with special moral force is the effort of prominent Armenian scholars to shoehorn the Armenian experience into the Holocaust paradigm; in other words, to redact the Armenian experience leading up to and during World War I so it resembles the Jewish experience leading up to and during World War II, with its hapless civilians murdered simply for who they were, innocent victims of a racist policy, evacuated of political context.[110] Muslim anti-Armenian sentiment comes to resemble antisemitism, and the genocide is seen as the outcome of decades if not centuries of ever-intensifying hatred in the name of Turkish ethnic purity. Rather than casting the war as the context in which ethnic difference became fatally politicized, it is merely a pretext for a carefully nurtured intention to kill off the Armenian minority whose aspiration for independent nationhood is unquestionably legitimate, whatever its implications for the Turkish homeland.

What is more, such accounts play down the notion of an Armenian rebellion or security threat to emphasize the agentlessness of Armenians; for the more passive the victims, the less likely they can be found guilty of treason, as the Turkish side effectively accuses. If Armenians were politically and militarily active, so the reasoning goes, they cannot have been passive victims of genocide, because the Ottoman state would have been guided by legitimate considerations of military necessity.[111] In this way, treating genocide as a nonpolitical hate crime blinds us (and politically and legally ties our hands) when faced with mass criminality that contains political dimensions; it obscures the reality that all such criminality is saturated with political logics.[112]

---

[109] Direnc Balik, "EU Court Rules in Favour of Turkish Politician Over Armenian Genocide Denial," *Middle East Eye*, October 15, 2015, www.middleeasteye.net/news/echr-rules-favour-turkish-politician-over-armenian-genocide-denial-240050098.

[110] Vahakn N. Dadrian, *Warrant for Genocide: The Key Elements of the Turko-Armenian Conflict* (New Brunswick: Transaction Publishers, 1998); Sossie Kasbarian, "Denial of the Armenian Genocide Should Concern Us All," *The Conversation*, 24 April 2017, https://theconversation.com/denial-of-the-armenian-genocide-should-concern-us-all-76537. On how redaction as distortion, see Alexander Laban Hinton, *Man or Monster? The Trial of Khmer Rouge Torturer* (Durham and London: Duke University Press, 2016). On how this dynamic works in Germany memory culture, see Christine Wilke, "Remembering Complexity? Memorials for Nazi Victims in Berlin," *International Journal of Transitional Justice* 7 (2013): 136–56. Also see Stuart D. Stein, "Conceptions and Terms: Templates for Analysis of Holocausts and Genocides," *Journal of Genocide Research* 7, no. 2 (2005): 171–203.

[111] Dadrian, *Warrant for Genocide*.

[112] Ryan Gingeras, *Sorrowful Shores: Violence, Ethnicity, and the End of the Ottoman Empire, 1912–1923* (Oxford: Oxford University Press, 2009).

The same logic obtains in Kurdish uses of the genocide concept to frame the Saddam Hussein regime's al-Anfal attacks on Kurdish communities in northern Iraq in 1988 in the context of the Iran-Iraq war. Soon after Middle East Watch published its influential report, *Genocide in Iraq*, in 1993, Kurdish groups adopted the term, noting that the report derived its model of how genocide unfolds – first, definition of the victim group, then its concentration, third, annihilation – from Raul Hilberg's landmark book, *The Destruction of the European Jews*. "The Kurdish genocide of 1987–1989," the report averred, "fits Hilberg's paradigm to perfection." Nazi analogies then abounded. "Like Nazi Germany, the Iraqi regime concealed its actions in euphemisms," the report proceeded, playing down Kurdish political agency.[113] The chain of association ran from genocide to the Holocaust to the Anfal campaign and back, meaning, as one Kurdish author put it, that: "The Anfal must ... be compared with the annihilation of the Jews by the German Nazis. Hitler managed to kill six million Jews, and Saddam had the same intention."[114]

The analogical challenge is that the Armenian and Kurdish cases in fact differ in significant respects from the Holocaust: in the absence of the Holocaust's iconic symbols, namely concentration and extermination camps, in the abduction and assimilation of women and children into Turkish Muslim families, in the presence of direct Armenian and Kurdish political and para-military agency, not to mention the fact that sections of the Armenian political organizations were allied to the Young Turks after 1908.

The same applies to the German campaign against the Herero people in German Southwest Africa in 1904 when colonial troops smashed a rebellion by a combination of massacre, isolation from water sources, and incarceration. It was a scandal then and continues to be so because recognition and compensation by the Federal Republic of Germany remains outstanding. Yet, according to some historians, journalists, and Namibians of German descent, genocide is not the applicable concept because the campaign does not resemble the Holocaust in its systematic, planned, and total nature.[115] This problem

---

[113] Middle East Watch, *Genocide in Iraq: The Anfal Campaign against the Kurds* (New York: Human Rights Watch, 1993), 5, 7–8. The report uses Hilberg's bare structure without mentioning that he added a further element: dismissal of employees, labor exploitation, starvation measures, and property confiscation: Raul Hilberg, *The Destruction of European Jewry*, 3rd ed. (New Haven: Yale University Press, 2003), ch. 3.

[114] Andrea Fischer-Tahir, "Searching for Sense: The Concept of Genocide as Part of Knowledge Production in Iraqi Kurdistan," in *Writing the Modern History of Iraq: Historiographical and Political Challenges*, ed. Jordi Tejel et al. (Singapore: World Scientific Publishing, 2012), 232–39.

[115] Bartholomäus Grill, "Gewisse Ungewissheiten," *Der Spiegel* 24 (June 11, 2016). Grill's title echoes Brigitte Lau's earlier, skeptical article, "Uncertain Certainties: The Herero-German War of 1904," in *History and Historiography. 4 Essays in Reprint*, ed.

of genocide means that its special stigma conceptually distinguishes it from political violence more generally. By the time Helen Fein realized in 2000 that a relationship between genocide and civil war existed after all, it was too late. The conceptual sundering was well and truly entrenched in Genocide Studies and international law.[116] Subsequent conflicts could be interpreted and downplayed accordingly.

Darfur

The challenges posed by the nonpolitical understanding of genocide was never so apparent as in the report of the United Nations International Commission of Inquiry on Darfur, delivered in 2007. It was established pursuant to a Security Council resolution to "investigate reports of violations of international humanitarian law and human rights law in Darfur by all parties, to determine also whether or not acts of genocide have occurred."[117] In 2003, militias attacked government outposts in Darfur in western Sudan as part of a rebellion against Khartoum's policies and neglect of the region. The state attempted to crush the rebellion by utilizing other militias, which destroyed hundreds of villages, killing hundreds of thousands and displacing millions. The five-person UN team, led by the distinguished jurist, the late Antonio Casesse, visited Sudan twice and met with all parties there and in Geneva. Its conclusion that the Sudanese government had not pursued a policy of genocide, but was guilty of crimes against humanity, was greeted in Khartoum and by African leaders. Western activists, by contrast, welcomed US Secretary of State Colin Powell's determination that genocide was in fact taking place, and argued that Western intervention was therefore warranted.[118] All parties held genocide to be graver a transgression than crimes against humanity despite the report's disavowal of any such hierarchy.

Annemarie Heywood (Windhoek, Discourse/MSORP, 1995), 39–52. First published in *Mibagus* 2 (1989): 4–8. Lau was the Namibian national archivist. Gunter Spraul, "Der 'Völkermord' an den Herero: Untersuchungen zu einer neuen Kontinuitätsthese," *Geschichte in Wissenschaft und Unterricht* 12 (1988): 713–39. The best analysis is Jürgen Zimmer and Joachim Zeller, ed., *Genocide in German South-West Africa: The Colonial War of 1904–1908 and Its Aftermath* (London: Merlin Press, 2008).

[116] Helen Fein, "Civil Wars and Genocide: Paths and Circles," *Human Rights Review* 1, no. 3 (2000): 49–61.

[117] Report of the International Commission of Inquiry on Darfur to the United Nations Secretary-General, Pursuant to Security Council Resolution 1564 of September 18, 2004 (Geneva, January 25, 2005), 2.

[118] Samuel Totten and Eric Markusen, eds., *Genocide in Darfur: Investigating Atrocities in the Sudan* (New York: Routledge, 2006); Amanda Grzyb, ed., *The World and Darfur: International Response to Crimes against Humanity in Western Sudan*, 2nd ed. (Montreal: McGill-Queen's University Press, 2011).

The controversy about how to label the violence in Darfur goes to the heart of how the upper threshold of state and para-state criminality is set in the international system. To clearly identify the salient issues, consider some revealing statements from the report. While recognizing that some elements of genocide were present, it stated that:

> ... one crucial element of genocidal intent appears to be missing, at least as far as the central Government authorities are concerned. Generally speaking the policy of attacking, killing and forcibly displacing members of some tribes does not evince a specific intent to annihilate, in whole or in part, a group distinguished on racial, ethnic, national or religious grounds. Rather, it would seem that those who planned and organized attacks on villages pursued the intent to drive the victims from their homes, primarily for purposes of counter-insurgency warfare.[119]

At the same time, the report continued, the Darfur government "also entertained the intent to drive a particular group out of an area on persecutory and discriminatory grounds for political reasons." This intention manifested itself in "systematic attacks" by Arab militias and government forces "on villages inhabited by civilians (or mostly by civilians) belonging to some 'African' tribes ... the systematic destruction and burning down of these villages, as well as the forced displacement of civilians from those villages attest to a manifestly persecutory intent." These acts, the report concluded, meant the government may be held responsible for crimes against humanity for murder and persecution. But not for genocide.[120]

The distinction between genocide and counterinsurgency warfare, the report implies, is based on two elements. First, that genocide requires the physical annihilation of a victim group; in Darfur, the UN commission noted, "the attackers refrained from exterminating the whole population that had not fled, but instead selectively killed groups of young men." It therefore concluded that:

> This case clearly shows that the intent of the attackers was not to destroy an ethnic group as such, or part of the group. Instead, the intention was to murder all those men they considered as rebels, as well as forcibly expel the whole population so as to vacate the villages and prevent rebels from hiding among, or getting support from, the local population.[121]

Despite the seeming permanence of this solution to the state's security emergency and its striking resemblance to the circumstances of the Armenian genocide, the destruction of these communities by the murder of the men,

---

[119] Report of the International Commission of Inquiry on Darfur, para 518.
[120] Ibid., para 519.   [121] Ibid., 130–131.

violent driving off of the remaining population, and torching of their villages was not genocidal.

Genocide is also depoliticized and distinguished from civil war via the legal requirement of genocidal intent. Genocide requires an aggravated form of criminal intention – the *mens rea* – called *dolus specialis*: a special intent. According to the Dafur report, special intent "implies that the perpetrator consciously desired the prohibited acts he committed to result in the destruction, in whole or in part, of the group as such, and knew that his acts would destroy in whole or in part, the group as such."[122] This abstract and convoluted statement is usually taken to mean that genocidal intention must be driven by racial or ethnic hatred. Thus, in 1999, the Jelisic Trial Chamber of the International Criminal Tribunal for the Former Yugoslavia presumed that a hateful motivation was intrinsic to genocide.[123] The words "as such" – that is, the intention to "destroy in whole or in part, the group *as such*" – are also usually taken to mean that the motive is a nonpolitical one of ethnic antipathy. The commissioners implied that the killing of suspected rebel men, the ethnic cleansing of the surviving population, and destruction of their villages were carried out "for political reasons" as part of the state's counterinsurgency. The relevance of these recondite points is that genocide is distinguished from counterinsurgency and civil war because its goals are "racial, ethnic, national or religious" (in the words of the Genocide Convention), and therefore irrational – that is: nonpolitical – while the latter's goals are explicable, understandable, and therefore political. In private, a member of the ICC investigation team said the issue was land and displacement, not race, and therefore it was not genocide but a crime against humanity. Darfuris were not destroyed as a group "as such."[124]

Holocaust Analogies

The report's determination effectively negated the intense pro-Darfur campaign in the US that makes direct Holocaust analogies. The director of the Committee on Conscience of the United States Holocaust Memorial Museum,

---

[122] Report of the International Commission of Inquiry on Darfur, 124.

[123] Prosecutor vs. Goran Jelisic, Judgement, December 14, 1991, para 79, www.icty.org/x/cases/jelisic/tjug/en/jel-tj991214e.pdf; Nina H. B. Jorgensen, "The Definition of Genocide: Joining the Dots in the Light of Recent Practice," *International Criminal Law Review* 1 (2001): 285–313; William A. Schabas, "The Jelisic Case and the Mens Rea of the Crime of Genocide," *Leiden Journal of International Law* 14 (2001): 125–39.

[124] John Hagan and Wenona Rymond-Richmond, *Darfur and the Crime of Genocide* (Cambridge: Cambridge University Press, 2009), 34; Eyal Mayroz, *Reluctant Interveners: America's Failed Responses to Genocide from Bosnia to Darfur* (New Brunswick: Rutgers University Press, 2019); David Patrick, *Reporting Genocide: Media, Mass Violence and Human Rights* (London: Bloomsbury, 2017).

for example, depicted the attacks on Darfuris as hate crimes in order to place them in the Holocaust analytical frame: "simply stated," he said, "in the western Darfur region of the country, people are being attacked because of their racial and ethnic identity." He explicitly focused on identity rather than civil war to link Darfur and the Holocaust: "Holocaust remembrance," he continued, "can play an important role in breaking this circle of inaction" that he decried in international complacency about Sudanese actions in Darfur. He hoped that "Holocaust remembrance can help create a 'constituency of conscience' that is aroused by threats of genocide in the present and future, that demands action to stop mass murder, that holds to account policymakers who temporize."[125] That is how the Committee on Conscience sought to shock the conscience of mankind. And that is why it took the authority of Elie Wiesel, the archetypal Holocaust victim, to shame the Clinton administration into action in Yugoslavia at the opening of the USHMM in 1993.[126]

Significant political implications are entailed by such classifications. Despite the assurance of the UN Commission of Inquiry on Darfur in 2007 that crimes against humanity and war crimes are coequal in gravity with genocide, it is hard to dispute the common assertion that the stigma attached to genocide is greater, as the "crime of crimes," when newspapers around the world reported that the UN's determination meant that the violence fell short of genocide, and the authorities in Sudan breathed an audible sigh of relief that they had been accused of crimes against humanity rather than genocide: "We have a copy of that report and they didn't say there is a genocide," exulted the Sudanese foreign minister.[127]

---

[125] Jerry Fowler, "Education about the Holocaust: How Does It Help Build a Better World?" Address to Annual Conference of the Association of Holocaust Organizations, June 8, 2004. USHMM Committee on Conscience, www.holocaust-trc.org/education-about-the-holocaust/. See also Arlene Stein, "Whose Memories? Whose Victimhood? Contests for the Holocaust Frame in Recent Social Movement Discourse," *Sociological Perspectives* 41, no. 3 (1998): 519–40.

[126] Elie Wiesel's Remarks at the Dedication Ceremonies for the United States Holocaust Memorial Museum, April 22, 1993, www.ushmm.org/research/ask-a-research-question/frequently-asked-questions/wiesel; Mark Chmiel, "The Political Varieties of Sacred Remembrance: Elie Wiesel and United States Foreign Policy," *Journal of Church and State*, 40, no. 4 (1998): 827–46; Power, *"A Problem from Hell"*, 604.

[127] "Sudan's Darfur Crimes Not Genocide, Says UN report," *The Guardian*, February 1, 2005; Rebecca Hamilton, "Inside Colin Powell's Decision to Declare Genocide in Darfur," *The Atlantic*, August 17, 2011; David Luban, "Calling Genocide by its Rightful Name: Lemkin's Word, Darfur, and the U.N. Report," *Chicago Journal of International Law* 7, no. 1 (2006): 303–20; William A. Schabas, "Genocide, Crimes against Humanity, and Darfur: The Commission of Inquiry's Findings on Genocide," *Cardozo Law Review* 27 (2005): 1703–21.

As a consequence, the temptation is great to analogize with the Holocaust and/or Nazi regime to gain attention for mega-human rights violations, spanning cases as diverse as the French Revolution, Belgian Congo in the nineteenth century, to the mass killing of communists in Indonesia in 1965 and the Khmer Rouge's cleansing of its cadres and own population.[128] Of the Indonesian case, the well-known film-maker-activist, Joshua Oppenheimer, went further than applying labels by matching Indonesian actors with Nazi ones.

> And so, I went back and started to realize, this is – it's as though I am in Nazi Germany 40 years after the end of the Holocaust, and it's still the Third Reich, the Nazis are still in power. So the official history says nothing about the killings. But, and yet, the aging SS officers have been allowed to boast about what they've done, even encouraged to do so, so that they've become these kind of feared proxies of the state in their communities, in their regions, and also perhaps that they can justify to themselves what they have done. And I realized at that point that this was a reality so grave, so important, that I would give it whatever it took of my life.[129]

Certainly, such projections can pay off, as the attention Oppenheimer has drawn to the 1965 killings demonstrates.[130]

However, resisting the Holocaust analogy is equally possible. In 1981, in a much-publicized case, the leftist Jewish-Argentine journalist Jacobo Timerman (1923–1999) claimed that Argentina was a fascist state and that his torture was motivated by antisemitism, thereby delegitimizing a US ally. In response, neoconservatives suggested that Timerman was persecuted for supporting leftist terrorism: in other words, Timerman suffered because of his actions, not his identity, thus receiving his just desserts.[131] The neoconservatives rejected the Holocaust analogy when it did not suit their anticommunist agenda.

---

[128] See the analyses in David Bell, "The French Revolution, the Vendée, and Genocide," *Journal of Genocide Research* 22, no. 1 (2020): 19–25; Sarah De Mul, "The Holocaust as a Paradigm for the Congo Atrocities: Adam Hochschild's *King Leopold's Ghost*," *Criticism* 53, no. 4 (2011): 587–606; Sean O'Hagan, "Joshua Oppenheimer: Why I Returned to Indonesia's Killing Fields," *The Guardian*, June 7, 2015. Symptomatic is Ben Kiernan, *The Pol Pot Regime: Race, Power and Genocide in Cambodia under the Khmer Rouge, 1975–1979* (New Haven: Yale University Press, 1996).

[129] "'The Act of Killing': New Film Shows US-Backed Indonesian Death Squad Leaders Re-enacting Massacre," interview with Joshua Oppenheimer, *Democracy Now*, July 19, 2013, www.democracynow.org/2013/7/19/the_act_of_killing_new_film.

[130] Jess Melvin, "Film Exposes Wounds of Denial of 1965 Violence," *Jakarta Post*, September 30, 2014.

[131] Irving Kristol, "The Timerman Affair," *Wall Street Journal*, May 29, 1981, 24; "Timerman's Critics Reply," *Jewish Veteran*, September–October 1981, 13. Thanks to Federico Finchelstein for pointing me to this controversy.

In response, human rights advocates redoubled their genocide pitch by presenting a long-term plan to exterminate a dehumanized and persecuted minority, thereby distorting the complex political dynamics that led to the mass killing.[132] As a consequence of these categories, Holocaust victims are also invested with an authoritative voice in world affairs. For example, US policy elites invited a Holocaust survivor to address them about the Syrian conflict and the perfidy of the Assad regime: "I find it most disheartening that again, 80 years after the end of World War II," she said in 2015, "the world is faced with a regime that targets its own people for discrimination or destruction."[133] As in the intense US interest in the Darfur case, the Holocaust analogy could be put to work when politically convenient and evacuated of political context. The categories with which all parties organized their thinking meant they wrangled about Holocaust analogies instead of recognizing permanent security in these cases.

After Genocide

A frank concession of the genocide keyword's limitations is the need to couple it with "extermination" in a world history of human destruction "from Sparta to Darfur" or abandoning it for "political violence" and "reigns of terror."[134] To all intents and purposes, prominent advocates of humanitarian intervention have abandoned or supplemented the genocide concept because its impossibly high threshold of proof deters lawyers, while its stigma inhibits states from using the term lest they be accused of genocide or compelled to prevent it.[135] Others propose "demographic surgery" or simply "mass killing" as broader, alternative concepts.[136] Sharing these reservations about genocide,

---

[132] An exemplary critical self-reflection is Alex de Waal, "Writing Human Rights and Getting it Wrong," *Boston Review*, June 6, 2016, http://bostonreview.net/world/alex-de-waal-writing-human-rights.

[133] United States Holocaust Memorial Museum, "Holocaust Survivor Margit Meissner's #WithSyria Remarks," July 20, 2015, www.youtube.com/watch?v=F-66adb5KUY.

[134] Ben Kiernan, *Blood and Soil: A World History of Genocide and Extermination from Sparta to Darfur* (New Haven: Yale University Press, 2007); Donald Bloxham and Robert Gerwarth, eds., *Political Violence in Twentieth Century Europe* (Cambridge: Cambridge University Press, 2011); Patricia Marchak, *Reigns of Terror* (Montreal and Kingston: McGill-Queens University Press, 2003). Adding crime against humanity of extermination to the UN genocide convention is the suggestion in Luban, "Calling Genocide by its Rightful Name."

[135] Gareth Evans, "Crimes against Humanity: Overcoming Indifference," *Journal of Genocide Research* 8, no. 3 (2006): 325–39.

[136] Antonio Ferrara, "Beyond Genocide and Ethnic Cleansing: Demographic Surgery as a New Way to Understand Mass Violence," *Journal of Genocide Research* 17, no. 1 (2015): 1–20; Stein, "Conceptions and Terms"; Mark Mazower, "Violence and the State in the Twentieth Century," *American Historical Review* 107, no. 4 (2002): 1158–78.

some commentators propose "atrocity crimes" to cover the infractions listed under genocide, crimes against humanity, and war crimes, thereby exemplifying Lawrence Douglas's thesis about the "atrocity paradigm" in international criminal law.[137] In doing so, they followed the Rome Statute of the International Criminal Court, which bundles genocide, war crimes, crimes against humanity, and crimes against peace under the rubric of "most serious crimes of concern to the international community as a whole."[138]

The new United Nations Office of the Special Adviser on the Prevention of Genocide has effectively institutionalized this approach by stating its "duty to prevent and halt genocide and mass atrocities."[139] The office's "Framework of Analysis for Atrocity Crimes" released in 2014, elaborated this point by positing a new category of "atrocity crime" to refer to genocide, crimes against humanity, war crimes, and ethnic cleansing. Because of the genocide concept's narrow national-ethnic-racial definition of a targeted group excludes so many other categories of people, the framework has atrocity crimes cover the more general "protected groups, populations or individuals" included in crimes against humanity and war crimes. In doing so, the framework runs counter to the monumentalization of genocide in popular discourse:

> Atrocity crimes are considered to be the most serious crimes against humankind. Their status as international crimes is based on the belief that the acts associated with them affect the core dignity of human beings, in particular the persons that should be most protected by States, both in times of peace and in times of war.[140]

This innovation by scholars and diplomats working at the coalface of international politics represents a major critique of the legal architecture to protect civilians and combatants that culminated in the UN Genocide Convention and Four Geneva Conventions after World War II. It implies that the hierarchy of these various crimes is inimical to their prevention, and that large-scale atrocity is their common denominator. But is it?

The "atrocity paradigm" criminalizes the outcome but not the intention of policy. That is an understandable approach given the difficulty of proving intentions. However, to understand why states (or states-in-the-making)

---

[137] David Scheffer, "Genocide and Atrocity Crimes," *Genocide Studies and Prevention* 1, no 3 (2006): 229–50; William A. Schabas, "Crimes against Humanity as a Paradigm for International Atrocity Crimes," *Middle East Critique* 20, no. 3 (2011): 253–69.

[138] Rome Statute of the International Criminal Court, Article 5(1), www.icc-cpi.int/nr/rdonlyres/ea9aeff7-5752-4f84-be94-0a655eb30e16/0/rome_statute_english.pdf.

[139] Office of The Special Adviser on The Prevention of Genocide, "The Responsibility to Protect," https://www.un.org/ar/preventgenocide/adviser/pdf/osapg_booklet_eng.pdf.

[140] United Nations, Framework for Analysis of Atrocity Crimes, 2014, https://www.un.org/en/genocideprevention/documents/about-us/Doc.3_Framework%20of%20Analysis%20for%20Atrocity%20Crimes_EN.pdf. Thanks to Jennifer Welsh for discussions on this point.

commit atrocities, let alone to cultivate a political imperative to prevent them, one needs to attend to the strategic logic that leads to their perpetration instead of resorting to the Responsibility to Protect doctrine of humanitarian intervention as a default solution.[141] Moreover, as we have been arguing, positing large-scale atrocities as the new threshold of the unbearable screens out other forms of state violence that are motivated by the same logic. This occlusion is also abetted by flawed "lessons of history." Political – that is, security – logics *did* drive Ottoman policy and practices against Armenians and other Christians during World War I. But the current emphasis on context-less atrocities prevents recognition of the escalation of policy from security to permanent security. Imagine the conceptual freedom to consider all such episodes in terms of their underlying strategic logic of permanent security rather than trying to stuff them into historically contingent categories?[142]

---

[141] Symptomatic: David Scheffer, "Atrocity Crimes Framing the Responsibility to Protect," *Case Western Reserve Journal of International Law* 40 (2008): 111–35.

[142] Mazower, "Violence and the State in the Twentieth Century."

12

Holocaust Memory, Exemplary Victims,
and Permanent Security Today

This book is about the problems of the term genocide: what they are and how they developed. It argues that these problems are as much conceptual as empirical: that the crowning of genocide as the "crime of crimes" depoliticizes the language of transgression; and that depoliticization means screening out how genocide, crimes against humanity, war crimes, and the wanton infliction of collateral damage are driven by the permanent security imperatives of states and political movements seeking to found states. As a consequence, the connections between the postwar order of nation-states, the violence with which they were founded, and the international legal order are largely hidden from view.[1]

The grand drama of the last century was the Allied victory over the fascist and militaristic Axis Powers with their illiberal permanent security aspirations: autarkic empires based on resource monopoly and the destruction of enemies. This victory and the legal regime of the "human rights revolution" established by the newly founded United Nations (UN) represented an incomplete global victory of liberal permanent security due to the subsequent Cold War rivalry between former allies. Western international lawyers at the time were acutely conscious of the international system's reshaping since 1900: transformed from a pluralistic, Eurocentric, and exclusive "family of (Christian) nations" that recognized core norms under the umbrella term of "civilization" to an ideologically divided and highly rule-bound system governed by the UN Charter on the other. Both the West and the Soviet Union purported to represent "humanity."[2] Both sides routinely broke the new UN rules, especially those prohibiting interventions in other states, to suit their interests. The Soviet bloc destabilized the system by supporting national liberation movements, while the Western powers intervened to suppress them, often

---

[1] Rare exceptions are Balakrishnan Rajagopal, "Counter-Hegemonic International Law: Rethinking Human Rights and Development as a Third World Strategy," *Third World Quarterly* 27, no. 5 (2006): 767–83, and Martin Shaw, *Genocide and International Relations* (Cambridge: Cambridge University Press, 2013).

[2] Odd Arne Westad, *The Global Cold War: Third World Interventions and the Making of Our Times* (Cambridge: Cambridge University Press, 2005).

supporting right-wing dictators in the process. The nuclear standoff made a nonsense of propositions about just war principles and proportionality in international humanitarian law.[3]

The end of the Cold War, with the collapse of the Soviet Union in 1991, enabled the liberal permanent security project to break through while the Chinese sleeping giant was yet to fully awaken. The UN established international criminal tribunals to prosecute perpetrators in Rwanda and the former Yugoslavia; NATO bombed Serbian forces to rescue Kosovo in 1999; an International Criminal Court was finally established in 2000, UN peacekeeping missions multiplied, and the UN General Assembly passed the Responsibility to Protect resolution in 2005, thereby making humanitarian intervention an ostensibly global rather than Western prerogative.[4]

Always unrealized in the eyes of liberal internationalists, this US-led order was challenged in the conditions of globalized modernity. Nationalists attempted to found ethno-states or secessionist enclaves – genocracies – in all corners of the world amid mass murder and expulsions, while Islamists tried to expel the US presence from the Middle East with spectacular terrorist attacks in 2001. In response, the US launched its "global war on terror" that gave rise to a debate about "American empire," a "permanent state of emergency," and "forever" or "endless" wars.[5] One of these wars, the invasion of Iraq and destruction of its state in 2003, eventually led to the insurgent *Daesh* (Islamic State) movement, comprising former Iraqi personnel who attracted Sunni recruits from abroad to found a murderous self-styled "caliphate" in Syria and Iraq between 2013 and 2019.[6]

---

[3] Percy E. Corbett, *Law in Diplomacy* (Princeton: Princeton University Press, 1959); Josef L. Kunz, *The Changing Law of Nations: Essays on International Law* (Columbus: Ohio State University Press, 1968); Louis Henkin, *How Nations Behave: Law and Foreign Policy*, 2nd ed. (New York: Praeger/Council on Foreign Relations, 1979); R. P. Anand, *New States in International Law* (New Delhi: Vikas, 1972).

[4] Gregory H. Fox, *Humanitarian Occupation* (Cambridge: Cambridge University Press, 2008); Lise M. Howard, *UN Peacekeeping in Civil Wars* (Cambridge: Cambridge University Press, 2007); Jennifer M. Welsh, ed., *Humanitarian Intervention and International Relations* (Oxford: Oxford University Press, 2004); Alex J. Bellamy, "The Responsibility to Protect – Five Years On," *Ethics & International Affairs* 24, no. 2 (2010): 143–69.

[5] Aniceto Masferror, ed., *Post 9/11 and the State of Permanent Legal Emergency: Security and Human Rights in Countering Terrorism* (Dortrecht: Springer, 2012); Celeste Ward Gventer, David Martin Jones, and M. L. R Smith, eds., *The New Counter-Insurgency Era in Critical Perspective* (New York: Palgrave Macmillan, 2014). Stephen Wertheim, "The Only Way to End 'Endless War': First, America Has to Give Up its Pursuit of Global Dominance," *New York Times*, September 14, 2019, and the Quincy Institute for Responsible Statecraft, https://quincyinst.org/.

[6] Simon Mabon and Stephen Royle, *The Origins of ISIS: The Collapse of Nations and Revolution in the Middle East* (London: I. B. Tauris, 2016); Fawaz A. Gerges, *ISIS: A History* (Princeton: Princeton University Press, 2017).

This dialectic operates within states as much as between them. The appeal of making the world "safe for democracy" and "saving strangers" in the name of humanity has waned with the election of populist nationalists who express disdain for "globalism" and emphasize national – and cultural – security, that is, genocratic rule. Even so, whether in the name of an "international rules based order" or making one's country "great again," subaltern actors that challenge US geopolitical domination are subject to permanent securitization in its liberal modality. US President Trump escalated his country's forever war despite his rhetoric to the contrary, and his successor will likely do the same. "Full spectrum dominance" remains US Department of Defense policy.[7] That entails military and humanitarian interventions justified in terms of the putative "lessons of history" of World War II and the Holocaust: defeating totalitarian enemies and preventing a "second Holocaust," namely defending the West's ally, Israel.[8] The fatal dialectic between illiberal and liberal permanent security regimes thus constitutes the contemporary scene. If "Genocide is a continuation of genocracy by other, more murderous means," as Yassin El-Haj Saleh declares, "The greatest political evil of our times is by no means terrorism; it is this global genocratic-genocidal tendency we experience today."[9] In this concluding chapter, I elaborate how these lessons operate as a mnemonic technology of permanent security that metastasizes the problems of genocide.

The Holocaust as Hate Crime

A basic problem of genocide, I have been arguing, is the popular conception of its archetype, the Holocaust, as a nonpolitical mass crime. Well-known historian Deborah Lipstadt expressed the distinction most starkly in criticizing the US president's attitudes to Jews in 2017:

> The Holocaust was something entirely different. It was an organized program with the goal of wiping out a specific people. Jews did not have to do anything to be perceived as worthy of being murdered. Old people who had to be wheeled to the deportation trains and babies who had to be carried were all to be killed. The point was not, as in occupied countries, to get rid of people because they might mount a resistance to Nazism, but to get rid of Jews because they were Jews.[10]

---

[7] Edward Wong, "Americans Demand a Rethinking of the 'Forever War,'" *New York Times*, February 3, 2020. Maria Ryan, *Full Spectrum Dominance: Irregular Warfare and the War on Terror* (Stanford: Stanford University Press, 2019).

[8] China's challenge to this order is a subject I will take up in another publication.

[9] Yassin al-Haj Saleh, "Terror, Genocide, and the 'Genocratic' Turn," *Aljumhuriya*, September 19, 2019, www.aljumhuriya.net/en/content/terror-genocide-and-%E2%80% 9Cgenocratic%E2%80%9D-turn.

[10] Deborah E. Lipstadt, "The Trump Administration's Flirtation with Holocaust Denial," *The Atlantic*, January 30, 2017.

This argument is partly intended to counter antisemites who contend that Jews provoked Germans and were thus coresponsible for their fate. Its consequence is to separate the Holocaust from other instances of permanent security: it is not "just one in a long string of inhumanities," as Lipstadt insisted.[11] As we saw in the previous chapter, the Holocaust's distinctive and unpolitical conceptualization – as a massive hate crime – became genocide's archetype in Comparative Genocide Studies. By this conceptual operation, the realm of the political is confined to civil wars and insurgences, and the unpolitical to genocide and the Holocaust.

International law reflects this consensus by insisting that genocide requires "that the victims of genocide must be targeted by reason of their membership in a group."[12] It compounds this depoliticization of genocide in another way, too. In their singular focus on individual criminal responsibility, courts are uninterested in the structural factors and contexts that shaped and enabled perpetrator decision-making. Causality is thought to emanate from individuals' minds in a way inimical to historical and social scientific explanation: individualization and decontextualization is intrinsic to these legal proceedings. In doing so, the complex state mechanisms in which individuals are caught up and the field of relations that prefigured their ability to commit crimes is shielded from view and naturalized.[13] Mass crimes are thus seen as extreme and rare irruptions of violence into an otherwise healthy normality rather than as the manifestations of potentials immanent in hierarchical and exploitative relationships.[14]

This depoliticization is deliberate because it diminishes the possibility of criminalizing the communities from which perpetrators come and on whose behalf they claim to act. It was Slobodan Milošević (1941–2006) who was on trial at the International Criminal Tribunal for the former Yugoslavia (ICTY), for instance, not the Serbian nation. In making these necessary distinctions – for it would be analytically and politically untenable to criminalize nations – legal scholar Martti Koskenniemi has pointed out, the courts prioritize a thin legal truth of individual responsibility over contextually richer historical truth,

---

[11] Deborah E. Lipstadt, "Not Facing History," *New Republic*, March 6, 1995.

[12] Prosecutor v. Krstic, Judgment, No. IT-98-33-T, para. 561, August 2, 2001, www.icty.org/x/cases/krstic/tjug/en/krs-tj010802e.pdf.

[13] Immi Tallgren, "The Sensibility and Sense of International Criminal Law," *European Journal of International Law* 13, no. 3 (2002): 561–95; Tor Krever, "International Criminal Law: An Ideology Critique," *Leiden Journal of International Law* 26, no. 3 (2013): 701–23; Karen Engle, "Anti-Impunity and the Turn to Criminal Law in Human Rights," *Cornell Law Review* 100 (2015): 1069–127. Thanks to Sophie Rigney for these references. See the discussion in her "Fairness, the Rights of the Accused, and Procedure in International Criminal Trials" (PhD diss., University of Melbourne, 2016).

[14] Brad Roth, "Retrieving Marx for the Human Rights Project," *Leiden Journal of International Law* 17 (2004): 31–66.

namely "structural causes, such as economic or functional necessities, or a broad institutional logic through which the actions by individuals create social effects."[15] Legal truth has trumped historical truth in popular and much academic understanding of genocide and the Holocaust. Analysis is limited to the moral drama of identifying the perpetrators and their evil designs, defeating, and prosecuting them. Then all will be well in the land.

By disembedding genocides from the ubiquitous geopolitical and military contexts in which mass violence against civilians always takes place, the legal truth of genocide–as–Holocaust effectively depoliticizes them as the outcome of senseless hatred.[16] The previous chapter showed how depictions of contemporary civil wars and counterinsurgencies must resemble the Holocaust by portraying civilians akin to Jewish victims of the Nazis, namely as passive and innocent victims of murderous racial persecution. The cultural reasons for this occlusion of permanent security require further elaboration

After the Holocaust: A Single Archetype, an Ideal Victim

In the Introduction to this book, I observed that the "transgression effect" in the West had belonged to the fate of Armenians until the early 1940s (it was of course not then called a genocide); thereafter, it became Holocaust, just as the Holocaust has become the template for understanding the Armenian genocide, leading ultimately to the conceptual muddle that plagues understanding about state criminality today.

There are two reasons for this tectonic shift in the transgression effect. The first is that both the genocide concept and the Holocaust evoke themes of group survival. They resonate broadly because they reflect widespread experiences of homeland belonging, exile, and endurance. The second reason is the temporal coincidence of the Holocaust with the coining of the genocide concept in 1944, meaning that these two keywords coexist in a complex – part enabling, part competitive – relationship. Because the Holocaust is also a genocide, it cannot totally dominate a discursive terrain that has to name and respond to contemporary atrocities. The Holocaust refers to a specific event (or series of events) in the past while genocide is a generic term for current application. Even so, the Holocaust has gradually supplanted genocide as

---

[15] Martti Koskenniemi, "Between Impunity and Show Trials," *Max Planck Year Book of United Nations Law* 6 (2002): 1–35.

[16] Mark Levene, "A Moving Target, the Usual Suspects and (Maybe) a Smoking Gun: The Problem of Pinning Blame in Modern Genocide," *Patterns of Prejudice* 33, no. 4 (1999): 3–24; Martin Shaw, *War and Genocide: Organized Killing in Modern Society* (Cambridge: Polity, 2003); Shaw, *What is Genocide?*, 2nd ed. (Cambridge: Polity 2015). As we saw in Chapter 7, the Nazis consistently depicted Jews as an active threat to Germany: their dehumanization in Nazi propaganda derived from an ascribed status as enemy people.

modernity's icon of evil: when Holocaust became a capitalized proper noun to refer to the Shoah rather than a lower-case adjective with no specific referent.[17] With the rise to prominence of Holocaust memory, especially in the West, the Holocaust simultaneously stands above genocide while investing it with charged significance because of their sibling relationship – as Lemkin effectively intended in confecting his term as we saw in Chapters 4 and 5. The Holocaust thus became genocide's archetype. A recent statement by a senior British barrister and Labour peer exemplifies this complex nexus:

> The word genocide should never be invoked too readily. For most the term will be forever associated with the atrocities of Nazi concentration camps and the deliberate effort to exterminate Jews. The horrors were so unspeakable that the language to describe that carefully orchestrated attempt at annihilation has to remain undiluted.[18]

She went on to plead for categorizing Daesh's persecution of Yazidis as genocide, the chain of association running from the Holocaust (the particular) to genocide (the universal) to a contemporary case.

Sociologist Jeffrey C. Alexander has explained how this complex process of symbolic transference and inversion originated in the construction of the Holocaust as a "cultural trauma" of universal appeal.[19] The "Holocaust" did not exist as a discursive category when the concentration camps were liberated. Western, largely Christian, publics were appalled by Nazi crimes, but regarded them simply as a very large atrocity and identified with the Allied soldiers rather than the liberated Jewish survivor inmates. Nazism, not the Holocaust, was the symbol of evil, and its polluting presence was to be expunged by the worldwide victory of liberal democracy. In this way, Nazi crimes were narrated into a progressive philosophy of history and left behind.

The inner logic of symbolic association, however, undermined this exculpatory narrative. For, if Jews had been Hitler's primary target, as became clear in the postwar period, then they must be of a piece with liberal democracy, and therefore the task was to expunge antisemitism and racism from Western societies. Moreover, by deriving abstract moral criteria from the World War II experience, the ethical foundation of the West could be held up to scrutiny by

---

[17] Jeffrey C. Alexander et al., *Remembering the Holocaust: A Debate* (Oxford: Oxford University Press, 2009); Sara Buttsworth and Maartje Abbenhuis, eds., *Monsters in the Mirror: Representations of Nazism in Post-war Popular Culture* (Santa Barbara, CA: Praeger, 2010).

[18] Helena Kennedy, "Isis is Committing Genocide: It is Indefensible for Britain Not to Say So," *The Guardian*, March 21, 2016.

[19] Jeffrey C. Alexander, "On the Social Construction of Moral Universals: The 'Holocaust' From War Crime to Trauma Drama," *European Journal of Social Theory* 5, no. 1 (2002): 5–85.

domestic critics. And, in doing so, elements of Nazism could be found there by analogy, a process that Alexander calls "symbolic extension" – that is, identifying apparent analogies between Nazism and situations, circumstances, and policies that obtained in one's own polity. Simultaneously, with the acculturation of the Jewish community and the popularization of "accessible" Jewish Holocaust victims like Anne Frank, psychological identification with Jewish victims became possible for non-Jews – as we will see with Samantha Power below. Consequently, the Jewish experience could be singled out from that of other victims of Nazism (and other demographic calamities like the victims of Stalinist and Maoist policies) and invested with "extraordinary gravitas" as "radical evil" and a unique "world historical" event: it can function as a "trauma drama" for everyone. The drama of Jewish victimization was de-historicized and became an emblem for the disastrous consequences of racism and intolerance generally. Henceforth, the Holocaust was a proper, not a common, noun: the "archetypal sacred-evil of our time."[20] The progressive narrative of military victory was supplanted by a tragic one of innocent victims and damaged survivors, the memory of whose fate must be kept alive to prevent such suffering from recurring.[21]

The view that the Holocaust is unprecedented, unique, or central to "Western civilization" thus does not preclude its contemporary applicability. Consider Great Britain's government-sponsored Holocaust commission, launched in 2014, which begins its terms of reference with this telling statement: "The Holocaust is unique in man's inhumanity to man and it stands alone as the darkest hour of human history."[22] Although this is a state-run rather than Jewish institution that is proclaiming the Holocaust's universal significance, both types of institution claim that this status shines the light of moral urgency on other genocides and thereby represents a potent source of humanitarian mobilization to protect civilians from genocidal violence. In this way, so the reasoning goes, Holocaust memory motivated and now reinforces the achievements of the human rights revolution after World War II.[23]

---

[20] Alexander, "On the Social Construction of Moral Universals," 31.

[21] Ibid., 30–3. Emphasis in original.

[22] "Prime Minister Launches Holocaust Commission," www.gov.uk/government/news/prime-minister-launches-holocaust-commission. Prime Minister's Holocaust Commission: Terms of Reference: www.gov.uk/government/uploads/system/uploads/attachment_data/file/275198/Terms-of-Reference-PM-Holocaust-Commission.pdf.

[23] Akira Iriye, Petra Goedde, and William I. Hitchcock, eds., *The Human Rights Revolution: An International History* (New York: Oxford University Press, 2012); Jim Ife, *Human Rights from Below: Achieving Rights Through Community Development* (Cambridge: Cambridge University Press, 1993), 69. Critique: Marco Duranti, "The Holocaust, the Legacy of 1789 and the Birth of Human Rights Law: Revisiting the Foundation Myth," *Journal of Genocide Research* 14, no. 2 (2012): 159–86; and Stephen Hopgood, *Endtimes of Human Rights* (Ithaca: Cornell University Press, 2013), ch. 3.

While the Holocaust's archetypal effect is palpable, there are good reasons to question this claimed humanitarian payoff. As discussed in the previous chapter, a consequence of the Holocaust–genocide relationship is that violence needs to resemble the Holocaust in crucial respects to be legible as genocide in the language of transgression.[24] To qualify as genocide, the status of the victims is as important as the perpetrator: they must be innocent and agentless.

This imaginary of the victim has Christian and Jewish theological roots. The Christ figure voluntarily takes on the sins of humanity in an act of sacrifice, while in Jewish religious discourse, Jewish victims are called *Kedoshim*, literally "holy ones": martyrs of the Jewish people because they were murdered solely on the grounds of their religion, not for anything they have done. In the case of the Holocaust, they are the "six million *Kedoshim*."[25] By voluntarily accepting their fate and resisting the temptation to convert – during Christian pogroms in the Middle Ages for instance – Jewish victims died *Al Kiddush Ha-Shem*, "for the sanctification of the divine name." Rabbis in the Warsaw Ghetto paraphrased medieval Jewish theologian Maimonides to rule that a Jew killed "simply because he is a Jew, is called *Kaddosh*."[26]

Conversion would not save Jews in the Holocaust, of course, and the notion of *kiddush ha-hayim* (sanctification of life) – the will to live and resist – became legitimized as an alternative Zionist response, and has predominated in Israel.[27] In reaction, Ultra-Orthodox Jews there have established their own Holocaust archive called *Kiddush Hashem* to emphasize, among other things, the traditional religiosity of Jewish victims, thereby linking those who perished in the Holocaust to the 10 martyrs of the Mishniac era executed by the Romans and remembered in a poem called *Eleh Ezkera* and in other rabbinic literature.[28] This theological interpretation has permeated general commemoration, which thereby constitutes a political theology. The terminology of "for the sanctification of the divine name" is used in the *El Maale Rachamim* memorial prayer chanted, among other occasions, on Holocaust and Heroism Remembrance Day (*Yom HaShoah Ve Hgevurah*).[29] All Jews

[24] Becky Jinks, *Representing Genocide: The Holocaust as Paradigm?* (London: Bloomsbury, 2016).

[25] Rabbi Ahron Lopiansky, "The Six Million Kedoshim," *Jewish Observer*, September 1980, reprinted at *Aish.com*, www.aish.com/ho/i/48955481.html.

[26] Pesach Schindler, "The Holocaust and *Kiddish Hashem* in Hassidic Thought," *Tradition: A Journal of Orthodox Jewish Thought* 13, no. 4 (1973): 88.

[27] Yisrael Gutman, "*Kiddush ha-Shem* and *Kiddush ha-Hayim*," *Simon Wiesenthal Center Annual*, ed. Alex Grobman, Vol. 1 (Chappaqua, NY: Rossel Books, 1984), 185–202.

[28] Yair Ettinger, "New Bnei Brak Center to Focus on Haredi-Style Shoah Commemoration," *Ha'aretz*, May 2, 2011.

[29] Haviv Rettig Gur, "The Many Holocausts of the Jews," *Times of Israel*, May 6, 2016; JewishGen Hungarian SIG, "Hungarian Holocaust Memorial Database," *JewishGen*, www.jewishgen.org/databases/Hungary/HolocaustMemorials.htm.

murdered in the Holocaust thus died *"al Kiddush Hashem."*[30] As one observer noted, "In contemporary times, the moral of the poem *Eleh Ezkera* has taken on a new meaning with the deaths of millions of Jews during the Holocaust."[31] The traditional interpretation of Holocaust victims as martyrs has prevailed because the Nazis murdered Jews as Jews.

Their innocence is vouchsafed by the motivations of their murderers: "the longest hatred," as Robert Wistrich described antisemitism in a phrase that has caught on. In its popular rendering, antisemitism possesses ontological status. It is groundless antipathy towards Jews. "All of these centuries of hatred were exploited by the Nazis and their allies during World War II," he wrote, "culminating in the Holocaust, the systematic murder of Europe's Jews."[32] In this vein, two British historians refer to antisemitism as a "virus" that takes "so many forms . . . that it may be impossible ever to eradicate."[33] Whatever its garb, antisemitism is posited as an independent and active force in history, irrational hatred incarnate, adapting itself to time and place; in the past, Christians did the hating, then fascists, and now – so it is commonly thought – it is Muslims and their naïve fellow travellers, leftist anti-Zionists.[34]

The Talmudic notion of "senseless hatred" (*sinat chinam*) that is supposed to account for the destruction of the Second Temple provides a ready template for understanding about how hatred is thought to function in genocide.[35] While referring to intra-Jewish conflict (that is, hatred of one's own people is not justifiable), the paradigm is readily transferrable. Whether involving gentile hostility or Jewish infighting, hateful motivation is gratuitous because the victims were blameless and the consequences were catastrophic. In some

---

[30] Yad Vashem, Remembrance: The Shoah Victims' Names Recovery Project. Community Outreach Guide, www.yadvashem.org/yv/en/remembrance/names/torah_world_activities.asp#!prettyPhoto.

[31] Joseph Scutts, "Ten Years Later, the Ten Martyrs, and 'Dying Al Kiddush Hashem'," *Jewish Voice New York*, June 12, 2013.

[32] Robert Wistrich, *Antisemitism: The Longest Hatred* (New York: Schocken, 1994). The United States Holocaust Memorial Museum (USHMM) uses it to head a page on the subject: "Antisemitism: The Longest Hatred," www.ushmm.org/confront-antisemitism/antisemitism-the-longest-hatred.

[33] Brendan Simms and Charlie Laderman, "The Longest Hatred," *New Statesman*, May 9, 2016. J. J Goldberg observes how the rhetoric of "virus" and "pathology" is deployed in this discussion in reviewing Daniel J. Goldhagen, *The Devil That Never Dies: The Rise and Threat of Global Antisemitism* (New York: Little Brown, 2013), in "Hatreds Ancient and New," *Democracy Journal*, November 30, 2013, http://democracyjournal.org/magazine/30/hatreds-ancient-and-new/.

[34] Deborah E. Lipstadt, *Antisemitism: Here and Now* (New York: Schocken, 2019); Bari Weiss, *How to Fight Anti-Semitism* (New York: Random House, 2019).

[35] Michael Laitman, "Why Are There Anti-Israel Jews?" *Jerusalem Post*, August 25, 2016; James Kirchick, "On Linda Sarsour's Politics of Hatred and the Pathos of Her Jewish Enablers," *Tablet*, June 14, 2017, www.tabletmag.com/jewish-news-and-politics/237149/linda-sarsour-jewish-enablers.

strains of Jewish memory, antisemitism binds Jewish victims of violence into a single, continuous line of martyrdom: the 10 martyrs, victims of the crusaders in Medieval Europe and of the Nazis 1,000 years later, Israeli soldiers, and those murdered by Islamists today "all died *Al Kiddush Hashem*" – because they were hated as Jews.[36] That is to say, the Jewish victim is innocent irrespective of agency: from Israeli soldiers to the Jewish-French children shot in front of their school by a Daesh terrorist. They all embodied the "virtuous martyr" as Norman Podhoretz memorably put it.[37] Whether killed from *sinat chinam* or *Al Kiddush Hashem*, victims died as passive victims because of undeserved hatred.

Given the status of genocide as the crime of crimes, and of the Holocaust as the archetypal genocide, the image of the largely agentless and innocent – that is, unpolitical – Jewish victim represents the "ideal" or "exemplary" victim: that socially constructed status by which sympathy and legitimacy are conferred on certain objects of violence and not on others. As martyrs, the dead were sacrificed for membership of their group, targeted because of their despised identity, bereft of political agency.[38] This victim is the innocent, depoliticized one. The Holocaust is not only the archetypal and universal genocide, then, a figure of "global memory."[39] Jews represent the archetypal and universal form of victimhood. This status becomes a "sacred alter" that "fosters identification with victimhood," even though – or perhaps because – most people are members of persecuting majorities rather than victims.[40]

---

[36] Scutts, "Ten Years Later, the Ten Martyrs, and 'Dying Al Kiddush Hashem'"; Rosally Saltsman, "Sisters of the Phoenix," *Jewish Press*, April 20, 2012,
   www.jewishpress.com/sections/magazine/potpourri/sisters-of-the-phoenix/2012/04/20/.

[37] Norman Podhoretz, "Hannah Arendt on Eichmann: A Study in the Perversity of Brilliance," *Commentary*, September 1, 1963, 201.

[38] Christine Schwöbel-Patel, "Nils Christie's 'Ideal Victim' Applied: From Lions to Swarms," *Critical Legal Thinking*, August 5, 2015, http://criticallegalthinking.com/2015/08/05/nils-christies-ideal-victim-applied-from-lions-to-swarms; Nils Christie, "The Ideal Victim," in *From Crime Policy to Victim Policy*, ed. Ezzat A. Fattah (Basingstoke: Palgrave Macmillan, 1986), 17–30. Allen Feldman uses the term "exemplary" for this effect. Feldman, *Archives of the Insensible: Of War, Photopolitics, and Dead Memory* (Chicago: University of Chicago Press, 2015), ch. 6.

[39] Daniel Levey and Natan Sznaider, *The Holocaust and Memory in the Global Age* (Philadelphia: Temple University Press, 2005). Innocence is inferred to victims of natural as opposed to humanly made disasters. See Hanna Zagefka and Trevor James, "Psychology of Charitable Donations to Disaster Victims and Beyond," *Social Issues and Policy Review* 9, no. 1 (2015): 155–92. Thanks to Eyal Mayroz for pointing out this parallel. See his *Reluctant Interveners: America's Failed Responses to Genocide from Bosnia to Darfur* (New Brunswick: Rutgers University Press, 2019), 74.

[40] Alex Cocotas, "Blow Up the Memorial to the Murdered Jews of Europe," *Tablet*, April 21, 2017, www.tabletmag.com/jewish-arts-and-culture/230085/memorials-yom-hashoah.

Ironically, however, the Israelites were mostly not senseless victims in the Old Testament. Each calamity has a theological explanation, supported with socio-political arguments. It is the New Testament ethos of Christ's willing sacrifice, with references to prophetic images of the suffering servant who carries the sins for others, which embodies the innocent victim. Christian and Jewish themes can thus be blended, as in Alfred Hrdlicka's Memorial Against War and Fascism in Vienna, which depicts a modern Jewish man occupying Christ's role in the sacrificial drama by wearing a crown of thorns.[41] Remembering the suffering of victims can be a vehicle for the redemption of the community and/or nation, as the former atone for the sins of the latter, thereby serving as "redemptive sufferers."[42]

Whether Jewish or Christian, or both, this image of the exemplary victim has proven irresistible to those seeking recognition as innocent victims of persecutions who deserve protection and/or compensation. Victims of various conflicts routinely construct themselves as Jews: killed for their identity rather than for their deeds, likewise virtuous martyrs.[43] Sometimes this recognition is easy. "Who if not the Jewish people should have a particular understanding for the persecution of the biblical Yazidi minority?" said Deidre Berger, director of the American Jewish Committee in Berlin, of the Iraqi minority attacked by *Daesh*.[44] Similar connections are made with Tutsis in Rwanda, whose cause has also been popular in Israel and with Jewish groups in other countries; Hutu Power was predictably called "tropical Nazism."[45]

This analogizing is usually unsuccessful. Not every persecuted group can convince others that they, too, are innocent victims, because most civilian destruction takes place during armed conflicts. Biafrans, we learned in the previous chapter, styled themselves as the "Jews of Africa" in their independence struggle with the Nigerian state in the late 1960s. While evoking sympathy in Israel, most states did not believe Biafrans were victims of an impending Holocaust. Similarly, various nationalists made bids during the

---

[41] Matti Bunzl, "On the Politics and Semantics of Austrian Memory: Vienna's Monument against War and Fascism," *History and Memory* 7, no. 2 (1995): 7–40. Thanks to Frances Tanzer for this insight and reference.

[42] Avril Alba, *The Holocaust Memorial Museum: Sacred Secular Space* (Basingstoke: Palgrave Macmillan, 2015), 161–4. Thanks to Avril Alba and Gili Kugler for discussions on these points.

[43] The temptation affects non-Jewish individuals, who style themselves as Jews. Sue Vice, "Binjamin Wilkomirski's Fragments and Holocaust Envy: 'Why Wasn't I There, Too?'" *Immigrants & Minorities* 21, nos. 1–2 (2002): 249–68.

[44] Toby Axelrod, "Shoah Educator to Help Yazidis Document Their Own Tragedy," *Jewish Chronicle Online*, April 26, 2016, www.thejc.com/news/world-news/157368/shoah-educator-help-yazidis-document-their-own-tragedy.

[45] Noah Schimmel, "Rwanda and the Jewish People," *Jerusalem Post*, June 23, 2009; Jean-Pierre Chrétien, "Un 'nazisme tropical' au Rwanda? Image ou logique d'un genocide," *Vingtième Siècle: Revue d'histoire* 48 (1995): 131–42.

post-Yugoslav conflagration to style their group as the victimized Jews, invariably without much success.[46] Continuing its campaign for international recognition, the Armenian Genocide Museum and Institute in Yerevan declared Armenian victims of the Ottoman deportations and massacres during World War I to be holy martyrs, converting all 1.5 million into "saints."[47] They were victims of Turkish racism and hate, it is claimed. Although most scholars are prepared to affix the genocide label, many states do not.

Scapegoating as Depoliticization

In the field of Genocide Studies and human rights education, a group becomes a victim by classification beyond the "boundaries of the universe of obligation," as Helen Fein put in an influential formulation; they are not members of "the circle of individuals and groups toward whom obligations are owed, to whom rules apply, and whose injuries call for amends."[48] The social dynamic determining this hierarchy of caring is the notion of auto-generated hatred: hatred is not a reaction to attributes of the hated group but a product of the hater's internal psychodrama.[49] This hatred is embodied by racial prejudice, above all by antisemitism – "the longest hatred" and the "blood libel" – that is deeply rooted in Western culture.[50]

In the most influential – and I argue misleading – approach, antisemitism is activated by the "scapegoating" mechanism, a term famously employed in 1939 by the literary scholar, Kenneth Burke, in analyzing Adolf Hitler's

---

[46] Robert M. Hayden, "Genocide in Bosnia," in *The Historiography of Genocide*, ed. Dan Stone (Basingstoke: Palgrave Macmillan, 2008), 487–516; Christian Axboe Nielsen, "Surmounting the Myopic Focus on Genocide: The Case of the War in Bosnia and Herzegovina," *Journal of Genocide Research* 15, no. 1 (2013): 21–39.

[47] The Armenian Genocide Museum and Institute, www.genocide-museum.am/eng/index .php; "Armenian Church Makes Saints of 1.5 Million Genocide Victims," *The Telegraph*, April 23, 2015.

[48] Helen Fein, *Accounting for Genocide: National Responses and Jewish Victimization during the Holocaust* (New York: Sage, 1979), 4, 33; Fein's term is widely used in toleration pedagogy: Facing History, "Defining Community: The Universe of Obligation," www .facinghistory.org/resource-library/defining-community-universe-obligation; The World as it Should be: Human Rights Program, "The Universe of Obligation and Why It Matters to Me," www.theworldasitcouldbe.org/?p=1573; OneIFoot: Jewish Texts for Social Justice, "Universe of Obligation," http://on1foot.org/sourcesheet/universe-obligation-0.

[49] Robert J. Sternberg, "A Duplex Theory of Hate: Development and Application to Terrorism, Massacres, and Genocide," *Review of General Psychology* 7, no. 3 (2003): 299–328.

[50] David Nirenberg, *Anti-Judaism: The Western Tradition* (New York: W. W. Norton, 2013), 468–70; Wistrich, *Antisemitism*; Hannah R. Johnson, *Blood Libel: The Ritual Murder Accusation at the Limit of Jewish History* (Ann Arbor: University of Michigan Press, 2012).

manifesto and biography, *Mein Kampf.* Drawing on Freud's notion that civilizational order requires repression and thus produces frustration, Burke saw in the operation of Nazi ideology a "vicarious victimage" purification ritual whereby a subject's guilt and inadequacies are projected onto an external vessel (the scapegoat) that becomes a sacrificial offering, leading to the community's "symbolic rebirth."[51] Although he was writing two years before the German mass shootings of Soviet Jews and the operation of the death camps, he understood the genocidal logic of Nazi victimage: "The 'Aryan' is 'constructive'; the Jew is 'destructive'; and the 'Ayran,' to continue his *construction*, must *destroy* the Jewish *destruction*. The Aryan, as the vessel of *love* must *hate* the Jewish *hate*."[52] French writer Alain Finkielkraut echoed this view when, referring to Nazi persecution of Jews, he wrote that "*Scapegoats* from time immemorial were rudely cast into an unrecognizable world, subjected to total war and treated as the *absolute enemy*."[53] Such an enemy was not merely to be ghettoized, but to be completely exterminated.

The attraction of the scapegoating concept to explain the Holocaust is heightened by the fact that it is taken from the Hebrew Bible: from Leviticus 16:1–34, which presents the expiation ritual at the center of the Yom Kippur ("Day of Atonement") service. God tells Moses to instruct his brother Aaron to take two goats; one will be presented to the Lord, the other "marked for Azazel," that is, for removal (the scapegoat). As verses 21 and 22 depict the drama, the goat takes on and carries off the community's sins, further purging and purifying it by the sacrifice of the other goat.

Although Freudian models of repressed psychodynamic conflict have fallen out of favor in social psychology, the scapegoating notion remains popular as a

---

[51] Kenneth Burke, "The Rhetoric of Hitler's Battle," *Southern Review* 5 (1939): 1–21, reprinted in Burke, *On Symbols and Society* (Chicago and London: University of Chicago Press, 1989), 211–31. He had already written briefly on scapegoating in 1935 in *Permanence and Change: An Anatomy of Purpose* (Berkeley: University of California Press, 1984 [1935]), 14–6, and then applied it explicitly to the Nazis: Burke, *A Grammar of Motives* (Berkeley: University of California Press, 1969 [1944]), Burke, "Dialectic of the Scapegoat," *A Grammar of Motives* (Berkeley: University of California Press, 1969 [1944]), 406–8. For more on "victimage," see Burke, "Interaction: Dramatism," in *International Encyclopedia of the Social Sciences*, 19 Vols., ed. David I. Sills (New York: Macmillan and The Free Press, 1968), 7: 445–452. The scapegoating category is used more recently by Dominick La Capra, *Representing the Holocaust History, Theory, Trauma* (Ithaca: Cornell University Press, 1994). The notion was also popularized by René Girard, *The Scapegoat*, trans. Yvonne Freccero (Baltimore: Johns Hopkins University Press, 1986).

[52] Burke, "The Rhetoric of Hitler's Battle," 204. Emphasis in original.

[53] Alain Finkielkraut, *The Imaginary Jews*, trans. Kevin O'Neill and David Suchoff (Lincoln and London: University of Nebraska Press, 1994), 46. Emphasis in original.

metaphor.[54] For instance, the United States Holocaust Memorial Museum explains in its online entry on antisemitism that "In more desperate times, Jews became scapegoats for many problems people suffered," thereby continuing venerable theories popular from the 1930s about social frustration and the displacement of aggression onto hapless minorities.[55] Significant for our discussion is that the goat is innocent, as is the human scapegoat; it is the agentless victim of a community's mythic drama of redemption, an object of pent-up frustration. Hannah Arendt rightly observed of scapegoating explanations of the Holocaust that they presume "the perfect innocence of the victim, an innocence which insinuates not only that no evil was done but that nothing at all was done that might possibly have a connection with the issue at stake."[56] Arendt's point is not that victims are guilty and coresponsible for their fate, but that victimage explanations evacuate the murderous context of interactions between victims and perpetrator. One does not need to accept Arendt's figuration of that context to agree that positing an "eternal antisemitism" as the explanation for the Nazis' choice of scapegoat ignores how and why "Jews were driven into the storm center of events" in the first half of the twentieth century.[57]

The problem in the prevalent view of the victim, then, is that it is apolitically religious rather than political. It is a secularized theology about the origins of evil: groups are victims of prejudice that arises within evil people.[58] This is the faith of Western liberal internationalists whose intense empathy with ideal victims drives the interventionist temptation to "do something" for them. Samantha Power embodies this subjectivity. Encounters with the terrible fate of Anne Frank and the Holocaust drove her resolve to personally make the US a global force to realize the maxim of "never again," thereby implicating Holocaust memory in a new civilizing mission, as I discuss below. Rather than messy conflicts of multidirectional violence, she, like other sentinels of liberal permanent security such as French philosopher Bernard-Henri Lévy, who lobbied his president to bomb Libyan forces in 2011, sees the Holocaust drama

---

[54] Peter Glick, "Sacrificial Lambs Dressed in Wolves' Clothing: Envious Prejudice, Ideology, and the Scapegoating of Jews," in *Understanding Genocide: The Social Psychology of the Holocaust*, ed. Leonard S. Newman and Ralph Erber (Oxford: Oxford University Press, 2002), 113–42.

[55] United States Holocaust Memorial Museum, "Antisemitism," www.ushmm.org/outreach/en/article.php?ModuleId=10007691. See the discussion in Glick, "Sacrificial Lambs Dressed in Wolves' Clothing."

[56] Hannah Arendt, *The Origins of Totalitarianism*, new ed. (New York: Harcourt, 1968), 5. She may have been relying on Bohdan Zawakzi, "Limitations on the Scapegoat Theory of Prejudice," *Journal of Abnormal and Social Psychology* 43 (1948): 127–41.

[57] Arendt, *The Origins of Totalitarianism*, 7.

[58] Sara Buttsworth and Maartje Abbenhuis, eds., *Monsters in the Mirror: Representations of Nazism in Post-War Popular Culture* (Santa Barbara, CA: ABC-CLIO, 2010).

of innocent victims and evil perpetrators unfolding before their eyes; it demands their intervention. When they destroy a state, as they did Libya's, the consequent anarchy – which unleashed far more violence than the Western intervention was designed to prevent – are disavowed and ascribed to the strange locals, their meddling neighbors, and the absence of still more US intervention: "Whatever our sincerity," Power wrote in her exculpatory memoir of the Libya debacle, "we could hardly expect to have a crystal ball when it came to accurately predicting outcomes in places where the culture was not our own."[59] The academic-cum-state official, Power embodies humanitarian intervention in theory and practice, making it difficult for its proponents to maintain that the Libya debacle was an illegitimate instrumentalization of their doctrine by cynical states.[60] What is more, she does not mention drone strikes, Obama's favored form of intervention, because it obviates the need for deploying US ground forces, although just under 10 percent of the 3,797 they killed in the 542 strikes he authorized were civilians – entirely legally.[61] At the end of the day, the discourse of the ultimate, innocent victimhood empowers activists to generate more violence and kill more innocent victims in the name of saving the world from violence against innocent victims.

A New Civilizing Mission

The fascination with non-Western victims of non-Western barbaric regimes reinscribes colonial rescue fantasies, especially of subject women who can

---

[59] Samantha Power, *The Education of an Idealist: A Memoir* (New York: Dey St, 2019), 45, 61, 118–20, 306, 310; Richard Brody, "Did Bernard-Henri Lévy Take NATO to War?" *New Yorker*, March 25, 2011. For a biting critique of such thinking, see Rajan Menon, *The Conceit of Humanitarian Intervention* (Oxford: Oxford University Press, 2016), and the forum on this book in the *Journal of Genocide Research* 21, no. 1 (2019): 96–130. Power may have profited from reflecting on David Kennedy's work on humanitarianism and power in his *The Dark Side of Virtue: Reassessing International Humanitarianism* (Princeton: Princeton University Press, 2004), and David Rieff, *At the Point of a Gun: Democratic Dreams and Armed Intervention* (New York: Simon and Schuster, 2005). See also Stephen Wertheim, "A Solution from Hell: The United States and the Rise of Humanitarian Interventionism, 1991–2003," *Journal of Genocide Research* 12, nos. 3–4 (2010): 149–72.

[60] The question remains whether the American and French intervention exceeded UN Security Council Resolution 1973 of May 17, 2011 that approved a no-fly zone over Libya and called for "all necessary measures" to protect civilians. Alex J. Bellamy, "Libya and the Responsibility to Protect: The Exception and the Norm," *Ethics and International Affairs* 25, no. 3 (2011): 263–9, and Aidin Hehir and Robert Murray, eds., *Libya, the Responsibility to Protect and the Future of Humanitarian Intervention* (Basingstoke: Palgrave Macmillan, 2013).

[61] Micah Zenko, "Obama's Final Drone Strike Data," Council on Foreign Relations, January 20, 2017, www.cfr.org/blog/obamas-final-drone-strike-data.

only feel pain and who are bereft of agency: help must come from the West.[62] In the words of one critic, Westerners thereby "steal the pain of others."[63] Indeed, non-Western political agency would preclude it from empathy because it could imply political responsibility, even guilt. Didier Fassin coined the term "humanitarian reason" for such moral sentiments that motivate remedial action for far-off victims while concealing its redemptive emotional investment and the asymmetrical power relations between the West and the Global South. When imagining the Third World, the militant resistance fighter has been replaced by the passive sufferer.[64]

The genocide keyword is thereby conscripted into a civilizing mission for the Global North to spread to the Global South. Thus, a prominent Genocide Studies academic can reassure his readers that "genocide contradicts traditional Western norms and approaches to law and morals,"[65] thereby projecting criminal mass violence outward. And no cognitive dissonance is experienced by Western leaders like former British prime minister David Cameron who engaged in gratuitous Holocaust piety while telling Jamaicans to "move on" from slavery's legacy and describing asylum seekers as "swarming" towards his country, whose wealth was built on slavery and that offers a paltry refugee quota for Syrians.[66] They do not qualify as victims

---

[62] Lila Abu-Lughod, *Do Muslim Women Need Saving?* (Cambridge, MA: Harvard University Press, 2013); Leti Volpp, "Saving Muslim Women," *Public Books*, August 1, 2015, www.publicbooks.org/nonfiction/saving-muslim-women. Thanks to Neil Levi for sharing this article. Western humanitarian sentiment is predicated on the "social and political death of the African citizen": Heike Härting, "Global Humanitarianism, Race, and the Spectacle of the African Corpse in Current Western Representations of the Rwandan Genocide," *Comparative Studies of South Asia, Africa and the Middle East* 28, no. 1 (2008): 61–77.

[63] Sherene Razack, "Stealing the Pain of Others: Reflections on Canadian Humanitarian Responses," *Review of Education, Pedagogy and Cultural Studies* 29, no. 4 (2007): 375–94.

[64] Didier Fassin, *Humanitarian Reason: A Moral History of the Present* (Berkeley: University of California Press, 2012); Kristin Ross, *May '68 and Its Afterlives* (Chicago: University of Chicago Press, 2002), 167. Thanks to Jess Whyte for this point and reference.

[65] Irving L. Horowitz, *Taking Lives: Genocide and State Power*, 5th rev. ed. (New Brunswick, NJ: Transaction Publishers, 2002), 29–30.

[66] Rowena Mason, "Jamaica Should 'Move on From Painful Legacy of Slavery,' Says Cameron," *The Guardian*, October 1, 2015; "Prime Minister Pledges Prominent Holocaust Memorial for Britain," Prime Minister's Office, January 27, 2015, www.gov .uk/government/news/prime-minister-pledges-prominent-holocaust-memorial-for-brit ain; "David Cameron Criticised Over Migrant 'Swarm' Language," BBC News, www.bbc .com/news/uk-politics-33716501. "David Cameron Says Britain Will Accept Just 'a Few Hundred' More Syrian Refugees Despite 4 Million Displaced by the War," *The Guardian*, August 5, 2015. To their credit, British-Jewish leaders criticized the prime minister for this stance: Liam Maguire, "Your Response to Migrant Crisis is Appalling, British Jews Tell Cameron," *Evening Standard*, August 12, 2015, www.standard.co.uk/

because they are fleeing a civil war where roughly symmetrical violence obtains; only the truly agentless and innocent deserve our pity. A politics of pity excludes a politics of justice as the optic.[67]

To be pitiable, refugees must "stop being specific persons and become pure victims in general," according to anthropologist Liisa Malkii, who observes that the praxis of aid delivery "dehistoricizes" the refugees' context. Accordingly, "it is difficult for people in the refugee category to be approached as historical actors rather than simply as mute victims."[68] To be included in the humanitarian narrative, potential objects of empathy now depend on their proximity to the protocols of exemplarity.[69] When they do qualify as objects of humanitarian intervention, Western trampling on national sovereignty and local autonomy is not understood as political, because the intervention becomes akin to a modern colonial occupation, establishing humanitarian regimes via expertise and technocracy that operate according to protocols of rationality to bypass the seemingly irrationality of local politics.[70]

Central to the civilizing mission of liberal permanent security is the promotion of toleration, antiracism, and human rights as a world-redeeming ideology. By positing intolerance as the cause of genocides that are necessarily committed by non-Western enemies of the civilized West, the promotion of toleration and human rights becomes an imperial ideology of cultural superiority – a "humanitarian melodrama" of good and bad guys – that licences

news/politics/your-response-to-migrant-crisis-is-appalling-british-jews-tell-cameron-a2487361.html. For the term Holocaust piety, see Gillian Rose, "Beginnings of the Day: Fascism and Representation," in *Modern, Culture, and "the Jew,"* ed. Bryan Cheyette and Laura Marcus (Stanford: Stanford University Press, 1998), 242–55.

[67] Considerations of context are essential in making this claim. It is one thing for, say, Palestinian women in Palestine to make a documentary criticizing so-called honor killings of women in their communities (even if funded by the UN), and quite another if Western-based feminists make such a film. See the frank exchange between various parties on the subject: Lila Abu Lughod, and Maya Mikdashi, "Tradition and the Anti-Politics Machine: DAM Seduced by the "Honor Crime"," *Jadaliyya*, November 23, 2012, www.jadaliyya.com/pages/index/8578/tradition-and-the-anti-politics-machine_dam-seduce; Tamer Nafar, Suhell Nafar, and Mahmood Jrery (DAM), "DAM Responds: On Tradition and the Anti-Politics of the Machine," *Jadaliyya*, December 26, 2012, www.jadaliyya.com/pages/index/9181/dam-responds_on-tradition-and-the-anti-politics-of; Lila Abu-Lughod and Maya Mikdashi, "Honoring Solidarity During Contentious Debates… A Letter to DAM From Lila Abu-Lughod and Maya Mikdashi," *Jadaliyya*, December 26, 2012, www.jadaliyya.com/pages/index/9249/honoring-solidarity-during-con tentious-debates. Thanks to Nida Alahmad for drawing my attention to this exchange.

[68] Liisa Malkki, "Speechless Emissaries: Refugees, Humanitarianism, and Dehistoricization," *Cultural Anthropology* 11, no. 3 (1996): 378.

[69] Feldman, *Archives of the Insensible*, 337–8.

[70] Vasuki Nesiah, "The Specter of Violence That Haunts the UDHR: The Turn to Ethics and Expertise," *Maryland Journal of International Law* 24 (2009): 135–54.

"humanitarian violence" in the name of a common humanity and cultural diversity.[71]

The drama is populated by the stock figures of the savage, the victim, and the savior.[72] The Western self is constructed as the authentic embodiment of caring, universal humanity on the basis of posited non-Western abjection (the brown victims) and criminality (the brown perpetrators). The fully human is contained in the Global North, and barbaric potentials split off and located in the Global South: genocide names a horror that cannot be reconciled conceptually with civilization.[73] The international community's remedy for the "scourge of genocide" is transitional justice, a tutelary regime of peace, reconciliation, and legal measures that transfer the attributes of civilization to the barbarous.[74]

Paradoxically, and fatally, assumptions about nationhood and belonging implicit in the rhetoric of toleration compound the structures of identity that enable genocide in the first place. The talk of toleration is a logical corollary of the ethnically defined nation-state that constitutes the geopolitical imaginary of the UN: each "people" housed in "its" state.[75] The genocide discourse does not challenge this ethnic construction of the state and its divine cartography: the assumption that a *Volk* governs and reproduces itself through the state, and that others are to be tolerated. These assumptions presuppose that outsiders remain outsiders, foreign bodies in the body politic to be at best tolerated and, if they seem to develop their own collective will and are perceived as threatening, to be suppressed, expelled, or destroyed.

These assumptions have several sources. One goes back to John Locke and the English *Toleration Act* of 1689, and to other Christian theorists who attempted to end the Wars of Religion by advocating tolerance of religious

---

[71] Robert Meister, *After Evil: A Politics of Human Rights* (New York: Columbia University Press, 2011), 66; Neda Atanasoski, *Humanitarian Violence: The U.S. Deployment of Diversity* (Minneapolis: University of Minnesota Press, 2013); Wendy Brown, *Regulating Aversion: Tolerance in the Age of Identity and Empire* (Princeton: University of Princeton Press, 2006).

[72] Makau Mutua, "Savages Victims, and Saviors: The Metaphor of Human Rights," *Harvard International Law Review* 42, no. 1 (2001): 201–45; Christine Schwöbel-Patel, "Spectacle in International Criminal Law: The Fundraising Image of Victimhood," *London Review of International Law* 4, no. 2 (2016): 247–74.

[73] David Kazanjian, "Re-flexion: Genocide in Ruins," *Discourse* 33, no. 3 (2011): 372.

[74] Alexander Laban Hinton, "Transitional Justice Time: Uncle San, Aunty Yan, and Outreach at the Khmer Rouge Tribunal," in *Genocide and Mass Atrocities in Asia: Legacies and Prevention*, ed. Deborah Meyersen and Annie Pohlman (Abingdon: Routledge, 2013), 86–98; Hinton, ed., *Transitional Justice: Global Mechanisms and Local Realities after Genocide and Mass Violence* (Piscataway, NJ: Rutgers University Press, 2010).

[75] Michael Walzer, "The Moral Standing of States: A Response to Four Critics," *Philosophy & Public Affairs* 9, no. 3 (1980): 209–29.

minorities. Another precedes the West by centuries in the Muslim empires after the Islamic wars of expansion. In both Islamic and Christian worlds, toleration was as a state policy intended to regulate relations between various religious communities. In neither did toleration imply equality. Under Muslim rule, the *dhumma* status of Christians and Jews justified discriminatory measures aimed to establish the superiority of Islam. The "tolerated ones" were to wear special clothing; were forbidden to ride horses or to carry guns; build new churches or synagogues, or practise their religion publicly before Muslims. The situation was similar in the Christian West. The Toleration Act in England discriminated against nonconformist Protestants and, above all, Roman Catholics. Tolerance had its limits and implied intolerance.

The logic persists in the idea of multiculturalism today. In 1994, British Columbia's Lieutenant-Governor, David See-Chai Lam, of Chinese descent, said Canadians should celebrate rather than tolerate cultural diversity, explaining that "tolerance is a slightly negative word ... it's like saying, 'You smell, but I can hold my breath.'" He recognized that toleration implies an unequal relationship in which the tolerators endures the other but does not accept them as full members of the political community, still less the ethnically conceived nation. Tolerance is a uni-directional discourse that presumes the normativity and hegemony of the dominant society that defines itself against "others" – usually ethnic others. It presumes that, for example, "Canadians" and "minorities" are mutually exclusive categories. The power to tolerate or not to tolerate is not challenged; that power remains.[76]

If this toleration discourse continues the structures in which minorities remain outsiders, it is also implicated in "ethnic caging." Minorities are constructed as a demographic threat when the members of the majority reach the limits of their toleration and declare there are "too many" of the minority and that they should integrate or leave. They should subject themselves to the national will and not express a threatening independent one of their own.[77] In this way, the discourse produces the insecurity that is the background precondition for genocide.

Holocaust Education as Liberal Permanent Security

A related problem of genocide is Holocaust- and genocide-prevention pedagogy: promoting toleration and combating of prejudice and discrimination. It

[76] Kiran Mirchandani and Evangelia Tastsogloui, "Towards A Diversity Beyond Tolerance," *Studies in Political Economy*, no. 61 (2000): 49–78; Sara Ahmed, *Strange Encounters: Embodied Others in Post-Coloniality* (London and New York: Routledge, 2000).

[77] Ghassan Hage, *White Nation: Fantasies of White Supremacy in a Multicultural Society* (Melbourne: Pluto, 1998); Evan Osnos, "The Fearful and the Frustrated," *New Yorker*, August 24, 2015.

is exemplified in the Simon Wiesenthal Museum of Tolerance in Los Angeles, recipient of the "Global Peace and Tolerance Award from the Friends of the United Nations," which challenges "visitors to understand the Holocaust in both historic and contemporary contexts and confront all forms of prejudice and discrimination in our world today."[78] The UN bestowed the prize after a General Assembly resolution on Holocaust remembrance in 2005 that led to an outreach initiative called The Holocaust and the United Nations Outreach Program (UNHOP). It aims to prevent genocide by mobilizing "civil society for Holocaust remembrance and education" and by condemning "all manifestations of religious intolerance, incitement, harassment or violence against persons or communities based on ethnic origin or religious belief, whenever they occur."[79] To this end, the UN mounts commemorative events on the International Day of Commemoration in Memory of the Victims of the Holocaust via its global network of information centers (UNICS) – from Accra to Yerevan.[80] This is an education project of planetary proportions.

The UN Educational, Scientific and Cultural Organization (UNSECO) followed suit in 2007 with a resolution to contribute to the Holocaust and United Nations program with its own focus on education.[81] A particular target of its efforts are African states, with whose education ministries it organizes advocacy meetings that include "important institutions specialized in the teaching of the Holocaust and other genocide," like Yad Vashem from Israel, the Shoah Memorial from France, and the German Georg Eckert Centre for International Research on Textbooks.[82] At the regional consultation in Cape Town in 2012, for instance, representatives of 14 Sub-Saharan African countries were entreated to include genocide in their curricula, and make the Holocaust a catalyst or the prism through which it is understood.

The Holocaust can function in this way because it is the "universal contemporary reference for extreme violence" by echoing "fundamental questions affecting the whole of humanity: racism, identity driven conflicts, the position of minorities, conformism in violence, solidarity in the face of oppression, the

---

[78] Museum of Tolerance, A Simon Wiesenthal Center Museum, Our History and Vision, www.museumoftolerance.com/about-us/our-history-and-vision. See the excellent analysis of the Wiesenthal museum in Brown, Regulating Aversion, ch. 5.

[79] Holocaust and United Nations Outreach Program, www.un.org/en/holocaustremembrance/index.shtml.

[80] International Day of Commemoration in Memory of the Victims of the Holocaust. 2019: Holocaust Remembrance Week Activities Around the World, www.un.org/en/holocaustremembrance/2019/UNICs.shtml.

[81] UNESCO resolution 34c/61on Holocaust Remembrance, www.un.org/en/holocaustremembrance/docs/UNESCO%20res.shtml.

[82] UNESCO Regional Consultation in Sub-Saharan Africa, "Why Teach about Genocide? The Example of the Holocaust," Cape Town, South Africa, September 10–11, 2012, https://unesdoc.unesco.org/ark:/48223/pf0000220858.

role of ideologies, justice and reconstruction, etc., which are relevant issues in many contexts." Human rights would be promoted by understanding genocide as the "result of deeply rooted situations of stigmatization and discrimination" that escalate into the "actual killings of targeted populations," as occurred exemplarily in the Holocaust.[83]

By rendering the particular European events of the Holocaust as a massive hate crime and as the most extreme human rights violation, the international community offers a universal model to African states. Indicating the unstable conceptual relationship between the Holocaust and genocide, let alone non-genocidal violence, the African delegates were warned by Georges Bensoussan from the Shoah Memorial not to forget the Holocaust's singularity – "unprecedented in the history of humanity, marking a radical anthropological rupture."[84] Given the unclear links between such an unprecedented crime and the presumably precedented events that occurred in Africa, the question remains: what was the intended point of the exercise?

The choice of Holocaust-as-exemplar appears incongruous only if universalism is confused with universality. Katz, Bensoussan, and the Western institutional instructors at these meetings explained that the conflicts in Africa did not resemble the Holocaust, with the possible exception of the Rwandan genocide. Instead, they imparted two Holocaust lessons to Africans and Muslims: don't engage in racist hatred in general, and especially not against the exemplary victim – Jews and Israel – whose particular experiences bear a universal message. Moroccan-born Bensoussan has long worried about anti-semitism among Arab citizens of France, and about anti-Israel sentiment in Europe and the Arab and Muslim worlds.[85] His concern is shared by the Aladdin Project, a Paris-based NGO founded in 2009 by the *Fondation pour la Mémoire de la Shoah* to combat Holocaust denial. Its executive director is Abe Rabkin, who previously led the UK Human Rights Foundation. Further indicating the tightknit network of organizations and interests, Samuel Pisar, the UNESCO Honorary Ambassador and Special Envoy for Holocaust and

---

[83] "Genocide is the radical outcome of a gradual escalation of human rights violation." UNESCO, "Why Teach about Genocide?" 11–2.

[84] UNESCO, "Why Teach about Genocide?" 13. Cf. Georges Bensoussan, "The Civil and Political Challenges of Holocaust Education," in *Holocaust Education in a Global Context*, ed. Karel Fracapane and Matthias Haß (Paris: UNESCO, 2014), 172–6.

[85] Matti Friedman, "It Began with Students Denying the Holocaust," *Jerusalem Report*, December 13, 2004; Georges Bensoussan, "History Aside," in *Perceptions of the Holocaust in Europe and Muslim Communities*, ed. Gunter Jileki and Joelle Allouch-Benayoun (Dordrecht: Springer, 2013), 13–8; Georges Bensoussan, *Juifs en pays arabes: le grand deracinement 1850–1975* (Paris: Editions Tallandier, 2012). See also Kimberly A. Arkin, "Historicity, Peoplehood, and Politics: Holocaust Talk in Twenty-First-Century France," *Comparative Studies in Society and History* 60, no. 4 (2018): 968–98.

Genocide Education, sat on the project's board. Pisar was a Polish Holocaust survivor and lawyer who directed the *Fondation pour la Mémoire de la Shoah* and cofounded the French Society for Yad Vashem.[86]

The Aladdin Project works with UNESCO, the French Ministry of Foreign Affairs, the International Holocaust Remembrance Alliance, the USHMM, and Anne Frank Fonds in Switzerland to spread the word about Holocaust education and ending "hatred of Israel" to Muslims by organizing conferences on the Holocaust in the Middle East and Africa.[87] The conference in Dakar, Senegal, in June 2015, for example, featured the usual Western specialists, and its rapporteur was none other than Steven Katz, who has devoted a long career to distinguishing the Holocaust from what he seems to regard as mere tribal conflicts in Africa.[88] Internalizing the message, antislavery campaigner Karfa Sira Diallo linked the history of slavery to pedagogy about racism and antisemitism.[89] The US-based Ghanaian scholar, Edward Kissi, concurred in the discussion paper he produced for the UNESCO Holocaust and United Nations Outreach Program. Confusingly, "The Holocaust as a Guidepost for Genocide Detection and Prevention in Africa" argued that the Holocaust provided lessons for the continent – his main example was Rwanda – although he conceded that "Armed conflicts between governments and armed antigovernment groups have been the greatest causes of crimes against civilians in contemporary Africa."[90] The imposition of the Holocaust template onto Africa conceals more than it reveals, then, and even leads to a new civilizing mission: "The twenty-first century requires a 'global war on genocide' with as

---

[86] Dr Sameul Pisar, www.unesco.org/new/fileadmin/MULTIMEDIA/HQ/ERI/pdf/S.Pisar-Biography.pdf; Yad Vashem Mourns Passing of Samuel Pisar, "A Deep Understanding of Humankind," July 30, 2015, www.yadvashem.org/yv/en/about/events/event_details .asp?cid=239.

[87] The Aladdin Project, www.projetaladin.org/en/the-aladdin-project.html; "Holocaust Education in the Non-Western World": www.projetaladin.org/en/holocaust-education .html; "The Director-General celebrates the 10th anniversary of the Aladdin Project against racism and anti-Semitism," UNESCO Media Services, May 30, 2017, www .unesco.org/new/en/media-services/single-view/news/the_director_general_celebrates_ the_10th_anniversary_of_the-1/.

[88] Liz McMillen, "The Uniqueness of the Holocaust," *Chronicle of Higher Education*, June 22, 1994.

[89] International Conference in Dakar Groundbreaking International Conference in Dakar Adopts Roadmap for Holocaust and Genocide Education in Africa, www.projetaladin .org/en/en-95.html. Thanks to Alex Hinton for alerting me to the Aladdin Project and this conference, which he attended.

[90] Edward Kissi, "The Holocaust as a Guidepost for Genocide Detection and Prevention in Africa," Holocaust and United Nations Outreach Program, 2009, 51, www.un.org/en/ holocaustremembrance/docs/paper5.shtml. For scholarship on such conflict, see Philip Roessler, *Ethnic Politics and State Power in Africa: The Logic of the Coup-Civil War Trap* (Cambridge University Press, 2016).

much commitment of resources and attention as the ongoing 'global war on terrorism.'"[91]

The message stretches to the Far East. The Hong Kong Holocaust and Tolerance Centre likewise seeks to impart the "lessons of history to prevent anti-Semitism, discrimination and genocide, as a way to advance tolerance and understanding among people."[92] To prevent genocide, then, it is necessary to end hate by teaching tolerance, a lesson that continues the tradition of Jewish organizations of ascribing antisemitism and racism to psychological causes that can be treated in educational programs and visiting Holocaust museums.[93]

The two incentives for developing states to appropriate these lessons are clear. First, they can join the society of civilized states, vouchsafed by subscription to the agenda of the International Holocaust Remembrance Alliance. Second, they benefit from the hegemonic language of transgression, in which their own civil war-like conflicts can be easily distinguished from Holocaust-like violence, and thus be treated as a less pressing problem for the international community.[94]

Empire and Civilization

The commonly drawn lesson of the Holocaust and genocide, namely "never again," not only contains the potential for illiberal permanent security practices by states that destroy perceived particular threats. It also licenses liberal permanent security to ensure that "humanity" is not menaced by universal enemies in the name of preventing genocide. In fact, those lessons embody liberal permanent security. Those entities that arrogate to themselves the new global morality of Holocaust/genocide remembrance wage "virtuous wars" and police the world with unassailable technologies to make it "safe for democracy" and international commerce by permanently destroying terrorism.[95] In doing so, the US in particular continues Britain's nineteenth-century

---

[91] Kissi, "The Holocaust as a Guidepost for Genocide Detection and Prevention in Africa," 47.

[92] Hong Kong Holocaust and Tolerance Centre, "Our Mission," www.hkhtc.org/mission .php.

[93] Stuart Svonkin, *Jews against Prejudice* (New York: Columbia University Press, 1999).

[94] This function is elaborated in Chapter 1. The International Holocaust Remembrance Alliance is the successor to the Task Force for International Cooperation on Holocaust Education, Remembrance, and Research, which was founded to implement the international Holocaust education agenda of the Declaration of the Stockholm International Forum on the Holocaust (the Stockholm Declaration). www.holocaustremembrance .com/about-us.

[95] Anthony Burke, *Beyond Security, Ethics and Violence: War against the Other* (London and New York: Routledge, 2007); Hopgood, *Endtimes of Human Rights*, 57; Douglas R.

imperial "war on terrorism" against indigenous insurgents, pirates, and slave-traders who violated the precepts of civilized, free trade.[96]

The justification for destroying noncombatants as the by-product of con-quest has been refined since the Spanish invasion of the Americas in the late sixteenth century. Savage wars of peace carried out by *razzia*, reprisal, reloca-tion, incarceration, and massacre were the vehicle of imperial conquest and spread of Western civilization since Rome.[97] Although the current "responsi-bility to protect" doctrine eschews the language of imperial humanitarian interventionism, its declarations about competent governance and implication in the overthrow of the Libyan government in 2011 embody familiar colonial assumptions about Western preeminence while screening out the dependence of Western state-building on imperial domination.[98] This regime-changing utopianism has its predecessor in the British practice of partitioning non-Western regions to permanently secure ethnic peace – genocide prevention *avant la lettre* – having largely disturbed the peace in the first place. As this book details, tensions in Mandate Palestine were caused by a British sponsored settler-colonial project that then necessitated further imperial, League of Nations, and later UN intervention with disastrous consequences for the indigenous population. This is the lesson of Chapter 8.

Since the 1970s, states pursuing liberal permanent security projects eschew targeting entire populations as enemies in this manner. Instead, when they target supposed threats preventatively – whether by snipers, drones, missiles,

Burgess, "*Hostis Humani Generi*: Piracy, Terrorism and a New International Law," *University of Miami International and Comparative Law Review* 13 (2005–2006): 293–341; William O. Walker, *National Security and Core Values in American History* (Cambridge: Cambridge University Press, 2009); Ryan Goodman, "Humanitarian Intervention and Pretexts for War," *American Journal of International Law* 100, no. 1 (2006): 107–41; Marina Espinoza, "State Terrorism: Orientalism and the Drone Programme," *Critical Studies on Terrorism* 11, no. 2 (2018): 376–93. The preoccupation with noble intentions to qualitatively distinguish so-called civilized from un- or antici-vilized violence – to prevent "moral equivalence" – is apparent in Sam Harris's attempted dialogue with Noam Chomsky: Sam Harris, "The Limits of Discourse," May 1, 2015, www.samharris.org/blog/item/the-limits-of-discourse. Thanks to Neil Levi for alerting me to this exchange.

[96] Isaac Land, ed., *Enemies of Humanity: The Nineteenth-Century War on Terrorism* (Basingstoke: Palgrave Macmillan, 2008).

[97] On the French tactics in North Africa, see William Gallois, *A History of Violence in the Early Algerian Colony* (Basingstoke: Palgrave Macmillan, 2013), and Benjamin Claude Brower, *A Desert Named Peace: The Violence of France's Empire in the Algerian Sahara, 1844–1902* (New York: Columbia University Press, 2011). Generally: A. Dirk Moses, ed., *Empire, Colony Genocide: Conquest, Occupation and Subaltern Resistance in World History* (Oxford and New York: Berghahn Books, 2008).

[98] Jess Whyte, "'Always on Top?': The Responsibility to Protect and the Persistence of Colonialism," in *The Postcolonial World*, ed. Jyotsna G. Singh and David D. Kim (Abingdon: Routledge, 2017), 308–24.

or bombs – they kill noncombatants as "collateral damage," incidental deaths caused in attacking military targets. Although governed by norms of proportionality, the outcome remains that killing large numbers of civilians is legal and acceptable.[99] Likewise, for liberal settler regimes, permanent security need not entail the total destruction commonly associated with genocide. It can be achieved by permanent deterrence in collective punishment practices that Israeli security analysts call "mowing the grass." This policy is conceived as an enduring solution to asymmetrical conflict against a colonial Other whose civilian population can be indefinitely killed at will in the name of security.[100] For liberal internationalists like Samantha Power, the prevention norm trumps the norm against wars of aggression, thus allowing partitions and wars of aggression to be fought in the name of preventing or ending genocide, as in Libya in 2011.

Other American liberal internationalists are more explicit about the imperial dimensions of liberal permanent security. The US Council of Foreign Relations pundit, Max Boot, enjoins the virtually permanent stationing of US troops in the Middle East and Central Asia, invoking genocidal colonial history:

> Think of our Indian Wars, which lasted roughly 300 years (circa 1600–1890), or the British deployment on the North West Frontier (today's Pakistan-Afghanistan border), which lasted 100 years (1840s– 1940s). US troops are not undertaking a conventional combat assignment. They are policing the frontiers of the Pax Americana.[101]

He has form, having made "The Case for American Empire" and invoked English imperial poet Rudyard Kipling, evidently without irony, in his book *The Savage Wars of Peace: Small Wars and the Rise of American Power* in the immediate aftermath of the 9/11 terrorist attack.[102]

---

[99] Bruce Cronin, *Bugsplat: The Politics of Collateral Damage in Western Armed Conflicts* (Oxford: Oxford University Press, 2018); Geoff Martin and Erin Steuter, *Drone Nation: The Political Economy of America's New Way of War* (Lanham, MD: Lexington Books, 2017); Ian G. R. Shaw, "Predator Empire: The Geopolitics of US Drone Warfare," *Geopolitics* 18, no. 3 (2013): 536–59; Andrew Blake, "Obama-Led Drone Strikes Kill Innocents 90% of the Time: Report," *Washington Post*, October 15, 2015.

[100] Daniel Byman, "Mowing the Grass and Taking Out the Trash," *Foreign Policy*, August 25, 2014; Michael Shkolnik, "'Mowing the Grass' and Operation Protective Edge: Israel's Strategy for Protracted Asymmetric Conflict with Hamas," *Canadian Foreign Policy Journal* 23, no. 2 (2017): 185–9.

[101] Max Boot, "Why Winning and Losing are Irrelevant in Syria and Afghanistan," *Washington Post*, January 30, 2019.

[102] Max Boot, "The Case for American Empire," *Weekly Standard*, October 15, 2001; Boot, *The Savage Wars of Peace: Small Wars and the Rise of American Power*, rev. ed. (New York: Basic Books, 2003).

The Soviet collapse in 1991 led many commentators to speak hubristically of American empire in terms of Rome and Britain. "People are now coming out of the closet on the word 'empire'," exulted columnist conservative Charles Krauthammer (1950–2018) 10 years later: "The fact is no country has been as dominant culturally, economically, technologically and militarily in the history of the world since the Roman Empire."[103] Other journalists could not resist the analogical temptation either. Robert Kaplan drew on imperial history to draw inspiring lessons about "warrior politics" and the "pagan ethos," while Cullen Murphy asked outright, *Are We Rome?*[104] Even critics spoke of the US as "a new Rome,"[105] although distinguishing between good and bad empires, that is between liberal and illiberal permanent security. Thus, historian Thomas Madden identified the US with Rome as "empires of trust" based on informal systems of alliances and devoid of excess – a revival of the defensive imperialism thesis – which he distinguished from empires of conquest or commerce.[106]

Robert Kagan, a foreign policy commentator at the Brookings Institution in Washington, DC, explains what is at stake in such security thinking is nothing less than the fate of civilization. "The downfall of the Roman Empire brought an end not just to Roman rule but to Roman government and law and to an entire economic system stretching from Northern Europe to North Africa," he reminded readers of the *Wall Street Journal*. "Culture, the arts, even progress in science and technology, were set back for centuries." The same fate portends today if American empire declines and falls. Accordingly, he urges that the US should embrace its global mission and relinquish the bashfulness of defensive imperialism, for its hegemony benefits all.[107]

Such arguments repeat those of the German legal theorist, Carl Schmitt (1888–1985), who supported the Nazi regime until he fell out of favor in the later 1930s. He was a proponent of the European nation-state, whose secular

---

[103] Emily Eakin, "It Takes an Empire Say Several US Thinkers," *New York Times*, April 1, 2002; Gregg Easterbrook, "Out on the Edge: American Power Moves Beyond the Mere Super," *New York Times*, April 27, 2003.

[104] Robert D. Kaplan, *Warrior Politics: Why Leadership Demands a Pagan Ethos* (New York: Vintage, 2001); Cullen Murphy, *Are We Rome? The Fall of an Empire and the Fate of America* (Boston: Houghton Mifflin, 2007).

[105] Andrew J. Bacevich, *Washington Rules: America's Path to Permanent War* (New York: Metropolan Books, 2010), 162.

[106] Thomas F. Madden, *Empires of Trust: How Rome Built – and America Is Building – a New World* (New York: Penguin, 2008). This general discussion is analyzed in Eric Adler, "Post-9/11 Views of Rome and the Nature of 'Defensive Imperialism,'" *International Journal of the Classical Tradition* 15, no. 4 (2008): 587–610.

[107] Robert D. Kagan, *The World America Made* (New York: Vintage, 2013), and "Why the World Needs America," *Wall Street Journal*, February 11, 2012. Also critical of this style of reasoning is John Tirman, *The Deaths of Others: The Fate of Civilians in America's Wars* (Oxford: Oxford University Press, 2011).

status he reasoned had ended the destructive wars of religion, and whose "discovery" of the New World in the late fifteenth century had imposed international order on the globe. The Christian empires (*respublicana Christiana*) thus followed in the tradition of Rome in acting as the "restrainer" (*katechon*) of the "Antichrist," who threatened its internal order with limitless violence, literally the "end of the world" in the Christian worldview.[108]

Is this just a self-serving fable? Schmitt famously postulated the existence of dichotomous spheres in which different rules of violence obtained. War was limited inside Christian Europe: "They were feuds in the sense of assertions of right, realizations of right, or confirmations of a right of resistance, and they occurred within the framework of one and the same total order encompassing both warring parties." By contrast, no such restraint was normative in "wars against non-Christian princes and peoples" and among Europeans when they competed for land and booty beyond amity lines.[109] Fatally, the Eurocentric order that he prized crumbled as the center of the West moved to the US, whose liberal internationalism postulated the criminality of all warfare. Europeans began to treat one another as they treated non-Europeans: not according them status as legitimate belligerents (*justis hostis*), but as "rebels, criminals, and pirates," with the resulting coarsening of war. In his famous book, *The* Nomos *of the Earth*, published shortly after World War, II Schmitt conveniently omitted the Nazi regime's egregious violations of internal European norms in its version of the *Grossräume* (geopolitical spheres of influence) that he saw replacing classical nation-states. Instead, he directed his ire at the moralizing US that criminalized Germany and now occupied Europe while threatening him with de-Nazification proceedings. The Anglo-powers' aerial destruction of German and Japanese cities during the war drew his attention to how the development of air power compelled international law to criminalize entire populations because strategic bombing entailed violating the principle of distinction.

> Bombing pilots use their weapons against the population of an enemy country as vertically as St. George used his lance against the dragon. Given the fact that war has been transformed into a police action against trouble-makers, criminals, and pests, justification of the methods of this "police bombing" must be intensified. Thus, one is compelled to push the discrimination of the opponent into the abyss.[110]

As the Cold War intensified and decolonization unfolded, however, Schmitt became less hostile to US hegemony. Whatever his reservations about its

---

[108] Carl Schmitt, *The* Nomos *of the Earth in the International Law of the* Jus Publicum Europaeum, intro and trans. G.L. Ulmen (New York: Telos, [1950] 2003), 59–60. Thanks to Elliot Neaman for conversations on this point.
[109] Ibid., 58–9, 93.   [110] Ibid., 309, 321–2.

liberal internationalism, he saw now that the US protected the West from the communist-sponsored revolutionary anticolonialism of Third World national liberation movements whose guerrilla warfare and notion of "people's war" threatened to undo the civilizational work of the early-modern European nation-state. Consequently, he admired the antirevolutionary counterinsurgency of the French military officers who cast the partisan as an absolute enemy in a cosmic struggle between good and evil – much like Kagan and his ilk today. In doing so, Schmitt internalized the exterminatory logic of limitless warfare into his defense of Western civilization.[111]

It was as if Schmitt had read Robert Jackson, who in his 1945 *New York Times Magazine* article repeated the arguments of interwar air power theorists that workers and housewives were part of the enemy's "war-potential." Consequently, it was necessary in future wars "to kill and maim the enemy and to destroy all that shelters him and all that he lives by not only in the field but at home."[112] Jackson's doctrine is borne out by the evidence that democratic regimes are more likely to countenance civilian casualties because they think they represent humanity, thereby demonizing their opponents as its enemies; because domestic public opinion will not allow them to countenance sustained troop casualties, thus preferring to inflict extensive civilian destruction on enemies to defeat and impose on them a friendly government; and because democracies think they abide by international law and represent universal values, they are likely to think they can wage war incessantly but humanely, thus accumulating civilian casualties *seriatim*.[113] All these modalities are manifestations of liberal permanent security. Where the "realism" of illiberal permanent security regimes has long been recognized as transgressive, the connections between the anti-"realism" of liberal internationalism and the violence entailed in attempting to permanently pacify the globe are less well understood. It ought to be brought into any frame proclaiming the welfare of people.

---

[111] Carl Schmitt, "Die Ordnung der Welt nach dem Zweiten Weltkrieg" in Carl Schmitt, *Staat, Großraum, Nomos: Arbeiten aus den Jahren 1916–1969*, ed. Günter Maschke (Berlin: Duncker und Humblot, 1995), 592–618; Carl Schmitt, *Theory of the Partisan: Intermediate Commentary on the Concept of the Political*, trans. G. L. Ulmen (New York: Telos Press, [1963] 2007). See Peter Hohendahl, *Perilous Futures: On Carl Schmitt's Late Writings* (Ithaca, NY: Cornell University Press, 2018).

[112] Robert Jackson, "The Worst Crime of All," *New York Times Magazine*, September 9, 1945, 89.

[113] Benjamin Valentino, Paul Huth, and Sarah Croco, "Covenants Without the Sword International Law and the Protection of Civilians in Times of War," *World Politics* 58, no. 3 (2006): 339–77; Alexander B. Downes, *Targeting Civilians in War* (New York: Cornell University Press, 2008); Hugo Slim, *Killing Civilians: Method, Madness and Morality in War* (London: Hurst, 2007). Displaying a touching faith in the efficacy of democratic norms to inhibit such violence is R. J. Rummel, "Democracy, Power, Genocide, and Mass Murder," *Journal of Conflict Resolution* 39, no. 1 (1995): 3–26.

The "Supreme" (Humanitarian) Emergency

It is no accident that both regimes of permanent security refer to emergencies to justify their violence. Where the "supreme emergency" is asserted by revolutionary cliques that seize power, the "supreme humanitarian emergency" is the required threshold for humanitarian intervention. Liberal permanent security's justification to kill the civilians of belligerent actors is made in these terms. The "supreme emergency" is a term coined by Winston Churchill to legitimize the terror bombing of German cities as the only means to prevent defeat by Nazi Germany. The influential political philosopher, Michael Walzer, took this phrase to name the exception to the principle of distinction, namely that noncombatants cannot be deliberately killed. In moments of existential crisis, when the "survival and freedom" of the one's community is imperiled – like Lemkin, Walzer regards such communities as representing "the highest values of international society" – the rule of "necessity" comes into play, meaning "that one has also been forced to kill the innocent."[114] To be sure, this is an argument about last resort, and Walzer rejects preventative attacks in the name of an illusory "perfect security," as he does the continued terror bombing of German cities after the emergency of 1941 subsided.[115] For him, humanitarian interventions can be justified in response to "acts 'that shock the moral conscience of mankind,'" consciously recalling what he calls the "old-fashioned language."[116] Even so, his reasoning lends itself to permanent security justifications. For regimes always claim – and believe – that they are attacking civilians at moments of existential crisis. And since the state guarantees the survival of its nation, people or race – the supreme human value we hear from Lemkin and Walzer – what limits can really be imposed on its mission?

Although Axis regimes – Italy, Germany, and Japan – initiated strategic bombing in the 1930s, their Allied enemies perfected the destruction of civilian centers far behind enemy lines. The most famous interwar theorist of this practice was the Italian officer and writer, Giulio Douhet (1869–1930), whose book *The Command of the Air* was published in 1921 and translated into various European languages during the 1930s. Ironically, before his support for Mussolini in the 1920s, he had been a liberal who proclaimed that bombing civilians would be barbaric and violate the "conscience of mankind."[117] Like his contemporaries who came independently to the same conclusion about

---

[114] Michael Walzer, *Just and Unjust Wars: A Moral Argument with Historical Illustrations* (Boston: Basic Books, 1977), 253, 260–1.

[115] Ibid., 77, 80, 261.   [116] Ibid., 107.

[117] Thomas Hippler, *Bombing the People: Giulio Douhet and the Foundations of Air-Power Strategy, 1884–1939* (Cambridge: Cambridge University Press, 2013), 28, 38, 42, 84.

strategic bombing, Douhet eventually reasoned that targeting the enemy infrastructure would prevent disastrously drawn-out conflict like World War I, and thus ultimately serve "humanity." What is more, his democratic instincts eroded civilian immunity by identifying civilians with their nations in an age when nations and not just armies went to war. Finding the bombing intolerable, citizens would pressure their governments to sue for peace.[118]

Behind this reasoning lurked a colonial logic, however. From the outset, aerial bombing had been unleashed by European colonial powers to conquer and then police territory, which destroyed the locals' means of subsistence as well as terrorizing them. Indigenous societies were treated as totalities, in other words, thereby eliding the civilian-combatant distinction. This was perfectly legal at the time, as The Hague rules did not apply in colonial contexts. In importing this logic into the so-called civilized warfare of advanced states, strategic bombing returned to the "savage and barbarian" status of warfare before its gradual codification since the early-modern period.[119] Ironically, Walzer advanced this argument in the name of civilization, thereby laying bare the logic of liberal permanent security. It is no accident that the British and Americans were the most committed to command of the air and atomic weapons during and after World War II.

Studying the self-understanding of states that target civilians, even if incidentally, reveals that they imagine their project as the rescue of themselves and their people from imminent destruction. Where Walzer juxtaposes the civilized British with evil Germans to justify self-defensive measures that violate the principle of distinction, humanitarian interventionists transfer his logic to third parties. Political scientist Nicholas Wheeler, for example, famously coined the phrase "supreme *humanitarian* emergency" to underline the element of a "horrifying" threat so grave that no other course of action seems possible, in this case rescuing others from harm by violating the international norm of nonintervention.[120] Whether knowingly or not, both he and Walzer are effectively making a case akin to Schmitt's "state of exception," in which a political emergency licenses the sovereign to suspend the constitution and

---

[118] Ibid.; Tami Davis Biddle, "Strategic Bombardment: Expectation, Theory, and Practice in the Early Twentieth Century," in *The American Way of Bombing: Changing Ethical and Legal Norms, from Flying Fortresses to Drones*, ed. Matthew Evangelista and Henry Shue (Ithaca, NY: Cornell University Press, 2014), 27–46.

[119] Thomas Hippler, *Governing from the Skies: A Global History of Aerial Bombing* (London: Verso, 2017), 114.

[120] Nicholas J. Wheeler, *Saving Strangers: Humanitarian Intervention in International Society* (Oxford: Oxford University Press, 2000), 34, 50. The phrase was quickly taken up by advocates of humanitarian intervention: Alex J. Bellamy, "Whither the Responsibility to Protect? Humanitarian Intervention and the 2005 World Summit," *Ethics and International Affairs* 20, no. 2 (2006): 143–69.

established norms to eliminate the threat.[121] Despite the fact that Schmitt was referring to the rules of a state – in his case, the Weimar Republic and eventually the Nazi regime – all three presume the right to determine the state of emergency and authorize a violent response. These rules constitute what sociologist Craig Calhoun calls the "emergency imaginary," which in addition to rationalizing violence, naturalizes the structures of the globalized economy and system of states rather than seeing their contradictions as sources of the putative emergency.[122]

Endless Occupation

The majority of UN delegates who formulated the Genocide Convention thought that population expulsions and cultural genocide were the stalking horse of the discredited League of Nations' minorities protection regime. They deliberately excluded these liberal measures of geopolitical security from the definition of the "crime of crimes." While the Nuremberg Trials indicted and prosecuted Nazis for deportation as a war crime and crime against humanity, the Allies deemed deporting enemy civilians legitimate if undertaken in the name of establishing a human rights order. Although the Nazis' mass deportation of Jews and Slavs was roundly condemned in the early 1940s, the Nazis' ultimate crime came to be considered mass mortality by the second half of the decade, and this is what was proscribed as the new threshold of "shocking the conscience of mankind" in the Genocide Convention: population transfer and forced assimilation were held to be not so shocking when carried out in the name of "mankind." If the new democratic order of "fundamental freedoms," as President Roosevelt's 1941 state of the union speech articulated the norms for which the Allies were fighting, was the beginning of the international rights regime we know today, it was also a blueprint for ethnic homogeneity and population expulsions in Europe and eventually also in South Asia and the Middle East. For many policymakers and politicians, transferring civilians did not violate the "standard of civilization": if anything, it was done in its name.

If the future of this order is a question that historians are unable to answer, we can at least better understand its fundaments. In 2013, the Czech foreign minister and presidential candidate, Karel Schwarzenberg, depicted the

---

[121] Carl Schmitt, *Dictatorship* (Cambridge: Polity, [1921] 2014); Schmitt, *The Concept of the Political* (Chicago: University of Chicago Press, [1932] 1976). The idea is taken up by Giorgio Agamben, *State of Exception* (Chicago: University of Chicago Press, 2005).

[122] Craig Calhoun, "A World of Emergencies: Fear, Intervention, and the Limits of Cosmopolitan Order," *Canadian Review of Sociology* 41 no. 4 (2004): 373–95. A nuanced version of R2P that tries to deal with state-centred measures is Alex J., Bellamy and Edward C. Luck, *The Responsibility to Protect: From Promise to Practice* (Cambridge: Polity, 2019).

expulsion of Czech Germans after the war as a "grievous violation of human rights" (*schwere Verletzung der Menschenrechte*) such that "today the government, including President Beneš, would probably find themselves in the Hague (international criminal tribunal)."[123] A few months later, Israeli journalist Gideon Levy remarked similarly of the 1948 expulsion of the Palestinians "that today such acts would be clearly defined as war crimes, and those responsible for them would be put on trial: In Jerusalem or the Hague."[124] They were half right. In 1948, many people thought expelling Germans and Palestinians furthered the new human rights order, whatever others' misgivings at the time. Norman Bentwich, who we encountered in Chapter 8, wrote in 1948 in favor of an international court at the UN that could protect individuals' "human rights and fundamental freedoms," plainly not considering Palestinian Arabs as bearers of rights with standing to participate in such a regime.[125] Losers of ethnic civil wars could not enjoy human rights lest they disturb the stability of the ensuing order.[126] That view was contested then as it is now. But highlighting the postwar order's founding violence still provokes resistance. Heavily criticized for his statement about the German expulsions, Schwarzenberg lost the election, and Levy was spat on as an "Arab lover."[127] Even as the era of liberal permanent security is challenged by an illiberal one, the violent potential of state sovereignty continues to threaten civilian destruction of people securitized as threatening.

Although the right to settle uninhabited land is no longer a legitimate ground for imperial expansion, its cultivation and improvement still possess a powerful hold over the Western imagination. The Israeli colonists trump the Palestinian right of self-determination in the minds of those who identify the Palestinians with "red Indians" and associate the colonists (many of whom are US citizens) with their forebears who conquered the North American interior. It is no accident that both sides in Israel/Palestine invoke this frontier analogy. "We are not red Indians," declared Yasser Arafat, implying that Palestinians could not be exterminated or driven off their ancestral land.[128] Others averred

---

[123] "Schwarzenberg: Beneš käme heutzutage nach Den Haag," *Frankfurter Allgemeine Zeitung*, January 18, 2013.

[124] Gideon Levy, "Ben-Gurion's Dark Side," *Ha'aretz*, May 31, 2013.

[125] Norman Bentwich, "The Judicial Committee of the Privy Council as a Model of an International Court for Human Rights," *International Law Quarterly* 2, no. 3 (1948): 392–401.

[126] See the concluding comments in Avi Shavit, "Lydda, 1948: A City, a Massacre and the Middle East Today," *New Yorker*, October 21, 2013, 40–6.

[127] Gideon Levy, "It's Spit, Not Rain," *Ha'aretz*, May 26, 2013.

[128] Graham Usher interview with Yasser Arafat, "Not Red Indians," *Al-Ahram*, November 4–10, 2004, http://weekly.ahram.org.eg/2004/715/re17.htm; cf. Karma Nabulsi, "Out of the Carnage of Gaza a New Spirit: We Are All Palestinians," *The Guardian*, August 12, 2014.

the contrary: "Even the great American democracy could not have been created without the annihilation of the Indians," Israeli historian Benny Morris told an interviewer in 2004. "There are cases in which the overall, final good justifies harsh and cruel acts that are committed in the course of history."[129] Echoes of the nineteenth-century North American discourse about savage Indians and manifest destiny are not difficult to hear.

The Palestinians can indeed be dispossessed and, as before, international law will help the occupiers dispossess the indigenous people by not standing in their way. When Israeli leaders say that their punitive measures are responses to the terroristic resistance of the occupied people, international law largely justifies them and their various transformative occupation regimes – West Bank, Gaza, and Israel itself – in the name of security and self-defense.[130] For this reason, critical observers like Richard Falk propose a new international convention that ensures occupiers withdraw as soon as possible and do not inhibit the self-determination of the occupied; and, in the case of prolonged occupation, that mechanisms are institutionalized – like a 10-year limit – to ensure such a withdrawal.[131]

We know that Raphael Lemkin addressed the relevant lacuna in international law already in 1944 in *Axis Rule in Occupied Europe*. His broad definition of genocide there more closely resembled permanent security than the internationally agreed definition in the UN Genocide Convention. His recommendations were accordingly broad. The Hague Regulations protected individuals rather than peoples whose protection, let alone right of self-determination or autonomy, was unaddressed. The regulations did not proscribe the "various ingenious measures for weakening or destroying political, social, and cultural elements in national groups."[132] We recall that he urged that they be amended in two ways:

> in the first should be included every action infringing upon the life, liberty, health, corporal integrity, economic existence, and the honor of the inhabitants when committed because they belong to a national, religious, or racial group; and in the second, every policy aiming at the destruction or the aggrandizement of one such group to the prejudice or detriment of another.[133]

---

[129] See Benny Morris and Ari Shavit, "Survival of the Fittest," *Ha'aretz*, January 9, 2004.

[130] I leave to one side the legal issues surrounding the UN Charter's conferral of the right to self-defense against other states, as distinct from international humanitarian law's license for states to engage in security actions against a people it is occupying.

[131] Richard Falk, "Some Legal Reflections on Prolonged Israeli Occupation of Gaza and the West Bank," *Journal of Refugee Studies* 2, no. 1 (1989): 45–6.

[132] Raphael Lemkin, *Axis Rule in Occupied Europe: Laws of Occupation, Analysis of Government, Proposals for Redress* (Washington, DC: Carnegie Endowment for International Peace, 1944), 92.

[133] Ibid.

Herewith, he hoped to proscribe genocide, which, he then defined broadly as a technique of occupation that destroyed, disintegrated, and weakened another nation. Accordingly, in *Axis Rule*, he posited genocide as a settler-colonial formation:

> Genocide has two phases: one, destruction of the national pattern of the oppressed group; the other, the imposition of the national pattern of the oppressor. This imposition, in turn, may be made upon the oppressed population which is allowed to remain, or upon the territory alone, after removal of the population and the colonization of the area by the oppressor's own nationals.[134]

Lemkin also called for international supervision of occupations in the form of an agency that could inspect occupied countries for how "the occupant treats nations in prison."[135]

While the Fourth Geneva Convention provides a machinery for supervision by the Red Cross, it seems impotent.[136] That is no accident, as this book argues. The attenuated definition of genocide and accompanying memory regime constitute central pillars of postwar liberal permanent security that is designed to enable conquest, occupation, settlement, and resource extraction – as it has for 500 years. Today, this regime ascribes Palestinians the role of the villains in a global drama about preventing genocide and a "second Holocaust" for resisting colonization of and expulsion from their land. They are criminalized as indigenous people have been since the Spanish set foot in the Americas in 1492.

The impoverished language of transgression, with a depoliticized genocide at its apex, also works to their disadvantage. Whereas once the conscience was shocked by the denial of self-determination and oppression of a people, as we saw in Chapters 1 and 2, now it is shocked only by genocide-as-mass-killing: by the Holocaust. The trauma of outright extermination overshadows the trauma of exile and occupation and their antidote, self-determination. Zionists like Lemkin used to appeal to both. With the marginalization of expulsion from the vocabulary of transgression, its creative pluralism has dissipated. Violent occupations – which are akin to military dictatorships – can endure for decades with relative impunity without shocking consciences like they used to. And the law allows the mass killing of thousands of civilians as a by-product of resistance to them.[137]

---

[134] Ibid., 79.   [135] Ibid., 94–5.

[136] International Committee of the Red Cross, Israel and the Occupied Territories, www.icrc.org/en/where-we-work/middle-east/israel-and-occupied-territories. Also see the UN Office for the Coordination of Humanitarian Affairs (OCHA) in Palestinian Territories, www.ochaopt.org/.

[137] Noura Erakat, "The Sovereign Right to Kill: A Critical Appraisal of Israel's Shoot-to-Kill Policy in Gaza," *International Criminal Law Review* 19 (2019): 783–818.

The hope of this book is to promote civilian protection by a revaluation of international law and the dominant memory regimes. That would entail making permanent security a crime to discourage states from exceeding legitimate security concerns: so they do not engage in civilian destruction, try to impose ethnic or religious homogeneity on diverse populations, or attempt to dominate regions, indeed the world, with the attendant extreme violence. The signs are, though, that the crises inaugurated by the global hegemony of liberal permanent security are calling forth illiberal permanent security projects as its negation, both within and against the West.[138] We are experiencing an "apocalyptic conjuncture": fears of group destruction that terrorize national and religious sects whose perceived permanent security entails dominating or destroying neighbors. A pernicious "security theology" that denounces as heretical any questioning of "national security" is universalizing itself. Entire peoples are criminalized as legitimate military targets with the same arguments used to bomb civilians, from European colonies and mandates, to the Spanish Civil War, to Germany and Japan, to Korea and Vietnam, and to Yemen and Gaza.[139] Everyone regards themselves as the victims, or potential victims, of inner or adjacent enemies, which licenses preemptive attack to forestall secession, genocide, or a "second Holocaust." In these circumstances, more, rather than less, civilian destruction is likely, meaning that it is all the more important to confront aspirations for permanent security in all its forms.[140]

---

[138] Stephen M. Walt, *The Hell of Good Intentions: America's Foreign Policy Elite and the Decline of U.S. Primacy* (New York: Farrah, Straus and Giroux, 2018).

[139] Nadera Shalhoub-Kevorkian, *Security Theology, Surveillance and the Politics of Fear* (Cambridge University Press, 2015). Symptomatic is Thane Rosenbaum, "Hamas's Civilian Death Strategy: Gazans Shelter Terrorists and Their Weapons in their Homes, Right Beside Sofas and Dirty Diapers," *Wall Street Journal*, July 21, 2014.

[140] The "apocalyptic conjuncture" and "terror of history" are the subject of my next book. Some of its ideas are trialed in A. Dirk Moses, "Paranoia and Partisanship: Genocide Studies, Holocaust Historiography and the 'Apocalyptic Conjuncture,'" *Historical Journal* 54, no. 2 (2011): 553–83; Moses, "Genocide and the Terror of History," *Parallax* 17, no. 4 (2011): 90–108; Moses, "'White Genocide' and the Ethics of Public Analysis," *Journal of Genocide Research* 21, no. 2 (2019): 201–13.

INDEX

Abdülhamid II, 80–81
abjection, 251, 494
abolitionism, 74, 83, 85–86, 88–89,
    91–92, 124–125
  in American colonies, 69–70
  as birth of human rights justice, 72
  British, 68–73, 125–127
  Christianity and, 86–87
  colonialism and, 69–70, 87–88
  humanitarianism and, 68–73
  imperialism and, 71–72, 87–88
  as justification of imperial mission,
    71–72
  language of transgression and, 70–71
Aborigines, 76–77, 87–88, 264–267
Aborigines Protection Society, 87–89
Abrahams, Elliot, 461–462
Abyssinia, Italian invasion of, 167–168
Academic Liaison against Renewed
    Militarism, 458–459
Acadians, 398–399
accountability, 425–426, 428–430,
    432–438, 451–452, 471–472, *See
    also* responsibility
Aceh, Indonesia, 114–116
Ache people, 445–447
Aden, 391–392
administrative separation, 335–336, *See
    also* partitions
Adorno, Theodor W., 134–135, 415–416
aerial warfare, 18, 26, 40–41, 129, 167,
    231–237, 396–397, 438–439,
    511, *See also specific bombings;
    specific conflicts*
  in Africa, 128–129, 408–409
  air power theorists, 504–505
  as barbarism, 167–168

Britain and, 152, 506
  civilian destruction and, 1, 151–152,
    167–168, 230–232, 236, 238,
    439, 504–506
  collateral damage of, 1, 238
  colonialism and, 506
  debate on, 18
  desensitization to, 432–433
  drone strikes, 1, 3–4, 439–440,
    490–491
  erosion of distinction between
    combatants and civilians and,
    503–507, 511
  excluded from definition of genocide,
    18–20
  France and, 152
  international law and, 503
  liberal permanent security and, 506
  missile strikes, 1–2, 439–440
  Nazi regime and, 505
  principle of distinction and, 503,
    506–507
  terrorization of civilians by, 164–166
  United States and, 1–2, 36, 232, 237,
    396–397, 416–418, 424,
    430–433, 438–439, 457–458, 506
  Vietnam War and, 424
  World War II and, 231–237, 432–433,
    451–452, 457–458, 460–461,
    503, 505–506
Afghanistan
  British bombing of, 103
  US bombing of, 1–2
Africa, 80–81, 85–86, 243, 447, *See also
    specific countries*
  aerial warfare in, 128–129
  British colonialism in, 121–123, 408

512

CPSIA information can be obtained
at www.ICGtesting.com
Printed in the USA
LVHW050027020221
678041LV00015B/343